THE LAWFUL REVOLUTION

Istvan Deak, Seth Low Professor Emeritus at Columbia University, specializes in central and east central European history. He received his Ph.D. from Columbia in 1964.

ALSO BY ISTVAN DEAK

Weimar Germany's Left-Wing Intellectuals

Assimilation and Nationalism in East Central Europe During the Last Century of Habsburg Rule

Jewish Soldiers in Austro-Hungarian Society

Politics of Retribution in Europe: World War II and its Aftermath (ed. with Jan T Gross and Tony Judt)

THE LAWFUL REVOLUTION

Louis Kossuth and the Hungarians
1848–1849

Istvan Deak

PHOENIX PRESS

5 UPPER SAINT MARTIN'S LANE
LONDON
WC2H 9EA

A PHOENIX PRESS PAPERBACK

First published by Columbia University Press in 1979
This paperback edition published in 2001
by Phoenix Press,
a division of The Orion Publishing Group Ltd,
Orion House, 5 Upper St Martin's Lane,
London WC2H 9EA

A CIP catalogue record for this book
is available from the British Library.

Printed and bound in Great Britain by
Clays Ltd, St Ives plc

ISBN 1 84212 148 0

To my father

who served Emperor Francis Joseph in the Great War

and to the memory of my great-grandfather

who served Louis Kossuth in 1848

Contents

Illustrations

Maps

Acknowledgments

I CONCEIVED THE idea for this book in 1970, and I completed the manuscript in 1978. During these years, while I was teaching and lecturing, taking care of the needs of a research institute, and engaging constantly in other forms of writing, many people, friends, colleagues, and students helped me in this major effort. I thank all who supported me. Some names, unfortunately, I cannot even recall. I remember with pleasure my research trips to Hungary, in 1971, 1972, and 1973, when I received most valuable assistance from György Ránki, Péter Hanák, György Spira, Domokos Kosáry, József Borus, Zoltán Szász, Károly Vörös, and other members of the Historical Institute of the Hungarian Academy of Sciences at Budapest. Győző Ember, Director of the Hungarian National Archives, received me hospitably; Mrs. István Baracka, archivist, helped me select the proper dossiers, and Aladár Urbán of the University of Budapest taught me the history of 1848 while working next to me in the Archives. I also want to thank Mrs. Zoltán Rády of the Pest County Archives, and Magda Rabati, a teacher, who did specific archival research for me.

At Columbia University, I was assisted in my research and writing by János Latin, a teacher of Hungarian language and literature, and by such excellent Ph.D. candidates in history and political science as Otto Krengel, Milissa Sedar, George Deak, Michael Silber, Claire Nolte, John Micgiel, and Eugene Kisluk.

The completed manuscript was read by foremost authorities in the field; I cannot thank them profoundly enough for their detailed commentaries and many corrections. I am particularly grateful to the late C. A. Macartney, the eminent British historian who, despite his advanced age and a painful accident, filled dozens of pages with his notes. No less helpful were R. John Rath of Rice University, Edsel Walter Stroup of the University of Akron in Ohio, László Deme of the New College of the University of South Florida at Sarasota, Béla K. Király of Brooklyn College, and Kathrin Sitzler of the Südost-Institut in Munich. Special thanks are due to George Barany of the University of Denver for his excellent corrections, and for his having recommended me to Columbia University Press. Robert A. Kann, dean of Habsburg historiography in the United States, read my manuscript with devoted care, and so did Domokos Kosáry and Aladár Urbán in Hungary. Two amateur historians: my father, who is a mechanical engineer, and my brother-in-law, who is a painter and a journalist, also read the manuscript and made useful suggestions.

The typing of my manuscript received the careful attention of Dorothy Roseman, Constance Dickerson, Kirk Astroth, Andrea Merényi, and Miriam Levy. The editing of the manuscript was undertaken, privately, by my wife, Gloria Gilda Deak, herself a writer and an editor, and by Miriam Levy, a Ph.D. candidate in history. Copy editing was the work of the talented Ann Jacobs at Columbia University Press. Bernard Bellon, a Ph.D. candidate in history, helped me read the galley proofs and prepare the index. Publication itself was the task of Bernard Gronert, Executive Editor, and Joan McQuary, Managing Editor, both of Columbia University Press.

Research and writing require time and money. I was fortunate enough to benefit from grants by the John S. Guggenheim Memorial Foundation, the International Research and Exchanges Board (IREX), the Fulbright-Hays program, and the Dunning Fund of Columbia University: to the officers of these institutions I give my heartful thanks.

Istvan Deak
New York City
November 1978

Introduction

IN THE FIRST half of the nineteenth century Hungary, with its underdeveloped economy and hierarchical society, experienced a powerful modernizing movement led by noblemen. Louis Kossuth, who was born in 1802, well before the unfolding of this reform effort, joined the liberal reformers as a young man, and through a supreme talent for journalism and oratory as well as an indomitable will, rose to a position of leadership shortly before 1848. In the spring of that year he and his fellow liberals among the nobility seized the opportunity presented by the European revolutions to legally restore the sovereignty of their country under the Habsburg Crown. They also introduced many administrative, social, and economic reforms. The ratification of Hungary's new constitution led the country's leaders to Great Power ambitions, and it reinforced an already vigorous drive to convert multinational Hungary into a truly Magyar state. The goals of the reformers ran into the combined opposition of the Habsburg Court, the new liberal Austrian government (equally a product of the spring events), and the non-Magyar peoples of Hungary who feared Hungarian nationalism. In the ensuing war, which must be judged inevitable, the country was led by Kossuth. The Hungarians lost the war. Given Hungary's diplomatic isolation as well as its economic, technological, and numerical inferiority within the Habsburg Monarchy, this, too, must be seen as unavoidable. In August 1849 Kossuth fled, never to return to his homeland.

Though the Habsburg Empire won, the Hungarians did not suffer an unqualified defeat. After 1849 the Hungarian nobility, which had adopted the 1848 spring reforms and had led the War of Independence, quickly adjusted to defeat and continued to dominate Hungary economically and socially. In 1867, in the Compromise Agreement with the House of Austria, the nobles added complete political hegemony to their already exalted social and economic position. Kossuth, the exile, opposed the Compromise Agreement, but though he refused to admit it, the Compromise had brought the realization of most of his goals. Politically, Hungary's Slavs, Germans, and Romanians gained nothing from the conflict. But economically, socially, and culturally they, too, benefited from the reforms of 1848 and from the Compromise that provided for Hungary's spectacular development. By the late nineteenth century it was a rapidly industrializing and prosperous country.

The revolution of 1848 is Hungary's most celebrated historic event: generations of Hungarians have lived in the aura of that unforgettable year. It unites the people as much as it divides them. It is the source of national pride but also of self-doubt and questioning. Was the constitution of the spring too progressive or not progressive enough? Did it benefit the lower classes or only the ruling class? Was there a social revolution in 1848 or only an aristocratic *Fronde?* Was it perhaps merely a peaceful change of guards that, through misunderstandings and much senseless suspicion, degenerated into a war? Could the war have been avoided or, if not, could it have been won? Social background and ideological convictions have profoundly influenced the responses to these questions, and among nineteenth-century commentators there was as little agreement as there is today.

Hungary's War of Independence was the bloodiest conflict of a European revolutionary era, and it excited nationalist passions that have not yet been stilled. When the last Hungarian fortress lowered its flag in October 1849 (later than any other revolutionary stronghold in Europe), the surrender came as a welcome relief to the peoples of the Habsburg Monarchy—even to many Hungarians—for it marked the end of an ethnic conflict unparalleled in Central European history. The principal actor of the drama was Kossuth, and the story of the revolution is told here in terms of his towering personality. In him, Hungarians recognize their spokesman and their hero but also the symbol of much that they see as calamitous in the national character: pomposity, excessive pride, a penchant for theatrical gestures, naiveté, and easy enthusiasm. Those who emotionally identify with Hungary's historic nobility often feel that Kossuth betrayed his estate, while those who see the nobility as the bane of the country often feel that he betrayed the people. Radicals believe that he was not sufficiently forceful, and moderates that he was reckless.

The collaborators of Kossuth who knew him best saw his strengths and shortcomings—and they expounded on them in their memoirs—yet they were unable to fathom the personality of their leader. They perceived him alternately as dynamic and forceful or as hesitant and weak; as a realist or a dreamer; as bright and well read but also ignorant of the world beyond the national frontiers; as a relentless advocate of a clearly outlined political program and as a diligent borrower of other people's ideas. Some found him open, kind, and friendly; others (hardly less devoted to Kossuth, the statesman) found him secretive, cold, and selfish. Many pointed to his intrigues, his false modesty, and his predilection for playing the uncrowned king of his country.

Because Kossuth kept no diary (or none has been found) and because he confided in no one (unless in his wife, but of that we know nothing), it is difficult to tell when he was sincere. Certainly, he was capable of deception when it served his interest or that of the nation—interests he considered to be identical. He lived modestly and simply, but he did not disdain the glitter of his high office as governor-president of Hungary. He made great efforts to provide for the wounded, the veterans, the widows and orphans, and he helped those who had sent him individual petitions. He sincerely wanted all citizens to be prosperous in a prosperous and progressive Hungary. He was not bloodthirsty, and he was incapable of massive revolutionary terror (for which marxist historians have found him wanting). But in his assiduous pursuit of victory in war he squandered the lives of soldiers, and he did not restrain his itinerant commissioners in their desire to hang rebellious peasants. Above all, Kossuth was a supreme organizer and a relentless worker, qualities that predestined him for leadership of the nobility, an estate not noted for diligence and assiduity.

Kossuth emancipated the peasants and the Jews; he did away with most remnants of feudalism in his country; he defended private property; and he favored banks and industrial entrepreneurs. As a lesser noble he despised the titled nobility, but he protected them in the name of national unity. He promoted Hungarian nationalism and he supported the European nationalist movements, but he tried to muzzle the nationalist aspirations of the non-Magyar peoples of Hungary. He held assimilation into the Magyar nation to be the duty and the *summum bonum* of the country's national minorities. In brief, Kossuth was a child of his age: a liberal and a nationalist for whom the two ideologies were not incompatible.

Amazingly, there is no modern scholarly work on the revolution and the war. The best recent general study of the era, György Spira's *The Hungarian Revolution,* is informative and valuable, but its only footnotes indicate the sources of quotations from such authors as Marx, Engels, Lenin, and Mao; and as the book was written in the 1950s, it is already dated. The public itself hinders the writing of a comprehensive history of the revolution. In Hungary almost everybody is a historian and an expert on the revolution: to make even the most cautious statement on the period is to bring wrath upon the head of the writer. The same is true with regard to Kossuth. In his lifetime he was the focus of lively historic interest (he outlived several generations, dying in 1894 at the age of ninety-two); and recently he has come into focus again. Nineteenth-century biographies, however, have been mostly popular, adulatory, and undocumented; recent studies have either concentrated on specific problems in Kossuth's career or they are equally popular, respectful, and romantic, albeit often with a strange socialist twist. Perhaps it is the marxist predilection for collective authorship and for economic history that has prevented the emergence of a full-scale scholarly biography by one writer. Perhaps it is the marxist imperative to present Kossuth as an all-out bourgeois democratic revolutionary—and hence a forerunner of socialism—that turns away the younger generation of Hungarian historians. It must be difficult to deal with a government-ordained idol. Therefore, it will perhaps be understandable if, instead of a Hungary-based historian, an expatriate attempts the analysis of Kossuth's role in 1848 and 1849.

Original sources on Kossuth are abundant. He and his associates were diligent functionaries: they filed away their dossiers in perfect order and, if the Austrian police had not carted away some of the papers after the war, the files of his presidential cabinet would be complete. Most, though not all, of the confiscated documents have since been recovered. There are also many contemporary newspapers, memoirs, and printed documentary collections. Kossuth's own writings (including communications he merely initialed) and the speeches he gave were published in nearly complete collections. Literature on the Hungarian 1848 would easily fill a library, so that the historian's main task is to sift rather than to uncover. Still, it was a pleasure to examine hundreds of documents from the Budapest National Archives that, to the best of my knowledge, have not been used by other historians.

No one but a linguist could cope with the language problems of Hungarian and Central European history. Nor is it possible to write entirely without prejudice or preconceived notions. To satisfy one's conscience, and to broaden one's perspective, one ought to know Hungarian, Latin, German, French, Russian, Slovak, Romanian, Polish, Serbo-Croatian and Italian, and one ought to have done research in the archives of all the countries that were once the Habsburg Monarchy. One should also be able to forget one's background and upbringing. At least I have tried my hand at a few languages: the relative abundance of Hungarian, German, English, French, and Romanian sources will show where my language abilities lie and where there are shortcomings.

I have tried to tell the story logically and simply. This is not easy when we consider the rather complicated revolutionary situation within the Monarchy. The French made a republic in 1848 and clashed over the question of social justice. The Germans and the Italians strove for liberal reform and national unity. The peoples of the Habsburg Monarchy fought over such problems as a centralized or a federative monarchy; Austria's independence or her union with Germany; Hungarian, South Slav, Czech and Slovak, Polish, Romanian or Italian secession, independence or autonomy; absolute or constitutional monarchy or several monarchies; a republic or many republics; a Hungarian, or a German, or a South Slav, or a Polish, or a Romanian empire, all within or outside of the Monarchy; the desire of entire nationalities to defect from one province of the Monarchy in order to join another—as well as social, educational, economic, military, religious, administrative, and communal reforms in all their conceivable variety. If there was one emotion common to the forty million inhabitants of the Empire, it was bewilderment.*

* Perhaps a single example will suffice to illustrate what I am talking about. In the summer of 1848 a Habsburg army colonel named Blomberg—a German national at the head of a regiment of Polish lancers—was in charge of the defense of a district in southern Hungary inhabited mainly by Germans. Confronted by an attack of Serbian rebels, Blomberg turned to his commander for instructions. The commander, a Habsburg general of Croatian nationality, instructed

As no one but a native can easily pronounce or remember Hungarian names, I have tried to keep them to a minimum. Personalities and places surface, nonetheless, in my desire to develop the human dimension of this narrative. Few ages were more replete with individual tragedies, moral dilemmas, awkward situations, infantile ideas, and grandiose projects; contemporary speeches and writings were flowery, erudite, emotional, often hauntingly beautiful—all these factors were not dismissed.

This is a political history with brief excursions into social and institutional history. Military history cannot be completely neglected since Kossuth's role during the war often became subordinate to that of the army. I have endeavored to place local developments in the larger European context. Yet this is essentially a Hungarian history.

Note on Place Names and Proper Names

Students of Habsburg history are familiar with the insurmountable difficulties, academic, practical, and political, caused by geographic terms and proper names. I remember well the furious scolding I, a child, received from a stranger in a train somewhere in Slovenia when I referred to the country's capital as Laibach, its German name, and not as Ljubljana. In the former Habsburg Monarchy most towns, mountains, and rivers had two, three, and sometimes more names, and to choose one is to betray the vital interest of one or more nations. What, for instance, is one to call the city that the Slovaks term Bratislava, the Germans Pressburg, the Hungarians Pozsony, and the Croats Požun? It is today a Slovak-speaking town and the capital of autonomous Slovakia, but in the early nineteenth century it was inhabited by Germans, Magyars, and Jews; in Europe it was known as Pressburg, and it was the seat of the Hungarian Diet, whose language of deliberation was Latin (hence it ought to be called by its Latin name, Posonium, perhaps) and later Hungarian, and where, just to complicate matters, the Croats had official representation while the

---

the colonel to fight the Serbs, and so did the local Hungarian government commissioner, who happened to be a Serb. But the leader of the Serbian rebels, a Habsburg army colonel of Austro-German nationality, begged Blomberg to think of his duty to the emperor and not of his duty to the king (the two were the same person), whereupon Blomberg, easily persuaded, ordered his Poles out of the region, leaving his German conationals to the tender mercies of the Serbs (for further illumination see pp. 140–41).

Slovaks, then unrecognized as a nation, had none. Or what is one to do with the city which the Hungarians called Kolozsvár, the Germans Klausenburg, and the Romanians traditionally called Cluj but now, for some strange reason, officially designated by its alleged old Daco-Roman name Napoca (even though the medieval Latin name of the city was Claudiopolis)? In the nineteenth century this city was inhabited by a mixed population, a majority of them Magyars, and it was the capital of Transylvania, now a part of Romania, then a province under the Hungarian Crown. Transylvania was administered by the Habsburgs separately from Hungary, except for three short periods of union: under Joseph II (1780–90), during the 1848–49 revolution, and again from 1867 to 1918.

For the sake of a dubious practicality, I have opted for names that have been adopted in English or, short of that, have the best chance to be found in Anglo-American general history books. Thus the capital of Slovakia will be Pressburg, of Croatia, Zagreb, and of Hungary, Budapest (and not the then current Ofen-Pest). By the same token, the village where the Romanian nationalists of Transylvania assembled in the spring of 1848 will be given the Romanian name Blaj, and not the Hungarian Balázsfalva; and the major center of Slovak nationalist activity in Hungary will be Liptovský Svätý Mikuláš, and not the Hungarian Liptószentmiklós. On the other hand, for all such places in the old Hungarian kingdom where no version is likely to figure in Anglo-American general histories, or figures most inconsistently, the Hungarian term will be used, rather than the German or the present-day Slavic or Romanian term, the latter two often invented only after the territory's annexation following World War I by Romania, Czechoslovakia, or Yugoslavia. A detailed nomenclature to follow this copious apology will allow the reader to find his or her preferred place name.

Proper names are sometimes equally disconcerting because people in the early nineteenth century, especially aristocrats, changed the spelling of their names to fit their mood or their circumstances. Consistent spellers like Field Marshal Windisch-Graetz (not Windischgrätz) and Prince Pál Esterházy (not Eszterházy or Eszterházi) will be given their due. In other cases, arbitrary choices will be made: thus Jelačić and not Jellačić, Jelasics, Jellasics, Jellachich, or Jellaschich. First names will not be translated except in the case of Kossuth, known in the West as Louis and not as Lajos, and in the case of princes and archdukes, even though this will give birth to such unusual concoctions as Archdukes John, Francis Charles, and Louis, instead of Johann, Franz Carl (or Karl), and Ludwig. Following the example of the great British historian C. A. Macartney, I too shall refrain from translating Archduke Albrecht into Albert.

Place Names

H, Hungarian; G, German; R, Romanian; S, Slovak; Cz, Czech; SC, Serbo-Croat; Ru-U, Ruthene or Ukrainian; I, Italian; P, Polish.

Agyagfalva H.	Lutiţa R.	
Beszterce H.	Bistritz G.	Bistriţa R.
Blaj R.	Blasendorf G.	Balázsfalva H.
Branyiszkó H.	Branisco S.	
Brassó H.	Kronstadt G.	Braşov R.
Buda H.	Ofen G.	
Debrecen H.	Debreczin G.	
Eperjes H.	Prešov S.	
Eszék H.	Esseg G.	Osijek SC.
Fehértemplom H.	Weisskirchen G.	Bela Crkva SC.
Fiume I.	Rijeka SC.	
Győr H.	Raab G.	
Gyulafehérvár H.	Karlsburg G.	Alba-Iulia R.
Karlóca H.	Karlowitz G.	Sremski Karlovci SC.
Kassa H.	Kaschau G.	Košice S.
Kolozsvár H.	Klausenburg G.	Cluj-Napoca R.
Komárom H.	Komorn (or Comorn) G.	Komárno S.
Kremsier G.	Kroměříž Cz.	
Lemberg G.	Lwów P.	Lviv Ru-U.
Lipótvár H.	Leopoldstadt G.	Leopoldov S.
Liptovský Svätý Mikuláš S.	Liptószentmiklós H.	
Marosvásárhely H.	Neumarkt G.	Tîrgu Mureş R.
Munkács H.	Mukachevo Ru-U.	Mukačevo S.
Nagyvárad H.	Grosswardein G.	Oradea Mare R.
Nagyszeben H.	Hermannstadt G.	Sibiu R.
Naszód H.	Năsăud R.	

Olmütz G.	Olomouc Cz.	
Orsova H.	Orşova R.	
Pétervárad H.	Peterwardein G.	Petrovaradin SC.
Pressburg G.	Pozsony H.	Bratislava S.
Segesvár H.	Schessburg G.	Sighişoara R.
Szatmárnémeti H.	Satu-Mare R.	
Szeged H.	Szegedin G.	
Szenttamás H.	Srbobran SC.	
Temesvár H.	Timişoară R.	
Tisza (River) H.	Theiss G.	Tisa SC.
Turócszentmárton H.	Turčianský Svätý Martin S.	
Turopolje SC.	Turmező H.	
Újvidék H.	Neusatz G.	Novi Sad SC.
Világos H.	Şiria R.	
Zagreb SC.	Agram G.	Zágráb H.
Zimony H.	Zimún SC.	

The Lawful Revolution
Louis Kossuth and the Hungarians, 1848-1849

1 / Road to Reform: Kossuth and Hungary before 1848

King and Nation

AS ONE OF the many kingdoms and provinces that constituted the domain of the House of Austria, Hungary had come under Habsburg rule in 1526. Perhaps because theirs was the largest unit in this multiple domain, Hungarians were able to maintain a measure of autonomy and, at least in theory, were governed constitutionally. The institution of a monarchy was at first elective, but in 1687, as a result of the country's liberation from the Turks, the assembled estates recognized the hereditary right of the Habsburgs to the Throne. This monumental concession was reinforced in 1722–23, when the Hungarian Diet accepted the so-called Pragmatic Sanction extending the right of hereditary succession to the female branch of the Austrian dynasty. Yet Hungarian Diets seldom granted a favor without wresting some favors in return. The kings had to consent repeatedly to their coronation in accordance with ancient rites which obliged them to swear to the rights and liberties of Hungary.

According to Hungarian legal theory, king and nation were both sovereign under the Holy Crown of Saint Stephen, Christian Hungary's founder. These joint sovereignties imposed specific rights and obligations on each partner. Hungary, as seen by her jurists, was an independent state that could be governed only by her own laws, unlike the other provinces of the Habsburgs, and in return the nation was under obligation to give aid and comfort to the monarch.

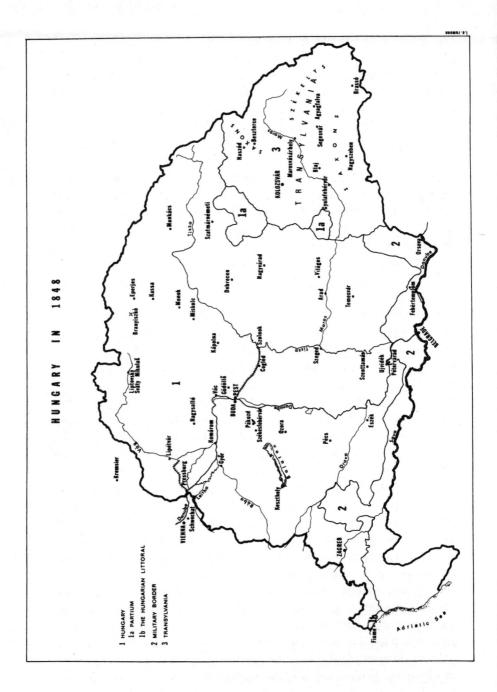

HUNGARY IN 1848

1 HUNGARY
1a PARTIUM
1b THE HUNGARIAN LITTORAL
2 MILITARY BORDER
3 TRANSYLVANIA

Because of their inclination toward absolutism, Habsburg rulers often tried to ignore their coronation oath; in exchange, the nation just as often resorted to passive resistance or to open rebellion. Thus the three centuries that preceded the birth of Louis Kossuth were marked by periodic clashes between the Hungarian nation and its foreign ruler. But mutual intransigence was mitigated by the threat of foreign aggression and domestic lower-class unrest. In consequence, the clashes between king and nation were invariably followed by reconciliation. The Vienna Court needed Hungarian taxes and blood to fight its European wars; the nation needed Austrian protection against the Turks and, increasingly, against the peasants and the non-Magyar nationalities. The bloody rebellion of Prince Ferenc Rákóczi early in the eighteenth century led to a compromise and to many decades of peace between king and nation. A new rebellion, this time bloodless but more effective, against the enlightened despotism of Joseph II between 1780 and 1790 was followed by the compromise of 1791, when Leopold II and the Diet codified in detail the rights and duties of both sovereign parties. The Napoleonic wars extended this compromise, partly because of the Habsburgs' and the Hungarians' identical hatred of Jacobin agitation, and partly because the Hungarians, or rather the wealthy landowners among them, profited enormously from the war. But the final defeat of Napoleon brought the excessively indebted Habsburg treasury to near-bankruptcy, and the parallel economic depression put an end to Hungarian prosperity. Yet, while income declined, the king demanded more revenue and more soldiers in order to play the policeman in Europe. Metternich's and Emperor-King Francis' international policy of law and order, although approved in principle by the Hungarian estates, led to a near-rebellion as this policy was implemented. To avoid an open clash, Francis reluctantly convoked the long-delayed national Diet in 1825.[1]

The Hungarian nation—a term, a concept, or a convenience of nomenclature so often mentioned in the preceding paragraphs—did not, by far, include all the inhabitants of the country. The "political nation" or *natio Hungarica* was understood to mean the nobility, the Catholic clergy, and the burghers of the free royal towns only. They were the *populus*, while the rest of the inhabitants constituted the *plebs* or *misera plebs contribuens,* the "poor tax-paying populace" of Hungary. Within the political nation the most important element, and the most numerous, were the nobles. Around 1820 the nobility

numbered some half million persons, close to 5 percent of the kingdom's total population. Since the Grand Principality of Transylvania,
legally under the Hungarian Crown, was governed separately from
Hungary, the inhabitants of this province were not included in the
above statistics. The relatively large proportion of nobles in Hungary
becomes all the more significant if one considers that in neighboring
Bohemia the nobility formed only a bit over one-tenth of 1 percent of
the population; and even in Galicia, where the "noble" Polish nation
reigned supreme, the nobility accounted for less than 2 percent of the
inhabitants.[2]

To be a nobleman in Hungary was a good thing; to be a commoner was bad by any reckoning. The basic privileges of Hungarian
noblemen included the right of habeas corpus; the right to be subject
to nobody but the legally crowned king; the right to the free ownership of personal domains; freedom from service to the king except in
arms; and exemption from taxes. The last was true in theory although, in the case of the lowest stratum of the nobility, taxes were
sometimes collected.

In contradistinction to the noblemen, the commoners could be
arrested at will; the peasants among them were direct subjects of the
noble landowners and only indirect subjects of the king; commoners
paid taxes and (the ultimate injustice) they had to perform military
service according to the wishes of the king and the Diet. The nobles,
who justified their privileges in terms of their duty to fight for the
king, owed no military service. Their only obligation was to rise up
in arms in defense of an endangered fatherland. They had done this
for the last time in 1809, when Napoleon had invaded Hungary. This
noble *insurrectio,* undertaken with great fanfare, had ended in defeat
at Győr in western Hungary, and the rapid flight of the noble army.

Again according to Hungarian legal theory, all nobles were
equal in their duties and rights. But in reality some nobles were con-
spicuously more equal than others. Ever since 1608 the nobility had
been legally divided into two estates: the aristocrats or magnates
(Latin: *barones*), who used such un-Hungarian, Habsburg-given titles
as prince, count, or baron, and the lesser (or common or untitled)
nobles. The aristocracy consisted of a few hundred families, about
two-thirds of whom were not even Hungarian by birth but so-called
indigenae, foreigners with landed property in Hungary. The aristocrats had a monopolistic claim to the highest offices of the state, and

the approximately 800 adult males of this estate had the right to attend the exalted Upper Table (or Upper House) of the Diet, where they sat together with the Catholic diocesan bishops and the lord-lieutenants of the counties. On the other hand, the lesser nobles had to be satisfied with sending their elected representatives to the Lower Table of the Diet, where they sat together with all the other Roman Catholic prelates, the judges of one of the king's highest courts, the representatives of the free royal towns as well as of certain privileged provinces and "nations," and finally the deputies of absentee aristocrats. The differences in wealth and influence within the aristocracy were as striking as they were between the aristocracy and the lesser nobles, or within the lesser nobility itself. Some aristocrats had automatic access to the king's presence; others had no access at all. Some aristocrats owned fabulous estates; others owned almost nothing. The Esterházy family, whose senior member bore the title of a prince of the Empire (whereas the rest of the Esterházys were mere counts), owned close to 1 million acres of land, with over a hundred villages, forty towns or markets, and 30 castles or palaces.

The lesser nobility's stratification was even greater. On top of the heap lived the so-called *bene possessionati,* landowners with a few thousand acres of land who usually wielded great influence in politics, national as well as local. Below this small stratum, constituting perhaps three thousand families, were those who owned enough land to live according to their status but generally did not produce for the market. Below them, in ever more numerous strata, were the poorer nobles. At the bottom were those who were generally referred to as sandaled nobles—they could not afford a pair of boots—or as tax-paying nobles, because they lived and worked on a single serf section and consequently were obliged to pay a land tax to the county, and sometimes even to the state. In addition, there were the privileged "nations," such as the Cumans (*Kunok*), Jazygi (*Jászok*), and Heyducks, who were generally peasants but who enjoyed some of the traditional liberties of nobles. All in all, to be a noble meant to be a free person, which was decidedly better than to be unfree.

The proportion of nobles relative to the total population was the largest in Europe, yet nobility was not equally distributed in Hungary. In some counties there were only a few dozen noble families, generally well off. In other counties one-fourth of the population called itself noble. In more than a thousand villages every single person was noble, no matter whether he or she was far poorer than some serfs in the neighboring villages. Village claims to collective nobility were based on ancient charters and donations usually awarded for military valor. These documents were often nowhere to be found, and the law courts as well as the lawyers had more than enough to do in settling disputes between the state or some large landowner, on the one hand, and such a village community, on the other. The state claimed taxes and recruits; the landowner claimed dues and services; the villages refused to contribute either.

To be a nobleman in Hungary was thus a vocation, and for many a full-time occupation. This does not mean that the nobles, even the wealthiest among them, were parasites; nor can they be compared with the useless dandies among the blue-blooded aristocracy of France toward the end of the Ancien Régime. It is true that the majority of the Hungarian aristocrats occupied titular rather than real offices at the Court or in the administration of Hungary; that, if they became officers or diplomats, the aristocrats tended to resign after a few years of glory in a cavalry regiment or in a foreign Court; and that many aristocrats, especially the foreigners among them, had nothing or little to do with the running of their estates. But there were enough aristocrats engaged in some kind of important activity to justify (at least in part) the existence of their estate. Hungarian aristocrats filled the top posts of the Royal Hungarian Court Chancellery in Vienna and of the Vice-Regal Council at Buda; aristocrats were increasingly active in national politics, and aristocrats were the first industrial investors and entrepreneurs as well as the first agrarian modernizers in the country. The post–World War I saying—that in Hungary not even revolutions could be made without the aristocrats—was based on the country's experience with the democratic revolutionary regime of Count Mihály Károlyi and a hundred times more applicable to early nineteenth-century Hungary. Nothing could be undertaken without the financial, political, and moral support of the aristocracy. Even the revolution of 1848, which (as we shall see) marked the triumph of the lesser nobility over the conservative court aristocracy, would have been inconceivable without the active assistance of rebellious members of the greatest aristocratic families. Nor did the aristocracy lag culturally behind the times. In the eighteenth century they brought the Enlightenment, especially its French variety, into the country. In the nineteenth century individual aristocrats were in the forefront of the struggle for a bourgeois-liberal transformation and the triumph of nationalism in Hungary. It was indeed fascinating to witness haughty magnates taking hesitant notice of Magyar culture and the political movements agitating the rabble, which, as far as the aristocrats were concerned, began somewhere at the level of the *bene possessionati*.

The lesser nobles were the core of the political nation, as well as the country's administrators. Of course, innumerable nobles merely sat in their manors, cut off from the rest of society by the abominable condition of the roads, eating, drinking, smoking, playing cards, pestering their serfs; haughty, indifferent, obstinate, incurably old-fashioned and selfish. But there were probably just as many small nobles imbued with a classical Latin culture (in contrast to the aristocrats, whose culture was generally French and German), nationally conscious, politically active, and committed to the management of their estates. Lack of capital, of credit, of technological training, and of incentive (because of the absence of profitable markets) prevented most of the lesser nobles from improving their land. Still, almost without exception, these petty and middle landowners were the real managers of their properties, as well as the governors, the tax collectors, the recruiting sergeants, the judges and sometimes even the welfare workers and educators of the serfs living on their estates.

Having dealt with the aristocracy and the lesser nobility, relatively little need be said about the Catholic prelates and the burghers of the free towns. While every Catholic clergyman enjoyed the privileges of a nobleman, only the high officials of the Roman Catholic church sat in the Upper or Lower House of the Diet. They drew tithes from all the serfs of the kingdom, whether Catholics, Orthodox, or Protestants; they controlled the education even of non-Catholics; and last but not least, the Catholic prelates were immensely rich. As large landowners they formed part of the aristocracy, from which they had been largely recruited in any case. Appointed by the grace of an "apostolic king" rather than by the pope, the prelates were very loyal and conservative. But ever since Joseph II their authority and prestige had been declining, and the prelates played only a minor role in the events of 1848.

There were in Hungary as many free royal towns as there were counties, namely about fifty. The towns (and mining cities) had corporate nobility, that is, they communally enjoyed liberties that the nobles enjoyed individually. Still, there were enormous differences between the economic and political influence of the towns on the one hand, and the nobles on the other. The free royal towns paid taxes, unlike the nobility; they were under the direct authority of the Royal Hungarian Treasury; and even though each free town had the right to send two deputies to the Diet, the total combined votes of all the town representatives counted only as a single vote. This was in contrast to the votes of the noble counties, which were each counted separately. Finally, the inhabitants of the towns were mostly non-Magyars, in the majority Germans, whose assimilation into Magyardom had scarcely begun by 1820. It is an apt commentary on the social and economic backwardness of Hungary that not a single town had 100,000 inhabitants, and that the majority of the urban dwellers in the free towns were in reality agriculturists. Only one-fourth of the dwellers in the free towns were burghers, and the majority of burghers had no part in city government. Municipal rule was in the hands of minuscule oligarchies. Once fairly prosperous and powerful, the free royal towns had become increasingly defenseless between the sixteenth and eighteenth centuries against the rising power of the landowning nobility. Only in Poland were there similar developments; only there, and in Hungary, did the nobles count for everything and the burghers for next to nothing, a fact stretching well into the nineteenth century. How, indeed, were the towns to develop an independent policy if, in the national Diet, they could muster only one vote against the fifty-odd votes of the noble counties? Dietal representatives of the free towns counted among the most conservative, and they rarely went along with the liberal reformers' attempt to modernize Hungary. It is an overriding factor of Hungarian history that the "Third Estate" in the French sense was made up of the landowning gentry, and that the burghers in no way resembled the bourgeoisie of Western Europe. In feudal Hungary the artisans and tradesmen were perhaps the most feudal stratum of all.

One more social group must be mentioned, a group that lacked official constitutional status but was nevertheless increasingly important: the *honoratiores,* commoners who, because of their higher education, were admitted to some privileges. These physicians, writers, journalists, Protestant clergymen, and professors had no political rights but exercised a marked influence in politics through their public activities. More importantly, the nonnoble *honoratiores* tended to blend with those nobles who exercised a profession. Kossuth, a landless nobleman, lawyer, and journalist, was for all practical purposes one of the *honoratiores*. This rising intelligentsia played a decisive role in the events of 1848, and one of the first acts of the new government was to grant voting rights to nonnobles with a higher education. Unfortunately for bourgeois development in Hungary, both the town burghers and the *honoratiores* tended then, and for a hundred years thereafter, to embrace the values and lifestyle of the landed gentry.

Child of Mediocrity

Where did Louis Kossuth fit into this complex social hierarchy?

He was a nobleman, of a very modest sort, born on September 19, 1802, at Monok in Zemplén county.

An average-sized village, Monok was located close to the center of the Kingdom of Hungary, but now it would be described as lying in the northeastern corner of post-1918 rump Hungary. The village is surrounded by gentle hills teeming with vineyards; Tokaj, the world-famous wine-producing region, is not far away.

Monok is not the ancestral home of the Kossuth family. It was where Kossuth's father, a lawyer, found employment as legal adviser to the wealthy estate-owning Count Andrássy's family. The Kossuths originated in the northernmost part of Old Hungary, in a tiny village which they owned and which bore their name. Kossuth village has recently fallen victim to urban development and has disappeared from the face of the earth, together with the Kossuth family cemetery. Before its disappearance, Kossuth was not easy to locate on the map, nor was Turóc county, the territorial unit to which Kossuth village belonged. Turóc was the smallest of Hungary's fifty-five counties. It had always been inhabited by Slovaks and today it forms part of Slovakia. In the nineteenth century its capital, Turócszentmárton, although similarly small, was a center of Slovak nationalist and cultural activity.

Austrian and Czechoslovak historians have maintained that the Kossuths were a Slovak family and that, consequently, Hungary's greatest revolutionary nationalist leader was a turncoat and a renegade. Since Western historians are more apt to read German, or even Czech, than Hungarian, Kossuth's Slovak background has been accepted in Western accounts. Kossuth's alleged conversion would not have been unusual in an age when thousands upon thousands of Slovaks, Germans, Jews, Serbs, and Romanians assimilated with fervor into the ruling Magyar nobility (Hungary's greatest revolutionary nationalist poet, Sándor Petőfi, for instance, was of purely Slovak origin), but the fact is that the Kossuths were not Slovaks.[3] They had been Hungarian nobles as far back as the documents take us, which is respectably far. The earliest document mentioning their name dates from 1263, when King Béla IV of the Árpád dynasty confirmed an earlier land grant to the family. Since that century the Kossuths have had the noble predicate *udvardi*. It is conceivable that prior to the thirteenth century, the Kossuths had been Slovaks: *košut* means billygoat, or buck, in Slovak, and the family coat of arms, designed in the fifteenth century, carries the replica of a goat. However, what counts is that almost the entire family had considered itself Magyar during the five centuries preceding the birth of Lajos Kossuth. This large clan of undistinguished petty nobles would have been rather foolish not to call itself Magyar; it was their protection against submersion into the sea of Slovak peasants that surrounded them.

Kossuth himself devoted some attention to his origins, but it never even occurred to him that he could have been a Slovak. He looked for a more glorious ancestry. When in exile, old and bored, he did extensive research on the subject and concluded that there had been some famous Kossuths in the Roman Empire. What is more, a Kossuth had built "one of the Acropoleis" in ancient Athens. Later he himself found such speculations a bit far-fetched and settled for a more modest "Scythian" origin, an ancestry popular among the Hungarian nobility.

Reality was, however, even more modest. Part of the Kossuth clan had been no better than glorified peasants; others had occupied uninfluential positions in various county administrations of northern Hungary. Some branches of the clan, including Kossuth's own, were Lutherans; others had remained loyal to Catholicism or had reconverted. Members of the clan were often unaware of each other's existence unless they met in court during the many lawsuits so characteristic of the life of the landowning nobility.

Kossuth's father, László, born in Kossuth village, left the ancestral domicile out of his need to earn a living. Kossuth's mother, Karolina Weber, came from a more secure background. Her ancestors had been German colonists and had lived mostly in Eperjes, a wealthy and civilized "Zipser-German" city in northernmost Hungary. One of Karolina's ancestors had been a respectable citizen and a militant Lutheran: he had been executed by General Caraffa, head of the Habsburg Counter-Reformation in the seventeenth century. The Webers were burghers; Karolina's own father was a postmaster in a small community. Thus Kossuth was half-German; he spoke and wrote German as well as he knew Hungarian.

Northern Hungary or Slovakia, then called the Hungarian Highlands, was a cosmopolitan region; untouched by the Turkish invasions of the sixteenth and seventeenth centuries, it harbored numerous villages and towns inhabited by many nationalities. The peasants were mostly Slovaks and poor (the region is mountainous); the burghers were Germans or Hungarians; most landowners belonged to the Magyar nobility. Since they lived so close to Poland as well as to the rather refined Zipser-German settlements, the Hungarian nobles of the Highlands generally traveled more and acquired a greater awareness of the outside world than their wealthier, more isolated fellow-landowners in the Great Plain of central Hungary.

When Kossuth was born, his father was about forty and his mother about eighteen. The family was still comparatively well off and occupied a spacious building owned by the Andrássy family. Restless and more often than not on bad terms with his employers, László Kossuth would soon be without a job. Eventually entirely dependent upon his son, he died in 1839 at the presumed age of seventy-six, a ruined and disappointed man. The mother was to see Louis Kossuth through the War of Independence and then follow him into exile, where she died in 1853 in Brussels on her way to her world-famous son in England.

Kossuth received a good education. Like many nobles, his father was indifferent to religious education and he sent his son to the best Catholic and Protestant schools of the region. An only child for a long time (later he was to have four sisters) Louis was adored by his family and repaid parental care by becoming an eminent student. Aside from Latin and Greek taught in the schools, and Hungarian, German, and Slovak spoken at home, Kossuth learned passable French from a private tutor. He was also taught to play the flute, and he played not only for his own delight but allegedly for those around him. Graduating from the excellent Lutheran high school in Eperjes, Kossuth acted as class valedictorian. He delivered his address in

Latin and was applauded both for his elegant diction and his melodious voice. His fellow classmates later remembered him as of medium height, lean, with light brown hair, dark blue eyes, regular features, an oval head, a fine Greek nose, and an intelligent forehead that was soon to become inordinately high. Kossuth was not a "typical" Hungarian, usually noted for a stocky build and round "Turkish" head, but a Western gentleman, a burgher, delicate and refined.

Law was the key in Hungary to practically every career outside the church, engineering, and medicine, but the latter two professions were neither respected nor very much practiced in this traditionalistic country. Kossuth entered the faculty of law at Sárospatak College, an ancient institution close to his birthplace. The school was militantly Calvinist, and this made it far more "Hungarian" than the other colleges in Hungary. Theoretical training in jurisprudence could not have amounted to much at that time, for Kossuth was able to graduate from college in one year. This was in 1820, when he was eighteen. What he had learned in college, and his attitude as a student, we know mostly from his later reminiscences. His esteem for his teachers did not preclude a fight with his favorite professor over the question of respect owed to the students. According to Kossuth, he emerged the victor from this encounter, but not without his professor predicting a seditious career for his pupil. The language of teaching at Sárospatak was Hungarian, a remarkable breakthrough in an age when all higher education was still in Latin, and when all laws and books pertaining to law were printed in that language.

For the aspiring jurist, his real training began after graduation from college, in the Eperjes office of a practicing lawyer. Following a year of this, Kossuth went to Pest, where he was to remain from 1821 to 1824. As one of the most talented of the city's innumerable apprentice lawyers, he soon landed a rare, paid position in the office of one of the country's highest judges. As an "expeditor," he did independent work by preparing legal briefs for his employer, and in 1823, at the age of twenty-one, he passed the bar exam. Although not yet the capital of Hungary (Pressburg was no less important, with its national Diet), Buda and Pest, not yet united, were already the seat of most of Hungary's highest courts and central administrative offices; and Kossuth, the full-fledged lawyer, tried but failed to set up his own law practice there. He was too poor for such a mighty enterprise. In the fall of 1824 he returned to Zemplén county, at first working under his father and, a year later, setting up his own practice. He was talented and lucky enough to become a legal adviser to important landowning families, an ideal start for a young and penniless lawyer.

For a while, Kossuth lived modestly and in relative obscurity. Instead of entering local politics, as was expected of him in terms of background and profession, he tried his hand at literature. There are a few extant manuscripts from this period, testifying to his diverse interests and to his determination to make a name for himself as a scholar or a playwright.

He first turned to history. A chronological account of the Great French Revolution, incomplete and unpublished, shows his admiration for the anti-absolutist tendency of the early revolutionaries, but also his hatred for the "monsters" of the Terror. Then came a few Western-language plays translated and rewritten in Hungarian. At least one of the plays was accepted and presented by a traveling company and even found its way on stage in a Pest theater. Finally, there was an attempt at a universal history. The introduction—on questions of methodology, historiography, and historical philosophy—although far from being original, deserves to be mentioned. Inspired by German historians, Kossuth made a serious attempt at historical periodization and at a "philosophic-pragmatic" interpretation of history. One notes his complete rejection of the Bible as an authority, his anticlericalism and his opposition to obscurantism. Such views were not unexpected from the educated youth of the period; for Kossuth they represent the first step in his steady development as a liberal politician.[4]

But Kossuth could not bury himself in his literary ventures for long. The revival of national political activity in 1825 and the parallel revival of local politics stirred his activist blood, and he became a member of the county's political and administrative machinery. He was to be a thoroughly committed politician from then until his death in 1894.

County Politician

Hungary's ancient laws gave immense power to the king. Although in the Middle Ages this power had often been more theoretical than real, the king, whether native born or foreign born, could initiate and execute laws; appoint the highest officials of the land; act as supreme judge or delegate such authority to his appointees; make war and conduct foreign policy; regulate public education and the affairs of the church; create new nobles and charter free royal towns; mint currency; grant monopolies; determine customs duties, and collect revenue from taxes and from the so-called *regalia*: the king's monopoly on the exploitation of salt and other mines, customs and the Crown's own vast properties. Only in two essential areas could the estates in an assembled Diet curb royal power: in voting taxes and recruits.

Understandably, the Habsburg rulers wished not only to preserve but to enlarge the rights of Hungarian kings. Fortified by current theories on monarchial absolutism and centralism, and by an ever-expanding state bureaucracy, the Habsburgs' striving for more power would have been irrepressible had it not collided with concurrent theories regarding human rights and national independence, as well as the very real rising power of the landed nobility. The result was that, in the seventeenth and eighteenth centuries, both king and nobility constructed mighty political institutions for the defense of their respective interests.

With clever manoeuvering, the Habsburg rulers succeeded in gradually shifting a great part of the country's government from specifically "Hungarian" royal offices to Imperial institutions charged with the affairs of the entire Monarchy. To this end they exploited the need of the Hungarian nobility for Austrian assistance against the Turks, peasants, and national minorities, and they used the Counter-Reformation as a political weapon. By the early nineteenth century most fundamental decisions were taken by such "all-Austrian" institutions as the Secret State Chancellery (*Geheime Haus-, Hof-, und Staatskanzley*), the head of which was in practice the foreign minister; the Court War Council (*Hofkriegsrath*); the General Treasury (*Allgemeine Hofkammer*); and the Highest Police and Censorship Office (*Oberste Polizey- und Censur-Hofstelle*). These all-monarchial bureaus left relatively little decisionmaking power to the offices specifically charged with Hungarian affairs, but that does not mean the latter had become negligible. The Royal Hungarian Court Chancellery (*Königliche Ungarische Hofkanzley*), located in Vienna, acted as an intermediary between the monarch and the local Hungarian authorities. Its chancellor, two vice-chancellors, and twelve major councilors performed very important advisory roles. The Hungarian Vice-Regal Council (*Königliche ungarische Statthalterey* or *Consilium Regium Locumtenentiale*) handled all domestic affairs with the exception of finances and justice. It was located in Buda under the presidency of the palatine or viceroy, who, since the end of the eighteenth century, had been a Habsburg archduke. The higher officials of the Hungarian governmental institutions were drawn from the Magyar aristocracy. But more important for further Hungarian developments were the minor bureaucrats of the royal offices in Hungary. When the first constitutional government was formed, in March 1848, it inherited prerevolutionary Hungary's twenty-five hundred functionaries. Without them the new, indigenous administrative machinery would have been unable to budge.

The Hungarian nobility, especially the lesser provincial nobility, viewed this state of affairs as anything but satisfactory. Painfully aware of their fatal underrepresentation in the all-important all-Austrian offices of the Monarchy, and the irregularity and inefficiency of their representation in the Hungarian offices of the state, the lesser nobles devised special means to make their influence felt in the executive branch. This means was the "noble" county. Originally bolstered by the kings as a counterweight to the power of the great medieval oligarchies, the fifty-five counties, plus the free districts and other privileged territories, under the Habsburgs had become the foremost bastions of lesser noble interests against the king. As explained earlier, each county was entitled to send two deputies to the national Diet. Bound by strict instructions emanating from the county assembly, the two deputies had to vote identically in the Diet, and their combined votes were counted as one.

Not only in the Diet, but in domestic administration as well, the counties were mighty fortresses of the provincial nobility. Their highest official, the lord-lieutenant (German: *Obergespann;* Latin: *comes;* Hungarian: *főispán*) was a royal appointee, but inasmuch as in many counties the lord-lieutenancy was held in hereditary tenure by aristocratic families or by the local bishop, not all lord-lieutenants were subject to royal pleasure. Furthermore, because the lord-lieutenants were almost invariably large landowners, they could feel themselves pretty independent from the Crown. Even worse for the king, all the other county officials were elected by the local nobility in triennial or, occasionally, in yearly elections. They received their pay from the county. And while the lord-lieutenant exercised supervisory functions, by no means unimportant, everyday affairs were firmly in the hands of the elected deputy lord-lieutenant (*Untergespann, vicecomes, alispán*) and his underlings. The deputy lord-lieutenant and the other important officials usually came from the ranks of the *bene possessionati,* the wealthiest segment of the middle landowners. Consequently, the counties were governed by well-established local oligarchies, the interests of which were as divergent from those of the Crown and the aristocracy as they were from the interests of the poorer nobility.

The counties were not merely self-governing; they claimed virtual sovereignty by rather arrogantly asserting their right to accept or reject the ordinances of the king. And even when they refrained from open rejection, as was most often the case, the county officials easily found the way to boycott royal edicts they found unconstitutional or harmful to the interests of the *bene possessionati.* The main reason for Emperor-King Francis' calling the national Diet in 1825 was that, in the preceding years, more than one county had defied his decrees with regard to taxes and recruits.[5]

Local preparations for the Diet of 1825, the first one to be held since 1811–12, created considerable excitement. Zemplén county put itself clearly in the camp of the opposition when it instructed its deputies to press in the Diet for the punishment of all Hungarians who had participated in the previous absolutist regime, to ask for the abolition of the discriminatory tariff system that separated Hungary from the rest of the Monarchy, and to promote the use of the Hungarian language in public affairs. Of the three instructions, the last one was relatively new; the first two had been part and parcel of the Hungarian nobility's time-honored grievances. The king's person being inviolable, it was customary to call for the indictment of the king's evil advisors—a device that was to remain current well into the revolution of 1848. The customs barrier between Hungary and the so-called hereditary provinces had been erected by Maria Theresa in the eighteenth century as an inevitable consequence of the Hungarian nobility's refusal to pay taxes on their demesne lands. The demand that the Hungarian language replace the customary Latin in public life was, however, the symbol of an unfolding new age, that of liberalism and nationalism with all its sins and virtues. Agitation for the compulsory public use of the Magyar tongue was to become the alpha and omega of Hungarian liberal politics and the main cause of the civil war that wrecked the Hungarian War of Independence in 1848–49.

The Diet sat in session until 1827 but with meager results. As usual, the king promised to call the Diet every three years and to let the Hungarians vote on taxes and recruits. But again, there was no guarantee that the king would abide by his promises. Francis I, Metternich, and their representatives at the Pressburg Diet, played a shrewd game: whenever the Hungarians brought up their grievances, the authorities threatened to bring up the plight of the serfs. They even indicated a readiness to lighten the intolerable feudal burdens of the peasantry by administrative fiat. The alarmed nobles thereupon moderated the tone of their polemics and reverted to the magnificent, empty oratory that had characterized Hungarian parliamentary politics for centuries. However, there were a few minor breakthroughs. The principle of the taxation of any nobleman living on a peasant tenure was accepted by the Diet, as was the provision for the legal census of the taxable population: a measure that the nobility had always tried to sabotage. Also accepted was the decision to form a postdietal commission to discuss the proposals for reform originally outlined by the Diet of 1790–91. The results of the commission's work were to be submitted to the Diet, but only after they had been thoroughly debated by the county assemblies. This provision guaranteed that county politics would not be dull in the next few years.

The fervor of renewed political life caught up with Kossuth. In 1826 he became attorney and notary of the local Lutheran church, a post not as politically insignificant as it might seem. The Lutherans in Hungary were mainly Slovaks and Germans: Kossuth and his Magyar noble Lutheran colleagues pressed for the introduction of Hungarian in church services. A year later he was appointed a *táblabíró* or judge of the county court in Zemplén. The office was an historical curiosity, soon to be the butt of liberal attacks. By 1848, the office would become associated in reformist minds—and thus in the mind of Kossuth—with everything backward and reactionary in Hungary. But in 1827 Kossuth could only rejoice over his appointment. While hundreds of judges in each county considered their title honorific, an ambitious young man would make something of it. Kossuth would not only sit in court, he would be charged with all sorts of temporary assignments which carried remuneration. It was the means to a career.

Y IN 1848

RUSSIA'n EMPIRE
(POLAND)

•Lemberg

G A L I C I A

SIA

H U N G A R Y

Buda• •Pest

Tisza

Tisza

Maros

BUKOVINA

MOLDAVIA

Kolozsvár
•

T R A N S Y L V A N I A

VONIA

Danube

MILITARY BORDER

Danube

WALLACHIA

Sava

SERBIA

OTTOMAN EMPIRE

i.e. romann

Kossuth was now hard at work. In 1829 he became city attorney of the county seat; in the following year he took an active part in the deliberations of the county assembly. By 1830 the national commission charged with preparing proposals for political reform had completed its work. Now it was up to the counties to discuss the *operata* of the national commission. Meanwhile, however, the international situation had suddenly worsened as a result of the overthrow of the Bourbon dynasty in Paris. Anxious to wrest more taxes and more recruits from the Hungarians as well as to avoid a national debate on reforms, the king quickly called a Diet, for October 1830, merely to vote on higher taxes and additional soldiers.

The Zemplén county assembly had met some two months before the opening of the new Diet to elect its deputies and to prepare their instructions. Kossuth was a member of the relatively large committee preparing the instructions, and in that committee he made his first known political address. While the speech itself was of no great interest, its oppositionary tone led Kossuth to a clash with the county's newly appointed lord-lieutenant and, by extension, with the aristocracy. While Kossuth would never lack aristocratic friends and protectors, his hatred for the institution of titled nobility was to become a permanent feature of his politics.

The Diet of 1830 again accomplished little, if anything. It voted the requested number of peasant recruits; in exchange, it received further concessions with regard to the use of the Hungarian language in public life. The pattern was established for many years to come. While both government and nobles knew that economic and social reforms were necessary, they feared a revolution and used the call for economic and social reforms to frighten the opposition camp. Magyarization, on the other hand, was a sop thrown to the nobles by the king in exchange for favorable votes on taxes and on the army. The losers were the non–Magyar-speaking majority of Hungary.

In the course of the dietal debates, when the liberal opposition finally began to show some cohesion, the two deputies of Zemplén county turned on one another. While one voted in conformity with his instructions, the other voted to grant the king's request, thus canceling out each other's vote. The king's friend was rewarded by a top appointment in another county. His "treason" caused immense excitement in Zemplén. When in January 1831 the county assembly called the two deputies to account, Kossuth made a fiery address excoriating the behavior of the unreliable deputy. Conservatives who were present described Kossuth as a "furious Catiline," and "arrogant attorney," eloquent and most dangerous. Kossuth's speech on this occasion is extant. One is struck by the Latin-inspired ornateness of his Hungarian style, while he eschewed the use of Latin words.[6] It would take him another decade to develop the direct, simple yet elegant style that revolutionized Hungarian political oratory, and even Hungarian speech.

The years 1830–31 were not wanting in great events. There was the French revolution; there was an anti-Russian uprising in Poland; and soon thereafter came a cholera epidemic in northeastern Hungary. The Polish uprising, begun in November 1830, met with widespread Hungarian sympathy. The Polish revolutionary nobles resembled their Hungarian counterparts in everything but speech, and their Russian overlords were easily compared with the Austrian overlords of Hungary. The Poles were fighting for their constitutionally guaranteed autonomy. While the Vienna government and the Hungarian conservatives grew increasingly worried about Polish development, the Hungarian liberals, especially the young among them, became more and more enthusiastic. After the Poles were defeated in 1831, revolutionaries fled en masse to Hungary, where they were hidden on the estates of the provincial nobility. When the authorities began to arrest and extradite the Poles, Kossuth was among those who protested most vehemently. The Polish issue was to remain alive in Hungary for many decades, as it did in the France of Louis Philippe. In 1848 all European revolutionaries toyed with the idea of making war to bring freedom to Poland, the "Martyr of Europe."[7]

Cholera came to Hungary in 1831 from the north. It had originated in India but had been dragged into Europe by the Russian armies fighting the Poles. Habsburg authorities combated the disease by closing the frontier (which had the additional advantage of keeping out Polish refugees), by putting the afflicted regions in quarantine, and by distributing quantities of bismuth and chloride of lime. The consequences should have been predictable. The dirt-poor Ruthene (Ukrainian or Little Russian), Slovak, Romanian, and Magyar peasants of northeastern Hungary, threatened by a horrible disease, were prevented from going south, as had been their custom, to help with the harvest on the rich Great Plain. They needed bread but got none. They were ordered to swallow pills, and they watched as officials dumped some white stuff into the wells. For the peasants the situation was clear: grain would no longer sell abroad but wool would; therefore the landowners wished to convert their land into sheep pasture. But for that the "gentlemen" had to get rid of the serfs, so they were sending doctors, priests, officials, and Jews, the traditional middlemen in the region, to poison the people. Cholera had led to starvation; starvation was now leading to *Jacqueries*. Landowners, priests, county officials, and Jews were hunted down by the peasants and many were killed.

Zemplén county, whose boundary reached the Polish border, was among the hardest hit. Instead of distributing food and promoting cleanliness, as the Hungarian government was wisely to do in 1848, county officials ordered the blockading of entire districts. But the cholera broke through the quarantine lines and entered the county seat.

Kossuth became one of the commissioners dealing with the plague there. While the older officials fled, Kossuth and a number of other young men sought to shelter noble refugees arriving from the provinces and to set up hospitals. After the city proletariat revolted, Kossuth and his colleagues helped to form a militia to maintain order. All in all, the young commissioners used far more persuasion than violence.

By the end of 1831 the epidemic had abated and the peasant revolt had been put down by Imperial-Royal troops. Noble courts in Zemplén and elsewhere ordered the hanging of over a hundred rebels and would have executed more had Metternich not put an end to the repression. But the nobles never forgot the year of 1831. From that time on, the figure of the wild peasant, armed with a pitchfork, axe, or torch, was to haunt the dreams and inflate the parliamentary oratory of the nobility. For some these nightmares pointed the way to reform; for others, to further repression.

Kossuth himself emerged from the affair with his reputation enhanced. He was now a respected official and well paid as well, for he had become a legal adviser to several of the county's richest landlords. Then, at the height of his success, his enemies managed to mount an efficient campaign against him. The campaign was to last many months and it was to ruin Kossuth locally but, paradoxically, it would thrust him into the midst of national politics and trigger his career as a statesman.

Kossuth had many enemies in Zemplén. He was young, handsome, a bit arrogant, conceited, smooth, and overly polite. Although his family was not from the county and he had no inherited wealth, he occupied increasingly important positions in local administration. He belonged to a club of noisy young liberal intellectuals whose aristocratic leaders provided the club with money and books. They read and discussed seditious works and ferociously attacked the county's conservative lord-lieutenant. On top of that, Kossuth's name was romantically linked with the beautiful wife of Count Andrássy which, if nothing else, would have enveloped the young upstart in a cloud of enmity. County life required that Kossuth attend dances and banquets, that he drink (which he did without passion), and that he play at cards. The result of all this was a mound of debts and, on one demonstrable occasion, Kossuth used public funds to pay off his gambling obligation. The incident occurred in the fall of 1831, when the orphans' court of Zemplén county formed a commission to make an inventory of the estate of one of the victims of the peasants' revolt. As a member of this commission, Kossuth sold seventeen barrels of wine to a Jew at an unduly low price, without immediately notifying the head of the commission and without handing over the money. Even worse, he temporarily left for western Hungary, perhaps to find a creditor. The ensuing scandal far surpassed the level of scandals normal in such cases: similar abuses were usually overlooked as long as the guilty official was ready to repay the money in a short time. Kossuth had no intention of permanently absconding with the money; yet, in his case, an investigatory commission was formed.[8] By contracting fresh debts, Kossuth was able to return the revenue from the wine sale as well as compensate the merchant whose wine had been seized. He defended himself before the commission with eloquence and skill. The result was that the commission branded his behavior as immoral, but neither deprived him of his positions in the county nor remanded him to a regular court. However, Kossuth's situation had become impossible. First he lost his lucrative position with his most important aristocratic employer; later he was dismissed as city attorney. By the autumn of 1832 he had no money and no future in the county. Then, in order to save him, several of his liberal aristocratic protectors designated Kossuth as their "absentees' deputy" at the national Diet, which was about to reconvene. (Hundreds of aristocrats customarily failed to show up at the sessions of the Diet. Instead they sent a representative, usually a young lawyer, to take their place in Pressburg.) The *ablegatus absentium* was not paid; he sat in the Lower House and not in the Upper; he had no right to vote; and it was expected of him that he would keep quiet. Kossuth was to provide some surprises on the latter score; but what counted for the moment was that in December 1832 he arrived in Pressburg, there to mingle with the grandees and the most illustrious politicians of the realm.

There is no reason to assume that Kossuth in that year was very different from the thousands of young noblemen who aspired to a career in politics. He was a liberal; so were most of the other young men. He had spoken publicly on behalf of the freedom of the press and against the archaic feudal system. So had the other young politicians. What may have distinguished him from most of his peers was his determination. He would never gamble again, nor would he drink. He would never fight a duel. His only known attempt in this direction had taken place in 1829. To a friend who had offended him he wrote at that time: "Like the lover awaiting the arrival of his beloved one, I await the hour, panting, when either I shall see your life evaporating in your blood, or else my own life will evaporate." But there had been no duel. Nor does it seem that Kossuth ever spent time on women. The rumor linking him with the beautiful countess in Zemplén was probably only a rumor. Kossuth was later to marry a penniless, hard-working, and passionately dedicated woman. No one knew anything concrete about Kossuth's intimate life in 1832 or later. The only reasonable explanation for this is that Kossuth had little intimate life. He was wrapped up in politics.

At the Diet

The Diet meeting in session in December 1832, one of the so-called Reform Diets, lasted four years and was to prove important. Those present seethed under the impact of the French and Polish revolutions, the recent cholera epidemic, and the peasant revolt in northeastern Hungary. But what agitated the estates most was the appearance of two books: *Credit* (Hungarian: *Hitel*) and *Light* (Hungarian: *Világ*), written by a little-known aristocrat, Count István Széchenyi, and published in 1830 and 1831 respectively. These polemical works went far beyond the force of all the world and national events combined in awakening the nobles to their responsibilities.

Széchenyi requires more than a casual presentation, though this is no place to write his biography. He was to become Kossuth's bitterest antagonist and, next to Kossuth, prerevolutionary Hungary's greatest political personality. His writings fill dozens of volumes and he has been the subject of infinite historical debate. The hostility between him and Kossuth divided the Hungarians into two camps, roughly defined as moderates (or pragmatists) and radicals (or idealists).[9]

Born in 1791, Széchenyi was Kossuth's elder by eleven years. He came from a devoutly Catholic western Hungarian family that had made its fortune in the seventeenth century through faithful service to the Habsburgs. István Széchenyi's father, Ferenc, was the founder of the National Museum and of the National (Széchényi) Library. He was a wealthy landowner, lord-lieutenant of a western Hungarian county, deputy lord chief justice of Hungary, and wearer of the Habsburg Order of the Golden Fleece. István Széchenyi spent his youth in the army, of course in a cavalry regiment. Having distinguished himself at the Battle of Leipzig in 1813, he rode with the allied armies to Paris and then, as "Count Stefi," became the darling of the Congress of Vienna. He went to bed with the fairest countesses and consorted with Metternich and Tsar Alexander. Soon thereafter he began a long series of travels. Although his regiment was stationed in Hungary, he hardly ever set foot there but traveled instead to Italy, the Middle East, France, and most importantly England. Poorly educated, Széchenyi now began to educate himself. Introduction to Western civilization, and especially to British parliamentarism and industrialization, turned him into a Hungarian patriot determined to relieve his country from its backwardness and misery. He underwent a religious and moral regeneration, mostly under the influence of the French religious philosopher Lamennais. He fell lastingly in love with the wife of a fellow aristocrat and finally married her in 1836 following the death of her husband.

An exalted and troubled soul, haunted by pessimism, Széchenyi filled the pages of his diary with meditations, expressions of self-doubt, and horrifying prophesies. He laced these with vitriolic comments about his political competitors. Characteristically, he wrote his diary in German, often in French or English, and only seldom in

Hungarian. He had recurring depressions and in 1860 was to end his life a suicide, in an insane asylum. Yet this perturbed and fiercely passionate man was also a patient planner and organizer who helped enormously in the economic and cultural development of Hungary. His active role in the amelioration of Hungarian conditions began in 1825, when he offered one year's income from his estates (around 60,000 gulden) toward the founding of a Hungarian Academy of Sciences. Other aristocrats followed his example and soon the Academy was inaugurated. Then came, successively, the National Casino (a debating and reading club for aristocrats), the first Hungarian association for the breeding of horses, the first company for steamship navigation on Lake Balaton, the first rolling mill, and the first commercial bank. Széchenyi assisted in the planning and erection of the first shipyard at Buda, promoted the growing of silkworms, the improvement of wine production, the regulation of the Tisza River and of the impassable cataracts on the Lower Danube, and to crown it all, the construction of the first permanent bridge spanning the Danube between Buda and Pest. Built by an Englishman and called the Széchenyi or Chain Bridge, this famous suspension bridge was to do good service until 1945, when it was blown up by the Germans. Paradoxically, the bridge was first used by the Austrian army, in the winter of 1848/49, when its troops marched across to pursue the Hungarian revolutionaries.

In 1825 Széchenyi was the first among the magnates to address the Diet in Hungarian, mainly because his Latin was even worse than his Hungarian. The oppositionary tone of his speech, and the fact that he spoke in Magyar, caused such suspicion in Vienna that Emperor-King Francis saw to it that this captain of the hussars would not be promoted. Nor was the suspicion ever to cease. Széchenyi resigned his commission and devoted himself to public life. Distrusted by the central administration, he also suffered the distrust of the Hungarian lesser nobility. Although they admired him, they considered Széchenyi too much of an aristocrat and far too moderate in his patriotism. Alone of all his great reformist contemporaries, Széchenyi insisted on tying the modernization of Hungary to that of industrialized Austria. Almost alone, he refused to treat the non-Magyar nationalities as children. He too wished the Slavs and the Romanians to assimilate into Magyardom, but only through the attraction of a good life, and not through the force of laws. Such convictions made his eventual clash with Kossuth and the other liberal nationalists inevitable.

Széchenyi's *Credit* was a clear enumeration of Hungary's ills, together with recommendations for reform. It asserted that the backwardness of agriculture was not due to ill fate or to Austria, but to old-fashioned methods and reliance on the unpaid labor of serfs. It called for the introduction of hired labor, which in turn necessitated the creation of credit. Credit, on the other hand, could not be made available as long as the laws on entail prevented the free sale of land. In *Credit* as in his subsequent works, Széchenyi turned against every aspect of feudalism: the common use of grazing lands and woods; the indivisibility of many hereditary properties; the immunity of nobles from taxation; the lack of civil rights for the vast majority of the population and their inequality before the law; the lack of the peasants' right to free ownership of land; the guild and pricing system. He demonstrated that the backwardness of trade was not due to discriminatory Austrian tariff laws but to domestic social and economic ills. In his *Light,* written in response to a fellow aristocrat's claim that the reforms Széchenyi had proposed would ruin the heavily indebted large landowners, he argued forcefully that serfdom was the main obstacle to development. In his most progressive work, *Stadium,* which had to be printed abroad and was smuggled into the country in 1833, Széchenyi formulated his reform demands in twelve clearly defined articles. His idea of reform was one from above, led by the central government and the Hungarian aristocracy and proceeding step by step on the firmest of grounds.

The Reform Diet of 1832–36 was not guided by Széchenyi, who was never able to attract a political following, but by the poet Ferenc Kölcsey and the Transylvanian landowner Baron Miklós Wesselényi. Both were more radical than Széchenyi. Imbued with the sense of mortal Slavic and Romanian danger threatening the isolated Magyars—a constant theme in Hungarian politics—they wished to create a modern and powerful nation by coopting the lower classes into the body politic. Kölcsey wrote in his diary: "The constitution must make room for the people, so that ten million will regard it as their own and not merely the affair of seven hundred thousand privileged individuals." This was a race against time. Unless a dynamic, enlarged nation was created, Hungary would founder. But the race was fraught with danger; in the eyes of the Hungarian liberal nobles, the evil government was ever ready to direct the rising expectations of the lower classes against the Hungarian nobility. In fact, this was what seemed to happen at the beginning of the Diet of 1832. When the deputies proposed to put a trade bill at the head of the agenda, the government put forward the reform of the peasant legislation. Whether or not the government's intentions were serious, the liberal nobles risked looming unmasked as enemies of the peasants. It needed all the magnificent oratory of Wesselényi to persuade his followers in the camp of the opposition to accept the government's agenda. For the next four years there was endless wrangling. When the Lower House took the initiative on the reform of peasant dues and rights, it was blocked by the Upper House or by the king. On the other hand, what the latter proposed was regularly voted down by the lower chamber. Still, there were a few significant changes. The serfs were relieved of some minor burdens; the enclosure of common pasture was facilitated; the nobility assumed the costs of the Diet; the law on the permanent bridge connecting Buda with Pest stipulated that tolls be paid by everyone, thus also by the nobles. These and such other laws as (for instance) the one authorizing the state to expropriate land needed for the construction of railroads infringed on noble privilege and on feudal property, but again, the most significant law concerned language. Magyar was to be the exclusive, or at least the first, language in legislation, the courts, and the church. Step by step, the Hungarian political leadership was driving the country toward a showdown with the nationalities. True, Latin was a dead language, dreadfully ill-used in Hungary, and modernization was impossible without getting rid of such an anachronism. But it occurred to no one, not even to Széchenyi, to try the multilingual approach. (It is also true that such a thing as a multilingual modern bourgeois state was unheard of outside of maverick Switzerland, and true that it would have contradicted the sacred *Zeitgeist* then hovering over young and striving Europe.)

One of the major questions plaguing the Diet was whether or not to publicize its debates. In a country without a free press but with a free assembly, immediate publication of the minutes of the sessions would have been of capital importance. But the majority of the deputies feared such a move no less than did the government. The meetings of the two chambers were open to the public, and the parliamentarians had already more than enough trouble with the apprentice lawyers and other spectators who cheered the liberals and jeered the conservatives. As a result, the deputies had adopted the habit of addressing the galleries that certainly did not improve the quality of the discussion. It was a testimony to the laxity, or tolerance, or inefficiency of the Metternichian system that while the personal authorization of the monarch was needed to set up even a single printing press, and censorship was both extensive and irrational, a few hundred young men in Pressburg were allowed to outshout the king's friends in parliament and to hold almost daily parades in honor of the king's opponents.

No sooner had Kossuth arrived at the Diet than he rose to speak on behalf of the freedom of the press at one of the so-called circular or district meetings of the Lower House: crucial but unofficial gatherings of the deputies, held in the absence of court-appointed Diet officers. This unheard-of intervention on the part of an "absentees' deputy," and a nobody to boot, was met with stony silence and Kossuth sat down in great embarrassment. But Kossuth did something far more consequential than to try to address the deputies. With the approval of Wesselényi, Kölcsey, and others, he began writing daily résumés of the meetings of the Lower House. He sent these reports, at first to his friends in Zemplén, and then to anyone interested. He recruited young jurists to copy and mail his reports. He was able to pay his employees from the substantial subscription fees he collected for his friendly correspondence. By the fall of 1833 some seventy handwritten copies of Kossuth's *Parliamentary Reports* (Hungarian: *Országgyűlési Tudósítások*) were mailed to every corner of Hungary. Later the number rose to one hundred, with the government among the most assiduous subscribers. Private correspondence was uncensored in Hungary (although the secrecy of mail was violated by the police), but Kossuth's mailing campaign clearly contradicted the laws on the press. Even worse, Kossuth used no shorthand when in the chamber. He took copious notes, dictating his account in the evening to his scribes. What came out was quite biased. Liberal speeches were reported on in detail and, if necessary, embellished; conservative addresses were recounted superficially, or spiced with venomous comment, or simply forgotten. In the summer of 1833 Kossuth secretly purchased a lithographic press in Vienna and used it for his reports. This was too much for the authorities, and in October the master of the horse (who was in charge of order at the seat of the

Diet) confiscated Kossuth's press. But the government was so timid, or so generous, that it amply paid Kossuth for his financial loss. Later the authorities bought the services of a young oppositionary journalist, who undertook to send out his own dietal reports. But few people were interested in the government's version of parliamentary events and the enterprise soon collapsed. Kossuth maintained the monopoly of written reporting until the end of the Diet.

Kossuth was then in his early thirties and he had suddenly become nationally known. For the first time he had given widely noted evidence of his unbelievable energy and dedication. Five or six hours spent in the chamber led to many hours of follow-up work: recruiting scribes, dictating, correcting spelling errors, and attending private parties where the most exciting news was to be heard. While most others played at politics, Kossuth tipped toward professionalism. Széchenyi's performance was erratic; Wesselényi, Kölcsey, the rising new leader Ferenc Deák, and most others were landowners who could (and did) retire to their estates at will. Kossuth had no such choice. Among other factors, it was the basic reason for his triumph in 1848 over his competitors. An unheard-of capacity for hard work and total dedication were necessary requisites for success then as now in the game of politics.

Altogether, Kossuth sent out three hundred and thirty-four lengthy reports in four years, with unmeasurable effect on the provincial nobility that circulated each copy until it was worn out.[10] He lived modestly. The subscription fees were barely enough to keep the reports going, and he had to provide for his parents and his four sisters. When the Diet closed in 1836 and his enterprise was over, Kossuth was completely familiar with the ins and outs of Hungarian politics. He knew now how to look for new ways to earn a living and to remain conspicuous on the national political scene.

Kossuth Martyr

Following the Pressburg episode, Kossuth moved to Pest, and there he immediately launched a new manuscript journal. Entitled *Municipal Reports* (*Törvényhatósági Tudósítások*), it was to be a biweekly account of the activities of the *municipia* (the noble counties).[11] Again, high subscription fees were charged to the one hundred and twenty-odd subscribers: mainly county assemblies, reading clubs, and individual provincial notables. Széchenyi, who had recently vetoed Kossuth's admission to the aristocratic National Casino, was among them.[12]

The journal was an excellent idea, for county politics were thriving, and through the *Reports* the assemblies could finally coordinate their activities. As liberal friends everywhere sent reports to Kossuth, his foremost job was a careful sifting, editing, and distribution of the information he had received from all parts of the country. Distribution was no easy matter, for the royal mail would no longer forward Kossuth's "correspondence," and every single copy had to be sent through traveling friends. The *Municipal Reports* were more militant than even the *Parliamentary Reports* had been: conservatives were denigrated, patriots glorified, absolutism and corruption unmasked. This time, however, Kossuth had it less easy with the authorities; the twenty-fourth issue of the *Reports* was confiscated and in the spring of 1837 he was arrested.

In the preceding two years drastic changes had taken place in Vienna's Hungarian policy. Emperor-King Francis had died in 1835, and the place of this narrow-minded but diligent, conscientious, and not unpopular bureaucrat was taken by his eldest son, the epileptic, retarded, gentle Ferdinand (I as Emperor of Austria; V as King of Hungary). Ferdinand certainly had his lucid moments but only rarely, and never when they were most needed. In putting Ferdinand on the throne, Metternich fulfilled the wish of Francis and upheld the sacred principle of legitimacy, but he also exposed the Monarchy to grave danger. Strangely, Ferdinand became rather popular among the Viennese, whom he charmed with his dialect speech and his fondness for the local cuisine.

The Hungarians had no objection to Ferdinand either, for they saw him as a puppet who could be manipulated as they wished. It was precisely to prevent such a catastrophe that effective government was assumed by a so-called State Conference (*Staats-Conferenz*) presided over by Archduke Louis (one of Francis' younger brothers) and composed of Archduke Francis Charles (Ferdinand's younger brother), Metternich, and Count Franz Anton Kolowrat-Liebsteinsky. As the two archdukes were only a bit wiser than the monarch himself, real power was exercised by Metternich, who specialized in foreign affairs but meddled in domestic politics, and Kolowrat, who left foreign policy alone but resented Metternich's interference with internal concerns. Unfortunately for the Monarchy, the two men did not get along at all. Metternich disliked the Hungarian nobles but, as it was not his intent to abrogate permanently Hungary's traditional liberties, he tried to win them over. Kolowrat, a Bohemian magnate less brilliant than Metternich, moody and constantly offended, despised the Hungarians, liked the Slavs (especially the Czechs), and was not at all averse to tampering with Hungary's ancient rights. And while Metternich in old age steadily gained in perception and foresight though he was less and less able to make decisions, Kolowrat understood little but was readier to act firmly. Finally, there was an unofficial adviser behind the throne: the Bavarian Princess Sophie. The wife of Archduke Francis Charles and the mother of the future Emperor Francis Joseph, Sophie was ambitious and ruthless as her poor daughter-in-law, Empress Elizabeth, was to learn later. A staunch believer in monarchial rights, Sophie abominated the unruly Hungarians. Her influence and the importance of the Hungarian question cannot be overestimated: there were years when four-fifths of the deliberations in the State Conference were devoted to matters concerning Hungary.

The new State Conference, both fortified and weighed down by a number of state ministers and by a vast, honest, and stubborn bureaucracy,[13] adopted a harsh Hungarian policy. Following the dissolution of the Diet in 1836, four young radical jurists in Pressburg were arrested and tried for treason. This action led to a storm of protest that Kossuth directed on the pages of his *Municipal Reports*. He assumed the unofficial legal representation of the principal defendant, László Lovassy, and he wrote widely circulated petitions for justice over the signature of Lovassy's father.[14] The government remained unimpressed, and in March 1837 a Hungarian royal court gave Lovassy ten years in prison, with two other youths receiving far lighter sentences. The government's *agent provocateur* also got ten years but was released immediately. Conditions of his imprisonment being horrible, Lovassy soon contracted scurvy and not much later went insane.

There were other measures. The moderate Hungarian chancellor was replaced by an ultraconservative aristocrat. The leader of the opposition, Baron Wesselényi, was charged with sedition and treason and, after a lengthy trial ending in 1839, was sentenced to three years in prison. As politics had meanwhile taken a new direction, and Wesselényi was going blind, he was called to serve only a very short term. He would never again play a crucial role in Hungarian politics.

In May 1837 Kossuth was arrested at Buda and charged with disloyalty and sedition. The ensuing storm of protest was so furious that the authorities relented to a degree. Hungarian law allowed the arrest of a nobleman only if caught *in flagrante delicto;* otherwise, he was to remain at liberty until his trial. Kossuth was first held in secret confinement, but gradually conditions eased in the Buda barracks that served as his prison. He was allowed to see his mother, to write and receive letters, to smoke, to read the text of his indictment, and to obtain books. It was here in his prison cell that he perfected—from the Bible and from Shakespeare—the magnificent English with which he would dazzle Anglo-Saxon audiences following the revolution.

Kossuth conducted his defense with such skill, attended by such national excitement, that it was two whole years before he was sentenced. His original sentence of a three-year prison term was subsequently raised by the highest Hungarian court to four years. Yet, in May 1840, precisely three years after his arrest, he was set free.

Imprisonment had worked to Kossuth's advantage: he was now a national martyr and hero; he had had time to read; he had proven himself supremely able to resist the stress of isolation, to work under duress, to prepare plans, and to develop trust in himself as well as in his many friends.

Kossuth's release was due to a new twist in government policy. Clearly, Vienna had overreached itself and had alienated many of its Hungarian friends. On the other hand, peaceful development was on the horizon with the emergence of a group of young aristocratic tories who, under the leadership of Count Aurél Dessewffy, proposed to take the wind out of the sails of the liberals by promoting reforms of their own. The reactionary Hungarian chancellor was replaced by a more moderate politician, and the Diet was recalled for June 1839. The political wrangle could begin again. In May 1840, at the same time as Kossuth, the wretched and mad Lovassy was also released from prison amidst general celebration.

Kossuth was thus still in prison when the newly elected Diet met in Pressburg. As usual, there was no agreement on the agenda. The government proposed, among other things, the creation of a credit bank, the launching of a national investment loan of 10 million gulden, and legislation permitting the peasants to buy off their feudal burdens. The opposition wanted to discuss the nation's grievances first, especially the political imprisonments. The clash led to the defeat of most of the proposals brought forward by either side, but again there were some concrete results in a liberal-national direction, as we shall see later.

The opposition was now led by Ferenc Deák, next to Széchenyi and Kossuth the brightest star in the Hungarian political firmament.[15] The three men could not have been more different. Széchenyi was very wealthy, Kossuth very poor, and Deák comfortably well off. Kossuth and Deák belonged to the lesser nobility (Kossuth's family was far older), but a wide social chasm separated the landless Kossuth from Deák, who owned over a thousand acres of good land. Széchenyi was neurotic and passionate; Kossuth calculating and flamboyant; Deák unassuming, patient, quiet, and very clever. Széchenyi worked in fits, Kossuth always, and Deák not much, for he was lazy, pessimistic, and depressive. Still, this nonorator, nonworker, and nonleader succeeded through intelligence, cunning, and a unique instinct for the possible and the practical to become one of Hungary's most important politicians before the revolution, and the country's undisputed leader in the two decades that followed the revolution.

Born in 1803 (one year after Kossuth), Deák came from a Catholic family in western Hungary that had served the Habsburgs well. Yet their reward was far more modest than that of the Széchenyis. Orphaned at an early age, Deák was brought up by an elder brother who ran the family estate, something forever beyond the competence of Ferenc. Trained as a lawyer, he rose quickly in the administration of his home county and was elected to the Diet in 1833. Three years later he became the recognized spokesman of the liberals, in which capacity he endeavored, unlike Wesselényi before him, to satisfy both the king and his own followers. Besides politics Deák's great passion was justice, and he developed excellent plans for the modernization of the judicial process and the penal code. In the growing controversy between Széchenyi and Kossuth, he tended to side with the latter without, however, losing the friendship of the former. It was due mainly to Deák that the political prisoners were released in 1840, and that the Diet passed a series of laws which further weakened the feudal structure. Serfs were allowed to redeem their dues; owners of capital were permitted to set up factories, which was a heavy blow dealt to the guild system; child labor was regulated; and Jews were entitled to engage in industry and trade. But the most significant laws were again in the field of language. All petitions by the Diet and by the counties to royal offices were to be written in Hungarian, a measure that threatened to drive non-Magyar bureaucrats out of the Hungarian offices in the Court; birth, marriage, and death certificates were to be written in Magyar, and no priest or minister was allowed to function unless he spoke the "language of the state." Finally—a major breakthrough—Imperial-Royal regiments originating from Hungary were to correspond with the Hungarian counties in the Magyar language.

Clearly, it was now only a question of time before the whole feudal edifice would be torn down by the liberal nobles, and before the unity of the Monarchy, as well as the coexistence of the many peoples of Hungary, would be threatened by the coercive language laws of the Diet. For the time being, the supranational and antiliberal Vienna establishment tried to cooperate with the Hungarian nobles. In January 1841 Kossuth received a sensational offer from a Pest printer. He was to start a newspaper, the *Pesti Hírlap* (*Pest News*), and fashion it according to his own taste. As the printer has since been proven a police agent, his offer would have been inconceivable without previous clearance in Vienna. It was commonly understood that Metternich himself wished Kossuth to edit a newspaper. Why the chancellor wanted this remains obscure. Perhaps Metternich hoped to make the Hungarian agitator more moderate and more responsible. As it was, the opposite happened. The *Pesti Hírlap* brought Hungary closer to revolution. By 1844, when Kossuth was finally removed from his post, he had turned the *Pesti Hírlap* into a vociferous instrument of his increasingly radical politics. The paper's circulation had surpassed five thousand, an incredible figure in a country where newspaper owners had been happy to sell a few hundred copies.

The Journalist

At the same time as he became editor of *Pesti Hírlap* with the respectable monthly pay of 100 gulden (the sum was to double with the paper's mounting popularity), Kossuth married Teréz Meszlényi. She came from an old and wealthy landowning family but she herself was poor. Having lost her father at an early age, she had devoted her youth to the care of an ailing mother. Eight years younger than Kossuth, she was considered a spinster at the age of thirty and, frankly, looked the part. Reserved, serious, well-read, intelligent, unexciting, and haughty, she was barely acceptable even to the penniless Kossuth family. Their wedding marked another political and social breakthrough, as Kossuth was a Lutheran and Teréz a Catholic. Not only did the law oblige couples of mixed religion to marry in a Catholic church, but the local archbishop had just recently ordered the conversion of the heretic partner before the marriage. Kossuth would not hear of such a concession and appealed to Pest county for protection. The county assembly declared the archbishop's pastoral letter illegal and threatened to try the parish priest who refused to legalize a mixed union. Here was another *cause célèbre* for Kossuth, one which would again end with his triumph. The church still refused the couple its blessing, but on January 9, 1841, in a Pest church following a perfunctory ceremony, a young priest grimly noted in the parish ledger the fact of Kossuth's matrimony. The marriage proved to be lasting and harmonious; Kossuth would always manifest the warmest affection toward his wife. Yet Teréz was not to become popular in Hungary: described as cold, conceited, and overly ambitious, she was seen as her husband's evil genius. The truth about her will never be known; perhaps the public simply assigned to poor Teréz the role of "the bad female influence" customarily assumed by the queens of tragic and unsuccessful monarchs.[16]

Kossuth's *Pesti Hírlap* was dedicated to a series of reform proposals, all interconnected and, if allowed to be put into effect, calculated to change Hungary. The first and perhaps most drastic proposal concerned rural conditions. Almost 90 percent of Hungary's inhabitants derived their livelihood from the soil.[17] Some of these agriculturists were burghers of the free royal towns; others were sandaled noblemen, still others belonged to such privileged communities as the Cumans or the Heyducks, who paid state taxes and performed military service but, not being tied to any master (not even to the noble county), owed no feudal services or dues. However, the vast majority of peasants lived under landowners who could be either individual noblemen or such legal personalities as a town, the church, or the Crown. Unlike Western Europe, where serfdom had all but disappeared by the nineteenth century, in much of Eastern Europe and thus also in Hungary serfdom had become more widespread, more rigorously enforced, and more burdensome to the peasants. In the Middle Ages Hungarian landowners had generally been content with relatively small servile dues, paid mostly in kind. In the early modern period increased dues and new labor obligations were enforced as an answer to the lords' quest for prosperity and their desire to maintain their privileged position. As the nobles shed one obligation after the other, they thrust them on the shoulders of the peasants. Wishing to raise cash, the landowners endeavored to expand their directly owned domain or demesne land at the expense of lands held by the peasants. Dues in kind or even in cash were not enough: now the lord's demesne had to be cultivated in the form of *robot,* the unpaid forced labor of peasants. Noble landowners stubbornly upheld the principle that all land belonged to them alone; peasants only held in usufruct land needed for their livelihood. In exchange for these holdings, they paid dues of all kinds and performed labor service. Dues ranged, in fantastic confusion, from periodic deliveries of such products as butter, eggs, milk, flax, and hemp to the "ninth" collected by the lord on the peasant's yearly crop and on the cattle the peasant raised. Labor service consisted of one or two or even more days spent weekly cultivating the lord's demesne, performing household duties in the lord's manor, and transporting goods over long distances for the lord's benefit. In addition, wood was to be cut and brought to the lord, estate roads and bridges were to be maintained, and other duties performed.

The landowner was not the only superior authority to exact services and dues from the peasant. The village community had its needs, as had the noble county, the church, and the state. County roads, bridges and waterways had to be built and repaired; county taxes had to be paid (the average county spent three-fourths of its income on salaries and only about 5 percent on public works); one-tenth of the peasant's crop, the so-called tithe, went to the bishop or to certain prelates; war taxes and other contributions were voted by the Diet, distributed by the counties, and collected by the landowners on behalf of the state; military service for life, reduced in 1845 to eight years, was the lot of the luckless peasant youngsters whom the village and the landlord had designated for such a catastrophic existence. Finally, the king's soldiers had to be fed, housed, and transported for nominal fees. Having fulfilled all these obligations, and having provided for his family and for next year's sowing, the peasant was still not free to dispose of his produce. Rather, peasant marketing rights were severely restricted. Neither was the peasant free to sell the land he held in usufruct, nor was he allowed to leave his holding to his heirs without the lord's interference.

In the hundred-odd years preceding the final emancipation of the peasants in 1848, the Habsburg government had done a good deal to alleviate the burden of the serfs and to give them security of tenure, chiefly in order to increase their ability to support the state financially and militarily. Maria Theresa's famous "urbarial" ordinances of 1767 regulated the size of serf holdings by geographic location and according to the quality of land. The ordinances also restricted the number of *robot* days owed the lord. Generally those peasants who held an entire servile section (*sessio*) and who were able to perform the *robot* with draft animals owed fifty-two days of labor annually to the lord; those peasants who held a full section but had only their hands to offer worked one hundred and four days on the demesne. Servile holdings that consisted of one-half, one-fourth, or even less of a section owed proportionally less labor. Maria Theresa's urbarium protected the serf against arbitrary jurisdiction by the nobility. It is true that the peasant's immediate judge was still his own master, and that the appellate court was the noble county but, at least in theory, it was possible to go from the noble county to the royal courts. All this was an unheard of, and much resented, governmental interference with the sovereign rights of the landowner. No wonder then that the urbarial ordinances were not everywhere put into effect, least of all in Transylvania, a backward and far-away province.

In 1785 Joseph II legally freed the peasants. The term "serf" (Hungarian: *jobbágy*) was made illegal; peasants were enabled to migrate, to marry, to learn a trade, and to dispose of their movable property without permission from the lord. Peasant holdings were put under the protection of the Crown. Unlike Maria Theresa's very practical ordinances, Joseph's decrees achieved little, aside from bolstering the self-respect of the peasants. Dues and services were not abolished, and while it became easier for individual peasants, especially youngsters, to break out of the village community, the farmer and his family were still tied to the land that they were not allowed to sell. Nor were they free to redeem their dues and services in cash.

In the feudal order, the peasant was chained to the lord by the land he held in usufruct. But the lord was also chained to the peasant whom he could not legally evict, whose holding he could not sell, and to whom he owed justice (often very costly) and such rudimentary services as existed: a pittance for old age, assistance in case of illness or accident, timber to rebuild the peasant's cottage, and relief in case of a natural disaster. If one were to believe the landowners, their obligations would be unbearable, and the services they received almost useless. And truly, the peasant on *robot* worked little and stole much. He secretly grazed his cattle on the lord's demesne: a practice that the lord's shepherds reciprocated in kind. Abuses on communal pastures and woodland were a perpetual source of aggravation for both sides.

Peasants who held an entire section of good-quality land were relatively well off. They fulfilled their labor obligation by sending their own servants to work; their produce often competed on the market with that of the lord. But peasants holding an entire servile lot formed only a small minority, and the number of those who had to make a living on fractional sections was constantly increasing. Also, peasant holdings were usually widely dispersed on the lord's estate, or several estates, and countless working hours were wasted in traveling from one narrow strip to another. Finally, an ever-increasing number of peasants held no land at all. These cotters or cottagers (Hungarian: *zsellérek*) and subcottagers (peasants who did not even have a hut) worked as farmhands for rich peasants and landowners, or as so-called contractual peasants rented pieces of land on the lord's demesne, where their security of tenure was nil.

Servile land was not readily expandable, yet the population increased rapidly. Less than one-third of the country's arable land was inscribed in the urbarial registers, meaning that the remaining two-thirds formed part of the lords' demesnes. It is true, however, that relatively little of the lords' demesnes was actually under cultivation at mid-century. In 1847 there were about 620,000 peasant families with land, while 920,000 families were registered as landless. Even though only a fraction of the latter were really without land, these holdings were inadequate or insecure. The 920,000 families formed a rural proletariat that would receive little or no help from the reformers of 1848, and that would grow in size until 1945.

As land could not be mortgaged, credit at usurious rates was available only to the rich, who could raise cash on their movable property. The landowners longed to hire labor but, with the exception of the magnates, they could not afford the cost. Thus with a vast labor reserve available, much good land was left untilled or was only badly tilled.

Because of the bad roads, indifferently maintained by forced labor, there was ruinous glut of agricultural products in some regions and starvation in others. Productivity was low even by contemporary standards, but because of the general lack of capital, machinery and technological know-how it was impossible to increase productivity, except on the large estates of enterprising aristocrats. Progress on these estates was the first sign of an agricultural revolution that was drastically to transform the Hungarian economy in the second half of the nineteenth century.

All impartial observers agreed that lord and peasant should be liberated from one another, and that land and labor ought to be made marketable commodities, but no one quite knew how to achieve this without ruining both landowners and peasants, and without risking peasant upheavals. Kossuth in *Pesti Hírlap* was among the few who faced the question with little fear. He advocated the introduction of what would be called today agricultural capitalism, which, he was confident, could be achieved peacefully—provided that it took place under the leadership of the lesser nobility, within the framework of the ancient counties and in a new, self-governing Hungary. Once the Hungarians were masters in their own house, Kossuth predicted, domestic reconciliation and general prosperity would follow inevitably.

Kossuth demanded in *Pesti Hírlap* that the landowners be obliged to emancipate those peasants who wished to be independent, at a compensatory price set by the state and with the state's financial assistance. This was a farreaching program, although the constitutional government of March 1848 would go farther. Kossuth also demanded that an end be put to the nobles' immunity from taxation—another radical program in Hungary but not in the rest of the Habsburg monarchy, where universal, although unequal and unfair, taxation had long been introduced.

The *Pesti Hírlap* fought obscurantism and requested humanitarian improvements. Bastinadoes (beatings), then most popular in the judiciary system and in the family, were condemned, as were prison conditions. An institute for the blind was clamored for, as were orphanages and a children's hospital. Again, as usual, Kossuth operated with the help of provincial correspondents. He had a few able editorial assistants, but he wrote almost all the editorials (the very genre was an innovation in Hungary).[18] His purpose was to awaken the public and to prepare a comprehensive opposition program for the next meeting of the Diet. Today his style would strike us as pompous and sentimental; in contemporary eyes it was simplicity itself, free of baroque tirades and of overly rich adjectives.

How could Kossuth allow himself the luxury of an almost free press? Perhaps the answer lies in the temporary though ill-planned leniency of Metternich and in the sympathy of the censors, who, as teachers and ecclesiastics, were not immune to the liberal and nationalist sentiments sweeping the educated public. Only Széchenyi understood the true implications of Kossuth's agitation. Disturbed by what he perceived as demagogic journalism, convinced that he, Széchenyi the reformer, had been responsible for the rise of Kossuth and jealous of his rival's popularity, Széchenyi attacked Kossuth mercilessly in *The People of the Orient* (*Kelet népe*), a book printed in June 1841. Rejecting anarchism, fanaticism, the *Zeitgeist,* and all blueprints for the future, Széchenyi warned that Hungary was not England or the United States, and that Hungarian democracy and nationalism as heralded by Kossuth would lead to a class war and a race war. Széchenyi's sensational declaration led to the birth of a vast polemical literature that kept Hungarian public opinion on edge for several years. Kossuth's *Reply* (*Felelet*), a book printed in September 1841, cleverly mixed an almost servile admiration for Széchenyi the statesman with a relentless condemnation of Széchenyi the politician and tactician. Széchenyi's battle was hopeless from the start: his program of leniency, moderation, and patience cost him sympathizers, except for the reluctant support of the "cautiously progressive" aristocrats. On the other hand, Kossuth's popularity was mounting. Clearly, a politician's fame now rested on the extent of his nationalist and reformist ardor.

Hungarian nationalism was almost as old as the state itself. Ancient Hungarian chronicles prove that the Magyars had always thought of themselves as superior to others. "Important components of Magyar self-consciousness can be traced back to the medieval Hungarian state," writes George Barany, an American-Hungarian historian specializing in Hungarian nationalism.[19] Barany points out that as far back as the fourteenth century, Hungarians considered themselves the "Bastion of Christianity" (as did, of course, the Germans, the Serbs, the Croats, the Poles, the Russians, the Bulgarians, the Romanians, the Greeks, the Portuguese, and the Castilians). It is true that preromantic and preliberal Hungarian nationalism was caste bound: it was the privilege of the "political nation." But it is also true that extraordinary political events often transcended the boundaries of class interest. In the fifteenth-century struggle against the Turks, in the sixteenth-century rise of Protestantism, and in the late seventeenth and early eighteenth-century uprisings against Habsburg absolutism, peasants and nobles were temporarily united in the pursuit of common national goals. The decline of patriotism among the aristocrats, but not among the lesser nobility or the peasants, set in during the eighteenth century as the result of Habsburg military and political triumphs and of the Enlightenment. As the titled nobility fell increasingly under German and French cultural influences, it all but forgot the Hungarian language, which it left to women, children, and servants. The lesser nobility would not embrace the foreign cultures (to which they had only limited access in any case), but in all official transactions, and even in personal correspondence, they used Latin in preference to Hungarian.

Paradoxically, the hegemony of Latin as the official language dated from the eighteenth century. During the religious struggles of the sixteenth and seventeenth centuries, both Prostentants and Catholics had used a vigorous and flamboyant Hungarian. It was the Counter-Reformation, and especially the Jesuits, who had put Latin in the place of Hungarian. This antique language made the "political nation" tolerant toward the linguistic minorities (about 10 percent of Hungary's nobles considered themselves Slavs and another 5 percent Germans and Romanians), but it also made modernization all but impossible. The linguistic crisis would have come much later had Joseph II not opened the Pandora's box of nationalism with his language ordinance of 1784, which stipulated the introduction of German as the official language in all parts of the Monarchy. Authorities in Hungary, whether central or municipal, were given one year to adopt German as their language of communication; lay and clerical courts were given three years to accomplish the same goal. Knowledge of German was made a prerequisite for admission to public service, to higher schools, and even to membership in the Diet.[20]

There is no doubt that Joseph II was driven by purely rationalist and enlightened, not German nationalist considerations. As the historian Gyula Szekfű has pointed out, Joseph was no different from the French *philosophes* who believed (as reflected in the entries of Diderot and D'Alembert in the *Grande encyclopédie* under the headings *"nation," "état," "langue"*) that political and linguistic boundaries had to coincide if a state was to flourish; that language would and must adjust to the requirements of state interest; and that the use of "dialects" was justified only where the nation was divided into many states, as was the case in Germany.[21] However, in those states where there was a central administration (the writers of the *Grande encyclopédie* insisted), language had to be centralized and unified. Joseph and his advisers, nay even the much less dogmatic Maria Theresa and her advisers, were unable to differentiate between state and nation. For them, patriotism was identical with love of the state.

Up to the 1780s nationalism was so little known in the Courts of Europe that Frederick the Great never once mentioned the nationalities of the Habsburg Monarchy in his voluminous writings. Maria Theresa's enlightened councilors saw no difference between France and the Habsburg Empire, and they rejected as foolish the suggestion of the Hungarian Chancellery that a separate Hungarian academy of sciences be established. An all-Austrian academy in Vienna was all the Hungarians needed.

If German had become the official language, foreign bureaucrats would have taken control of the country: Joseph's linguistic ordinances therefore threatened the autonomy of Hungary and the hegemony of the nobles. The ensuing national political resistance ruined most of Joseph's enlightened reforms. Hungarian national costumes and Hungarian speech had suddenly become fashionable, and the Hungarian intellectuals who, like Joseph's own councilors, were also keeping their eyes on Paris, began to apply the tenets of the *philosophes* to the Hungarian situation. They too found centralization and unification necessary, not in a pan-Austrian but in a pan-Hungarian framework.

Hungarian nationalist enthusiasm was short lived, however. Under the impact of the French Revolution, mainly out of fear of Jacobin agitation, the nobles made their peace first with Leopold II in 1791, and then with his successor, Francis I. German was dropped as the official language, and Hungary returned to the use of Latin. Only very gradually, and mostly after 1825, did Hungarian attention turn again to Magyar culture; this time, however, not under the influence of the *philosophes* but under that of the German romantic writers.

Modern nationalism in Hungary began, as everywhere else in Central and Eastern Europe, in the form of a cultural and linguistic revival, soon to be turned into a political and social reform movement. Almost from the beginning, the positive elements of hope and faith in progress were juxtaposed with elements of fear and hopelessness. The nation on the rise was also a nation threatened by extinction. Expanding and dynamic Hungary was seen as menaced by German and Slavic expansion. Fear became the dominant motive of Hungarian nationalism: a fear powerfully nourished by the German writer, Johann Gottfried Herder. Instead of identifying nation and language with the state, Herder investigated the spiritual roots of nationality. He saw language as the repository of a people's tradition, culture, history, religion, wisdom, heart, and soul. Turning to Central Europe, Herder predicted that the Magyar language, and hence the Magyar people, would soon disappear in the sea of Slavic peoples. His prophecies caused the Magyar leaders to advocate the spreading by law of Magyar culture. These leaders were neither more nor less naive than Joseph II had been when they believed that by teaching Hungarian in the schools, they would achieve the universal acceptance of Magyar as the state language. After all, they argued, Hungarians had founded the state; they had consistently proved themselves the leaders in the Carpathian Basin, and they possessed the superior warlike qualities that alone entitled a nation to lead others.

Worried Hungarian politicians witnessed the parallel and often more dynamic rise of nationalism around them. Slavic nationalism seemed to exude far more optimism. As Czech, Slovak, Croatian, and Serbian authors never ceased to emphasize: theirs was a vast movement bound to unify millions upon millions of people now artificially divided by political boundaries and anachronistic "dialects." A Pan-Slav empire appeared to the Slavs—and to the Hungarians—a distinct possibility. The warning of the German writer Ernst Moritz Arndt resounded in Hungarian ears: For a nation-state to exist, it must have a sea coast, and its inhabitants must speak the same language. Kossuth made Arndt's program his own.

Kossuth's nationalism was neither original nor was it extraordinary. The radicals to his left were more chauvinistic, just as the conservatives to his right were more tolerant toward the nationalities. Kossuth was convinced that a stagnant, stationary nationality would be doomed. The nation, he taught, must expand and develop. He therefore advocated unification with Transylvania and the introduction in Hungary of Hungarian as the official language. With regard to Transylvania, it was not the presence of a Romanian majority that worried him; he did not even mention the Romanians in the context of unification. It was the backwardness of Transylvania's political and social institutions which threatened progress in Hungary unless remedied prior to unification. As for the state language, it required urgent action before it was too late.

In 1842 Kossuth wrote in *Pesti Hírlap:*

In Hungary, Magyar must become the language of public administration, whether civil or ecclesiastic, of the legislative and the executive, of the government, of justice, of public security, of the police, of direct and indirect taxation and of the economy.[22]

"To accept less," he stated, "would be cowardice; to insist on more would be tyranny; both would mean suicide on our part."[23]

Kossuth was perfectly willing to grant the use of minority languages in private life, and he spoke up repeatedly against forceful assimilation. He saw the Slavs, Romanians, and Germans in Hungary as comparable to the Bretons in France, the Welsh and Irish in the United Kingdom, and the Kashub in Prussia. Let these people cultivate their quaint customs and language, as long as they recognize that there is only one nation under the Holy Crown: the Magyar.[24]

Kossuth was particularly vehement on the Slovak question. Originating in a Slovak region, and reacting as a functionary of the militantly assimilationist Lutheran church, Kossuth rejected all Slovak claims to autonomous cultural development. His argument was that the Slovaks had had no history of their own and that they had never formed a distinguishable territorial unit. His views on the other nationalities were somewhat more tolerant. The Germans and Romanians he saw as potential allies against the Slavs; the Jews, who were showing signs of voluntary Magyar assimilation, he was ready to receive with open arms.

Only in the case of one nation was Kossuth (like most other Hungarians) willing to make an exception. Croatia had been for many centuries a *corpus separatum* under the Crown of Saint Stephen: the Croats had had their own history, nobility, and administration. They had always been treated by the Hungarians as a privileged and somewhat separate entity. Now the Croats, under the impact of a South Slav or Illyrian movement born under Napoleonic occupation, were clamoring for the same rights that Hungary wished to obtain from Vienna. Following an Illyrian victory in Zagreb county elections in 1842, Kossuth proposed, for the first but not for the last time, the complete separation of Croatia from Hungary. It was a proposition that not even Széchenyi was willing to consider. On the other hand, Kossuth rejected as ridiculous the Croatian demand that the Hungarian Diet continue to debate in Latin. If Croatia was to stay as an associated part of Hungary, the Croats had to make adjustments to the new realities. Kossuth knew that while Kolowrat encouraged Illyrian separatism, Metternich and Archduke-Palatine Joseph were opposed to it, but he was now too far gone in his anti-Vienna posture to accept Metternich as an ally. And yet, in 1843, the Vienna court forbade the Croats to use the term ''Illyrian'' and dissolved the Illyrian party.

When even Rotteck's and Welcker's famous liberal *Staatslexikon* predicted the Slavic conquest of Hungary, Kossuth decided that a final clash with Slavdom was inevitable. He foresaw the rise of a majestic alliance of the German nation (not of course of the German princes), France, England, Hungary, and perhaps Poland against Russia and the other Slavic nations. One of the reasons underlying his campaign for the immediate construction of a railroad line connecting the Hungarian Adriatic port Fiume with the heart of the country was that Kossuth hoped to see Western troops make use one day of that line in a combined anti–Pan-Slav campaign. Only in such a way, Kossuth argued, could Hungary recover her historic mission as the bastion of Western civilization.

The Diet of 1843 was preceded by wild agitation. The government and the conservatives belabored the sandaled nobles, who had nothing to gain and everything to lose from the equality heralded by the opposition. These poor nobles resorted to preelection violence in several counties: many reform candidates were chased away or defeated while others, like Deák, withdrew from the battle. Still, there was a strong reformist-oppositionary camp in the Diet which, as usual, forced through a series of progressive resolutions but failed to provide for their implementation. Actually, the main problem was not the equality of taxation or the peasant question, but customs and tariffs. The opposition, egged on by the *Pesti Hírlap,* reversed its previous position on trade, and instead of asking for the abolition of the customs barrier separating Hungary from the rest of the Monarchy, now demanded the strengthening of the customs barrier. However, this was to be no longer under Austrian but under Hungarian control. Protective tariffs had become Kossuth's latest campaign issue. The customs problem was not resolved by the Diet, and it was to become a bone of contention between government and opposition in the ensuing years. The Diet made progress in the question of religion by extending the rights of Protestants, and it finally and definitely established Magyar as the official language of Hungary. [25]

When the Diet closed in the fall of 1844, Kossuth was no longer in a position to guide the opposition from the pages of the *Pesti Hírlap.* His tariff agitation and his brazen calls for the boycott of Austrian goods in Hungary caused Metternich to give up experimenting with Kossuth. Through his Hungarian councilors, the Austrian chancellor ordered the Pest printer to get rid of Kossuth. Incident after incident was provoked until Kossuth resigned in a rage, but first he brought his complaint to Vienna, where he was received by Metternich. According to Kossuth's old-age reminiscences and the chancellor's own notes, Metternich made a last attempt to buy Kossuth, an offer turned down with indignation. In May 1844 Kossuth was again without a job and without money. Never discouraged, he now launched himself on a new career as founder and head of a national industrial and trade association.

For a National and Nationalist Economy

When still the editor of *Pesti Hírlap,* Kossuth had begun founding industrial and trade associations, and after his ouster from *Pesti Hírlap* in 1844, it was from the dais of association banquets and in a small trade journal that he elaborated upon his political and economic theories. His thoughts on the economy were not original; nor did he show much consistency in switching almost overnight from the advocacy of free trade to that of economic autarky and defensive tariff barriers; but at least his customary feverish dedication created unheard-of interest in the *embourgeoisement* of Hungary. His schemes were grandiose and impractical, mirroring the incurable optimism, chauvinistic conceit, and economic ignorance of the lesser nobility. Yet the amateurish Kossuth succeeded where the far more erudite and pragmatic Széchenyi had failed: Kossuth made the industrial revolution a popular subject, and he gathered adherents for his schemes among both nobles and commoners. The leagues he formed were the first in Hungary where members of various estates worked together for a common national goal. Thus in a very practical sense Kossuth promoted egalitarianism.

As has been indicated earlier, Hungary's economy was most backward by contemporary Western standards, although certainly no more so than the economies of the neighboring Polish or Balkan lands. Even worse, the Hungarian economy had a poor reputation abroad or, rather, it had no reputation at all. When Kossuth sent some friends to London to inspect the new machines or to Paris to invite French entrepreneurs to Hungary, the results were disheartening. As one of these agents wrote to Kossuth: "In the opinion of the French we are on the same level with the Kalmuks."[26]

The Napoleonic wars had brought a measure of prosperity to agriculture. When food prices were high during the Continental System, the big landowners enlarged their patrimony, breaking up virgin lands, enclosing commons, hiring wage labor, and introducing (whenever they knew how) more intensive methods of cultivation. In the deflationary and depressed period that followed upon the wars, a few large estates continued to flourish; others sank deep into debt. With the decline of grain prices, many a landowner could no longer satisfy his creditors, who were either wealthy individuals or such institutions as a monastery, a convent, or a religious trust fund. Some magnates had debts of several million gulden, yet not even the interest on the debts could be collected from estates that were of course entailed. The resulting scandal ruined the credit of even the richest landowners, that of Széchenyi among them.[27]

When low-grade Hungarian grain could no longer compete with Russian and North American imports on the reduced European market, big landowners turned to raising sheep for the wool industry. This brought new wealth to some aristocrats in the 1820s and 1830s, but the enclosed pastures deprived thousands of peasants of their livelihood; and when the coarse Hungarian wool failed in the competition against imports from overseas, many aristocrats were ruined. Statistical data, no matter how incomplete, indicate the extent of the trouble; but they also show that, in the long run, Hungarian agricultural production rose nevertheless. In 1818 Hungary exported over 100,000 tons of wheat and more than 10,000 tons of wool. By 1827 wheat export fell well below the 100,000-ton mark, but wool export rose to 19,000 tons. By 1845 wheat export approached 250,000 tons, the export of wool 25,000 tons. Statistics on the total volume of agricultural produce do not exist; but it has been estimated that in the 1830s Hungary exported between 5 and 10 percent of all cereals, and about 80 percent of the raw wool produced in the country.[28]

The *bene possessionati* (the wealthiest segment of the lesser nobility) generally did better than the titled nobility, for these owners of a few thousand acres managed their own property, drew considerable salary—modestly called ''honorarium''—from the counties they administered; and rather than producing for shifting foreign markets, the *bene possessionati* tended to produce for the needs of the growing Hungarian cities.

Even the petty nobles had been affected by the prosperity of the Napoleonic years. For the first time in history, small landowners dressed fashionably, bought furniture instead of ordering it from their own serfs, and sent their sons to school. Later, however, many petty nobles were unable to resist the effect of deflation and sank back into the near-peasant life that had been their pattern since time immemorial.

The servile condition—that is, the peasants' way of life—varied so greatly as to defy generalization. Western travelogues, very fashionable at that time, devoted a good deal of attention to peasant life in Hungary, but their portraits ranged from one of near-starvation to relative wealth and satisfaction. The rich peasants (holders of full ''sections'') were often depicted as wallowing in the accumulated flour and lard that these peasants could not, or would not, bring to market; cotters and day laborers were described as subsisting on coarse rye bread or, when that ran short, on tree bark or on roots found in the forest. The peasantry of the mountains, mostly Slovaks, Ruthenes, and Romanians, were seen as particularly brutish and depressed. Filthy, drunken, and often ill, these mountaineers survived in hovels or in holes dug in the ground. Paradoxically, the Slovaks were alternately described as gay, contented, and well-fed or as rebellious and ground down by misery. The secrets of good house-keeping and of a healthy diet were closed to all but the wealthiest peasants and to the German colonists, who were uniformly described as clean, healthy, and industrious.[29]

One thing is certain: in the early nineteenth century the land-owners did their best to increase the peasants' servile burdens and to acquire more demesne land. And the state's appetite for taxes showed no decline. And while it is impossible to prove that the peasantry's condition as a whole deteriorated in this period, it is clear that the peasant was less and less in sympathy with the demands of the lord, with the system of patrimonial jurisdiction, and with his own lack of landownership. Revolts were rare, but refusal to perform labor service (*robot*) was frequent; and so was general sloth and thievery.

The solution to all problems lay in the modernization of agricul-ture, in industrialization and urbanization. In all these areas remark-able progress was being made: progress, however, that was still too slow in the eyes of the patriots.

At the beginning of the nineteenth century, the total population of the fifty-odd free royal towns amounted to about 400,000, a bit over 5 percent of the kingdom's population. But then migration to the towns began in earnest; and by 1840 Pest, the country's most indus-trialized city, had 64,000 inhabitants, a figure which was to increase to over 100,000 by 1848.

Around 1800 the bulk of the urban population consisted of day laborers, domestics, and small artisans. Later the factory worker made his appearance and so did the skilled journeyman employed in large manufactories. In 1828 there were only 63,000 skilled workers in the country; by 1848 they numbered 150,000. Well before that year the first steam-powered paper mills, flour mills, leather tan-neries, sugar refineries, and factories producing machine tools, and silk and other textiles appeared in Hungary. Still, out of the aggregate number of capitalist enterprises in the Habsburg empire, only 10 per-cent were in Hungary, and there were fifteen times as many steam engines in Austria as in Hungary. By the 1830s Hungary's annual pig- and cast-iron production reached 30,000 metric tons, which was perhaps one-sixth of the Austrian production. Hungary had to import a considerable amount of iron to satisfy her modest needs. Now, fi-nally, efforts were made to improve the roads; the first canals were constructed and the arrival of the steamship heralded a new age in river transport. Well before 1848, thirty-two steamships plied the Hungarian section of the Danube.

The financing of the industry came mostly from the West, especially from the Rothschilds, but considerable capital was also raised by Hungarian aristocrats. The entrepreneurs, engineers, and skilled workers were mostly Germans; trade was increasingly taken over by Jews from the formerly dominant Greek, Serbian, and Armenian merchants.

Back in 1785 Hungary's Jews had numbered 75,000, less than 1 percent of the total population. As a result of a relatively high birth rate, a rapidly declining death rate, and immigration from both West and East, the number of Jews increased by 1848 to 250,000, thus forming about 2 percent of the population. By 1848 there were far more Jews in Hungary than in Bohemia and Moravia, the traditional homes of the Habsburg Monarchy's Jewry.

Excluded from most professions and from many urban areas, the Jews thrived nevertheless. They rented the taverns of the large estates; they dealt in grain and wool; they settled without permission in the cities, there to practice illegally the professions formally protected by the Christian guilds. The overwhelmingly German-speaking burghers fought this immigration tooth and nail, but nationalist-liberal public opinion and the local administrative machinery sided with the Jews. Besides, Jewish skills were badly needed. By 1848 there were 1,500 Jewish artisans in Pest, many of them practicing without authorization.[30]

The credit law of 1840 increased the amount of capital available to entrepreneurs. While before that year there had not been a single operating savings bank in Hungary, by 1848 there were thirty-five. The year 1841 saw the creation of the Pest Hungarian Trade Bank, to be followed by the founding of other large financial institutions. In 1843/44 trade bank deposits had amounted to only 670,000 gulden; by 1847/48 deposits totaled almost 5 million. The president of the Trade Bank was a Hungarian aristocrat; its general manager was the converted Jew Móric Ullman, a division of labor that foreshadowed a subsequent general practice. Ullman had been ennobled by the king in 1828 and he had bought an estate—another practice that was to become common among successful businessmen. The new Hungarian bourgeoisie tended to copy slavishly the lifestyles and the ideals of the landed nobility.

The railroad reached the country at the end of the 1830s, after the Vienna Rothschilds had obtained the right to build a short, horse-drawn railroad line in western Hungary. By 1848 Rothschild and Sina money (another great Vienna banking firm) had helped build the first steam-powered railroads. In January 1849 Kossuth and his fleeing fellow-revolutionaries made good use of the 60-mile-long railroad extending from Pest eastward into central Hungary.

The impetus to modernization had come to Hungary from Western capitalists and from the patient labor of Count Széchenyi; the popularization of industrial growth was almost entirely the result of Kossuth's often blundering activities.

Kossuth's initial enterprise, a Hungarian trade association, had as its first president a young Fiume sea merchant, Pál Szabó, who soon boasted of having established firm and fruitful relations with the "greatest houses in the world from Cadiz to St. Petersburg, from Odessa to Liverpool, and from New York to Rio de Janeiro." This was a lie, as it later turned out; but Kossuth unthinkingly celebrated the association's "achievements" as firm proof of Hungary's indomitable energy and business acumen.

Kossuth's second enterprise, a Trade Defense League, was both more ambitious and potentially far more dangerous to the unity of the Empire.[31] Its creation was due to the Vienna government's attempt to abolish the customs barrier separating Austria from Hungary. Kossuth's was to be a truly national organization "with one million, or at least with five hundred thousand members," and with a basic capital of 150,000 gulden to be contributed by the members.

The Trade Defense League was solemnly launched in October 1844, in the meeting hall of the Lower House of the Diet. The league's president, Count Kázmér Batthyány, and its vice-president, Count László Teleki, both progressive opposition politicians, belonged to Hungary's first families. During the War of Independence they would become Kossuth's close associates. The manager of the league was Kossuth himself, endowed with the decent annual wage of 1,000 gulden. The board of directors included all the great names in the liberal camp but not Széchenyi's. With the founding of the league, Kossuth had definitely swung from the advocacy of free trade to that of economic autarky. His mentor in the subject was the popular German economist Friedrich List, who had recently launched a campaign of economic protectionism in the German states against the invasion of British goods. List's arguments had their merits, and it is understandable why the Germans, most of them recently united in a *Zollverein,* wished to protect themselves against British competition. But Kossuth had not even attempted to analyze Hungary's economic potentials before he launched the slogan: "Buy Hungarian!" As it soon became painfully clear, the infant Hungarian economy could not possibly grow without Western (especially Austrian) assistance. Had Kossuth succeeded in his protectionist campaign, he would have ruined the nascent Hungarian economy. For a while upper-class women paraded in stylized Hungarian peasant garments, and aristocrats appeared disguised as shepherds or cowboys; but to "buy Hungarian" meant more or less to buy nothing, which the fashion-hungry public was not willing to endure for long. Even the lapel buttons exhorting Hungarian economic self-sufficiency were manufactured in Vienna.

On a visit to Hungary, Friedrich List found Kossuth's schemes "sanguine, overconfident and damaging," a criticism which did not deter the Magyar politician from launching a third enterprise called Association for the Creation of Industry. In this new endeavor Kossuth's main goal was to create the railroad connecting Buda-Pest with Hungary's Adriatic coast, but the necessary 18 million gulden were nowhere to be found. "Unto the sea, Magyar!" Kossuth thundered; yet the only Magyar to take to the sea was Pál Szabó, who in October 1846 sailed from Fiume to France, leaving behind a deficit of 150,000 gulden. The Trade Association and the Trade Defense League collapsed, and Kossuth himself resigned his directorship—not before seeing his minuscule savings melt away in an attempt to satisfy some of the shareholders. Undaunted and indomitable, Kossuth now returned to pure politics, an endeavor in which he was to become more successful than ever. One of the most popular leaders in the liberal camp, in 1846 he began a new political career.

Head of the Opposition

By 1846 Metternich had renewed his counterattack in Hungary. Following the failure of his policies of repression and of leniency, the chancellor now experimented with methods that, if carried to completion, would have amounted to a revolution from above. Metternich knew well what was wrong with Hungary: an increasingly aggressive liberal opposition; the resistance of the counties that made a mockery of royal legislation; oppressed peasants and national minorities who were less and less willing to bear the oppression. Here was an opportunity for forceful action! At Metternich's instigation, the brilliant Count Emil Dessewffy launched a Conservative Party in November 1846. Now, finally, there were a number of young, rich, and educated aristocrats ready to save Hungary for the Throne and for themselves. The Conservatives' social and economic program hardly lagged behind Kossuth's. And, unlike Kossuth, they were willing to take notice of the existence of national minorities. No wonder that Széchenyi joined the party! Founding a political movement in such a traditionalist place as the Habsburg Monarchy created a dangerous precedent, but, at least for once, the government was ahead of the opposition. And there was an even more significant development: Széchenyi and a number of other independent politicians decided to enter the internal administration of Hungary, thus creating the country's first unofficial cabinet.

That was not all. Ever since 1845 the government had experimented with the system of "administrators" aimed at recapturing the recalcitrant counties. These functionaries were meant to replace or to assist the many lord-lieutenants who had proved unable or unwilling to represent Vienna's interests. The administrators were paid the royal sum of 6,000 gulden yearly and, even though the opposition howled at this violation of the constitution, the undertaking brought results. Local resistance was broken by cajolery and bribes or, if necessary, by the force of arms. The administrators speeded up the handling of affairs and introduced many useful reforms. In Vienna itself direct power over Hungary was handed over to the vice-chancellor of the Hungarian chancellery, Count György Apponyi, a ruthless and talented politician. In November 1847 Apponyi was appointed chief chancellor of Hungary. To frighten the Hungarians, Apponyi openly flirted with the Croatian nationalists. At the same time he reinforced the police intelligence service in Hungary, the reports of which showed that a showdown with the opposition had become inevitable.

The question was whether Metternich would dare discard the constitution and, in so doing, win the dispossessed masses over to the Austrian cause. That the masses were not necessarily behind the liberal nobility was shown by the Galician events of February 1846. In that month a violent national revolt had been planned in all parts of partitioned Poland. The risings in Prussian and Russian Poland came to nothing, but in the Free Republic of Cracow the revolutionaries did actually take over and had to be crushed by Russian, Prussian, and Austrian troops. The result was the annexation of Cracow by Austria. In a vastly surprising development, the Galician uprising was nipped in the bud, not by the Habsburg army, but by the serfs. The Polish revolutionary nobles had promised sweeping reforms to the serfs and had incited the peasants to kill the Austrian officials. Instead, the Polish and Ukrainian peasants massacred over a thousand noblemen. Contemporary—and later—Polish and Hungarian accusations to the contrary, the Vienna government or the local Austrian officials had not driven the Galician serfs against their noble masters. Nor is there any evidence to show that grateful Austrian officials paid a premium (allegedly salt, a government monopoly) for the head of every Polish revolutionary. The hatred of the Galician serfs for their lords and their traditional faith in the "good emperor" was enough. The peasant revolt was spontaneous, and it preceded the Polish noble revolution by a few days.

The effect of the Polish disaster on Hungary was immeasurable, especially as the international economic depression had now reached that country and as the Galician peasant revolt itself had spread to northern Hungary. From now on the Hungarian nobility lived in heightened fear of a *Jacquerie*: a threat that Kossuth and his friends unhesitatingly attributed to the machinations of the tsar and Metternich. Clearly, it was now up to either Metternich or the Hungarian opposition to exploit the discontent of the peasants.

In this decisive moment Metternich shied away from action. Instead of emancipating the peasants by royal decree, he instructed King Ferdinand to convoke the Diet for the fall of 1847. There Metternich intended to introduce reform bills that, he hoped, would take the wind out of the sails of the liberals. Thus he threw away his one great opportunity to win the battle against the nobles. During the many months left before the new Diet, the opposition created its own political party with Kossuth as its most influential leader. The Party of United Opposition formulated a program that was at least a few hesitant steps ahead of the Conservatives.

Making a liberal party was no easy matter, for the opposition was deeply divided between "municipalists" and "centralists," and also between moderates and various shades of radicals. The municipalists—in the first place Kossuth—wished to build new Hungary on the time-honored institution of *municipia*, i.e., the noble counties run by the provincial lesser nobility. Such centralists as József Eötvös abominated the oppressive and backward county system and demanded a strong reforming national government, as well as the democratic self-government of the cities and the villages. The centralists were the more progressive, but they were also far too intellectual and bourgeois to win a mass following. In any case, the provincial nobles (soldiers of the opposition movement) could never have been persuaded to destroy their stronghold, the county system. Kossuth knew well the realities of the Hungarian situation: if the lesser nobility was to reform and modernize Hungary, the counties had to be preserved.

It took almost a year's wrangling for the Opposition to arrive at a common platform. The final Declaration launched in June 1847 had been drafted by Kossuth but had been substantially edited—or rather toned down—by Deák, the eternal conciliator. It included all the liberal demands in the area of national sovereignty under the Habsburg dynasty, unification of all the lands under the Crown of Saint Stephen, economic and social progress, and a bill of rights. Only the nationality question was left unmentioned and this for the simple reason that, in the eyes of the liberals, the nationality question did not exist. All subjects of the Hungarian kingdom, without regard to status, race, or religion, were to benefit from the introduction of Magyar as the compulsory language of state education (as opposed to German or Latin), freedom of the press and religion, the extension of suffrage, a cabinet responsible to the National Assembly, equality before the law, general taxation, modernization of the city charters, equal voting rights in the Assembly to the free royal cities, and the abolition of entail and of peasant servitude. Although rather unclear on such crucial issues as whether the abolition of lord-serf relationship should be made compulsory or voluntary, and when and how the lords should be compensated, the Declaration became the basis for the sweeping reform legislation of March 1848. For the time being, the government forbade the printing of the Oppositionary Declaration. Nevertheless, it was printed clandestinely and distributed all over the country.[32]

The major reason for the government's interdiction of the Declaration was that for the first time—but certainly not for the last—in the history of the Monarchy, the Hungarian liberals expressed the desire to see a liberal constitution introduced not only in Hungary but in the other Habsburg lands as well. Magyar insistence that the absolutistically governed Austrian and Bohemian provinces adjust their political system to that of Hungary, as a *conditio sine qua non* for Hungary's remaining in the Empire, was to determine developments in 1848 and again in 1867. In fact, it was to govern the domestic affairs of the Monarchy until its collapse in 1918.

The national election campaign was the fiercest ever, its most sensational event Kossuth's candidacy in Pest county. This penniless and landless journalist, a newcomer in the county, was to represent in the Diet Hungary's most important territorial unit, which often dictated policy to many others. Against this nightmarish development Chancellor Apponyi mobilized all his forces: the secret police, the Conservatives, the Catholic prelates, the big landowners. But, as it soon turned out, the government had neither the machinery nor the money to defeat Kossuth, whose candidacy was supported not only by Pest county's largely progressive middle nobility, but by such liberal aristocrats as Count Lajos Batthyány, later Hungary's prime minister. It was rumored that Batthyány alone had spent 100,000 gulden on his protegé's election. Even if this figure was an exaggeration, Batthyány was not the only nabob to finance the campaign. The liberal aristocrats financed the printing of pamphlets and the organizing of demonstrations; and they wined and dined the poor sandaled nobility, who were often their clients. Of course, Kossuth helped his own cause mightily with his magnificent oratory.

As usual, the election campaign resembled a patriotic orgy. At mass banquets and parades the Kossuth supporters (aristocrats, poets, and journalists) appeared dressed up as swineherds, cowboys, or shepherds. Noble ladies wore diamonds on their peasant costumes. While many a landowner abominated the parvenu Kossuth, others were dedicated Kossuthists, as were a large part of the Catholic lower clergy as well as almost all the Protestant and Orthodox clergy (Pest county had a substantial Greek and Serbian merchant population). The results were decided by the sandaled nobles, whose votes had to be bought, and by the *honoratiores,* who were allowed to vote in Pest county. For the first time in Hungarian history, nonnoble clerks, notaries, ministers, elementary school teachers, and even some barbers participated in the election process. Kossuth's egalitarian political efforts in the national trade associations had now paid off: his party was supported by the new middle class in Budapest and other cities.

Hungarian elections were held openly, as was then the custom everywhere. There were only a few polling stations and the voters always went there in closed ranks, wearing the insignia of their favorite candidate. On October 18, 1847, the Kossuth faction marched to the polls sporting red, white, and green feathers—Hungary's new national colors—on their caps. Supporters of his conservative opponent wore white feathers. In the city of Pest the liberal charade was led by Batthyány and other magnates, all dressed in peasant garb but riding magnificent mounts. The results were predictable: Kossuth's ballot boxes contained 2,948 pellets, those of his opponent 1,314. The total number of votes was considered phenomenal, yet only a minority of those legally entitled to vote had cast their ballots. In Pest county with its 600,000 inhabitants, there were 14,000 adult male nobles, all entitled to vote.

Because of the participation of the commoner *honoratiores,* Kossuth's election was constitutionally doubtful. Yet no power on earth, short of a military dictatorship, could now prevent his going to the Diet.[33] Metternich had failed.

The government did not give up the fight, nor had the liberals been successful everywhere. Deák had been elected but, out of indolence, he refused to serve. He appeared at the Diet only in March 1848. Eötvös and a number of other leading liberals had been defeated. But the increasingly anxious Széchenyi had been himself elected though not without difficulty, and thus Kossuth's greatest antagonist now moved from the Upper House into the crucial Lower House. According to a secret police report sent to Vienna at that time, deputies of twenty-one counties at the Diet were considered absolutely loyal to the Crown, those of eight counties could be won over, seven were doubtful, and the deputies of fourteen counties were hopelessly oppositionary.[34]

Kossuth's fame was overwhelming. In the words of an exasperated conservative official from Pest county: "Kossuth is an agitator and not a peaceable and quiet character as had been recommended by His Gracious Majesty in his letter of convoking [the Diet]. He is of the kind who alone will cause more trouble than the rest of the Diet combined."[35]

On November 11, 1847, King Ferdinand opened the Diet in

Pressburg with a few painfully learned Hungarian words. A friendly gesture to the Magyar patriots, this was an insult to the Croatian deputies, who still insisted on their right to use Latin.

The king's legislative proposals proved to be massive and nearly revolutionary. They included almost all the Opposition's demands with an additional proposal that the customs barrier between Austria and Hungary be lifted. The progressive character of the governmental program swayed many a hesitant deputy, which was all the more surprising as the galleries—filled with hundreds of wildly cheering and booing students and young barristers—made it almost impossible for a deputy to take the government's side. Kossuth argued exasperatedly for the rejection of the royal agenda. But only because it was traditional did the deputies finally decide that national grievances ought to be discussed first, and only then the government's proposal. Kossuth put the system of county administrators at the head of Hungary's list of grievances. Again, because it was a tradition, the Upper House promptly rejected the Lower House's recommendation that the Diet's reply to the king insist on a reversal of the agenda. Thus many weeks were again wasted in debating the content of the Diet's reply. In the end, at Kossuth's suggestion, the Lower House introduced a surprising innovation: for the first time in history there was to be no Address to the Throne. Without an agenda, diverse issues were taken up in no particular order. Universal taxation was discussed as was the compulsory emancipation of the peasants. Incessantly, Kossuth reminded the deputies that the "nobility could no longer lord it over Hungary; they could, however, assume the nation's leadership."[36] But, as it turned out, the Opposition itself was divided on these issues and the resolutions adopted in principle were worthless. Meanwhile, Chancellor Apponyi, Széchenyi, and the Conservatives worked on the deputies and, in an almost conspiratorial action, won the temporary support of several leaders of the Opposition. On February 5, 1848, when Kossuth insisted that the Diet ask for an immediate end to the system of administrators, he was voted down at the unofficial meeting of the Lower House. The tally was 24 to 23, the decisive vote having been cast by the deputies from Croatia.[37] This was a stunning reversal for Kossuth and a bad omen for the coming confrontation with the Croats, whom Apponyi had been courting for years and whom Kossuth had constantly irritated. It is noteworthy that the liberal leaders who on that occasion sided with the government would form the Peace Party during the War of Independence: a moderate nationalist group that was searching for a compromise with the dynasty and disliked Kossuth.

Kossuth did not give up the fight, and he soon passed to the offensive again. All in all, the struggle had been a draw, with the Lower House being about evenly divided between the two camps. Then international events came to the rescue of Kossuth.

In January 1848 a revolution had broken out in Sicily. Soon most of the peninsula was in turmoil and Austrian troops had to be hastened to Lombardy to defend the integrity of the Monarchy. Everyone knew that the Italian revolt was only a beginning, especially as the international and domestic economic situations were terrible and as the Treasury clearly could not afford a war. The Court was worried; liberals were seething with excitement. A Prussian diplomat wrote from Vienna on February 29:

Every day the Italian mail brings news of constitutions, rebellions and political murders. To see Metternich weak, deaf, reduced to a shadow, senile, is to make one sense that he will not have the strength to brave the storm. I saw the Emperor recently at a Court ball: I would never have believed him in such a terrible condition. The Empress spends all her time with her confessor, but she will not pray away the trouble. Archduchess Sophie cries the whole day. It seems that she is the only one to sense the danger. . . . Bankruptcy is upon us. The thirty million [gulden] sent by the Russians is a drop in the bucket. The fact that no one buys tobacco or plays the lottery has caused a deficit of ten million gulden in the Italian provinces alone. The army in Italy costs three million gulden monthly. . . . Today everyone is talking about the resignation of Louis Philippe. Will this bring peace? Only a war can save Austria and Germany now.[38]

On the same day, Metternich wrote to a Prussian general: "We are looking forward to the most horrible events. . . . The world is being taught a grave lesson."

News of the Paris revolution reached Vienna on February 29. A day later the Pressburg Diet also learned of the event. From that time on changes were to follow upon each other in bewildering succession, with the large cities in the Empire interacting decisively. Reformers and revolutionaries in Vienna, Milan, Prague, Pressburg, and Buda-Pest drove each other ahead in a brief exaltation of national and international solidarity. In the drama the two Hungarian capitals,

Pressburg and Buda-Pest, played a major role, and in the two capitals Kossuth's influence was greater than anyone else's. Because Hungary had her own Diet and administration; because the Hungarian liberals were organized and represented the interests of a large and powerful social class; because Hungary had a tradition of political independence; and because Kossuth was a Hungarian, that country in March 1848 was to influence greatly the future of the dynasty and of the monarchy's peoples.

The rise of Hungary in less than a quarter of a century had been phenomenal. Legally always in an exalted position, after 1815 it had been completely in the shadow of Austria and politically as well as economically almost inconsequential. With the Diet unconvoked, its political life retrenched in the counties, its national tongue unused except in colloquial speech, its agriculture medieval, its trade in crisis, its society old-fashioned and rigid, Hungary could have been accurately described as one of the more backward and less influential provinces of a prestigious and victorious Habsburg Monarchy. Then change came, at first gradually, later rapidly. Starting with the Greek revolution of the early 1820s, which Metternich wanted to suppress but could not, Austria suffered one diplomatic humiliation after another. Nor was the Court more successful in its domestic policy. Meanwhile, the Hungarians forged ahead relentlessly. By the 1840s the Diet was frequently in session, and it was an exciting forum for debate and reform proposals; political parties had been constituted, and they were now combating the central government as well as each other; newspapers poured out social criticism and political programs; the country's internal administrative machinery had become almost entirely Magyar; Hungarian literature was thriving; assimilation into Magyardom was progressing (at least in the cities); the Catholic church and education were becoming Hungarian; the social structure had become less rigid; feudalism was about to die a natural death, and Hungary was getting ready to impose its modernistic ideas on the other provinces of the Monarchy, as well as to wrest a new constitution from the Court. Meanwhile, political and cultural ferment had made its appearance among the Slavic and Romanian inhabitants of Hungary also: in part it was the direct result of the Hungarian ferment. Thus, quite unwittingly, the Magyar nobility had helped the nationalities prepare for their own national rejuvenation.

But Hungary's new-found greatness was built on a shaky foundation. Created not by a rising industrial bourgeoisie but by the land-owning nobility, Hungarian progress lacked solid economic backing. In fact, despite some modest successes in agriculture, in trade, in transportation, and in industry, Hungary's economy was falling behind the western parts of the Monarchy. For the time being, Kossuth and his fellow-reformers could hide the country's economic weakness behind the facade of modernistic slogans and an excellent political organization, but this cover-up could last only as long as neither the Court nor the Austro-German (and Czech) ruling circles were able to adopt similar slogans and political organization. Thus the rise of Hungary was due, at least in part, to Metternich's inactivity and conservatism, and it would face powerful odds shortly after the chancellor's fall. The year 1848 would give the Hungarians virtual independence within the Empire, but it would also teach their opponents to counter Hungarian progressivism with their own progressivist propaganda and political institutions. In the confrontation that developed in 1848–49, Hungary was the inevitable loser.

Széchenyi was right and Kossuth was wrong: Hungary ought not have embarked on its great political adventure without having first developed economic strength and a bourgeois society. On the other hand, once the Empire showed signs of falling apart (as it would in 1848), it is hard to see how the Hungarians could have abstained from trying to secure the greatest advantage from this political turn. Yet, in an understandable reach for independent development, Hungary helped to bring about the great crisis of the Empire.

More than anyone else, Kossuth fostered the crisis. His program was Hungarian sovereignty within the Monarchy, and he worked consistently to achieve this goal. Unlike Széchenyi, his much greater contemporary, Kossuth was never disturbed by self-doubt, partly because he cared little for the opinion of others, partly because of the intensity of his aims. He borrowed ideas liberally, but he set out his own program. His determination was unique and so was his pragmatism, at least with regard to his country's immediate problems. His vision of the future and his understanding of the European situation were hazy. This combination of the realistic and the utopian endowed him with the qualities of a perfect leader in an epoch when the Hungarian nation—and not only the Hungarian nation—strove simultaneously for practical reform and for an ideal state of affairs.

2 / Reform Triumphant: March–April 1848

The First Hungarian Journées

FOLLOWING HIS NEAR-DEFEAT in parliament in February and his sudden resurgence in March, Kossuth led Hungary's spring drive for constitutional reform. Exploiting the revolutionary events in Paris, Italy, Berlin, and Vienna but acting without violence and with only rare illegality, Hungary achieved in five weeks what it had been unable to accomplish in all the previous decades: royal consent to its long-claimed independence, to its right to unite with Transylvania and the Military Border, and to its revolutionary economic and social legislation. But the new constitution, while it settled many questions, left just as many unanswered and opened many new ones. The Hungarians' and Kossuth's ability to handle the problems of March, but not the problems that arose as a consequence of March, led to a civil war in the summer and to a national war with Austria in October.

The March successes and shortcomings were mostly Kossuth's doing; yet his leadership was not unconditionally accepted. He was allowed to lead because his courage and determination were needed; but well before the ratification of the new constitution on April 11, his colleagues made certain that Kossuth would not become dictator. Admired by all liberals, he was still the penniless journalist and landless upstart in their eyes; once the situation became stabilized, the liberal politicians reasoned, more substantial figures would have to take over. Kossuth bowed to the inevitable: he was not to assume complete leadership again until the next emergency arose, in September.

Hungary's March drive for independence cannot be understood without a quick glance at the Habsburg Empire of which this forceful maverick was a member.

It is a historical truism that the Monarchy was a traditionalist state, next to Russia and the Ottoman Empire the most traditionalist in Europe. Its provinces were the private domain of the House of Austria, and all its *Völker* were the children of the emperor. But it was not the "China of Europe," no matter what many historians tell us. Unlike Russia and the Ottoman Empire, the Habsburg Empire was marked by legalism and civilized conduct. Here administrative power was mitigated by custom, local privilege, and the celebrated *Schlamperei,* that carefree and salutary neglect exercised by those in command positions. The trouble was that following the failure of Joseph II's reforming efforts in the 1780s, the Empire had given up the will to move with the times. Metternich had resigned himself simply to "getting along" without major domestic disturbances and without unleashing upon the Throne the wrath of any one nationality or stratum. Concessions were made to all, but no one was completely mollified. Despite this relative immobility, or perhaps because of it, the system endured. The aristocrats, although simultaneously indifferent to state service and indignant over the gradual loss of their political power, were mostly loyal; and so were the city burghers who had made a virtue of their political impotence by creating the comforts and sentimentalities of Biedermeier culture. The students and intellectuals were more bothersome but, being few in number, they could be kept in check by the police. The officers and the civil servants, although constantly complaining about low pay and slow promotion, were the most reliable: their careers depended on the grace of the emperor, and they looked upon themselves as the only true Austrians. As for the peasants, they were too uneducated to care or, if they did, they still cherished the image of the emperor as their father-protector.[1]

Yet disaster was just around the corner—something that Metternich knew well. There was no way to deal with the rising nationalisms, or with the growing aspirations of the new business class and the quite opposite desires of the artisans and workers. The appetites of the nationalist leaders were becoming insatiable. An individual bourgeois could be dazzled with manifestations of Imperial grace; but it was difficult, if not impossible, to satisfy both protectionist and free trade interests. Nor was it possible to conciliate the antagonism of artisans and factory workers, who were united only in their anticapitalism.

The worst problem was finances, always the Achilles heel of the Habsburgs. The budget was hard to balance because of local privilege, the backwardness of the economy, and the Empire's desire to police Europe. Recently the financial situation had grown worse, with the state debt rising to astronomical heights. And even though the government tried to squeeze its tax-paying subjects for all they were worth, income rarely matched expenditures. Direct taxes, principally a land tax, brought in about one-half of the revenue; the other half came from customs duties, from the Crown's monopoly on salt and tobacco, and from the turn-over tax, the last three burdening mainly the lower classes. Expenditures were divided into almost equal thirds among defense, administration, and the debt service. As revenue was inadequate, more state loans had to be contracted at an exorbitant cost. The only solution was to improve the economy, but this was not easy. Over 70 percent of the population was still engaged in the production of food; the population was generally ignorant of modern technology; raw materials were widely scattered; and the few seaports were difficult to reach. Besides, industrialization was politically dangerous, for it strengthened the middle class; and a strong and ambitious middle class was understood to mean revolution. Emperor Francis, in particular, had mixed emotions about industry and had alternately fostered and hampered economic growth.

Yet, especially in the early 1840s, there was remarkable progress. Between 1840 and the end of the decade, Austrian railroad mileage had multiplied fourfold, the total horsepower of the Empire's steam engines had grown from 30,000 to 580,000; the annual production of hard coal had increased from .5 million tons to 2 million tons, and the production of pig iron had shown significant gains. But this was still very little compared to the 19 million horsepower mustered by Britain's steam engines, or the 65 million tons produced annually by the British coal mines. Instead of keeping pace with the West, the Monarchy was falling farther and farther behind.

The worst feature was that, just when industry had begun to show a spurt, public opinion despaired of the Metternichian system.

There was growing discontent—even in the best of circles—with censorship, with bureaucratic inefficiency, with the unbridled proliferation of cities and the parallel growth of urban disorder. Vienna and its suburbs now had a population of 400,000; they swarmed with immigrant peasants in search of factory jobs. Housing conditions in the cities, most notably in the new suburbs, were as bad as anywhere in Europe; factory wages in Vienna ranged from 50¢ to $4 a week, and when the international economic crisis of 1845–47 hit Austria, half the factory population was thrown out of work. Simultaneously, the price of wheat in Vienna had nearly doubled, and the price of potatoes had multiplied by a dizzying fourfold. The government tried in vain to contain the price of bread and meat: there was widespread hunger and, in the years before the revolution, bakeries were regularly plundered in Vienna, Prague, and other cities. The state's indebtedness did not help matters: it needed only the first bad news from abroad for the public to lose confidence in the government's credit.[2]

The Austrian revolutions of 1848 began with the public's rush on the state exchange counters to convert paper bills into specie. On March 1, prompted by the panic, Deputy Kornél Balogh demanded in the Lower House at Pressburg that Vienna finally issue an official statement on monetary policy. Kossuth, who, unlike Balogh, had not yet heard of Louis Philippe's fall in Paris but who knew about the precipitous decline of government bonds in Vienna, seized the occasion to announce that, instead of fussing over monetary problems, he would now discuss all the major issues confronting Hungary. Two days later, on March 3 at an unofficial "circular" meeting of the Lower House, he delivered a speech that led directly to the upheavals in Vienna and in Hungary. This "inaugural address of the revolution," to use C. A. Macartney's phrase,[3] was translated by sympathizers into German the next day and distributed in Vienna, creating extraordinary excitement.

In his March 3 address, Kossuth put all the blame on the government for the financial ills of the Monarchy. He demanded a separate Hungarian financial system; the taxation of the nobility; the suppression of feudal dues and services, with compensation to be paid the landowners; political rights for the urban middle class and the urbarial peasants; the reorganization of the Imperial-Royal army to fit Hungarian national interests; a Hungarian ministry responsible to a newly elected parliament; and the revision of Hungary's relations with the other Habsburg lands. The Austrian half of the Monarchy was to get a constitution similar to that which in Hungary was being refashioned. Kossuth's speech contained an ultimatum to Vienna: "The dynasty must choose between its own welfare and the preservation of a rotten system."[4]

On March 4, Kossuth's propositions were acclaimed at the official meeting of the Lower House and were adopted as an Address to the Throne. The text of the Address was then sent to the Upper House, where it got stuck for a while. As the palatine and his chief assistants were away in Vienna, there was no one in Pressburg legally entitled to convoke the Lords. It is nearly certain that the high officials had left precisely to prevent the calling of such an emergency meeting. Assembled at Court, the greatest dignitaries of the realm—with a vehemently anti-Kossuth Széchenyi among them—swore not to let the seditious Address reach the Throne. But it was impossible to stop Kossuth. Moved by his oratory, the Lower House now issued a threat: without waiting for the Upper House, as constitutional procedure required, it would send the Address directly to Vienna.

There was no need for such an unconstitutional move, either then or later. On March 13 revolution broke out in the Imperial capital, forcing the government to make immediate concessions to the Hungarians. On that single day the already highly agitated meeting of the Lower Austrian Estates was invaded by Vienna University students, forcing the Estates to send a mass delegation to the Imperial palace with a petition for reform; workers revolted in the suburbs of Vienna, destroying the hated machines and setting fire to the factories of unpopular owners; demonstrators clashed with Imperial grenadiers both inside and outside the city walls, leaving behind forty-five victims; the arming of the burghers and the students was authorized by a cowed Court; and in a veritable palace coup the archdukes dismissed Metternich, whom they hoped to turn into a scapegoat. Also dismissed were Police Minister Sedlnitzky and Hungarian Chancellor Apponyi. All these tumultuous happenings had begun with the repeated reading of Kossuth's March 3 speech to delighted crowds in the streets of Vienna and in the Aula of the university.[5]

After that day, the revolutionary infection of one Central European city by another continued unabated. On March 14 the Viennese obtained arms from the Imperial arsenal for their Academic Legion and their burgher-dominated National Guard; censorship was lifted, and Emperor Ferdinand offered to grant a constitution in the near future. On the same day in Berlin there was a bloody clash between demonstrators and the Prussian soldiers. Again on the same day the Pressburg Diet took further forceful action.

Duly impressed by the Vienna revolution, Archduke Stephen, who was the palatine of Hungary and a younger cousin of the emperor, hastened back to Pressburg to convoke the Lords. Meeting on March 14, the Upper House accepted Kossuth's proposed Address to the Throne without a debate. It also accepted Kossuth's request that the Address be brought before the king by a mass deputation made up of members of both Houses. On the same evening, the "dietal youth" held a torchlight parade for Kossuth. To them he presented his friend and protector, Count Lajos Batthyány, as future prime minister of Hungary.

March 15 was to become the most important revolutionary *journée* of Central Europe. On that day new demonstrations erupted in Vienna because the emperor's vague promises had satisfied no one. The terrified archdukes now promised, through the mouth of Ferdinand, to grant a real constitution. The Viennese were jubilant and cheered the good kaiser; but on the same day in Prague, a hastily constituted Czech National Committee felt so exalted over Metternich's fall that it voted to heighten its demands for civil rights and a Bohemian constitution. The Czech petition was to be brought to Vienna by a mass delegation. Also on March 15, the Pressburg Diet decided to increase its own demands and, simultaneously, a revolution broke out in Buda-Pest.

On the morning of that day, the Diet voted to institute all Kossuth's reform proposals. It also decided, at the request of Kossuth, that the parliamentary delegation to Vienna should now ask for the immediate appointment of a Hungarian prime minister, and that the king be forced to give the palatine, who was held to be pro-Hungarian, plenipotentiary powers in Hungary.

All this haste would have been inconceivable without alarming news from Buda-Pest. So far, Pressburg had experienced only vigorous parliamentary action and a few noisy street meetings; reports from Buda-Pest spoke of an intoxicating but dangerous revolution.

The February events in Paris had infected not only Pressburg but also Buda-Pest, and ever since early March the legislative and the executive capitals of Hungary had vied with one another in political agitation. And as Buda-Pest was more radical than Pressburg, the first city spurred the second city ahead, while the second manoeuvered to control and restrain the first. And as Kossuth was in Pressburg, not in Buda-Pest, it was natural that the first city should emerge victorious from the contest!

Buda-Pest (the two cities were to unite only in 1873, but it was already customary to write the names together or to join them with a hyphen) was not only the official capital of Hungary, but also its administrative, cultural, and business center. The two cities had recently begun to develop differently. Buda, the seat of the Vice-Regal Council and many other governmental institutions and once the seat of the kings, had not changed much in the preceding decades: it was a pleasant, rather quiet place, built on hills and in valleys and populated mainly by German burghers. In 1848 Buda had about 35,000 inhabitants. Pest, on the left bank of the Danube, was on the edge of the Great Hungarian Plain; its expansion met with no natural obstacles, and it was rapidly becoming a boom town.

In the 1780s Pest had 25,000 inhabitants and was in fourth position behind Debrecen, Pressburg, and Buda. By the 1830s, with 70,000 people, it was well ahead of the other Hungarian cities. By 1848 the population had grown to 110,000. More importantly, Pest was becoming a Hungarian city through the largely spontaneous assimilation of its German inhabitants and the influx of Magyar nobles and peasants. Pest had Hungary's only university, its Academy of Sciences, its National Museum and Library, its National Theater, its largest printing presses, and its important newspapers and journals. Pest's artisans (masters, journeymen, and apprentices) numbered over 11,000; its new factories employed about 900 workers, by far the greatest concentration of factory population in the country. The city's professional population consisted mainly of lawyers—twice as many as all the lawyers of Bohemia, Moravia, Galicia, Styria, and Dalmatia combined.[6] There was also a herd of poets, journalists, dramatists, and actors (mostly unemployed or underpaid), who constituted Hungary's most subversive element. For years young intellectuals had been meeting in the Pest cafés, passing along forbidden literature while they debated the arts, politics, and the future. They were, without regard to religious, ethnic, or social origin, culturally avant-garde, religiously indifferent, politically Magyar nationalist, and socially progressive, although their progressivism ranged from the advocacy of mild liberal reforms to republicanism and communism. By 1848 their undisputed spokesman was the twenty-five-year-old Sándor Petőfi: a lyricist, patriot, and political radical who hated feudalism, the kings, the aristocrats, the bureaucrats, and burgher philistinism. He loved the "people," by whom he meant the Magyar peasants (whose life he knew well) rather than the mostly foreign-speaking urban journeyman and workers, of whom he knew little. In 1846 Petőfi had formed the Society of Ten, a club of young democratic writers who called themselves Young Hungary and dreamed of a revolution.[7] As part of all the "young" movements in Europe, Young Hungary wanted to create a free, democratic, and thoroughly magyarized nation, one that would live in perfect harmony with the other progressive nations of the world. It had occurred to no one in the group to seek contact with other radicals in Europe. The revolution would come by itself, arising simultaneously everywhere. March 1848 became the moment of truth for Young Hungary.

Following his March 3 speech, Kossuth had turned to the Pest branch of the Party of Opposition with the request that they reformulate his own program and submit it to the Diet as a popular petition. The Pest Oppositionary Circle knew where talent lay and, on March 9, it asked the Society of Ten to draw up such a petition. Petőfi and his friends obliged in haste, for there was to be a popular fair in Pest at which some 40,000 peasants were expected; and Young Hungary hoped to put pressure on Pressburg by organizing a reform banquet for the occasion and thereby rouse the peasants. These 40,000 peasants were to become a decisive factor in the coming political events. Even though the fair was not held until March 19 and the peasants—when they came—were mostly interested in buying and selling, the political leaders in Pressburg and Vienna were convinced that the peasants had arrived in Pest earlier, that they were armed, that Petőfi was their leader, and that they were in an ugly mood. The chimera of a Petőfi-led *Jacquerie* drove the Court and the Diet to make concession after concession to the popular-nationalist cause. Kossuth was one of the few who kept a cool head in Pressburg: he used the threat of the peasant uprising to further his political goals.

Young Hungary's program was ready by March 11, but it was not a petition: it was called "Twelve Demands," and it included several radical *postulata* not suggested by Kossuth. Besides Kossuth's reform proposals, it requested freedom of the press; an independent Hungarian ministry residing in Buda-Pest and responsible to a popularly elected parliament; the setting up of a National Guard; complete civil and religious equality; trial by jury; a national bank; a Hungarian national army; the withdrawal from Hungary of foreign (i.e., Austrian) troops; the freeing of political prisoners; and union with Transylvania. Typically, not even this radical program proposed to do anything for the landless or contractual peasants, nor anything for the workers and journeymen, but it offered to help the urbarial peasants by omitting any mention of compensation to be paid the landowners. Nor did the Twelve Demands have anything to say about Hungary's non-Magyar nationalities.

On March 14 the Danube steamship brought news of the Vienna revolution to Buda-Pest. Young Hungary now decided to abandon the idea of circulating the Twelve Demands for mass signature or of submitting it to the Diet; rather, the Demands were to be acted upon immediately. This revolutionary step was taken in the morning of March 15, when, in the Café Pilvax, the demands were read aloud and Petőfi recited the "National Song" he had written for the occasion.* The refrain of Petőfi's poem was simple and effective:

We swear by the God of Hungarians
We swear, we shall be slaves no more.

Having gathered courage in the café, the young radicals on March 15, 1848, went to the university, there to be joined by the students. Thousands of ordinary Pest citizens were also aroused. Petőfi and his friends now seized the largest printing shop in the city (that of Landerer, Kossuth's former employer and betrayer); leaflets containing the Twelve Demands and the National Song were printed on the spot and thrown to the multitude. Thus freedom of the press was established by one peaceful stroke. At 3 P.M. Petőfi spoke to some 10,000 demonstrators in front of the National Museum; it was a

* Petőfi's National Song became the anthem of all Hungarian radicals, just as the Twelve Demands became the symbol of Hungarian revolution and independence. During World War II left-wing demonstrators, meeting under the statue of Petőfi in Budapest, recited the National Song in defiance of right-wing Hungary and the Third Reich. On October 23, 1956, Budapest students and intellectuals drew up their anti-Soviet and anti-Stalinist demands in conscious imitation of Petőfi's program. They then marched across the city with the National Song on their lips.

rainy day and, instead of the eagerly hoped for weapons, Petőfi faced a sea of umbrellas. Still, the Pest burghers, caught in the *Zeitgeist,* celebrated the poet whom they would have ranked with circus performers a few days earlier. From the museum the crowd marched on Pest City Hall, invading the chamber of the council in session, mounting chairs and tables, and ordering the council to endorse the Twelve Demands. Then and there a Committee of Public Safety was formed to govern the twin cities, to spread the good word, and to set up a National Guard. This was a most revolutionary move, but in effect the composition of the committee presaged the rapid decline of Young Hungary. Understanding that they represented only themselves, the radical intellectuals put only four of their ranks on the committee, Petőfi included. The rest of the membership was made up of six liberals from the Pest City Council, all functionaries or master craftsmen, and three noblemen, all of whom were political friends of Kossuth. And even though Young Hungary dominated the Committee of Public Safety for a few days, Kossuth's colleagues would thereafter have the final say. As it soon became clear, Kossuth allowed the Pest radicals to push the revolution only as far as he, Kossuth, wanted it to go.

For the time being, all was success and joy. In the late afternoon of March 15, some 20,000 people crossed over to Buda on the pontoon bridge connecting the twin cities (Széchenyi's permanent bridge was not yet complete), and the Committee of Public Safety invaded the chamber of the Vice-Regal Council. This high body surrendered immediately, ordering the garrison not to meddle in the affairs of the citizenry, abolishing censorship, and signing the release of Hungarian political prisoners—of whom there was only one in the capital: Mihály Táncsics, a Hungarian nationalist radical political pamphleteer of Slavic peasant origin. He was carried in triumph across the city, and the day ended with a gala performance in the National Theater celebrating freedom.

Why had the Vice-Regal Council surrendered so easily on March 15? Because 20,000 demonstrators in a place containing 150,000 inhabitants was an unheard-of multitude, even though the people had no arms; because the 7,000-man garrison, composed mostly of Italians, could not be counted on absolutely, and because the old order was frightened—as it seemed to be frightened in those days everywhere in Europe. Petőfi was to write of the event that, while the demonstrators shouted outside the palace, the spokesman of the Committee of Public Safety (one of Kossuth's friends) presented the demands of the revolution "stammering in all humility and trembling like a pupil before his teacher." "Their Magnificences, the Vice-Regal Council, turned pale and were graciously pleased to tremble also. Within five minutes, they consented to everything."[8]

With March 15, the first of the Hungarian *journées* came to an end, not to be renewed until the end of the month.* In the following weeks the Diet and the Pest radicals worked—sometimes together, sometimes at cross purposes—to consolidate the gains of the revolution. On the very afternoon that demonstrators took over Buda-Pest, the delegation of Pressburg parliamentarians, accompanied by hundreds of apprentice lawyers, boarded two steamships to carry the Address directly to the Throne. The time had come for the customary hard bargaining that had always marked compromise negotiations between Crown and nation in critical periods. But, on this occasion, the nation was stronger than the king.

Vienna Success and Croatian Contretemps

From Pressburg to Vienna, travel on a steam packet took only a few hours: time enough for the Hungarian leaders to rethink their strategy. Clearly, the Address to the Throne, as composed by Kossuth less than two weeks earlier, was now outdated, requesting as it did a separate Hungarian cabinet only as a pious wish and not as an immediate need.[9] Yet the Diet, on the morning of March 15, had instructed the delegation to press for an immediate appointment.[10] Now it was resolved to create a fait accompli by drawing up in advance the king's reply. His Majesty would merely have to sign. This Royal Rescript was drafted by Kossuth himself, on the night of his arrival in Vienna.[11] If the king had signed the document as it stood, he would have instructed Count Batthyány to form a cabinet, appointed Palatine Stephen as royal plenipotentiary in Hungary, and promised to

---

* March 15 became a national holiday in Hungary. Every regime, whether of the left or of the right, celebrated it as its own. But March 15 also became the day of the opposition to any regime. In the early 1970s, for instance, Budapest University students ran along the streets on March 15 wearing national insignia and demanding freedom and independence for their country. But this time the demonstrators met with a far more efficient police than the volunteer municipal constabulary of 1848.

ratify any and all bills adopted by the Diet under the leadership of the palatine. This was the first—but not the last—instance when Hungarian reformers, in particular Kossuth, drafted a Royal Rescript for Ferdinand's signature. That they dared do such things, and that their drafts were sometimes accepted by the Court, testified to Hungary's sudden power and the near collapse of the old regime.

Resplendent in their gala national dress, girt with their richly studded swords, and bearing egret feathers on their caps, the arriving Hungarian nobles presented the Viennese with an unforgettable sight. Kossuth himself looked somber and dignified in his simple black national garb. The reception given the Hungarian "Argonauts" (as the Viennese press referred to them) went beyond their fondest dreams. The crowd may have numbered 100,000. Masses of armed students and National Guardsmen lined the streets; a myriad of hand-held lamps illuminated the dusk; weeping women rushed forward to touch Kossuth's cloak; his carriage was unhorsed and pulled by citizens, and forced to stop again and again for him to make a speech.

What struck most observers was the virility and elegance of the man. At forty-six, his brown hair was now lightly flecked with white; his beard—full and wavy and thereafter so much in vogue in Hungary—gave him dignity and enhanced the handsomeness of his face. He was frail, and when he began to speak, he always acted as though he were about to collapse. Then, as if overcoming with a superhuman effort his weakness, his exhaustion, and his many illnesses (of which he complained constantly), his voice rose gradually until it rolled into a rumbling storm. Kossuth was not only a brilliant speaker—alternately majestic, dignified, fearsome, mellow, flattering and humble, refined and direct in simplicity—but his voice carried farther than that of anyone else, an indispensable attribute for someone constantly addressing crowds.

While the Champion of Liberty and Hero of the People was thus being celebrated, the Imperial palace, tightly shut, was protected by several companies of soldiers. Members of the Imperial family were at the moment virtual prisoners. Writing in exile ten years later, Kossuth recalled with bitterness the events of the day:

As I arrived in front of the Imperial residence, behind whose dark and mute windows the offspring of proud emperors awaited the verdict of fate trembling, it flashed suddenly through my mind: what would become of the bungling masters of the Burg . . . what would become of them, within one-quarter of an hour, if I were to thrust the spark of the living word into the gaping mouth of the gunpowder-kegs which surrounded me from all sides; this on the very spot where even the written word [the German translation of Kossuth's March 3 speech] had sufficed to ignite a flame that had consumed the centuries' old edifice of absolutism? But I, who had come merely to seek justice for my fatherland, was not even tempted by the opportunity.[12]

Kossuth's claim that on March 15 he was master of Vienna and that, had he wanted to, he could have put a sudden end to Habsburg rule, is not quite borne out by historical evidence. Only a few hours prior to his arrival, the emperor had promised a constitution to Austria and the Viennese had applauded him for it. On that day, in the exaltation of the moment, both Ferdinand and Kossuth were popular and, in any case, the temptation for Kossuth to do away with the House of Austria did not loom large. Obviously, he enjoyed the adulation of the crowd, and he knew how to turn it to his own and to his country's advantage. But he had no desire to dissolve the Monarchy, nor to end the rule of the emperor-king. On the contrary, he had come to Vienna to secure Hungary's rightful position in the Empire and to repossess the monarch for his country.

If March 15 was the *journée* of revolution, March 16 was that of frantic bargaining. Early in the morning, Archduke Stephen hastened to Court to inform his relatives that unless there was accession to Hungarian demands, the country would secede and might well proclaim a republic. To his credit, the palatine did not mention that there was also a movement afoot in Hungary to make him king. Around noon Ferdinand received the Hungarian delegation and, in response to flowery speeches, mumbled a few words of acknowledgment. Besieged for days by councilors, delegations, and petitioners, the emperor was at the end of his strength: his face a deathly pale, his head lolling, he was almost unable to understand what was happening. "Peinlicher Anblick," Széchenyi noted in his diary, while Kossuth was to write later: "Once the official procedure was over, Emperor-King Ferdinand V turned to Archduke Stephen, and folding his hands as in prayer, begged the archduke with childish simplicity that now that the latter had become his vice-regent [in Hungary], he should remain vice-regent and not take away his throne (I' pitt' di,' nim mir meinen Thron nit!)."[13]

Soon thereafter the State Conference met in the Hofburg. With brief intermissions, it was to remain in session until dawn. The participants (the Archdukes Louis and Francis Charles; General Windisch-Graetz, commander-in-chief in Bohemia and an arch-conservative; a few Hungarian high officials; and a number of ministers of state as well as lesser councilors) were aghast at the arrogance of the Pressburg Diet. But as the day advanced and alarming reports kept coming in of turbulence everywhere—the 40,000 Pest peasants played a major role here—they agreed to consider Kossuth's draft Reply. The Royal Rescript, issued on the morning of March 17, was a verbatim rendering of the Hungarian text but with two crucial omissions: the name of Count Batthyány, and the promise of an unconditional ratification of the bills to be adopted by the Diet. This was not good enough for the Hungarian leaders; now not only Batthyány and Kossuth, but Széchenyi himself was adamant. The palatine thereupon rushed to his Imperial uncle and obtained his oral consent to the appointment of Batthyány. Immediately thereafter, as royal plenipotentiary for Hungary, Archduke Stephen wrote a note to Batthyány appointing him prime minister and instructing him to submit a list of cabinet members.[14] The Hungarians had won a great victory but there could be no doubt that the king's consent had been achieved by the palatine going behind the back of the State Conference. This was to constitute the grounds on which the Court would later repudiate the Hungarian constitution, send Archduke Stephen into exile, and condemn Count Batthyány to the gallows.

The events of March 16–17 had shown clearly that the highest governing circles of the Monarchy were not united in their Hungarian policy. Naturally, they all wished to save the Monarchy, and their own privileged positions in it, but they disagreed among themselves on tactics and strategy. For years the Hungarians had been insisting that the Vienna Court was dominated by the "Camarilla," a sordid conspiratorial clique that was as obscurantist and reactionary as it was anti-Hungarian. The existence and absolute power of the Camarilla (allegedly led by the fiendish Archduchess Sophie, mother of Francis Joseph) was an article of faith with Kossuth, one that he refused to abandon to his dying day. There was literally no political speech or writing in which he did not refer to the "murderous," "infamous," or "accursed" Camarilla as the dedicated enemy of everything that was good and noble. Kossuth and his compatriots saw themselves as innocent victims of Camarilla machinations: they, the Hungarians, had the law on their side while the Camarilla violated the law. Revolutionary Hungary's Paris envoy, Count László Teleki, assured the Polish Prince Adam Czartoryski in 1849: ". . . nous n'avons pas pris les armes que pour la défense de notre constitution légalement garantie et . . . c'est la Camarilla qui est en état de révolte contre nous."[15] Nationalist Hungarian historiography unconditionally embraced the same view and modern marxist historians fervently reiterated the accusations of Kossuth.[16] What neither Kossuth nor the nationalist radical historians ever made clear is who or what constituted the Camarilla. Some Hungarians use the term interchangeably with State Conference; others separate the "civilian" from the "military" Camarilla; again others a bit cavalierly identify the term with the entire Vienna Court, including the Austrian government.

Historical evidence does not support the Hungarian thesis. It is true, of course, that following Ferdinand's accession to the throne in 1835 a group of archdukes and Imperial bureaucrats had been taking all decisions in the name of the feeble monarch. It is also true that the secrecy surrounding all high-level deliberations fostered the creation of such legends. But the fact remains that there was no conspiracy, and that there were many factions at the Court which were formed and re-formed on important political issues. Of the twenty-five-odd persons who usually attended meetings of the State Conference, at least ten were Hungarian aristocrats; the rest were of diverse nationality, often Germans from outside Austria. By 1848 nationalist sympathies had begun to influence these people, and so had diverse ideologies. Some members had pro-Magyar or pro-German or pro-Slav leanings; others showed aristocratic-federalist or bureaucratic-centralist inclinations; some put their faith in a quick military solution of the Monarchy's problems; others favored temporary or lasting concessions to the liberal cause. The Imperial family itself was divided: Archduchess Sophie—"the only man in the Hofburg" but naturally not a member of the State Conference—was willing to introduce reforms and to sacrifice both Metternich and Ferdinand; Archdukes Louis and Francis Charles were generally rigid, as was Archduke Albrecht, a tough militarist; Archduke John had German liberal leanings, and Archduke Stephen, not a regular participant of State Conference deliberations, yearned to be both a loyal Habsburg and a loyal Hungarian. As for the Hungarian Court officials, their opinions ranged from absolute political orthodoxy to mild sympathy with Batthyány and the Diet, if not with Kossuth.

The strongest opposition to Hungarian demands on March 16 had come not from the conservative-aristocratic camp but from the camp of German-Austrian bureaucrats, who had pointed out with some justification that the emperor's March 15 promise of an Austrian constitution clashed directly with the king's March 16 concessions to the Hungarians. These functionaries saw the March 15 Rescript as the first step toward the creation of an all-Austrian cabinet supported by a soon-to-be-elected all-Austrian parliament. How would Hungary's separate constitution fit into such a scheme?

Hungary's later defeat lay in this German-Austrian opposition to separate Hungarian development. Conceivably, the Hungarians could have dealt with their conservative opponents alone: Habsburg traditionalists, like Windisch-Graetz, had always recognized at least some of Hungary's historic rights. It proved to be much more difficult for the Hungarians to combat a coalition of conservatives and bureaucratic centralists, especially as the latter came to be increasingly supported by German-Austrian liberal nationalist opinion, with only a few Vienna democrats remaining staunch supporters of the Hungarian cause. Finally, when the Czechs, Croats, and other Slavs joined this mighty coalition (for reasons of their own to be explained later), the fate of Hungary was sealed.

Why had the politically inexperienced Stephen, then thirty-one, overruled the State Conference? No doubt because he enjoyed his popularity in Hungary and because this was his way of saving the Monarchy. From that time on, all major Austrian leaders—whether archdukes, generals, or politicians—endeavored to save the Monarchy in their own way, and sometimes in violation of Imperial-Royal decrees. Finally, the generals were to save the Throne, often in defiance of the expressed wishes of the Crown. But, unlike the generals, Archduke Stephen was not to earn the pardon and gratitude of the Throne.

On March 18 the State Conference ruled that Stephen had overstepped his authority, but by then it was too late. Bowing to the inevitable, the Conference "temporarily" upheld the appointment of Count Batthyány. The Hungarian success was complete.

In those days the roof seemed to collapse on the Monarchy. On

March 17, while the palatine was pleading with the king, revolution broke out in Venice; the next day the same happened in Milan. On the same March 18, as if to show the Habsburgs that succor could not be expected anywhere, violent clashes occurred in Berlin between revolutionaries and Prussian royal troops.

On March 19 a Czech delegation came to Vienna to present its demands. Two days later, the Austrian commander in Venice capitulated to the rebels without having fired a shot: a republic was proclaimed there, with Daniele Manin as president of Venice and hopefully of Italy. One-third of the Austrian land forces in Venice and the majority of the Austrian fleet—manned mainly by Italians—declared for a united Italy. The rest of the fleet fled to Trieste. On March 22 the small Austrian garrison in Milan, headed by Field Marshal Radetzky, Austrian commander in Italy, evacuated the city. The Milan revolutionaries formed a provisional government and asked for brotherly help from the Kingdom of Piedmont-Sardinia. On March 23 the king of that country, Charles Albert, ordered his army into Lombardy: Austria was now at war with a foreign country. All Italy was in revolt; client princes of Austria had to flee their capitals; even the pope promised troops against His Catholic and Apostolic Majesty. Radetzky now withdrew to the Quadrilateral, the four great fortresses guarding the Alpine passes between Italy and Austria.[17] Meanwhile, there were demonstrations in Galicia and a revolt in Cracow.

The State Conference tried to save what it could. Troops and a little money were dispatched to Radetzky. In Vienna a further step toward consolidation was taken on March 20 with the formation of an Austrian cabinet, the first in the country's history. It consisted of old and trusted servants of the Crown; but it was not at all clear whether this ministry, headed by Kolowrat, an old-regime figure, would command any authority. Windisch-Graetz was sent back to Bohemia to keep order there and, on March 23, a Croat colonel, Josip Jelačić, was appointed *ban* (governor) of Croatia.* This was a fatal move, destined to lead to war with Hungary.

For nearly 700 years the Kingdom of Croatia-Slavonia had been associated with the Kingdom of Hungary: both formed integral parts of the Crown of Saint Stephen. Although theoretically equal, small

* The official name of the country was Croatia-Slavonia, but it was customary to call it Croatia. According to Hungarian legal theory, the three Slavonian counties, unlike Croatia proper, were part and parcel of the Kingdom of Hungary.

and backward Croatia-Slavonia had less than 1.5 million inhabitants
to Hungary's more than 10 million (the latter without counting Transylvania), and it was definitely in a subordinate position. Moreover,
ever since Turkish times, Croatia-Slavonia had been divided into two
parts: Civil Croatia and a much larger and more populous Military
Border. Originally established as a line of defense against the Turks,
the Military Border was not administered, like Civil Croatia, by the
Hungarian Chancellery in Vienna, but by the Court War Council.
Thus the Military Border, while legally part of the Crown of Saint
Stephen, was not the concern of either the Hungarian or the Croatian
authorities. The Military Border, incidentally, extended well beyond
the boundaries of historic Croatia-Slavonia into Hungary proper and
into Transylvania, thus infinitely complicating matters to contemporary jurists and presumably to readers of this work. Still, the bulk of
the Border was in historic Croatia-Slavonia, and its peasant-soldiers
were either Croats or Serbs. These were the famous *Grenzer,* similar
to the Cossacks of Russia, and the pride and joy of the Habsburg
army.[18]

Civil Croatia was a small country with, however, its own diet
(the Sabor), its landed nobility, and some measure of autonomy.
Relations between the Hungarian and Croatian nobility, once frater-
nally united in opposition to the centralizing and reforming endeavors
of Vienna, had lately become envenomed. Hungarian nationalism
was seen in Zagreb, the capital of Croatia, as a mortal danger to the
historic rights of their country. Naturally, the Croats were also divided among themselves. Some—mainly young middle-class intellectuals—belonged to the Illyrian movement: they dreamed of the unification of all South Slavs in one sovereign country, perhaps under the
nominal rule of the Habsburg dynasty. Other Croats, mostly from the
nobility, simply wished to strengthen Croatian rights under the
Crown of Saint Stephen. Again others, especially a distinct group of
Croatian peasant-nobles, were ardent followers of Kossuth.

The status of Croatia greatly worried Vienna. There were thousands of Croatian and Serbian soldiers under Radetzky in Italy, constituting the best part of that army. If the Hungarians were satisfied
but not the Croats, there was real danger that the latter would refuse
to fight for Austria. To avoid giving the Croats the impression that
they had been delivered, bound hand and foot, to the whims of their
Hungarian overlords, it was imperative that the governorship of Croa-

tia be offered to a man whom both the Croats and Vienna could trust. This man was Jelačić. The son of a two-star general in the Habsburg army, he became an officer in 1819. He counted as a Croatian patriot because of the heroic poems he wrote and read aloud to his soldiers in camp; he was the commander of a Croatian regiment; he was a conservative and his loyalty to the Throne was absolute; finally, Jelačić hated the ''lawyers' clique'' in Pressburg and Buda-Pest. His appointment, of doubtful legality, was hurriedly passed lest the Hungarian government (not yet constituted) be able to prevent it. After all, the *ban* of Croatia was one of Hungary's highest dignitaries. Characteristic of the disunity in Imperial circles was the fact that while some Austrian officials saw Jelačić's appointment as a peaceful measure and an inevitable consequence of the great concessions made to Hungary, at least one Imperial official, not a member of the State Conference, wrote to Jelačić: ''Austria will have to reconquer Hungary, and therefore you must at all costs retain the loyalty of the Military Border.''[19]

Within two weeks Jelačić was promoted to a two-star general, and in an unprecedented move the new governor of Civil Croatia was also put in charge of the armies of both Civil Croatia and the Croatian-Slavonian section of the Military Border. In September 1848 he was to invade Hungary, precipitating the war between the Habsburgs and Kossuth.[20]

Seen from Vienna, Hungary still posed a serious problem, but for the time being not of catastrophic proportions. It appeared that the country would remain in the Monarchy, something that could not be said of northern Italy. Nor could it be said of German-Austria proper, where radical agitation was growing for unification with the rest of Germany at any cost—even, if necessary, by discarding the Habsburg dynasty.

Left to their own devices for a few days, the Hungarians now proceeded to create a new country. In this effort Kossuth took leadership.

Making a New Constitution

The delegation's dazzling success in Vienna swept all Magyars, except for archconservatives, off their feet. Now even Deák troubled himself to leave his estate in order to attend the Diet. Széchenyi, cynic and eternal worrier, suddenly felt elated. On March 6, when he had still been advising firmness to the government, he had written his secretary:

We must decide what is more important: *gentle treatment to Louis* [Kossuth] or the *welfare of fatherland!* I believe it is high time to imitate the French— not *in proclaiming the republic* but in kicking our own Louis in the ass.[21]

By March 17 Széchenyi was of a different opinion:

My friend, we have lived through miracles! Our national destiny hung by a thread. Act One of the drama was a magnificent success! I am full of the greatest expectations. . . . I cannot doubt that things will develop for the best of our nation; and since I am only delighted by the tremendous roles played by Batthyány and Kossuth and since, as God sees my soul, I enter-tain not the slightest envy towards them, I indulge in the sweet conviction that the sole motive force of my politics is "devotion"! . . . As far as I am concerned, I shall serve Batthyány and Kossuth most sincerely! . . . My policy was certain but slow. Kos[suth] staked everything on one card, and has already won as much for the nation as my policy could have produced over perhaps 20 years![22]

On the afternoon of March 17 Pressburg celebrated the returning Hungarian Argonauts: Kossuth was again the main speaker, and, this time, he sounded a note of law and order. The next day the Diet sat down to work—in haste—for the lawmakers were as worried about the further radicalization of the public as the Court was of the radica-lization of the lawmakers. Fear of extremism marked the times as much as exuberance and drive. March 1848 meant an indefinite number of interconnected, overlapping, and feverishly busy political groups, each trying to put pressure on the group to its right and to neutralize or coopt the one to its left. Reactionary Court aristocrats were under pressure from moderate conservatives, the latter by liberal nobles, these again by radical nobles, and the last by plebeian radi-cals. All believed that those to their left were going dangerously far, and all attempted to mellow "the extremists" with calculated conces-sions and by luring extremists into their own camp. The Court dis-trusted Archduke Stephen but was willing to work with him because it was better to have a Habsburg as palatine of Hungary than to have someone else, or to have a republic, or to see the archduke proclaimed king of Hungary. The palatine distrusted Batthyány but made him prime minister because Batthyány was less dangerous than Kossuth. Batthyány feared Kossuth but had supported the latter's election to the Diet in 1847 so that Kossuth would become a member of the legislature rather than a demagogue at large; now Batthyány was preparing to entrust Kossuth with a responsible but not too influential cabinet post. Kossuth distrusted the radical intellectuals, but he suffered their activities because he needed their support. He also endorsed the Committee of Public Safety, and infiltrated it with his own friends because it burdened the intellectuals with responsibility for maintaining order in Buda-Pest. Finally, Petőfi with his friends had little respect for the peasant-agitator Táncsics, but they supported him so as to secure the loyalty of peasants to the radical and national cause.

In this nerve-racking situation, the noble Diet, or rather its liberal majority, set itself the task of drawing up in rough outline the maximum reforms it was ready to adopt before quickly dissolving itself, lest more extreme measures be imposed on it by the street. The new Hungarian government, it was hoped, would then execute the reform laws as it saw fit and would restrain the radicals with the might of the state.

For the next two weeks, including Sundays, there were to be daily meetings of both Houses: with unofficial "circular" sessions preparing the work of official ones, with incessant debate and voting, and with almost all important bills originating from Kossuth.

On March 18 Kossuth proposed, and the Lower House accepted, equal voting rights to be given during the remainder of the session to the hitherto practically voteless town representatives and clerical chapter delegates. On the same day both Houses voted in favor of a number of other proposals by Kossuth, among them those on general taxation and the abolition of feudal dues and services. Now that the landowning noble estate had made such a supreme sacrifice, it was high time for the members of the clerical estate to give up something, too. All eyes were turned to them, but the deputies of the chapters kept silent. In one of his reminiscences Kossuth tells us what happened next:

The emancipation of the serfs having been voted in . . . I stole quietly to the stand where the deputies of the chapters were sitting and, addressing them in a gentle low voice, I said: "Gentlemen: the tithe of the landlords has just ceased to exist; it is natural therefore that the tithe of the clergy cease also. Secure for the Hungarian Catholic clergy the glory of surrendering it yourselves; do not wait for me to make the proposal. You must take the initiative yourselves." Thereupon one of them replied: "Thank you for the warning; I shall do so immediately." . . . I still laugh when I recall how some of the reverend colleagues of this gentleman tugged at his cassock. "Per amorem dei," he should not be a fool. But the good man wanted to be. He announced, in the name of his chapter, that he would renounce the tithe, on behalf of the people, in perpetuity, and without any compensation. His example was followed by his colleagues, all making enthusiastic statements; not one spoke against it, not even the cassock tuggers. . . . Such was the genesis of the eternally glorious Law XIII of 1848 [on the abolition of tithes due the clergy].[23]

To reassure the worried priests, Kossuth immediately guaranteed state financial support to the lower clergy, a promise he kept as long as he was in power.[24]

With the Batthyány-Kossuth faction standing somewhat left of center in the political spectrum, it was inevitable that clashes would occur with opponents on both the left and the right.

The first such confrontation took place on March 19, when delegates of the Buda-Pest Committee of Public Safety appeared at the circular meeting of the Lower Table to present the Twelve Demands and to request that the Diet immediately remove itself to the nation's capital. Széchenyi happened to be in the chair at this meeting and—with all his loathing for hotheads—he could not help but admire these young revolutionaries, particularly twenty-two-year-old Pál Vasvári, a historian and one of Hungary's few revolutionary theoreticians, who was to die at the hands of Romanian guerrillas a year later. "Charmant garçon," Széchenyi noted in his diary, adding that Vasvári reminded him of Saint-Just.

Less sensitive souls remained unimpressed by the beauty of youth. Delivering the reply of the House, Kossuth mixed flattery with threats. Neither then nor after did he refer to March 15 in Buda-Pest as a revolution; it was for him simply another manifestation of the "national movement." He told the youth delegation that the Diet would not budge: not with the few weeks of urgent work left; the

Twelve Demands were laudable but unnecessary, as most of them were already included in the Diet's program. Kossuth then stated:

I recognize the inhabitants of Buda-Pest as inexpressibly important in this fatherland; I recognize Buda-Pest as the heart of the country, but I shall never recognize it as [this country's] master . . . just as the word ''nation'' cannot be arrogated by one caste, so it cannot be arrogated by any one city; the 15 million Hungarians, as an entity, constitute the fatherland and the nation . . . this nation is so strong in the awareness of its rights, its vocation and its mission, that it can crush anyone who entertains the notion of indispensability to the nation.[25]

Kossuth's message was understood clearly by everyone, especially the moderate-conservative elements in Pressburg to whom the speech was really addressed. Their newspaper bannered Kossuth's threat to the youth as a headline. There was to be no second revolution in Hungary; Buda-Pest would not be allowed to play the role of Paris; commoners ought not to try to wrest power from the nobles; all changes would be made by the legally constituted Diet, and not by plebeian revolutionaries.

With this address, Kossuth achieved two aims. By simultaneously complimenting and warning ''Young Hungary,'' he made it clear that they were to remain loyal to him: they had, after all, no one else to whom they could turn. But by not advocating the dissolution of the Committee of Public Safety, he also served notice on the conservatives. Without Kossuth in the cabinet, there could never be peace in Hungary.

The following days saw feverish activity in the Diet. On March 20 the annual convening of the new National Assembly was decided, together with the creation of a national bank. On the same day, the new press bill was presented, abolishing censorship but setting strict limitations on the freedom of the press by severely punishing press delicts and by requiring publishers to deposit a high bond before starting a newspaper. The youth in Pest later burned the bill in public, and in its final form the press law became somewhat less stringent. On March 21 decisions were made, among others, on the charters of the cities. This gave some urban elements the opportunity to demonstrate their own interpretation of freedom. The bill would have granted voting rights at municipal elections to every city inhabitant, otherwise qualified, without regard to religion. In other words, it would have granted suffrage to financially secure Jews. Members of the guilds, both masters and journeymen, had long resented the illegal immigration into the cities of Jewish shopkeepers and artisans. On the very day the city bill was debated in the House, Jewish shops were broken into and Jews beaten up in Pressburg. The pogrom, once begun, spread rapidly to other cities and it was to culminate in April.

Kossuth condemned the pogrom in the House; but as the government, not yet formed, had practically no means to control the mob, the majority of liberals favored delay in the emancipation of Jews. The city bill was therefore modified, over the lukewarm protestations of Kossuth, to deny suffrage to the Jews.[26]

March 22 saw the presentation of the bill on the National Guard system. Guards were the great fashion of the Springtime of Peoples: no revolution was considered complete without these armed and uniformed civilians, charged with defending property and the new regime. In Hungary, the first Guard companies sprang up on March 15 in Pest; from there, the movement spread rapidly to other cities and even to the countryside. The formation of a militia was inevitable, but it was also dangerous: for what if the armed peasants should turn against the landowners or, as one deputy put it, the peasants should become "the tools of emissaries heralding communistic doctrines"? It was decided to set rather high property qualifications for entry into the Guard; for instance, no peasant holding less than one-half of a serf section was allowed to serve, which meant that most peasants were excluded. Speaking on the issue, Kossuth again struck out in two directions: he challenged the conservatives by declaring that "whatever the people have acquired cannot be taken away from them; rather, one must legalize and organize it";[27] and the radicals by categorically rejecting the idea that Guard officers above the rank of captain be elected democratically.

As it turned out, the Guard companies blithely ignored the Diet's decision with regard to property qualifications; after the national minorities revolted, the government needed all the men it could get anyway. On the other hand, the Diet's initial fears proved unwarranted: the Guards became the willing though inefficient tools of the new regime.

On March 23 the two Houses adopted no less than seven major laws, among them one on the abolition of entail and one on compen-

sation to be paid the landowners who had lost feudal dues and services. It was a major tribute to Kossuth that the deputies, unlike himself almost all landowners, consented to wait for compensation
without a deadline and without any better guarantee of payment than
that "the compensation of private landowners will be placed under
the protective shield of national honor."[28] True, no one could rea-
sonably expect the peasants to pay, nor did anyone have the slightest
notion where the state would get the money from, in the near future.

On the same March 23 Batthyány submitted his proposed cabinet list to the Lower House, and thus Kossuth, when he spoke on the
issue of compensation, was already addressing his audience as future
minister of finance. Unlike the new constitution, the first Hungarian
government was not Kossuth's brainchild but that of Batthyány. Two
days earlier Kossuth had been invited to Batthyány's house, there to
be told who the ministers would be and to be offered the portfolio of
finance. Formally, he had shown himself reluctant but there could be
no doubt about his accepting the nomination: everyone knew that if
he insisted on such a crucial post as that of minister of interior, the
king would reject the cabinet list; and if he refused to enter the government, the Diet and the people would turn against Batthyány. Yet
Kossuth had also suffered an outright defeat on that day when he had
failed to get either one of his two collaborators, Count László Teleki
and Pál Nyáry, on the list.

For the first but certainly not for the last time during their
friendly rivalry, Batthyány emerged stronger than Kossuth. As a
result of Kossuth's defeat or magnanimity, the first Hungarian government was a durable one; unlike the weak Austrian cabinet, whose
composition was to change constantly, Batthyány's ministry truly
governed Hungary for the next six months. Yet Batthyány had started
under very bad auspices: Court circles tended to regard him as a radical revolutionary, an egomaniac, a tool of Kossuth, and a fool; Hungarian radicals saw in him an enemy of Kossuth and a cunning agent
of the Camarilla.

Batthyány was neither a radical nor a reactionary; least of all
was he a fool or anybody's tool. He was a fine statesman, next to
Kossuth the most remarkable political product of the revolutionary
year. Unfortunately, relatively little is known of him, for he still
awaits a biographer; nor have his papers yet been collected. Two

valuable historical works, dedicated to his memory by the reliable and highly sympathetic Árpád Károlyi, deal mainly with his activities in 1848, and not with his life or personality.[29]

At forty-one, Batthyány was one of Hungary's richest land-owners and the bearer of an illustrious name. Like the Széchenyis, his ancestors had been good Catholics and good Habsburg loyalists. Batthyány himself had begun as a soldier, then returned to manage his estates, traveled to Western Europe, and later helped create the liberal-oppositionary faction in the Upper House. He had participated in Kossuth's nationalist-economic undertakings, and in October 1847, as noted earlier, he had secured Kossuth's election to the Diet. Handsome and elegant, Batthyány enjoyed women and luxurious living; he was intelligent though indifferently educated, and while he was a poor speaker, he proved to be a first-class administrator and political organizer. He failed, in the end, because he had attempted the impossible: to reconcile the interests of the House of Austria with Hungary's Great Power aspirations. Batthyány wished to build a strong Hungary within the Habsburg Empire or, if the latter disappeared, without the Empire but still, he hoped, with Ferdinand as king. He desired to act legally but had no hesitation in imposing the law on the king or bending the law in a national emergency. In social and economic questions he was close to Kossuth; in politics the major difference between the two was that Batthyány was not ready to take so many risks vis-à-vis Vienna, and that he refused to resort to open rebellion against the ruler. In foreign policy, both the well-traveled aristocrat and the poor country lawyer proved to be naive: neither could understand that the foreign powers were indifferent to the independence and greatness of Hungary.

Batthyány's cabinet list was comprised of the brightest stars in the Hungarian political firmament, their ideologies ranging from the conservative to the very liberal, but with the pre-1848 liberal opposition forming a six-member majority over two conservatives and one without party affiliation.

Prince Pál Esterházy, at sixty-two the doyen of the new government, became "minister near His Majesty." The wealthiest man in Hungary and the head of the country's greatest family, he was an outright conservative. He had worked with Metternich and had been for many years Austrian ambassador to the Court of Saint James. Although Batthyány had offered him the post in order to reconcile the aristocracy with the lesser nobility, and the Court with Hungary, Esterházy agreed to serve only at the solicitation of his own friends at Court. He conceived of his role as a mediator between king and country, or as a substitute Hungarian Court chancellor. Within the cabinet he hoped to "neutralize that deadly poison": Kossuth. Yet even this dynastic aristocrat saw Buda-Pest as "the future and natural center of gravity in the Empire," and he signed every document as foreign minister of Hungary. Amazingly, the new Austrian Foreign Minister Ficquelmont and other high officials respected this title and repeatedly addressed Esterházy as "königlich ungarischer Minister des Äussern."[30] How the "Imperial-Royal Austrian Ministry of Foreign Affairs" and the "Royal Hungarian Ministry of Foreign Affairs" were to conduct the international affairs of the Monarchy was obscure to both Ficquelmont and Esterházy. In any case, the diplomatic service—both foreign and Austrian—continued to recognize only the Austrian ministry.

Széchenyi was made minister of public works and of transport. More depressed than ever, he accepted the portfolio because he could not bring himself to say no to his friend Batthyány, and because he too hoped to neutralize Kossuth in the cabinet. On March 23, when he accepted the post, he noted in his diary: "I have just signed my death sentence! My head will certainly land on the block!" To which he added: "I shall be hanged with Kossuth," a dire prospect for Kossuth's bitterest enemy.[31] But even Széchenyi was to do his best as minister until madness clouded his mind early in September 1848.

One more cabinet member stood outside the liberal opposition in the Diet: the minister of war, Colonel Lázár Mészáros. Batthyány himself had not been able to find a suitable candidate for the post, all the Imperial-Royal generals of Hungarian origin having declined his offer. It was Kossuth who remembered this fifty-two-year-old colonel of the hussars. He had been a former subscriber to Kossuth's *Pesti Hírlap* and had been in the habit of submitting his own articles, principally on the growing of silkworms. Mészáros was assigned the portfolio in absentia for he was at the moment fighting in Italy. He had spent all his life in the army, where, for a very minor Hungarian nobleman, he had carved out a respectable career for himself. The king reluctantly released him from service in May and the "Old Man," as Mészáros came to be called, entered the cabinet as a moderate liberal and a loyal soldier. As one of the many soldiers who had acquainted themselves with modern ideologies before 1848, he earnestly tried during the revolution to reconcile his progressive ideas with the oath he had taken to the monarch. Distressed by the growing conflict between king and country, Mészáros sent in his resignation to the revolutionary Hungarian government again and again, but his entreaties were always rejected. Out of discipline and patriotism, he was to shoulder various important tasks even after the deposition of the dynasty in April 1849. In the end, he went into exile with Kossuth. A dutiful administrator, Mészáros may very well have been a good regimental commander in the old army; as a general in the Hungarian revolutionary forces he proved to be uninspiring, uninspired, and a steady loser.[32]

The other ministers came from the liberal camp in the Diet: Batthyány as prime minister, Kossuth as minister of finance, Baron József Eötvös as minister of cults and education, Ferenc Deák as minister of justice, Bertalan Szemere as minister of interior, and Gábor Klauzál as minister of agriculture, industry and trade. In age they ranged from thirty-five (Eötvös) to forty-six (Kossuth); politically they were all experienced. All had been trained in law; all had once served as county administrators; with the exception of Batthyány and Eötvös, who because of their titles sat in the Upper House, all had been or were at that time deputies in the Lower House. With regard to the Court, Kossuth was the most militant, Eötvös the most moderate. In domestic policy, Eötvös was theoretically a radical; all the other liberals favored the cautious reforms of Kossuth. Again with the exception of Eötvös, all believed firmly in noble supremacy.

Eötvös, a poet, journalist, and Hungary's first successful novelist, was the leader of the centralist movement mentioned earlier, which wished to destroy the rotten counties, unconditionally emancipate all peasants, and build political democracy on the basis of communal self-government and a strong central executive. In his novels he belabored the nobles, the cruel county jails, the corrupt county administrators, and everything that was antiquated and feudal in the country. He was a true humanitarian and, in 1867, when he would again become minister of cults and education, he was to create an excellent state school system and give an enlightened nationalities' law to Dualistic Hungary. Before 1848 he had been Kossuth's friend and ideological opponent and, like Deák, he had reluctantly sided with Kossuth against Széchenyi. Now he entered the cabinet very much against his best convictions, for he was persuaded that, in order to save noble political and economic supremacy, Kossuth was driving Hungary to war. Still, he agreed to serve, out of loyalty to his colleagues. Only after war had broken out did Eötvös seek (in September 1848) more peaceful pastures.[33]

Szemere seemed ideologically closest to Kossuth, although he often spoke like a centralist and his convictions were difficult to fathom. He was to prove an energetic, petulant, and ruthless wartime administrator; like Mészáros and Kossuth, he did not quit with the other ministers in September 1848. Rather, he carried on till the end of the conflict, finally as prime minister. Thereafter, he too went into exile.[34] Of the two other liberals, Klauzál belonged to the moderate faction; and the well-known Deák, also a moderate, was one of those who accepted his post only reluctantly.

This then was the first constitutional cabinet of Hungary: four titled and five untitled nobles and, with the exception of Mészáros, all well-known political figures. Unlike the new Austrian cabinet, which was composed mainly of bureaucrats, the Hungarian ministry included only one servant of the Crown. Unlike the French revolutionary government, which consisted of middle-class lawyers, journalists, businessmen, and one worker, this was almost entirely a government of noble landowners. In fact, Kossuth alone owned no land. The cabinet faithfully reflected the opinions of the Hungarian ruling class; it also bore witness to the fact that the lesser nobility was now much stronger than the titled nobility. Of all these men, Eötvös alone closely resembled the Western bourgeoisie in his political convictions, and Kossuth in his need to work for a living. Yet this government of the nobility became the great hope of all the revolutionaries in Europe.

The April Laws

The Diet's drastic reform bills caused agony at the Court, especially as no one in Vienna knew what to do about them. In a confidential memorandum to the king, dated March 24, the palatine explained that for the time being there was no way to stop the Hungarians. This famous note (a copy of which the Hungarians were to find following the palatine's resignation and departure from the country in Sep-

tember 1848, causing the parliament to brand the archduke a traitor—
in Habsburg eyes he was a traitor already) outlined three alternatives
open to the king. First, he could order his troops out of Hungary,
abandoning the nobility to the tender mercy of the peasants. "One
could then," the archduke wrote, "look on passively while the country
is being burned to the ground." Second, the king could collaborate
with Batthyány, make compromises, and "save whatever can be
saved." Third, the king could dismiss the palatine, appoint a royal
commissioner with power over life and death, send an army into
Hungary, disperse the Diet, advance on Pest and place the country
under martial law. The first alternative the palatine found immoral; he
also knew well what a sobering effect such a proposition would have
on the Magyar aristocrats at Court. The third alternative he considered unfeasible in view of the Monarchy's multiple military commit-
ments. There remained the second alternative, namely collaboration
with Batthyány; this the palatine considered "the sole guarantee of
the preservation of the province," adding that, "with the arrival of a
more favorable time, much can be changed which at present would
cause secession."[35]

Archduke Stephen was no traitor to Hungary or to anyone else.
He was an embattled leader trying to mediate (as did almost everyone
else in those days) between two hostile camps. Naturally, when he
talked to the Hungarians he emphasized the benefits of moderation,
and when he talked to the Court he held out the possibility of later
improvements. What counted was that he had managed to persuade
the State Conference to agree with him; for the time being, it was
necessary to negotiate with Batthyány. And in truth, when the palatine's second alternative was finally abandoned early in the fall of
1848, the Court adopted his third alternative, complete with an army
of invasion, a royal commissioner, and a state of siege.

Of course, the palatine did not mean the king to surrender without bargaining. A golden opportunity to weaken Kossuth's position
presented itself with the agitation of nobles over the bill on the abolition of serfdom. This measure, which Kossuth had driven so easily
through both Houses of the Diet on March 18, exasperated many landowners, and not only those of conservative persuasion. It was an
open scandal that there had been only seventeen members present
when, in a surprise meeting, the bill had been introduced in the
Upper House. Without immediate redemption payments, how were

the landlords to hire workers who would cultivate the suddenly abandoned demesne land? What would become of the countless small
nobles, especially in northern Hungary, who owned no demesne land
and were entirely dependent on income derived from feudal dues?
Count Antal Szapáry, a well-known liberal, turned on Batthyány at a
meeting of the Upper House: "If there is no compensation, I shall
shoot you dead." To which the prime minister replied: "That won't
be necessary because in that case I shall do it myself."[36] Estimating
his annual losses at over .5 million gulden, Prince Pál Esterházy was
prepared to ask the assembly of the county of which he was lord-lieutenant to petition the king not to sign the bill that Esterházy's own
cabinet had submitted.[37]

Most of the emperor's advisers did not personally object to the
idea of improving the condition of the peasants which had been part
and parcel of Metternich's own program; but in order to exploit dis-
sension in Hungary, on March 26–27 the State Conference decided to
request that the Diet suspend the bill until means were found to compensate the landowners. Simultaneously, the Conference expressed
its very understandable satisfaction with the taxation of nobles.[38]

A day later, and thus without waiting for Vienna's rejection of
the peasant bill to take its propaganda effect in Hungary, the State
Conference issued a second Royal Rescript attacking the bill on the
separate Hungarian government. True, this bill was far more dangerous to the unity of the Monarchy; still, by suddenly adding a nationalist issue to a socioeconomic issue, the Court defeated itself. In the
ensuing tumult the peasant question was nearly forgotten, especially
as Kossuth wisely combined the two problems into one great national
cause.[39]

The Rescript of March 28 stipulated (1) that the Hungarian
Court Chancellery be preserved, with powers of supervision over the
government; (2) that when the king was not resident in Hungary
(which the Austrians hoped would continue to be a permanent arrangement) plenipotentiary powers be exercised by the present palatine only and not by all palatines, the danger being very real that future palatines would not be of Habsburg blood and could even be
rebels; (3) that all royal revenues should be paid into the central
treasury whence, after deducting all royal expenditures, the money
would be redirected to Hungary—meaning in essence that there was
no need for a Hungarian ministry of finance, and that the Hungarians

would not be permitted to dispose of their own revenue; (4) that the king not be deprived of his monopoly over the commissioning of army officers and the employment of troops, and that such rights should not be exercised by the palatine even during the king's absence from Hungary—meaning that there was no need for a ministry of war either, and that the Hungarian government would have no say over wars; and (5) that Hungary should shoulder a part of the state debt.

The Royal Rescript was read aloud at a joint meeting of the Diet's two Houses on March 29, creating consternation. The second major confrontation between king and nation had begun. Batthyány, feeling personally cheated by the Court, announced his resignation but then changed his mind, trusting that the palatine would take immediate action with the monarch. There was general bewilderment: "Terror panicus an vielen Gesichtern," Széchenyi noted in his diary.

The storm erupted at the next circular meeting of the Lower House, where, free from the palatine's august presence, Kossuth "raised his thundering voice: more thundering and forceful than ever before." Already at a morning meeting Kossuth had threatened revolution: "It seems that God will not grant us the joy and pleasure of realizing our transformation without our citizens having to shed their blood." Now he announced that the Hungarian government was "no toy, no puppet, no useless post office," and he moved that the Royal Rescript should be rejected in toto. This the House then proceeded to do in two fiery resolutions, repeating verbatim what Kossuth had said.[40]

In reality Kossuth's fury was as calculated as it was political: in the same two speeches where he had asked for revolution and for the indictment of the king's evil Hungarian councilors as traitors, he had urged the palatine to see to it that the king kept his word. Thus relations with the Court were not to be broken off; rather, the bargaining was to continue.

Now it was for the street to help out the Diet. As early as March 27 the Buda-Pest Committee of Public Safety had held a mass meeting, where Petőfi and others had demanded the immediate convocation of a national convention, the repudiation of the Batthyány ministry, and the proclamation of a republic; and where the two ministers-designate, Klauzál and Szemere, had had a hard time calming the crowd.

In the ensuing days, the second set of Pest *journées* continued. It is certain that Kossuth had encouraged these manifestations with his passionate speeches, and by stressing to the delegate of the Pest radicals that the "March Youth" ought to "risk everything for fatherland." But it is also very probable that the *journées* would have occurred even without Kossuth. On March 29 the agitation in Pest reached its crescendo with a massive march on City Hall to demand arms and with barricades erected in the streets—no one quite knew against whom. On the same night the acting chairman of the Vice-Regal Council, Count Ferenc Zichy, sent an urgent message to Vienna: "If, within a few days, favorable decisions are not taken, especially with regard to the ministries of war and finance, Hungary is lost to the dynasty."[41] On March 30, 20,000 people assembled in front of the Pest National Museum to hear Petőfi proclaim the coming of a world revolution.[42]

By then the Pest commotion had achieved its desired effect, the more so as news of it had arrived in Pressburg and Vienna, tremendously inflated. On March 30 the State Conference, where Archduke Francis Charles had taken over from Archduke Louis, urgently summoned the Hungarian leaders to Court, and following an all-night debate dropped almost all of its restrictions on Hungarian self-government. What remained was the not-so-important reservation that inviolability apply only to the person of the present palatine and not to all palatines, and the soon-to-be-very-important reservation that the king alone be empowered to commission officers as well as to employ the Hungarian army "abroad," i.e., outside the boundaries of Hungary. The king was left with his ancient privilege of appointing the Catholic prelates and the (often titular) high dignitaries of the realm. The matter of Hungary's participation in servicing the state debt was left to the next Hungarian parliament. For all this, the palatine had secured the personal consent of Kossuth.[43] On the same March 31 this drastically modified Royal Rescript was read in the Diet amidst tumultuous cheering. Kossuth spoke again, "reaching one of the highest summits of his oratorical career," and now, when victory was complete, sounding a conciliatory note. He promised a generous civil list to His Majesty, all the while reminding the monarch that he was on the throne only through the courtesy of Kossuth.

Gentlemen! I am a simple citizen. I had no other power, no other influence in this world than that which justice, instilled by God in my soul, gave me. And yet, such are the ways of providence that I, the simple citizen, one of the fatherland's lowest, was—because of the munificence of circumstances—in such a position, during a few hours [on March 15], that this hand of mine was able to decide whether the House of Austria should stand or not stand.[44]

Thus the Hungarians had won again, or rather, Kossuth had won because it was he who had taken the greatest risks: he alone had dared call the bluff of the Court and had mobilized the street. Whether the price ultimately paid by Hungary was not too high is another matter. The unfortunate Pest radicals, who (unlike the Court) remained permanently powerless and whose bluff had been called earlier by Kossuth, now celebrated "Citizen Kossuth." Forgetting about a second government, a national convention, a republic, and a war, the radicals built bonfires in Pest to hail their hero. Only Petőfi and one or two of his friends knew that not only the Court but they, too, had been defeated. Petőfi wrote on April 1: "No, the revolution is not over: this was only the First Act. Au revoir." But there were to be no new Buda-Pest *journées* until May 10, and then the scenario of March would be repeated.[45]

It remained only for the Court to accept Batthyány's cabinet list. Kossuth's name was a bitter pill to swallow, but the argument prevailed that his appointment was inevitable and that, as minister of finance, he would have little power and a lot of responsibility. And truly, no portfolio could have been less enviable than his: while the peasants were no longer paying taxes and the nobles not yet, he was expected to balance a still nonexistent budget; send an annual 3-million-gulden stipend to the king; pay the ministers, the administration, the army in Hungary; and, *horribile dictu,* contribute to the Austrian debt payments. For the time being, Kossuth was satisfied. He summed up his views of past events in an address on April 1 to the palatine: "The nobility, this first-born of the fatherland, has decided to share with all others the treasury of rights and liberty. Instead of privileged classes, Your Highness is now surrounded by a free nation, one that has become master of its fate and its future."[46]

The king having set April 9 as the closing date of the Diet, feverish activity began again. On March 31, the day the king's modified Rescript was read aloud and celebrated, the legislators finally settled the question of suffrage reform, which they had debated ever since the fall of 1847. Although drafted by several hands, the bill again bore Kossuth's imprint. Providing for an annual parliament in Buda-Pest, the bill confirmed the rights of those who already possessed the franchise (that is, noblemen and the burghers of free cities) and extended the franchise to all those who were born in Hungary, were at least age twenty (for the passive franchise the age limit was set at twenty-four), were free from the control of parents or that of a master, had not been convicted of major crimes, belonged to a "received" religion, and met specific property, residence, and employment qualifications. As to the latter, fairly substantial property and a secure income were required from the inhabitants of free cities, and possession of at least one-fourth of a servile "section" with corresponding income was required from the inhabitants of towns and villages. Manufacturers, shopkeepers, and master-artisans also had to be solidly established, with the latter employing at least one worker. This meant in practice that, in addition to dependent children, domestics, servants, and other wage earners, the law excluded all the landless and contractual peasants, as well as many of the urbarial peasants (thus extending voting rights to about one-third of the entire peasantry) and the urban poor. As the "Mosaic faith" was not yet a "received religion," the law also excluded the Jews. On the other hand, specifically included were the *honoratiores:* scholars, artists, surgeons, lawyers, engineers, teachers, ministers—in brief, all educated people of a commoner background. The ballot remained open (but several cities were eventually to resort to secret balloting); and the Upper House was left unchanged, which would not prevent the latter from steadily losing influence. Finally, knowledge of Magyar was made obligatory for all legislators, "the language of legislation being exclusively Hungarian."

The most controversial issue, which ended with Kossuth's resounding victory over the radical deputies and their centralist allies, was the nobility's continued franchise. No matter how destitute or uneducated, the nobles preserved their ancient rights and would succeed, through sheer numbers and even more through prestige and force, in maintaining their hegemony in parliament. The new House of Representatives, elected in June, was to consist almost exclusively of noblemen, which is precisely what the March legislators had in mind. Ironically, this new "popular assembly," which remained in session until the end of the war in August 1849, would accomplish infinitely less in terms of social and economic reforms than the old feudal Diet was now accomplishing in a few weeks. But this, too, was the legislators' wish in March, for with them the great reform age was to come to an end, and the age of consolidation was to begin. Then, too, the old Diet was not presiding over a war-torn country as the new National Assembly would do.

All in all, the franchise provisions were very progressive, raising the proportion of qualified voters to about 6 percent of the population, or one-fourth of all adult males, a proportion not to be surpassed in Hungary until after World War I. It was more progressive than the French electoral law of 1830 had been; or the British Parliamentary act of 1832, which had increased the proportion of voters to about 5 percent of the population; or the famous liberal Belgian constitution of 1831, which had set the lower age limit at twenty-four and was more stringent in other respects, too; or the Austrian constitution of April 25, 1848, with its provisions for indirect voting. And while both the Prussian law of April and the French electoral decree of March were definitely more democratic, the Prussian Assembly turned out to be not much more "popular" than the Hungarian, while the French National Assembly, elected on the basis of almost universal suffrage, became quite conservative.[47]

The debate on the national electoral law was followed by a debate on the reform of the county structure. Kossuth wished to extend the national suffrage system to the counties, with the proviso that the elected county assemblies would then choose the county officials; but, on this question he was surprisingly defeated. Now that the political emergency was over, an unlikely alliance of conservatives, centralists, and radicals came into being, with the conservatives wishing to save noble privilege and the left wing hoping to destroy the counties through the rejection of reforms. Despite all his eloquence and his insistence that his whole purpose was to guarantee the economic and political hegemony of the nobility, Kossuth was voted down on April 2 and 3. Finally, nothing was changed: the nobles alone had the franchise in the counties, and the problem was passed on to the new parliament, which in turn would prove unable to deal with the issue. There would be no new county elections, and during the war, power over the counties would pass gradually into the hands of government commissioners, similar to Metternich's much-hated "administrators," who were to exercise near-dictatorial power.[48]

One more major clash with the Court occurred before ratification of all the bills; but as this took place behind closed doors in Vienna, not even the legislators heard much about it. At issue was the inclusion of the Military Border in the national electoral law and thus in the new parliament. Correctly understanding that this was the first step toward the reincorporation of the Border into the Hungarian administrative and military systems, Archduke Francis Charles categorically refused his consent. The danger to the Court was indeed enormous, for it would have meant subjecting the Monarchy's best soldiers to the whims of the Hungarian minister of war and risking an anti-Habsburg revolt of the *Grenzer*. Even though Batthyány and Kossuth immediately rushed to Vienna offering major concessions, nothing had been achieved by April 8. Then, suddenly and inexplicably, the archduke surrendered in exchange for a written promise that for the time being the Border's military system would not be changed.

It was all over. In the final days before the closing of the Diet, the State Conference approved a whole series of bills, virtually without argument; and on April 10 the king arrived in Pressburg in the company of Francis Charles and the latter's son, young Francis Joseph. On the following day, the king solemnly closed the Diet: ''I wish from the depths of my heart the happiness of my loyal Hungarian nation, for I find therein my own. . . .''[49] Soon thereafter the deputies went home with printed copies of the thirty-one April Laws in their luggage. It seemed to them that a miracle had happened.

The New Constitution: An End or a Beginning?

As the Hungarian liberals saw it, theirs had not been a revolution at all, but a peaceful adjustment to the times and the legal reconquest of Hungary's historical freedoms. Their actions had been forceful, dignified, and magnanimous: his Majesty's ancient rights had not been curtailed, only the dual sovereignty of king and nation under the Crown of Saint Stephen had now been reconstituted. The king could still appoint and dismiss the prelates and the high officials of the realm, commission officers, make war, suspend or dissolve parliament, veto legislation, grant pardon, and create nobles. He was given a generous civil list, the right of his family to succeed to the Throne was not questioned, and his person remained sacrosanct. The very law guaranteeing freedom of the press made it a crime to incite against the king or to agitate against the ties linking the nation with the Crown, against those linking Hungary with the other parts of the Monarchy, and against the hereditary rights of the Habsburgs.

Many extralegal institutions having been abolished, Hungary now possessed its own government, responsible to a parliament meeting annually with deputies elected for three-year terms; it also had—as it always should have had—its own army, militia, administration, and judiciary. The counties and the cities were free; all citizens enjoyed equality before the law, and almost all enjoyed religious freedom; taxation was proportional and general; all privileged estates, churches, nations, and corporations had ceased to exist; the franchise was given to all who by virtue of their profession, position, or income had a stake in ordinary progress and the stability of society; all peasants were free and former urbarial peasants were granted full ownership of their tenure; patrimonial jurisdiction, labor services, the tithes to the church and to the landowner, as well as payments in kind and cash on former servile lands, were abolished; entailment and other feudal restrictions on the free flow of goods and labor were suppressed; citizens could live where they wished and engage in any profession; the hitherto church-controlled university was placed under state supervision; provisions were made for the establishment of a national land-credit institution, as well as for the building of canals, highways, railroads, and harbors; arbitrary arrest and detention were forbidden; trial by jury for political crimes was introduced; and the state guaranteed the security of life and private property. In brief, theirs was now a free and modern country where dedication, talent and patriotism were the sole avenues to career and prestige.

Moreover, Hungary was finally on her way toward unification! The *Partium,* those small districts on the Transylvanian border and until now illegally administered from there, were finally returned to the mother country. The same could be expected of Transylvania proper, although in this case Hungary had generously consented to wait for the Transylvanian Diet to pronounce for unification and to adjust its antiquated political and social legislation to that of progressive Hungary. The Military Border remained under Austrian military control; but it too eventually would have to be placed under the legal authority of Hungary. Last but not least, Croatia-Slavonia was guaranteed her traditional liberties, but the new *ban* would be watched, lest he attempt to defy his own government.[50]

Writing from post-revolutionary exile, Bishop Mihály Horváth, a companion of Kossuth and the revolution's first great historian, summed up the events of March–April 1848:

This nation: so full of healthy, youthful and sparkling energy; so full of enthusiasm and of fervent yearning for all that was good, beautiful and just— accepted these magnificent reforms with complete satisfaction and exuberant joy. Having been, through the practice of centuries, accustomed to freedom, it knew how to live with freedom. In political sophistication and in constitutional experience, it incomparably surpassed all the other peoples of the Monarchy.[51]

Seen from Vienna or through the eyes of the Jews, the poor, the radicals, or the non-Magyar nationalities, things looked a bit more complicated. The king's privileges were gravely threatened by the special status granted the palatine and by the necessity of a ministerial countersignature to all royal or palatinal decrees; the competences of the "minister near His Majesty," the minister of finance, and the minister of war were ill-defined or not defined at all. The responsibilities of the Hungarian minister of war were particularly obscure: was this minister to control the Imperial-Royal troops stationed in Hungary, or the regiments originating from Hungary no matter where they happened to serve, or was he to control both? How was he to coordinate his functions with his Austrian counterpart? Did he have authority over the Hungarian regiments now fighting in northern Italy? What would become of the General-Militär-Commandos into which the Empire was divided, with five out of a total of twelve finding themselves in the lands under the Hungarian Crown? What was the precise meaning of that ominous sentence in Law III of the constitution: "The employment of the Hungarian army beyond the frontiers of the country will require the counter-signature of the responsible Hungarian minister"? This sentence went directly against another clause in the same law granting sole rights to the king over the deployment of the Hungarian army beyond the frontiers of the country. What, in any case, was the Hungarian army? Did "beyond the frontiers" include the other provinces of the Monarchy? What if the

Hungarian government chose to disapprove of a domestic or foreign military action of the king? Would the minister of finance help pay for such action? And how about the state debt? Clearly, even if the Hungarian government would wish to observe its own laws—and chances were that it would not—it could interpret them in a way fatal to the unity and greatness of the Monarchy.

As far as the Jews were concerned, nothing good had happened so far. On the contrary, things had become worse, with innumerable peasants having the franchise but even the wealthiest Jewish business-men not having it; with city authorities suddenly cracking down and expelling "illegal residents," and with the mob thirsting for the blood of "Yids." Still, there was hope. The sympathies of Batthyány and Kossuth could not be doubted; in Buda-Pest, where Jews had volun-teered en masse for the militia only to be thrown out bodily by their Christian fellows, no lesser heroes than Petőfi and Vasvári had since created their own all-Jewish National Guard company. No wonder that the Jews rallied to the new Hungarian tricolor: the red, white, and green.

There is evidence to show that the peasants appreciated the abolition of dues and services, especially the *robot;* but it seems that in the other material aspects of their emancipation (at least in the ini-tial confusion) many peasants saw little progress, or no progress at all. The same law that granted full ownership to urbarial peasants also raised the possibility that former seizures and forced enclosures by the landlords might be validated by the courts. The "grape-tithe" on vineyards—a special category of land under the old tenure system—remained, and ownership of the vineyards was still withheld from their peasant cultivators. Nor were any of the so-called *regalia* abolished: the noble landowner's exclusive right to sell wine and other produce in certain periods of the year, as well as to hold fairs, to hunt, to fish, and to fowl. Peasants were still required to do public work for the county and to pay county dues. And as for the hundreds of thousands of peasants who held parts of the lord's demesne in private contract, nothing was done for them; nor was there anything for the landless cotters, the houseless, the day laborers, or the estate servants. Demesne lands were considered private not feudal property: their distribution among the poor was unthinkable to the nobility and, as a matter of fact, even to the peasantry. But since there were so many disputed rights and so much disputed land, the outbreak of peasant disturbances could be taken for granted—and they would follow shortly.

The radicals resented the lack of complete national independence, the hegemony of the nobles, the restricted suffrage and militia laws; but mainly they resented the punitive press law. The urban workers missed the regulation of wages and working hours, and finally the non-Magyar nationalities (for the moment mildly sympathetic) could not help but notice that their existence went unrecognized in the April Laws, or was recognized only negatively with the stipulation that Magyar be the language of legislation and administration.

The Habsburg problem, the Croatian problem, the Jewish problem, the peasant problem, the worker problem, the radical problem, and the nationality problem: the Hungarian cabinet would have to face them all, intertwined as they were in a bewildering fashion, and would have to face them simultaneously. There would be many more triumphs, both political and military, but the liberals' policy as a whole was not destined to bring its promised results. Kossuth's dream—that a better age would follow now that everyone from king to beggar had been given his due rights—would prove precisely that: a dream.

Hungarian historians have never ceased to question whether, in March 1848, the nobility acted out of idealism, fear, or economic self-interest. The historian Mihály Horváth was the first to formulate clearly the idealistic interpretation: "The former noble class, even though it had lost its privileges and urbarial benefits . . . not only shouldered, with dignified resignation, the sacrifices made to justice and to the common good, but, with a few exceptions, was genuinely pleased with the fact that the walls separating social classes had fallen into dust and the nation now melted into one big and robust body."[52]

The "fear" theory was best explained by the early twentieth-century radical socialist critic of Dualistic Hungary, Ervin Szabó, who wrote that "not revolutionary enthusiasm, but fear of the revolution coalesced the hitherto acrimoniously fighting parties in the Estates' Diet into that 'selfless' unity, of which the nobility has never since ceased to boast," an interpretation ironically corroborated to an extent by the conservative historian Gyula Szekfű, who affirmed in his classic *Hungarian History* that not only magnanimity but also "the pressure of foreign news" had driven the nobles to embrace laws "which cast a doubt on the future of their families.''[53] Finally, the theory of economic motivation was best propounded by the marxists, in the first place by that insightful historian and rigid stalinist cultural tyrant József Révai, who stated that economic circumstances—the superior productivity of the large estates—drove the market-producing, middle landowning nobility to cast away the feudal system and to opt for the bourgeois-capitalist reorganization of Hungary. Thus, far from casting doubt on the future of the nobility, the April Laws saved the middle and lower nobles from economic decline and consequent political extinction.[54]

It is hard to see how the motivation of such a large and disunited body as the nobility could ever be penetrated. Kossuth himself was so unsure of what the nobles wanted, or wanted to hear, that he appealed simultaneously to idealism and to patriotism, ambition and the thirst for power, fear and the instinct for survival, normal economic self-interest and greed, common sense and emotionalism. Nor can it be argued that Kossuth said one thing in public and another in private: everything that issued from his mouth or his pen was meant for public consumption. Even the delightfully candid and hesitant Széchenyi used a rich variety of arguments to convince himself, and those more conservative than himself, that the April Laws were a good thing. It is an easy answer, but not necessarily a wrong answer, that a multiplicity of motives caused the nobility to submit to the new constitution.

Ervin Szabó writes in his revisionist history of the revolution that after an auspicious radical beginning in the 1830s, Kossuth became more and more conservative in the 1840s, until finally there was no significant difference between his social program and that of Metternich. József Révai says exactly the contrary, and so do all modern marxist historians: it is an article of faith with them that Kossuth considered the April Laws only a first step toward the complete democratization of Hungary. Kossuth alone understood (Révai argues) that the interests of the nobility and of the peasantry had to be "equalized." "The equalization of interests . . . was the only possible program of the national unity front." Thus (according to Révai) Kossuth's seeming moderation was in reality a revolutionary act, national independence being a must for the establishment of democracy.[55]

It is difficult to agree with Szabó on Kossuth's gradual retreat toward conservatism. On the contrary, he moved from an old-fashioned "estates" nationalism in the 1830s to a modern liberal nationalism in the 1840s, one that was energetic and progressive enough to allow the creation of the most significant reform laws in Hungarian history. Many of these laws were not immediately translated into reality, as legislation alone never changes society; but the April Laws did become the basis of later progressive developments. And while it is true that there was no fundamental difference between Kossuth's and Metternich's socioeconomic programs, the fact remains that Metternich did not dare introduce these changes whereas Kossuth dared.

But Révai's view that for Kossuth the April Laws were only a beginning does not stand up to historical scrutiny either. By the early 1840s Kossuth's *Weltanschauung* was firmly established, and he was not to change it to his dying day. There is no evidence to show that after April 1848 Kossuth wished to go further to win over the lower classes. All signs indicate that for him, as for most other nobles, the great reform age had come to an end in April 1848.

After April, only a few radicals wished to extend the reform measures. Further progressive legislation was widely seen as dangerous to the stability of society, and the last thing Kossuth and his friends wanted was to endanger that stability. History, measured not in years but in decades, proved Kossuth successful. Neither war, nor defeat, nor the subsequent Habsburg absolutism was able to dethrone those who had consolidated their rule in March–April 1848. The National Assembly, elected in June, was made up almost exclusively of nobles, and so was the officer corps of Kossuth's national army; Czech and German-Austrian commoners, whom the Bach regime imported in the 1850s to administer subjugated Hungary, were gotten rid of in the 1860s, and the parliament of 1867, the one of the Compromise Agreement between King and nation, consisted entirely of the traditional elite. The only victims of 1848 were those who had sided too closely with Metternich, or who, in the summer of 1849, had failed to desert Kossuth. Yet, even from among these loyal fools a good many eventually returned to the political stage.

Hungary was led by noblemen, or by ennobled commoners, until almost the middle of the twentieth century, and even though Kossuth died in exile he had realized his dream of a country modernized under the guidance of the noble estate.

The historic significance of the Hungarian Spring was enormous: it guaranteed the economic and political survival of the landowning class; it opened the way to spectacular economic and cultural development; and it provided the Magyar nation with an eternal romantic legacy. Since agreement has never been reached as to what exactly happened in March–April 1848, short of a national consensus that it was something magnificent, Hungarians of all persuasions—extreme nationalists, fascists, orthodox conservatives, liberals, democrats, even Communists—have looked back at the Hungarian Spring with pride and have derived from it a profound source of inspiration. The Hungarian Spring has become all things to all people in that country.

3 / Between Legality and Rebellion: Kossuth Minister of Finance (April–August 1848)

Troubled Beginnings

ROYAL SANCTION OF Hungary's April Laws was followed by six months of constitutional government: a period marked by peasant and worker unrest, anti-Semitic mobs, revolt of the nationalities and grave trouble with Croatia, Austria, the Imperial-Royal army, and the Court. Yet it was not an entirely fruitless or hopeless period. The government held on, which made it more or less unique in revolution-torn Europe; a new parliament was elected and it quickly proved capable of great determination; the workers and at least the Magyar peasants, if not the peasants of other nationalities, were quieted; the pogroms were stopped; finances and the administration were organized. But the regime proved unable to handle the nationality problem, the Croatian problem, or the Austrian problem. Ultimately, Hungary could not avoid a crisis. In September the country slid into a revolutionary dictatorship and into a war with its several enemies.

Between April and August Kossuth had to share the limelight with others; still, as minister of finance, as spokesman of the government in the National Assembly, as a dabbler in the affairs of the other ministers, and as editor and publisher of a popular newspaper in which he criticized his own cabinet, he exercised political influence far beyond his official status. In September he would emerge again as his country's undisputed leader.

Government policy during these months was characterized by efforts at complete administrative centralization; a strong although not entirely inflexible stance toward the monarch and the non-Magyar nationalities; ambition and naiveté in foreign policy; and a firm commitment to the constitution, something that distinguished the Hungarian from other newly formed liberal regimes.

Hungary's political situation differed fundamentally not only from that of Western Europe and Germany but also from that of Austria. There, the new ministry was as subservient to the Court as it was passive when confronted with popular pressure. The makeup of the Austrian cabinet changed whenever the Court or the crowds desired it; political concessions were made to the Viennese every time they decided to stage one of their famed *Katzenmusik* happenings (noise-making under the windows of unpopular politicians); and the existence of parallel second and third "governments" composed of Viennese students, National Guard, and burghers was tolerated. Despite everything, or perhaps because of it, the Austrian government survived—if not quite in power, then at least as a constituted body, a model for the future. The contrast between Austria and Hungary is even more striking if we consider that the Austrian cabinet had to weather an almost permanent revolution in its own capital, while it had relatively little trouble with the provinces, except for the grave but not fatal trouble in Lombardy-Venetia. The Hungarian cabinet, on the other hand, was firmly ensconced in Buda-Pest; but it had grave, ultimately fatal, trouble with the provinces, at least where South Slavs and Romanians lived.

As for the Court, another point of contrast in our story, its position deteriorated at first to such a degree that it had to flee from Vienna to Innsbruck; by the end of the summer, however, the Court overcame some of its difficulties and returned to the capital.

It is customary for historians of the Habsburg Monarchy to apologize for their inability to account cohesively, and in a logical sequence, for the events of this period. In the words of Robert A. Kann: "The revolution in the Habsburg empire took place in several theaters and on several levels. All were interrelated. This factor can never be fully shown in a historical presentation, which cannot tell all at the same time."[1] If this famous Austro-American historian could make such a frank admission, then it should be enough to remind the reader here that in Hungary all issues—constitutional, national, social, and economic—were more sharply accentuated and more closely interrelated than anywhere else; that all issues were fought out to the bitter end; and that, while Western Europe and the German states were gradually moving toward law and order, conflicts in Hungary kept increasing in vehemence, with the Hungarians defying the centralizing efforts of the Court and the Austrian government, and the Slavs and Romanians defying the centralizing efforts of the Hungarian regime.

What makes these events so difficult to fathom is the existence of several power centers in the Monarchy, with each center seeking the support of the enemies of its enemies. The Court in Innsbruck allied itself with the Czechs against the Vienna liberals, the latter with the radicals in the capital against the Court; the Imperial army with Slavic peasants against Hungary, and the latter with German burghers and peasants in southern Hungary against the Serbian revolutionaries. Some centers, such as Innsbruck, Buda-Pest, Zagreb, and Karlóca (the seat of Serbian nationalist agitation) were relatively cohesive and stable; other centers such as Vienna and Prague were divided into many competing groups; again others were not tied to any one city but represented circles around powerful leaders or important institutions, such as Radetzky's army in Italy, Windisch-Graetz's army in Bohemia, or the Romanian National Committee in Transylvania. Weakened by internal dissent, desperately confused on the issue of loyalties, generally loath to shed blood but still feeling duty-bound to fight, these power centers struggled for widely divergent objectives; but, at least in this period, they unanimously and exclusively struggled in the name of the emperor-king. Thus dynastic loyalty and adherence to the concept of legality survived long after the ruler had ceased to exercise supreme control and had himself become one of the many competing forces. Ultimately, it was this concept of loyalty and legality which saved the Habsburgs—not their policy of *divide et impera,* not the British desire to see the Habsburg Monarchy intact, not the Russian intervention in Hungary, not the economic interest of the ruling classes, not the betrayal of the revolution by the bourgeoisie. The history of the Habsburg Monarchy in this era presents not only a case study of conflicting ideologies and interest groups, both new and old, but also a fascinating case study of the desolate confusion of good men caught in a turmoil of which most understood nothing. This confusion explains why so many people held on, so long, to the one idea which they comfortably shared: devotion to the near-mythical figure of the emperor-father.

Minutes of the Hungarian cabinet's first official meeting, on April 12, tell almost all there is to know about the policy of the new government: assertion of virtual independence vis-à-vis the ruler; meddling in the domestic affairs of Austria, and ambition in international relations. The day's agenda included debate and decision on Slovak nationalist activity, on Jelačić, on Hungarian soldiers in Austria and on Austrian soldiers in Hungary, on famine in some areas of the country, on the use of the Hungarian flag by the merchant fleet, on the Hungarian Court Chancellery, on Polish autonomy in Galicia, and on foreign affairs, especially relations with Great Britain.[2]

By April 12 reports had reached the Council of Ministers regarding "Russian-initiated Pan-Slavic" agitation among Slovak students and intellectuals in northern Hungary. This agitation was all the more worrisome because of even more alarming news received from the southern parts of the country: the Croats reportedly wished to secede completely; the Serbs were rebellious; and beyond the Ottoman border the Bosnians were arming themselves for an invasion of Hungary. But no reliable troops were available to nip the Slovak movement in the bud, so local authorities were ordered to watch the Slovaks closely; and Prince Esterházy was instructed by mail (for he was in Vienna near the king) to request from His Majesty that the Hungarian soldiers in Galicia (three regular infantry regiments and four cavalry regiments) be dispatched immediately to northern Hungary. The instructions to Esterházy were drafted by Kossuth; and as the center of Russian Pan-Slavic agitation was thought to be in Galicia, Esterházy was also told to prevail upon the Austrian government to set up, without delay, a purely Polish (and thus not mixed Polish and Ukrainian) militia in Galicia, and to emancipate the peasants there. Clearly then, the Batthyány cabinet was intent—in its own interest—to follow up on its original plan to impose reforms, similar to those instituted in Hungary, on the other provinces of the Monarchy.

The Hungarians saw the Galician issue as particularly important. Paralleling the French and Prussian revolutionary desire for the resurrection of Poland, the Hungarian leaders insisted on April 12 and later that the Emperor grant a constitution to Galicia. From Galician autonomy a unified anti-Russian Poland might arise one day. On this

question there was absolutely no difference between Kossuth, Batthyány, or the others.

Again on April 12, "Prince Esterházy Foreign Minister" was or-
dered to get in touch with Lord Ponsonby, the Vienna envoy of the
British government, and, "in harmony with the Austrian Foreign
Minister," inform him of certain developments interesting to Great
Britain, Austria, and Hungary. Lord Ponsonby was to be told that the
recent political changes would not weaken the Habsburg Monarchy;
on the contrary, the situation now favored peace in the Empire. But
Ponsonby was also to be informed that revolutonary agitation and
Russian influence in the "Lower Danubian Provinces" (Moldavia,
Wallachia, and Serbia) were likely to endanger the security of
Hungary and thus the security of the entire Monarchy, as well as
British interests in the area. Revolutions in the Ottoman Empire
might follow, with a European war as a probable consequence. The
Hungarian cabinet expressed its hope that Her Britannic Majesty's
government would adopt a pro-Hungarian policy, which meant a pro-
Austrian policy. Hungary was, after all, "the strongest pillar of the
House of Austria."

The Hungarian note to the British was drafted by Kossuth, and it
was a clear reflection of his old foreign policy scheme of a joint military crusade by the British, French, Germans, Austrians, and Hungarians against Pan-Slavism and Tsarist Russia. The Hungarian move
proved to be unsuccessful: British Foreign Secretary Lord Palmerston
responded to Ponsonby's communication on April 28, expressing his
pleasure with

the satisfactory state of the mutual relations of Hungary and the Austrian
Govt. With regard however to the danger of revolutionary movements in
Moldavia, Walachia and Servia, . . . Her Majesty's Govt. would . . . on
every account be desirous of preventing any such outbreak from happening,
but they scarcely know in which way and by what means they can have it in
their Power to assist in doing so.[3]

British reluctance to intervene in the Balkans was for the moment only a minor problem for Hungary; far more dangerous was the
presumption of the Batthyány cabinet that it could influence British
policy, and the cabinet's resolve to treat Esterházy as foreign minister. Even if the Austrian and Hungarian chiefs of diplomacy would

try to act in harmony, a great power could not possibly operate with two foreign ministers.

In its further resolutions, the cabinet council of April 12 asked the palatine to order Jelačić to Buda, there to hear the remonstrations of the Hungarian government; were he to refuse, punitive measures would be taken against him. Upon hearing the complaint of the head of the Buda military General-Commando, Baron Lederer—that some units under his command could not be transported out of Hungary because of the reluctance of the Danube Steamship Company to rent him a boat without orders from the responsible Hungarian minister— the cabinet council decided to dispatch a ship in secret to the Austrian commander. Secrecy was to be maintained so as not to agitate the public in Buda-Pest. Detailed measures were drafted for the total liquidation of the Hungarian Court Chancellery; relief was voted for the famished population in northern Hungary (where the money was to come from was not specified); and finally, after Kossuth had reported that because of the Italian revolution ships from Hungary's Adriatic ports were unable to sail while flying the Austrian flag, it was decided that from now on these ships should fly the Hungarian flag. The Hungarian foreign minister was told to ask his Austrian colleague to secure recognition for the Hungarian tricolor in every harbor where there was an Austrian consul. Thus the government provided for Hungarian independence in foreign trade as well as in diplomacy. But the Austrian foreign minister did nothing about the request.

Life was not to be dull in Buda-Pest, where the government finally settled in the middle of April. First of all, there was trouble in the cities. From the middle of March to at least July, workers in Pest and miners in the northern Hungarian mining towns agitated for improved living conditions. Journeymen and apprentices demanded the suppression of the guilds, the reduction of the work day from 13–15 to 10–12 hours, higher remuneration on piece rates, and the right to collective bargaining. When their demands were not met, the workers in many places struck. Yet the labor movement in Hungary never became as active as in Vienna, Prague, or Berlin: there were far fewer workers in Hungary, with no real contact among the several crafts; skilled workers were mostly German and skilled miners mostly Czech; the latter in particular had had long experience with workers' organizations, but as foreigners they had little in common with the generally unskilled Hungarian workers; journeymen tended to regard

Jewish competitors as their enemies and not the masters; and, last but not least, the government handled labor agitation with skill, and without much emotional involvement. Strikes were broken with force, or the threat of force; but since the landed nobility in power neither felt threatened by the workers nor had much sympathy with the mostly German employers, the government ordered the reduction of working hours for journeymen to 11 a day, granted higher rates for overtime, and (among other measures) allowed a limited number of journeymen to attend guild meetings. In Hungarian industry, printing shops were the most technically advanced and the printers the best organized; because the regime badly needed the printers, it convoked a joint meeting of owners and workers on May 13, where collective bargaining in the printing industry was agreed on—the first in the country's history. Because of such enlightened policies, there was to be little trouble with the workers, who would profit handsomely from the production of weapons. Labor morale would never be very high; but after Kossuth had assumed dictatorship in the autumn of 1848, he made sure that as many workers' demands as possible were met. Without their contribution, the War of Independence could not have been fought.[4]

The most frightening aspect of urban disorders was the pogroms. On April 24 ten Jews were killed and about forty wounded in Pressburg. There is evidence that the rioters, mainly apprentices and journeymen, had been incited by their masters. The government used the regular army against the rabble; but as soon as the soldiers turned their backs, lynchings and looting started again. The city council took no action until Gentile property also began to suffer; meanwhile the Jews were ordered out of the city within twenty-four hours. The Pressburg riots were the worst; in Pest, where anti-Semitic disturbances had been unintentionally triggered by a radical drive against the payment of rents to houseowners, the militia and army grenadiers were able to stop the excesses. In general, German-inhabited western Hungarian cities saw the most vicious riots; other cities were much quieter, and the whole affair died down in a few weeks.

Batthyány was aghast at the pogroms; but when even Kossuth argued that unconditional promotion and defense of Jewish rights would mean sending the Jews to the slaughterhouse, the prime minister, as commander-in-chief of the National Guard, "excused" the Jews on April 25 from the by then compulsory militia service. Thus besides being unable to vote, financially qualified Jews were not allowed to bear arms for their country. In the same decree Batthyány also ordered strict enforcement of the municipal immigration laws, which meant attempts to evict the Jews from the free royal towns. Petőfi, Táncsics, and other radicals bitterly protested against the government's surrender to what they termed German bourgeois pressure; and their newspaper, *Márczius Tizenötödike* (*March Fifteenth*), commented that a government which forbade its citizens to do their duty (to serve in the militia), that allowed the people to disobey the law and itself disobeyed its own laws, was a government of cowards.[5] Actually, the government's caution was understandable and tactically not unwise. Jewish emancipation was a novel concept, not uniformly popular even in left-wing circles, where Jews were often identified as exploiters. As enlightened a measure as Joseph II's famous 1783 Edict of Toleration had excluded most Jews from the free royal cities, had kept them under the strict control of the Treasury, and had obligated them to pay a toleration tax. The Hungarian reformers were divided on the question of this emancipation. Széchenyi (who disliked the Jews more than was customary for an aristocrat) was particularly agitated by the massive influx of the poverty-stricken East European Jewry. He wrote in 1844: "The English or the French can afford to liberate them because a bottle of ink will not spoil the taste of a great lake, yet it would certainly spoil a plate of Hungarian soup." Kossuth's views were those of a typical liberal nationalist: for him a drastic reform of the Jewish religion and the modernization of Jewish communal life were prerequisites to legalized assimilation: "The emancipation of European Jewry, in society and politics, can be achieved only if the Jews, abiding by Napoleon's directives, prepare for emancipation through a great Synedrium." Or as he wrote in 1844 in *Pesti Hírlap:* the Jews must prove through proper reform and a solemn ecclesiastical proclamation "that the social institutions of the Mosaic laws do not constitute an essential part of the Jewish religion."[6] Eötvös was more militantly liberal, arguing that once free in a free land, Jews would develop their own healthy version of Magyar nationalism. But even Eötvös hoped that emancipation would lead to religious conversion.

The contemporary nationalist press, while championing the cause of Jewish artisans against the German-dominated guilds, abounded in anti-Jewish clichés: in tales of usury, immorality, and ritual murder. Emancipation, many a liberal journalist feared, would mean Jewish parliamentary deputies, Jewish officers, Jewish civil servants, and, horror of horrors, Jewish noblemen.

Jews were the true middlemen of the countryside: they were the innkeepers and store managers of the large estates and played an important role in grain trade; but to assert, as some contemporary journalists did, that Jewish speculators had been responsible for the rise in grain prices during the famine years 1846–47, was wide of the mark.

Now, in the spring of 1848, the not unjustified claim of Jewish revolutionary radicalism was added to the old accusations. The young Hungarian-born medical doctor, Adolf Fischhof, was only the best known of the many Jewish intellectuals who spearheaded the Vienna revolution. The Jewish historian Salo Baron states with considerable exaggeration: ". . . as head of the Committee on Security, which maintained public order in Vienna during the breakdown of all governmental authority, Fischhof became practically the uncrowned emperor of Austria."[7] The commitment of some young Jewish intellectuals to revolution led to a vast anti-Semitic reaction in Austrian ruling circles and in the perpetually anti-urban Austrian countryside; in Hungary it increased the unease of the liberal nobles, who liked revolutions to occur outside, not inside, the country. Jewish journalists in Pest and in Pressburg were among the foremost radical agitators but they were less dangerous than their Vienna compeers, being fewer in relative numbers and totally devoted to Hungarian nationalism.

The patriotism of many Hungarian Jews was truly amazing, not explainable solely by their attraction to liberal programs. The seemingly irresistible appeal of Hungarian gentry life to the urban middle class must also have played a role. When war came, some Orthodox rabbis even violated the Sabbath for the sake of fighting. A young Buda-Pest rabbi, Ignác Einhorn, was to write in 1851:

Common Asiatic origins, the great similarity in the destinies of the Jewish and Magyar peoples, the conspicuous lexicographic and grammatical affinities of the Magyar and the Hebrew languages, etc., may have contributed their share to that affection . . . Purely material consideration may have added their weight: The Jew lived off the nobility, from whom he purchased for resale grain, wine, wool and other agricultural produce, while selling to them in turn industrial products which he imported from abroad . . . In contrast thereto the poor Slav could not be a lucrative customer, whereas the German burgher was an outright competitor.[8]

Scholarship knows nothing of the affinities of the Magyar and Hebrew languages; but the business interests tying individual Jews to Hungarian landowners was a very real thing, as was the resulting Slav and German hostility to Jews.

Faced by the massive military attack of their numerous enemies in the autumn of 1848, the Hungarian public quickly relented on the Jewish question. Minister of War Mészáros now accepted Jewish volunteers in the national army and commissioned many Jewish officers. The response of Jews was massive enlistment, enormous financial contributions to the war effort, spying on behalf of Kossuth behind enemy lines, as well as religious conversions and name changes. By the spring of 1849, there would be quite a few Jewish army captains and middle-level Jewish civil servants. If no Jew rose to colonel or general, or to a high government position, it was because in revolutionary Hungary no commoner, whether Jew or Gentile, was ever awarded such a promotion. The Jews were to pay a heavy penalty for their patriotism after the war: their leaders would be imprisoned by the Austrians, and their communities fined. As for the Slavs, they would for a long time identify the Jews with aggressive Magyar nationalism.

Workers and Jews were a problem, but not an insurmountable one, to the Batthyány cabinet. Far worse was the trouble the regime faced with the peasants.

Rumors of impending peasant emancipation had naturally preceded the enactment of the law. The most widespread rumor was also the most traditional: the good king wished to free the peasants and give them all the land that was rightfully theirs, but the officials, the priests, the Jews, and the landowners were hiding the truth. The outcome was rioting in many places. Formerly expropriated lands were re-seized by peasants; commons that had been enclosed by the landowners were now enclosed by the village; the tithe on vineyards was not delivered because the peasants could not perceive the fine distinction between feudal customs and proprietary rights; contractual peasants stopped paying rent on their dominical land parcels; *regalia* were ignored; dominical forests were denuded and the hitherto sacrosanct game were slaughtered. Often peasants would not even hire themselves out as wage-laborers for fear that paid work would soon be turned into a gratis obligation. Here and there manor houses were torn down and noble families attacked, but the rioters' main thrust was against the hated legal papers.

As all this affected the nobility's vital interest, the regime acted with swiftness and efficiency born of long experience. Local clergy were enlisted to remind the peasants of the gratitude owed their self-sacrificing landowners; a government-subsidized peasant newspaper was founded; ringleaders were arrested; and where things really got out of hand, regular troops, the militia, or noble vigilante squads were used. On June 21 Minister of the Interior Szemere proclaimed a state of siege for the entire country, which led to ten publicly acknowledged executions. The repression and the concurrent Serbian insurrection calmed at least the Magyar peasants.[9]

The question had been raised repeatedly whether more far-reaching agrarian reforms would have prevented the peasants from rioting and subsequently would have caused the Magyar peasants—and even the Slavic and Romanian peasants—to rally en masse to the flag of Kossuth. Polish, German, and Italian historians have been asking the same question about their countries, where liberal revolutions took place repeatedly amidst the indifference, nay the hostility of peasants. Answering the question with a categorical "yes," the radical Ervin Szabó argues that the lack of a truly progressive agrarian policy lay behind the ultimate defeat of the War of Independence. But the stalinist József Révai points out rightly that even the most farreaching concessions could not suddenly have turned the dirt-bound serfs into flaming patriots; that total agrarian reform, including the distribution of the lord's demesne, was unthinkable and that the mere mention of such a possibility is unhistorical and therefore unmarxist; and that total reform would have driven the country's entire military, political, and economic elite back to the bosom of the dynasty. A fully contented peasantry, Révai continues, would probably have followed the example of the French peasants in the late 1790s, entrusting all power to a Bonaparte.[10] To all this must be added that, because of the dearth of meticulous studies on the social background, living conditions, and aspirations of the early peasant rioters, or of the later peasant army volunteers, we simply do not know how the peasantry felt and behaved in 1848–49. The practice of Hungarian historians, citing isolated cases to prove either the hostility or the enthusiasm of peasants, tells very little. This much seems to be clear: the riots did not generally start among the very poor, who were probably too downtrodden to care and who would not have known what to ask for in any case. The rioters were urbarial peasants clamoring for what was historically theirs, or contractual peasants who wished to be treated in the same way as the urbarial peasants.

As for the militia, its good companies were made up of urban not peasant elements. Rural militiamen had the annoying habit of going home when their enlistment was up, even if they were in the middle of a campaign; and they fought far better for their home district than for the country. The national standing army, based at first on voluntary enlistment and later on conscription, lends itself to very few generalizations. There are no data on the proportion and performance of former urbarial peasants among the soldiers, and even if there were, such statistics would prove little. Are landowning peasants more likely to leave everything behind and go to war than peasants who own no land? What is more important to a farmer: to attend to his property or to fight the distant enemy who might threaten this property? What led men to volunteer in 1848: patriotism, gratitude to their noble benefactors, the king's call (as opposed to the emperor's call), a not unjustified fear of the rapacious South Slav border guards, the subtle or not-so-subtle pressure of the local authorities, good pay, the lure of travel and adventure, the charisma and rhetoric of Kossuth, the contempt of Catholic or Protestant Magyar peasants for the Orthodox Serbian or Romanian peasants? The motivation of Magyar peasant volunteers is as hard to determine as that of the nobles who had voted for peasant emancipation and would soon take commissions in the national army. It is certain, however, that the South Slav and Romanian (but not the Slovak, Ruthene, or German) peasants of Hungary were at least as willing to fight against the Hungarian regime as the Magyar peasants were prepared to defend that regime. The only conceivable explanation for this willingness is that, while the Slovaks and Ruthenes were politically and socially less well developed and the Germans were divided among themselves on the issue of loyalty, the South Slavs and Romanians had reached the same level of national political consciousness as the Hungarians. In fact, it was easier for a Serb, a Croat, or a Romanian to identify the Magyar noble as his oppressor, than it was for a Hungarian peasant to perceive the Austrian bureaucrat or officer as his enemy and the Magyar noble as his comrade-in-arms. Clearly, then, we must now cast a glance at the non-Magyar nationality movement in Hungary.

A Majority of Minorities

The 5.4 million Hungarians in the lands of the Hungarian Crown made up less than four-tenths of the population. Their proportion was somewhat higher than that figure in Hungary proper or Inner Hungary, somewhat lower in Transylvania, and insignificant in Croatia-Slavonia. Listed in descending order of numerical importance, the major ethnic minorities were Romanians (about 17 percent of the total), Slovaks, Germans, Croats, Serbs, Ruthenes or Ukrainians, and Jews, the last constituting about 2 percent of the population.[11]

It is difficult but not impossible to generalize about the non-Magyars. Some, like the Slovaks and Croats, had probably been in the Carpathian Basin when the Hungarians came from the East in the ninth century; others, like the Germans, Serbs, and Jews, were more recent immigrants. Romanian settlement in Transylvania and eastern Hungary is a hopelessly debated issue. Most non-Magyars lived in homogeneous groups, but in such areas as the Banat in southern Hungary there was a bewildering mosaic of peoples. Germans and Jews were both urban and rural, the others overwhelmingly rural. In living standard, education, and cultural level, only the German surpassed the Hungarians. Except for the Slovaks, all the minorities had fellow nationals outside Hungary, even outside the Empire. Romanians, for instance lived in Inner Hungary, Transylvania, and the Military Border as well as outside Hungary in Austrian Bukovina, Russian Bessarabia, the Ottoman Balkans, and Moldavia and Wallachia—the two "Danubian Principalities" subject to the Ottoman Empire but in reality controlled by the tsar.

The Croats had their own so-called Triune Kingdom, made up of five distinct parts (Croatia, Slavonia, the Croatian-Slavonian part of the Military Border, the Hungarian Littoral, and Austrian Dalmatia), each part with its own historico-legal and practical-political status. Serbs under the Holy Crown had no political existence of their own, but their autonomous Serbian Orthodox church formed a base for national life—and for imperial ambitions. Romanians had no national-political rights either; and they were split into Greek Orthodox and Uniates (or Greek Catholics), with the former being subjected to the Serbian Orthodox, and the latter to the Hungarian Catholic hierarchy; but at least in Transylvania the Uniate bishop and some Romanian property owners had their seats in the provincial Diet. The Germans ranged from the privileged Transylvanian Saxon (in reality Rhinelander or Alsatian) Nation or *Universitas* to the politically unrecognized but personally often free and prosperous *Schwaben* (very few genuine Württemberg Swabians among them) in Inner Hungary. The Slovaks (who were either Catholic or Lutheran) and the Ruthenes (who were either Orthodox or Uniate) had no corporate legal existence; the Jews had it, but whether such an existence can be counted a privilege is doubtful.

The level of national self-awareness reached by each nationality before 1848 was tied less to economic development than to history and geography. The Croats were relatively poor but possessed their tradition of self-government, their nobility, their military system. And with their many brothers in neighboring countries, it is no wonder that they nurtured both Croatian nationalist and Illyrian imperial aspirations. The Serbs and Romanians were similarly nationalistic, possibly because of their conationals in the nearby autonomous principalities. The Slovaks, Ruthenes, and Hungarian Germans were less ambitious: they concentrated on cultural goals and (principally the Slovaks) on gaining official recognition as a nation.

The nationalist demands of 1848 were guided by the pre-1848 situation: Croats, Serbs, and Romanians sought to emulate the Hungarians in creating their own strong state under the Holy Crown; or if not under it, then still within the Empire; or—if conditions warranted—even outside the Empire. The Slovaks followed haltingly behind; the Germans and Ruthenes did not follow at all. Yet despite these variations, the nationalities' mood followed a chronological sequence: first sympathy for the Hungarian reforms with only modest national demands added; later a more energetic striving for autonomy under the Hungarian Crown; and even later alliance with Austria in an all-out war against Kossuth's Hungary. But while the Croats and the Serbs jumped to the third stage without waiting for Austria to start a war on Hungary, the Romanians moved gradually (only to adopt neutrality in the summer of 1849); and the Slovaks, Ruthenes, and Germans ranged all the way from those who met the Hungarians in armed combat to those who formed some of the Hungarians' best battalions.

Nationality policy was decided by the elites, and the policy of the elites depended on their composition. Croatian nobles, army officers, functionaries, and intellectuals; Serbian and Romanian priests, officers, teachers, and writers; Slovak Lutheran ministers and students —the larger and the more traditional the elite, the greater the initial nationalist ambition, but also the quicker the abandoning of autonomist or separatist aspirations for the sake of a military alliance with and subjection to Austria. All nationalities started out with democratic political and social demands; most changed the emphasis to national autonomy; and all ended up as cogwheels in the Austrian or the Hungarian military machinery.

The programs and attitudes of the non-Magyars were profoundly influenced by events in the neighboring countries. The Serbs looked to Belgrade, the Slovaks to Prague, the Romanians to Bucharest and Jassy; and all looked to Austria. Events there were decisive for the policy of Hungary's minorities.

On April 11, the day the king ratified the Hungarian constitution, the Czech liberal leader František Palacký notified the German Vorparlament in Frankfurt that his nation would neither send delegates nor join in a united Germany; rather, the Czechs would stay in the Monarchy: "Truly, if it were not that Austria had long existed, it would be necessary, in the interest of Europe, in the interest of humanity itself, to create her." Palacký's repudiation of Great German nationalism and his declaration in support of a renewed Habsburg Monarchy comprised of politically equal nations—in essence a Slav-dominated Monarchy—set many Hungarian Slavs against Great Hungarian nationalism and in favor of Austria. On April 25 the emperor issued a constitution for Austria. His Patent envisaged a centralistic state with a powerful ruler, and it was immediately and vociferously rejected by the Viennese. Still, it contained a phrase which, despite its vagueness, was good enough for many Slavs and Romanians in Hungary: "All peoples of the Monarchy are guaranteed the inviolability of their nationality and language." Since Hungary's constitution had given no such guarantee, her minorities now had another reason to turn to Austria. Finally, the abortive Prague Slavic

Congress in June, with its lack of commonly agreed on goals but with its Austro-Slav majority, confirmed the belief of most Hungarian Slavs that their salvation lay with Austria and the dynasty.[12]

The Hungarian government's answer to nationalist demands varied according to the historical-political status of the nationality that had presented the demands. The legalistic Hungarian nobility could recognize claims based on ancient constitutional privileges; it rejected claims based on nationalism. The historically autonomous Croats were offered concession after concession, until their very right to secede from the Hungarian commonwealth was recognized. Negotiations were also attempted with the historically privileged Serbs; but there was really no way to satisfy them, for the Serbs escalated their demands to the point of wanting most of southern Hungary for themselves despite its ethnically mixed population. With the other nationalities there was practically no question of compromise: their agitation was to be stopped categorically.

The Hungarian liberals were unable to fathom the depth of national sentiments among the non-Magyars. Why should free citizens of a free country suddenly be granted special status? Why should collective privileges be bestowed on a specific nationality, shortly after all corporate or caste privileges had been abolished? "The true meaning of freedom," Kossuth preached to a Serbian delegation on April 8, "is that it recognizes the inhabitants of the fatherland only as a whole, and not as castes or privileged groups, and that it extends the blessings of collective liberty to all, without distinction of language or religion. The unity of the country makes it indispensable for the language of public affairs to be the Magyar language."[13] Neither Kossuth nor any other Hungarian liberal or radical was ever willing to concede that the agitation of the national minorities was not necessarily reactionary.

Slovak nationalists held their first meeting on March 28, when they drew up a modest petition asking, among other things, that they be permitted the use of their vernacular in the assemblies of those counties where they formed a majority of the inhabitants, and that Slovak be taught in the elementary schools of such counties. Labeling the petition "a manifestation of Pan-Slavic activity," the Hungarian government rejected the demands. The next Slovak meeting, larger and better prepared, took place on May 10–11 at Liptovský Svätý Mikuláš in northern Hungary. Its Fourteen Demands included land ownership for all, not just for the urbarial peasants; complete freedom of the press; the federative reorganization of Hungary with a central parliament of all nationalities; regional parliaments for each nationality to be elected on the basis of universal suffrage (but renegades were to be excluded from the Slovak Assembly); the flying of red and white Slovak national colors next to the Hungarian flag; the release of all Slovak political prisoners—there were two; a national militia with Slovak officers; national administration and education, including a university, in the Slovak autonomous territory. As the Slovaks too liked to play at foreign policy, they insisted that neighboring Galicia be given to the Poles for self-government. The tone of the petition was conciliatory: the Slovak nation was willing to forgive the Hungarians for "900 years of oppression"; the brotherhood of the peoples of Hungary was on the horizon.[14]

The Hungarians, for whom the name *tót* ("Slovak" was not a term used in Hungary) conjured the image of a meek, dumb, often drunk lumberjack or village tinker, were convinced that such arrogance could stem only from foreign, tsarist sources; and they took immediate punitive measures. Royal commissioners were appointed in northern Hungary, and *lettres de cachet* were issued for the arrest of the three Slovak agitators: L'udovít Štúr, Jozef M. Hurban, and Michal M. Hodža. The three fled to Prague, there to participate at the Slav Congress in June. But even there they refused to ask (although prompted to do so by their Czech friends) for the secession of the Slovak-inhabited counties from Hungary. Maybe they knew that the majority of the Slovak people could not care less; maybe they were reluctant to see Slovakia joined to the new Czech state—the inevitable consequence of secession. When an anti-Austrian revolt broke out in Prague on June 12, the Slovak leaders were on the barricades. Only after the revolt had failed and they were faced with a choice between Austria and Hungary did the Slovak leaders follow the Czechs in opting for Austria. Thereafter their political role was minimal: their guerrilla incursions into Upper Hungary met with peasant indifference, and they ended up as mere propagandists for the Habsburg cause. Like the Polish Democratic Society in exile, the Slovak leaders found themselves in an impossible situation: their radical democratic program had alienated the conservatives without winning over the peasants. The Austrian generals regarded Štúr and his friends as communists, and so did the Hungarians. Persecuted in all its manifestations, devoid of a native ruling class, the Slovak national movement failed in 1848–49.[15]

There were only about 1.8 million Slovaks in the world, and despite their many Slavic cousins, they felt a sudden sense of isolation. The Romanian nation was far larger, almost 2.5 million under the Holy Crown alone; still, the Vlachs, as people called them in those days (the Hungarian term was *oláh*) faced the same impossible odds. They were without ethnic relatives in Eastern Europe; they lived under many sovereignties; they were poor; their small native nobility in Hungary and Transylvania tended to assimilate into Magyardom; their two churches were at odds with one another; their intelligentsia of priests, students in theology and law, journalists, army officers, civil servants, and merchants was relatively new and of many views. The fortunes and dilemmas of the Romanians in Inner Hungary and in Transylvania were so different that there could be no cooperation between the two groups. Those in Hungary proper had no recognized national or religious existence, yet their main grievance was not Hungarian oppression but the servitude imposed by the Serbian Orthodox hierarchy on the Romanian Orthodox church. The April Laws having made the Orthodox equal with the others, the Romanians hoped for religious autonomy; instead, the Serbian metropolitan at Karlóca, who was in revolt against Hungary, attempted to increase his authority over the Romanians. Thus Magyars and Hungarian-Romanians became natural allies, a development which made it easy for the Buda-Pest government to ignore the requests of Eftimie Murgu, the Hungarian-Romanian leader, for national political autonomy.

The Hungarian-Romanians, these enemies of Buda-Pest's enemies, gave little trouble in 1848–49; rather, they tried to act as intermediaries with their Transylvanian brothers.[16] Here the situation was different and, for Hungarians, fatal. The Grand Principality of Transylvania was a curious mixture of democracy and oligarchy. It had a Court Chancellery in Vienna, a governor in Kolozsvár, and a Diet in which sat, not the nobility as in Hungary, but representatives of Transylvania's three "political nations": the Hungarians, the Székelys, and the Saxons. The first was made up of nobles, burghers, and peasants, with political representation the privilege of the first two estates; the second was an ancient Magyar tribe in which, because of the tribe's traditional border guard service, everyone had once been free and where even in 1848 the upper classes did not have final say; the third consisted of German burghers and rather prosperous peasants, led by a partriciate. The Romanians, who constituted an absolute majority in Transylvania, had no recognized "national" status, nor were their churches equal with the others. Since the sixteenth century there had been religious freedom in Transylvania, but only for the religions of the political nations: Catholic, Calvinist, Lutheran, and Unitarian. Then, too, the Romanians constituted four-fifths of the peasantry in the Grand Principality; and they were badly off because (unlike Hungary) Maria Theresa's urbarial reform laws had never been put into effect there. Thus the Romanians had an abundance of national, religious, and social grievances; still they were not powerless. There were two Romanian Border Guard regiments in Transylvania, which were to play a crucial role in later events; their merchants had greatly profited from commerce with the Danubian Principalities; and their intellectuals collaborated with those of Moldavia and Wallachia in renewing Romanian culture and in propagating Romanian nationalism.

The Transylvanian Romanian intelligentsia was delighted at first with the news from Hungary; at urban demonstrations in March, Hungarian and Romanian students (among them the later guerrilla leader, Avram Iancu) marched arm in arm, hailing reforms and union with Hungary. In fact, at the beginning everybody but the suspicious Saxons and the highest aristocracy embraced the idea of union; the question was under what conditions the unification would take place. The hesitation of the Saxons and the landowners was understandable: the Saxons feared for their 600-year-old privileges; the landowners feared the peasant emancipation that was to precede unification. Without cash and credit, without technical know-how, and in an anarchical situation where no one knew what land belonged to the serfs and what to the lords, it was indeed hard to see how a smooth transition from feudalism to the bourgeois order could be achieved. On the other hand, if emancipation was inevitable (as it obviously was), then it was far better for the aristocracy to be under the protection of Hungary than of the far-away and seemingly powerless emperor. Therefore the aim of the Transylvanian Magyar nobility was to maneuver the union without much domestic change. The aim of the Romanians was the opposite: liberation of the serfs and the recognition of the Romanian nation and churches were for them preconditions to union with Hungary. To that effect they held meeting after meeting, in vain besieging the Transylvanian authorities with their petitions. On May 15–17 a mass congress was held at Blaj with as many as 40,000 participants, mostly peasants. A petition was adopted, not only for the eyes of the Magyar nobles at the Transylvanian Diet but also for those of the emperor. Drawn up by a forty-year-old law student, Simion Bărnuţiu, the "National Petition" asked for extensive civil rights, the abolition of serfdom without indemnification, free industry and commerce especially with the Danubian Principalities, Romanian schools and a Romanian militia, a separate national parliament, Romanian participation at the Kolozsvár Diet, and an all-Transylvanian constitutional assembly to work out the when, how, and if of union with Hungary. Tha Blaj congress then formed a Romanian Pacification Committee, made up of various elements, which was to guide Romanian fortunes throughout the war. And a Romanian National Guard was created immediately.[17]

The delegation that brought the petition to Ferdinand in Innsbruck received no satisfaction; rather, it was told to bring its grievances to the Buda-Pest National Assembly, which had not even met. The royal refusal was a major triumph for Batthyány.[18] Well before this June 23 event, on May 30 the Transylvanian Diet had voted unanimously for union with Hungary, having put pressure on the Saxon deputies and having eschewed consultation with the Romanian leaders. Feudal dues and services were abolished at the same time. On June 10, under pressure from Batthyány, the king ratified the Act of Union. The palatine was now plenipotentiary in both Hungary and Transylvania, and Transylvanian deputies (Hungarians, Székelys, and Saxons from the old Diet) were invited to attend the soon-to-be-convened Buda-Pest National Assembly.[19]

The Romanian delegation thereafter made the pilgrimage to Buda-Pest but obtained only the admonition that as free citizens of a free country they ought to be contented. The result was their growing alienation from the Magyars and attempts to form a separate Romanian principality under the Crown, perhaps even a Romanian empire in personal union with the Monarchy. Soon there was a ferocious guerrilla struggle against the Magyar landowners in Transylvania, a civil war with the Székelys, and a Romanian alliance with the Austrians against Kossuth.[20]

It was to be a terrible ethnic conflict: the most terrible in Hungarian history and the worst in contemporary Europe. The Romanian revolt in Transylvania was pivotal, for while Hungary had to defend itself against the aggressor Serbs and Croats, the war with the Romanians should and could have been prevented. Romanians in Inner Hungary were opposed to it, and so were the Romanians in Moldavia and Wallachia for whom Turks and the Russians were the problem and not Kossuth. Even the Transylvanian-Romanians were no dedicated Habsburg followers, and timely Hungarian concessions could have saved the situation; but these concessions were never made because the Transylvanian nobility feared such reforms and because the Hungarian government feared the anger of the Transylvanian nobility. Further, the Magyar leaders despised the Romanians at least as much as they despised the Slovaks. Judged incapable of thinking for themselves, the Romanians were seen as marionettes of the Camarilla and of the tsar. One of the more vociferous in this respect was Kossuth, who had fallen into his own propaganda trap. He knew nothing about the Romanians; he hoped that repression combined with minor concessions would quiet these unruly peasants.

Transylvania never became safe; the Hungarian army always had an enemy in the rear; retreat into that province became difficult; money, troops, and the best general were wasted there. The Hungarians lost the war, partly because of Transylvania, but the Romanians also gained nothing: an unhappy story that will be recounted later.

Serbs were merchants, craftsmen, and peasants; a substantial portion of the last group doubled as *Grenzer,* so there existed a large complement of trained Serbian soldiers. Serbs had many things to be proud of and they had the reputation of a proud race: their ancestors had come to Hungary from the Balkans in 1690 to escape Turkish servitude; their brothers south of the Danube had just achieved virtual independence by defeating the Ottomans; their language had been recently reformed and their modern literature established; and there were prosperous Serbian settlements in Inner Hungary. The Serbs jealously guarded their religious autonomy, and they had been less than enchanted by the Magyarization process of the Reform Age. Still, like all the other peoples of Hungary, they were at first joyous over the April Laws that not only promised to free them as peasants but held out the possibility of an end to the onerous border guard service. Meeting on March 17–19 at Pest and on March 27 at Újvidék, the Serbian leaders greeted the Hungarian achievements and asked for the same limited national rights that the Slovaks and the Hungarian-Romanians were demanding for themselves.[21] In his April 8 reply to the Serbian delegation (as already mentioned), Kossuth categorically rejected their petition. The Serbs were made of a tough fiber: they had soldiers and weapons, and they received immediate encouragement from the Croats and from Belgrade. At the Karlóca congress on May 13 (Karlóca was within the Military Border and thus safe from Hungarian authority) 8,000 Serbians, including emissaries from the Principality of Serbia, adopted an ambitious national program. There was no more talk of social reforms, only of political rights: Metropolitan Josef Rajačić was acclaimed "Patriarch of all the Slavs, Serbs and Vlachs," and the creation of an autonomous Serbian province called Vojvodina was announced. It encompassed all of southern Hungary, including parts of Croatia-Slavonia. A Serbian colonel of the frontier guards, Stevan Šupljikac, was proclaimed *vojvoda* or prince of the new Serbian province. It is true that Šupljikac was in Italy fighting His Majesty's enemies; but then, so was Colonel Mészáros, the Hungarian minister of war. The two brothers-in-arms would soon lead troops against each other. The Karlóca congress declared itself ready to conclude a close alliance with the Triune Kingdom of Croatia-Slavonia and Dalmatia, and it elected an executive committee, the Glavni Odbor, to govern the Vojvodina. Its president, a twenty-six-year-old lieutenant of the Imperial-Royal cavalry, Djordje Stratimirović, assumed temporary command of the Serbian army. Finally, the congress proclaimed its undying loyalty to His Majesty but not, of course to His Majesty's Hungarian government.[22]

Subsequently the Odbor established its effective rule over large tracts of southern Hungary, ousting the Hungarian officials and encouraging the Serbian peasants to attack not only the Magyar landlords but also the Hungarian, Romanian, or German settlers of the region. Within a few weeks, southern Hungary was in a turmoil.

The Serbs, who proclaimed their allegiance to the Empire, in reality defied its multinational concept. Southern Hungary was not theirs; they did not even constitute a majority there. Almost uninhabited following the expulsion of the Turks early in the eighteenth century, the area was gradually settled by the hardiest of peasants from Hungary and Europe. Its soil was rich and its inhabitants became prosperous. For over a century, Serbs (or Raitzen [Hungarian *rácok*], as they were called then), Magyars, Germans, Romanians, Bulgarians, Croats, Slovaks, and others had lived there in relative harmony. Now this great enterprise was ruined.

Rajačić, whose promotion to patriarch was of course illegal, led a delegation to Innsbruck, having at first consulted with Jelačić. Ferdinand turned him down, but this did not stop the Serbs from proceeding with their state building. On May 24, having secured Belgrade's support, the Serbs raised the standard of revolt against Hungary.[23]

The Hungarian government did not remain idle. Early in June it ordered the head of the Pétervárad General-Commando, Baron János Hrabovszky, a Hungarian, to put down the Serbian revolt. On June 12 Hrabovszky's regulars attacked the Serbian camp at Karlóca, but, surprisingly, they were defeated by Stratimirović.[24] Now that a Habsburg lieutenant had defeated a Habsburg general, there began a bizarre war in which officers and men of the Habsburg army, aided by irregulars and in the Serbian case also by volunteers from abroad, carried the same Habsburg flag, along with either the Hungarian or the Serbian national flag; His Majesty's border guards shot down His Majesty's regulars, and each side accused the other of rebellion. Soon there were about 30,000 men in each camp, all proclaiming their loyalty to the king.

To say that in the spring of 1848 the Hungarians missed the chance to conciliate all their nationalities and therefore could not but lose everything, would be as wrong as to assert that there were no chances whatsoever. Newly triumphant Hungary could not be expected, voluntarily, to divide the realm into self-governing territories, with the whole inevitably coming under the control of the non-Magyar majority, but the government could have arrived at a *modus vivendi* with some nationalities. The suppression of the Slovak movement, though immoral, was successful; the war against the Serbs and the Croats—as we shall soon see—had to be fought; the attempt to vanquish the Romanians was a terrible mistake.

Jelačić Woes

Among the non-Magyar nationalities in the lands of the Holy Crown before 1848, the Croats were politically the most mature. Desperate over Magyar expansionism, and expansionist in turn, they now asked for complete independence. Nationalist parties had dominated Croatian politics for many years; the humiliations suffered by Croatian deputies at the Pressburg Diet and Hungarian incursions into Croatian self-government had created deep resentment, demonstrations, and riots; their most remarkable leader, Ljudevit Gaj, had been working on the creation of a great South Slav–Illyrian state since the early 1830s. But the same Gaj had also been a paid agent of the Austrian government—and he had offered his services, and the "Crown of Illyria," to the tsar.[25]

March 1848 caused the same excitement in Croatia as it did in Austria and Hungary. The peasants themselves abolished serfdom. A national congress hastily assembled in Zagreb on March 25 only ratified this fact, and the mood of this assembly was as threatening to Vienna as it was to Pressburg. In its Thirty Demands the congress asked for the convocation of a Croatian-Slavonian-Dalmatian parliament; the incorporation of the Croatian-Slavonian sector of the Military Border into the Triune Kingdom; a national army, university, and bank; a ministry responsible to their own parliament; separate finances and separate conduct of foreign affairs (which would have given the Habsburg monarchy three foreign ministries!); the removal of foreign (i.e., non-Croatian soldiers) from the Triune Kingdom and the return of Croatian troops from Italy; civil rights; the abolition of the remnants of feudalism; the suppression of internal customs; the use of the vernacular in the Croatian Catholic church; and an end to clerical celibacy. In brief, the Croats wanted for themselves what the Hungarians were bargaining for in Vienna.[26] A delegation then took the resolutions to Vienna. During the folk festival that Vienna turned into in March 1848, the Croatian team must have been the most dazzling. In the words of one delegate: "All members of our deputation, four hundred people, were dressed in national costumes, the *šurka* [embroidered shirt] and white or blue trousers, with *kolpaks* [hats] or red caps and swords. A few national guardsmen wore their uniforms and the clergy were dressed in their habits." A smaller group from the full deputation presented an abbreviated version of the Thirty Demands to the monarch: His Majesty was gracious but reminded the Croats of their subordination to Hungary.[27]

It was mainly in order to defuse this type of agitation that Ferdinand appointed Colonel Jelačić governor of Civil Croatia and then also commanding general of the Zagreb General-Commando. No matter what the Hungarians thought then, and have been thinking ever since, Jelačić's appointment and promotion were a blow aimed both at the Illyrian party and at Hungary. One had to assure the loyalty of the Croats, especially of the *Grenzer* fighting in northern Italy; without the latter's help the Italian war would have been lost. The April Laws, almost simultaneously ratified, guaranteed the loyalty of Hungarian soldiers in Italy. The choice of Jelačić was both brilliant and fateful. Without granting the slightest concession to the Croats, the appointment of a popular hero made Croatia at one stroke a bulwark of the Monarchy. Jelačić diverted the Croatian independence movement into a hate campaign against Hungary. Surrounded by crowds of mounted peasants and by Croatian and Imperial flags, he toured the country exhorting the populace to give up their lives for emperor and country. Jelačić knew that only anti-Magyar propaganda could unite Croatian nobles and peasants, conservatives and progressive Illyrians. In the words of Gunther E. Rothenberg: "Animosity toward Hungary . . . was the only unquestioned fact of Croatian politics."[28]

The emperor-king had not asked Jelačić to campaign against Hungary although some people at Court undoubtedly rejoiced over it: the method was the *ban*'s own. The result was war between Croatia and Hungary and between the Monarchy and Hungary.

Jelačić's first act was to deny that the Hungarian cabinet or even the archduke-palatine had any authority over Croatia-Slavonia. After the government had tried to introduce Magyar administrative language in Slavonia, Jelačić instructed all the officials under him to ignore orders from Buda-Pest and took punitive measures against the Turopolje nobility, a group of free Croatian peasants who were fiercely pro-Magyar.[29] Letters from Buda-Pest he returned unopened; he mobilized the reserves among the Border Guards and, on May 2, alleging the threat of Turkish invasion and domestic disorder, he proclaimed martial law.

The Hungarians attempted conciliation, then retaliation, then conciliation again. In the Diet on March 28, Kossuth promised that the historic rights of Croatia would be scrupulously respected. Losing patience, on April 15 he suggested that the *ban* be dismissed—which was easier said than done as Jelačić would not accept Hungarian orders even if they came from the king, and he had reliable troops while the Hungarians were not sure of their own. Worrying over

Jelačić day and night, Batthyány devised a three-pronged strategy: (1) put pressure on the *ban* through the king, (2) secure the loyalty of the Imperial-Royal regulars in Hungary, and (3) create a national army. These goals were more or less reached in the coming months; only the overthrow of Jelačić could not be accomplished.

All through April, May, and early June, the Court and the Austrian government cooperated with Batthyány. Whether this was done out of weakness, desire to gain time before a counteroffensive, or sincere good intentions will never be known. Since there were many wills at Court and no one had the final say in the Austrian cabinet, it is more than likely that all three motivations prevailed.

The dynasty was unquestionably in a precarious position. The April 25 Patent contained no reference to Austria's union with Germany, it provided for an Imperial veto over legislation, and it envisaged a conservatively structured legislature. The Patent's proclamation was therefore followed by immediate *Katzenmusik* concerts in Vienna, which in turn led to the resignation of the Ficquelmont cabinet on May 4. The new ministry, headed by Pillersdorf, was the third in the history of this institution. Its new franchise law, based on indirect voting, led to new demonstrations in Vienna on May 15 and to new concessions from the regime: universal suffrage and a unicameral parliament. But now the Court had had enough of the turmoil: on May 17 the emperor, his family, and his entourage (but not the Austrian government) fled to Innsbruck and were received joyously by the faithful Tyroleans. In Vienna the *journées* continued until, at the end of May, the Executive Committee of the "Committee of Security of Burghers, National Guards and Students" took charge of the city. The *Kaiserstadt* was now in revolutionary hands, but with one light in the darkness: early in May Radetzky had won his first victory over the Sardinians and Italian revolutionaries—the turning point in that war had come.

It is against this Austrian background that we must now look at the doings of the Hungarian government. Harassed from all sides, the Batthyány cabinet understood well that it desperately needed to arrive at a *modus vivendi* with the monarch and the Austrian cabinet. That there was such a possibility in the spring and early summer is denied by most historians, with Hungarian nationalists insisting on the Camarilla's determination to undo the Hungarian constitution, conservatives pointing to the intransigence of the Kossuth camp, and marxists elaborating on the counterrevolutionary conspiracy of the ruling classes in Austria and Hungary. There is a bit of truth in all these contentions. But a young Budapest historian, Aladár Urbán, has recently asserted that a lasting accommodation between Austria and Hungary was not out of the question; that the Court, the Austrian cabinet, Batthyány, and even Kossuth were striving toward such an end; and that the failure of their combined endeavors was due not to hostile acts but to unfriendly gestures, mutual suspicion, and the propagandistically overblown disturbances caused by minor Austrian officers and radical pranksters in Buda-Pest.[30] But even Urbán fails to touch the essence of the problem. While he is right in showing that the major partners in negotiation tried hard to come to an agreement, he underplays the difficulties built into the constitution. No amount of mutual good will could have eliminated these difficulties short of changing the constitution itself: something that the Hungarian liberals refused to consider. Two foreign services, two armies, and two fiscal administrations were simply too much for a European great power.

Aside from the duplication of essential state institutions, there were also the problems left unsettled by the constitution. The king tried to abide by the law, but there were not always laws to abide by: the military command structure and the servicing of the state debt were sources of perpetual disagreement. Convinced that the Monarchy was doomed unless Hungary chose to save it (in exchange, of course, for Hungarian preeminence in the Monarchy), the Hungarians were less forthcoming on these issues than the king. Following Ferdinand's flight to Innsbruck they immediately invited him to place himself under the protection of his faithful Magyars at Buda: an invitation that would be repeated assiduously.[31] In all this, Kossuth played a major but not a decisive role. Alternately supportive of Batthyány, critical of him, or neutral, he maneuvered to preserve the confidence of the palatine and the prime minister on the one hand, and of nationalist public opinion on the other. He ended up almost losing the confidence of both. Only after the final emergency in July and August—an emergency he himself had helped create with his maneuvering—did Kossuth again become all-important.

On April 7, before the constitution was sanctioned, the king had asked the Hungarians to shoulder one-fourth of the interest on the state debt: 10,000,000 gulden a year. In view of Hungary's size, population, and the state of its economy, this was a reasonable request:

after 1867 the country would easily pay over 30 percent of the Monarchy's common expenditures. Yet the Royal Rescript was neither brought before the Diet nor was it answered; instead, at the end of April, the *Pesti Hírlap* (by then the semiofficial newspaper of the government) stated categorically that not a single kreuzer would be paid. The Hungarian government's justification—that the debt had been contracted without the country's consent and not to its benefit—was politically and morally indefensible, and clashed with the endlessly repeated assertion that Hungary was the strongest pillar of the Monarchy. No wonder that the hitherto so friendly Viennese bourgeois press now complained of Hungary's virtual declaration of war on Austria.[32]

Army matters were handled in a less cavalier fashion, and in this respect there was more cooperation than hostility between Hungarians and Austrians. The Buda-Pest cabinet's repeated requests for the return of all Hungarian regiments from Galicia were never met; but other troop exchanges did take place, in bits and pieces and without much fanfare. The Austrian Ministry of War allowed Hungarian agents to purchase weapons in Vienna or to import them through Austria; the Hungarian ministry did not try to purge the Imperial-Royal command in Hungary; technical information was readily exchanged by the two partners, and neither side neglected the provisioning of garrisons in Hungary. On April 26, when the Hungarian government decided to set up ten permanent National Guard battalions and thus created the nucleus of a standing national army, the Austrians did not protest. On April 16 and again on April 26, the government informed the heads of the Hungarian-based General-Commandos in Buda, Temesvár, Pétervárad, and Zagreb that, from May 1 on, they would have to take all their orders from the Hungarian minister of war.[33] Attempting to have this crucial move ratified, the palatine and Batthyány journeyed to Vienna on May 1; to everyone's surprise, they returned less than a week later with the royal consent. On May 6 the king authorized the palatine to send a royal commissioner to Croatia to bring Jelačić to heel. The palatine thereupon signed a series of orders declaring all Jelačić's decrees null and void, appointing General Hrabovszky (who would attack the Serbs at Karlóca in June) royal commissioner in Croatia-Slavonia, and authorizing him to start trial proceedings against Jelačić for treason, if necessary.[34] It is true that Hrabovszky achieved nothing, but this was not his fault nor that of the king or the palatine. Jelačić refused to obey and Hrabovszky had no means to enforce his will. Because of this, the king would soon take even stronger measures against the *ban,* again at the insistence of the Hungarian government.

Not even the so-called Lederer incident in Buda-Pest could thwart military collaboration between Austria and Hungary, although it undoubtedly poisoned the air.

On May 10, the same day that the cabinet informed the public of the king's consent that the regular army in Hungary be placed under the control of the Ministry, a bloody clash erupted between soldiers and civilians in Buda-Pest. Responsibility for this third set of Buda-Pest *journées* lay with the Pest radicals and with a few junior army officers: the political ambitions of one and the violence of the other caused a serious crisis.[35]

The aristocratic Batthyány was not in the habit of informing the public of his doings: the Pest radicals were convinced that he was doing nothing; or if he was doing something, it was to prepare a counterrevolution in cohort with the Camarilla. The few outward signs of government activity, such as the apparent filling of the new ministries with bureaucrats of the old regime (actually a wild exaggeration, for the best jobs were given to members of the former liberal opposition), did nothing to soothe radical hearts. Jelačić was about to attack Hungary, or so it was rumored; the Austrian soldiers were traitors; and the National Guard was unarmed; yet Baron Lederer, the head of the Buda General-Commando, refused to hand out weapons, claiming that he had none. A commission appointed by the government found 14,000 rifles lying about; at this news the radicals planned a *Katzenmusik* concert in honor of the "traitor" Lederer. On May 10 a crowd estimated at a mere 2,000 walked over to Buda in the direction of Lederer's residence; but when they arrived, they were attacked by curassiers and grenadiers who had been kept in hiding by their officers. Many people were wounded, and at least one demonstrator, a Jewish medical student, was killed. The result was more demonstrations and demands: that the officers and Lederer be tried; that Austrian troops in Hungary be obliged to take an oath to the constitution; that Magyar troops be immediately returned from Italy; that German officers of Hungarian-speaking regiments be thrown out; and finally that the government cede its place to a new cabinet led by the radical nobleman Pál Nyáry and by Kossuth. These mass meetings were addressed by Petőfi, who announced that he "would not trust his dog to this government, even less the fate of the fatherland!"

Batthyány refused to be intimidated: he coldly dismissed a delegation of radicals led by Petőfi, and he appointed a commission to look into the incident. The latter came up with an indictment of the junior officers and of Lederer, but meanwhile the eighty-year-old Austrian general had fled to Vienna.[36]

The incident increased the stature of the government and diminished that of the radicals. Petőfi's "wild outburst" was widely interpreted as incitement to treason, declarations of loyalty to Batthyány poured in from all sides, and Lederer's flight was seen as a victory for the cabinet. Thus the radicals failed again: they had not overthrown the cabinet and they had unwittingly strengthened the ministers' hands. Now Batthyány took action. He ordered that all regular troops stationed in Hungary take an oath to the constitution, that no more soldiers or equipment be allowed to leave the country, and that the setting up of the ten standing battalions, soon to be named *honvéd* ("defender of the fatherland"), be hastened. The National Assembly was convoked for early July; and on May 19 the prime minister launched an appeal to the Székely nation, and especially to the Székely Border Guards, to rush to the aid of the endangered fatherland.[37] The appeal was illegal. Although Batthyány issued his manifesto as acting minister of war (Mészáros had still not arrived from Italy) and expressed his hope that His Majesty would retrospectively ratify the emergency measure, he was really asking soldiers to desert their posts. Amazingly, even this measure was later approved by the king.

Because Batthyány was martyred after the war, politically moderate Hungarian historians and many Austrian historians argue that he was no rebel. Incidentally, this view is corroborated by Hungarian nationalists and marxists, who, following in the footsteps of the 1848 radicals, accuse Batthyány of weakness and subservience to the Court. Again, Aladár Urbán is almost alone in pointing out that the prime minister, who abhorred the very idea of revolution, did in reality stretch the law to the breaking point in order to meet the national emergency.[38]

There is no evidence to show that Kossuth was behind the Lederer incident, or that he incited the radicals during the ensuing *journées*. On the contrary, he complained later that the May 10 affair had caused deep embarrassment to himself and the whole cabinet. Still, his behavior during the crisis was bizarre. While the crowd shouted for him to help form a new government, he suddenly pleaded sickness and refused to receive anyone. When the crisis blew over, he reappeared without showing a trace of the grave illness he had previously publicized by issuing medical bulletins. In all likelihood, Kossuth had at first washed his hands of the cabinet only to return to his post after Batthyány had refused to let himself be overthrown. No one reproached him for it: there was no time for quarrels.

Having established his authority over the army—no general would dare disobey him for a while—Batthyány again tackled the Jelačić problem. Through a letter issued by the king, he invited Jelačić to meet him in Innsbruck. The same letter forbade the meeting of the Croatian parliament, planned for early June. In those days the palatine, the archdukes, the king himself, functioned as mailmen between Buda-Pest and Zagreb: the Hungarian cabinet decided that the king should denounce the *ban;* Kossuth wrote the royal proclamation; it was sent to the palatine, who sent it to the archdukes, who gave it to Ferdinand for his signature; Jelačić then gaily cast the whole thing away. He refused to meet the Hungarian prime minister in Innsbruck, or rather he was deliberately late. On June 10 the king stripped him of all his political and military positions, ordering the Croats and the Border Guards in particular to obey only Hrabovszky and under no conditions to obey the traitor Jelačić. These latest royal manifestoes had also been written by Kossuth.[39] Although unenforceable and legally invalid (the suddenly recalcitrant Esterházy had refused his countersignature), Jelačić's dismissal was a major victory for Hungary, one of the greatest in a long series of diplomatic triumphs that had begun in March. The June 10 manifestos depicted Jelačić as the devil, and the Hungarians as Croatia's benefactors. Yet the *ban's* refusal to obey his king was not such a bad idea on his part. A few months later, other royal manifestos would depict him as His Majesty's faithful and obedient servant, while the framer of the June manifestos would be cast in the role of the devil. How it would come to that will be told shortly. For the time being, the Hungarian government's tasks were clear: organize resistance against the Serbs and, if necessary, against the Croats; at the same time, organize elections for the National Assembly.

The Months of Confusion

In June, just when the conservative Court was at its most conciliatory toward Hungary, the liberal Austrian cabinet members turned against their Hungarian colleagues over the question of Transylvania's union with Hungary. The Austrians lost, but they were to remember their defeat.

Ever since April, the Court and the Austrian ministry had been debating the planned union, with the latter increasing its objections after the emperor's flight to Innsbruck. Distance seems to have lifted the morale of the Pillersdorf cabinet members: with no power over the very city they were residing in, but removed from the sagging spirits at Court, the ministers became more militant. They saw the proposed union as a disaster that would dry up revenues from Transylvania, give too much power to Hungary, alienate the Saxons ("the Eastern bulwark of the dynasty"), and cause the Romanians to attempt secession in order to form an independent state. On the other hand, the ministers argued, if the king vetoed the project, there was a good chance for the grateful Transylvanian Romanians to bring Moldavia and Wallachia under the Habsburg Crown. The Austrian cabinet particularly objected to the palatine extending his plenipotentiary powers to Transylvania: this would have meant, among other things, Hungarian control of the entire Military Border. If the border guards fell under the authority of the palatine, the Austrian cabinet wrote to Ferdinand on May 27, Archduke Stephen "would be able to paralyze the Croatian *ban's* efforts to defend the rights of the emperor, and he [the palatine] could suppress the widespread Croatian upheaval."[40]

The Austrian protests were in vain and the king (as we have seen) sanctioned both the union and the dismissal of Jelačić. But at least the ministers made sure that there be no more major Hungarian diplomatic triumphs. From early June on, the Court—that is, Archduke Francis Charles and his immediate advisers—paid more and more attention to the opinion of the Austrian cabinet in Hungarian matters. Not that this opinion was always clear and unanimous. Only in the autumn would the Austrian cabinet solidify its centralistic policy with regard to Hungary; until then, it may have been possible for Batthyány to come to an agreement with his Austrian colleagues. For this, however, he would have needed the unconditional support of his own colleagues, something that he could no longer count on. As Austrian hostility increased, so did the impatience of Kossuth: during the summer he repeatedly allied himself with the radicals against Batthyány, while, at the other end of the political spectrum, moderates in the cabinet pressed on for compromises with Austria. Riddled by doubt, Batthyány had to pursue—sometimes quite alone—his dual goal of negotiations plus armed defense. He was not even sure of the backing of the National Assembly, where the majority followed Kossuth. Had he been a political genius (which he was not), Batthyány still would have had little chance of success.

In June the political situation worsened. The Zagreb assembly, meeting despite royal interdiction, declared its readiness to join Austria and to secede from Hungary; it rejected the dismissal of Jelačić and entrusted him with dictatorial powers, thus defying the king's will. The Croats were acting revolutionary, not the Hungarians, but they were making a revolution on behalf of the emperor. As in response to these declarations, on June 24 the Austrian minister of war, General Count Baillet von Latour, sent Jelačić 100,000 gulden to replenish his war chest. Latour even had the cheek to request reimbursement from his Hungarian colleague.

True, Kossuth as minister of finance had, on June 1, stopped provisioning the Zagreb General-Commando (which was now legally under Hungary), and Jelačić had no money for his troops. But how could the Hungarians be expected to send money to the *ban?* As Kossuth wrote: "I would not deserve to breathe the air; nay, I would merit to be spat upon by the nation, if I had given money to the enemy."[41]

Kossuth's attitude was logical yet, paradoxically, so was Latour's. It was the personal union between Austria and Hungary—an arrangement which placed the interests of each part as high as the interests of the whole—that dictated Latour's peculiar action. The welfare of the *Gesamtmonarchie* required that the Imperial-Royal army, and thus also the army in Croatia, be preserved; as this coincided with Austrian interests, Latour was glad to support Jelačić. But the welfare of the *Gesamtmonarchie* also required that the army in

Hungary proper be preserved; as this did not coincide with Austrian interests, Latour both supported and obstructed the army in Hungary. He gave ample evidence during the summer of his ability to pursue these contradictory goals simultaneously. This was no Machiavellianism on his part, nor a manifestation of bureaucratic stupidity: it reflected his effort to obey laws that could not be obeyed because they were contradictory.

Consider the Serbian revolt where the brunt of fighting was borne by Imperial-Royal regulars on both sides. The first major Hungarian campaign on July 14, against the fortified Serbian camp at Szenttamás, was led by General Baron Philip Bechtold, whom the Hungarians had put in charge of their Field Army of the South. The campaign was a failure, not because of Bechtold's treason as the Hungarians thought, but because of his modest talent and the unreliability of the National Guard who made up one-half of his forces. When Mészáros took over for a short while in August, he also failed; in fact, no one could defeat the heroic Serbs until late spring 1849. What is amazing is that Bechtold held out as long as he did on the Hungarian side. What went on in his mind is rather clear from his correspondence. Born in Hungary but a German, he had been serving the emperor since the age of fifteen. He was sixty-two and in command of a military district in Hungary, when in June 1848 he was ordered to take the oath to the Hungarian constitution and lead an army against the Serbs. For a while, there was no dilemma. He saw ample evidence of the brutality of the Serbs against Magyar, German, and Romanian villagers; he knew that thousands of men had invaded the Monarchy from the Serbian Principality; as a Habsburg officer he disliked the idea of an autonomous Serbian province in southern Hungary that would surely have joined the Serbian Principality one day. But by late July Bechtold had received plenty of letters from his army comrades reproaching him with being a toady of Kossuth; simultaneously, the Hungarian press berated him as a traitor. He knew that many Habsburg officers, not only those from the Border Guard regiments, were fighting against him. He turned repeatedly to Latour for advice but was alternately told to obey the Hungarian minister of war or to obey his conscience. Latour consistently refused counsel to Habsburg officers in Hungary, and thus each officer had to make up his own mind: an inhuman task for men who had been taught never to think independently. Bechtold resigned and left for Vienna at the end of August; other generals, who were not of Hungarian origin, stayed longer.[42]

If the generals were confused, how much more confused must have been Ferdinand's poor subjects in southern Hungary! "Your Imperial-Royal Majesty," intoned a plaintive appeal on July 11 from "the loyal German and Wallachian inhabitants of Fehértemplom," a prosperous little town that served as headquarters to the Illyrian-Banat Border Guard regiment:

Hitherto we were accustomed to seeing Your Very Highest orders and laws executed by the authorities without opposition; the population of these regions vied with one another in furnishing proofs of loyalty and attachment to the Monarch. . . . All this has completely changed in recent times, and the old order and security of things are no more. . . . What in one place is right and legal, in another place appears as betrayal of the good cause, and no matter what one does, one is bound to violate Your Majesty's laws by the very act of obeying them.[43]

History records no Imperial reply to the Fehértemplom burghers, who soon opted for Hungary and thereby formed a small island in a hostile Serbian sea. For a while they were protected by troops of the Temesvár General-Commando; but when the commander of their immediate region, a Baron Blomberg, announced that he would fight the Serbs who had come from beyond the border but not the *Grenzer* and withdrew his Polish lancers from the area, the Serbs attacked the town on August 19. Many people were killed, and half Fehértemplom was set on fire, but the center resisted the assault. Next day, the enraged *Schwaben* and Romanians made a sally, massacring the Serbs of their town with whom they had lived in perfect peace until then. "Have pity on us," Blomberg now wrote to Latour, "recall us from this place of uncertainty. We can no longer bear this terrible dilemma."[44] It is noteworthy that Vienna learned about the Fehértemplom massacre from Lieutenant-Colonel Mayerhofer, who, though His Majesty's consul at Belgrade, was in effective charge of the Serbian rebels in that region. It is also noteworthy that the then Austrian Prime Minister Wessenberg (who received the report on September 12, that is, at a time when the die had already been cast against Hungary) strongly disapproved of Mayerhofer's active participation in the Serbian rebellion. Yet, not much later, the emperor made Mayerhofer a general.[45]

Such events and such dilemmas were commonplace in southern Hungary: both sides were certain that Ferdinand was with the enemy, yet both sides swore by Ferdinand.

Nor was the situation much clearer in the rest of Hungary. Impatient with the slow return of the Hungarian regiments from Austria, Kossuth appealed to them directly to come home on their own. A few hundred hussars made it to Hungary in June and later. Kossuth's colleague, Mészáros, publicly deplored this act of insubordination and promised to punish the deserters. But his protest was swept away by the surge of nationalist enthusiasm.[46] In fact, even though Hungary would not allow a single Austrian regular to leave, the organized return of Hungarian regulars continued until the fall. Altogether almost seven regiments of Hungarian origin were sent back by the Austrian Ministry of War; without these troops the war against Austria would have been much more difficult to fight. And to give another example of continued cooperation between the two ministries of war at a time of growing hostility—or is this another example of the prevailing anarchy?—early in August, Latour allowed Hungarian *honvéd* troops, thus not regulars, to cross Austrian territory en route to the Adriatic port Fiume, which was being threatened by Jelačić.[47]

In July one more major problem in military collaboration was added to the others, that of Hungarian assistance to Austria in the Italian conflict. As this assistance was officially requested by Austria, it was for the Hungarian parliament to decide whether or not it would be granted. To understand the Assembly's vote on the question, we must first find out how the new House of Representatives was elected and what its general agenda was like.

It had taken some time to prepare for the elections, mostly because the government wanted to make sure that power would not slip from its hands. The electoral committees were made up almost exclusively of nobles and, in the cities, of respectable burghers. They followed the advice of the county lord-lieutenants, favoring candidates who were at least nominally behind the government. The elections lasted over a month, from early June to almost mid-July, but not all qualified people cast their votes. In the south elections could generally not be held; in other areas many people, especially peasants, had not bothered to register; again in other areas peasants and other commoners had been systematically excluded from the ballot. There was only one polling station in each electoral district: people from outlying areas were often unable to get there or, if they did, they often found the polls closed. On the other hand, wagons were dispatched to fetch reliable voters. All these practices were hallowed by tradition, with the only difference that there was now only one party, the former Opposition. Sixty percent of the candidates were elected unanimously (those who had made a poor showing usually yielded before the closing of the polls), but in many districts candidates representing the same party had fought a brave battle against each other. Altogether 414 deputies were elected.

The composition of the Lower House brought no surprises. There were many familiar faces, and even more well-known family names. The only important changes were the virtual disappearance of the Conservatives, the absence of the Croats, and the presence of the Transylvanians. The radical faction within the Government Party numbered between thirty and fifty, which meant no proportional change from the past. Seventy-four percent of the deputies were noble landowners; the rest were classified as "bourgeois" (*bürgerliche*) even though most of the latter also had noble predicates. Thirty percent of the total were county officials (with or without landed property); most of the professional people were lawyers. Only two deputies came from the former servile class, and there were a few other commoners. Petőfi, who ran as a radical, was defeated in scandalous circumstances, having almost been killed by his drunken opponents. Another famous poet, János Arany, did not fare much better. But the radical peasant leader Táncsics (the one whom Young Hungary had liberated at Buda on March 15) was elected in two rural districts and could have easily been elected in more.

All in all, this was an assembly of the untitled nobility (there were twenty-six titled nobles in the Lower House, a few of them radicals) as had been true of all previous parliaments and as would be true of all the following assemblies in the next several decades. Of the nationalities there was almost no trace, except for three Romanians from Inner Hungary, the Saxons from Transylvania, and a handful of others.[48] The old ruling class was solidly in power.

The two Houses of parliament were solemnly opened by the palatine on July 5. The king being "gravely ill," it was Archduke Stephen who informed the deputies and members of the Upper House (which was, of course, unchanged except for the 130-odd members who failed to show up from a total of about 800) that His Majesty profoundly deplored all Hungary's troubles, especially the "evil agitation" in southern Hungary, and that he wished the parliament to discuss finances and defense. The Address from the Throne included the briefest reference to the Italian war, "which was not yet over." This seemingly innocuous sentence was the result of bitter wrangling in the Hungarian cabinet that had penned the king's Address. Kossuth wanted not a word on Italy, where the nation's sympathies clearly lay on the side of the enemy; the other ministers insisted that the Address ask for Hungarian assistance in that war. Not that Deák or Széchenyi or Eötvös were keen on sending Hungarian recruits to Lombardy—on the contrary; but the Austrian request was real, and the public had to be warned. The sentence, as finally formulated, was a compromise solution.[49]

Thus Hungary's first postfeudal parliament met: it was to prove a long and assiduous one. Meetings would be held almost every day, often several times a day, with the Lower House never losing its importance. It would seize executive power in September through the formation of a National Defense Committee; it would then entrust power to Kossuth, the head of that committee; in April 1849 it would reassert its power; and finally it would adjourn itself when the war was over. It was a one-class and one-nation Assembly but, precisely because it was so homogeneous, it became the only parliament in revolutionary Europe never to submit to resurgent monarchial absolutism.

The deputies set to work with gusto. The first important meeting of the Lower House, on July 11, was also one of its most theatrical. It was the day when Kossuth presented his budget report and his Motion on National Defense.

Kossuth was ill again. He entered the hall supported by friends, haggard, deathly pale, his eyes on fire. The deputies begged him to speak while seated, but he dragged himself to the rostrum; and his voice, at first a mere whisper, soon rose to dazzling heights. Judging by the length of his address, he must have spoken for hours—on Croatia, the Serbs, the Russian menace, the king's hoped-for coming to Hungary, relations with Austria, England, France, and the new German state, national defense and the budget. This is how William

H. Stiles, the U.S. chargé in Vienna, translated Kossuth's opening lines (with a few corrections, based on the Hungarian original, by this author):

In ascending the tribune to demand of you to save our country, the awful magnificence of the moment weighs oppressively on my bosom. I feel as if God had placed into my hands the trumpet to arouse the dead, that—if still sinners and weak—they may relapse into eternal death, but that they may wake for eternity, if any vigor of life be yet in them. Gentlemen! Thus, at this moment, stands the fate of the nation. With the decision of my motion, God has confided to your hands the decision affecting the life or death of the nation. You will make your decision. But it is because this moment is so magnificent, that I am determined, Gentlemen, not to have recourse to the weapons of rhetoric. . . . Gentlemen! the fatherland is in danger!

All in all, Kossuth asked that the country's armed forces be increased to 200,000, of whom 40,000 should be mustered immediately; and that, to provide for this army, the deputies vote 42 million gulden in taxes, of which from 8 to 10 million would be due in the first year. He had not yet finished when the deputies sprang to their feet to roar their approval. He concluded: "This is my request! You have risen to a man, and I prostrate myself before the nation's greatness. If your energy in execution equals the patriotism with which you had made this offer, I will make bold to say, that even the gates of hell shall not prevail against Hungary."[50]

Two days later, on July 13, the cabinet council discussed the question of aid to the king in the Italian war. The majority of members favored assistance, hoping that in exchange the king would move to Buda-Pest, making it the capital of the Monarchy, and that once there, the Court would put an end to Jelačić's activity. Kossuth shared this view, except that he was not satisfied with hope and insisted on firm guarantees from the king. Following violent debate during which Batthyány and others threatened to resign (a practice that was becoming frequent), the cabinet deferred to Kossuth's wish; and it was he who on July 20 presented the government's motion in the House. This motion, to be included in the Assembly's Reply to the Throne, was fraught with if's and when's. Yes, Hungary would send recruits to Italy (up to 40,000 had been requested) but only if thereby the cause of peace and understanding with the Lombardo-

Venetian people would be promoted, simultaneously guaranteeing the dignity of His Majesty and the "rights, freedoms, and just demands of the Italian nation." Moreover, not a single recruit could be dispatched until peace had returned to Hungary, and its sovereignty fully respected. As the radicals would not hear of even such an obviously theoretical offer of aid, Kossuth turned on them:

If we demand that those who attack the Hungarian Crown should not be able to boast of the Protection of the Austrian ministry; if we justly desire, and demand, that every member of the dynasty, together with the Austrian Emperor, give us aid as faithful allies in defending the integrity of the Hungarian Crown and the rights and sovereignty of this nation, then the ministry of the Hungarian King must have equal regard for the position of the Austrian Emperor, and we must not say that, if the Austrian Emperor is attacked by a foreign power, then that is of no interest to the ministry of the Hungarian King.[51]

Spokesmen of the Left, especially the radical Count László Teleki, tore into Kossuth's reasoning, pointing out that the Italians were fighting for universal freedom and Jelačić was not; that the Camarilla would never take forceful action against the *ban* and that, once the war against the Italians had been won, there was no guarantee that Austria would respect Italian rights as requested by the Hungarian cabinet. Radical attacks made Kossuth uneasy. No one was to be a better patriot than he, and the next day he delivered a scathing indictment of Austria, adding—without consultation with his colleagues—a further governmental stipulation to the offer of Hungarian assistance: Austria must consent to the division of Lombardy-Venetia, with only the northern part remaining under the Crown, and with even that rump receiving complete self-rule.[52] Batthyány was furious and again threatened to resign, a gesture which Kossuth did not consider advantageous at that time. So on July 22 he recanted publicly, reverting to the government's original motion, which of course had been his very own. Over the furious opposition of the radicals, and amidst great confusion—for in the torrent of his words, no one quite knew what Kossuth really wanted—the House passed the government's initial motion, 233 to 36.[53]

The consequences of the Italian affair were momentous: the split in the cabinet had been aired in public; all sensed that Kossuth could overthrow the cabinet any time he wished; the radicals gathered fresh courage and, trusting in Kossuth's sympathy, began to think of a coup d'état. As for the Austrian government, it understood perfectly that more Hungarian recruits for the Italian war could not be expected.

The Hungarians were pursuing illusory objectives. The radicals wanted to make the country completely independent and then fight a war (if necessary with all their neighbors) until the international revolutionary movement could rush to their assistance. Batthyány and Kossuth thought nothing of international revolutionary solidarity and of course they were right. By July there was not the slightest chance of a European revolutionary war, with the French workers' revolt drowned in blood in June, the Czech revolt suppressed, the Italians losing their war against Austria, the German radicals and liberals powerless, and Poland quiescent. Batthyány and Kossuth pinned their hopes on the Great Powers, no less of an illusion than the illusion of the radicals. Their primary aim was alliance with Great Britain; but Palmerston, who took an active interest in the Italian freedom movement, was not at all interested in the independence of Hungary. He would not even send a representative to Buda-Pest. As a second-best possibility, Batthyány had dispatched two Hungarian liberals—Dénes Pázmándy and László Szalay—to Frankfurt.[54] The two had been there since May, and there was some hope that the German parliament would establish diplomatic relations with Hungary.* More important, the Frankfurt Assembly had asked Austria to join the new German union. The precondition for this new kind of Austro-German union was that those parts of the Monarchy which had not belonged to the Holy Roman Empire be tied to the German parts of Austria only through a personal union. Hungary never having belonged to the Holy Roman Empire, the Frankfurt stipulation meant that it could become free. The Hungarians, for whom the Pragmatic Sanction of 1722/23 was the source of their legal existence, felt that if Austria became part of a united Germany, the Pragmatic Sanction would become null and void. Hungary could then dispose of its own fate, most

---

* It is not without interest that both the Austrian government and Archduke Francis Charles originally approved of the Hungarian mission to Frankfurt, probably because in May the Austrians too believed in the necessity of a German-Austrian-Hungarian anti-Slav alliance. See István Hajnal, *A Batthyány-kormány külpolitikája*, pp. 49–59; Árpád Károlyi, *Németújvári gróf Batthyány Lajos első magyar miniszterelnök főbenjáró pöre*, I, 314, and Ladislaus Szalay, *Diplomatische Aktenstücke zur Beleuchtung der ungarischen Gesandschaft in Deutschland* (Zürich, 1849).

preferably with the Habsburg king in Buda-Pest. Thus, if there were no great Habsburg Empire with Hungary as its pivot, then there could be an independent Hungarian Monarchy. It was on this new prospect that Batthyány and Kossuth placed their bets, delaying a final accord with Austria in the expectation that the latter would unite with Germany. On this issue, as on so many others, there was no fundamental difference between Batthyány and Kossuth, though it did not mean that their disagreements were superficial. They hated each other's methods, a hatred that threatened the survival of the cabinet.

Széchenyi alone knew that all was illusion. He, with his excellent Western contacts, sensed keenly that the union would not take place, that the great German state would not be born, and that the Italians would lose the war. He agreed with the radicals that the offer of military assistance to the emperor, even if it were unconditional, could no longer appease the Austrian government. On the contrary, Austria's coming victory in Italy meant that the Croatian units there would soon be free to join the army of Jelačić. Széchenyi's solution was reconciliation with Austria at any price, even by drastically altering the Hungarian constitution. He planned some kind of direct action of his own, but physically and mentally he was unable to go ahead. On July 18, during a testing of his beloved Chain Bridge, a cable snapped, throwing him and some other people into the Danube. He swam ashore unharmed but experienced a new depression: "We are lost," he wrote in his diary, "sunk back into barbarism; we are being ruined not by Kossuth and his associates as I have said, but by a greater power, by Nemesis." He went on opposing Kossuth in the cabinet and in the House, but his confidence was waning rapidly. "We cannot get anywhere with that madman," he noted in another diary entry.[55]

With Széchenyi dejectedly remaining on board, Batthyány and Kossuth were free to pilot Hungary's troubled ship. At the end of July, they both knew that their partnership could not last.

"The Government in Vienna . . . Could Never Count on Hungarian Assistance."

It was mid-July when Széchenyi learned from influential friends that the fortunes of war were changing in northern Italy: a week later at

Custozza, Field Marshal Radetzky annihilated the Piedmontese army. His Germans, Croats, Serbs, and Hungarians had fought bravely: there was no disharmony among the men whose brothers at home were preparing to slaughter one another. On August 6 the Austrians entered Milan, and shortly thereafter King Charles Albert asked for an armistice. The Empire's foreign war was over: it could now deal with its only remaining domestic enemy, the Republic of San Marco at Venice, and with the Hungarian problem.

Hungarian political circles underestimated the importance of Custozza. Yet the victory bolstered up Austrian morale, freed troops for action elsewhere in the Empire, and gave even more influence to Radetzky, the dynasty's savior. The old man could not budge from Italy, where the situation remained tense, but he put great pressure on the Austrian ministers to liquidate the Hungarian question.

In Vienna, too, things had vastly improved for the dynasty. The same burghers who in the spring had cheered the revolutionary students, now bemoaned anarchy, democracy, and especially the absence of the Court, which hurt their pride and their business. Delegation after delegation appeared in Innsbruck, begging Good Ferdinand (*Ferdinand den Gütigen*) to come home. At first, only the popular liberal Archduke John was sent to Vienna to test the atmosphere, but he had to leave almost immediately to take up his post in Frankfurt as elected president of the German Reich. He returned to Vienna in July to open the Austrian parliament, the constitutional Reichstag. Now all hopes were centered on the popular assembly: revolution was no longer in fashion. When the emperor arrived in the capital on August 12, he was given a hero's welcome. Meanwhile, the economy had worsened considerably; and between August 21 and 23 the workers of the city struck against the proposed lowering of wages. Their movement was put down with remarkable ferocity by the Vienna National Guards, who were radical in theory but not when the pocket-books of the bourgeoisie were threatened. The Academic legion remained neutral even though dozens of workers were killed and hundreds more wounded. The revolutionary Committee of Security was forced to disband itself; order had returned to Vienna. There was to be one more major revolutionary upheaval, in October, but the present peaceful interlude gave the new Wessenberg cabinet time to take steps with regard to Hungary. Its ministers went about the task of centralizing the Monarchy (Metternich had been a federalist, by

comparison) with patience and assiduity. On August 14 they caused
Ferdinand to withdraw the authorization he had given the palatine in
June to ratify, in the king's name, all bills adopted by the Buda-Pest
Assembly. This was only a beginning: all through August the minis-
ters were preparing a series of measures that were to prove decisive
for Austro-Hungarian relations.

The Hungarian parliament, having voted in favor of a 200,000-
man national army and a huge outlay of money, had to decide where
the money should come from and what ought to be done with the
recruits. These were not easy questions, especially as of money there
was hardly a trace.

When he created the Ministry of Finance in April, Kossuth
found a mere .5 million gulden in the treasury: not enough to pay the
civil service, not enough for anything. Up to the end of October, the
closing of the military fiscal year, another 5 million in revenue was
expected, but this was a theoretical expectation. Few people bothered
to pay taxes; commerce was in decline; Jelačić had sequestered all the
state moneys found in Croatia, so no revenue could be expected from
there; the Hungarian mints continued to send to Vienna the gold and
silver coins they produced, while the Austrian Bank of Issue was
hoarding silver—which it had been buying at preferential rates. As a
result, silver coins all but disappeared from Hungary.

Kossuth proved a determined and conscientious finance administrator. The major budget address he presented to the House in July
has been called a masterpiece by modern experts.[56] Once in office,
Kossuth ordered that revenues collected by provincial state agencies
be dispatched to Buda-Pest continually and not (as in the past) only
once a month; he sent the ingot reserves of private banks to the mint
for conversion into coins; and on May 24 he launched a state loan to
create the collateral for the issuing of Hungarian banknotes. These
bonds, carrying an annual interest of 5 percent, could be purchased
only against gold or silver. Altogether, Kossuth hoped to collect from
a number of sources 5 million gulden worth of bullion, which would
have permitted the printing of banknotes with a nominal value of
12.5 million. The loan drive was a failure; only a small part of the
expected sum was collected, and not until August could the new 2-
gulden notes be issued at the total face value of about 4 million. To
prevent the ratification of this unconstitutional measure (the constitution had said nothing about a Hungarian Bank of Issue), on August

14 the king withdrew the palatine's right to sanction bills. On the following day Kossuth placed severe restrictions on the export of silver, and, as the Austrian ministry had placed an interdict on Kossuth's banknotes in Vienna, he made the Austrian 1- and 2-gulden notes unacceptable in Hungary—adding one more major item to the list of mutual grievances.[57]

Kossuth practiced drastic economy in all sectors of the administration (not that the administration was very big; the ministries employed a total of 1,800 persons, including customs officials and servants), but he was not prepared to save on national defense. He kept reassuring his colleagues that money for defense would be made available somehow. He later wrote:

When I was asked for money for the fatherland's defense . . . the only thing I wondered about was which solution was better, which more purposeful, but my answer was always the same: "Go ahead! Go ahead! There is money for the country's defense; there will be money; the nation will not abandon us, or if it does, we shall find the money in heaven; and if even heaven abandons us, we shall find the money in hell."[58]

Somehow Kossuth succeeded. The same public that would not subscribe to the state loan and that donated little or nothing of its wealth, readily accepted the banknotes that Kossuth was to print throughout the war. With his stable assignats that people called "Kossuth notes," he built up a great national army and fought a long war.

If the Assembly let Kossuth take care of finances, it had to face the problem of recruits: whether the new soldiers would be added to the Imperial-Royal army in Hungary, or whether they would be used to bolster the ranks of the *honvéd*. Kossuth's July 11 address in parliament had failed to mention the issue, for the simple reason that the ministers had been unable to agree among themselves. Kossuth favored the idea of strengthening the *honvéd* forces; Batthyány, Mészáros, and most others favored the regular army. Kossuth's proposal was unconstitutional (the *honvéd* were legally still part of the amateur National Guard system), and its practical value was doubtful; for the *honvéd*, although reliable, constituted a raw and inexperienced body of twelve incomplete battalions, led mainly by pensioned officers who had joined out of patriotism and for the good pay. The regular army in Hungary, on the other hand, was well organized and professionally commanded, although politically suspect.

The question of recruits was supposed to be debated in parliament on August 1; but Batthyány, who knew the mood of the House and who wished to delay a potentially fatal clash with Austria until the latter had made a decision on the union with Germany, obtained a postponement. On August 3 he requested that the House send a message of warm sympathy to the Frankfurt Assembly: it was to show that Hungary favored German-Austrian union. A few weeks earlier, through their Frankfurt delegate Szalay, the ministers had proposed a German-Hungarian military alliance against the Serbs, the Croats, and the Russian Empire, with each partner contributing an army of 100,000. Upon Austrian protest, this proposal was withdrawn.[59] The August 3 message was considerably meeker, causing the radicals and Kossuth's followers, on that day, to turn against Batthyány; they changed his minor gesture into a major policy statement. Arguing that the message was too weak, Kossuth's political friend, Pál Nyáry, caused an addendum to be adopted. It stated bluntly: "The House of Representatives declares, in the name of the Hungarian nation that, should the Austrian government in Vienna find itself at war over the question of German unity with the united German power, it could never count on Hungarian assistance."[60]

The addendum was much more hostile to Austria than the House's resolution on the Italian war had been. Unlike the latter, it was a breach of Hungary's constitutional obligations, or it was seen to be so in Vienna. Kossuth's parliamentary speech of that day, together with his newspaper articles on the subject, prove that he was fully behind the radical resolution. Surprisingly, Batthyány, who had been absent from the House on August 3, showed no anger when informed of the developments. Only Széchenyi and Mészáros were shocked: "The decline and humiliation that Hungary and the Hungarian nation will suffer are unprecedented in history," noted Széchenyi in his diary.[61] He now felt that not only Kossuth but his other colleagues too were insane. The only possible explanation of Batthyány's positive reaction to the addendum was that he thought the gamble worthwhile: by threatening Austria, the Hungarians could hasten the German-Austrian union.

On August 6 the debate on the recruits was again postponed for a week; and on the same day Count Latour ordered that Austrian regiments hoist the red, black, and gold flag of the German Reich next to the black and gold flag of the Habsburgs. But the Hungarians were given no time to rejoice: having made his symbolic gesture for the unity of Germany, Latour ordered the removal of the German flags the next day. The Great German Reich lasted twenty-four hours: it would be recreated only by Hitler.

The deputies still had to decide the fate of the Hungarian recruits. On August 16 Mészáros put forward his motion that all recruits be added to the regular army. He was attacked ferociously. Three days later, again in the House, Kossuth lashed out against the minister of war and thus indirectly against Batthyány. On August 21 the House adopted, 226 to 117, a motion that Kossuth considered a compromise but that hardly could be called that. According to this resolution, the great majority of recruits would be employed to create new *honvéd* battalions. The rest were to be used to fill the third battalions of regular regiments originating from Hungary. This meant in practice that the trained first and second battalions, now mostly in Italy, would receive no reinforcements; only the reserve third battalions, which acted as training units in the regimental depots (that is at home), would receive them.[62]

For several weeks Kossuth had been systematically defying Batthyány in Council, in the House, and in his own newspaper, the "Journal of Kossuth" (*Kossuth Hírlapja*) which he had been writing, editing, and publishing since July 1. And yet, the prime minister could not get rid of his former friend, for he knew well that it would cause a revolt in the House and in the streets. In desperation, Batthyány resolved to develop a major plan to conciliate the Court at the last minute: it was to mark a complete break with the government's previous stand on Croatia. But while Batthyány was preparing to extend a friendly hand to Vienna through Zagreb, the Austrian cabinet was taking decisive steps against Hungary.

Had Batthyány been more resolute and more consistent, he could have salvaged much of the sovereignty of his country. But he could not rid himself of the chimera of Hungary being a great independent state, entitled to pursue its own Great Power foreign policy. Loyal to the king but disloyal to the emperor, if such a thing were possible, Batthyány lost the confidence of both. But Kossuth was no more consistent. He took up a propaganda position to the left of the prime minister, which caused Batthyány no end of trouble, yet the political aims of the two were almost identical and similarly confused. Only the radicals and Széchenyi knew what they wanted; but as they had no power, they made compromises. By August the optimism of the spring had evaporated: a magnificent new age had turned into a quagmire of resentments and infinite trouble.

4 / The Month of Defiance: September 1848

The Turning Point

ON AUGUST 26 a secret emissary from Vienna called on Jelačić at Zagreb. Two days after the visit, Jelačić wrote to the Serbian Metropolitan Rajačić:

I am in a position to tell you, under the cloak of greatest secrecy, that the Imperial Court has recognized the righteousness of our cause—not only of the Croats but also of the Serbs—and that the Court will soon make the appropriate statement. Among other things, the insulting June 10 Manifesto [depriving Jelačić of his positions] will be revoked. But they prefer to wait until after we had left for the battlefield [against Hungary]. As soon as we begin the operations and the fighting, the Court will step in openly to restore peace on the basis of the principles I outlined in my latest manifesto, namely on the basis of equal rights to all nationalities. Moreover, an Imperial commissioner has already been appointed to undertake such mediation.[1]

Jelačić well deserved the confidence of the Court. Despite his dismissal in June, he had consistently advocated absolute loyalty to the emperor and had exhorted the *Grenzer* in Radetzky's army to go on fighting for the preservation of the state.[2] Yet the Vienna emissary was not telling Jelačić the truth; or perhaps in his letter to Rajačić, Jelačić was embellishing the Vienna message. Of an Imperial commissioner for Hungary there was as yet no trace at the Court, and the Royal Rescript rehabilitating the *ban* was issued before and not after he set out for Hungary with his soldiers. Writing on September 4, the king merely expressed the pleasure of "his paternal heart" with the proven loyalty of Jelačić, revoked the June Manifesto, and exhorted the *ban* "to labor to promote the welfare of the collective monarchy, to maintain the integrity of the Hungarian crown, and to aid the beneficial development of the Hungarian dependencies."[3] Only a faction at the Court, led by Minister of War Latour and Baron Kulmer (the Zagreb National Assembly's "delegate near His Majesty") believed firmly that Jelačić ought to invade Hungary. Others in the Austrian leadership feared Jelačić, in whom they suspected a fanatical nationalist.[4]

Jelačić himself was unsure of the situation and, although he sent his troops into the Hungarian Adriatic port Fiume on August 31, he wanted direct orders from Vienna before beginning the military campaign against Hungary.[5] He got none: only admonitions from his Viennese friends that he act quickly before Batthyány could reassert his influence at Court. So when Jelačić marched into Hungary on September 11, he did not know whether the king would again brand him a rebel. After he had been in Hungary for ten days, he told his officers:

Since my appointment as Ban I have received 21 memoranda (*Handbillete*) from His Majesty the Emperor. To my regret, I was not able to obey any of them. Now, finally, His Majesty has approved of my actions. But were His Majesty the Emperor to send me another 21 memoranda, all meant to divert me from my goal, I would still not obey them. I must act on behalf of His Majesty, if necessary against His Very Highest Will.[6]

The rehabilitation of Jelačić and Rajačić (but not necessarily the invasion of Hungary) were part of the Austrian ministry's program to put an end to Hungarian independence. On August 31, the day Jelačić's soldiers seized Fiume, the king addressed a stern letter to the palatine, supplementing it with a lengthy memorandum prepared by the Austrian cabinet. The memorandum outlined the history of Austro-Hungarian relations, assuring the Hungarians that they had drawn only benefits from this relationship, and accusing the Batthyány cabinet of the violation of the letter and spirit of the Pragmatic Sanction, which had tied Hungary to the rest of the Monarchy "indivisibly and inseparably" (*indivisibiliter ac inseparabiliter*). The king's Rescript ordered that the aggressive plans between Hungary on the one hand and Croatia and the Military Border on the other be abandoned; that the Hungarians heed the Austrian cabinet's call for Hungary to surrender her independent finances and war ministry; and that the Hungarian ministers come to Vienna to meet with the Austrian ministers and with Jelačić.[7]

The Vienna documents mixed the reasonable with the irrational, as would most governmental manifestoes on both sides in the coming weeks. Whether or not Hungary benefited from its long association with Austria is still a matter of heated controversy. Of course, Hungary was constitutionally tied to Austria, but the April Laws had considerably loosened these ties. The accusation that Hungary was planning aggression against Croatia, its own subordinate kingdom, was nonsense. The Hungarians had no idea how they would defend themselves against Jelačić, let alone invade his territory. As for the Serbs, the king had sent his own generals and troops against them. Jelačić and Rajačić were Hungarian dignitaries, and whatever the Hungarian government planned to undertake against them was constitutionally no business of the Austrian government. Finally, it was rather ironic for the Austrian cabinet, which had come to power through revolutionary demonstrations, to reproach the Hungarian cabinet for being revolutionary. But while all these arguments neatly favor the Hungarians, it remains true that in the spring of 1848 the Hungarians had forced the Court into excessive concessions, that they had subsequently evaded discussing a modification of the new constitution or the settlement of such common concerns as military affairs or the state debt, and that they had been unable to maintain peace in their country.

And the supreme irony of it all: just when the Austrians took these drastic steps, the Hungarians came forward with a most conciliatory proposal on the Croatian question. Meeting on August 27, the Buda-Pest council of ministers agreed on a bill granting extensive autonomy to the Croats; or if the Croats failed to accept this, offering them complete secession from Hungary, provided only that Croatia remain an ally of Hungary, and that Fiume plus the Hungarian Littoral remain under the Holy Crown with free Hungarian access thereto. The author of this bill was Minister of Justice Ferenc Deák, who in 1867 was to conclude the Compromise Agreement with the king. Kossuth supported the bill at the cabinet meeting—whether sincerely or only to prove that concessions would lead nowhere, is not known.[8]

Thus the Hungarians offered far greater concessions to the Croats than the Austrian cabinet had asked for, but their concessions came too late and they were not in the right area. Croatian secession from Hungary was not in the interest of the Habsburgs, who feared the Croatian independence movement almost as much as they feared the Hungarian independence movement. The Court sincerely wished to maintain the integrity of Hungary but, of course, only under the control of Vienna. It was in the realm of common affairs that substantial concessions were expected from the Hungarians, but when Batthyány and Deák came to the Court, they merely reiterated the old Hungarian demands that the king come to live in Buda-Pest and that he sanction the army bill and the bill on army financing. No wonder then that the two ministers were sent from pillar to post in Vienna, of which they complained bitterly in letters home.[9]

Thus the die was now cast, which (in the customary Central European manner) did not mean that the negotiations were over or that arms alone would speak. There were to be many more efforts at a conciliation and many more contradictory pronouncements. Batthyány resigned, then decided to stay, resigned again, and once more remained at his post; the Court and the palatine continued their routine correspondence but also exchanged desperate appeals; the palatine attempted a coup d'état in Buda-Pest but also accepted command of the Hungarian army facing Jelačić. The Hungarian parliament was the scene of feverish activity and the streets of the capital teemed with demonstrators. In the crisis, the political center slowly melted away and, at the end, only the intransigents were left: Jelačić, Latour, Kossuth, the Hungarian Roundheads. By late September Hungary was a different country: a constitutional monarchy in name only, it had become a parliamentary dictatorship. September was a turning point in Hungarian history.

The central figure in all this was Kossuth. He dominated the cabinet and public opinion, and he dictated all the major parliamentary decisions. His assiduity was amazing: he seemed to be everywhere at the same time. Between September 1 and 15, Kossuth drafted at least thirteen decrees, five other rather lengthy communications, and several newspaper articles. He also made at least sixteen parliamentary speeches.

No sooner was Ferdinand's Rescript of August 31 read aloud in the Lower House on September 4, than Kossuth asked for permission to speak. He had again arrived ill on that day and now he began by protesting his inability to stand or speak audibly. While deputies begged him to think of his health, he sat down, rose again, and remained standing till the end of his address. Speaking passionately but with great self-mastery, he asked the House to prepare a manifesto to the peoples of Europe proclaiming Hungary's innocence and the purity of her aims. More ominously, for the first time he raised the specter of dictatorship "based not on law but on the fatherland's peril." Then he mitigated the stunning effect of his proposal by recommending that the National Assembly send a giant deputation to the king. One hundred members of the Assembly were thereupon delegated to Vienna.[10]

While the deputation was en route, Kossuth published a decree on the immediate issuance of new 5-gulden banknotes to be covered by a government loan of 61,000,000 gulden, which the National Assembly had authorized late in August but which the king had obviously no intention of ratifying.[11] This was the Hungarian government's first truly unconstitutional act.

In Vienna the mass deputation presented an ultimatum to the king insisting as usual that he come immediately to Buda-Pest. They were turned down with firm words.[12] A Hungarian observer in Vienna noted that the deputies, who had eschewed the glittering costumes of Hungarian noblemen and were dressed for the occasion in somber black with unadorned swords, departed from the king's presence with only a deep bow. Nation and king were not to meet again. By the time the delegation reached the steamboat anchored near the Vienna Prater, some deputies were sporting a red plume on their caps. When the ship arrived in Pest, it was decorated with the red flag of defiance and rebellion.[13]

On September 10 Batthyány handed in his resignation. He had returned with the deputies on the same ship and immediately hurried to the palatine. The following day proved to be the most exciting, and the most important, of the "September *journées.*"

On September 11, the day Jelačić crossed the Drava River separating Croatia from Inner Hungary, the palatine attempted to seize power in Buda-Pest. In a letter to the National Assembly he announced that since the cabinet had resigned, he would take the government into his own hands. The palatine could not have chosen a worse day for his move. The young archduke (he was then thirty-one) had grown desperate over developments in Hungary. He had sincerely tried to serve both his family and the country, but had soon discovered that his authority and popularity were commensurate with his approval of each and every Hungarian measure. And he had turned down all Hungarian suggestions that he become king. Just a few days earlier, Kossuth had offered him the crown.[14] The palatine felt neglected by Vienna and isolated; he feared that Kossuth and the radicals would drive the country into communism and anarchy. To prevent this he had ordered reliable troops to Buda to reinforce the ridiculously weak and blatantly unreliable garrison. (There were only around a thousand regular troops in Buda fortress at the end of August.[15]) Grenadiers had torn off their black and yellow Imperial insignia and had cut the hated tails off their white waistcoats. They clamored for admission into the *honvéd,* where the language of command was Hungarian, the pay better, the discipline less barbarous— no corporal punishment there—and the chances of advancement excellent.

By the time the troops finally arrived in Buda around September 10, the local National Guard and the *honvéd* had also been reinforced and were in an ugly mood. The archduke could not possibly enforce his decision, which was immediately understood to be what it was: an attempted coup d'état. The National Assembly indignantly branded the palatine's action unconstitutional and, at Kossuth's recommendation, urged Batthyány to remain temporarily in office.

The constitutional consequences of the prime minister's resignation were so obscure that not all the ministers had resigned with Batthyány. Nor had they all been in a position to do so. Mészáros was with the troops in southern Hungary; Esterházy was in Vienna with the Court (he wished to have nothing to do with the Buda-Pest clique in any case), and Széchenyi had lost his reason.

Madness had haunted Széchenyi for many weeks; the final blow to his health came from the king's letter of August 31. "Within 48 hours all will be in fire and flames," Széchenyi wrote in his diary. "In the entire universe I am unable to find a single flicker of light." Again, he blamed himself for all of his country's misfortunes. He spent the nights wrestling with his conscience. His attempts at suicide were averted with difficulty. He was hastened out of Buda-Pest by his doctor and on September 7 he entered the insane asylum in Döbling, where he was to stay until he killed himself in 1860.[16] Following his disappearance from the capital, the radical press accused him of cowardice and desertion.

In the Lower House on September 11, Minister of the Interior Szemere refused to budge from his seat. Kossuth, who had at first resigned, now reoccupied his ministerial chair and challenged anyone to doubt his right to be there. Amid tumultuous patriotic demonstrations in the streets and in the galleries of the Assembly, Kossuth easily persuaded the deputies to approve his measures with regard to the issue of the 5-gulden notes and to enact the government's proposal on military conscription—a bill that the Assembly had previously approved but that the king would not ratify. To give a show of legality, the deputies decided that the conscription should begin with the recruitment of volunteers; only when that failed would lots be drawn. The House also ruled that the new recruits should be employed in the *honvéd* battalions and not in the regular regiments stationed in Hungary. To all this was added the pious clause that these measures were only temporary "until the day His Majesty sanctions the bill": a formula which was attached to every law or decree for many months to come.

Kossuth's parliamentary address was again endless, passionate, poetic, and convincing. As a tribute to his eloquence and to the crowds demonstrating in front of the Assembly, not a single deputy raised his voice in opposition. On that day Kossuth could easily have had himself proclaimed prime minister. That he did not do so showed his self-discipline and political flair. He gave Batthyány and the moderates further opportunity to prove themselves unable to master the crisis.[17]

The Coming of a Friend

On September 11, that day of days, precisely five months after the ratification of the Hungarian constitution, Jelačić entered Hungary with the bulk of his forces. In his first manifesto to the soldiers in Hungary, he assured them that he had come, as a friend, only to restore the unity of the Imperial-Royal army and of the Monarchy.[18] But although the river had been crossed without incident and the troops opposite those of Jelačić had withdrawn to avoid a clash, there was no surrender. This was the bloodless beginning of the only internecine struggle known to the Habsburg army. In the preceding months on the battlefields of southern Hungary, Habsburg officers had already fought one another, but with the clear understanding that those on the Hungarian side were upholding the law, however grudgingly, whereas those on the Serbian side were acting in the name of some higher *raison d'état* superseding the laws of a weak and misguided emperor. Nor had there been any Austrian generals in the Serbian camp. Now Habsburg generals were leading troops against Habsburg generals.

The Croatian army of over fifty thousand men was a mixed lot, as were all the armies during the first months of the war. Regulars, Border Guards, Croatian National Guards mingled in colorful confusion. The main force was the *Grenzer,* but their quality was uneven. Their trained first and second battalions were in Italy; to the reserve third battalions had recently been added *arrière-garde* fourth battalions and even fifth battalions: elderly peasants shouldering scythes and pitchforks.[19] The *Grenzer* had been told to hate the Hungarians, who (it was said) wanted to rob the Croatian nation of the rest of its sadly diminished liberties; but mostly the *Grenzer* were fired by the prospect of booty, their time-honored reward for fighting in alien territory. Of all the descriptions of the emperor's South Slav soldiers, none matches in charm that of the American historian Priscilla Robertson. This is how she describes the entry of the *Grenzer* into Vienna in October of the same year:

The Croats marched in, quiet as cats, with none of the noise and clang of an ordinary army. Their beautiful scarlet cloaks, clasped at the neck with a large silver egg which opened into a drinking cup, their variety of Turkish weapons, the warrior women who marched at their sides, all made such a sight as Vienna had not seen for centuries. Europe's most urbane capital did not know what manner of men inhabited the edges of the Empire. Unfortunately, it was one of the historical privileges of the Seressan soldiers [a special border police force] to plunder. When they found the Emperor, whom they thought they were coming to save, was not in the city, they began to loot it like a Turkish frontier village, though they stole with no sense of value. They would sell a gold watch for a few florins, or even think they had the best of the bargain if someone gave them a few pieces of real silver money for a banknote worth a hundred florins.[20]

Loot the Croats did in Hungary too, as recorded in their own officers' letters, captured by the Hungarians during the campaign. "Our

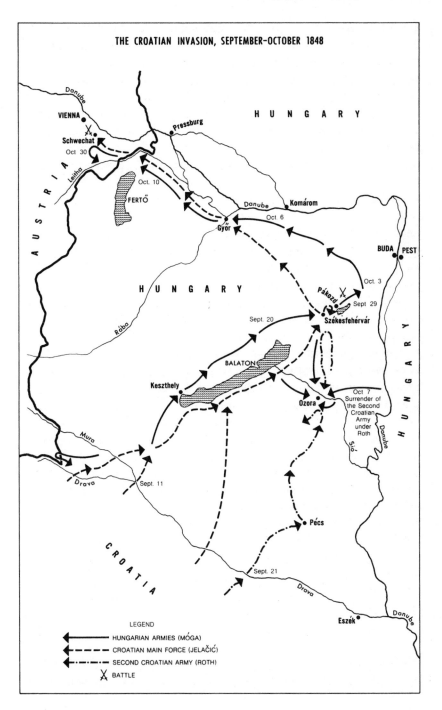

THE CROATIAN INVASION, SEPTEMBER-OCTOBER 1848

LEGEND
HUNGARIAN ARMIES (MÓGA)
CROATIAN MAIN FORCE (JELAČIĆ)
SECOND CROATIAN ARMY (ROTH)
BATTLE

Border Guards . . . loot and steal without shame. We distribute 1,000 cudgellings every day, but to no avail. God himself could not stop them, even less an officer. . . . I am quite exasperated over this robbing expedition and begin to think of myself as a bandit chief,'' one officer wrote to a friend in Italy. "Our army is a band of robbers; they steal and loot, even though they suffer no want in anything. . . . Since yesterday four dead Border Guards were found on the highway by Hungarians. I am told that the Hungarians revolted in our rear . . . ,'' another officer wrote to his wife.[21] He was well informed.

The Croats' behavior infuriated the Hungarian peasants, who armed themselves to hunt for isolated Guards. Croatian atrocities and, even more, the atrocity stories diligently propagated by the Hungarian government united the people of Transdanubia against the invaders, and spun the bloodless invasion into a series of wild skirmishes that contributed to Jelačić's ultimate defeat.

If the Hungarian peasants were ready to fight, the Hungarian army was not. It was a small army (the German regular regiments having deserted it on the spot), consisting of two hussar regiments, two regular infantry and two freshly formed *honvéd* battalions, and two batteries of artillery, each with eight guns. There were 6,000 men all told, to whom must be added the so-called Mobile National Guards, poorly armed peasant youngsters whom the regular officers despised.[22] The commanders of the Hungarian army viewed the whole affair as a ghastly mistake soon to be clarified through rational negotiations between comrades-in-arms. A few weeks before Jelačić's entry into Hungary, the then commander of the Hungarian troops, Major General Franz Ottinger, ordered his soldiers not to resist the Croatian invasion but to open immediate negotiations. If these were to fail, "the troops must act as if they were at army maneuvers and withdraw without using their weapons.''[23] Why army maneuvers should consist only of withdrawal and not also of advance was not explained to the troops. Ottinger was immediately recalled by the Hungarian government (he subsequently went over to Jelačić and participated in the latter's campaigns), but his replacement proved to be equally disloyal and was also recalled. The third commander, Major General Count Ádám Teleki, a brother of the radical László Teleki, had commanded a Hungarian hussar regiment before 1848. He, too, was reluctant to fight. Instead of army maneuvers, he hit upon the idea of neutrality and proposed to remove his troops from the scene. This again was prevented by the government's commissioner in the army and by Teleki's own underlings. Short of wisdom, the officers of the first battalion of the 60th Wasa Infantry Regiment sent a delegate to Vienna to inquire about His Majesty's wishes. The emissary got as far as Latour, who gave the reply—astonishing under the circumstances—that, as Austrian war minister, he had no right to issue orders to officers of a Hungarian regiment: that, he said, was the responsibility of his Hungarian colleague.[24] Hungarian historians have consistently called Latour's action, and others similar to it, a subterfuge. But it is hard to see why such a subterfuge was necessary at a time when Jelačić was deep inside Hungary. Rather, Latour's reply must be ranged alongside the many contradictory moves that characterized Austrian policy between March and September.

Teleki still tried to negotiate but was overruled by his officers, who on September 20 issued a manifesto asserting that, if Jelačić continued to advance, they would stop him with arms.[25] Now Teleki was also recalled (he later went over to the Austrians but instead of being rewarded for his deeds, was deprived of his rank) and was replaced by *Feldmarschalleutnant* (two-star general) János Móga, who, although no less loyal to the monarch, was determined to fight. Meanwhile, Jelačić had crossed half of Transdanubia in the direction of Buda-Pest, where equally momentous events were taking place.

The National Assembly Prepares for a Take-Over

Batthyány's reappointment by the National Assembly encouraged him to attempt a counteroffensive aimed simultaneously at the Court and at Kossuth. He drew up a new cabinet list of moderate liberals and Kossuth announced triumphantly in his newspaper that he was now a mere journalist "no longer tied by the shackles of ministerial collegiality. I have been freed from the suffocating fumes of Court intrigues. Grant me only one week's rest to restore my somewhat crippled health."[26]

Batthyány launched an appeal to the people of Transdanubia to rise up in arms against the Croatian invaders. He forbade soldiers in the regular units to transfer into *honvéd* battalions, thereby spreading terror among the unfortunate men who had cut off their coattails and now expected to run the gauntlet. He ordered reliable, that is non-Magyar, troops into Buda-Pest. Most important, he prevailed upon the palatine, who was ex officio captain general of Hungary, to take command of the army facing Jelačić. This was a brilliant stroke, for now a Habsburg archduke was marching against a Habsburg general, a situation from which Hungary and Batthyány could only profit. Unfortunately for Batthyány, as we shall see, the archduke was willing to play the game for only a few days.

Meanwhile, Kossuth—the journalist with the "crippled health" —was scarcely resting. He spoke in the House of Representatives every single day, sometimes two or three times a day, driving through a series of measures that fortified the country's defenses and his own position. He also found time to write articles and to address delegations or the crowds demonstrating in favor of his prime ministry. He insisted that the Imperial-Royal soldiers be allowed to enter the *honvéd* battalions; he protested the arrival of foreign soldiers in Buda-Pest; he assured the palatine and Batthyány of his loyalty to them; he presented a detailed plan on compensation to be paid to landlords for losses suffered through peasant emancipation; and he persuaded the House to dispatch a delegation to the Austrian Reichstag. Finally, on September 15, the day Batthyány announced his intention to send the palatine to the army, Kossuth prevailed upon the House to appoint three of its members, all nominated by him, to follow the palatine to the army.

Kossuth could now make no proposal that the House would not have applauded. He knew how to flatter the deputies and how to assuage their fears. A semblance of legality was strenuously maintained; the king's name was invoked in tones of deepest respect; the king's evil advisers were held up for contempt and ridicule; the landowning nobility was comforted with the promise of financial compensation, although in the obscure future; the power of the House was enhanced by the appointment of three itinerant commissioners. Clearly, these men were sent out to control the palatine. Batthyány immediately sensed the danger to the archduke and to himself, but his protests were brushed aside.[27] From that day on, and until May 1849, Assembly members sent out by Kossuth would govern an increasing number of counties and cities, administer justice, recruit soldiers, feed, equip, and advise the armies. The power of the parliamentary commissioners was to become absolute in the provinces, with one crucial exception: unlike the *représentants en mission* during the French Revolution and the Red commissars in the Russian Civil War of 1919–21, effective command of the armies would never pass into their hands. It would be exercised by the generals, who in turn would meddle in administration and in politics. The power struggle between the generals and the commissioners was to mark the history of the War of Independence.

On September 15 in a unanimous vote and again at Kossuth's advice, the House decided to abolish the tithe levied on vineyards.[28] This is as far as the liberal majority, and Kossuth, were willing to go to win over the peasants. When in the following days the radical deputies pressed for other measures on behalf of the cotters or of the peasants holding a section of manorial land, the House suspended its decisions until "the day that the danger threatening the country disappeared." Since the danger never disappeared, there were (with one exception in April 1849) no further agrarian reforms.[29]

In the days following September 15 Kossuth asked the people of Buda-Pest to build ramparts against the enemy, and called upon the country to rise in general insurrection. The situation was truly terrible. The Austrian Reichstag had refused to receive the Hungarian delegates. On September 18 the news arrived that the Slovak patriot Jozef Hurban had crossed the Carpathians from Moravia with some armed men—as it turned out mainly Czech and Slovak students. Their mission would fail, but this could not be known in Buda-Pest at the time. On the following day the six Saxon deputies from Transylvania resigned from the rebellious Assembly and were immediately branded as traitors by Kossuth.

On September 21 Kossuth took a long step toward the establishment of a revolutionary government in Hungary. He had broached the issue twice before, but now he carried through a concrete proposal: the House consented to elect a committee of six to assist the prime minister permanently and to discuss with him such military questions as could not be aired in public. On the following day the House elected Kossuth, one other liberal deputy, and four radicals as members of the new committee. The radical László Madarász, the bogy of the moderates, was among them.[30] This was not an assumption of executive power by the legislature, but it was a crucial move in that direction. Within a short time the committee, soon to be called the National Defense Committee, was to become the government of Hungary.

For the time being, Batthyány was still forcing the issue of a cabinet composed of moderate liberals. He had asked for some guarantees from the king before he formed a new government. The king allowed Batthyány to make the attempt, but would give no guarantees; instead, His Majesty insisted on seeing the list of cabinet members before making a decision. Batthyány chose to play the game of resignations but it got him nowhere. In any case, his future now depended on the palatine's ability to stop the Croatian army. As long as the country was in mortal danger, Kossuth would have the final say in all matters.

Hungary's Valmy

Archduke Stephen left Buda-Pest on September 16 together with General Móga, who was to replace Ádám Teleki. Trying to negotiate on armistice, the palatine invited Jelačić to meet him on the first and at that time only steamboat that plied the waters of Lake Balaton. What followed was rather comical. The *ban* came on September 21; but when he saw the ship, decorated with Hungarian flags and presumably hiding many Hungarians, he suspected an ambush. He asked that the archduke alight from the ship and that the two meet in separate rowboats. But there was only one rowboat. Would the palatine come to the shore then? No, his officers would not allow that, nor would it have been worthy of his title and position. As for the less-than-eager Jelačić, his officers would not let him board the steamboat. Amid tumultuous cheers by the Croatian officers, the planned armistice negotiations fell through.[31]

By then the palatine must have received the king's letters forbidding him to fight a battle with Jelačić, for "that would be incompatible with your position as an archduke."[32] Archduke Stephen, who in any case had had no desire to fight, immediately returned to Buda-Pest and on September 23 informed Batthyány of his decision to resign as palatine. As he explained in his letter to the prime minister, he would do his best at the Court to support the cause of Hungary.[33] And even though the Hungarians of his own and of all subsequent generations never forgave Archduke Stephen for his "cowardly flight and treachery,'' his self-appointed mission had not been completely in vain. The king's appointment of General Lamberg as royal commissioner was partly the archduke's doing, as we shall see. Nor did the Court forgive the palatine. He was sent into exile on his estate in Germany; although there was a later reconciliation with Emperor Francis Joseph, he remained abroad until he died in 1867.

The Austro-Croatian army continued its advance on Buda-Pest. Finally, toward the end of September, the Hungarians decided to make a stand. General Móga had chosen his position well; near the village of Pákozd about thirty miles southwest of the capital, he arranged his troops between some marshes and a lake. Jelačić's army, at that point over 30,000 strong, enjoyed a great superiority in numbers and in arms; it attacked on the morning of September 29 and, following a battle of two hours, was brought to a halt. On the Hungarian side there were, besides the hussars, only three battalions of trained regular infantry. Three out of five soldiers belonged to the *honvéd,* the volunteer units or the National Guards. The lion's share of the victory was taken by the Czech cannoneers of the Fifth Prague Artillery Regiment (they far outclassed their colleagues from the same regiment who fired from the Croatian side), but the *honvéd* and the militia also fought very well. The new national army saved Buda-Pest and, like the French at Valmy in September 1792, allowed the revolution to continue.[34]

Jelačić now asked for, and immediately obtained, a three-day armistice between ''the Royal Hungarian and the Imperial-Royal Croatian armies.'' He used this respite to turn his troops around and to withdraw in the direction of Austria. The Hungarians followed him, but reluctantly.[35] Shortly thereafter, a second Croatian army suffered defeat, this time totally. On October 7 at Ozora, Generals Roth and Philippovich surrendered between 6,000 and 10,000 famished and isolated Border Guards and peasants to a far smaller army of Hungarian National Guards and Transdanubian peasants. Suddenly the Hungarians were inundated with Croatian weapons and prisoners of war. The peasants were let go but the Border Guards were kept in Hungary, giving a lot of headaches to the Hungarian authorities, who could never decide whether the prisoners of war, especially their officers, should be kept under guard or treated as visitors paid by the host country.

The victory at Pákozd should have enabled Batthyány to consolidate his position and to seek renewed negotiations with the Court. But the battle came too late. The day before Pákozd, a conciliatory move on the part of the king had ended in tragedy. There was to be no reconciliation, nor any salvation for the prime minister.

The Assassination

The day after the palatine's final departure from Buda-Pest, Kossuth also left the capital "to call on the people to rise in arms . . . to save themselves, and to save this orphaned fatherland." He traveled on the brand-new railroad line to Cegléd, a large peasant town on the Great Hungarian Plain, then he journeyed to all the great settlements of central Hungary. Surrounded by local officials and by young men on horseback, he spoke to masses upon masses of peasants, success-fully exhorting tens of thousands to volunteer for the war. The volun-teers had few arms, of course, and the state had no spare weapons. Those among the volunteers who had wandered in the direction of the enemy found that the Croats were gone; those who had been organ-ized into more or less coherent units found that service was a bore, and most of them returned home. The immediate result of Kossuth's recruiting effort, then, amounted to little in military terms. The real Hungarian army was to be made up of systematically recruited or conscripted young men. But the political and psychological effect of Kossuth's pilgrimage was inestimable. For the first time, the peasants had laid eyes on their already legendary liberator. The magic of his oratory, his charm, and his sincerity roused the customarily dour and suspicious peasants of the Great Plain to paroxysms of an enthusiasm that was to last a century. Kossuth became a saint, the god of the peasants. From that time on, he was immune to public attacks from his political opponents. He was one with the people in these halcyon days of his life. Kossuth made the most of the success of his tour; and Hungarian writers, historians, and artists have done the same. Many Kossuth statues—and there is one in every self-respecting Hun-garian town—show him addressing the people of the Great Plain while the peasants, young and old, male and female, sit at his feet with arms upraised in eternal gratitude.[36] Even New York City resi-dents can gaze on Kossuth in this immortalized posture on Manhat-tan's Riverside Drive.

While the revolutionary leader was thus on tour, Ferdinand issued a series of new manifestos aimed at stopping the war in Hungary. The most important, that of September 25, announced the appointment of *Feldmarschalleutnant* Count Ferenc Lamberg as royal commissioner and commander-in-chief of all armed forces in Hungary; he was to bring about an immediate armistice on all battlefields. Simultaneously, the king entrusted the right-wing liberal politician, Baron Miklós Vay, with forming a new government.[37]

Most Hungarian historians have condemned Lamberg's appointment as unconstitutional and counterrevolutionary. They see it as another base trick played by the Vienna reactionaries. It was perhaps unconstitutional, but the appointment was also in the interest of peace and the autonomy of Hungary. When the manifestos were published on September 25, Jelačić was still moving leisurely toward Buda-Pest: it was expected that he would take the city in a day or two. Why then the appointment of a new supreme commander with authority over both the Hungarian and Croatian armies, and with the specific task of enforcing an immediate armistice? This could have stopped Jelačić. And if the aim was entirely anti-Hungarian, then why appoint a moderate Hungarian? Lamberg had participated in the Reform Diet of 1847–48 as a member of the Upper House; and as commander of the Pressburg army corps he had shown himself as patriotic as his uniform allowed him to be. His *Ungarns politische Zukunft,* published anonymously in 1842, proved him a conservative reformer; Batthyány himself respected the general. The king's move represented a last effort to save the Monarchy in its old decentralized form. But Lamberg's appointment was totally misunderstood in Hungary.

Who had dictated the king's decision with regard to Lamberg is fairly well known. We must remember that Ferdinand himself never decided anything; he was seldom even consulted. When we talk about his letters, his manifestos, his decrees, they are always to be understood in terms of that relatively large group of advisers who were, however, divided among themselves. The moderate constitutionalists had grown temporarily strong toward the end of September. Frightened by radical agitation in Vienna and the hatred of the Viennese for Jelačić, the Austrian ministers feared a new insurrection and a civil war. Wessenberg had always disliked the military-dictatorial faction at the Court, and especially its leader, Latour. In their memorandum of September 21 to the emperor, Wessenberg and his ministers argued that Latour and his friends were endangering the future of the Monarchy by setting the Serbs and the Croats against the Hungarians. The ministers asked that Jelačić be stopped by the appointment of a commander-in-chief with authority over both the Hungarian and the Croatian forces. Otherwise "a victorious general [Jelačić], carried forward by nationalist fanaticism, would be likely to do away with the constitutional liberties."[38]

For once the conservative Hungarian magnates in the Court agreed with Wessenberg. It was decided that a royal plenipotentiary would be sent to Hungary to suppress the Kossuth clique and force Jelačić to return behind the Drava River. Lamberg's name was supplied by Archduke Stephen, who wholeheartedly supported Wessenberg's proposal.

The news of Lamberg's and Vay's appointments created tremendous excitement in Buda-Pest. Kossuth, who was recalled from the countryside but would set out again shortly, violently condemned the king's move in a parliamentary speech on September 27. He called it unconstitutional (the manifesto lacked the countersignature of Batthyány, the acting prime minister), and he demanded that Lamberg be treated as a rebel and a traitor. The resolution was unanimously adopted by the House, and the people of Buda-Pest were duly notified, through posters, of the enemy general's expected arrival.[39]

Batthyány himself was willing to ignore the slight to his person in the appointment of another prime minister, and he set out to meet Lamberg. But where was the general? Batthyány searched for him in the Hungarian army and even among the Croats. Meanwhile, Lamberg had arrived in Buda-Pest, in turn looking for Batthyány.

When on September 28 he learned that Batthyány was not there, Lamberg tried to meet with other officials. He was in a hired cab and in civilian clothing. By then the Buda-Pest radical press had asked for his head, and excited crowds were searching for him. When he crossed the pontoon bridge connecting Buda and Pest, Lamberg was recognized. Although eyewitness accounts differ on the details, it is clear that he was dragged out of the cab, beaten, led away, and then slashed to death by a mob composed of soldiers, artisans, and students. His body was dragged along the streets; the hanging of his corpse was prevented by some National Guardsmen.[40]

The National Assembly's resolution deploring the murder of

Lamberg was drafted by Kossuth. It put the responsibility for the tragedy squarely on the shoulder of those in the Court who had "usurped the name of the King" in devising this unconstitutional appointment.[41]

Lamberg's death was a terrible blow to Batthyány. Still, he did not give up. He went to see Jelačić and, referring to the Royal manifesto, asked the *ban* to stop the fighting. Jelačić claimed never to have heard of the king's orders and insisted on leading his troops wherever he pleased. But in fact, the *ban* had little choice, for his army had been stopped at Pákozd the day before. Batthyány then went to Vienna but met only with hostility because he was suspected of having played a role in the murder of Lamberg. On October 1 he again resigned, this time for good.

The Lamberg affair strengthened the position of the military faction at Court. It seems that Latour wished to provoke not only war with Hungary but also a popular insurrection in Vienna, so as to deal militarily with all the radicals. Yet Latour was not to have his way completely. His plan—to start an immediate military campaign against Hungary and to outlaw all the members of the National Assembly—was opposed by Wessenberg and by the Hungarian magnates. Instead, it was decided to delegate another Royal plenipotentiary and to name a new prime minister. After enormous confusion, with names popping up left and right, with appointments announced and withdrawn, the worst possible choices were made. Instead of someone acceptable to Batthyány (Baron Vay, who had been appointed earlier, refused to serve), a seventy-three-year-old soldier, General Baron Ádám Récsey, a completely apolitical Hungarian, was made prime minister of Hungary. Since Batthyány would not countersign this document, Récsey reluctantly countersigned his own appointment, fully aware that his name would become anathema in his country. Even worse, Jelačić was made Royal plenipotentiary and commander-in-chief of all the armies in Hungary. After all, so the argument went, Lamberg had been equipped with only a piece of paper. Jelačić had an army. The trouble was that Jelačić's army was no longer moving toward Buda-Pest; rather, it was moving steadily in the opposite direction. Finally, it was decided to dissolve the Hungarian National Assembly and to subject the country to martial law. On October 3 the king announced these decisions in a manifesto addressed to the Hungarian parliament. The document, reprinted in seemingly innumerable copies, was sent to every official and military commander in Hungary. Those who persisted in their rebellious attitudes after October 3 were to be treated as traitors to their king.

A few days after the promulgation of the Royal manifesto, the National Assembly unanimously rejected the king's decrees, again at Kossuth's recommendation. Now war alone could decide whether or not Hungary would retain its independence.[42]

"Second Revolution"

Some historians characterized the Hungarian September not only as a turning point but also as a second revolution. Taking one's cue from the events of August 1792 and October 1917, a second revolution would imply the overthrow of the revolutionary government and its replacement by a new, more radical revolutionary authority. Batthyány's government was revolutionary neither in action nor in philosophy. It had come to power in March 1848 with the assistance of mass demonstrations and local seizures of power, but it had determinedly clung to the idea of legality. Moreover, Batthyány's cabinet was not overthrown; it resigned when it could no longer handle the crisis of the state.

And yet, the September events led to the assumption of power by forces that constitutionally had not been entitled to assume power; forces that were willing to act illegally to save the country. This is what makes the Hungarian September experience unique among the 1848 revolutions in Europe: the readiness of the parliament to shoulder the onus of illegality.

Everywhere in Europe, when threatened by a popular revolt or by the necessity of acting unconstitutionally, liberal reformers had allied themselves with absolutists. In Paris, in Berlin, in Vienna, the threat of a proletarian revolt had driven the liberals into the arms of soldiers and princes. The June barricades in Paris led to the military dictatorship of General Cavaignac and ultimately to the rule of Louis Napoleon. The need to organize an army and a navy against Germany's enemies, something that the Frankfurt Assembly was not empowered to do, drove the German liberals to submit to the king of Prussia. But the Hungarian liberals refused to seek the protection of the king against the domestic radicals or the foreign invaders.

The Hungarian marxist historian György Spira points out that in Hungary—unlike France—there was no danger of the proletariat "expanding the revolution beyond the boundaries held to be desirable and acceptable" by the ruling stratum of the state.[43] There was no working class worthy of its name, and the peasants were potential petty capitalists. On the other hand, Spira continues, the revolutionary ruling stratum had much more to fear from outside forces that threatened it with destruction. This is true, but Spira disregards the fact that Jelačić could have been stopped through concessions made to the king. After all, Jelačić had not come to Hungary entirely of his own volition, but as a result of considerable prodding on the part of Count Latour and other politicians. Nor does Spira's analysis take into consideration the importance of myths, of dangers imagined rather than real. It was the imagined threat of a mass peasant revolt, led by the radical poet Sándor Petőfi, which had caused the Diet in March–April 1848 to go farther in its social and economic legislation than most of its members had wished to go. The specter of rebellious peasants sacking and burning, raping and killing, haunted the imagination of the nobles, and not only those in the conservative camp. And while in reality peasant revolts had constituted only isolated incidents—the revolt of the Serbian and Romanian peasants falls into the category of threats from the outside—the radicals in Buda-Pest did their best to fan the fears of the liberals.[44] Petőfi himself repeatedly conjured up the image of mass executions.

> The death sentence to them!
> Even if the executioner must strike
> a hundred thousand blows,
> Even if the blood which flows
> Would flow through the windows of
> the houses from the streets.[45]

Nor could it be lost on the liberals that Petőfi and his friends were constantly talking of a revolution and the need to proscribe the liberals. Petőfi wrote on August 16 in a private letter: "I believe us to be on the eve of a great revolution, and you know that I make no false predictions. Then our first task will be to erect an immense gallows and [hang] nine people on it."[46] The nine were unmistakably the members of the government of Hungary, which included Kossuth.

Petőfi was not alone to raise the threat (rather grandiosely) of gallows and guillotines. Other radicals repeatedly proclaimed their desire to imitate the Jacobin terrorists. And in fact there was a plan afoot, or rather several plans, to overthrow the government and establish a radical dictatorship. The plans were hardly a secret to anyone—no secret is ever kept in Hungary—but they must have sounded all the more ominous for being so widely discussed. The Society for Equality, set up in Buda-Pest in July, was the largest organization the radicals had ever brought into being: it included at least thirty deputies and had a total of perhaps a thousand members. It controlled most of the Buda-Pest newspapers and it had some weapons. When at the end of August it appeared that the government would surrender to the Court, the society began to prepare for political banquets, demonstrations, and a possible seizure of power. But the plans were vague and were made dependent on the attitude of the government toward the Austrians. More important, the plans hinged on the attitude of Kossuth. Petőfi in his wildest dreams may have hanged Kossuth alongside the other ministers; in public he advocated loyalty to Kossuth in solidarity with the other radicals. When Kossuth asked the Assembly to wait—for the return of a delegation from Vienna or for the success of one of Batthyány's missions—the radicals waited too. When Kossuth became impatient, the radicals became impatient with him. When Hungary was invaded and Kossuth called on the people to rise in arms, the radicals felt duty-bound to propagandize for the war or to join the *honvéd,* dropping along the way their plans for antigovernment demonstrations. By the end of September the Society for Equality was falling apart: Petőfi, the historian Pál Vasvári, scores of young radical intellectuals went off to war while the radical nobles in the parliament busied themselves in the committees set up by Kossuth.

What had happened to circumvent a radical revolution in Hungary—or a return to the protective arms of the Court? The disintegration of the Society for Equality points to one clue: the radicals themselves were no socialists; and they too were mesmerized by Kossuth. There was no urban working class, at least part of the peasantry was satisfied, and the peasants idolized Kossuth. The enemy was at the door. But Hungary's swing in either a radical revolutionary or in a conservative pro-Austrian direction was prevented chiefly by the realism of the liberal deputies. They had been disturbed by the specter of peasant and radical insurrections and had made some concessions to it, but their major actions reflected an indomitable will to stay in power. In 1848 their leader was Kossuth. They gave him full authority because he alone could tame the radicals without resort to arms, and because he alone could mobilize the lower classes in defense of the country. It was a mutual need; the liberals needed Kossuth and he needed them to achieve his aim: a free and powerful Hungary with himself at the helm. The love affair between the liberals and Kossuth was as ardent as it was rational and therefore it was not unbreakable. When, toward the end of 1848, the situation appeared hopeless, a good part of the deputies deserted Kossuth. And when, in the spring of 1849, the national army won major victories and it looked suddenly as if Hungary had won the war, those among the liberals who had held out with Kossuth withdrew their unconditional support from him and deliberately weakened his dictatorial powers. And when, finally, all was lost in the summer of 1849 and there was a parting of the ways, Kossuth was left only with his most dedicated followers.

As soon as the immediate threat of a Croatian invasion waned, the House of Representatives put an end to the radicals' numerical domination of the National Defense Committee. In the original committee, as we have seen, four out of six members had been radicals. On October first the House added the names of Mészáros and Szemere, and a few days later four magnates from the Upper House were delegated to the committee. They were all followers of Kossuth.[47]

Subsequently, the Assembly expanded the powers of the committee. On October 8 the deputies vested all executive authority in the National Defense Committee and elected Kossuth its president.[48] On that day, the reign of Kossuth began.

5/From Defiance to Near-Disaster: Kossuth Dictator, Part One (October–December 1848)

The Road to Austria—and Back

THE EXHILARATING SEPTEMBER *journées* soon gave way to months of hard work and to an acute crisis. As the year drew to an end, Hungary seemed lost: the army continued withdrawing, most of the territory was in enemy hands, and the government was abandoning the capital. That Hungary survived at all and went on to win victories in the spring was due above all to the superhuman efforts, superb self-confidence, organizational talent, and administrative experience of Kossuth and his collaborators.

Outside observers held out scant hope for Hungary in those months. In September British Ambassador Ponsonby reported to his government that Hungary would not resist Jelačić, and that Kossuth had already fled abroad; in October the ambassador informed Palmerston that Kossuth had only 2,000 regulars; in November he wrote that all the hussars in Hungarian service would soon desert, and that Kossuth had sent his family to Hamburg (which was of course untrue). A dedicated supporter of the House of Austria, Ponsonby described the Hungarians to his government as "the authors and actors of attempts to create and to make successful a system of social war, under the name and pretence of men seeking political liberty."[1]

With Lamberg assassinated and the Royal manifesto of October 3 rejected, it was only a question of time before the combined forces of the Monarchy would attack Hungary. Against them, Kossuth had but a ridiculously small, untrained, ill-equipped, and less than reliable army. He needed time to organize, and it was granted to him by unexpected events in Vienna. The October upheaval in that city gave the Hungarians a reprieve of several weeks: not enough to prevent their army from suffering one defeat after another, but enough to prolong the revolution.

The Viennese rebelled against Imperial authority on October 6, because of economic depression, hunger among the poor, and fear of a counterrevolution. But the immediate reason for this most dramatic of all Viennese revolts was Latour's decision to send Austrian units to the aid of Jelačić. One of these units, the Richter Grenadier Battalion, which had been stationed in the capital for fourteen years and among whose German-speaking soldiers liberal nationalist propaganda had made some headway, was reluctant to go. While the Richters dragged their feet, Viennese students and workers, who idolized Kossuth and abominated Jelačić, clashed with the cavalry that had been sent out to "protect" the grenadiers. In the shooting, the Richters fought on the side of the demonstrators. This famous Tabor Bridge incident was probably the only time in the history of 1848–49 that men of the Habsburg army fired on one another without orders from their officers.[2]

The Vienna revolt succeeded immediately. Within a few hours the 14,000 Imperial troops were driven out of Vienna and its suburbs, and on the same night Latour was hanged from a lamppost. The emperor, the Court, and almost the entire ministry fled to Olmütz in Moravia. Only the Reichstag remained behind. But the Viennese revolutionaries were not united: there were at least six competing authorities, with the majority advocating continued loyalty to the emperor. Revolutionary Vienna petitioned Ferdinand to return to his good city, just as Hungary had begged him to seek the protection of his good Hungarians; the finance minister, who had lingered to protect the Imperial Treasury, gave handouts to the revolutionaries but also sent money to Jelačić; the attack of the counterrevolutionary forces was expected any day, yet the railroad tracks were not torn up around Vienna, and the trains were running on time; finally, the Austrian parliament (minus the Czech deputies who had left when the emperor did) held its sessions and maintained decorum. The commander of the Vienna National Guard and commander of the city, Wenzel Cäsar Messenhauser, may have been a good novelist, but he had no plans, little authority, and hardly any military talent.

By October 10 the Hungarian army had reached the Austrian border but crossed the Leitha River only briefly. Reluctant to enter His Majesty's other possessions, General Móga and his officers found their little army of almost no use. The entire Hungarian force had only one and a half cases of reserve infantry ammunition.[3] Kossuth first ordered Móga to cross the frontier, then qualified the order making the officers personally responsible if they endangered the army. Insisting that the Hungarians were not rebels but defenders of the fatherland, Kossuth asked that the proper Vienna authorities invite the Hungarian army into Austrian territory. "We are not entitled," he wrote, "to force our aid upon people who do not express their willingness to accept it."[4]

Ferenc Pulszky, who was in Vienna as state secretary of the Hungarian Foreign Ministry, went from one governing body to another demanding that they call in the Hungarian army. The Central Committee of the Democratic Clubs was most willing, but its members were too radical for Hungarian taste. The other Vienna authorities denied competence in the question. Not even Messenhauser (to be shot after the Imperial occupation of the capital) was willing to disappoint His Majesty by calling in His Majesty's Hungarian opponents. The unbelievable situation arose where the Hungarian rebels refused to aid their allies, and the Vienna rebels refused to call upon their allies for fear of offending their enemy's sensibilities. Friedrich Engels wrote four years after the event:

> Under these circumstances it was the clear duty of Hungary to support, without delay, and with all disposable forces, not the Diet of Vienna, not the Committee of Safety or any other official body at Vienna, but the *Viennese Revolution.* And if Hungary should even have forgotten that Vienna had fought the first battle of Hungary, she owed it to her own safety not to forget that Vienna was the only outpost of Hungarian independence, and that after the fall of Vienna nothing could meet the advance of the Imperial troops against herself.[5]

Finally, Kossuth went to the Hungarian camp, bringing with him some 13,000 volunteers. On his orders, the army marched into Austria for the second time, then returned quickly. While the revolutionaries hesitated, the counterrevolutionary forces had been organized under Prince Alfred Windisch-Graetz, the former head of the Prague General-Commando and suppressor of the June revolt in Prague. He had been promoted to field marshal on October 16 and appointed commander-in-chief of all the Habsburg armies operating outside of Italy. For the next six months this sixty-one-year-old aristocrat, the haughtiest among the haughty, would be Kossuth's chief military antagonist.[6]

In a supreme effort Windisch-Graetz collected over 70,000 soldiers—mainly Croatian, Czech, Moravian, and Galician regiments, but also many Germans. The spirit of the soldiers was good; they did not mind fighting the Viennese students and workers. Mostly of peasant origin, the troops seemed satisfied with the Imperial emancipation law promulgated a month earlier. They were grateful to the emperor, not the Austrian parliament—still a rather mysterious body—which had driven through the bill on emancipation.

By the end of October Messenhauser and almost everyone else in Vienna was willing to surrender. The revolutionaries asked for and received a brief truce; and all would have ended peaceably had not some observers in the tower of the Stefanskirche noticed a flash of guns from the direction of Hungary. The Hungarian army had crossed the border for the third time and was attacking, this time seriously. Not since the time of Matthias Corvinus in the fifteenth century had the troops of independent Hungary approached the Habsburg capital. Forgetting their prior discouragement, the Vienna radicals again rushed to the ramparts; Windisch-Graetz answered with massive bombardment and on October 31 stormed Vienna amid scenes of fierce fighting and even fiercer brutalities committed by his troops. When the field marshal occupied the city, he was given a tumultuous welcome by the capital's fickle residents. Revolutionary beards and Carbonari hats were quickly discarded, nine revolutionaries were executed, and law and order returned to Vienna for another seventy years.

The 25,000 men and 40 guns of General Móga clashed with a far superior Austro-Croatian army on October 30 at Schwechat, today the site of Vienna's airport. The Hungarian regulars fought well; but when the first artillery shots hit the National Guards they panicked and fled, dragging the entire army with them. Ready and willing to make a stand at Pákozd in defense of their homeland, these peasants were totally unprepared to offer battle far away from their villages. Hungarian losses—killed, wounded, and taken prisoner—amounted to about five hundred. The Austro-Croatian losses were far smaller.[7]*

The scenario of Pákozd was now reenacted at Schwechat, and the Austrian army did not pursue the Hungarians. The Habsburg officers on the Austrian side were determined to stop the attack of a hostile army; but they were not prepared to go after, and cut down, their comrades-in-arms. It would take several months before the war became truly brutal. During the battle General Móga fell from his horse and injured his leg. He used this welcome opportunity to resign his command a few days later.

On November 1 Kossuth promoted a thirty-year-old former first lieutenant of the hussars, Arthur Görgey, to major general and commander-in-chief of the Hungarian army facing Windisch-Graetz. With his seemingly radical militancy, obvious determination, and talent, Görgey had endeared himself to the president of the National Defense Committee. It was a decision of doubtful wisdom, for Görgey was to become the most celebrated Hungarian general and Kossuth's greatest domestic opponent.

Arthur Görgey

The prehistory of 1848 was marked and symbolized by the rivalry between Széchenyi and Kossuth, the history of the War of Independence by that between Görgey and Kossuth. Time has only aggrandized the size of this conflict: the "Görgey question" has continually agitated Hungarian public opinion, splitting families and friends, labeling parliamentary parties, and marking each successive political generation. It was—and it still is—a subject of drama and poetry. Kossuth the revolutionary has been contrasted with Görgey the reactionary; the national hero with the traitor to the fatherland. Conversely, the irresponsible demagogue has been compared with the wise statesman; the man of impossible dreams with the man of attainable goals. The generation which followed upon the War of Indepen-

---

* A Hungarian participant wrote of the battle that "not even at Vaterló [sic] was there a more terrifying cannonade than here" (Lajos Árkossy to Imre Krausz [Kattendorf, Nov. 16, 1848]; printed in Deák, *1848*, p. 268).

dence generally swore by Kossuth, if not in action then in words; that of the Compromise Agreement of 1867 leaned in the direction of Görgey, although a vociferous opposition to the Compromise identified him with abject submission to Germanic imperialism. Following World War I, Admiral Horthy's regime rehabilitated Görgey while it still paid lip-service to Kossuth; finally, the post–World War II stalinist regime idolized Kossuth, who "had risen above his class," while it abominated Görgey, "who was unable to rise." The statue of Görgey erected under Regent Horthy on Buda fortress disappeared after World War II, and there is not even a plaque commemorating modern Hungary's greatest military genius. Only recently has Hungarian marxist historiography begun to blunt the sharp edges of the Görgey image.[8]

Of the two men, Kossuth was undoubtedly the greater figure. He had been a national leader for many years when the far younger Görgey appeared on the scene. Kossuth was a statesman with an interest in military affairs; Görgey was a brilliant soldier. Following the War of Independence, Kossuth played an important role in international affairs and deeply influenced his countrymen for another forty-five years. Görgey's star shone brightly for ten months; during the next sixty-seven years (he was ninety-eight when he died in 1916) he did nothing. Kossuth was warm, passionate, elegant, and flamboyant; Görgey was cold, sarcastic, overly modest, puritanical, and contemptuous. Kossuth had long hair and wore a fashionable round beard; Görgey wore a conservative crew-cut and a goatee. Yet the two men also had many things in common: a talent for organization and leadership; a profound belief in their country and in their own mission; and the power to win followers dedicated to them unto death. Kossuth and Görgey loved and hated each other with a passion that only a romantic age could produce—and phrase in ornate sentences. Their correspondence, especially Kossuth's letters to Görgey, reads like *Wuthering Heights*.

In reality, both men pursued idle fancies: Kossuth imagined that he could maintain Hungarian independence in a Europe where even such liberal powers as England were working for its suppression. Görgey thought that he could fight for limited goals: the preservation of Hungary's April constitution and its dignified place within the Monarchy at a time when the Habsburgs were no longer willing to grant Hungary its constitution or its dignity. Kossuth believed that the peasants would fight to the last man in defense of liberty, if necessary without weapons; Görgey hoped that a small professional army, without the support of guerrillas and peasants, could defeat the larger professional army of an industrially stronger country. Briefly put, they personified two totally different concepts of war and of revolutionary politics.

Hungary's fate had been consummated with the defeat of the Vienna October revolution; thereafter the country fought only a delaying action. But the glories of this struggle, and the contrasting revolutionary concepts of Kossuth and Görgey, profoundly influenced Hungarian political development in the following century.

"Hungary's Judas," (these are Kossuth's words) was born in 1818 in a small village in northernmost Hungary.[9] His family was old, respectable, and mostly poor, as was Kossuth's. The Görgeys were Lutherans, as were the Kossuths, a denomination relatively rare among Hungarians but not among the gentry of Upper Hungary. Görgey's mother came from a Zipser-German burgher family, as did Kossuth's. Relative material ease in Görgey's early years was followed by dire want, mainly because of a ruinous family lawsuit which had begun in the eighteenth century and was settled only after the War of Independence. Meanwhile, Görgey's father had gone bankrupt. Arthur and his three brothers had to learn a profession. In 1834, at the age of sixteen, Görgey entered the engineering cadet school at Tulln in Austria, a liberal institution by comparison with the Monarchy's two more hallowed military academies, where students lived like monks and were literally held incommunicado for seven or eight years.[10] Görgey was a good student with a special interest in chemistry, but he never ceased to dislike the army and its discipline. In 1837 he joined the Hungarian Noble Guards in Vienna, a free school founded by Maria Theresa for members of the Hungarian petty nobility. Four years later he was ready to enter field service as a first lieutenant. He chose the cavalry and, following a desperate borrowing campaign among members of his family, he raised enough cash (2,000 gulden) to purchase the horses, equipment, and uniforms necessary for a cavalry officer. From among the twelve Hungarian hussar regiments he selected the 12th, the palatine's own, for the simple reason that here the decorative braids on officers' uniforms were entwined with silver, and not with the more expensive gold.

Görgey was a good enough horseman, soldier, and comrade to

win the respect of his fellow officers, but poverty remained his tragedy. To redeem his debt to the family, he was forced for years to eat
"a piece of bread for breakfast and for dinner nothing." The pay of a
subaltern officer in the Imperial-Royal army was ridiculously low: on
a monthly income of 32 gulden—less than the salary of a skilled
worker—a first lieutenant had to provide for his food, his furniture,
his horse, his many uniforms, the regimental library and regimental
band, and even the debts incurred by his fellow officers.[11] Discipline
was strict and the tedium of peacetime service unbearable, at least to
Görgey. He read a good deal and tried to subscribe to newspapers,
for instance to Kossuth's *Pesti Hírlap,* but the Court War Council
refused its permission. In 1845 he was made regimental adjutant,
which brought him prestige and the privilege of eating at the colonel's table; but it also carried with it "luxury" expenditures which he
was unable to shoulder. As he was also unable to get permission to
marry, both he and his fiancée being impoverished, Görgey resigned
his commission in 1845, "without retaining the character of an officer," as the official terminology would have it. He had to sign a
pledge never to take up arms against his monarch. He then studied
chemistry at Prague University, graduated with honors, and was appointed an assistant at the University of Lemberg; but he never occupied the post. Instead, he returned to Hungary in a vague attempt
to manage his aunt's estate. Then came the events of spring 1848, a
godsend to Görgey as it was to many other junior officers. He volun-
teered for the new national army and was promoted to captain in June
1848; in the same month Batthyány sent him to Austria to study the
manufacture of percussion caps and to order them for Hungary.

The Croatian invasion found Görgey a major, in command of
the Mobile National Guards in the area between the Danube and the
Tisza rivers. Following the battle of Pákozd, Görgey refused to abide
by General Móga's armistice agreement and repeatedly denounced
his superior to the National Assembly for incompetence and suspected treason.[12] This was Görgey's first act of insubordination, to be
followed by several others. Yet he himself never tolerated insubordination. At the end of September one of Görgey's patrols captured
Count Ödön (Eugen) Zichy, a conservative Hungarian magnate who
traveled with a safe-conduct from Jelačić in his pocket, and with a
bundle of Imperial manifestos. Görgey tried the count with all the
decorum of an Austrian military court and had him hanged on Sep-

tember 30. Zichy's execution, the first and perhaps the only act of revolutionary terror directed against an aristocrat during the war, created almost as much furor in Vienna and in Buda-Pest as did Lamberg's assassination. Görgey's motivation remains unclear, for he was no radical by any stretch of the imagination. Unlike Kossuth, he did not resent the titled nobility, and he never flinched in his own special variety of loyalty to the king. The explanation he offered for this act in his postwar memoirs was manifestly untrue: he claimed to have granted a "dignified death," the rope, to Zichy, who would otherwise have been lynched by a mob. In all probability he wished to impress Kossuth and the National Assembly with his iron determination.[13] Certainly by executing Count Zichy he had burned all bridges behind him, a fact which did not escape Kossuth.

Early in October 1848 Görgey was instrumental in the encirclement and capture of General Roth's Croatian army corps. Kossuth now decided to make Görgey supreme commander at the earliest opportunity. This came after the battle of Schwechat in which Görgey (by then a full colonel) had distinguished himself. On November 1 came his promotion to major-general and to commander of the main Hungarian army.[14]

Kossuth had had no choice but to promote the most resolute of the junior officers. He and Mészáros had been begging the older generals of Hungarian origin to assume command of the Hungarian armies.[15] But the few who came out of retirement proved to be incompetent because of age, the conflict of loyalties, or their conservative military training. Even among the staff officers of the Imperial-Royal army, colonels or majors, there seemed to be no one with enough bravado to shoulder the crushing burden. Despite his meteoric advancement, Görgey soon acquired great prestige among the officers and men. His simplicity, his calm, his intelligence, his contempt for civilians, and his obvious talent turned his army into a band of devoted followers. It is no exaggeration to say that most of his officers fought throughout the war because of Görgey and despite the National Defense Committee. Imperial-Royal officers who would not serve Kossuth, the civilian and the revolutionary, obeyed Görgey, the soldier and the constitutionalist. But his independent course also divided the army. Ultimately Görgey, too, was a Magyar patriot; and as the Austrians refused to guarantee the April constitution, he fought the war to the end. When they had to choose between flight and capture, all his top officers obeyed Görgey. They went into captivity with him, and from there to the gallows without him.

There was more than a month, as it turned out, between Görgey's appointment and the concerted Austrian military attack in December 1848. During that time, Görgey and Kossuth clashed over the nature and composition of the army, with Kossuth wanting a regular army permanently supported by a large body of National Guards, peasant insurrectionists, and guerrillas; and Görgey wanting to operate with only a small but efficient professional army. He had no use for the "drunken louts" in the auxiliary forces and he sent them home as soon as he could, first confiscating their weapons.

In the controversy, both sides were inflexible. An all-professional army would require time to organize and train, and Kossuth was correct in insisting that there was no time to spare. But the auxiliary forces were unreliable; they wasted weapons and ammunition. Yet again, a revolutionary war must be fought by a revolutionary army: soldiers and populace, side by side. A professional army inevitably becomes an alien body in the country. Kossuth pointed insistently to the occasional heroism of the auxiliary forces, and Görgey to their frequent inefficiency.[16]

It came down to this question: Would the new Hungarian state be able to provide Görgey with the needed officers, recruits, uniforms, food, and weapons? Early in November the state had very little to offer. The crucial task was shouldered by Kossuth, the National Defense Committee, and the itinerant commissioners of the National Assembly. Together, they accomplished wonders.

Of the Old Army and of the New

If one is to understand the history of the Hungarian revolutionary army, one must look first at the history of the Habsburg army which gave the *honvéd* its cadres, many of its men, and much of its spirit and tradition.

By 1848 the Imperial-Royal forces had had long experience as a standing army.[17] The need for frontier defense against the Turks led to the creation, in the sixteenth century, of a permanent Military Border on the Monarchy's southern approaches and the founding of the Court War Council. The crushing demands of the Thirty Years'

War led the Habsburgs to set up the first regular military units under mercenary captains and colonels. But only in the eighteenth century were the different detachments organized into a coherent whole, and only then was state financing of the army established on a fairly solid basis. Under Maria Theresa all regiments were assigned serial numbers, all soldiers were given uniforms, standardized weapons, and regular pay; and all were subjected to identical drill and discipline.

But not even Maria Theresa or her successors were able or willing to do away with territorial divisions in the army. These divisions were reflected in the very names of the regiments, so units from the various provinces were easy to tell from one another. However, from the point of view of 1848 only four fundamental territorial divisions mattered: Hungary and Transylvania as one major sector, Lombardy-Venetia as another, the Military Border as a third, and the rest of the Monarchy (commonly referred to as Austria) as the fourth. This is not to say that regiments from the major divisions had particular difficulty in communicating with each other. The language of command was uniformly German; in addition, commissioned and noncommissioned officers had to learn the language spoken by the majority of their men. Common territorial origin did not mean ethnic or linguistic uniformity in any case. In many a so-called Hungarian regiment hardly anyone spoke Hungarian, and regiments from different historic provinces often had less trouble understanding one another than regiments originating from the same province. The Court War Council had long engaged in the practice of *divide et impera*—dispatching the two line battalions from each regiment into areas inhabited by another nationality—but this practice was never consistently pursued. Early in 1848 there were in the Hungarian Kingdom as many soldiers originating from Hungary as there were soldiers originating from elsewhere.

Because of the high number of foreign subjects serving as officers, the Habsburg officer corps was even more cosmopolitan than the troops.[18] Most of the foreigners were Germans (one-third of the highest ranking Habsburg generals were born in German states other than Austria) but there were also many Spaniards, Frenchmen, Walloons, Danes, Irishmen, and Englishmen. A contemporary Austrian observer noted that "the Hungarian hussar regiments have virtually become English colonies."[19] One of Kossuth's most devoted generals in the War of Independence was the Englishman Richard

Guyon, who had been a first lieutenant in a Hungarian hussar regiment and who, possibly because of his marriage to a Hungarian lady, had become an ardent Magyar patriot and a radical.[20] When the Hungarian rebel officer Count Karl Leiningen-Westerburg, a Hessian German by birth and a Hungarian through marriage and through personal predilection, advanced too far in the course of a battle in the War of Independence, there was a curious encounter. Landing among enemy Austrian soldiers—whom Leiningen mistakenly took for Hungarians because they wore the same uniform and almost the same distinguishing collar patches as his own men—he was finally recognized and captured by an old friend,* the Englishman Digby, who was an officer in a Croatian hussar squadron fighting on the Austrian side.[21] And in May 1849 when Görgey was besieging Buda fortress, he sent a message to the fortress commander, the Austrian General Heinrich Hentzi, asking for the latter's surrender; Görgey argued among other things that surrender was Hentzi's patriotic duty, for he too was a Hungarian. To which Hentzi replied that even though he was born in Debrecen, a Hungarian city, he was no Hungarian but a former Swiss subject from Bern. Not that this mattered very much, Hentzi added, for he was not a Swiss patriot either, only a patriot for the emperor.[22]

The relatively high number of foreigners in the Habsburg army must be attributed to the unique cosmopolitanism of the House of Austria, the particular attraction it exercised on young gentlemen everywhere—and not only on the Catholic aristocracy—and the reluctance of part of the native nobility to serve in the army. The old Austro-German aristocracy neglected its duty to the Crown because of indolence; the Hungarian nobility because it persisted in regarding the army as a foreign institution. Thus, aside from its complement of foreigners, the Habsburg officer corps consisted mostly of Germans from Bohemia and Hungary, Slavs (particularly Croats), Romanians, and Italians, a great majority of whom were commoners.

During the aristocratic reaction that set in all over Europe following the defeat of Napoleon, the aristocracy regained some ground in the high command of the Imperial-Royal army (four out of five top-ranking generals were noblemen during the Napoleonic wars and nine out of ten before 1848), and in the cavalry the nobles had always predominated; but in the infantry, the artillery and the technical units,

---

* Leiningen's captivity was not to last long, for he was soon liberated by his soldiers. He went on to become a general in the *honvéd* and was sent to the gallows after the war.

nobles constituted a small minority. Of the 230 generals and 10,800 officers of the Habsburg army in 1837, only 4,224 held patents of nobility, and a great proportion of the latter did not belong to the old nobility (*Altadel*) but had been ennobled in service or their fathers had been ennobled (*Neuadel*). All this mattered little from the point of view of the dynasty: the commoners and service nobles were even more loyal (*habsburgtreu*) than the noble officers, and even less inclined to be nationalistic. Only an insignificant number of Hungarian officers of nonnoble background joined Kossuth's forces in 1848, and the single rebel general who was a commoner, András Gáspár (a hussar officer of peasant origin) resigned in April 1849 when Kossuth proclaimed the deposition of the House of Austria from the Hungarian throne.[23]

Descended for the most part from families where military service had become a tradition, educated in the isolation of military schools, separated from much of the civilian population by status, pride, poverty, and the language barrier, the officer tended to spend his active life among his fellows. Advancement was excruciatingly slow (the average officer ended his career as a captain), and transfer to another regiment was the privilege of those with money or the right connections: no wonder then that the regiment became the officer's fatherland and his home. He knew loyalty only to his regimental flag and to the emperor. Discipline was strict; but life was not necessarily unbearable, for the officers ran their own lives and assumed moral and fiscal responsibility for each other. The regimental officers' assemblies functioned democratically and they were to play a crucial role in 1848, when they often overruled their commanders.

The officers' isolation from the public had even increased in the years before 1848. Minister of War Mészáros noted in his memoirs written in postwar exile that, beginning around 1825, the officer's lot had become difficult in Hungarian, Polish, or northern Italian garrisons. As nationalist passions grew, officers stationed in rural areas were less and less welcome in the better households. No longer the celebrated victors over Napoleon, they were upbraided for not being good Hungarians, Poles, or Italians, and for serving a foreign master.[24] Understandably then, the officers clung ever more stubbornly to the idea of unselfish and sacrificial service to the emperor. The term "His Majesty's uniform commands" pops up invariably in their correspondence and memoirs.

Because of financial troubles constantly plaguing the Habsburg government, military expenditures decreased year by year. In 1817 the army had received one-half of state revenues, in 1847 only 20 percent,[25] which meant that thousands of enlisted men had to be furloughed regularly with the instruction that they fend for themselves. Maneuvers were rarely held and infantrymen were issued only twenty rounds of ammunition a year with which to practice. Exceptions were the army in northern Italy, which under Field Marshal Radetzky was on a permanent war footing, and the Military Border, where soldiers divided their time between guard duty and tending their land.

Certainly, discontent existed among the officers: in 1840 some Polish officers were arrested for conspiracy, and "Young Italy" was active among the army's Italians. But the actively discontented were only a small minority and most officers tumbled into the turmoil of 1848 without the slightest knowledge of politics.

In January 1848 the Habsburg army had a total of 400,000 men, at least on paper. As the Empire had less than forty million inhabitants, 400,000 seemed a respectable figure; but, because of the furloughs, actual army strength did not exceed 250,000. Also, the quality of soldiers was very uneven. The length of service had been gradually reduced from life to eight years in 1845, but there were so many exceptions allowed and so many paid substitutes that in practice only poor people served. The situation was particularly bad in Hungary, where the fiction of voluntary enlistment meant the impressment of the least desirable elements from the estates and villages.

The principal arm of the military was, of course, the infantry, consisting of 59 regular and 18 *Grenzer* regiments, as well as 20 independent grenadier battalions (they performed mainly domestic peacekeeping duties) and 12 fast-moving *Feld-Jäger* battalions. The cavalry was made up of 37 regiments, and the artillery of 5 regiments. Out of this force, 35 infantry, 25 cavalry, and all 5 artillery regiments counted as Austrian; 15 infantry and 13 cavalry regiments as Hungarian or Transylvanian; and 8 infantry regiments as Italian. The balance was thus heavily weighted in favor of the Austrians.[26]

In the spring of 1848 large parts of the four Italian regiments stationed in Lombardy-Venetia, and most of the Austrian navy, joined the Italian revolution. But the other Imperial-Royal troops in Italy fought for the ruler, including some 30,000 Hungarians. Despite repeated Piedmontese appeals, almost no Hungarian soldier deserted the army of Radetzky. In the other trouble spots of the Monarchy—Vienna, Prague, Cracow, Lemberg—there were no defections either, with the single exception of the Vienna Richters. Only in Hungary was the situation vastly different, for the simple reason that in Hungary, unlike elsewhere, there were not only conflicting nationalist ideologies but also conflicting constituted authorities. By the time a Habsburg officer in Hungary discovered that he had been obeying the wrong authority, it was often too late. He had taken an oath to the Hungarian constitution; he was receiving his pay from Buda-Pest; he had been promoted by the palatine or Batthyány or Kossuth, and he was being watched by Hungarian political commissioners and by his own men. Until the autumn resignation or retirement was relatively easy; afterwards the officer trying to resign risked arrest by the Hungarian authorities. Or, if he succeeded in going over to the Austrians, he risked arrest by the Austrian authorities. Besides, even after the promulgation of the October 3 manifesto, it was not quite clear whether staying in the Hungarian army was truly illegal. The Buda-Pest government assured the officers that the October 3 manifesto was a forgery perpetrated by the Camarilla, or that it had been coaxed out of the king by the Camarilla; and General Mészáros, by then a member of the National Defense Committee, continued to sign his communiqués to the troops as "His Majesty's Minister of War." Many an officer of the Hungarian army, clutching at straws, addressed Mészáros by that title, never reporting to the committee itself. Commissions and promotions were being awarded with the proviso "pending gracious approval by His Majesty," even after His Majesty's regulars had invaded Hungary.

All through the summer and the fall, individual commanders, officers' assemblies, mixed officer–enlisted man committees, and even genuine soldiers' councils made decisions for or against the Hungarian authorities. Entire regiments turned against their commanders in the name of the emperor, the king, the National Defense Committee, or the Serbian or Romanian national committee. Some regiments tried to steer a neutral course; others dutifully obeyed their commanders who, in turn, defied their own superior officers. In Transylvania, where the two Romanian Border Guard regiments spearheaded the Romanian revolution against Kossuth, the two Székely Border Guard regiments gradually got rid of their pro-Habsburg officers and fought for Kossuth under the command of Székely officers. In the Transylvanian 31st Graf Leiningen-Westerburg Infantry Regiment, the Romanian-speaking majority opted for the emperor, the Magyar-speaking minority for the king. In Hungary proper, units of the several Italian infantry battalions stationed there changed sides repeatedly.

Even more important than the field regiments from the point of view of the war were the fortresses of Hungary. Their saga is a perfect illustration of the Habsburg army's dilemma. Successive commanders tried to hand over the gigantic and virtually impregnable fortress of Komárom on the Upper Danube to the Austrians, but they were overruled by civilian commissioners and assemblies of officers. Komárom remained Hungarian until October 1849, two months after the surrender of the field armies, when it was finally abandoned in return for amnesty. In another impregnable fortress, Pétervárad on the Lower Danube, Magyar soldiers of the 39th Hungarian Dom Miguel Regiment rebelled against their pro-Habsburg fortress commander in October 1848 and hoisted the Hungarian flag. At the end of December garrison officers again tried to turn the fortress over to the Austrians, but the enlisted men and National Guards saved it for Hungary. Pétervárad, too, stayed Hungarian until September 1849. In the fortress of Eszék in Slavonia, elements of the 16th Italian Zanini Regiment petitioned the Hungarian government in October to be allowed to remain neutral or to be transferred out of the country. The government thereupon dispatched reliable troops to Eszék, who saved it for Hungary for a few more months. But in February 1849 the officers of the garrison succeeded in surrendering the fortress, with all its vast supplies, to Jelačić. In the fortress of Temesvár in southeastern Hungary, an officers' assembly took power in October 1848, overruling the commander and organizing for defense against Hungary. The officers' manifestos contributed mightily to the continued Serbian and Romanian peasant revolts in the area. Temesvár suffered incessant Hungarian siege during the war but never surrendered. The nearby fortress of Arad, on the other hand, gave up to the Hungarian troops in June 1849. Its garrison was allowed to return to Austria in exchange for the promise never again to take up arms against Hungary. Gyulafehérvár in Transylvania remained Austrian throughout the war; Munkács in northeastern Hungary remained Hungarian.[27]

If one can draw any conclusions from what happened in the forts, it is that energetic individuals or groups dictated developments. In some fortresses the traditional hierarchy survived under resolute commanders, whether pro-Hungarian or pro-Austrian. In others the traditional command structure broke down and officers' assemblies or united officer–enlisted men's committees assumed power, whether for or against Hungary. Decisions were usually, although not always, made on the grounds of nationality.

At the end, about 50,000 regulars—among them almost 1,500 career officers—found themselves on the Hungarian side in the war: 20 infantry battalions of the line (with the exception of some Italians, they were all Hungarian or Transylvanian battalions), 6 complete and 4 incomplete hussar regiments (all Hungarian or Transylvanian), 2 Székely Border Guard regiments, a part of the Fifth Prague Artillery Regiment, and assorted other units. The best element was the hussars, all unconditionally loyal to the Hungarian government—provided that they happened to be in the country when the war began. Unfortunately for Hungary, 2 entire hussar regiments and parts of 4 others were not in Hungary in the fall, and they continued serving the emperor in Italy or elsewhere all through 1848–49.[28]

The regulars were gradually incorporated into, but not amalgamated with, the *honvéd* forces.[29] Regulars kept their uniform, their unit numbers, and names; only the language of command was changed to Hungarian, wherever possible. The presence of Imperial-Royal units in the *honvéd* forces led to tragicomic incidents: soldiers dutifully obeyed well-known trumpet signals coming from the enemy, or obeyed enemy officers whom they knew and thought to be their own; commanders spent a considerable time at the battlefield trying to distinguish between friend and foe. Not until Windisch-Graetz's forces adopted a white ribbon on their shakos did the misunderstandings cease.[30]

Fifty thousand regulars, dispersed from one end of Hungary and Transylvania to the other and often blissfully ignorant of their new status as rebels, were clearly insufficient to resist the coming Austrian onslaught. A genuine national army was desperately needed.

The foundations of the national army had been laid in the spring by Batthyány, as we have seen, through the introduction of compulsory National Guard service and the creation of the first ten *honvéd* battalions. National Guards thrived in the cities and larger towns, but they were remarkably less popular among the peasants, who tended to view them as another evil invention of the "gentlemen." By September there were 400,000 National Guards inscribed on the rolls; only about 150,000 of them had received a modicum of training or owned some sort of arms. This fell far short of the original goal of 1 million envisaged by Batthyány, but was still a formidable force.[31] The main problem with the Guards was that they had been set up to perform local police duty only. Consequently, as early as the summer of 1848 the brunt of the fighting against the Serbs had been shouldered by the regulars, the *honvéd,* and the so-called Mobile National Guards (volunteer battalions whose members had agreed to serve, not for the usual seven weeks, but for several years). Eventually the Mobiles were amalgamated with the *honvéd;* and in the course of this expansion, the socially and physically elite character of the first *honvéd* disappeared.[32] And even though volunteers kept flocking into service (the pay of 8 kreuzers daily was double that of the Habsburg regulars' 4 kreuzers, and the minimum commitment was for four years instead of eight), compulsory military service was introduced in September. The aim was to sign up two recruits for every 127 inhabitants—a goal the government never achieved.

As time went on, the auxiliary forces (although they never disappeared) gradually diminished, while the *honvéd* army continually increased. In September there had been only 16 *honvéd* infantry battalions; by the end of October there were 42; by December their number was up to 62; in January they totalled 72; in April, 91; and in June 1849 there were 140 *honvéd* battalions. Simultaneously, incomplete hussar regiments were filled with recruits and new cavalry regiments were created, so that by the end of the war there were eighteen hussar regiments. Even though several of these regiments were untrained, the hussars were the pride and joy of the national army. Compared with the infantry, they had a far larger complement of old professionals; and the white-mustached, worldly-wise veteran hussar became part of popular legend. The hussars were fabulous horsemen, tough, proud, and steeped in national tradition; and while the uniform of the *honvéd* infantry was simple brown, the horsemen were resplendent in blue, gold, and silver (even if somewhat less resplendent than in the days of yore).

In the summer of 1848 the artillery situation looked hopeless. The fortresses had over 1,200 guns, but the field artillery consisted of only a few batteries. (A formidable *honvéd* artillery force would soon spring up with several hundred guns, but of this later.) In the summer of 1848 there had been no Imperial-Royal technical units in Hungary whatsoever; a few months later there were 5 *honvéd* pioneer battalions, manned chiefly by Slovak miners.[33] The number of troops in the standing army reached 100,000 by December and by June 1849 they totaled 170,000.

The experience of centuries facilitated the enlistment of new soldiers. The requested quota of recruits had always been voted on by the Diet and proportionally distributed among the several counties. The counties in turn had assessed the local communities. In 1848 the county administrator had an even easier task; for unlike past recruitment efforts, service was now universal and compulsory and the cause was national. Nowhere in Europe was the situation more favorable for a revolutionary authority than in the Magyar-inhabited areas of Hungary. In Berlin, Frankfurt, Vienna, Venice, or Rome—where tradition and the bureaucracy were against the revolutionaries—everything had to be improvised. Only in revolutionary France were conditions similar to those in Hungary but, in 1848, the French were not fighting a war.

If there were enough men to build an army, there were not enough trained leaders. Batthyány, Kossuth, and Mészáros personally solicited the titled aristocrats and other noblemen to become officers. As a result, almost 10,000 officers were commissioned during the war. But the promotion policy was never settled. Many of the new officers turned out to be shirkers, which caused Kossuth constant headaches. And there was great confusion when the right to commission and to promote was arrogated by almost everyone: the generals, the itinerant civilian commissioners, the minister of war, and Kossuth. Such a nonsystem of commission and promotion resulted in a running battle, on the one hand between the successive ministers of war and Kossuth, on the other between Kossuth and the generals.

The new officer corps was largely democratic in style but not in origin. Even though hundred of commoners were promoted to junior rank, especially from among the noncommissioned officers of the old army, the chances of a commoner becoming an officer were remarkably less than those of a nobleman. While noblemen and especially titled aristocrats were routinely given command positions, often without any training, it was virtually impossible for commoner civilians to rise above the rank of captain. Such a situation was at least in part a reflection of the commoners' high rate of illiteracy and lack of authority and prestige to be commanders; whereas the noble landowners usually had the required experience to organize and to lead men. And though the Hungarian nobility was relatively well educated and was anything but a small stratum of the population, it is an apt commentary on the "gentlemanly" character of the Hungarian revolution that its army was less open to talent than the Habsburg army.

Recruits were found and delivered by the administration of the counties; the battalions were organized; and the commanders were appointed, at first by Batthyány and then by Kossuth. These two men were Hungary's subsequent war ministers in all but name, with General Mészáros acting as their trusted servant. Mészáros complained that his ministry was "only a post office," and he resigned an average of once a month but was always prevailed upon to stay. He would indeed have been unable to handle the task alone, but his Ministry of War provided Batthyány and Kossuth with statistics, recommendations, and expert opinion as needed. According to the papers of the Prime Ministry and of its successor, the National Defense Committee, it was in these offices that all military matters—and all too many of the unimportant ones—were decided. Military logistics became Kossuth's responsibility. "Arms, we must have arms," he wrote Görgey at the end of November; "I am moving hell to obtain them, but it is very difficult."[34] Commanders and government commissioners swamped Kossuth's office with calls for arms; and as everyone knew that there were too few weapons, local emergencies were magnified until it must have looked from Buda-Pest as if the whole country was in flames.

Where, indeed, were weapons to be found? Since 1836 many first-line units of the Habsburg army had gradually been equipped with percussion muskets, and even with special percussion rifles.[35] But in 1848 most of these troops were in Italy; the regiments stationed in Hungary had mainly old-fashioned, smooth-bore flintlock muskets. Between March and September the Austrian war minister had shipped as many arms out of Hungary as he could lay his hands on, while others were in the hands of soldiers fighting against Hungary. Kossuth urged the civilians to surrender their hunting rifles or shotguns; he asked the county administrations to part with the rusty weapons left over from the time of the nobles' unfortunate "insurrection" against Napoleon's army; and the Croatian army became another, involuntary, contributor. But most of the arms from these sources went to the National Guards, and the yield for the *honvéd* was meager. One county offered Kossuth 92 pistols, 10 cavalry sabres and about 50 swords, mostly broken; another county contributed 70 sabres and 16 swords.[36]

The purchase of arms from abroad was a much more reliable source of weapons. These had to be paid for in bullion, for Kossuth's banknotes were worthless outside the country; fortunately Kossuth had confiscated all the royal gold and silver left in Hungary when he was still minister of finance. More bullion came from the modest generosity of the aristocracy and the prelates, as well as from the greater generosity of less wealthy untitled nobles and commoners. Batthyány and Kossuth used commercial firms in Vienna as well as traveling Hungarian agents to purchase arms from England, Prussia, and chiefly from Belgium. Only the legal uncertainties of the time, and the plodding shortsightedness of the Austrian bureaucracy, can account for the fact that foreign weapons were brought to Vienna and from there transported to Buda-Pest at a time when the Austrian and Hungarian armies were already at odds with one another. For example, on October 3 the Hungarian commander of Komárom fortress received a shipment of 2,000 modern muskets that the Vienna firm Wodianer had bought in Prussia. The weapons had reached Vienna by rail and were then taken to Komárom on the Austrian steamship *Johann*.[37] Arms legally continued to arrive in Buda-Pest from abroad; and later, when the Austrian embargo became more efficient, it was still possible to smuggle in weapons. For a relatively long time even Austrian manufacturers were allowed by the Vienna minister of war to work for Hungary. On September 7, 1848, Herr Anton Stuwer, "Burgher and Proprietor of an Imperial Royal Monopoly for the Fabrication of Fireworks in Vienna," signed an agreement with Ferenc Pulszky, the Hungarian plenipotentiary, providing for the manufacture of rocket weapons for Hungary. This is less surprising if we consider that all through September, Croatian and Hungarian recruiting booths operated next to each other in Vienna, and that recruits of both armies were observed drinking away their press-money in perfect harmony.[38]

Ultimately, Hungary had to equip itself, and Kossuth personally directed the endeavor. He dealt with the question daily, his concern ranging from the production of cannons to tiny quantities of undershirts. Only such an incurable optimist as he could take up this seemingly impossible task. At a time when Bohemia and Styria each produced 45,000 tons of iron annually, Hungary produced only about 30,000 tons[39] and domestic iron production had not even been able to satisfy Hungary's very modest peacetime needs. Copper production amounted to less then 2,000 tons, and lead less than 200 tons. Other metals were almost nonexistent; the first sulphur mine, militarily so important, had been opened only in 1848. And the country's only armaments plant, in Pest, had produced little until November when it was nationalized by the government; thereafter it delivered up to 500 muskets a day.[40] There were several good powder mills; but with that, the list of military plants is complete. Hungarian industry as a whole had made great strides in the preceding two decades, but there were few machine tools and even fewer skilled mechanics or trained workers.

Kossuth offered factory owners large loans to shift to war industry, he sent government commissioners into the plants to control production, and he directed the skilled workers from among the *honvéd* and thousands of Croatian prisoners-of-war into industry. Skilled mechanics (including a few Englishmen) were imported from abroad. Inventors (domestic and foreign) made their appearance; and the inevitable patent for an armed airplane was submitted to Kossuth, while the French engineer Château alone assured the manufacture of up-to-date cartridges.[41]

On October 24 Mészáros informed Kossuth that because of the lack of gunpowder the war would have to end very shortly; a few days later he complained about the excessive demands of some generals upon mortar reserves in Buda-Pest; one of them had the cheek to ask for ten in one breath, which meant that the capital would soon be without mortars.[42] In the middle of November Kossuth announced that 30,000 soldiers were still without arms; but toward the end of the year the situation improved noticeably, and by the spring the *honvéd* enjoyed not only numerical superiority over the Austrian army fighting in Hungary but, miraculously, a superiority in weapons. Toward the end of the war the national army of 170,000 men had between 120,000 and 140,000 muskets: taken from Imperial arsenals, received from civilian donors, captured from the enemy, purchased abroad, or repaired, refashioned, or manufactured. Artillery pieces were being cast in brand-new plants as well as in small workshops. By July 1849 the army had 508 field guns: 60 of them had been taken over from the old Fifth Artillery Regiment, 236 had been repaired and refashioned from confiscated Imperial stock, and 187 had been cast by the Hungarians.[43]

In the early months of the war entire battalions wore rags and went barefoot; but here too the situation improved gradually. Uniforms were turned out chiefly by the country's relatively advanced textile mills; underwear and boots were made mainly by petty artisans. Toward the end of the war the *honvéd* were dressed almost as respectably as any regular army.[44]

There was never a food shortage during the war. Government commissioners bought up the surplus for the military and requisitioning was practiced only rarely. A black market was practically unknown and the price of grain did not increase significantly. The soldiers ate the coarse staples they had been used to as peasants, but generally they ate better than they had at home. War Ministry records show that the Komárom garrison commander requested for its troops bread, flour, rice, barley groats, peas, beans, lentils, sauerkraut (excellent to ward off scurvy), beef, smoked meat, garlic, onions, salt, wine, vinegar, pepper, and tobacco. The men in Komárom were given almost a pound of meat and a pint of wine every day. Such luxuries as white rolls, mutton, "good wine," spirits, dried fruit, and sugar were set aside for the sick.[45] Potatoes, coffee, or tea were not on the list.

Somehow, time was found to set up a military academy, a number of homes for military invalids, and scores of field hospitals. The medical corps of the *honvéd* army was exemplary for the period. Repeated outbreaks of cholera were handled successfully, and there were no other epidemics. Amazingly, the military hospitals cured more wounded and sick than they buried. According to one contemporary hospital record, only about two out of every hundred patients treated there died.[46] Before the main fighting had started, the major medical worry had not been epidemics but venereal disease. In No-

1. Kossuth: the earliest known portrait (1841). Elegant and reflective. It was all ahead of him.
Lithograph, Franz Eybl.

The illustrations are drawn from various sources. Most of the originals are in the Historical Art Gallery of the Hungarian National Museum; others are in the Hungarian National Gallery, the Budapest Historical Museum, and the Kossuth Museum at Cegléd.

2. Kossuth in 1848, the year of destiny. Majesty and flamboyance are now evident.
Lithograph, August Prinzhofer.

3. The great reformer—Count István Széchenyi in 1842.
Lithograph, Franz Eybl.

4. The eternal conciliator: Ferenc Deák in 1842.
Lithograph, Franz Eybl.

5. The magnates in action—the Upper House during the "Long Diet" of 1832–1836.
Drawing in India ink, A. J. Groitsch.

6. The Lower House during the "Long Diet."
Copper engraving, A. J. Groitsch.

7. Where "Young Hungary" met: the Café Pilvax at Pest. If there are any radicals here, they are obscured by the dandies. *Water color, from a pen-and-ink sketch by József Preiszer.*

8. Archduke Stephen, palatine of Hungary, in the uniform of a Hungarian hussar general, with the Order of the Golden Fleece around his neck (1847).
Lithograph, Josef Bekel.

9. The future martyr: Count Lajos Batthyány in 1839.
Water color, Friedrich Lieder.

10. The first constitutional cabinet in 1848. Standing, from left to right: Baron Eötvös, cults and education; Szemere, interior; Kossuth, finance; Deák, justice; Colonel Mészáros, war. Seated, from left to right: Batthyány, prime minister; Count Széchenyi, public works and transport; Klauzál, agriculture, industry and trade; Prince Esterházy, "minister near His Majesty." As Esterházy was with the king in Austria, the artist left him *sans tête*. The ministers being busy men, the artist—as was conventional practice—first drew the figures, then, working from real life, he portrayed and attached the heads. Archduke Stephen and King Ferdinand look down on the Hungarians from the wall. *Lithograph.*

11. The opening of the National Assembly on July 5, 1848, at Pest. The ministers are on the rostrum with Archduke Stephen in the center. In the midst of the glittering assembly, there is a lone peasant deputy in the lower left of the scene.
Lithograph, József Borsos and August Pettenkofen.

12. ''The rebel leader'': General Arthur Görgey.

13. Field Marshal Prince Alfred Windisch-Graetz in 1848.
Lithograph, August Prinzhofer.

14. Kossuth exhorting the Magyar peasants of Cegléd to take up arms against Jelačić (September 1848).
Drawing, Franz Kollarz(?).

15. The first battle of the revolution at Pákozd on September 29, 1848. Jelačić's Imperial-Royal Croats launch an attack on General Móga's Royal Hungarians. The mountains supplied by the artist are in reality small hills.
Lithograph, Franz Xaver Zalder.

16. A sally of Hungarian hussars from the fortress of Komárom, February 24, 1849. *Lithograph, Vincenz Katzler.*

17. The Austrian siege of Komárom, March 31, 1849.
Lithograph, Josef Lanzedelli and Eduard Weixlgärtner. From a sketch by Fritz L'Allemand.

18. Görgey's *honvéd* assault Castle Hill at Buda on May 21, 1849.
Lithograph, József Winezky.

19. The last major battle of the Revolution: Haynau's Austrian heavy cavalry are about to ride over Bem's Hungarians at Temesvár, August 9, 1849.
Lithograph, Vincenz Katzler.

Er wiegt mehr, als sie alle!_

A.Paternos W: 5 Sohn in Wien

20. The hat of Kossuth weighs more than all the monarchical crowns of Europe, 1848.
Lithograph, Josef Lanzedelli.

21. An autograph of Kossuth, dating from before the Revolution. Above his signature, the autographs of Count Kázmér Batthyány, Hungary's foreign minister in 1849, and Count László Teleki, Kossuth's envoy to Paris.

vember, when it turned out that two-thirds of the patients in the field hospitals were there because of such infections, the Ministry of War issued a strict order to the counties to put the "ladies of pleasure" under medical surveillance.[47]

The spring 1849 victories of the *honvéd* army were to prove that an economically undeveloped country could at least challenge an economically superior opponent. The Monarchy's renewed Italian troubles in 1849 would play a role in this turn of events, as would Hungary's outstanding military leadership. The revolutionary enthusiasm of the Hungarian national army has also been heralded as the major factor. But the Hungarian organization of war production was decisive, and this was mainly Kossuth's work.

We have here a somewhat premature overview of the entire war. In November 1848, where we interrupted the chronology of events, the national army had just been born. On the other hand, the Imperial forces had begun careful political and military preparations for their supreme offensive. In fact, political changes in Austria had preceded the military campaign, matching in character the Hungarian political measures. By the time Windisch-Graetz's army attacked Görgey's army in mid-December, both Austria and Hungary had strong men as leaders.

From Ferdinand to Francis Joseph

For a few weeks following the capture of Vienna, Windisch-Graetz was the dictator of Austria. The Wessenberg cabinet, theoretically still in office, had been too discredited by the October events to command much authority. The Reichstag, now sitting in the Moravian town of Kremsier, lived in the shadow of the Court in Olmütz; it devised an excellent constitution but it could not interfere in politics. Therefore it was Windisch-Graetz, not the Reichstag, who selected the next Austrian prime minister: his own brother-in-law, General Prince Felix zu Schwarzenberg.

If Windisch-Graetz was Kossuth's chief military antagonist in the winter of 1848–49, Schwarzenberg was to become Kossuth's principal political enemy until the end of the war. Long after Windisch-Graetz's dismissal for military incompetence, Schwarzenberg would preside over the defeat of Hungary and the complete reorganization of the Monarchy. From the standpoint of Windisch-Graetz's political philosophy, the choice of his brother-in-law was a grave mistake. The field marshal was an ultraconservative who wished to restore traditional rule within each of the Monarchy's historic kingdoms and provinces; the much younger Schwarzenberg (he was forty-eight at that time) wished to modernize, centralize, and (up to a point) Germanize the Monarchy. Windisch-Graetz was willing to grant the Hungarians their pre-1848 feudal liberties, which would have entailed some form of self-government for Hungary. Schwarzenberg saw himself as the prime minister of a *Gesamtmonarchie* united by a single constitution.

Whether or not Schwarzenberg was a true liberal is a matter of historical debate: his biographer, Adolph Schwarzenberg (a scion of the same family), the Austrian historian Friedrich Walter, and the British historian C. A. Macartney see the new Austrian prime minister as a friend of constitutions and of popular liberties; the older Habsburg historians saw him as a tyrant.[48] The two brothers-in-law disagreed in temperament, in political philosophy, and perhaps most importantly in the degree of their respective aristocratic conceits. In the words of Macartney:

Windisch-Graetz abhorred only the middle and lower classes; he conceded to Counts and Barons a right to exist, and wished to base the new political structure of the Monarchy on an oligarchy of these classes. Schwarzenberg despised even his fellow-nobles; it would indeed be desirable, he wrote to his brother-in-law in January 1849, to see the aristocracy governing the Monarchy, were they capable of doing so, but there were not among them a dozen men of sufficient political insight or experience to justify entrusting them with real authority.[49]

The Schwarzenberg ministry was appointed on November 21. It included Count Franz Stadion as minister of the interior, a true constitutionalist and a centralist who would become the most important cabinet member next to Schwarzenberg; and Dr. Alexander Bach as minister of justice, an ex-revolutionary who would later give his name to an absolutistic era. The other cabinet members were officials, officers, or former liberal members of the Wessenberg government. Several of the ministers were of *bürgerliche* background (for instance, Bach and Minister of Commerce Karl Bruck). In revolutionary Hungary every single member of the National Defense

Committee was a nobleman; but then (to emphasize a point already made in this book) Austria had long had an influential bourgeoisie, whereas in Hungary the bourgeoisie was without influence, and it was mostly non-Magyar. The Austrian nobility's indifference to public affairs was noted by Schwarzenberg himself; the Hungarian landed nobility was highly politicized and it held all the country's political power in its hands.

For his complete disregard of Hungarian national interests and his revengeful postwar brutality toward the revolutionaries, Schwarzenberg was much hated in Hungary. Széchenyi called him a "cold-blooded vampire" after the war, and Hungarian historians have made much of his lack of political education, his aloofness, and his conceit. They also made much of Schwarzenberg's sensuality, which, while he was a diplomat, had involved him in several scandals.[50] Yet Schwarzenberg had definite aims: he wished to uphold the greatness of the Empire; he would not allow it to merge into a united Germany—on the contrary, he wanted Austria to dominate the Germanic confederation; he would not let the Italian provinces secede; and he was determined to crush the Hungarian revolution. Hungarian arrogance had to be taught a lesson once and for all. Hungary was to be redivided into its historical provinces and the country as a whole downgraded to the same level as the other provinces of the Monarchy.[51]

Windisch-Graetz's next move was to replace Ferdinand with Archduke Francis Joseph. This took place on December 2 and is too well known to be recounted in detail. Ferdinand was persuaded to sign his resignation and to bless his young nephew. The reason for the emperor's dismissal was not only his feeblemindedness: in the hands of a strong prime minister he would have been a perfectly flexible tool, and he had been dangerous only as long as there were too many people to tell him what to do. The eighteen-year-old Francis Joseph could not command more respect and authority than Ferdinand who, despite all his weaknesses, was beloved by many. The reason for the change of rulers was something rather unworthy of a dynasty whose *raisons d'être* were legality and historical continuity: the argument in Court circles was that Francis Joseph would not be bound by the unfortunate laws his predecessor had sanctioned.[52]

Ferdinand's abdication ceremony demonstrated the decline of both Hungarian aristocratic and Austrian parliamentary influence at

Court: no Hungarian, not even the most loyal was invited, and the president of the Reichstag was also snubbed.

The change of rulers caused a storm in the Hungarian parliament. Kossuth wanted immediate and categorical disavowal; but for the first time since the outbreak of the war, he was openly challenged.

For some time a new political movement had been growing in parliament with the aim of bringing about a reconciliation with the dynasty. The movement, soon to be called the Peace Party, had proven its strength in mid-November in connection with Kossuth's attempt to transform the National Defense Committee into a real ministry. The Peace Party had acted discreetly at that time, through private correspondence with Kossuth. Its spokesman, Bertalan Szemere, was not even a member of the group, being too much of an individualist to attach himself to any political faction. But Szemere could not have opposed Kossuth had he not been aware of the support of many politicians in the Assembly. In the National Defense Committee decisions were supposed to be made by all the members at regularly held meetings, but some members never attended the meetings or participated in any real sense; others, like Mészáros, busied themselves within their particular competences. Gradually the meetings were abandoned and most of the governing fell on Kossuth's shoulders. This burdened him inordinately and also aroused many suspicions. Moderates feared the dictator's close alliance with the radical faction; the radicals suspected that Kossuth—no radical himself—would desert them one day and thus deprive them of all political influence. In November, realizing the awkwardness of the situation, Kossuth tried to constitute a cabinet with regular portfolios and with himself as prime minister; but every one of his combinations was rejected by Szemere and others because of Kossuth's insistence on having the radical László Madarász as minister of the interior. There was endless haggling over the other appointments as well,[53] and Kossuth wrote dejectedly to Szemere:

Your first letter is based on the contention that it is wrong for the cause of the fatherland to be tied to my person. . . . Is this my fault? Have I asked for it? Have I wanted it? Have I taken a single step in this direction? Do you believe that I enjoy this accursed life? If what you have written is true then you yourself have written a satire on this country and on everyone in it.

Why don't you do everything in your power to arrange that the fate of our poor fatherland be not tied to one unfortunate individual? How is it that you know me so little as to believe me ambitious? Me, who would rather be a dog than a minister or prime minister.[54]

Rhetoric and some dishonesty aside—for he was obviously very ambitious—it is true that Kossuth had indeed tried to share with others the burden and responsibility of government. He failed, not merely because of jealousies and intrigues but chiefly because a number of politicians had begun to see in Kossuth and Madarász the principal obstacles to an honorable settlement with the dynasty. The Peace Party wished to negotiate with the Court but knew that negotiations were impossible if Kossuth and Madarász occupied key positions in a regularly constituted cabinet. The Court hated Kossuth and Madarász more than any other Hungarians. Of the four revolutionaries against whom Austrian officials issued a rather symbolic warrant at that time, two were Kossuth and Madarász. The other two were Ferenc Pulszky, by then one of the National Defense Committee's principal agents in Western Europe, and the Vienna radical Dr. Karl Tausenau.[55]*

The Peace Party was in a quandary, for even though it wished to get rid of Kossuth, it needed him in the national crisis. It seemed best therefore to let the National Defense Committee and Kossuth's dictatorship continue. The committee and the dictator were clearly stopgap measures, an expression of the national emergency, to be replaced at an opportune moment by a cabinet of moderates with which the Austrians would perhaps negotiate. But proof at least had to be furnished that not all Hungarians were unequivocally behind the dictator; therefore Kossuth was to be criticized, albeit cautiously.

The Peace Party made its first public attack on Kossuth at the parliamentary session that followed the resignation of the emperor-king. On December 6, at a closed meeting of the deputies, Dénes Pázmándy, president of the Lower House, recommended that Francis Joseph's accession to the Throne be recognized. This alone, Pázmándy argued, would enable Hungary eventually to seek a reconciliation with the dynasty.[56] But Kossuth's usual eloquence swayed the majority of the deputies to adopt his proposal. On the following day in an

---

* The warrant put Kossuth's age at younger than it really was and it described him in most flattering terms; the name of Madarász was misspelled and there were numerous other errors; and the "oriental" (i.e., Jewish) features of Dr. Tausenau were strongly emphasized.

open session, the parliament solemnly branded the accession of Francis Joseph as unconstitutional. In a decision inspired by Kossuth, the deputies pointed out with irony that the news from Olmütz had reached them only through private communications. (Since the king had dissolved the parliament on October 3, he was in no position to send official notice to the deputies.) The parliamentary proclamation further explained that, according to Hungarian constitutional practice, the king could not resign without first consulting with the Diet of Hungary; that the Pragmatic Sanction obliged the nation to recognize only the rightful heir of a dead ruler and not of a living ruler; and that, even if the nation had been consulted in due time, the heir to the throne was no king until he had taken the oath to the constitution and had himself crowned with the Crown of Saint Stephen. In brief, as far as Hungary was concerned, Ferdinand was still king and Archduke Francis Joseph was a usurper. Or, if Ferdinand insisted on resigning, then the contract between people and prince was broken and the nation could do as it pleased.[57]

The Assembly's proclamation was a masterpiece but it was useless outside Hungary, for neither the other peoples of the Monarchy nor any foreign power raised the slightest objection to the new emperor. Francis Joseph began his sixty-eight-year rule in a strong position.

The Peace Party was not alone in worrying about Hungary's military situation. At the same time that Kossuth had tried to form a cabinet, he had also attempted to reach an armistice with the Austrians. On November 20 and again a few days later, he wrote to William H. Stiles, chargé d'affaires of the United States in Vienna, requesting that Stiles open armistice negotiations on behalf of Hungary. According to Stiles, the second message had been brought to him in great secrecy by a "young female" who was "a most beautiful and graceful creature and, though attired in the dress of a peasant, the grace and the elegance of her manner, the fluency and correctness of her French, at once denoted that she was nearer a princess than a peasant."

The American diplomat, whose *Austria in 1848–49* was to become an important historical source and who was a friend of revolutionary Hungary, took up the matter immediately, first with Schwarzenberg and then with Windisch-Graetz, who was plenipotentiary for Hungary. Stiles was turned down politely but firmly, as he had ex-

pected, with the reply that Hungary would have to surrender unconditionally. He communicated the bad news to Kossuth and with that his
diplomatic role, and that of the U.S. government, in the Hungarian
war was over.[58] It was a clear sign of Hungary's complete diplomatic
isolation that Kossuth's appeal for an armistice had to be channeled
through the representative of the United States, whose influence on
Austria was obviously nil. Kossuth's démarche also showed that he
was no fanatic ready to drag his country into an abyss for the sake of
an ideal. On the contrary, he had always fought for limited goals. All
in all, despite some vague and premature attempts in parliament to restrain Kossuth, he was very much in power in December 1848.
Against him, the Austrians had finally marshaled a strong team, that
of the two princes. From that time on, there was to be no political
hesitation in Vienna, no change of cabinets, no weak ruler. The war
could begin in all seriousness.

The Triumphant March of Prince Windisch-Graetz

The Austrian military offensive against Hungary started not in the
West but in the faraway domains of the Monarchy. Early in December the dynamic and talented *Feldmarschalleutnant* Count Franz
Schlick entered Hungary from Galicia with his army corps, dispersed
the hastily organized Hungarian resistance, and on December 11 occupied Kassa, an important city in northern Hungary.[59] Another
small Austrian force, that of *Feldmarschalleutnant* Baron Balthasar
Simunich, had come from Moravia and was operating in northern
Hungary. Since the National Defense Committee was short of troops,
it could do little else but to outlaw Simunich, put a price of 100 silver
gulden on his head, and call his troops a horde of bandits.[60] The earliest and gravest threat, however, came from Transylvania, where the
onset of the Austrian campaign coincided with the Hungarian advance toward Vienna in October, and the defeat of the Austrian campaign coincided with Windisch-Graetz's conquest of Buda-Pest in January.

Of all the confused situations in the lands of the Crown of Saint
Stephen, the Transylvanian situation was the most confused. There
the old Imperial-Royal authority, represented by the Nagyszeben
General-Commando, competed with the still-functioning Kolozsvár

Vice-Regal Council (Gubernium), the plenipotentiaries and military commanders of the Buda-Pest government and parliament, the Saxon Universitas, the Romanian National Committee (then still called Pacification Committee), and numerous other institutions, all of which claimed extensive authority and all of which were split into moderate and militant factions. Yet by October a certain unity of purpose began to bind the Saxon and Romanian leaders with some members of the Vice-Regal Council and with the Imperial-Royal army. Their common aim became to drive out the "Kossuth clique" and to reverse the Union. It was a curious alliance: Austrian regulars and Romanian Border Guards; conservative Saxon burghers; reactionary Hungarian magnates; Orthodox and Uniate clergymen; conservative, liberal, and radical Romanian intellectuals; and Romanian peasant guerrillas. The Romanians constituted by far the greatest numerical force in this alliance, but by the fall most Romanian leaders were no longer pursuing their own national objectives. In order to rid themselves of the Hungarians, they had gradually subjected themselves to the Austrian military command.

The Imperial commander, to whom the Romanians (especially the Pacification Committee and the Orthodox Bishop Andreiu Şaguna) were becoming increasingly subservient, was *General der Cavallerie* (three-star general) Baron Anton Puchner, head of the Transylvanian General-Commando. He vaguely thought of himself as a Hungarian; at least he had been born in Hungary and was a friend of the Transylvanian Magyar aristocracy. Almost seventy at that time, Puchner was sickly, peaceful, rather indolent, but imbued with a strict sense of duty to his prince. He had obeyed the Hungarian minister of war as long as he felt this to be His Majesty's desire; he reversed himself when he began to sense that this was no longer the emperor's wish. His position was not easy: both the Hungarians and the Romanians reproached him with weakness toward the other side.[61] By late September Puchner was engaged in strengthening his strategic position. When he learned of the emperor's October 3 manifesto, he immediately began preparations for a military takeover. But rather than being able to isolate Kossuth's relatively few emissaries and soldiers, he was confronted with a desperately complex situation.

The continuous Romanian agitation, and the openly anti-Hungarian stand of the Austro-Romanian regular troops, had triggered the Székely nation into action. At their Agyagfalva assembly held in mid-October, perhaps as many as 60,000 Székelys affirmed their loyalty to Hungary and proclaimed the general insurrection of their nation.[62] Soon about 30,000 Székelys, including the Székely Border Guards, were armed. On October 18 Puchner issued a proclamation to all the officials and peoples of Transylvania. Referring to the Emperor's manifestos, he announced that he had now taken over civilian authority; he declared the Hungarian National Defense Committee illegal and forbade the activities of the Hungarian emissaries; he ordered an immediate end to recruitment into the *honvéd;* and he placed all National Guard units under his own command. Generously sprinkling his proclamation with exhortations to peace, order, and discipline, Puchner also called on the loyal inhabitants of Transylvania to arrest and deliver to the authorities all those who would disobey his orders. Finally, he requested the people "to rise to the last man, one for all and all for one," to arm themselves and to fight courageously for the emperor.[63]

The October 18 proclamation put an end to Puchner's association with most Hungarians. It brought him into close alliance with Lieutenant-Colonel Karl Urban who, as commander of the 2nd Naszód Romanian Border Guard regiment, had long been rallying the Romanian national forces around his flag. It also brought Puchner in line with the Saxons and with the Romanian Pacification Committee. The latter immediately issued its own proclamation exhorting all Romanians both to preserve law and order and to fight to the death against the Hungarian officials.[64] Finally, Puchner's proclamation inevitably associated him with the Romanian peasant guerrillas. The peasants had been restive for a long time; now they felt that the emperor himself had ordered them to take up arms against the Hungarians. Ever since March 1848 these mostly illiterate and desperately poor people had been deluged with promises from all sides. As the promises had in no way improved their condition, they became convinced that the emperor had meant to liberate them and to give them land, but that the landlords and officials had hidden the emperor's good laws from them. No Romanian peasant had ever laid eyes on His Majesty, yet he was for them the only stable figure in a disordered world. Back in September, when the Hungarian county authorities had attempted to conscript the peasants for service in the *honvéd* army, the Romanians had resisted; one young peasant explained to the recruiting official that he and everyone else in the village would go anywhere at the orders of the emperor, but never at the orders of the Hungarians, for the latter had too often cheated the peasants and had kept them in slavery.[65] The Hungarians had been doing their conscripting in the name of the king: and as happened elsewhere, some peasants did not even know that emperor and king were one and the same person.

Following Puchner's manifesto, the Romanian rebellion erupted and engulfed almost the entire province. The peasants systematically hunted down the Magyar nobles and officials. The lucky ones were turned over to Imperial officers; others were slaughtered together with their families. The number of victims is unknown, but it must have reached several thousand. The Hungarians naturally defended themselves, and soon Székely National Guards, noble *Jäger* corps, and *honvéd* companies were hunting down the Romanian peasants. Again hundreds were killed and many villages were wiped out. And instead of presiding over a disciplined and chastised province, Puchner now found himself in the middle of a war which he himself had helped to precipitate.

Early in November Puchner set out for Hungary with 12,000 trained soldiers (mostly Romanian Border Guards), about 20,000 fairly well-armed Saxon and Romanian National Guards, and an indeterminate number of armed Romanian peasants. The Hungarian army was much smaller and even less well trained, except for the Székely Border Guard regiments.[66] Coming from several directions, Puchner's troops converged on Kolozsvár and occupied it on November 17. The Imperials had met with very little resistance and now moved in the direction of Nagyvárad, in Hungary proper, with the aim of attacking Kossuth's forces from the rear. By late November almost all of Transylvania was in Imperial hands. The only thing that slowed Puchner down was the resistance of a part of the Székely territory far behind his advancing troops. Most of the Székely lands had surrendered to Puchner; but the county of Háromszék (Trei Scaune) had held out, forcing the general to return some of his troops there. This brief breathing space allowed Kossuth to organize resistance and reverse the situation within a few weeks.

When all seemed lost, Kossuth, in a stroke of genius, appointed General József Bem (a Polish emigré who had come to Hungary from Paris via the Vienna October revolution) commander-in-chief in Transylvania. Simultaneously, Kossuth assembled a small army for

Bem to start a counteroffensive, and he appointed the most energetic Hungarian politician, László Csányi, government plenipotentiary in Transylvania.

Between December and January Bem reconquered most of the province with his troops: some 8,000 infantry and 1,500 cavalry, plus 5,000 National Guards and 21 guns.[67] His army would never grow much bigger, explaining why the Polish general could win battles but never secure the entire province for Hungary. Still, the importance of his victories cannot be overestimated: once the Transylvanian war had started—a capital mistake on the part of Hungary—Bem alone could secure the rear of the Hungarian forces facing the Austrian main army. He proved that the Imperials could be defeated in a regular campaign, and he gave courage to a despairing public. Kossuth made the most of Bem's successes, glorifying the Polish general. But this turned out to be a dangerous move; for while the public, and his own soldiers, came to idolize "Father Bem," Görgey and the other Hungarian commanders grew jealous of the foreigner. Kossuth would have liked to make Bem commander-in-chief, but the Pole would not be moved from Transylvania. This again led to bitterness. Yet what counted for the time being was that Puchner had been stopped and that the Hungarians were free to oppose the main Austrian army.

In mid-December Windisch-Graetz finally crossed the Hungarian border from Austria. He had 52,000 trained regulars and 210 guns against Görgey's 30,000 mostly inexperienced soldiers and about 80 guns.[68] Görgey withdrew along the banks of the Danube and offered only minor resistance, in which his soldiers behaved bravely. Kossuth was in despair, for the general explained very little and promised nothing. By then, the president of the National Defense Committee and the commander of the Army of the Upper Danube were at odds with one another. Görgey had complained of the lack of supplies, the plethora of untrained and pitifully dressed recruits, constant interference on the part of the government commissioners, and—above all—interference on the part of Kossuth. The president complained of Görgey's unwillingness to make a stand or to win at least "a tiny little victory," so sorely needed for national morale. It is true that Kossuth issued several contradictory orders: alternately, he agreed with Görgey that withdrawal was inevitable; or he demanded a decisive battle, but "without endangering the safety of the army."

In the controversy between Kossuth and Görgey over strategy, the latter seems to have been right.[69] For even though Kossuth sounded convincing when he wrote that Hungary was no Russia and that they would soon run out of space, Görgey had a better understanding of Austrian military mentality or, rather, of Windisch-Graetz's mentality. Görgey had sensed that Windisch-Graetz only wanted to take Buda-Pest and then rest in the conviction that the Hungarians would voluntarily abandon the fight. Görgey also knew of the Austrian generals' desperate preoccupation with supply lines. The fortress of Komárom on the Danube stood firm; the Austrians surrounded it but would not dream of taking it by storm. With Komárom defiant in his rear, the field marshal would advance beyond Buda-Pest only with the greatest caution.

Görgey was discerning in wanting to conserve the best of Hungarian troops for a later counteroffensive. However, there were some political considerations behind his strategy. By late December Görgey and his officers had nothing but contempt for the "lawyers and scribblers in Buda-Pest," whom they considered selfish fanatics and irresponsible radicals. Görgey had developed a concept of the political role his army was to play. If he succeeded in keeping his divisions intact, he would hold a major weapon in his hands with which eventually to force the Hungarian and Austrian leaders to negotiate. A compromise peace could then guarantee the honor of the army, the safety of the officers, the sanctity of the April Laws of 1848, and Hungary's return to the Habsburg fold.

This then was the situation toward the end of December: a growing Peace Party in the parliament; the Hungarian armies in retreat everywhere except in Transylvania; the capital in danger; and the military commander preparing a political role for his army.

On December 30 Kossuth's concept of "attack is the best defense" suffered a major blow when General Perczel was defeated at Mór, some fifty miles west of Buda-Pest. Perczel had not been attached to Görgey's army but had operated independently. For several weeks now, he had been withdrawing from southwestern Hungary—not because of enemy pressure, but in order to maintain contact with Görgey's army. At Kossuth's urging, Perczel had finally made a stand at Mór and had lost almost all of his 6,000 men. Perczel was a political radical, a brave soldier, and a megalomaniac. He hated Görgey, with whom he had quarreled earlier; and he suspected Kossuth. Now he heaped all blame on Görgey and Kossuth, both of whom returned the compliment in kind: a bad omen and a clear sign of many more devastating quarrels to come.

After the disaster at Mór and faced with Görgey's determination not to sacrifice his army, the politicians could either start negotiations or flee. On December 31 at a closed session of the National Assembly, they adopted both alternatives. Kossuth exhorted the deputies to continue the fight and announced that he would withdraw to Debrecen in eastern Hungary. In a stormy session the Peace Party agreed to the departure of the National Defense Committee, but it demanded that the Assembly stay put and that negotiations be opened with Windisch-Graetz. If this recommendation had been adopted in its entirety, the National Defense Committee would have been completely isolated—which was just what the Peace Party wanted. But with the help of the left-wing deputies, Kossuth again prevailed. It was decided by a majority that the committee and the parliament would both go to Debrecen, and that a peace delegation would seek out Windisch-Graetz. Kossuth supported the latter move, for he knew from his bitter November experience that the mission would fail.[70]

In the Assembly the attack on Kossuth had been led by no less a personality than Batthyány. He had been a National Guard for a while, then had allowed himself to be sent to the House of Representatives in a by-election; and his express purpose in coming to Buda-Pest was to defeat Kossuth. It was at his behest that the peace delegation was formed. Batthyány had no more illusions than Kossuth about the success of this mission, but he felt duty-bound to try everything to save the country. "Sometimes I feel as if I were in a madhouse," he wrote earlier from Buda-Pest to his wife, "here I am being called a traitor, and in Vienna they believe that I killed Count Latour. Apparently, extremes attract one another."[71]

The peace delegation, consisting of Batthyány, Deák, an archbishop, and two conservative former high officials in the pre-1848 administration, was the best that revolutionary Hungary could offer in respectability and in dynastic loyalty. The delegation reached Windisch-Graetz's headquarters west of Buda-Pest on January 3 and was immediately received, except for Batthyány, who was not allowed in the presence of the prince. The delegates asked for the recognition of the laws of 1848 and in exchange offered an armistice in the name of the National Assembly. The field marshal was friendly but insisted on unconditional surrender; he demanded that the Hungarian army parade in front of him before surrendering its arms and that it take the oath of loyalty to His Majesty.

The delegates were only able to notify the Assembly in writing of the failure of their mission, for although they were free to return to their estates, they were not allowed to go to Hungarian-held territory.[72] In truth, they had no desire to follow Kossuth. Batthyány went to his palace in Pest, where he was arrested a few days later on the orders of the prince. He remained a prisoner until he was executed in October 1849.

The evacuation of Buda-Pest began on December 31. In the parliamentary session of that day, one angry deputy demanded that a roll call of deputies be held at the railroad station; those who failed to show up were to be hunted down and hanged. János Pálffy, a member of the Peace Party, later noted with regret that not a single deputy had dared to raise his voice in protest against such humiliating threats. "Yet I am as sure as I am here," Pálffy wrote, "that neither Kossuth, nor anyone else, would have hanged any of us."[73] Pálffy knew Kossuth well: no disloyal deputy was ever executed, yet their number was legion.

Evacuation was not easy. Everything had to go within two or three days: the offices and the officials; the deputies and their families; the newspaper presses and the one and only banknote press; the arsenal and the entire armaments industry; the machines and the workers; the Holy Crown and the cash reserve. The latter, totaling almost 2 million guldens in gold and silver, was somehow left behind by Ferenc Duschek, the undersecretary of the Finance Ministry, who later prided himself on having been a confidential Austrian agent all through the war. Evacuation had to proceed on the single railroad line connecting Buda-Pest with Szolnok, about half way to Debrecen; from there the evacuees could either ride in peasant carts or walk. And many walked the entire 140 miles from Buda-Pest to Debrecen. The railroad line was brand-new but functioned badly because of the extreme cold and—as it was rumored then—because of sabotage by the railroad management.

On New Year's Eve Kossuth, his family, his friends, the deputies, and other politicians met at the railroad station to wait for the train. At midnight they toasted the new year with punch and at three in the morning they finally boarded the train. It was a pitiful pilgrimage, with throngs storming the cars and locomotives constantly breaking down. Few of these Hungarians expected to return to the capital under the national flag.

6 / Recovery and Ecstasy: Kossuth Dictator, Part Two (January–April 1849)

Refuge in Eastern Hungary

DEBRECEN, WHERE THE National Defense Committee, the ministries, and the Assembly were to sit from January to May 1849, was the city farthest away from the advancing Austrian armies. By happy coincidence it was also the center of Hungarian Calvinism and thus symbolized national resistance to Habsburg-Catholic imperialism.* In all other respects, Debrecen was a bad place for a temporary capital. Like the other major towns of the Great Plain, it was not an urban center but a gigantic village. It had no pavement, no sewers, and no street lights; its houses were no more than mud cottages; its low city walls were useless except to enforce customs regulations. On its vast municipal pastures roamed the horses and longhorn cattle of the wealthier burghers. It was these prominent citizens who governed the city's 27,000 inhabitants—mostly peasants whose pride, stubbornness, conservatism, suspiciousness, and greed were (and still are) legendary. There were in Debrecen fewer than a hundred shopkeepers or merchants, only a few dozen clerks, lawyers, or engineers, and one doctor in private practice.[1]

---

* Debrecen became the temporary capital once more in 1944, when the Soviet army created Hungary's first anti-fascist government there. Meeting in the same buildings where the 1849 National Defense Committee and Assembly had met, and assiduously invoking the name of Kossuth, the new provisional government and assembly laid claim to the ideological heritage of the War of Independence and its leader.

Debrecen as temporary capital made the revolution more national and less social. Here strikes were unthinkable, as were street orators and demonstrating crowds pressing for reform. There were no coffee-house intellectuals and no organized journeymen. The students of the Protestant college and the Catholic lycée proved impervious to democratic and republican programs. The left-wing members of the parliament found themselves in a political vacuum; without support from the street they gradually lost influence, which ultimately weakened the position of Kossuth.

All through the bitterly cold days of January the evacuees converged on Debrecen.[2] Huddled together in peasant carts and ruthlessly exploited by their peasant drivers, some refugees felt themselves in a land as alien as the frozen Asiatic steppes. Those without valid travel documents were turned back at the gates; Kossuth alone was not asked to show his passport. When he entered the city on January 7, the gatekeeper's logbook simply noted the arrival of "Kossuth, the Moses of Hungarians."

Eventually, all made it into the city: some two thousand evacuees from Buda-Pest and a thousand others from Transylvania. Together with the soldiers, the patients of the five new military hospitals, and the Croatian prisoners of war, they swelled the city's population by almost ten thousand. For a few days this disgruntled mass tramped the frozen or muddy streets of Debrecen; but eventually they all settled down, more or less comfortably and expensively. The National Defense Committee, the Holy Crown, and Kossuth and his family installed themselves in the City Hall; the House of Representatives, the banknote press, and the Ministry of Finance crowded into the Protestant college. Gradually the evacuees returned to their old routine: the majority of the deputies and many officers without troops to their nightly card games in the taverns; Kossuth and his friends to back-breaking labor.

No sooner had everyone arrived in Debrecen than the National Assembly was called into session, with its first tasks the counting of heads and the painful decision as to what ought to be done about the defectors. Clearly, not all deputies would show up in Debrecen; there were persistent rumors that Kossuth himself had lost heart and was preparing to escape abroad. Rumor also had it that while they were still back in Buda-Pest Kossuth and his colleagues had asked for their passports and had planned to flee to the United States.[3] Bertalan

Szemere, then government plenipotentiary in northern Hungary, so despaired of the situation that he pressed for surrender. "When making your plans for the future," he wrote to the National Defense Committee on January 12, "do not count on a popular insurrection and the power of the masses. . . . People are unspeakably tired of the war. . . . 'Liberty and Nationality' are mere lyrics to them of which they understand nothing. . . . In the entire country there are no more than five people dedicated enough to do their duty."[4] The commander of the Polish legion in Hungary, *honvéd* Major (later General) Józef Wysocki, begged Kossuth for a firm reply with regard to the Hungarians' determination to continue the struggle. The Austrians would show no mercy toward the Poles, nor toward Kossuth either, Wysocki wrote. In the event of further negotiations with the Austrians, perhaps even against the will of Kossuth, Wysocki asked to be informed so that the poor Poles could start again on their wanderings.[5]

At the first Debrecen meeting of the House of Representatives on January 9, only 145 deputies out of a total of 415 attended. Gradually they grew to 300; but not all representatives had come out of sheer patriotism. Some were just passing through Debrecen on their way to Transylvania or eastern Hungary; others had not dared to return to homes in Austrian-occupied western Hungary; others again needed their salaries. With Buda-Pest lost, many deputies considered the Assembly de facto dissolved and their own roles terminated. Even those who had come often left again under various pretexts. There was a constant coming and going, and only Kossuth's will and prestige kept the Assembly together.[6]

Logically, those who had made it to Debrecen should have been the more militant and radically inclined, but this was not the case. The Peace Party emerged stronger than before, and the parliamentary radicals more isolated. It became clear that the majority of the deputies, especially the vast *marée* in the center, was made up of cautious and moderate individuals who had limited aims for the revolution. The Peace Party went to Debrecen with the express purpose of keeping the door ajar for negotiations with the Austrians. Those in the center, while often inconsistent, ended up by supporting the Peace Party on several crucial issues. The deputies understood that a compromise with Austria was impossible as long as Windisch-Graetz was advancing, but they wished to safeguard the chances of renewed negotiations following an eventual Hungarian military recovery. Thus both the radicals and the anti-radicals hoped for and worked toward the strengthening of the army. Until that was accomplished, the Peace Party wished to prevent Kossuth and the radicals from doing anything foolish and irreversible.

The House of Representatives in Debrecen became even more an assembly of the lesser nobility. Of the three peasant deputies, Táncsics alone was present, and he was treated by his colleagues as a clown. The Saxon burgher deputies were absent as were many aristocratic members of the Lower House. The Upper House was a mere skeleton of its former self; at first only twenty magnates showed up in Debrecen and their number never went above thirty-five. It is an article of faith among Hungarian historians that, by the winter of 1848–49, the titled nobility had deserted the revolution. Entire scholarly works are devoted to the *Treason of the Great Landowning Aristocracy* (Erzsébet Andics), but the truth is that the treacherous aristocrats cited in these works were all well-known ultraconservatives or high-ranking Habsburg functionaries. The absence of magnates from the Upper House proves simply that it had become an impotent body, and that the lesser nobility of the Lower House had seized power in Hungary. Meanwhile, sixty aristocratic members of the Upper House were serving as officers, and a simple perusal of the official Hungarian *Monitor* shows that in 1849 eighty barons and counts were commissioned or promoted in the *honvéd* forces. It is true that about the same number of Magyar aristocrats served in the Habsburg army in 1849, but this was inevitable with the high number of titled nobles in the professional officers' corps. The defection of the Catholic high clergy was more conspicuous: of all Hungary's bishops, only two came to Debrecen.

The meetings of the House of Representatives opened with an offensive move by the radicals, who on January 26 proposed that the absentees be deprived of their mandates. The radicals insisted that the people be allowed to hold by-elections in order to fill the vacant seats. This proposal, if accepted, would have strengthened the radicals, for it was generally assumed that the districts interested enough to hold by-elections would send left-wing deputies. The debate on absenteeism and on the by-elections went on for several months. At first the radicals seemed to have their way, but the Peace Party stole the fruits of their victory. The committee charged with examining the case of the absentees was filled with moderates who exonerated most of the absent deputies on the slightest pretext. By-elections were not only allowed but were made mandatory, which guaranteed that the more moderate districts, where there had been no drive for a by-election, would also send their representatives.

The twenty or thirty radicals assembled in the Club of Equality felt themselves more than ever the true heirs of the French Jacobins. Their ominous talk of revolutionary vigilance and terror spread fear among the members of the Peace Party, who now began to think of themselves as the future Girondist victims of László Madarász, the Hungarian Fouquier-Tinville. The Peace Party girded itself for the fatal struggle. When a law for the speedy creation of revolutionary courts was adopted, the Peace Party inserted a paragraph guaranteeing the immunity of the deputies. The revolutionary courts were quickly constituted; but they were not too eager to try traitors coming from the ranks of the nobility. Up to the end of the revolution, the courts pronounced 122 death sentences, almost exclusively upon members of the non-Magyar nationalities. Altogether, eight Hungarian nobles were executed for treason.[7]

Forgetting that Hungary was not France and that the nationalities constituted the majority of the population, the radicals imitated the French Jacobins in advocating a republic one and indivisible and in branding all requests for national minority rights as treason. Pál Nyáry raised his voice against the anti-Slav and anti-Romanian propaganda of the Left, pressing the point that the war was being fought against Habsburg absolutism and not against any one nation. But by then the once-radical Nyáry stood close to the Peace Party, and the House indignantly rejected his pleas for moderation. For once, the majority of deputies sided with the radicals: together they engaged in an orgy of chauvinism. Speakers likened the nationalities to a herd of cattle; they insulted the Romanian deputies, and they threatened entire nationalities, especially the Transylvanian Saxons, with collective punishment.[8] The xenophobia of the deputies made concessions to the nationalities impossible, at least until the summer of 1849, when it was too late.

The radicals were unable to exploit their propaganda victory on the nationality question because they got entangled in the "Affair of the Diamonds," which preoccupied the House all through the spring months. The treasure chest of Ödön Zichy, the count executed by

Görgey for treason in October, had been entrusted to László Madarász, who was in charge of the postal service and the national police. It seems that the National Defense Committee had repeatedly dipped into this treasure to finance the operation of its foreign agents. Accounts were not kept; and in February 1849, when *Esti Lapok,* the newspaper of the Peace Party, accused Madarász of embezzlement, the police chief found no valid defense. Nor was Kossuth willing to protect his close associate. The parliamentary committee charged with investigating the scandal finally declared the embezzlement unproven but not unlikely. Today, after a sea of ink has been spilled on the question, it is still impossible to prove Madarász's innocence. Yet dishonesty was not in keeping with the character of this dedicated radical.[9] An unattractive little man with a long red beard, Madarász was able and diligent, but his arrogance, impatience, and authoritarianism made him unpopular among the deputies. Following the scandal, he resigned his parliamentary mandate; although subsequently reelected by his district, he never again played an important political role. The fall of Madarász was a major victory for the Peace Party; indirectly it was a defeat for Kossuth, who had always been able to count on the support of the police chief.*

Kossuth's reluctance to help the embattled radical politician strengthened the conviction of both the Left and the Right that he was malleable and weak. Kossuth, the god of the people, could not be overthrown; but he could perhaps be influenced. Thus, all through the winter and spring of 1849, the time-honored practice was continued of trying to win Kossuth over to one side or another. Kossuth remained the pivot on which all politics turned. In the spring of 1849, as we shall see, both the radicals and the Peace Party were to test their strength on Kossuth. Neither group was to have its way, but the failure of the radicals proved more conspicuous than that of the Peace Party.

Between January 9 and May 31 the Debrecen House of Representatives held fifty-eight open and fifteen closed meetings. During all that time the deputies failed to adopt a single measure of social or economic reform. The radicals pressed vociferously and unsuccessfully for a wider suffrage, the abolition of all titles, and complete po-

* After the war Madarász fled to the United States, where he lived as a farmer in Iowa until his death in 1909 at the age of ninety-eighty. Longevity seems to have been a family trait; his brother, the equally radical József Madarász, lived to be one hundred and one.

litical democracy; but they did not demand the suppression of the last remnants of feudal land rights, nor the distribution of land to the landless. And again it became clear that the radicals had no social or economic program. It was a leader of the Peace Party, István Bezerédy, who consistently proposed the only true reform measure: the introduction of a graduated tax system. The House turned him down with the argument that it would hit hard the "already overburdened landowning class."[10] As Szemere explained in one of his many replies to Bezerédy, what the embattled country needed was "taxes, not reform."

The parliament in Debrecen accomplished little—far less than the parliament in Pest, and infinitely less than the last Diet in Pressburg. Still, the Debrecen National Assembly was not useless, for it served as a political forum and as a sounding board for the government. More important, by merely sitting and debating, the Assembly legitimized the government. Power continued in the hands of the National Defense Committee, which faced the gravest issues: the massive defection of officers and officials and the continued withdrawal and near-rebellion of the army. Amazingly, the committee and its itinerant commissioners were able to meet the challenge.

A Handful of Determined Men

The presidents of the two Houses of parliament had not followed Kossuth to Debrecen. They had submitted to the enemy instead and had become active in the Imperial camp. Accordingly, lesser dignitaries opened and presided over parliament. If the legislative branch in Debrecen was thus quite wanting, the executive branch was even more so.

In the early days of January when desperate efforts were being made to evacuate the banknote press, the key documents, the equipment of the factories, the skilled workers, and the guns, relatively little attention was paid to the government officials. They had been asked to move to Debrecen, but, unlike the deputies, they had not been threatened with death or national disgrace if they opted to stay in Buda-Pest. The functionaries had always been a somewhat alien lot among the noble politicians. Batthyány, while prime minister, and subsequently the National Defense Committee had filled the higher echelons of the central administration with their own appointees; but most of the lower officials had come from the old Vice-Regal Council, the Royal Treasury, and the customs service. Even though Hungarian-speaking in their great majority, these secretaries and clerks bore the mark of their training in the Habsburg bureaucracy. As bureaucrats they were the very antithesis of the semiprofessional nobles who administered the counties and filled the ranks of the National Assembly and the National Defense Committee. The county nobility viewed the officials with suspicion, and indeed most government officials had decided to stay put in Buda-Pest and continue their labors under Windisch-Graetz. The number of ministerial employees who made it to Debrecen bordered on the ridiculous.[11] After all the stragglers had trickled in and new appointments had been made, Hungary's central administration totaled a few hundred persons.* This was not such a bad thing if we consider that there was no office space in any case and that the fifteen departments of the Ministry of War had to be crowded into the same number of rooms.[12] Furthermore, many government officials in Debrecen found that there was nothing for them to do—or rather, they would do nothing. The business of governing was shouldered by a small minority.

Overlapping authorities and lack of clarity about individual responsibilities confused matters. Ever since the resignation of the Batthyány cabinet there had been no prime minister, and (with one exception) there were no ministers either. Batthyány was in Austrian captivity; Széchenyi was insane; Deák and Klauzál had withdrawn from public life; Prince Pál Esterházy was with the enemy; and Eötvös had fled abroad. Szemere had never resigned from his post as minister of the interior, but he was now a government plenipotentiary in northern Hungary. Kossuth had long left the Ministry of Finance to preside over the National Defense Committee. Only Mészáros continued as minister of war, except for the times when he was heading some invariably unsuccessful military campaign. The other ministries were headed by "state secretaries," that is, by deputy ministers once

---

* Thirty-one persons—attendants and messengers included—worked in the offices of the National Defense Committee. The Ministry of War employed 90 civilians, the Ministry of Finance 41 persons and the Postal Service and Police 73. The latter was not a ministry but a new, separate part of the Ministry of the Interior. The Ministry of the Interior proper and the other ministries had to be satisfied with about a dozen functionaries each.

appointed by Batthyány. The power and influence of the state secretaries varied a good deal, depending on whether or not they had Kossuth's ear.

The National Defense Committee continued as a collegial body despite Kossuth's repeated efforts to divide the tasks and to form a cabinet. Pál Nyáry acted as his deputy, while Count Mihály Esterházy developed great expertise in armament matters. Some other members continued to do nothing. Two members of the committee, Mészáros and László Madarász, headed ministries of their own, although only one of these, the Ministry of War under Mészáros, bore the title of ministry. But while Mészáros had only limited influence on military matters, Madarász exercised almost absolute authority over the postal service and the police until his resignation in April 1849 and the reincorporation of his office into the Ministry of the Interior. General Mészáros complained incessantly of being slighted by his colleagues and of encroachments upon his jurisdiction, yet he insisted on submitting the pettiest matter to Kossuth for a decision. (At one point he asked for Kossuth's permission to rent a room for the central military pharmacy.) Mészáros protested repeatedly against the generals' practice of commissioning and promoting officers without previous consultation with the Ministry of War, and Kossuth strongly defended the minister's right to control such matters. But Kossuth himself constantly promoted officers without consulting Mészáros. Kossuth delegated government plenipotentiaries to the army, issued large sums of money to the generals, and purchased arms either on his own initiative or on the advice of his own military cabinet. He kept a finger on the pulse of the army, and he was better informed on the morale, the whereabouts and the movement of the troops than the Ministry of War. Kossuth complained that the Ministry of War was not taking care of routine problems, yet he and his secretaries were constantly busying themselves with even the minutest military matters.

Confusion does not necessarily run counter to effective revolutionary government. The Jacobins of 1793–94, after they had put an end to the extreme decentralization practiced by their Girondist predecessors, engaged in a fierce power struggle within the new centralized administration. The National Convention, the Committee of Public Safety, the Committee of General Security, the Commune of Paris, the several political clubs—all claimed absolute authority and disputed the absolute authority of the others. It was precisely this confusion, the many overlapping responsibilities, and the threat of the guillotine that drove the French revolutionary committees to feverish and efficient activity. The harrassed and fearful Jacobin officials and generals accomplished miracles. It is perhaps because in Hungary there was somewhat less administrative confusion and almost no revolutionary terror that so many administrators became careless and lazy and so many generals rebellious. In revolutionary France no one, not even Robespierre, was allowed to establish a one-man rule; in Hungary the politicians permitted, nay they forced, Kossuth to govern. They wished to guide, not to replace Kossuth. As a result, all major decisions fell on the shoulders of this energetic but somewhat weak and irresolute leader.

In the winter and spring of 1849 the central authority of Hungary was Kossuth. He was assisted by a few dozen advisors and secretaries, but the bulk of the work had to be done by him. Of course, Hungary was smaller than France, its population less numerous, its economy more primitive, and its administrative structure simpler. But if we consider that the Hungarian army in the field approached 200,000 while revolutionary France (with a population almost three times that of Hungary) had about 500,000 men under arms in September 1793, and if we add to this the fact that Hungary produced about 500 muskets a day, which was equal to the French daily production in 1793,[13] then we cannot but admire Kossuth's achievement.

On an ordinary day, the president of the National Defense Committee received and replied to between thirty and forty communications. They ranged from lengthy and often heavily documented reports by government plenipotentiaries, generals, or county administrators to individual supplications, suggestions, or denunciations. Even though Kossuth's secretaries routinely prepared the material for the eyes of the president with brief summaries and background information, Kossuth read practically every item. He also drafted most of the replies and decisions, either through dictation or in his own hand. Thousands of documents bear his handwritten remarks, queries, or corrections.

The atmosphere of Kossuth's cabinet was formal and rather impersonal. Kossuth, his colleagues, and his secretaries usually communicated with one another in writing; and the documents betray almost no trace of levity, sarcasm, or individual sentiment. Only once did an unknown hand pen on the hair-raising financial request of a general: "He must have gone mad." All issues were handled with equal seriousness and efficiency. The documents were then registered and filed away with the customary precision of the Austrian-trained bureaucracy. Indeed, as explained in the Introduction, the papers of the National Defense Committee would be complete today had the Austrian police not removed a number of documents following the War of Independence.

The National Defense Committee would have been powerless without the traveling government commissioners. Curiously, these men, who for the most part had grown up in the world of liberal oppositional county politics, proved to be generally more disciplined than the officers, who had been trained in the harsh routine of the Habsburg army. Yet the responsibilities and functions of these civilian agents were less clearly defined than those of the generals.

The system of government commissioners harked back to tradition. Batthyány had revived it, and the number appointed had grown enormously under the National Defense Committee. By the end of 1848 the committee had appointed some eighty commissioners, and the system was to expand until a reaction set in and the institution was partly suppressed late in the spring of 1849.[14] The commissioners performed a variety of functions. Some were called government plenipotentiaries and exercised absolute authority over large sections of the country, others were in charge of individual counties or were assigned to army units, while still others had to provision the army or were sent out on special missions. The authority and functions of the commissioners often overlapped, which led to numerous clashes. Some commissioners, such as Szemere, Count Kázmér Batthyány, or László Csányi, were diligent, reliable, talented, and highly efficient; others were petty tyrants or incapable cowards. As a whole, the commissioners were invaluable; there was no day when Kossuth did not receive reports from a number of commissioners and when he did not send them instructions. He appointed and controlled the commissioners; he alone knew of their whereabouts; he arbitrated between their internal disagreements; and he acted as a buffer between them and the generals. The commissioners were all Kossuth's men, whether they belonged to the liberal or the radical parliamentary factions, and through them, Kossuth controlled the country.[15]

By the nature of their functions and the circumstances of their appointment, the Hungarian commissioners closely resembled the Jacobin *représentants en mission*. Both enforced the will of the central revolutionary authority; both mobilized the population, secured the fortresses, and organized and politically supervised the army. They combated counterrevolutionary activity and exhorted the soldiers to fight the foreign invaders. The French and Hungarian commissioners were the sine qua non of the two revolutionary upheavals. But as the marxist writer József Révai has pointed out, there was also a fundamental difference between the two groups.[16] The Jacobin agents built their authority on the militant support of the local Jacobin clubs; the Hungarian revolution could lean on no such clubs. Consequently, the Hungarian commissioners had to rely on the assistance of the old county administrations and the local nobility from which they themselves had descended. Many a county lord-lieutenant became a government commissioner in his own county. The county administrations were experienced and powerful; they were also cumbersome, particularistic, and often unreliable. And of course the county administrations, as well as most of the government commissioners, mirrored the social views of the county nobility.

Government commissioners operated not only in the free areas but also in some Austrian-occupied counties. This war knew no front lines; large sectors in the rear of the Habsburg armies never saw an Austrian soldier. Goods, merchants, and the mail crossed from revolutionary Hungary into Habsburg Hungary, and so did the representatives of Kossuth. Commissioners recruited soldiers for the *honvéd* army or purchased food under the nose of the Austrian authorities; they also reported to Kossuth on the mood of the population in the Austrian-occupied territory.[17]

Since the commissioners had to rely on the support of the county administrations, it was essential to secure the loyalty of the counties. Kossuth sent the county officials an avalanche of exhortations and tried to keep in touch with them all, but this was not easy. In some counties the personnel had practically disbanded by January and new staffs had to be appointed. In others the old administrative machinery continued to function, and it remained loyal to the Debrecen government—but only until the arrival of the Austrian forces. It was a terrible blow to Kossuth, an unrelenting advocate of "municipalism," to realize that most counties were perfectly willing to bend with the wind. Back in the days of Jelačić's invasion, the counties had adopted heroic decisions to arm against "the wild herds of Croatian bandits." Yet in reality, wherever the Croats had passed, the counties had submitted: the local officials had bought with food and fodder the lives of the inhabitants as well as their own.

This pragmatic behavior characterized most counties all through the War of Independence, casting a strange light on the patriotism of the lesser nobility. These deputy lord-lieutenants, clerks, county attorneys, treasurers, auditors, jurymen, and police commissioners before the revolution had been the most vocal advocates of Hungarian liberties. Now they often acted not as representatives of a free nobility but as bureaucrats ready to serve anyone powerful enough to command obedience. It was common practice for the counties to deliver to the arriving Austrians the food and the recruits originally gathered for the *honvéd* army. It was also common to send food and fodder to, and expect payment from, both armies.[18]

Again as in prerevolutionary times, the counties tended to follow the example set by Pest, the "head county." Pest, which in 1847 had elected Kossuth and had led the liberal opposition to Metternich's system, in January 1849 joyously submitted to Windisch-Graetz. Its officials worked diligently for the emperor. Kossuth was mortified by the abject behavior of his own county and he tried to encourage domestic resistance to the traitors. As a result of his efforts, the district of Solt, which was under only nominal Austrian military control, practically seceded from Pest county, organizing a local national committee and setting up a free corps to support the *honvéd* army.[19]

No task was more important for a government commissioner, or for the county officials, than the recruitment of soldiers. Volunteers had to be found; and if enough volunteers were not forthcoming, conscription was the alternative. No generalization is possible with regard to the fighting spirit of the population in the winter of 1848–49. Certainly, manpower was not lacking, nor did the officials lack experience in conscripting and recruiting. In some areas there were still more than enough volunteers; in others, conscription itself failed. A few counties found the ratio of two recruits for every 127 inhabitants excessive; others complained that the recruiters had exceeded the prescribed ratio. Conscription in the Romanian- and Serbian-inhabited counties continued to be almost impossible.[20] Because of the emergency, the authorities were not choosy: military and political convicts were accepted into service, and prisoners of war were forced into the *honvéd* if they belonged to regiments originating in Hungary. For example, Kossuth approved the impressment of eight officers and 200 enlisted men from the Second Romanian Border Guard Regiment, captured by Bem during the reconquest of Kolozsvár. The Romanians were distributed among reliable units.[21]

Kossuth did not underestimate the importance of the standing army, but he continued to insist on the creation of a vast people's auxiliary army equipped with scythes and pitchforks. On December 16 he issued a general order for a great mass insurgency. The new people's army was to be organized by counties and was to engage in guerrilla action in the enemy's rear. The best of the insurgents were to form mobile free corps units; unlike the people's army, these were to be paid by the government. The free corps were allowed to keep their booty and were to be independent of both the minister of war and the regular army command, with the sole obligation of reporting periodically to the National Defense Committee.[22]

It does not seem that the *levée en masse* was a success. There arose some guerrilla activity in the rear of the Austrian troops in Transdanubia; but in general the December *levée* was a failure, as it had been in October 1848 and as it was to be again early in the summer of 1849. Neither the country's physical geography nor Hungarian peasant tradition encouraged guerrilla activity, and it compared badly with the activity of the Romanian insurgents in the Transylvanian mountains, in the rear of Bem's army.

The free corps was more of a working reality. Led by petty landowners, younger county officials, or radical intellectuals, the free corps or *Jäger* companies were active in many parts of the country. Some operated in the enemy's rear; others fought against the Romanian or Serbian guerrillas. The free corps annoyed and weakened the enemy, but they also wasted weapons and money and were guilty of atrocities. Furthermore, the free corps hampered regular Hungarian military operations through their irresponsibility and insubordination. Mészáros and the other generals hated the free corps. What good had it done to disband one by one all the National Guard battalions if Kossuth was returning them through the back door in the form of free corps companies? Mészáros, usually so complacent, conducted a regular campaign for the suppression of the free corps, or at least for their subordination to the Ministry of War. At the end of February he called on the commander of the largest free corps unit to obey the orders of the commander-in-chief of the army or go to prison. Szemere, who himself had set up free corps units in the past, came around to the view that they were a waste of money and energy. Kossuth, who in December had still been dreaming of 10,000 organized guerrillas in Transdanubia alone, reluctantly accepted the reasoning of his military experts. Early in March 1849 he placed the free corps operationally under the minister of war and forbade them to recruit from the regular *honvéd*. Subsequently, the National Defense Committee ordered the gradual incorporation of the free corps into the army and, finally, all the county-based free corps were disbanded.[23] Only two privately organized companies remained, and they came to a sorry end in the hands of armed Romanian peasants.

The flight from Buda-Pest had inevitably aggravated the problem of military logistics. Unoccupied Hungary had very little industry, least of all any weapons factories; and arms production had to be based on the manpower and the machines evacuated from Buda-Pest. The National Defense Committee named Nagyvárad, a city southeast of Debrecen, as the center of military industry and put two expert officers and a civilian specialist in charge of the affair.

The peasant carts transporting the machines and equipment from Pest began to arrive in Nagyvárad on January 14, but they found the old fortress where the factory was to be set up unprepared for their reception. While future workshops were being emptied and cleaned, the machines were dumped into the courtyard snow. There was almost no help, no money, and no armed guards to protect the valuable equipment when the peasant carters left. The gunpowder and the cartridges, brought in another caravan, arrived with considerable delay. In Pest it had taken five months to get the weapons factory started; now twelve days were granted for the same thing to be accomplished in Nagyvárad.[24] Production began at the end of January; by then a whole month had passed before Hungary began turning out arms again.

The skilled workers brought over from Buda-Pest proved to be a problem: prices were high in the refugee town and the workers—not so much the Germans among them as the Hungarians—insisted on better pay. Kossuth authorized higher wages but demanded discipline and threatened the rebellious workers with court martial. When the civilian factory director dismissed a do-nothing smith, the others struck and intimidated the potential strikebreakers. Kossuth showed little admiration for the growing trade-union consciousness of the workers; he took further measures to improve living conditions, but he also supported all disciplinary actions proposed by the factory director.[25]

Somehow order was restored despite the lack of military discipline in Nagyvárad, and by mid-February production was up to Buda-Pest standards.[26] Soon new factories sprang up in Nagyvárad and elsewhere. Musket barrels were produced in great quantities but there was a great shortage of seasoned wood necessary for the making of musket stocks. Bayonets remained in short supply as did iron ramrods, but there were plenty of old cannon to be repaired and refashioned. The casting of swords was delayed by the shortage of steel, but silver plumb for bullets was found in the cellar of the county hall in Nagyvárad. To supply paper for making wads to keep the powder in place, Kossuth had to order the requisitioning of the "old useless protocols" in the county archives. Monsieur Château and his aides prepared 50,000 cartridges and 30,000 percussion caps a day, but the factory directorate was so suspicious of the Czech gunners of the Fifth Imperial-Royal Artillery Regiment who were employed in that process that (at least for a while) it posted a Hungarian artilleryman next to each Czech soldier. Clothes and shoes continued to be manufactured, mainly by artisans, all over free Hungary; and the National Defense Committee regularly received and accepted offers from merchants in Austrian-occupied Hungary.

The committee and the Ministry of War continued to provide for the care of the sick and wounded. Hospitals were set up in several towns of eastern Hungary. In a single week in May over 12,000 soldiers—close to 10 percent of the men in arms—received some kind of hospital care.[27] The gentle ladies of Hungary made bandages; drugs were manufactured in sufficient quantity; food was abundant as usual; only in the spring did some commissioners mention local shortages of wheat and flour. Thus the country continued to provide for the army; the latter, however, was still far from having overcome its own crisis.

Rebels, Renegades, and an Old Field Marshal

In January Lord Ponsonby reported to London: "It is clear that the resistance of the insurgents in the flat open country from Debreczin to Szegedin, can be of no very long duration, more particularly as the fortresses of Arad and Temeswar are in the possession of the Imperial troops." [28] The ambassador's judgment was logical although wrong, as usual; for, aside from the Tisza River and its marshes, nothing—not even a single fortress—protected the area that the National Defense Committee could call its own. Only General Bem was well ensconced in mountainous Transylvania. Moreover, the committee had very few troops.

Back on January 1, Kossuth had ordered Görgey to fight a "decisive battle" west of Buda without, however, jeopardizing the chances for the army's orderly withdrawal across the Danube and without endangering the physical safety of Buda-Pest. This supremely contradictory order was typical of Kossuth: now, whatever Görgey did, whether he fought and died or withdrew and evacuated the area, the responsibility for either disaster would be the general's alone. Görgey refused to engage in the big battle; instead, he used the chance given him by the president to make his army independent of the National Defense Committee. On January 2 a council of war was held in Buda-Pest, under the chairmanship of government commissioner László Csányi. The generals present were seething with anger, for they believed, not unjustly, that Kossuth had fled from the capital far too early and that they had been left with an impossible military situation. At Görgey's recommendation, the council of war accepted a plan developed by a young ex-Imperial-Royal lieutenant, Colonel (later General) György Klapka: a plan providing for the abandonment of the capital without a battle and the evacuation of the entire central region between the Danube and the Tisza rivers, as well as of southern Hungary. General Perczel was put in charge of the main defense line, which was to run along the middle and lower Tisza. His ridiculously small force of 10,000, composed partly of raw recruits, was to be reinforced by the two relatively strong army corps that had been operating against the Serbs in southern Hungary—if these corps could arrive in time to do any good. The best Hungarian unit, Görgey's original Army of the Upper Danube, was ordered to move away from and not toward the main defense line along the Tisza. He was to march from Buda-Pest in a northwesterly direction to campaign north of the Danube against the comparatively weak expeditionary force of the Austrian General Simunich. With Simunich defeated, Görgey was to secure the vital mining towns in northern Hungary.[29]

The strange decision regarding Görgey's army was the essence of the plan. It was a bold military decision and it would prove a wise one, but it was also a political measure. By moving away from the main front in the East and from the vicinity of Debrecen, Görgey became his own master and was able to keep his army intact for possible negotiations with the enemy. But negotiations could not be started as long as Görgey's army was falling apart, which is precisely what it seemed to be doing in those days because of the massive desertion of his officers. This, Görgey had to stop; and he accomplished it efficiently although, from Kossuth's point of view, most unsatisfactorily.

All through December and early January scores of his officers deserted Görgey and went over to the enemy, among them almost the entire officers' corps of the 10th Wilhelm Hussar Regiment. As one of the Wilhelms' officers explained to the general, they had sworn among themselves to "fight for the honor of the country, the regiment and their own name, but only until the retreating army reached the banks of the Danube." Now the game was over and their honor vindicated.[30]*

Fearing the eventual disappearance of all his officers and filled with contempt and hatred for Kossuth, Görgey resorted to a drastic measure. On January 5 at Vác north of Pest, the general issued a manifesto on the political position and the aims of his army. This famous Vác Proclamation, the first publicly aired compilation of the grievances of Hungary's moderate revolutionaries and of the soldiers, asserted that the "Royal Army of the Upper Danube" had always fought in accordance with its duty to His Majesty. The Proclamation attacked the National Defense Committee for its disastrous interference with the conduct of the war, its contradictory orders, and its hypocrisy with regard to the defense of Buda-Pest. The Proclamation affirmed that the Army of the Upper Danube would never become the military arm of a political party, but would remain loyal to the constitution sanctioned by the king, and to the principle of constitutional

* The rank and file of the Wilhelms did not submit alongside their commanders; they marched away from Buda-Pest in Görgey's host, under the command of four junior officers.

monarchy. The Proclamation insisted that the army would obey solely the orders of the "responsible Royal Hungarian Minister of War" or his deputy appointed by the minister himself (which meant that the army would not obey Kossuth and the National Defense Committee); it threatened to suppress "any kind of foolish republican agitation," and finally it made clear that the Army of the Upper Danube would accept a compromise with the enemy, but only if this compromise guaranteed Hungary's constitution and the honor of the army.[31]

Görgey's Vác manifesto saved his corps from dissolution, but it threw the gauntlet at the feet of the National Defense Committee. Back in Buda-Pest Kossuth had wished that, in case of a withdrawal, Görgey and Perczel jointly assure the defense of the Tisza line. The war council had decided otherwise; understandably, Kossuth interpreted the decision as the first step in the direction of a military rebellion. Why had Görgey chosen to march into northern Hungary, if not to leave Debrecen unprotected? Why the Vác Proclamation if not to make clear to those who would listen that Görgey was ready to surrender to the enemy independently of the committee but with the trump card of a battle-ready army in his hands? A few days after the Proclamation, Kossuth sent a bitter letter to Görgey refuting the latter's accusations, point by point. Somewhat later, Kossuth wrote to Szemere: "Görgey has come close to being a traitor—unless he is already a traitor."[32]

Kossuth, who had personally guaranteed to the National Assembly Görgey's absolute loyalty and dedication, now wished to get rid of the general and bring his army back to the main battlefront. But how was this to be done? Kossuth could not enforce his will on Görgey; he did not even quite know where Görgey had gone.

A second-best solution was to attempt to control Görgey. Unfortunately for the National Defense Committee, László Csányi, a friend of both Kossuth and Görgey, was no longer with the Army of the Upper Danube. He was on his way to Transylvania as government plenipotentiary. Kossuth sent two younger members of the House of Representatives, a liberal and a radical, as government commissioners to Görgey's camp. They could be counted on to report the general's every move, but they had neither the authorization nor the physical power to remove Görgey. Presently, they would also lack the will to do such a thing, for they fell under the general's magic sway.

Kossuth had misunderstood the Vác Proclamation, for Görgey had no intention of deserting. When, at the end of January, Windisch-Graetz sent an adjutant to Görgey's headquarters with an offer of immunity to the general and a request for the unconditional surrender of his army, Görgey simply handed over to the adjutant a copy of the Vác Proclamation. Görgey was ready to negotiate with the Austrians but not to surrender. Yet Kossuth was correct in interpreting the Proclamation as a political move against civilian authority.[33]

Kossuth was not alone in discovering the oppositional politician in Görgey. The Peace Party began to sense a man to their liking in the formerly much-feared radical, with whom plans could eventually be coordinated. In reality, the coordination would never materialize, for Görgey insisted on treating the Peace Party as yet another bunch of loud-mouthed civilians, while the Peace Party feared in him a would-be Bonaparte.

In January the military situation went from bad to worse. Two days after the war council meeting in Buda-Pest, the Hungarians suffered an unexpected blow. The council had not reckoned with the inability of the northern Hungarian army, a motley force led by Mészáros, to stop General Schlick. On January 4 Schlick, who had entered Hungary from Galicia, soundly defeated the minister of war near the city of Kassa. The Hungarians scattered in retreat, and the road was open for the able Schlick to march on Debrecen across the northern course of the Tisza.

This, then, was the military situation early in January. Both Windisch-Graetz and Schlick were in an excellent position to take Debrecen; the Austro-Serbian army was about to move north in the footsteps of the two withdrawing Hungarian army corps; the Tisza line was defended by extremely weak forces; and Görgey was gone. He and his corps were to disappear in northern Hungary, so that for several weeks no one in Debrecen would know Görgey's whereabouts.

Lázár Mészáros affirmed in his memoirs that a few regiments of Austrian cavalry and a handful of infantry battalions could have occupied Debrecen at that time.[34] Both the Buda-Pest council of war and Kossuth had reckoned with this possibility, and they envisaged continuing resistance in Transylvania under General Bem. This would at best only have prolonged the war. Perczel himself was so painfully aware of the weakness of his position that in mid-January he spontaneously abandoned the Tisza line and fell back in the direction of Debrecen.

Then, in the second half of January, the predictions of Görgey and Klapka were proven right. They knew Windisch-Graetz and his underlings too well to believe that the Austrian army would make haste to strike a decisive blow. In those crucial weeks neither the field marshal nor Schlick made a move. In January 1849 the Habsburg army lost a supreme opportunity to win the war.

Austrian military historians have generally been most critical of Prince Windisch-Graetz. Still, in their effort to understand the prince's failure they have pleaded such causes as the exhaustion of the troops and their extreme dispersion; the shortage of supplies; the need to surround the great fortress of Komárom and to guard the occupied cities; and the impossibility of obtaining reliable information about the disposition of the Hungarian troops. All this was true; for example, Windisch-Graetz was greatly hampered by the lack of light cavalry needed for reconnoitering. His troops also suffered from the peasants' hostility in the Danube-Tisza region.[35] But the Hungarians were troubled by many of the same ills, and to a far greater degree. They had plenty of light cavalry but they, too, were forced to expend soldiers fruitlessly on the siege of two fortresses, Arad and Temesvár; they had been defeated repeatedly in the recent past, and for several weeks to come they had fewer soldiers and weapons.

Windisch-Graetz had fallen into the trap set by the Hungarians. He had dispatched an entire army corps to pursue Görgey, fearing that the Hungarian leader would not only overwhelm Simunich but would also threaten Vienna. Windisch-Graetz's overestimation of the danger represented by Görgey's army of 15,000 was matched by the field marshal's simultaneous underestimation of Hungary's will to continue the war. Following the occupation of Buda-Pest and the unopposed advance of his cavalry detachments to the Tisza, Windisch-Graetz had judged the war practically over. Having reported in this vein to the young emperor, he turned his attention to the political and moral reconstruction of Hungary.

The inactivity of Windisch-Graetz and Schlick gave the Hungarians a brief breathing space from which they profited instantly. Suddenly aware of the Austrians' immobility, Perczel turned around. Recrossing the Tisza, he entered the Danube-Tisza region toward the end of January. He was forced to withdraw quickly; but with his move the Hungarians had regained the initiative, which they were not to cede for another five months. At the news of Perczel's unexpected advance, Windisch-Graetz underwent a sudden change of heart. He who had been so confident a few weeks earlier, now began to worry and fired off pessimistic reports to the emperor.

In the north, where Schlick had finally decided to advance, he was stopped by the hastily assembled forces of Colonel Klapka. Schlick was not only unable to march on Debrecen, he was caught between Klapka attacking from the south and Görgey advancing from the west. The latter had mysteriously appeared from the mountains of northern Hungary and was now threatening the rear of Schlick's forces.

Görgey's northern Hungarian odyssey belongs in a military history, which this account does not wish to be. It is enough to say that Görgey had soon given up his plan to defeat Simunich; he led his army instead into the high mountains of Upper Hungary, where he secured the cash and the mints of the gold- and silver-mining towns. This done, he ordered a long rest for his troops, all the while without troubling to notify the National Defense Committee or even the minister of war. "We had ordered Görgey three successive times," Kossuth wrote to Szemere on January 21, "to bring back his army and to lead one part of it to Kassa [where General Schlick was installed] but we have not even received a reply. With this man the nation will have a heavy account to settle one day, unless he surprises us with an unexpected great victory as a result of his obscure adventure."[36]

Görgey soon provided this unexpected victory. Finally acceding to Mészáros's insistent demands, he turned eastward and on February 5 broke through the fiercely defended mountain positions of the Austrians at Branyiszkó. The breakthrough was the work of the Englishman Richard Guyon, one of Görgey's divisional commanders, but the plan had been Görgey's own. He who had been between two fires in the preceding weeks, now threatened to overwhelm General Schlick's forces from the rear. Schlick had to decamp in haste; he evacuated northeastern Hungary and joined Windisch-Graetz's main army not far from Buda-Pest. A few days later Görgey reached Klapka's army corps, and the stage was set for a Hungarian counteroffensive.

Görgey's winter campaign, conducted under extremely harsh conditions, was justly considered a strategic masterpiece by contemporaries. That passionate military amateur, Friedrich Engels, called Görgey and Bem "the most gifted commanders of our time." This is how Engels described Görgey's adventure:

Görgey at the same time [as Bem in Transylvania] made a similar triumphal march in North-eastern Hungary. He set out with a corps from Pest to Slovakia, for two months kept in check the corps of Generals Götz, Csorich and Simunich operating against him from three directions, and finally, when his position became untenable against their superior forces, fought his way through the Carpathians to Eperies and Kaschau. There he appeared in the rear of Schlick and forced him hurriedly to abandon his position and his whole operational base and retreat to Windischgrätz's main army, while he himself was already marching down the Hernád to the Theiss [Tisza] to join the main body of the Hungarian army.[37]

Instead of taking revenge on Görgey, Kossuth now congratulated the hero. Never would Kossuth be able to solve the dilemma Görgey presented. The nation admired not only Kossuth but also Görgey; and the great majority of the officers were unconditionally devoted to the general. Perhaps Kossuth should have attempted to get rid of Görgey with the help of the few officers hostile to him. Yet the politics of coups, of arbitrary arrests and assassinations, was completely alien to Kossuth. And since this was the case, it would have been better to let Görgey assume supreme command and to conduct the war in his own way. For that, however, Görgey's politics were far too unreliable and dangerous to Kossuth's thinking.

Ultimately, Kossuth kept Görgey as a general but refused to make him commander-in-chief. It was the least satisfactory solution; it left Kossuth with a permanently dissatisfied general and with a persistent crisis in the supreme military leadership.

Görgey was still lost in the snowy reaches of Upper Hungary when Kossuth at last decided to give the Hungarian armies a permanent structure. He appointed a chief of staff to the *honvéd* and he divided the entire force into eight army corps.* Görgey's force thus

---

* The first was under Klapka and was to operate on the upper reaches of the Tisza; the second under Perczel was to assemble on the middle course of the same river; the two former army corps of the south were to gather near Szolnok, also on the Tisza, as the third and fourth corps of Hungary. The third was led by General Count Károly Vécsey, and later by the most able General János Damjanich. The fourth was commanded by Count Gusztáv Hadik. A fifth corps under Miklós Gaál was besieging the fortress of Arad. General Bem's Transylvanian army was called the sixth corps, and Görgey's former Army of the Upper Danube was the seventh. The garrison of Komárom was considered the eighth army corps.

became one of the eight corps and Görgey one of the eight corps commanders. On January 29 Kossuth appointed the Polish general Dembiński commander-in-chief of the several army corps, including Görgey's, assembling along the Tisza. In addition, Dembiński was made a two-star general, which meant he now outranked the Hungarian generals.[38]

Count Henryk Dembiński had come to Hungary with an extraordinary reputation. Educated in the Vienna Engineering Academy, he fought in the army of the Polish Grand Duchy created by Napoleon. After the battle of Smolensk the French emperor made him a captain; he earned the Cross of the Legion of Honor at the battle of Leipzig. Following the Napoleonic wars he lived on his father's estates in Poland, and in 1831 he joined the Polish revolution. He became a general and acted as the governor of Warsaw as well as generalissimo of the Polish army. After the Polish revolution he went into exile, and in 1833 he organized the troops of Mehemet Ali in Syria. Late in 1848 he was approached by Count László Teleki, Kossuth's delegate in Paris. Dembiński accepted Teleki's offer of an important appointment and by mid-January he was in Debrecen.[39]

Kossuth's choice of Dembiński as the leader of the planned Hungarian counteroffensive was understandable in view of the tremendous international reputation enjoyed by Polish emigré officers. The Poles were the heroes and the great strategists of the first half of the nineteenth century; no self-respecting revolution could be without a Polish commander. In truth, the Polish officers were free, available, eager to serve, and brave; they were the *condottieri* of the Romantic Age, fired on by a great idea: the liberation of Poland. And through the liberation of Poland, these revolutionaries also hoped to liberate humanity.

The choice of Dembiński was understandable, but it was a very bad choice. Now that the main Hungarian army and that of Transylvania (adjacent to Russian-occupied Moldavia) were commanded by Polish revolutionaries, the Habsburg propagandists made the most of it. They had an easy time persuading the world, especially Russia, that Hungary was fighting a war not of self-defense but of international revolution. Furthermore, the Hungarian nobles did not take kindly to the Polish nobles, in whom they recognized their own weaknesses: excessive pride and an inclination to intrigues, quarrels, and factional politics. Dembiński's appointment was a blow to all those in Hungary who still insisted on seeing themselves as faithful children of His Majesty and who felt that the war was an internal quarrel among the peoples of the Monarchy. Bem could be tolerated because he was the first Pole to assume an important command and because Bem had charisma. The fifty-five-year-old Bem was called "Father Bem" by his soldiers; the fifty-eight-year-old Dembiński was referred to as the "old fool." Dembiński was the enemy planted in the midst of the *honvéd* by the Debrecen civilians. A fool Dembiński was not; but he was conceited, dull, sensitive, and quarrelsome. Faced by a most delicate situation, he managed to alienate everyone, even Kossuth.

Görgey did not hesitate to react openly to Dembiński's appointment. Before his corps arrived on the Tisza line, he issued a manifesto to his soldiers: "I solemnly ask all senior and subaltern officers under my command to accept this apparent humiliation [the appointment of Dembiński] with the same indifference that leads me, the corps commander, . . . to place myself voluntarily under the orders of General Dembiński who, we are told, is an honorable commander, grown old in wars."[40]

Görgey was not satisfied with sarcasm. He meant to overthrow Dembiński and assume command in reality if not in name of the Hungarian offensive at the first opportunity. But before engaging in this story, we must first glance at the Austrian-held parts of Hungary. The events there, somewhat neglected in Hungarian historiography, were at least as important for later Hungarian and Central European developments as were the events in free Hungary.

The Other Hungary

Military occupation under Prince Windisch-Graetz was not particularly severe. Some highly compromised politicians, such as Batthyány, were brought to trial, as were a number of local officials, journalists, poets, and clergymen. A handful of Kossuth's followers were executed for acts perpetrated against the Austrian army. Rebel cities were heavily ransomed, as well as many Jewish communities accused of having lined up behind Kossuth. Food was requisitioned for the army of occupation and paid for in Hungarian currency of unstable value and dubious future. Unreliable functionaries were dismissed and the estates of the "rebel leaders" (*Insurgentenführer*) were seized, but there were no mass arrests and scores of rebel politicians were let go after signing a formal submission. The vast majority of the population was not penalized; many peasants were probably unaware that they had changed masters. After all (to bring up a point which must be made again), Windisch-Graetz's soldiers did not look very different from Kossuth's. Some of the Austrian officers were in reality Hungarians, and, most important, the Austrian authorities invoked the name of the king as often as Kossuth's generals.

Windisch-Graetz was anxious to restore prerevolutionary Hungary and to preserve its political integrity as far as possible. A central civilian commission that he appointed as an eventual replacement for the military government resembled in its structure and personnel the old Hungarian-dominated Vice-Regal Council. Transylvania, Croatia, and the Military Border were treated as separate bodies, but they had been separate before 1848 as well. The prince was most unenthusiastic about the Vojvodina, the new autonomous territory that the Austro-Serbian forces had set up in southern Hungary, but he could no longer prevent its formation. On December 15, 1848, Francis Joseph had solemnly promised the Serbs a national self-government.[41]

If it had been left to Windisch-Graetz, Hungary would have emerged from the war with the same administrative set-up it had had before 1848. Like Kossuth, the field marshal wished to preserve the counties, and he appointed a Hungarian Royal commissioner to head each county. Fortunately for the inhabitants, Kossuth's commissioners were no longer called "Royal" but "governmental"; consequently the politically educated were able to distinguish Kossuth's plenipotentiaries from those of Windisch-Graetz. The Royal commissioners were temporarily placed under the regional Austrian military commanders but were required to report directly to the prince.

The field marshal had simple political ideas and goals. As he explained in his numerous missives to Schwarzenberg, all the Monarchy's troubles came from the reckless agitation of democratic journalists and lawyers who had challenged all sacred values. Kossuth & Company were not the only irresponsible demagogues, although they were momentarily the most dangerous because they had succeeded in perverting a great part of the nobility in their own country. He, Windisch-Graetz, had broken the back of the German and Czech democrats' drive; but there were other democrats left lording it over the Slovak. Serbian, and Wallachian peoples. For the time being, these democrats feared Kossuth more than they feared the Habsburg power, but sooner or later they would make common cause with the Hungarian agitators. Therefore, the democrats must be suppressed everywhere.

Since the aristocrats were the democrats' natural enemies, Windisch-Graetz argued, it was essential to strengthen the aristocracy—even in Hungary, although far too many nobles there were blind enough to fight against their own interests. A hereditary aristocracy was unthinkable without the continued existence of the Monarchy's historic provinces: hence Windisch-Graetz's decision to preserve Hungary and to oppose such wild projects as an all-Imperial representative parliament, so dear to the heart of Windisch-Graetz's political rival, Count Franz Stadion.

The prince was grudgingly ready to grant recognition to the Serbian nation because the Serbs could at least refer to a tradition of religious self-government. He absolutely refused to recognize the existence of the Slovak people, who had no such tradition. He warned against the pernicious influence of Štúr, Hurban, Hodža, and other Slovak Lutheran ministers who paraded as His Majesty's loyal subjects but in the Prince's eyes were terrorists and communists.[42]

The field marshal heartily disliked and persecuted political and cultural coteries, the free press, and the institution of the National Guards. He was outraged when he heard that the Austrian commander in Bukovina planned to call for a *levée en masse* to oppose a threatened invasion from Transylvania by General Bem's Hungarian troops. The prince declared the National Guards and the *Landsturm* (people's insurrection) militarily useless and politically (as well as socially) dangerous, a view with which Görgey would have heartily agreed.[43]

Windisch-Graetz was wise enough not to want to undo the agrarian reform laws of the Hungarian parliament, because they had already been put into effect. On the other hand, he reintroduced the tithe levied on vineyards because the Hungarian National Assembly's earlier decision on that matter had not yet been implemented. The prince ordered that the Hungarian nobles be taxed, but warned his commissioners to be most cautious so as not to ruin the landowners. Out of respect for the territorial integrity of Hungary, he refused to

draw the boundaries of the Austrian military commands along na-
tional-linguistic lines, as had been suggested by the Court. But Windisch-Graetz granted the non-Magyar nationalities linguistic freedom
in the schools and in local administration. He preserved Hungarian as
the official language of the county administrations but allowed the
citizens to address the county authorities in their own vernacular and
obliged the officials to reply in the same language. All communications between the county commissioners and the free cities on
the one hand, and the Imperial Court as well as the Austrian government on the other, were to be in German.

The concessions Windisch-Graetz made to the linguistic aspirations of the nationalities aggravated many a loyal, conservative Hungarian; yet they were not enough to satisfy the political leaders of the
nationalities. The prince knew that the linguistic confusion in
Hungary permitted no judicious solution. He repeatedly pointed out
to the liberal reformers in the Court that while it was easy to promise
self-government to such a national group as the Serbs, it was almost
impossible to draw fair and reasonable boundaries for their autonomous territory. In truth, the Serbs were fighting among themselves as well as with their neighbors. The conservative wing of the
Serbian national movement, under the Patriarch Rajačić, waged an
extremely bitter political struggle against the liberal wing, led by the
new *vojvoda* Colonel Djordje Stratimirović (Colonel Supljikac had
died in December). At the same time, the Serbs clashed with *Feldmarschalleutnant* Baron Georg Rukavina, the commanding general in
Temesvár, over the territorial extent of the proposed Serbian autonomous region. The Croat Rukavina opposed the Serbs because he
feared for his own nation—and because he knew better than the politicians in Olmütz that the Serbs were Serbian nationalists first and
loyal Habsburg subjects after. Windisch-Graetz himself had protested
when he heard that the Serbian Border Guard had hoisted the tricolor
of the Belgrade Serbian Principality alongside the Imperial flag. The
prince was also made aware of the fact that the Serbs were a minority
in the region they demanded for themselves. If the Serbian demands
were granted (a conservative Hungarian official wrote to Windisch-
Graetz), then southern Hungary, "this granary of Austria and pearl of
the Monarchy would become a Serbian democracy." What, then (the
official asked), would become of the German colonists who had
turned southern Hungary into an agrarian paradise? In April Vienna

divided southern Hungary into two parts: the western part became the Serbian autonomous territory; the eastern part was left under the command of General Rukavina. In an arrangement closely resembling that which the peacemakers in Versailles painfully reached in 1919, the Germans and the Magyars, but not the Romanians of southern Hungary, were put under Serbian authority.[44]

The Vojvodina crisis again demonstrated that there were basically two types of officials in the Habsburg Monarchy: those who, like Windisch-Graetz, were too fearful of social and national upheavals to tamper with the historic inner boundaries and traditional social structure of the Monarchy; and those who, like Colonel Mayerhofer, consul general of Austria in Belgrade, dared to appeal to popular emotions to save and modernize the Monarchy. Windisch-Graetz and Mayerhofer had their counterparts in revolutionary Hungary, where Görgey and the Peace Party refused to stir up mischief by calling for a people's insurrection, while Kossuth or Bem did their best to foster such a movement. But while Kossuth's or Bem's appeals for a people's army backfired because there were always more anti-Hungarian than pro-Hungarian guerrillas, the appeals of men like Mayerhofer paid dividends. But the Mayerhofers also hastened the awakening of the nationalities and thus the ultimate dissolution of the Monarchy.

Scores of conservative Hungarians wrote to the prince on what had happened and what should be done in Hungary: these letters represent the first attempt to evaluate the causes and the consequences of the revolution, and to draw up plans for the future. The conservatives often contradicted one another, but they agreed in requesting harsher punishment for Hungary than that planned by the prince. Some Hungarian conservatives accused Windisch-Graetz outright of being soft on the revolutionaries. All conservatives insisted on a lengthy military dictatorship in Hungary. This was inspired by vengeance, but also by the realization that the new liberal and centralistic constitution being worked out in Olmütz threatened to incorporate Hungary into a united monarchy (*Gesamtmonarchie*). On the other hand, extended military rule would allow for the patient preparation of a conservative constitution guaranteeing aristocratic interests and the political integrity of Hungary.

One of the early and most diligent commentators was Count Emil Dessewffy, leader of the pre-March Conservative Party. Dessewffy, who began to write in October 1848, had addressed his early communications to Prince Schwarzenberg. Among other items, he prepared a long list of rebels to be punished or amnestied. He distinguished three basic categories of culprit ranging from those directly responsible for the revolution to mere fellow-travelers (*Mitläufer*). Dessewffy recommended the gallows for the first category, the threat of death with ultimate clemency for the second, and total amnesty for the third. Among those that Dessewffy wanted to see dead were Batthyány, Count László Teleki, Kossuth, General Perczel, László Madarász, Pál Nyáry, the radical journalist Albert Pálfi, the radical peasant Mihály Táncsics, the liberal Ödön Beöthy, the statistician Elek Fényes, as well as two other politicians who did not deserve such illustrious company.[45] The list was characteristic of the confusion on the Austrian side as to who was truly important and militant on the Hungarian side. It is because of such confusion that moderates like Batthyány would later be executed, along with some genuine revolutionaries.

Dessewffy had a low opinion of his own estate. He called the Hungarian aristocrats morally bankrupt, incorrigible, and rebellious by heredity. He asked for a permanent army of occupation of 65,000 to 75,000 men not only to control the nobles, but also to save them from the wrath of the peasants. As for the Catholic high clergy, Dessewffy called them traitors, especially Archbishop János Hám of Esztergom. It was a mistaken judgment, for while it is true that Hám and the other bishops had supported Batthyány's government, by January 1849 all the bishops had publicly submitted to Windisch-Graetz, except for the two who had followed Kossuth to Debrecen.

The case of the Protestant high clergy was different. None of their bishops had made obeisance to Windisch-Graetz. Dessewffy and even more Count György Andrássy, another conservative, directly identified the revolution with the spirit and tradition of Protestantism in Hungary. Andrássy saw an unbroken line leading from the "Protestant rebellions" of such seventeenth- and eighteen-century princes as Bocskai, Thököly, and Rákóczi to the "Protestant rebellion" of Kossuth. Andrássy went so far as to say that, with a few exceptions, all the rebel leaders were Protestants, as were most of the officers, the "corrupted" noncommissioned officers, and the enlisted men, especially the hussars.[46]

Where Count Andrássy got his information is a mystery, for

even today we know very little of the officers' religious affiliations and even less of the rank and file. My attempt to establish the denominational membership of the fifty-odd officers who became *honvéd* generals did not lead to a comprehensive list. All that can be asserted with certainty is that the overwhelming majority of the generals were Catholics, with a sprinkling of Lutherans, two Calvinists (the Englishman Guyon and the peasant offspring András Gáspár), and one Greek Orthodox (the Serbian János Damjanich). Of the thirteen generals executed at Arad on October 6, 1849, ten were Roman Catholics, two Lutherans, and Damjanich a Greek Orthodox.

By reviving the old Habsburg argument against the Hungarian Protestants, Andrássy provoked a controversy that raged between Catholics and Protestants for many years to come. Undoubtedly, Protestantism—especially in its Calvinist-Reformed variety—had been a religion of resistance to Habsburg absolutism. Undoubtedly also, the Protestant churches would again stand up for Hungarian national interests in the 1850s after the Austrian government had affirmed the Catholic church as one of the pillars of its absolutist system. Kossuth himself, when in exile, overestimated the role of religion in the clash between the dynasty and Hungary. In reality, religious denomination played almost no part in the events of 1848–49. The Hungarian liberals tended to be free-thinkers; they rarely referred to their religious affiliation; Batthyány and Kossuth tried carefully to balance the proportion of Catholics and non-Catholics in their cabinets. The Ministry of Cults and Education had Catholic, Lutheran, Calvinist, Uniate, and Greek Orthodox department heads. Batthyány was a Catholic; Kossuth a Lutheran; Eötvös, the minister of cults and education, a Catholic by birth but a free-thinker by conviction. Religion was neither a motive nor an important factor in the revolution.

Windisch-Graetz's idea of Imperial reorganization and reconstruction was simple and natural. He wished to restore the *status quo ante* the rebellion, and to build his state on the triune foundation of contented peasants, loyal burghers, and chastised nobles. Mixing lenience with rigor, he would punish the chief culprits and win over the lesser rebels. The prince took into consideration the inherent power and inner strength of Hungary within the Monarchy. He knew that this power could not be wished away by mere administrative fiat. But he failed to understand the irresistible drive of the peoples of the

Monarchy, especially of the Hungarians, toward the assertion of their nationality. Therefore the prince's plan, although rather fair, was doomed to failure. In fact, it could not even be attempted, for its implementation depended on the continued success of Windisch-Graetz's armies in Hungary, and this is precisely what the Hungarians were to deny the field marshal.

There were, among Windisch-Graetz's unsolicited advisers, two renegades from Kossuth's immediate circle of friends. Dénes Pázmándy and Kálmán Ghyczy had been prominent figures in the pre-March liberal opposition. In 1848 Pázmándy had been one of the two Hungarian delegates to the Frankfurt parliament. Later he had become the president of the Hungarian House of Representatives. Ghyczy had been a state secretary in the Ministry of Justice. The two had not followed Kossuth to Debrecen but had instead submitted to Windisch-Graetz. On January 29, 1849, they sent a lengthy memorandum to the prince on the future of Hungary; despite its servile tone, the memorandum contained noteworthy ideas. The authors protested against Schwarzenberg's plan of an Imperial parliament and ministry, and they submitted a twelve-point counterplan that included the creation of a Hungarian cabinet without the portfolios for war, finance, and trade; the convocation of a bicameral Hungarian parliament based on a restricted suffrage; the crowning of Francis Joseph as king of Hungary; the right of Croatia, Slavonia, the Serbian Vojvodina, and the Transylvanian Saxon community to decide whether they wished to belong to Hungary or, rather, the other half of the Monarchy; separate status for Transylvania with full equality guaranteed to the Romanian nation; Hungarian state secretaries in the Imperial ministries of war, finance, and trade; Hungarian parliamentary control over the administration and budget of their country; the formation of a joint Austro-Hungarian parliamentary commission to supervise the common ministries of war, finance, and trade; the abolition of the tariff barrier between Hungary and the rest of the Monarchy; Hungarian participation in the common expenses of the Monarchy; legislative and administrative support of the aristocracy in all parts of the Monarchy; official encouragement and public use of all the languages common to the peoples of the Monarchy; and, finally, a solemn promise by Francis Joseph that Hungary would be governed constitutionally.[47]

Windisch-Graetz forwarded the memorandum to Schwarzenberg

with favorable comments, but it does not seem to have created any great stir at Court. Pázmándy was court-martialed by the Austrians; and even though he was not imprisoned, he and Ghyczy were treated contemptuously. Meanwhile, the Kossuth camp referred to the two as traitors.

Much of what Pázmándy and Ghyczy suggested was more progressive and more tolerant toward the nationalities than anything that Kossuth would ever have conceded. Other points, especially those on the common Ministry of War and the joint parliamentary commission, were to figure in the Compromise Agreement of 1867. The Pázmándy-Ghyczy plan upheld Magyar hegemony in the Kingdom of Hungary. This may seem unjust today, but in view of nineteenth-century realities, it reflected a correct estimate of the situation. The only alternative—complete political freedom to all the nationalities—would have led to the rapid dissolution of the Habsburg Monarchy and of Hungary. The Pázmándy-Ghyczy plan took into consideration the interests of the dynasty, the Habsburg army and bureaucracy, and the Hungarian nobility; without their common consent no viable solution was possible. This is what Francis Joseph, Baron von Beust, Count Gyula Andrássy, and Ferenc Deák were to realize in 1867, eighteen years after Pázmándy and Ghyczy had submitted their memorandum.

But time was not yet ripe for a reasonable agreement. Toward the end of February, the fierce armed struggle began again. It was to lead to great Hungarian victories.

On the Road to Buda-Pest and Beyond

Less than two months after the *honvéd* army had fled from the capital to avoid complete annihilation, it began to move forward again. Despite some initial setbacks, it was not to stop until most of Hungary was liberated.

The commander-in-chief of the main army, General Dembiński, concentrated his forces northeast of Buda-Pest: he wished to strike a decisive blow in one massive attack for which he had some 35,000 men, about the same as Windisch-Graetz's and Schlick's combined forces. To support this principal offensive, Dembiński demanded that a lesser Hungarian force engage in a military demonstration farther to the south, at Szolnok on the Tisza River, Windisch-Graetz was to be misled into believing that the major Hungarian offensive would begin there.

Things did not go very well at first. If the Szolnok maneuver was to achieve its purpose, it had to precede the offensive in the north. But the units destined for that affair were still on the way from southern Hungary when, under pressure from Kossuth, the Polish general ordered his own army forward. Alarming news had reached the government: Bem reported the massive presence of Russian troops in Transylvania; the fortress of Eszék had surrendered to the Austrians; Komárom and Pétervárad were surrounded and their garrisons seemed less and less reliable. On February 26 Dembiński's advancing units unexpectedly met the Austrians, also advancing, at Kápolna about sixty miles northeast of the capital. But half of Dembiński's forces were too far behind to take part in the encounter. The battle lasted two days and ended with the withdrawal of the Hungarians, who moved back slowly until they settled behind the protective marshes of the Tisza. The *honvéd* had stood the test of its first major battle remarkably well; but it was a particular humiliation to Dembiński that the very unit he had led into Kápolna in the heat of the battle, a 1,000-man battalion of the Venetian 16th Zanini Regiment, had gone over to the Austrians almost to the last man. Their Italian commander was subsequently shot by the Hungarians.[48]

Kápolna had two momentous consequences, both favorable to the Hungarian cause. The first, though it had only psychological significance, was crucial. Following the battle Windisch-Graetz decided, not for the first but certainly for the last time in his career, that the Hungarians had been definitively beaten and that the war would soon be over. He reported to the Court at Olmütz: "The rebel hordes appeared at Kápolna in awesome numbers. I dispersed them and destroyed the large majority. The rest fled across the Tisza. I hope to be in Debrecen in a few days and take possession of the nest of the insurrection."[49] Encouraged by the prince's battle report, the Court decided to promulgate the so-called March Constitution, which in turn strengthened the Hungarians' determination to press on with the military campaign. The second consequence of the battle of Kápolna was an officers' revolt against Dembiński, which led to the latter's resignation and Görgey's assumption of the command of the army.

The March Constitution had not been the only one in prepara-

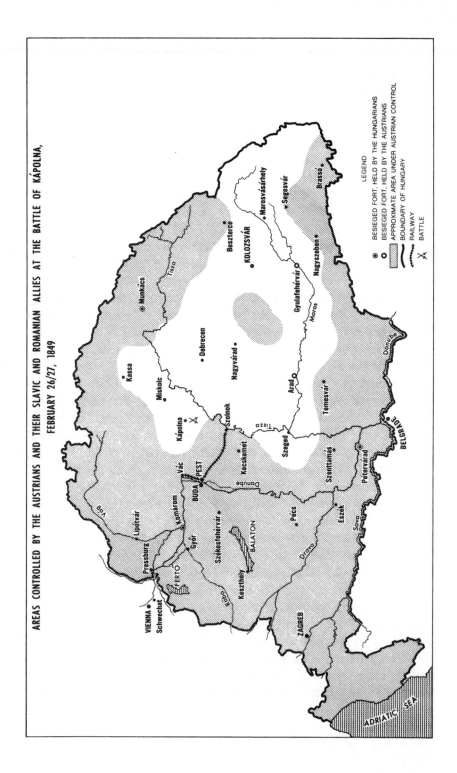

AREAS CONTROLLED BY THE AUSTRIANS AND THEIR SLAVIC AND ROMANIAN ALLIES AT THE BATTLE OF KÁPOLNA, FEBRUARY 26/27, 1849

LEGEND

⊙ BESIEGED FORT, HELD BY THE HUNGARIANS
○ BESIEGED FORT, HELD BY THE AUSTRIANS
▨ APPROXIMATE AREA UNDER AUSTRIAN CONTROL
⟋ BOUNDARY OF HUNGARY
⌇ RAILWAY
⚔ BATTLE

tion. While Schwarzenberg and Stadion were putting the final touches to their proposal, the Austrian parliament at Kremsier was busy completing its constitutional project. The Reichstag's proposal was most progressive for its time. It made the emperor absolute only in foreign policy; in all other respects his power was to be restricted. His ministers were to be responsible not only to him but also to the parliament. The Reichstag decided to abolish the titles of nobility and to end the Catholic church's role as the "dominant religion." The deputies introduced civil marriage, and they guaranteed to the citizens of united Austria a long list of civil rights. Finally, they offered equal linguistic rights to all the nationalities of the Monarchy. The Reichstag's proposal never became law, but as C. A. Macartney points out, it served as a model for all later constitutional projects: "In general, when peoples and politicians came to discuss constitutional proposals again, they took up their arguments exactly where the Reichstag had laid them down."[50]

No sooner had the deputies of the Reichstag come forward with their project than the Austrian government put its plan into effect to get rid of the parliament and introduce its own constitution. On March 4 Francis Joseph dissolved the Kremsier Reichstag and promulgated the new constitution (called the Stadion or *oktroyierte Constitution*). No longer protected by parliamentary immunity, some radical deputies had to flee Kremsier for their lives.

The Stadion Constitution did not lag far behind the Kremsier project as far as civil liberties were concerned. But the octroied (granted) document provided for a more unitary and authoritarian state. The Monarch had to swear allegiance to the Imperial constitution, but his powers were well in excess of those envisaged by the Reichstag deputies. He exercised his legislative power "together with" the parliament (still to be convoked) and the provincial diets; but he had an absolute veto and was authorized to dissolve the Reichstag at any time. Executive power was vested in the monarch, who was to exercise it through his ministers and his officials. Cabinet members were to be responsible to the emperor alone. The ministers had the right, but not the obligation, to address the meetings of the Reichstag. The monarch had sole right of decision over Imperial affairs—and almost everything was deemed an Imperial affair: foreign relations, the army and the navy, church and state relations, higher education, finance, trade, customs, money, transportation, and internal security. All powers not specifically delegated to the provinces remained the prerogative of the emperor. The Monarchy was proclaimed one and indivisible. But while the provinces were given very limited authority, the municipalities were guaranteed extensive self-government, a reflection of Stadion's concept in which the municipalities were to serve as the seeds of later liberal development. The constitution promised equality before the law to all citizens; it abolished all types of feudal subjugation; and it proclaimed the principle of ethnic and linguistic equality.

It was paragraphs 71–75 that made this constitution anathema to the Hungarians. Within the one and indivisible Monarchy, Transylvania, Croatia-Slavonia, Fiume and the Adriatic Littoral, the Military Border and the Serbian Vojvodina were to be completely detached from Hungary and subjected directly to the central government. The Hungarian constitution was to remain in force but only where it did not conflict with the new instrument. This in effect would mean the negation of the 1848 Hungarian constitution. Hungary would cease to be a sovereign kingdom tied to the monarch through a series of specific historical treaties: it would now simply be one of His Majesty's many possessions.[51]

The March constitution was never put into effect. First, there was the war with Hungary to be settled; and then, after the war, other political experiments would be tried. All that the octroied constitution achieved was to enrage the Hungarians. Kossuth protested in words both solemn and threatening. More important, he decided that time had come to proclaim Hungary's complete independence. Political preparations were begun immediately, but the actual declaration of independence was to await the first major victories of the Hungarian armies. And these were somewhat slow in coming.

The Hungarian army had recrossed the Tisza eastward in a turbulent mood. Almost all the higher officers turned against Dembiński, whom they detested as a foreigner (in the sense that Dembiński had not been an Imperial-Royal officer), the suspected agent of Kossuth, and as an inept, secretive, and haughty commander. On March 3 Görgey met with Szemere, who had just arrived at army headquarters in Tiszafüred as the delegate of the National Defense Committee. As the senior general under Dembiński, Görgey officially passed on to Szemere only the officers' dissatisfaction with the Polish general, but there could be no doubt about his own opinion. Overwhelmed by Görgey's arguments, Szemere did not defend the commander-in-chief and asked Kossuth to come to the camp. Meanwhile, he suspended Dembiński from his command.

Kossuth was outraged by the news of the officers' rebellion. "He [Görgey] is a traitor; he must stand trial," Kossuth told Szemere the day he, Mészáros, and General Vetter, the chief of staff, appeared in the camp. By then, Görgey's own chief of staff had posted grenadiers in front of Dembiński's tent. The Polish general was indignant; he threatened to return to Paris immediately. Kossuth persuaded Dembiński to stay (he was to play another important and most unfortunate role in the last stages of the revolution), but not even Kossuth was able to restore to Dembiński his command over the army. Kossuth had to leave the camp with Görgey temporarily in charge of the campaign.[52]

On March 8 Kossuth met with a parliamentary delegation in Debrecen. The majority of the deputies were in favor of making Görgey supreme commander, but Kossuth informed the deputies that he would appoint General Antal Vetter commander-in-chief of all forces outside of Transylvania, and that he (Kossuth) would stay with the army as a sort of supreme government commissioner during the campaign. The deputies applauded the decision (writes Mihály Horváth, a close associate of Kossuth). They forgot (Horváth continues) that these moves only reflected Kossuth's weakness and that Kossuth had given numerous proofs of his weakness in the past. The deputies also forgot (adds Horváth) that notwithstanding his many magnificent qualities, Kossuth had always lacked "physical courage."[53]

Kossuth's self-appointment and his appointment of Vetter as a *pis aller* was typical. It was also a poor decision. He could have attempted to place Görgey under arrest; alternatively, he could have bowed to the officers' wish and given the supreme command to Görgey. Vetter's appointment satisfied no one, not even Vetter, who was an experienced staff officer but lacked the self-confidence for such a trying position. To dismiss Dembiński and to pass over Görgey only proved the impotence of civilian authority when faced with a united army. Fortunately for Kossuth, Görgey did not rebel against the National Defense Committee's humiliating decision.

On March 9 Kossuth awarded high military honors to Vetter,

Bem, Görgey, and a few other generals. He also offered large sums of money to Vetter and Görgey, which the latter rejected contemptuously.

Mihály Horváth attributes Kossuth's self-appointment to the Hungarian army and his belief that he could henceforth bring the generals under his control to the adulation surrounding him. Horváth points to the catastrophic influence on the president of his "courtiers" and especially of his "haughty, conceited and demanding wife." It was she, writes Horváth, who drove Kossuth to behave like a crowned head of state. When a *Jäger* regiment was created in Debrecen under Kossuth's personal supervision, his wife did not rest until their two baby sons were made honorary officers of the regiment. The ensuing outburst of indignation in Debrecen forced Kossuth to withdraw the decision.[54]

The image of the evil wife—haughty, ambitious, and aggressive—is part and parcel of the folklore surrounding Kossuth, so Horváth's argument cannot be taken too seriously. Kossuth's consort had many unpleasant characteristics, but there is no evidence to show that she exerted any political influence on her husband. His grave mistakes must be explained in terms of himself, and the fault lay not in his conceit but in his hesitancy and opportunism. Where determined action was indicated, Kossuth often sought a compromise. More often, he declined to shoulder the responsibility for his decisions. This had been the case in October, when he had ordered the Hungarian troops into Austria but had put the responsibility for the army's eventual defeat on General Móga. Around New Year's Eve, he had ordered Görgey to fight a decisive battle in defense of Buda-Pest while at the same time warning him not to risk the army. He failed to stand up for Dembiński in whom he had unlimited confidence, just as he failed to defend his best collaborator, László Madarász, against the Peace Party. And in August 1849 Kossuth would make Görgey dictator of Hungary but would inhibit the General's exercise of power by blaming him in advance for the unavoidable surrender of the Hungarian army.

Early in March 1849, all depended upon whether Vetter would be able to lead the army to a speedy victory. Vetter changed Dembiński's plan and shifted the main emphasis to the southern prong of the Hungarian offensive. He concentrated the first, second, and third army corps near Szolnok, while further to the north Görgey's seventh army corps was given the task of a diversionary maneuver. But Vetter's attack at Szolnok on March 17 came too late, for Windisch-Graetz had also massed his forces in that area. Vetter abandoned the offensive and withdrew behind the Tisza. Now Görgey forced the resignation of Vetter, facilitated by the latter's genuine illness; and Kossuth bowed to the inevitable: he put Görgey in charge of the Hungarian campaign. But he withheld from him the supreme title and made Görgey "deputy commander-in-chief." This was on March 30; the Hungarian campaign now took a turn for the better.[55]

The attack started on April 1, according to a third plan. The main army was again concentrated in the north, and only a weak division was left near Szolnok. Now 52,000 Hungarians marched against 55,000 Austrians, but by then Windisch-Graetz was totally confused as to Hungarian plans. His reconnaissance service having failed him, the field marshal dispersed his forces all over the landscape.

The Hungarian battle plan was modified once more. On Klapka's advice, the seventh corps was ordered to make a frontal attack, while the three other corps attempted to encircle the enemy. It was an extremely risky plan, as were most of Klapka's projects, for it exposed the seventh corps to the fury of a massive Austrian counteroffensive. Yet Klapka's strategy turned out to be successful.

It would be extremely difficult to do justice to a military outline in view of the mountain of literature—expert and contradictory—on the subject. Suffice to say that the Hungarians won victories on April 2, on April 4, and on April 6. These were major encounters with significant bloodshed. Each victory brought the Hungarians closer to Buda-Pest and each demonstrated the increasing numbers and superior morale of the Hungarian troops. The battles were usually decided by the near-suicidal bayonet charges of the elite "red-cap" battalions, composed in their majority of urban artisans and intellectuals and in their minority of young Magyar or Slovak peasants. The Hungarian cavalry and artillery also proved superior to their Austrian counterparts. Yet Windisch-Graetz's army was not ill equipped or spiritless, and Field Marshal Radetzky's victorious second campaign against the Sardinian King Charles Albert, between March 20 and March 23, had in no way weakened Windisch-Graetz's forces in Hungary.[56] Kossuth followed the army wherever it went. On April 7 he installed himself in the royal castle in Gödöllő, only a few miles east of Buda-Pest. From there he announced to the population that he would sleep in the same bed vacated that very morning by His Highness the Austrian field marshal.[57]

Kossuth held an important council of war at Gödöllő on the same day. He asked Görgey to occupy the capital immediately, but he was persuaded by the general that the liberation of the besieged fortress of Komárom, northwest of Buda-Pest, was a far more important undertaking.[58] By that time Kossuth was full of admiration and enthusiasm for Görgey. Subsequently, the main Hungarian force moved in the direction of Komárom and, on April 10 at Vác on the bank of the Danube, it again defeated the Austrians.

On April 12 Windisch-Graetz was dismissed by the emperor and was replaced by General Baron Ludwig Welden, until then the military governor of Vienna. This was a terrible blow to Austria's former dictator and savior, and the prince hesitated before complying with the order. But then Windisch-Graetz proved himself the good Habsburg subject: he obeyed and left Hungary, never to reappear on the Austrian military or political scene.[59] With him ended the ultraconservative, traditionalist administrative experiment in Hungary; now the liberal centralists of Vienna would take over.

Görgey detached a small force to take Pest. By then the inhabitants of the city were in revolt: wide-brimmed revolutionary hats had made their appearance, together with red plumes and red, white, and green flags. The city, which had unconditionally submitted to Windisch-Graetz in January, was preparing to salute the triumphant Kossuth. It would be quite a few weeks, however, before the president was to appear in the capital.

The Hungarian army was able to defeat, but not to encircle or to annihilate the enemy. This may have been Görgey's fault: nationalist and marxist historians alike assure us that it was. The fact remains that Görgey won this campaign, and he would win others. He was a true captain; he usually stayed behind the battle lines, allowing his excellent corps commanders a good deal of liberty and coming forward only when his decisive intervention and magic personality were needed. He did not lack physical courage and the soldiers idolized him.

By April 14 the Hungarians were marching toward Komárom, the hussars were near Pest, and the Austrians were withdrawing everywhere. On that day, Kossuth proclaimed Hungarian independence and the deposition of the Habsburg dynasty from the throne of Hungary.

"The Perfidious House of Habsburg-Lorraine . . . Dethroned"

Toward the end of March, the rapidly improving military situation encouraged both radicals and Peace Party to attempt a political offensive in Debrecen. Convinced that final victory in the war was only a question of time and perseverance, the radicals wished to prevent a hasty conclusion of peace. The Peace Party, on the other hand, seeing a stalemate developing in the war, wished to negotiate with Austria from the strong base of recent battlefield victories. Since the success of either plan depended on Kossuth, both parties attempted to influence and to control him.

Fear of the opposite party guided both political groups as much as their long-term war aims. The Peace Party's vicious campaign againt László Madarász in the Affair of the Diamonds, Kossuth's partial surrender to Görgey at Tiszafüred, the arrival of moderate deputies in Debrecen (many a political deserter had rejoined the flag at the news of the Hungarian military counteroffensive), and the flagrant leniency of the parliamentary commission charged with examining the credentials of the absentee deputies, all convinced the radicals that they would be overwhelmed unless they acted promptly. On March 24 the leaders of the radical parliamentary faction appeared before Kossuth, demanding that he dissolve, or at least suspend, the National Assembly; that he order the court-martial of Görgey and other traitors; and that he appoint General Bem as commander-in-chief. This was a call for an open dictatorship which Kossuth rejected with the logical argument that the parliament would not go home graciously and that the army would not tolerate the court-martialing of Görgey. Besides (Kossuth pointed out to the radicals), the National Assembly was the National Defense Committee's only legitimate base, the source of its authority. It was unreasonable to expect the generals, so keen on maintaining at least a semblance of legitimacy, to obey an open dictatorship. And Kossuth had something else in mind, which he did not yet reveal to the radicals: he needed the National Assembly in session to approve the Declaration of Independence he was planning for Hungary.[60]

As to the Peace Party, it was no longer in a position to communicate directly with Kossuth. Therefore, it decided to intensify its press and parliamentary campaign against László Madarász. Clearly, the Austrians would never negotiate as long as such a wild radical was in the Hungarian government. The overthrow of Madarász would teach Kossuth a lesson and show him which way the wind was blowing. But the destruction of Madarász no longer seemed sufficient, for the Austrians would not negotiate with Kossuth either. By March a few members of the Peace Party had begun discussing the hitherto impossible idea of getting rid of Kossuth. This again was inconceivable unless the army supported the Peace Party; contacts were therefore sought with the military, especially with Görgey. A few meetings actually took place with Görgey, but led nowhere because both the Peace Party and the general were far too suspicious of each other.[61] Thus neither the radicals nor the Peace Party got closer to their political goals. What the radical faction could not achieve because of its isolation in Debrecen and its lack of military support, the Peace Party could not accomplish because of the hesitancy, suspiciousness, and basic patriotism of its members. As a result, both groups had to wait, more or less passively, for Kossuth's next move.

Kossuth answered the political maneuvers of both groups on March 25, in a long and masterly parliamentary speech. Announcing that he would now follow the army wherever it went, he begged and threatened the deputies not to deviate from the established political line while he was absent from Debrecen. Otherwise, he announced, he would resign immediately. Kossuth's warning was obliquely but unmistakably directed at the Peace Party; the president had reproached the party for packing the House of Representatives with previously absent deputies, and for leading a ruthless press campaign against László Madarász. But again, while he deplored the tone and style of the newspaper articles directed against the police minister, Kossuth did not defend Madarász. In the same address Kossuth announced that he would not suspend the parliament until the end of the hostilities.[62]

Kossuth was right, of course, in believing that the deputies

wished to remain in session during the war and would not go home
without vociferous protests. When, on the day of Kossuth's parliamentary speech, the radical deputy Dániel Irányi proposed that the
president of the National Defense Committee be empowered to remove the National Assembly to another place whenever he wished,
i.e., that he be allowed to move the parliament from Debrecen to the
soon-to-be-liberated Buda-Pest, the House of Representatives did not
even put Irányi's proposition on its agenda. The deputies understood
that this was an indirect way of allowing Kossuth to suspend the Assembly. The only thing that Irányi accomplished with his proposal
was to unmask the anti-parliamentarism of the radicals and their plan
to make Kossuth a dictator, not only in practice but in name as
well.[63]

Now Kossuth's mind was made up. On April 1 he informed
László Csányi in Transylvania that he would soon proclaim
Hungary's independence and then form a regular cabinet responsible
to parliament. After the war, a new *"constituant"* assembly would
frame the constitution of an independent Hungary.[64]

The most difficult task was to persuade the army. On April 7
Kossuth met Görgey at Gödöllő. Besides discussing military strategy, the two debated the country's political future. The only eyewitness accounts being those of the two participants, it is difficult to tell
exactly what happened. However, it is certain that Kossuth informed
Görgey of his intention to make Hungary totally independent. The
president insisted that final victory was near and that Europe was
waiting for an official Declaration of Independence to recognize
Hungary as a sovereign state. Hungary was faced with a holy task:
"We must do more than just help ourselves. We can and we must
fight for and win the freedom of all those peoples who wish us victory."[65]

Again, as so often in the past, Kossuth mingled international
revolutionary slogans with arguments borrowed from traditional diplomacy. He seemed to be convinced both of the good will of the European governments toward his country, and of the readiness of the
oppressed peoples to fight for their freedom in concert with Hungary.
He felt that the British, French, and Ottoman cabinets would recognize Hungary and that the British, French, German and Italian nations would sooner or later take up arms on her behalf. It was a his-

toric necessity that these cabinets, and these peoples should resist Habsburg reactionary absolutism and the pan-slav threat represented by Russia and her petty Slavic allies.

Görgey naturally objected to Kossuth's reasoning, or so he tells us in his memoirs.[66] The general pointed to Hungary's weakness and isolation and warned that secession from the Monarchy would make a just struggle unjust. It would become a fight against, and not in defense of, the law. Independence would upset the balance of power in Europe; neighboring countries would inevitably become Austria's allies against Hungary.

The debate ended inconclusively; but when, on the following day, Kossuth told his plans to the assembled generals, Görgey stood aside silently; he later explained that public disapproval would have split the unity of Hungary during a crucial military campaign. Kossuth, on the other hand, subsequently maintained that Görgey's silence had meant acceptance of the dethronement of the Habsburg dynasty.[67] In fact, Görgey never objected publicly to the Declaration of Independence. Why he did not remains a mystery, for there can be no doubt about his profound desire for a reconciliation with the dynasty. One must conclude that despite his outward determination and militant statements, this young career officer was confused and uncertain about nonmilitary matters. Lieutenant Görgey could master the art of war; he remained an amateur in the art of politics and palace revolutions.

On April 12 Kossuth returned to Debrecen. On the following day at a closed session of the House of Representatives, he introduced a four-point program. First, Hungary was to be proclaimed independent and sovereign: the Habsburg dynasty was to exercise no power over Hungary; members of the family were to be deprived of their civil rights and forever excluded from the country. Second, Hungary was to establish good-neighbor relations with the peoples who had lived under the rule of the same monarch. Third, Hungary was to "seek an alliance with the Italian provinces and the provinces of the Ottoman Empire." And finally, Hungary's future form of government was to be determined by the National Assembly, "according to the requirements of the day"; until that time, the country was to be led by a governor-president who, in turn, would form a ministry.[68]

Members of the Peace Party spoke out against Kossuth's plan, not on the basis of principle but on that of expediency. These moderates were simply afraid to condemn Kossuth openly. As a result, the House decided unanimously to hold an open meeting on the next day, when independence would be publicly proclaimed. At the same time and as a challenge to the radicals, the House ruled that it would remain in session "until the fatherland was completely safe."

Details of the secret meeting spread like wildfire in Debrecen, and on April 14 large throngs were clamoring for admission to the Assembly hall. It was decided to adjourn the meeting to the Great Church, the historic old Calvinist temple in Debrecen. Here the front pews were reserved for the deputies and the magnates, but the public filled the rest of the building. It was more of a mass demonstration than a parliamentary meeting. Amid tumultuous excitement, Kossuth rose to speak. He started out in a low and trembling voice, coughing profusely. Then, as was his custom, he gradually rose to dizzying oratorical heights. He spoke irresistibly and interminably. He listed all the past and present sins of the Habsburg dynasty, and he painted a rosy picture of the military and diplomatic situation. Finally, he repeated all the proposals he had made to the deputies a day earlier. László Madarász thereupon demanded that Kossuth's recommendations be accepted and that he be elected governor-president of Hungary. The other deputies interrupted Madarász, for they did not like this historic proposal to come from the mouth of the unpopular police minister: Kossuth was acclaimed unanimously. In his brief acceptance speech, Kossuth struck his usual modest note. He would wish to lead the country to victory and then remain governor no longer. "I swear to God Eternal, and by my honor, that after that moment [the moment of final victory], I shall become a modest and poor private citizen again."[69]

The National Assembly entrusted five of its members, Kossuth among them, with drafting the solemn Declaration of Independence. It was published on April 19, for the most part drafted by Kossuth. It was not a well-conceived statement. Unlike the American Declaration of Independence, which served as one of its models, the Hungarian Declaration lacks a theoretical justification.[70] It is mainly a treatise on Hungarian history, and as history it is enormously biased. Hungary's historic rights and grievances are enumerated from beginning to end; the House of Austria is made guilty of all the ills that had plagued the country in the preceding three centuries. The war is seen as a conflict between a perfidious dynasty and a very loyal but ruthlessly betrayed nation. The multi-ethnic composition of Hungary is nowhere mentioned, unless in a few crude references to cruel Serbs and ignorant, misled, but murderous Romanians. The Declaration of Independence, a gigantic essay running over twelve pages even in good-sized books, is a document written by Hungarian lawyer-politicians for Hungarian lawyer-politicians; its style is more feudal than modern; and its impact on the other peoples of the Monarchy and abroad could only be limited. Yet the government had it translated into many languages and distributed it everywhere.[71]

Even if it had been an exceptional document, the Declaration could not have broken through Hungary's diplomatic isolation. But Kossuth was so naive about foreign affairs that he may seriously have expected armed assistance from the Western powers. In addition, he may also have put excessive faith in the local revolutionary flare-ups then occurring in Germany and Italy. And the Declaration of Independence also had domestic political aims. Through it Kossuth attempted to weaken both the radicals and the Peace Party. Independence was a concession to the radicals and a gesture of defiance to the Peace Party; the new constitutional government under the prime ministry of Bertalan Szemere was a concession to the Peace Party and a hit at the radicals. Through the Declaration Kossuth wished to prevent both a negotiated peace with Austria and an antiparliamentarian dictatorship in Hungary.

It is necessary here to put right a number of historical misconceptions. First, Hungary was not made a republic on April 14. The future form of government was left open, and it was generally understood that sooner or later Hungary would again become a monarchy. When on April 13 a delegation of radicals asked Kossuth why he had not proposed the creation of a republic, the president explained that such a drastic move would have alienated most of the governments of Europe.[72] In the following months, both Kossuth and Prime Minister Szemere attempted repeatedly to offer the Crown to a foreign prince. This was not at all astonishing. Even though he was not a dedicated monarchist, Kossuth was perfectly willing to serve a crowned head of state as long as this would strengthen the country. Kossuth was ambitious for himself, but he was even more ambitious for Hungary.

The second misconception is that the Declaration of Independence brought about Russian military intervention in Hungary. In reality, Russian intervention had been decided on before April 14 and would have taken place in any case. It is true, however, that Hungary's secession from Austria strengthened the moral base of the Habsburg-Romanov alliance against Hungary.

Kossuth's domestic political misgivings were vastly exaggerated, and the Declaration of Independence was accordingly a great mistake. The radical group had been moribund before April 14; its demise was neither hastened nor delayed by the Declaration. On the other hand, the Peace Party was not deterred by April 14; it continued its activity in the coming months. But the Peace Party could never achieve its aims, for it remained the movement of an intelligent minority without a determined and aggressive leadership. Kossuth's greatest error was to make himself governor-president of a country now provided with a regularly constituted government. This enhanced Kossuth's prestige, but it also weakened his power—if not fatally, then temporarily.

Since a great many deputies, and almost all the generals, had never wanted the dethronement of the dynasty and bitterly resented it once it had been proclaimed, one must ask why they consented to Kossuth's moves on April 14. The answer must be sought in the disunity of the deputies and the political inexpertise of the generals. The only person who could have opposed Kossuth effectively was Görgey. But Görgey did not know how to lead a political movement.

Finally, the reason for the acquiescence of the opponents of dethronement must be sought in psychology. The dethronement of the Habsburgs, an unpopular measure, was combined with the affirmation of Hungary's independence, something that even conservative Hungarians had taken for granted and had considered compatible with dynastic loyalty. Kossuth, the brilliant lawyer, had once again outwitted his opponents.

If one is to measure a country's independence by the presence or absence of foreign garrisons, Hungary had only brief periods of genuine sovereignty during its association with the House of Austria: a few years under Prince Rákóczi early in the eighteenth century and a few months under Kossuth. In both cases independence was the result of rebellion, and in both cases national sovereignty failed to encompass the entire Kingdom of Hungary. Hungarian hegemony over the kingdom (but not complete sovereignty) was possible only under the tutelage of the Habsburg Monarchy.* This was recognized by the majority of Hungarian nobles in Rákóczi's time, and they consequently paid homage to the king. Following the Declaration of Independence in April 1849, the Hungarian nobles gradually arrived at the same conclusion, and, to save what could be saved of the state, they began to desert Kossuth just when he seemed most successful. This will be the story of the last few months of Hungary's War of Independence in 1849.

* Historical parallels and generalizations are usually fallacious; still, it is noteworthy that during Hungary's third and last period of independence, between 1918 and 1944, Hungarian rule did not extend over the whole kingdom, and it was the Horthy regime's striving for the reconquest of historic Hungary that led to the country's enslavement and ruin before the end of World War II.

7 / The Travail and Decline of Independent Hungary: Kossuth as Constitutional Governor-President (April–July 1849)

Toward Vienna or Castle Hill?

POLITICS AND WARFARE are more closely intertwined in a civil conflict than in wars waged by established states. In 1849 Hungary's military campaigns decisively influenced politics, and politics decisively influenced the campaigns. Generals became politicians, and politicians, especially Kossuth, interfered with the movement of troops. As battles were at first almost invariably won, and later almost invariably lost, Kossuth's politics became increasingly uncertain: he alternated between the heights of great self-confidence and the depths of profound depression, and there were times when he wasted time on piddling matters, neglecting national affairs. But he never stopped. He bore his burden until it was time to go into an exile from which he never returned.

Following the battle at Vác, the Hungarian army pressed onto the north of the Danube. On April 19, near the village of Nagysalló, the *honvéd* again ran into the enemy, among whom were many fresh troops. Now that the war against Piedmont was definitely over and the Austrians in Italy only had small Venice to worry about, they could marshal more of their military might against Hungary.

At Nagysalló over 20,000 troops fought on each side. Driven ahead by General Damjanich, the Hungarians overran the Imperial positions and for the first time since the Ozora surrender in October 1848, they took many prisoners, perhaps as many as a thousand. But unlike the Croatian peasants captured at Ozora, these Austrian prisoners belonged to first-line units, among them crack grenadier battalions. Görgey noted that the celebrated tall "bear-skin caps" cut a sorry figure as they trudged to the rear under the guard of a few diminutive *honvéd* lads.[1] The Hungarians were now free to move on to Komárom, where they arrived a few days later.

The liberation of Komárom was a tremendous feat yet Görgey refused to rest, and on the night of April 25/26 he sent 4,000 elite troops to the southern shore of the Danube on an improvised floating bridge. They were to destroy the main Austrian army, then withdrawing from Buda-Pest.[2]

Threatened with encirclement by the Hungarians at Komárom, the Austrian army had finally evacuated Buda-Pest on April 23. It was a great humiliation to the Habsburg military, but a wise move on the part of Baron Welden, the new Austrian commander-in-chief in Hungary.[3] Welden had ordered most of his troops to march west toward Komárom and Győr in an attempt to defend the Austrian border against Görgey's attack, but he had left four battalions under *Generalmajor* Heinrich Hentzi on Castle Hill, situated in the center of Buda.

On April 23 and 24 the Hungarian hussars and *honvéd* infantry entered Buda-Pest amid scenes of fierce patriotic exaltation. Castle Hill still flew the Imperial flag, but everyone expected the garrison to surrender. The withdrawing Austrian army met Görgey's advance forces on April 26 near the southern section of Komárom fortress. Had the floating bridge on the Danube been constructed earlier by the garrison of the fortress, and had the Hungarians had more artillery ammunition, the destruction of the Austrians would have been possible, with potentially catastrophic consequences for the defense of Vienna. Instead, the battle raged on, indecisive, until the Hungarians had used up their cannon balls and the exhausted but undefeated Austrians could continue their march toward the border.

For the Hungarians it was time to take stock of the situation. Even though the enemy had not been annihilated, the strategic plan formulated at Gödöllő proved to be a great success. Reports from other parts of the country showed that the Austrians were everywhere withdrawing. Hungary was almost completely liberated. The trouble was that nobody had made plans beyond Komárom: some because they had believed that luck could not be stretched farther; others because they had felt that with the liberation of Komárom and Buda-Pest, the war was over. Görgey and most professional officers were among those who thought that the army's capacity for further advances was exhausted; public opinion and most politicians were keen on enjoying what they felt was final victory. Kossuth himself was pessimistic and overconfident at the same time. He warned the nation that the greatest struggle was still ahead; yet at the same time he created the illusion of victory with his jubilant pronouncements. Worst of all, Kossuth believed that Castle Hill in Buda could be overwhelmed rapidly, without the main army, which should continue its advance to the Austrian border.[4]

Görgey seemed crushed by his multiple duties and his own prestige and power. On April 19 he had been notified in camp that Kossuth wished him to join the cabinet as minister of war.[5] Görgey accepted, for he felt that the post would allow him to reorganize the army and the provision of supplies, as well as do away with the corruption, shirking, and nepotism rampant within the military administration. At the same time, Görgey was reluctant to leave his soldiers in the midst of a major campaign. His staff had told him that the officers, desperate as they were over the Declaration of Independence, would not fight without their commander. One of Görgey's favorite subordinates, András Gáspár, an old professional and the only general of nonnoble stock in the honvéd army, had already resigned because of the Declaration of Independence. Görgey decided to delegate Damjanich to Debrecen as deputy war minister. Unfortunately for the country, Damjanich had just then smashed his leg in an accident and was out of commission for the rest of the war. Görgey thereupon sent Klapka to Debrecen to act as deputy war minister. All this meant that the best army corps lost their experienced commanders. Their replacements were no match for their predecessors.[6]

The army needed rest and ammunition. No supplies had arrived for several weeks, yet time was pressing because of the expected arrival of Austrian regiments from the Italian campaign and because of disturbing news with regard to a Russian intervention. By the end of April, Görgey had reliable information that the Russians would soon enter the war.

Görgey's chief of staff recommended an immediate Hungarian advance on both shores of the Danube toward the Austrian border; General Klapka favored a concerted attack on Castle Hill at Buda with the argument that its garrison was threatening central Hungary as well as traffic on the Danube. According to Klapka, the capture of the one-time residence of the kings of Hungary would bring world-wide recognition of Hungarian independence.

The final decision rested with Görgey, and he decided to take Castle Hill first and then move to the Austrian border. Almost the entire *honvéd* army was dispatched from Komárom to Buda-Pest; only a small force was sent westward to observe the withdrawing Austrians.

This was Görgey's worst decision, which all later apologies do not quite explain and certainly do not excuse. With this single move the general threw away his already slim chance of a final victory or even of a military stalemate. By moving to Buda the army not only separated itself from Welden's defeated forces, it actually withdrew. Had Hentzi surrendered immediately, which he did not, the Hungarians would still have lost precious time in getting their army on the move again. Castle Hill was too diminutive a target for an entire army; yet once it had become a target, it could tie down vastly superior forces for the simple reason that fortresses, no matter how ancient and inadequate (as was Castle Hill), were extremely difficult to overpower with weapons of that age. It is true that Castle Hill controlled the Chain Bridge, the only permanent construct across the Danube; but by moving to Komárom across the region north of the river, the *honvéd* army had solved the problem presented by the Danube. According to all evidence, Welden would have been unable to stop a resolutely advancing Hungarian army all the way to the Austrian frontier. The Austrian command took the Hungarian threat so seriously that it loaded the emperor's residence in Schönbrunn outside Vienna with soldiers and guns.

A Hungarian advance to the Leitha River on the Austrian border would not have won the war for Hungary. Austria had great potential for recovery; the morale of her troops was unbroken; several regiments were on the move from Italy to the Hungarian front; and the

Russians would have come to the aid of Austria. But a *honvéd* army on the Leitha, or perhaps in Vienna, would have raised Hungarian prestige to such heights, and would have lowered Habsburg prestige to such depths, that negotiations might have been inevitable. That is what Görgey was counting on, but his speculations were based on the wrong strategic premises. Arguing that April 14 had made a total victory indispensable but that total victory was impossible, he took what he himself called a political decision but what was in essence a misguided military decision. Through the quick capture of Castle Hill, Görgey hoped to raise the morale of his officers and persuade them to march as far as the Leitha River. There his army would stop and offer a dignified compromise to the Austrians. Since Russian intervention could not possibly please the Austrian government, Görgey told himself, the Austrians would decide to accept the 1848 Constitution of Hungary. The country would return to the Habsburg fold as an equal partner, and the nightmare of the civil war would be over.[7]

Görgey's timing was all wrong, because Castle Hill resisted for over three weeks. By then the main Austrian army had reinforced its position and was preparing for a counteroffensive. Russian intervention, too, had been firmly decided upon. The war was lost for Hungary.[8]

In his memoirs Görgey claimed that the siege of Castle Hill had been forced upon him by Kossuth and public opinion. There can be no doubt about Kossuth's views and about public opinion, but Görgey should have been the last person to succumb to such pressures. Kossuth had never ordered Görgey to turn his entire army against Hentzi; he had suggested the storming of Castle Hill, but he could have been persuaded to accept another solution. And Görgey had always known how to ignore, or to defy, an impractical civilian suggestion.

Writing almost ten years after the event, Friedrich Engels called Görgey's move "the turning point" in Hungary's War of Independence.[9] Let us state in Görgey's defense that when the event itself took place, the cofounder of marxism found nothing objectionable in Görgey's decision. The Hungarians, Engels wrote in the *Neue Rheinische Zeitung* on May 19, 1849, being menaced by fresh troops from Austria and Russia, acted very wisely when, instead of advancing swiftly on Vienna, they confined themselves to steadily forcing the imperial armies out of Hungary, enveloping them in a wide arc from the foothills of the Carpathians to the spurs of the Styrian Alps, dispatching a strong corps towards Jablunka [a mountain pass in the northern Carpathian mountains] and covering the Galician mountain passes, attacking Ofen [Buda] and rapidly proceeding with the recruitment of 250,000 men. . . .[10]

On May 4 Görgey's forces reached Buda and began to encircle Castle Hill. By then Klapka had realized his mistake and asked that the siege be abandoned before it had started. Görgey rejected Klapka's recommendation by saying that it would be interpreted as a sign of Hungarian indecision and weakness. The siege had begun.[11]

The Siege of Castle Hill and the Liberation of Hungary

While Görgey's army marched from central to western Hungary and then marked time under the walls of Castle Hill, other Hungarian forces were gradually pushing the Austrians out of the country. Southern Transdanubia and northern Hungary, two regions that saw no major opposing forces, were cleared by subaltern commanders operating with a few thousand men. Their bands of regular *honvéd*, free corps, and peasant insurrectionists harassed the even smaller Austrian forces out of the region. Hungarian control never became absolute in these areas, but neither had Austrian control ever been absolute.

Southern Hungary had been the scene of fierce fighting since the summer of 1848. In January 1849 the Hungarians had evacuated the entire region. Now they came back, redressing the havoc once caused by the Austro-Serbian forces with new havoc. The fact that the Serbian leaders were divided among themselves and that many were disillusioned helped the Hungarian campaign. The Serbs had begun to perceive that their union with the Serbian Principality south of the Danube was impossible, and that the autonomous Serbian Vojvodina would be abolished by Vienna at the first opportunity. On May 13 Patriarch Rajačić reported to the Austrian government that the Serbian nation had begun to doubt the solemn promise of the emperor and that it regretted having taken up arms against the Hungarians.[12]

On March 27 General Perczel, leader of the Hungarian campaign in the South, relieved the long-encircled fortress of Pétervárad on the lower Danube. From there he turned against the reinforced Serbian positions in the open country and took them one by one. Perczel accomplished near-wonders in the south, but only at a horrifying price and not without constant quarreling with Kossuth. Unlike Görgey's orderly campaign against the Austrian regular army, the war in the south had always been brutal. At the Serbian fortified camp near Szenttamás, the Hungarians gave no quarter: thousands of Serbian Border Guards and irregulars were killed, together with their families. The place itself was looted and burned to the ground.[13]

The nature of General Bem's campaign in Transylvania was quite different from that of Perczel, although no less successful. Bem proved that mutual massacres were not inevitable: under him the formerly terrible Transylvanian civil war had become an almost civilized affair. He secured at least a modicum of sympathy and understanding between the Romanian and Hungarian peoples in the following century. In fact, Romanian historiography now claims General Bem as one of their own, forgetting that, despite Bem's tolerant attitude, the war was still between him and the Hungarians on the one side and the Romanians, Austrians, Saxons, and Russians on the other.

All through the winter months, Bem clashed with Government Plenipotentiary Csányi on the question of nationality policy. Bem granted amnesty to the Romanian peasant rebels and the Saxon burghers; he recruited Romanian volunteers into his army; he opposed the punitive expeditions of the Hungarian free corps, and he tried to reorganize Transylvania on the basis of religious and national autonomy.[14] Csányi, who was also willing to grant some concessions to the Romanian peasants, was in other respects categorically opposed to Bem. In the dispute between the two, Kossuth sided unconditionally with Csányi. In his many instructions to Csányi and Bem, Kossuth rejected the idea of national and religious self-government. He demanded the dissolution not only of autonomous local bodies but of the entire governmental machinery of Transylvania; he insisted on the province's complete incorporation into Hungary; he condemned what he called Bem's mania for clemency; and he called for the merciless punishment of the guilty.[15] Kossuth, who alternately called the Romanian peasants ignorant and murderous savages or fundamentally decent but misguided children, was willing to forgive the peasants for their sins, but never the Saxon or Romanian leaders who had incited the peasants against Hungarian authority.[16]

In the controversy between Bem on the one hand, and Csányi and Kossuth on the other, justice was not always on the side of General Bem. Csányi's most powerful argument against Bem was that of civilian authority over the military: Bem had no business handing out amnesties or conscripting soldiers. Kossuth, who had more than enough trouble with Görgey and other generals in Hungary proper, would not hear of a Bonaparte in Transylvania. Using every means of persuasion, he flattered, begged, or ordered Bem to leave the administration to civilians.

There can be no doubt about Bem's obstinacy, his unfamiliarity with the country, and his occasional contradictory moves. At one point he ordered the wholesale expulsion of all Romanians from the territory of the Naszód Romanian Border Guard Regiment and their forcible replacement with Székely peasant colonists. Now it was Csányi's turn to protest against Bem's intolerance. Kossuth himself strongly disliked Bem's action and prevented its execution.[17]

Kossuth was not the most intolerant or the most impatient with regard to Romanian and Transylvanian affairs. The radicals to his left, and some soldiers, were definitely more intolerant.[18] Accounts of Transylvanian massacres poured into Kossuth's office. And even though reports of Romanian atrocities were understandably more numerous, there were enough complaints about Hungarian atrocities to give a balanced picture of developments. In answer to these reports, Kossuth showed no great humanity, but no great brutality either. He condoned and encouraged rigorous punitive measures, but he rejected such collective punishment as mass deportation.

By late March, Hungarian victory in Transylvania appeared complete. Ignoring the protests of his itinerant emissaries that the situation in the rear of the Hungarian armies was far from consolidated, Kossuth ordered Bem to leave the province for the war in southern Hungary.

Now that victory seemed final in Transylvania, Kossuth extended a friendly hand toward the Romanian peasant guerrillas. On April 14, the day independence was proclaimed, he instructed Ioan Dragoş, a Romanian member of the Hungarian parliament, to seek negotiations with Avram Iancu's insurrectionists in the western mountains of Transylvania.[19] Dragoş's mission failed and he himself was killed by the Romanian guerrillas; but at least Kossuth had tried to come to terms with the Romanians; and he would try again, a bit more successfully, in the summer. Unfortunately, by then it was too late.

In April Bem and Perczel joined forces in the Banat, in southernmost Hungary (although Bem refused to integrate his army with that of Perczel, whom he called a murderer and an arsonist[20]), and the two generals drove the Austro-Serbian forces into small defensive pockets. Thus by late April, with the exception of some fortresses and of limited areas of resistance, the whole country was in the hands of the *honvéd* army. And yet, at this unique juncture, the best and biggest Hungarian army concentrated its efforts on taking a small medieval fort.

Görgey completed the encirclement of Buda's Castle Hill early in May with close to 40,000 troops, among them 5,000 cavalry. But the army lacked mortars and siege guns, and when these were finally sent down the Danube from Komárom, the Hungarians had wasted almost two weeks at the foot of Castle Hill.[21] On May 4 Görgey asked Hentzi to surrender. He promised humane and dignified treatment to the garrison even if resistance continued, but only on condition that Hentzi abstain from damaging the Chain Bridge or the city of Pest. As already recounted, Görgey also appealed to the patriotic sentiments of Hentzi, allegedly a Hungarian; but Hentzi vowed in his reply to fight on to the end.[22] Görgey now ordered a direct attack on Castle Hill. It was repelled with heavy losses for the *honvéd,* as was a subsequent attack. Finally, the siege guns opened a breach in the wall, and during the night of May 20/21 the Hungarians successfully climbed the steep slopes of the hill. While Italian soldiers from the 23rd Ceccopieri Regiment lent the attackers a helping hand, the rest of the garrison fought in hand-to-hand combat to the end. Hentzi himself was mortally wounded; about one thousand Austrians were killed in the battle. The *honvéd* spared the survivors, despite Görgey's previous order that no quarter be given. Pest had been frightfully damaged by the Austrian guns, and at the last minute the Austrians had tried but failed to blow up Széchenyi's Chain Bridge.

The fall of Castle Hill was celebrated in the Debrecen parliament as Hungary's greatest victory. While the siege lasted, Kossuth had showered abuse on the Austrians: "The history of banditry has known no more awful robbers and arsonists . . . Damnation, hundredfold damnation upon the head of the tyrant and on the tyrant's devilish instruments!'' After the fall of Castle Hill, Kossuth praised the god of liberty and ordered that Görgey be promoted to a two-star general and that he be given the Grand Cross of the Military Order of Merit.[23] Görgey turned down all the honors, perhaps because he was a puritan, perhaps because he planned a decisive political action against Kossuth.

Görgey's behavior had become incomprehensible. He, who later claimed that his military moves had always been guided by politics and that his politics had always been based on the principle of eventual reconciliation with the Habsburgs, now chose to make a whole series of radical and international revolutionary pronouncements. Following the liberation of Komárom, he addressed a proclamation to his army asserting that the coming struggle ''would not be fought by Hungary alone against Austria. It would be fought by Europe as a whole for the sacred natural rights of all peoples against tyranny.'' During the siege of Castle Hill, Görgey informed Kossuth in an open letter that the Austrian bombardment of Pest could not but ''extinguish the last spark of reverence in the inhabitants of this country towards this perfidious dynasty,'' and that the fires burning in Pest were but ''torches lit at the funeral ceremony of the House of Austria.''[24]

Revolutionary ardor did not inspire Görgey to persist in the energetic pursuit of the Austrians after the fall of Castle Hill. Instead of his leading the army against Vienna, Görgey journeyed to Debrecen at the end of May, there to throw himself into the political fray. Life in Debrecen had hardly been quiet during the siege of Castle Hill. Politicians were jockeying for positions; and while some conspired against Kossuth, others were preparing to reap the fruits of victory.

The Dilemma of a Constitutional Presidency

Because of Kossuth's penchant for secrecy as well as the lack of a diary or of a truly intimate correspondence, it is difficult to know what he had in mind when he made political decisions. His behavior following the Declaration of Independence is particularly difficult to fathom. What seems certain is the following. After his election as governor, Kossuth hoped to remain the de facto prime minister of

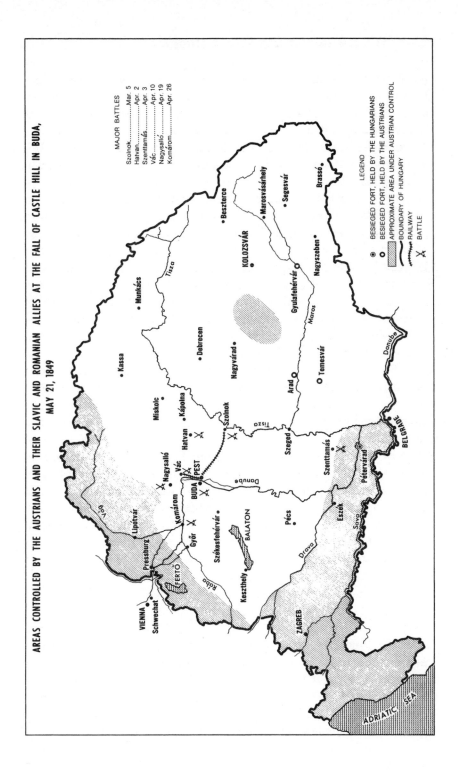

AREAS CONTROLLED BY THE AUSTRIANS AND THEIR SLAVIC AND ROMANIAN ALLIES AT THE FALL OF CASTLE HILL IN BUDA, MAY 21, 1849

MAJOR BATTLES

Szolnok............Mar. 5
Hatvan.............Apr. 2
Szenttamás........Apr. 3
Vác................Apr. 10
Nagysalló.........Apr. 19
Komárom...........Apr. 26

LEGEND

⊚ BESIEGED FORT, HELD BY THE HUNGARIANS
⊙ BESIEGED FORT, HELD BY THE AUSTRIANS
▨ APPROXIMATE AREA UNDER AUSTRIAN CONTROL
〜 BOUNDARY OF HUNGARY
‒‒ RAILWAY
✗ BATTLE

Hungary. He planned to govern, not only to rule. At the same time, he was anxious to share the burden of government with others. He literally begged the ministers-designate to hasten to Debrecen in order to assume their duties.[25] He initially planned to include such radicals as Count László Teleki and General Perczel in the new cabinet. But Teleki was in Paris and Perczel had lighted on Kossuth as the main target of his fury.[26] Thus Kossuth quickly gave up the idea of appointing radicals, if he had ever thought of it seriously. He had not offered a portfolio to László Madarász, the radical who would have served him best, and he soon settled on a cabinet of the center. The ministers he selected were, with one exception, dedicated to Hungary's armed struggle. They were efficient and experienced leaders; strong-willed and dynamic enough to take their roles seriously. Not one minister sympathized with the radicals; one or possibly two stood close to the Peace Party. Kossuth had chosen a respectable and energetic cabinet; sooner or later he would have to make concessions to his ministers.

The prime minister and minister of the interior was Bertalan Szemere, one of Kossuth's closest collaborators. Szemere had been a forceful minister of the interior in the Batthyány cabinet and an equally forceful government plenipotentiary under the National Defense Committee. His appointment was logical, for not only did Szemere represent legal continuity from Hungary's first constitutional ministry (as did Kossuth), but after Kossuth he was the best known political leader. Unfortunately, Szemere was also an intriguer and cynic: he shifted his views and his political pronouncements according to his own interest. He had long been maneuvering between Kossuth and Görgey and between the radicals and the Peace Party. He was Kossuth's friend but also his secret enemy. In his inaugural address to the House of Representatives on May 2, Szemere announced that his government would be "republican," "revolutionary," and "democratic"—a statement that in the eyes of many a moderate deputy was equal to saying that the cabinet would pursue communist policies. But when members of the Peace Party rushed to him and demanded an explanation, the prime minister remarked nonchalantly that his speech ought not to be taken seriously, and that it was sometimes necessary to out-demagogue Kossuth.[27] In general, Szemere showed himself rather moderate and cautious.

The other ministers were equally noteworthy. Intellectually a notch below those in the Batthyány cabinet, they were more determined and forceful. Count Kázmér Batthyány, foreign minister and acting minister of commerce; László Csányi, minister of transport; and Sebő Vukovics, minister of justice; all came from the ranks of the prerevolutionary liberal opposition. During the war they had been devoted government plenipotentiaries in southern Hungary or, in Csányi's case, in Transylvania. Kázmér Batthyány, a wealthy Catholic magnate and a relative of Lajos Batthyány, Csányi, a landowning noble, and Vukovics, a noble landowner and lawyer of Serbian origin, were loyal supporters of Kossuth. Batthyány and Vukovics would follow Kossuth into exile, as would Szemere; Csányi would be hanged by the Austrians after the war. The minister of cults and education, Mihály Horváth, was one of the two Catholic bishops who had gone with the National Assembly to Debrecen. He too was a Kossuth follower, a political liberal and a freethinker. Horváth would go into exile with Kossuth and make a name for himself as the foremost historian of the revolution. The minister of finance, Ferenc Duschek, came from a different background. An old civil servant of Bohemian-German origin, he had been secretary of state in Kossuth's finance ministry. He knew his trade well, but whether he acted in good faith is doubtful. Politically a conservative, Duschek was more interested in preserving Hungary's financial reserves, her mines and manufactures, than in serving the war effort. Even though he remained in Kossuth's camp to the end, the Austrians seemed to have appreciated Duschek's efforts on behalf of the common good of the Monarchy, for they punished him very lightly.

The appointment of Arthur Görgey as minister of war was undoubtedly the most problematical. Mihály Horváth argues in his history of the revolution that Kossuth made Görgey a minister in order to separate him from the army and to keep him under personal surveillance.[28] If this was indeed Kossuth's intention, then he failed very badly, but there is no convincing evidence that the governor had such a plan. It is true that all through May Kossuth begged General Bem, then operating in the Banat, to cross the Danube and join the main army in northwestern Hungary, and that Kossuth held out the possibility to Bem of making him commander-in-chief to replace Görgey. But this was only natural since it was impossible for Görgey to be simultaneously in the seat of government and with the main army. Kossuth did not hide his doubts from Görgey and indicated over and over again that some solution had to be found to this awkward situation. Instead of viewing the position of war minister as a "kick upstairs," as some historians maintain, Kossuth felt it to be a most important appointment, and he offered it to Görgey, the most outstanding military leader. He also gave the new minister of war all the power the latter requested. Unfortunately for Kossuth, there was to be no solution to Görgey's dual appointment, for Bem turned Kossuth down: the Polish general was unwilling to take his small expeditionary force so far away from Transylvania where, he correctly felt, it would again be needed. Bem's relations with Kossuth were becoming most unpleasant in any case; Bem disobeyed Kossuth as often as did Görgey, and in early June he was back in Transylvania where the Romanian revolt had erupted anew.[29]

By May Kossuth had far more confidence in Görgey than the general had in him. An emotional personality with almost unlimited belief in the essential goodness of man, Kossuth easily overlooked Görgey's past "mistakes." Under the impact of Görgey's brilliant victories and militantly radical pronouncements, he again began to see in Görgey the potential savior of Hungary and was therefore willing to have Görgey as both minister of war and acting commander-in-chief. Yet, at the same time, Kossuth still refused the general the coveted title of full commander-in-chief.

On May 8 Kossuth informed Görgey that as minister of war he should have full authority over all the armies of Hungary. Then, and in subsequent communications to Görgey, the governor upheld the right of the minister of war to confirm all important appointments and promotions and to exercise strict authority over the other generals.[30] The result was the resignation of a number of generals. Dembiński, who had recently been appointed commander of an army corps in northeastern Hungary, resigned immediately, as did Perczel—but neither without first heaping abuse on both Görgey and Kossuth. Since Klapka had meanwhile replaced the radical Guyon at Komárom, practically all the generals hostile to Görgey had been eliminated by June. This was what Görgey had wanted, and it was being accomplished with the full approval of Kossuth. Winning the war with a disciplined army was more important for Kossuth than his memories of a rebellious Görgey. The general now held the two most important military posts in Hungary, a status that was to inspire far less sincerity and devotion in him toward Kossuth then the governor had demonstrated toward the general.

Szemere's cabinet enjoyed the support of the center and of the Peace Party in the House, that is, it enjoyed majority support. Cabinet and House together trimmed Kossuth's power and instituted a parliamentary system of government. As soon as Kossuth was elected, the tug-of-war over the respective competences of the governor and of the government began. Since the concept of a governor-president was entirely new, everybody had his own interpretation. Kossuth saw himself in the role of an American president; Szemere saw him as a constitutional monarch. He insisted that Kossuth should not be allowed to oppose parliament, even less to govern on his own. The issue of gubernatorial power was debated in the House at several secret meetings toward the end of April, with the majority of deputies in favor of Szemere's position. Despite radical protests, the House insisted that it must retain ultimate authority.[31] Kossuth quickly gave in, and on May 2 he informed parliament that he would respect both cabinet and National Assembly. He recognized the right of cabinet members to countersign his decrees, decisions, and appointments, but he affirmed his prerogative in determining general policy and in making the most important appointments. He would appoint and dismiss the ministers, but he would leave administrative matters entirely to the cabinet. He would not declare war nor conclude peace and alliances without the consent of the National Assembly. In the following days the House discussed the oath that the governor and the cabinet should take before the National Assembly. Overruling the original recommendation of a left-wing member which had favored the governor's position, the majority of the deputies adopted an amendment obliging Kossuth to swear "to obey and uphold the laws and decisions of the National Assembly." On May 14 Kossuth took his solemn oath at a plenary meeting of the National Assembly, warning the parliamentarians in a subsequent address that he would disobey the Assembly if it deviated from the path of Hungarian independence and freedom.[32] Theoretically, a happy balance was thus established between the head of state on the one hand and the parliament and the cabinet on the other. In reality, Kossuth's power and influence fluctuated according to military and political developments: they alternately exceeded or fell behind his constitutional prerogatives.

On May 2, the day his cabinet was formed, Szemere ordered all counties and cities, government commissioners and other officials henceforth to address their communications to the appropriate ministries, and no longer to Kossuth. For a while, both the public and Kossuth ignored the order, but gradually they got used to the new system. The governor adopted the custom of forwarding to the ministries mail addressed to him, often without comment. He wrote fewer letters and often abstained from correcting drafts drawn up by his secretaries. He allowed the civilian and military members of his own office to issue communications in their own names. In May and June he often left important administrative and military matters to the ministries; but by July, when the danger to the country became most acute, he again made all the crucial decisions. Once more he became virtual dictator.[33]

Marxist historians maintain that following the Declaration of Independence Hungary moved toward the right, and that the increasingly conservative cabinet tore down, one by one, all the revolutionary institutions created by the National Defense Committee. The fundamental cause of Kossuth's failure (György Spira argues) was his unwillingness to go all the way with the radicals and, through the radicals, with the people. Kossuth did not dare decree the kind of drastic social reforms which alone would have mobilized the peasants and inspired the simple soldiers to wage a determined struggle. Because of the lack of massive social reforms, the lower classes grew increasingly indifferent to the revolution. Consequently (writes Spira), the War of Independence was lost.[34]

It does not seem that such generalizations can be made. It appears rather that, in the period after April, socially and politically progressive governmental measures mingled with governmental moves aimed at stabilization, the latter dictated by the false impression that the war had been won. Meanwhile, power gradually slipped from the grasp of the Hungarian regime. Between May and August 1849, all classes of society began to abandon the cause heralded by Kossuth. Emancipated farmers and unemancipated laborers, wealthy and poor burghers as well as nobles, grew tired of the war and of the increasingly theatrical manifestos of the government. The public still loved and admired Kossuth, as it always would; but it recognized, far earlier than the politicians, that the war was lost. No radical social reforms, outlined in hindsight, could have changed this basic fact.

Toward the end of the war Kossuth found himself at the head of a handful of civilian followers. What is astonishing is that the army, generally so critical of Kossuth, followed him down the path of destruction more loyally than did the masses.

On April 22 Kossuth initiated a bill to increase the army by 50,000 men. The bill was accepted by parliament but the new conscription failed disastrously. Almost all the counties reported a general lack of enthusiasm and even outright defiance. On June 1 the council of ministers complained to the government commissioners that enlistment had fallen far behind plans and that, for the first time in the war, there were more muskets than soldiers. This then was the history of Hungary's military effort: the barefooted and undisciplined volunteers of the autumn of 1848 gave way to the better equipped and enthusiastic regulars of the spring of 1849, to be replaced by a well-equipped army that was short of new blood in the summer.[35]

At about the same time that parliament passed the new army bill, Kossuth issued a momentous decree on the protection of the peasants. Ever since April 1848 peasants and landowners had been fighting over the rightful ownership of disputed pieces of land. Landlord abuses seem to have been particularly severe in the east Hungarian county of Szatmár; and while still president of the National Defense Committee, Kossuth had ordered a government commissioner to investigate conditions there. The commissioner's detailed report indicted the noble landowners; as a result, on April 19, 1849, Kossuth ordered that whenever the legal status of a given piece of land was in dispute (i.e., when it was not known whether the land had been dominical or urbarial), the benefit of the doubt would go to the peasants. It was for the landlord, to prove the dominical character of the land. If he failed to furnish satisfactory evidence of his ownership, he forfeited his right to dues and services from the peasants. This meant, at least in theory, that a great part of the contractual peasants would be liberated, for it was extremely difficult to prove traditional rights one way or another. In practice, Kossuth's decree was quietly ignored by most local officials, as was a subsequent governmental ordinance exempting the peasants from unpaid haulage in the period of summer labor.[36]

György Spira is correct in pointing out that Kossuth's decree on behalf of the peasants preceded the formation of the Szemere government and that the early measures of the Szemere cabinet tended to be conservative. But there would be another period of progressive governmental reforms toward the end of July. In any case, Kossuth's social measures did not lead to a popular insurrection against the enemy.

On April 20, when the House debated the special committee report on the alleged mishandling of Count Zichy's confiscated treasure and ended by condemning László Madarász, the sixty officials of the police department were also censured for not having kept more careful watch over the treasure chests. As a first measure toward consolidation and centralization, on May 11 the Szemere cabinet dissolved Madarász's separate police and postal department; it merged the police into the Ministry of the Interior and the postal service into the Ministry of Commerce. There was to be no more opening of private mail and no more spying. The police were not to act without orders from the prosecutor's office.[37]

Soon thereafter, the government proceeded to the consolidation of the judicial system. Summary courts of one kind or another had been operating in Hungary since the summer of 1848 trying rebels and traitors. There was much criticism of these revolutionary courts—the five judges, who had to come both from among the civilians and the military, could only acquit the defendants, relegate them to regular courts, or sentence them to death. The judges tended to be lenient with defendants from the noble estate, while they were noticeably harsher with peasants. Also, in the previous few months summary courts had multiplied until their respective jurisdictions overlapped. In order to protect the poorest of the defendants, on May 5 the minister of justice ordered that even paupers be provided with lawyers. He also ordered the summary courts to notify him regularly of every case. A few days later the government reduced the number of summary courts to ten and later, on June 8, to a single one in Pest. The minister of justice took strong steps to combat abuses against defendants' property. He forbade confiscation and allowed only the sequestering of property, and he forbade the sale of sequestered property without his express authorization. The private property of defendants' wives was to be protected; if left penniless, the wives and children of condemned defendants were entitled to enough income from the husband's property to live decently. All this clemency toward traitors may have weakened the war effort, but it stood in glaring contrast to the practices then increasingly adopted by the Austrian military judges, who condemned captured Hungarian rebels to death and confiscated their property.[38]

On May 12 the government began its campaign against the system of government commissioners by recalling the commissioners of fifteen counties and replacing them with regular deputy lord-lieutenants. Here, too, there had been many abuses; still, the system had functioned well, and the crackdown on the government commissioners was an error. It must be stated, however, that it was not only the Peace Party that had demanded the dissolution of this revolutionary institution: the radical Perczel had also blasted the government commissioners and requested their disbandment.[39]

The radicals were so exasperated by the government's law-and-order measures that some among them, for instance the Madarász brothers and Ödön Kállay, planned a mad plot to overthrow the government by calling on Perczel to occupy Debrecen with his army corps. Perczel declined, arguing correctly that the Left was too weak to seize power.[40] A somewhat more serious move against the government was planned by Görgey himself, but this too had to be dropped because the parliamentary Right felt itself no stronger against Kossuth than did the parliamentary Left.

When he was still besieging the walls of Castle Hill in Buda, Görgey was visited by General Klapka—or so Görgey tells us in his memoirs. Klapka presented his chief with a gloomy estimate of the general situation. The economic weakness of the country, he argued, would make it impossible to continue the war beyond the fall of 1849. In particular, Klapka referred to the shortage of funds and of gunpowder and lead to make bullets, and explained that Hungary could be saved only with foreign help. Such help would not be forthcoming, he felt, unless Hungary could withstand the concerted Austro-Russian attack until late fall 1849, an obvious impossibility. Continued struggle required unity of command that he, Klapka, as acting minister of war, was unable to secure, since the generals would not listen to him and Kossuth was no help either. Kossuth was a dangerous man, Klapka allegedly explained to Görgey, for the governor wished to exterminate the Serbs. Kossuth was also dishonest, Klapka went on, for he had talked the politicians into accepting the Declaration of Independence by referring to the enthusiasm of the army for such a step. He had equally misled the generals by alleging that the National Assembly was fully committed to independence.

Klapka then informed Görgey that there was a strong party in the House opposed to the dethronement of the Habsburgs and that he, Klapka, had already established contacts with this Peace Party.

All this came as a revelation to Görgey and led him to drop his plan for a military coup, or so again he tells us in his memoirs. He decided to go to Debrecen and attempt to put legal steps in motion for Kossuth's overthrow. The heads of the parliamentary delegation then visiting Görgey reaffirmed to him the deputies' hostility to Kossuth. Toward the end of May Görgey arrived in Debrecen and met with some fifteen or twenty deputies from the Peace Party, all of whom were unknown to him with the exception of General Mészáros. The meeting did not go well, for the politicians informed Görgey that just a few days earlier it had been decided to move the parliament to Pest and not to meet again until early in July. This legal avenue to removing Kossuth was therefore closed. Görgey then allegedly proposed a military coup, but that proposal was rejected by the Peace Party deputies with anguished cries: "We want no military revolution! We want no rule of the sword!" Görgey left the meeting "profoundly disappointed."

The general now decided on a new political strategy: to exert political influence by exhorting the officers faithful to him to stand for election in the House. Indeed, both Görgey and Klapka were soon given seats at local by-elections. The general also decided to get rid of the radicals in the army—a task in which, as we have seen before, he was more successful.[41]

To compound Görgey's dilemma, frightening news had been arriving from the Austrian side. On June 5 the new Austrian commander-in-chief in Hungary, *Feldzeugmeister* (three-star general) Baron Ludwig Haynau (who had replaced Welden), ordered the execution of two captured Hungarian officers for treason and rebellion. The two had been sentenced to death by one of Windisch-Graetz's military courts, but the sentence had not been carried out either under Windisch-Graetz or under Welden. Now Haynau, whose brutality was notorious, put the officers to death.[42]

The dual execution caused enormous excitement in Hungary, and especially in the army. The Hungarians had never executed an Austrian officer, nor did they keep the officers in close captivity. Officers among the prisoners of war were free to move around on parole in the city to which they were assigned, and the Hungarian government gave them regular peacetime pay. Now the executions ordered by Haynau showed that former officers of the Habsburg army could not expect clemency from Austria.

What was Görgey to do under these conditions? Kossuth, his cabinet, and the majority of the National Assembly would not negotiate: they were still hoping for victory. The army was ready to negotiate with the Austrians, but direct contacts were impossible. Not even unconditional surrender would guarantee the life of the officers. Yet the war was clearly lost.

For want of a better solution, Görgey still put his hope in a compromise peace. However, that could not be attempted without Kossuth's overthrow. Politics demanded that Görgey remain at the seat of the government, but his political aims could not be achieved without subjecting the Austrian enemy to a major blow before the massive arrival of the Russians. Hence Görgey also needed to be with the army. Finally Görgey decided to return to his army and commence military operations. This took place early in June, at least a month too late to defeat the Austrians.

The politicians continued to live in a fool's paradise. On May 31 Szemere requested the adjournment of the parliament and announced that the Assembly would meet again on July 2 in Pest.[43] On June 5 Kossuth left Debrecen for Budapest. Wherever he passed with his glittering retinue, he was met with speeches, flowers, and jubilation. Meanwhile the international situation had changed drastically, and an enormous Russian army was marching toward Hungary.

Decision in St. Petersburg

Habsburg-Romanov cooperation for European peace and the upholding of conservative principles dated from the end of the Napoleonic wars. Balkan developments in the 1820s temporarily disrupted this cooperation, with Russia playing an expansionist and international revolutionary role and Austria alone respecting the principle of legitimacy; but there never could be any doubt as to the two powers' readiness to assist one another in the event of a grave domestic crisis. In 1830–31, during the Polish revolution, Metternich stood by the tsar, earning the latter's gratitude and lasting confidence through his steadfast support. In 1833, at Austrian initiative, Francis and Nicholas met at Münchengrätz in Bohemia to conclude a formal alliance, joined in the same year by the Prussian king. The three rulers swore "in the name of the blessed and indivisible Holy Trinity" (as their subsequent manifesto revealed) to come to each other's aid, upon request, against all domestic and foreign enemies. The rulers and their ministers met again in 1835 at Teplitz, where Metternich addressed the tsar as his master and as Austria's protector, advisor, and savior. The Austrian chancellor and the tsar fully agreed in their hatred of the liberal bourgeoisie and of middle-class political agitation. In 1846 Nicholas and Frederick William of Prussia militarily supported Austria against the Polish revolutionaries in Galicia and in the annexation of the free city of Cracow. The tsar took a lively interest in Austrian domestic affairs, and he decided well before 1848 that Hungary would present the gravest threat to the integrity of the Habsburg Monarchy.[44]

No sooner did he receive the news of the February revolution in Paris than Nicholas ordered the partial mobilization of his army. He was preparing to send military aid to Ferdinand in Vienna when the surrender of the Austrian Court to liberal demands caused him to drop his plan. As the Austrian constitutional governments became successively less conservative, St. Petersburg's hostility to them grew commensurately. The case of Hungary especially worried the tsar, for he suspected the Hungarians not only of wishing to break away from the Habsburg dynasty, but also of planning to create revolutionary disturbances in the Danubian Principalities and plotting to occupy the mouth of the Danube.

Fully aware of the Russian threat to Hungary's autonomous development, the Batthyány cabinet did its best to reassure the tsar. It made clear in Vienna and thus, it hoped, also in St. Petersburg that far from fomenting revolt in Moldavia and Wallachia, the Hungarian constitutional government viewed with suspicion the Romanian national movement.[45] And indeed, a powerful Romanian nation could only be dangerous to Hungary with its large Romanian minority. In the summer of 1848 Kossuth himself made sure that Romanian refugees from the Danubian Principalities would not become politically active in Hungary.[46] Of course, this was rather embarrassing to Kossuth for it contradicted his professed enthusiasm, and that of the Hungarian liberal reformers, for freedom movements everywhere. But, as in Italy's case, Kossuth placed national interest above international liberal solidarity.

If Kossuth was caught in a painful dilemma, the Russian government's problem was no less acute. Suspicious of the Batthyány cabinet, St. Petersburg was even more suspicious of Hungary's domestic enemies. In the spring and early summer of 1848 Russian diplomats in Vienna consistently interpreted the anti-Hungarian agitation of Jelačić as a threat to the Monarchy, and to law and order in general.[47] When, at the end of July, a Croatian delegation appeared before Russian Chargé d'Affaires Felix Fonton in Vienna to ask for Russian aid against Hungary, the Russian diplomat categorically rejected the Croatian plea. Revolutionary movements, whether South Slav or Hungarian, were anathema to Russian diplomacy. Only when it became clear that Jelačić was above all the emperor's soldier did Russia's view of him change drastically. By September 1848 Jelačić was the celebrated hero of St. Petersburg political circles.

The formation of the Schwarzenberg cabinet in November 1848 was well received in Russia, for it was expected that the new prime minister together with Field Marshal Windisch-Graetz would quickly reestablish order in the Habsburg Monarchy. Schwarzenberg's liberal pronouncements were interpreted (rather inaccurately) as a smoke screen.

The tsar stood ready at all times to offer limited military assistance to Austria; and at the end of November 1848 the Russian government demonstrated this readiness. Windisch-Graetz was informed that the tsar had authorized his corps commanders near the Austrian border to rush to the aid of the Austrian generals upon the latter's request, without previous consultation with St. Petersburg. The aid was to be local but unconditional. When in the winter of 1848/49 General Bem drove most of the Austrians out of Transylvania and then entered Bukovina on January 5 with his troops, the tsarist government became alarmed; it could hardly wait for an Austrian appeal for military assistance. Such a step, however, was most painful to the Austrian leadership. Schwarzenberg repeatedly asserted that the Monarchy was perfectly able to deal with the Hungarian rebels and forbade General Puchner, the Transylvanian commander, to seek Russian intervention. But when Puchner nevertheless asked for help from the Russian commander in the Danubian Principalities, Schwarzenberg did not protest. He left it to Puchner to decide when the Russian auxiliary army would no longer be needed.

Called in by Puchner and by the Saxon burghers of Brassó and Nagyszeben, some six thousand Russian troops entered Transylvania on February 4. As it turned out, their stay was short and their campaign anything but glorious. On March 11 at Nagyszeben Bem completely defeated the united Austro-Russian army. Now Russia, too, was humiliated; and to make matters worse, the Ottoman Porte was becoming increasingly agitated. The Danubian Principalities were theoretically Turkish territory; it was the Turks who had subdued the Wallachian liberal revolt of June 1848; and now Russian troops were using Wallachia as a base for their invasion of Hungary, a country friendly to the Porte. When the Ottomans mobilized their army and navy against Russia, war was prevented only by the energetic intervention of Palmerston in Istanbul.

Curiously, Kossuth refused to take the Russian problem seriously. He—for whom the Russian and pan-Slav threat had always been Hungary's main dilemma, but only *in abstracto*—tried to ignore the Russian intervention in Transylvania. Rather, he insisted on believing in the tsar's good will. This can be understood only in light of Kossuth's unswerving optimism in foreign affairs, which embraced the conviction that Europe as a whole, governments as well as peoples, looked with sympathy on Hungary.

At first no one but the soldiers on the spot could or would believe that the Russians were in Transylvania. On February 13, 1849, Government Plenipotentiary Csányi reported to Kossuth that the Székely soldiers at Brassó had encountered some "miraculous troops dressed in Russian uniform." In reality, Csányi wrote, they were Romanian peasants dressed up by the "dastardly Saxon burghers" to look like soldiers from Muscovy. On February 23 Kossuth, still convinced that the Russians were Romanian peasants, ordered Csányi to get in touch with the Russian commander in Wallachia, and through him to send a friendly message to St. Petersburg. The message was to emphasize Hungary's loyalty to the House of Austria, and it was to point out that the war had been forced upon Hungary. In a separate confidential message Csányi was to indicate to the Russian government that the Crown of Hungary could be made available to Prince Leuchtenberg, a nephew of the tsar.

It is not known whether the Hungarian message ever was sent.

Csányi himself continued to argue, as late as March 10, that the Russian troops were not Russian and that Russian intervention was an *idée fixe* of old Bem. The next day Bem trounced the Russians and Austrians at Nagyszeben, and four days later the last of the Russian soldiers left Transylvania. Now at last Kossuth grew furious and threatened the Saxons with expulsion from Hungary after the war.[48]

Following their debacle in Transylvania, the Russians were no longer willing to intervene locally. Nicholas still wanted to help but only with a large and invincible army. While the Hungarians accumulated victories over the Habsburg army, negotiations dragged on between Vienna and St. Petersburg, with the former trying to make its appeal for help as unofficial and as inconspicuous as possible, and the latter insisting on an open and official petition. Nicholas envisioned himself the savior of Austria; he expected no gains or compensation but relished the expectations of an easy and popular victory. As things went from bad to worse for the Austrians, Schwarzenberg gradually acceded to the Russian point of view. It was the civilians in his cabinet who long opposed Austria's public humiliation, while the Austrian generals, especially Windisch-Graetz and Welden, pleaded for immediate Russian intervention under any conditions. Welden had still drawn an optimistic picture of the situation in Hungary at the end of March, but on April 20 he informed the Court that no hope existed outside the Russian army. On the following day Schwarzenberg asked the Russian minister in Vienna for military assistance. This was not good enough for the tsar: he wanted Francis Joseph to turn to him directly and publicly. This too was done, with the young emperor pleading on May 1 for armed assistance in "the holy struggle against anarchy." Following the publication of the appeal in the official *Wiener Zeitung,* the tsar immediately ordered Field Marshal Prince Ivan Paskevich, viceroy of Poland, to hasten preparations against Hungary. Schwarzenberg followed up with a series of urgent dispatches to the "Prince of Warsaw"; while in a memorable Warsaw scene, Austria's military emissary to Poland, General Count Johan Caboga, was genuflecting to kiss Paskevich's hands and tearfully imporing the Russian field marshal not to waste another hour. This, at least, is the story passed on by the Russians present at the scene.[49] On May 21 Emperor Francis Joseph himself appeared in Warsaw to meet with the tsar. He, too, went down on his knees and kissed the hands of his Imperial protector.

The Austrian panic was unwarranted. Because of the exhaustion of the *honvéd* army, its lack of artillery ammunition, its self-defeating strategy following the liberation of Komárom, and the hostility between Görgey and Kossuth, the Hungarian army was totally unable to take Vienna. Furthermore, Austrian strength was increasing constantly; Hungarian strength was declining. By the end of May Austria had a vigorous and determined new commander in Hungary in the person of Haynau. He would soon defeat the Hungarian main army with only minor Russian assistance.

Perhaps Austria's haste was due to fear of foreign political complications as a result of Russian intervention. If this was true, the anxiety was exaggerated, for no power in Europe—large or small, legal or illegal—was willing or able to lift a finger on behalf of Hungary. Admittedly, Vienna could not have judged this in the crucial months of April and May, what with terrified generals wringing their hands at Schwarzenberg's door. Still, it was a tragedy for Austria that cool heads did not prevail, or more properly, that cool heads were absent. Tsarist military intervention in the summer of 1849 destroyed Hungarian independence—something the Austrians could have taken care of by themselves—and destroyed as well the Great Power status and prestige of the Habsburg Monarchy.

It has often been asserted that Russian intervention was a result of the tsar's fear that the Hungarian revolution would spread to Poland. This is only partly true. The Russians naturally disliked seeing Polish generals at the head of Hungarian armies. They also resented the presence of a Polish legion in Hungary. But the Polish legion consisted of barely 3,000 men, many of whom were in reality Slovaks.* And even if the Russians had heard of General Dembiński's plan to invade Poland from Hungary, it is unlikely that they would have taken the plan seriously.

All through the spring of 1849 Dembiński had badgered Kossuth

---

* Western observers wildly overestimated the role of Poles in the Hungarian revolution. Typically, the British embassy in Vienna reported on April 24, 1849, that "the struggle has now acquired as much a Polish as a Hungarian character; Polish Generals, Dembinski, Bem, etc., direct all the military movements, and Polish infantry form the best though not the most numerous portions of the insurgent troops." Four days later the embassy informed Palmerston that Poles directed the artillery of the Hungarian army, and that the Polish infantry numbered 15,000 in Hungary, forming "the kernel of their best troops" (*Correspondence Relative to the Affairs of Hungary*, pp. 184–185, 189). In reality, there were practically no Polish artillerists, and the Polish legion, although brave, was unimportant as a military force. Officers of the legion, quarreling among themselves and with the Hungarians, caused Kossuth a lot of trouble.

with projects to carry the war into Polish territory, an idea unpopular among the Hungarian generals and politicians as well as among the Poles in Hungary. Bem rejected the project categorically, and so did Kossuth after some hesitation. In their joint resolution of May 5, the governor and the Council of Ministers argued that the Polish liberation movement was too weak, that the Galician peasants had not changed their murderous intentions toward the Polish nobility, and that a Hungarian invasion of Polish territory would bring both Russia and Prussia into the war against Hungary. Clearly, both Russians and Hungarians knew full well that the Polish people would not move: the wounds of 1831 and 1846 were still open in Polish hearts.[50]

In sum, the Russian invasion of Hungary was due less to the Polish problem than to the tsar's genuine desire to help his young fellow monarch, and to Nicholas's passion to extirpate "anarchy" wherever it presented itself. The tsar and his generals expected an easy campaign marked by heart-warming victories. The campaign was indeed easy, as it turned out; but it was not marked by many victories in the field: that job was done for Russia by Haynau's Austrian armies.

"Awake, O peoples and nations of Europe"

By late spring 1849 news from the outside was hard to come by in Hungary. There were a few captured newspapers and others were smuggled in; an occasional French paper reached the country through Turkey but with enormous delay. In contrast with the recent past, revolutionary Hungary was now efficiently guarded by its enemies. It took two weeks for the Hungarians to learn of the emperor's May 1 appeal to the tsar and the tsar's decision to invade Hungary; but when the news did reach Kossuth and the government, they reacted instantly. Typically, their measures were dictated less by despair than by renewed hope. Convinced that all Europe would be terrified by the forthcoming Russian invasion of Hungary, and that the British and the French would never consent to it, Kossuth and his colleagues conjured up the image of a great European anti-absolutist alliance responding on Hungary's behalf. Their immediate task, as they saw it, was to alert the Hungarian people and the world.[51]

On May 18 the Council of Ministers asked Kossuth to authorize a crusade against the coming invasion of Hungary. Setting the tone of all subsequent Hungarian proclamations, the council warned that the tsarist army would turn the country into a Russian colony and her inhabitants into slaves. "The Russian will extirpate the national identity of Hungarians, Germans, Romanians, Serbs and Slovaks alike, for he hates all who are not Russians. . . . He will suppress our religion, just as he is now persecuting Catholicism in Poland and torturing the Protestants in Livonia and Estonia." Against these horrors, the council proposed, and Kossuth accepted, a solemn protest addressed to all the nations; a people's insurrection at home; a whole series of divine services and processions; a national day of fasting on June 6; the incessant ringing of church bells; a scorched-earth policy with compensation to be paid later by the government; and a muster of bishops and clergy to lead the people against the enemy in their ecclesiastic garb. On the same day Kossuth and Foreign Minister Count Kázmér Batthyány formulated a solemn protest to the nations of Europe. Next, the foreign minister sent a lengthy memorandum to Lord Palmerston asking the British to prevent the Russian invasion, supporting his request with an inventory of the political and economic advantages that would accrue to England from an alliance with Hungary.[52]

All this was only the beginning of a series of Hungarian manifestos, protests, and appeals. The minister of cults devised a special crusade-prayer for the use of the clergy, women and children were given special auxiliary tasks, and senior citizens were asked to bless and exhort younger men on their way to meet the enemy.

The crusade was a failure from the start. There was no popular rise to arms (the number of draft dodgers increased constantly), the clergy did very little if anything, and granaries were not burned in the path of the Russian army. On June 27, with the Russians physically in Hungary, Kossuth issued an even more pathetic proclamation. He depicted the Russians as killers, rapists, and looters and warned all nationalities in Hungary that the Russians would kill them, or at best deport them to Siberia. Again, Kossuth ordered that all men arm themselves within forty-eight hours with axes and scythes, and that the countryside be devastated ahead of the tsarist armies. The following day the governor and the cabinet launched a new appeal to the peoples and governments of Europe: "You proud English nation . . . do you tolerate this assault on constitutional freedom? . . .

You French republic, have you forgotten the principles upon which your system had been built?'' And to conclude: "Awake, O peoples and nations of Europe! Your freedom will be decided on the fields of Hungary.''[53]

These appeals, often drafted in Kossuth's own hand, were a monument to his declining realism and perspicacity. He who in the past had used rhetoric as a subtle weapon to coax his supporters toward realistic and attainable goods, had now been overwhelmed by his own tactics. The constant harping on the theme of extreme Russian brutality tended to paralyze rather than activate the inhabitants of the country. The religious themes, repeated interminably, ran counter to the anticlerical and enlightened message of the Hungarian revolution. Yet it was precisely this latter message which had attracted many educated Hungarians to Kossuth.[54] The terrifying image of voluntary self-destruction could not possibly appeal to peasants who had just recently gained ownership of their land. Further concessions in terms of taxes or other benefits had been their expectation, not the burning of everything they had. Experience had clearly shown that the peasants were willing to fight for their homeland as long as armed defense offered more protection to their property than submission to the enemy would have.

The simultaneous appeal to the cabinets and the peoples of Europe, with its mélange of tactics, had the effect of neutralizing the appeal. The Hungarians, to attract the increasingly conservative European governments to their side, should have insisted on the legality of Hungary's fight and on Europe's need to check Russian expansion; and to attract the "oppressed peoples of Europe," that is, those in revolt, the tone of the manifestos should obviously have been different. In the final analysis, either tactic would have been hopeless.

The flow of Hungarian agents to foreign countries, begun under Prime Minister Batthyány, continued unabated under Kossuth. Following circuitous and adventurous routes, these representatives (some of them women) reached every major European capital. The Declaration of Independence and the protest against Russian intervention were printed in many languages and were smuggled abroad by various batches of agents. The emissaries knew little of one another and their commissions were vague and overlapping. Some of these agents were honest and talented patriots; others were swindlers.[55] Of all the Hungarian diplomatic representatives sent abroad by Kossuth, only two—Count László Teleki and Ferenc Pulszky—achieved international fame though no official diplomatic recognition.

László Teleki was the scion of a great Transylvanian family.[56] At the start of the revolution, Teleki was thirty-eight years old and one of Hungary's most controversial politicians. Unlike some of his relatives who served the dynasty faithfully, he was a radical and a republican. As a member of the Upper House he had belonged to the far-Left opposition. An unsuccessful dramatist, he was well read, intelligent, passionate, neurotic, given to fighting duels, and an incurable pessimist. He spoke several languages, and he had studied and traveled abroad. In 1848 he was elected to the National Assembly on a markedly progressive program. As a deputy he recommended extensive concessions to Croatia, and he violently opposed the idea of Hungary offering aid to the king against the Italian revolutionaries. At the end of August 1848 Prime Minister Batthyány sent him to Paris, some say to get rid of a bothersome radical, more probably in order to convert the French nation to the cause of Hungary.

Although the French government had asked Batthyány for a diplomatic representative and the French themselves had planned to send a chargé d'affaires to Buda-Pest, Teleki was not recognized in France as an official emissary. Austrian diplomats protested immediately against the French plan to send a special envoy to Hungary, and Prime Minister Cavaignac was hostile to the plan in any case. As a result, Teleki was received only as a "distinguished foreigner." Nevertheless he stayed, diligently trying to accomplish what he sensed to be hopeless. The French knew little about Hungary, and what they knew was mostly unflattering. Foreign Minister Bastide, a former lumber merchant, insisted that the Hungarians were "Catholic Slavs"; the French newspapers tended to identify the "Madjars" with the nobility, and the latter with extreme, barbarian chauvinist policy; Victor Hugo's journal, *Les Évènements,* celebrated Jelačić as a freedom fighter; only the *National* was somewhat friendly. It was much to Teleki's credit that he converted several journals to the cause of Hungary within a few months of his arrival.

In January 1849 Teleki was joined by Ferenc Pulszky, a very different sort of Hungarian. Cultivated, witty, charming, bright, and an opportunist, he was at home in the world of West European journalism and political intrigue. Pulszky came from the ranks of the middle nobility. A few years younger than Teleki, he was born in the same region of northern Hungary as Kossuth's and Görgey's families.[57] Pulszky's mother tongue was German, as was theirs, but he too embraced the Hungarian cultural renaissance at an early age. As a young jurist at the Diet of 1832–36, he became a radical, subsequently escaping arrest only by undertaking a study tour abroad. More than a dilettante in the fine arts, philosophy, and archeology, he met with the famous scholars of Europe. Returning to Hungary, he launched journalistic debates with the German critics of the reform movement at home. He supported Kossuth, and like Kossuth he strongly opposed the national aspirations of the minorities, especially of the Slovaks. In 1845 Pulszky married the daughter of an enormously wealthy Vienna banker (she later wrote a fine book on Hungary[58]), installed himself in a castle, and was awakened from a life of leisure only by the events of 1848. Because of his excellent Vienna connections, he was made state secretary to Prince Pál Esterházy. In reality it was Pulszky who led Hungary's unofficial foreign ministry. Following the resignation of Esterházy in September 1848, Pulszky became Kossuth's main agent in Vienna. There he learned how to bribe journalists, an experience that would serve him well in London and Paris. As we have seen (see chapter 5), he was in Vienna during the October revolution; he then returned home to become one of Kossuth's closest associates. After Windisch-Graetz's invasion of Hungary in December, Pulszky suddenly left the country. Despite his claims to the contrary in his memoirs, there can be little doubt that Pulszky took fright and escaped. But since he was both able and willing to serve his country abroad, Kossuth let him do so. The two Hungarian emissaries worked closely together: Teleki mainly in France, Pulszky mostly in Great Britain.

Teleki's best potential allies were the French radicals, who wished to start a European revolutionary war. Yet he generally avoided them for he sensed a turn to the right in French politics following the December 1848 election of Louis Napoleon as president. He preferred contacts with more moderate groups, among them the conservative royalists. The results were disappointing, and Teleki turned to those whose plight was similar to his and with whom he could at least discuss Central European affairs: the political emigrés. In the Hotel Lambert, the residence of the Polish Prince Adam Czartoryski, he met with the prince and many Poles and other refugees. They were different from their compatriots at home: more sophisticated and more tolerant. Members of the Lambert Polish coterie and the Romanian revolutionary emissary Alexandru Golescu dreamed of a federation or confederation of all nations between the Baltic and the Black Sea.[59] These were generous and grandiose plans that could have altered the course of history if anyone besides some emigrés had taken them seriously. The talk delighted Teleki, who developed the Hungarian side of the project. Arguing that Saint Stephen's Hungary was as dead as Austria, he would grant autonomy not only to the Croats, but also to the other nationalities. Yet even he insisted that the official language of federated Hungary be Hungarian. Furthermore, he imagined that Hungary would become "the center and queen of a future Danubian Confederation with power to crush forever the monster of absolutism and with borders extending from the Baltic to the Black Sea." All this magnificence demanded but "a little bit of self-sacrifice on our part." These Great Power dreams were contained in a letter to Kossuth, and thereby Teleki may have hoped to mitigate the painful effect at home of his proposed concessions to the national minorities.[60]

Prince Czartoryski, who in the past had regarded the Hungarians as oppressors of the Slavs and who could never overcome his dislike for Kossuth, agreed to work with Teleki. On May 19, 1849, in the Hotel Lambert, a number of leading emigrés—Teleki, Pulszky, a third Hungarian, the Czech František Rieger, Czartoryski, and other Poles—met and drew up a protocol according to which Hungary would grant complete territorial autonomy to Croatia, the Serbian Vojvodina, and the Romanian-inhabited areas of Hungary. Germans and Slovaks would enjoy local or municipal autonomy. This protocol had no binding value, but it was the first of its kind in Central European history.[61] Kossuth indignantly rejected the protocol, and there can be little doubt that the domestic leaders of the other nationalities would have rejected it too, had they ever been told of its contents. Pulszky, who had come to Paris at Teleki's request, considered the whole affair a comedy and wondered how grown-up men could have engaged in such senseless activity.[62]

The news of Russian intervention stirred both Teleki and Pulszky to feverish activity. Teleki's enthusiasm faded fast, however, especially when he learned of Kossuth's intransigence with regard to the nationalities. On June 10 and with Kossuth's blessing, Kázmér Batthyány sent a memorandum to all the Hungarian emissaries abroad, upbraiding them for undue promises some of them had made to the nationalities and insisting that the emissaries uphold the principle of unconditional Magyar supremacy in Hungary.[63] Nor was Teleki charmed by proposals coming from Kossuth that the Adriatic port of Buccari (which the Hungarians did not hold) be pledged to the British in exchange for their support, or that the Crown of Saint Stephen be offered to various princely houses in Europe, including the Bonapartes.

The government of Louis Napoleon, while not unconcerned about Russian intervention in Hungary, was too busy and harassed to take effective action. Parliamentary elections in May 1849 absorbed everyone's attention; in addition, French troops were preparing for their final assault on Mazzini's and Garibaldi's Roman Republic. It was therefore essential for France to secure the goodwill of Russia and Austria. Temporarily swayed by left-wing pressure, early in May Foreign Minister Drouyn de Lhuys declared in the parliament that if England would take measures to counteract Russian intervention, France would follow suit. Teleki congratulated himself on this development, but Russian and Austrian diplomats soon understood that these were mere words. Drouyn de Lhuys immediately apologized to the Russian chargé d'affaires; and in the same month in an unheard-of move, the tsar officially recognized the French Republic. After the French troops had attacked the Roman Republic early in June, the radical "Mountain" attempted to overthrow the French government, but it failed lamentably; and the leader of the radicals, Ledru-Rollin, was forced to flee to Belgium.

Fortunately for Teleki, he had not openly associated himself with the "Reds"; still, Hungary had lost its only real friends in Paris. Because of radical pressure, on July 12 the French Assembly termed the Russian invasion "dangerous to liberty," but this gesture was not followed by any action. In Eastern European affairs the French government generally followed Great Britain's lead, and in London Foreign Secretary Lord Palmerston, never too harassed to care, worked actively for the preservation of the Habsburg Monarchy.

Palmerston never wavered in his belief that Hungary "was a part of the Austrian Empire" and was to be treated accordingly. Teleki, who saw all this very well, moved to London in the summer of 1849 to help Pulszky. Both he and Pulszky had their private interviews with Palmerston; each time the foreign secretary explained patiently that his liberal sympathy for Hungary notwithstanding, the integrity of the Habsburg Monarchy was essential to European security. After the Russian invasion had begun, Palmerston publicly declared himself disturbed; but in personal conversation with the Russian ambassador he expressed the hope that the tsarist army would act swiftly. He added his desire that reason and magnanimity guide Austrian policy toward Hungary after the war.[64] Broken in spirit, Teleki sent his resignation to Kossuth on August 3, 1849: "I am sick, dying," he wrote.[65] By the time his letter reached home, an independent Hungary no longer existed.

Pulszky understood rapidly that his role was that of a lobbyist rather than a diplomat. In London since February, he had patiently built up a circle of political and journalistic friends. With the money put at his disposal by Teleki, he employed a few talented writers; and with his charm he won over such fairly influential liberal politicians as Bernwall Osborne and Lord Stuart Dudley as well as Richard Cobden, the apostle of free trade. The Russian invasion created a painful impression in England. Public opinion rapidly swung around to the Hungarian side, but the Russian ambassador was still able to reassure St. Petersburg that the British cabinet "believes it to be useful and necessary for Russia to hasten to the aid of Austria." Prime Minister Earl John Russell went beyond Palmerston's "balance of powers" reasoning and declared to the Russian ambassador that he, Russell, abhorred the "red color of socialism" wherever it presented itself. In his opinion Hungary was one of those red countries.[66] But the British wanted to prevent Austria's sinking to the level of a vassal state of Russia.

Of the other European powers, Prussia, by then thoroughly conservative, was definitely hostile to Hungary. In the spring of 1849, Berlin offered to send 20,000–30,000 Prussian and other German troops to aid Francis Joseph against Kossuth; but only if Austria would allow Berlin to conclude a military alliance with the other German princes. Schwarzenberg immediately rejected this offer, for he wished himself to sign a military alliance with the German princes with the aim of establishing Austrian supremacy in Germany. It was because the Prussian offer had been totally unacceptable that Schwarzenberg, in despair, turned to Russia for assistance.[67]

Of Italy's many principalities, Piedmont (Sardinia) was most friendly to Hungary, but only if and when it happened to be at war with Austria. The two countries exchanged chargés d'affaires in December 1848, and the Piedmontese were allowed to encourage Hungarian soldiers in Austrian-held Lombardy to come over to their side. Teleki and other Hungarians issued a manifesto to the Hungarian troops, but the results were most disappointing. Instead of the expected 20,000, only about 200 or 300 Hungarians escaped across the border to form a Hungarian legion. When in March 1849 Piedmont gave up the fight against Austria, Teleki had enormous difficulty preventing the Piedmontese from handing over the Hungarian deserters to Austria. The free republic of Venice, the Italian revolution's last stronghold in the summer of 1849, naturally considered itself an ally of revolutionary Hungary. Daniele Manin, dictator of Venice, was as much a hero to the Hungarians as Kossuth was to the Venetians. On June 3, 1849, the two powers concluded a formal defensive and offensive alliance, according to which the Venetians would equip a Hungarian Adriatic navy in exchange for Hungarian monetary aid.[68] Unfortunately for the signatory powers, the Hungarians were nowhere near the Adriatic, and Venice was under siege. Soon they would eat rats and dogs and grow pale from worries other than the creation of a Hungarian fleet. Communication between the allies became impossible, and the Republic of San Marco succumbed to the Austrian army at about the same time as did Hungary.

In the last months of the war, Kossuth made great efforts to create a Southeast European alliance among the Serbs, the Romanians, and the Turks. With the Serbs the result was nil, with the Romanians a little bit better than that. The Turks were sympathetic but powerless: Kossuth's chief envoy to Istanbul, Count Gyula Andrássy (the future foreign minister of the Dual Monarchy), was reduced to sending situation reports to Kossuth.

Kossuth also put much hope in an alliance with the United States. The American chargé d'affaires to Vienna, Stiles, was most accommodating, but he could do nothing. Late in the spring of 1849 one of Kossuth's emissaries to Paris, a certain Samu Vass, suddenly left for the United States. Whether he left on his own authority or at Kossuth's request remains unclear. Vass arrived in the United States sometime in June and established contacts with the tiny Hungarian colony in New York and with the U.S. government. By then the Hungarian emigrés had been active on behalf of Hungary, and on May 24 they had decided to sew a Hungarian flag and dispatch it to

Kossuth. The leader of the Hungarian-American community, Professor Leopold Breisach, wrote to President Zachary Taylor suggesting that he send a special agent to Hungary. The President obliged and on June 18 instructed one of his diplomats in Paris, A. Dudley Mann, to proceed secretly to Hungary in order to ascertain if Hungary was truly independent. True independence would win U.S. recognition. Meanwhile Kossuth had also written to President Taylor asking him for the diplomatic recognition of Hungary.[69] A follow-up letter by Kázmér Batthyány reached the United States only after the surrender of the Hungarian army. As for the U.S. agent Mann, he never got farther than Vienna, but in his reports to the State Department he presented a well-balanced account of Hungarian events.[70]

All this is a rather pathetic tale, and one must ask if it had been worth sending agents abroad in the first place. Undoubtedly Kossuth, a provincial who had never been in a foreign country, knew little of European diplomacy; and what he knew was marred by his national pride and optimism. Yet a more cosmopolitan statesman might not have achieved more. Kossuth was right in generally avoiding the noisy but impotent revolutionary groups; he was wrong in believing that the governments would help. He tried everything, from appealing to the mercantile spirit of the British to invoking the alleged republican dedication of the French. His agents were an uneven lot, but it is doubtful that more astute envoys would have achieved more. One thing his emissaries did accomplish. They prepared the ground for the delirious enthusiasm the West would manifest toward their country and its leader after Hungary was defeated and Kossuth had become a refugee.

In the summer of 1849 Kossuth and the government had less and less time for foreign affairs in any case: in June the Russians invaded Hungary.

March across Hungary

As agreed to by tsar and emperor, Paskevich's forces were to enter Hungary on June 17. While one strong Russian division would be lent to the Austrians, the bulk of the tsarist army would operate independently. Except for food and fodder, the Russians would receive nothing from Austria; and following the suppression of the Hungarian rebellion, the tsar's soldiers would depart immediately. Finally, all Poles in Hungarian service, whether from Russian, Prussian, or Austrian Poland, would be handed over to the Russian authorities.[71] These were generous terms indeed for Austria, with only one demeaning stipulation: the extradition of Polish revolutionaries who were Austrian subjects. A few years later, when Francis Joseph chose to support Russia's enemies during the Crimean war, the tsar would have ample opportunity to regret his previous generosity.

Undoubtedly, Schwarzenberg would have accepted far more humiliating conditions if these had hastened the Russian invasion. In reality, no amount of Austrian prostration would have made any difference, for at age sixty-seven Field Marshal Paskevich, the hero of the French, Persian (hence his title of Count of Erivan), Turkish, and Polish (hence his title of Prince of Warsaw) wars, had become rather circumspect. Unwilling to sully his reputation with reckless military adventures, he ordered the stockpiling of enormous supplies of food and ammunition along the Hungarian border. Even though he had quickly dispatched the single infantry division on loan to Austria, advance units of his army had barely crossed the Carpathians by the June 17 deadline.

Haynau, the Austrian commander-in-chief in Hungary, was far more eager to fight; and he soon did without waiting for the Russians. Four years younger than Paskevich, the Austrian *Feldzeugmeister* was a fearsome soldier. The son of the elector of Hesse from a morganatic and hence secret marriage (if the marriage took place at all), Haynau entered Habsburg military service in 1801 at the age of fifteen. He excelled in the Napoleonic wars, rose quickly in the ranks, and was a general stationed at Temesvár when the age of constitutions dawned upon the emperor's army. Haynau solved the dilemma of divided allegiance by simply abandoning his post in Hungary and joining the regiment he "owned" in Lombardy. He distinguished himself under Radetzky at Custozza, and again in the Italian campaign of March 1849. Then, in Brescia, he ordered the flogging of local Italian insurgents, among them women of noble birth. For this, history has never forgiven Haynau. His defenders claim that the women had been guilty of pointing out the Austrian soldiers among the wounded in the hospitals; the Italian revolutionaries then cut the throats of these unfortunates.[72] Be that as it may, this tall, aristocratic soldier, whose luxurious mustache was conspicuous even in an age of luxurious mustaches, was mean, suspicious, hysterical, and probably a sadist. But he was also a fine general, and although he lacked the patriarchal bonhomie and charm of the octogenarian Radetzky, who was adored by his soldiers, Haynau was not unpopular in his army. The Hungarians and Italians hated him, of course, as did the Western press, which came to call him the "Hyena of Brescia," a play on his name. On a visit to England following the war, Haynau was soundly thrashed and almost thrown into the Thames by enraged workers in Watney's Brewery. To his own men, Haynau represented the efficient organizer and the victorious general: a commodity the Habsburg army in Hungary had until then held in short supply.

When Haynau took over Welden's army at the end of May, the once dispirited little force was already on its way to a brisk recovery. Officers had come in droves from Lombardy, and so had a few good regiments; and the recruitment and training of new men proceeded without difficulty. In a period when the flow of *honvéd* volunteers and conscripts was slowing to a trickle, Austria easily enlisted thousands of young men, proving once again that it was capable of survival.[73]

Between June and August, Haynau's rejuvenated Army of the Danube fought a dozen important engagements, more than once against superior enemy forces. There were a few draws, but Haynau did not lose a single battle against the Hungarians. Ultimately it was the Austrians, not the Russians, who put an end to the Hungarian war of independence. This triumphant campaign, the last in the annals of Austrian military history, was due to the prowess of an old brute of a general and to the splendid determination of His Majesty's German, Slavic, and Romanian peasant soldiers.

Total Allied superiority over Hungary was crushing. The Austrian and Russian armies of invasion were more numerous, better equipped, and better led than the *honvéd* army. Haynau's Army of the Danube, consisting of four army corps and the Russian infantry division on loan from Paskevich, numbered about 83,000 men and 330 artillery pieces.[74] It was the Allies' best army. In the south of Hungary a mixed Austro-Serbo-Croatian force under Jelačić numbered some 44,000 men and 190 guns. In Transylvania the Austro-Romanian regulars were notably weak, with fewer than twenty battalions clinging precariously to a few forts and frontier passes. These

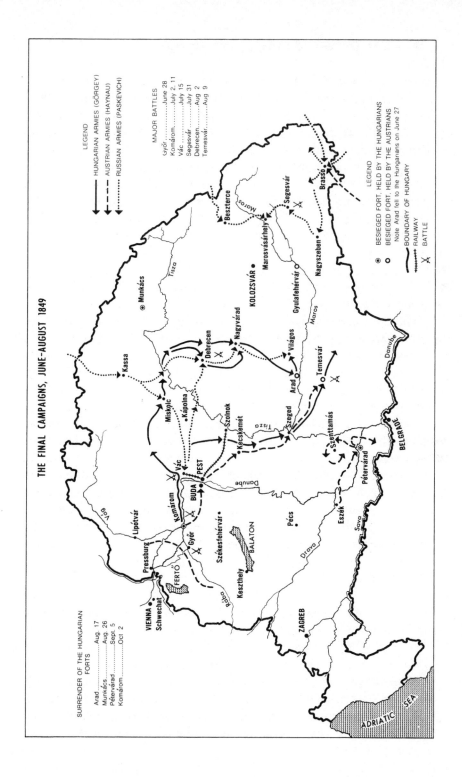

THE FINAL CAMPAIGNS, JUNE–AUGUST 1849

SURRENDER OF THE HUNGARIAN
FORTS

Arad..............Aug. 17
Munkács..........Aug. 26
Pétervárad.......Sept. 5
Komárom..........Oct 2

LEGEND

→ HUNGARIAN ARMIES (GÖRGEY)
- - → AUSTRIAN ARMIES (HAYNAU)
····· → RUSSIAN ARMIES (PASKEVICH)

MAJOR BATTLES

Győr..............June 28
Komárom..........July 2, 11
Vác...............July 15
Segesvár.........July 31
Debrecen.........Aug 2
Temesvár.........Aug 9

LEGEND

⊙ BESIEGED FORT, HELD BY THE HUNGARIANS
○ BESIEGED FORT, HELD BY THE AUSTRIANS
  Note Arad fell to the Hungarians on June 27
╫╫╫ RAILWAY
✗ BOUNDARY OF HUNGARY
✗ BATTLE

VIENNA
Schwechat

Pressburg
Lipótvár
FERTŐ
Győr
Komárom
Székesfehérvár
Keszthely
BALATON
Pécs
Vág
Rába
Dráva
Sava
ZAGREB
Eszék
BUDA PEST
Vác
Szolnok
Kecskemét
Miskolc
Kápolna
Kassa
Munkács
Tisza
Beszterce
Debrecen
Nagyvárad
Szeged
Szenttamás
Pétervárad
BELGRADE
Danube
Arad
Világos
Temesvár
Gyulafehérvár
KOLOZSVÁR
Marosvásárhely
Nagyszeben
Segesvár
Brassó
Maros
Maros

ADRIATIC SEA

troops had practically no contact with either Haynau in the West or with the Romanian peasant guerrillas in the mountains, and it was here, in Transylvania, that Russian military support was crucial. All in all, there were about 175,000 Austrians in Hungary in June 1849, and between 600 and 1,000 field guns.

The Russian army of intervention was larger than the Austrian: about 200,000 strong with almost 600 guns. The main force of three large army corps and other assorted units entered Hungary from Galicia through the passes of the northern Carpathian mountains. Another powerful group made up of two army corps supported the Austrians in Transylvania.

Against this super-army of over 360,000 men (many times the size of the later French-English-Sardinian expeditionary force in the Crimea) the Hungarians mustered a much smaller army. In the West Haynau's elite troops were faced by Görgey's own crack units. With five relatively small army corps and a couple of autonomous brigades, Görgey had about 62,000 soldiers. But he still held Komárom fortress and his soldiers were veterans. On balance, this made Görgey only a little weaker than Haynau. In the south two Hungarian corps represented a force inferior in numbers, but not in experience or determination, to Jelačić's Army of the South. Here both sides had to cope with recent peasant rebellions that no longer distinguished between nationality groups and denominations, and both camps manoeuvered to capture each other's fortresses: Eszék, Temesvár and Arad, which were in Austrian hands; and Pétervárad which was held by the Hungarians. In Transylvania Bem's recently gained numerical superiority ended quickly with the arrival of the Russians. Now Bem's 27,000 or so veterans faced a difficult future. Altogether, the armies of Hungary numbered about 170,000 soldiers and something like 500 field guns.

It is clear from the above that in the west, the south and the east the situation was grave for Kossuth's soldiers, but not hopeless. Only in the north were conditions appalling.

The northern front had always been a weak link in Hungary's defenses. Hastily collected and poorly equipped troops, and such luckless commanders as Mészáros, had always made this a near-disaster area. In the winter of 1848/49 General Schlick's aggressive little Galician corps could not be held in check until the main Hungarian army took over the defense of the north. But now the Hungarian

Army of the North, hopelessly dispersed, consisted of fewer than 17,000 men with 57 guns. Scurvy and cholera weakened the soldiers and they received little in clothing and in weapons. Led by the cantankerous and unpopular Dembiński, this pitiful force was expected to stop and defeat a Russian army almost ten times as strong.

For a while Dembiński continued to advance his plan for the invasion of Galicia, arguing that the Russians had to be beaten first, and after that the Austrians. He insisted that the majority of the *honvéd* be sent against the Russians, while a much smaller force, protected by Komárom, would be able to delay Haynau on both banks of the Danube. This was an interesting plan, and Kossuth at first leaned in the same direction; but it was not feasible because the troops were already engaged on every front, and because Görgey would not hear of it. When Dembiński learned that instead of getting further reinforcements his army would be subordinated to Görgey's Army of the Upper Danube, he resigned. It was neither the first nor the last time in his Hungarian career that he did so. His place was taken on June 18 by another Pole, General Wysocki, who subsequently did what all reasonable men would have done in similar circumstances. Leading his motley charge of Hungarians, Slovaks, Ruthenes, Poles, Romanians, and Austrian POWs pressed into Hungarian service, Wysocki withdrew almost incessantly. By the end of June the Russians were deep inside Hungary with neither the Army of the North nor the population offering serious resistance.[75]

Since the Russians were moving forward without engagement in major battles, why did the war last until mid-August, or in some places until the following month? Because Paskevich was inordinately slow and cautious, because the Russians were decimated by cholera, and because the Hungarian generals—Görgey in particular—managed to avoid the Russians almost completely in their determination to fight the Austrians. The main Hungarian army quietly maneuvered behind the back of the Russians in search of the Austrians. As a result, the war was not over until Haynau met and dispersed one *honvéd* unit after the other, or until the *honvéd* generals decided to surrender. The tsarist army moved across the country like a witless but benevolent giant. It inflicted only limited harm on its opponents and in turn suffered little harm from the Hungarians. Kossuth's scorched-earth policy was not even attempted in the path of the Russians; the population did not flee; and the tsar's Cossack, Tartar, or Circassian horsemen, as well as his myriad foot soldiers, were received with quiet resignation. On their part, the Russians often behaved with exemplary dignity. They were fair to their prisoners; they paid for the goods they requisitioned; with one or two notable exceptions they engaged in neither rape nor killing; and according to Russian and Hungarian historical legend, they openly sympathized with their victims. Russians and Hungarians vied with one another in their contempt for the "cowardly and rapacious Austrians."[76]

The simultaneous Russian and Austrian invasions threw the Hungarian leadership into disarray. There was simply no agreement on what to do next. In this extremity Kossuth was again recognized as the supreme leader. Generals and politicians looked to him for guidance, and he was willing to provide it, but his leadership became incoherent. Like other charismatic leaders in the face of defeat, Kossuth increasingly divorced himself from the problems of the day; he developed utopian diplomatic schemes, and he issued many orders only to revoke them a short time later. However, this behavior should not be exaggerated. Kossuth was still capable of wise decisions, and the central administration continued to function like the well-oiled machine that it was. But then it was perhaps this efficient handling of routine matters that proved Kossuth's growing weakness. Gone were the dramatic innovations of the summer, fall, and winter of 1848. Fully aware that military and political decisions had to be coordinated, Kossuth repeatedly proposed himself as supreme military commander but never summoned the audacity to carry out his proposal. Unwilling to admit that the situation was hopeless, Kossuth fooled not only himself, but his most devoted followers. In constant search for a "solution," he readily agreed to the most contradictory suggestions. His cabinet was divided between his own and the "Görgey faction," reflecting more than rivalry between the two leaders: it symbolized the struggle between those who still hoped for a compromise with the Austrians and those who did not. Kossuth knew that a compromise was impossible, but he was unable or unwilling to suppress the compromisers. He repeatedly gave in to Görgey for the simple reason that the general knew, or thought he knew, what he wanted; and he had the power to get his projects started. But Görgey was also Kossuth's arch-rival and enemy; his plans flew in the face of Kossuth's convictions about the war and the future of the nation and of the revolutionaries. Thus Kossuth felt impelled, again and again, to extricate himself from Görgey's influence and power. All this led to the bitterest intrigues and the greatest confusion in the history of the revolution.

On June 26, with the fighting already well advanced in western Hungary, Görgey took part in a cabinet meeting in Pest, the last attended by him as minister of war. At this conference Görgey proposed a plan according to which the government was to be made "mobile," i.e., it was to join the main army. Kossuth and the cabinet vaguely assented, or at least did not object. As Görgey explained to his colleagues, it was impossible to defeat both Russians and Austrians. Therefore, all available forces were to be concentrated on the Upper Danube to inflict a last great blow on the Austrians. If the *honvéd* won, the road was open to an honorable peace with the emperor. If they lost, army and government should lock themselves up in Komárom, there to resist the Austrians as long as possible. Meanwhile, let the Russians occupy the country.[77]

Görgey claimed in his memoirs that once he learned of Russia's intervention, he knew that the war would be lost regardless of the plans developed by the Hungarian side. However, this clairvoyance did not lead the general to the next logical step. In what he liked to call his "military-political activities," he could have decided either to arrest Kossuth and the cabinet and then beg forgiveness from the emperor in the name of a penitent nation, or else to so direct his campaign as to enable the most compromised or threatened soldiers and politicians to escape abroad. The campaign against Haynau and the proposal of Komárom as the ultimate refuge reflected Görgey's confused logic with its mixture of loyalist-legitimist and radical-revolutionary concepts. Perfidious and tyrannical Austria had to be bled white for the ambiguous purpose of achieving reconciliation or at least of "saving the honor of the *honvéd* army." The despised Kossuth clique had to be made a prisoner of the army so that both army and ruling clique could share in the same fate. For Komárom could have withstood encirclement only as long as its food supply lasted: with an ordinary garrison perhaps one year; with an entire army crowded within its walls, far less. And when Komárom fell, what then?

Görgey's plan to beat Austria into negotiations had made good sense in April or even in May, yet in that period the plan had not even been attempted. Now, at the end of June, it was too late.

Görgey's offensive on the Upper Danube met with Haynau's simultaneous and stronger offensive. The result was a series of defeats, the cruel bleeding of Hungary's best army, growing Austrian fury at the sight of continued Hungarian resistance, a belated Hungarian retreat to southeastern Hungary, and hence no escape from the gallows for many Hungarians.

Neither Kossuth nor the cabinet ever seriously contemplated committing collective suicide in Komárom, and why they had not immediately objected to Görgey's June 26 plan remains a mystery. Three days after that cabinet meeting and following a bad defeat at Győr on the Upper Danube, Kossuth threw away the plan to beat Haynau first; he then came forward with a new plan that required general withdrawal from all fronts in the direction of Szeged on the Tisza River, that is, in the direction of southeastern Hungary. There the combined armies were to make a final stand and hopefully demolish both enemies. Kossuth's "Szeged Plan" was presented to Görgey by a delegation of political and military leaders—all trusted friends of both Kossuth and Görgey—and the general publicly accepted the proposal. But he quietly sabotaged the order and in a bitter letter to Kossuth denounced the governor's attempt to devastate the country in Haynau's path. He threatened to make his army independent of the government and announced that he contemplated the negotiation of a separate armistice, "if the interest of the people so required." On July 1 at an enlarged Council of War from which Görgey was absent, Kossuth branded the general a traitor and recalled him from the command of the Army of the Upper Danube. As a sop to this traitor, Görgey was allowed to remain minister of war. At the same council, Kossuth made Mészáros commander-in-chief of all the Hungarian forces and Dembiński his chief of staff.[78] This led to a rebellion of Görgey's officers against the governor's orders and to Kossuth's abjectly backing down. Görgey was allowed to stay at the head of his army, but he finally resigned as minister of war.

While the politicians and generals battled with one another, the war went on in western Hungary with scant success for the Hungarians. First Görgey's division attacked, then Haynau's. At every one of these encounters Hungarian losses grew heavier, and the army had to withdraw farther. On July 2 Görgey was leading forty squadrons of hussars at Komárom in a thunderous and not unsuccessful charge against the Austrian lines when he received a sabre blow on his head;

whether it came from an enemy soldier or from one of his own will never be known. He was delirious for a few days. While he was ill, his deputy, General Klapka, combined Görgey's plan with Kossuth's, whereby Klapka would attempt to inflict a blow on the Austrians first and then withdraw the army (as had been scheduled some two weeks earlier) in the direction of southeast Hungary. On July 11 in a new battle at Komárom, Klapka was badly defeated. Dividing the army into two parts, he moved two army corps into Komárom fortress with himself as commander and sent the three other corps toward Szeged under the command of the barely recovered Görgey. The Austrians pushed ahead relentlessly, with Francis Joseph himself present at one of the battles. (Habsburg hagiography tells us that at Győr the young monarch crossed a burning bridge ahead of his soldiers.) Having left an army encircling Komárom, Haynau entered Buda on July 13 and the Russians subsequently occupied Pest. The revolutionary capital submitted, rather obsequiously, to the invaders.

The question was now whether Görgey could succeed in escaping from western Hungary. Obviously he could no longer move toward Buda-Pest. On July 15 at Vác, somewhat north of the capital, his army ran into a sizable Russian force and the two antagonists fought each other to a standstill. The road being cut off not only to the southeast but also to the east, Görgey now repeated his brilliant maneuver of January 1849. He marched toward the northeast; and again, as in the winter of 1848/49, he disappeared from sight. This time, however, he operated not behind the Austrians, but in the rear of the Russians. Two weeks later he emerged on the Upper Tisza River in eastern Hungary, having suffered almost no losses in the campaign. Again, Görgey manifested his military genius; he could accomplish miracles whenever politics did not obscure his judgment or thwart his strategy. His was a dramatic *anabasis* indeed: Görgey still quite ill; his no less brilliant chief of staff, Colonel Bayer, now almost permanently drunk; his tired and hungry soldiers marching without complaint. Although Görgey's generals were far from being united, the march was nonetheless a success. His monarchist and republican officers eyed one another with increasing distrust, and in their subsequent memoirs alternately praised or cursed their commander for this second *anabasis*. They were to describe him both in terms of saintly dedication and devilish cunning; even today, in Budapest theaters, in novels, or in histories, the image of Görgey in the last days of independent Hungary alternates between that of the wise soldier-statesman and the perfect blackguard. Like Görgey's image, that of Kossuth toward the end of the war is also twofold: either the superior leader weakened by warmth and good intentions, or the mediocre statesman whose pusillanimity, vacillation, pride, reckless ambition, and adventurism obscured his unquestionable qualities of leadership.

This, then, was the military situation toward the end of July: northern Hungary and most of western Hungary were completely in enemy hands; the main Russian army was flooding the Great Plain in the center of the country; and Haynau was marching on southeastern Hungary from the direction of Buda-Pest. The southernmost regions had been evacuated by the Hungarians; Görgey's army was moving southward along a line east of the Tisza River and more or less parallel to the Russian invaders; and a large Hungarian force was assembling around Szeged in preparation for the big battle. In Transylvania Bem had only recently broken into Moldavia in the hope of revolutionizing the Romanian peasants there; now he was fighting a rearguard action against increasingly hopeless odds. While the dead-tired, hungry, and often barefooted *honvéd* crisscrossed the country under the cold eyes of indifferent peasants, Kossuth and his cabinet engaged in a lot of wishful thinking. To their credit, they also engaged in a number of admirable *beaux gestes*. The last weeks of the war brought a few pieces of legislation of which Kossuth could justly be proud. In fact, the end of the war and the first years of exile lent more glory to Kossuth's name than anything he had done before. Yet this period was also marked by his customary lack of physical courage, his vacillation, and his egotism.

8 / Defeat

Toward Abdication

IN THE SUMMER of 1849 Kossuth, the government, the National
Assembly, the newspaper and money presses, the treasury, the
weapons factory, everything and all that formed the core of revolutionary Hungary were on the road again. But this time, unlike January 1849, the pilgrimage was final.

On June 5 Kossuth had reentered Buda-Pest in regal style. Riding with his wife in a gilded carriage and surrounded by adjutants, he
was greeted by heaps of flowers and by blushing maidens. He had
come with ambitious plans. Although the war was only a hundred
miles away, he and the ministers plunged into the work of postwar
reconstruction and planning. Prime Minister Szemere announced the
drafting of a new constitution and, at Kossuth's suggestion, asked the
president of the Upper House to prepare for the voluntary dissolution
of that body, giving the aristocracy fresh proof that the revolution
meant middle-class ascendency. The personnel of the ministries made
plans for the reform of their institutions and for the reconstruction,
beautification, and unification of Buda-Pest. The economy of independent Hungary was expected to develop rapidly; Kossuth himself
pressed for an immediate start on important railroad construction. As
part of the general work of consolidation, governor and cabinet were
keen to show that they could be as generous to the national minorities
as they had been strict during the war emergency. They worked on a
nationality law that was scheduled to be brought before parliament at
its July 2 meeting. As it turned out, on that day there was no time for

such complicated issues. At the end of June the Imperials had stormed Győr, a city barely ninety miles west of Buda-Pest; and the Russians were also approaching. At the one and only meeting of the parliament in the capital, Szemere informed the startled deputies that all would have to move south to Szeged. On July 8 the entire leadership left Pest and proceeded at a rather leisurely pace toward Hungary's new provisional capital, a large peasant town of the Great Plain and not unlike Debrecen.

At Szeged, Kossuth and Szemere continued to push for measures that would satisfy the national minorities. Things had been improving somewhat in this respect. Thanks mainly to the activity of Polish emigrés in Serbia, that principality had withdrawn its "volunteers" from southern Hungary; and the Hungarian Serbs were willing to make peace with Kossuth in return for the recognition of their autonomous Vojvodina. Kossuth refused and the Hungarian Serbs went on fighting, but with less ardor.

The most obvious ethnic group to negotiate with was the Romanians, who had gained little so far from their sacrifices and suffering. Vienna continued to regard Romanian nationalism with the greatest suspicion; the emperor would grant no autonomy to the Romanians in Transylvania or in Hungary.[1] Because of Bem's victories, the Romanian National Committee had fled to Wallachia in March, never to be resurrected again. The few fortresses that continued to resist Bem in Transylvania in the first half of 1849 were Austrian rather than Romanian strongholds. The only center of Romanian resistance was the Apuşeni Mountains in western Transylvania with about 25,000–30,000 peasant insurgents under the Tribune Avram Iancu. They had few weapons and little food; so whenever the Hungarians did not attack, the Romanian rebels cultivated their fields.

In April 1849 Ioan Dragoş, a Romanian deputy in the Hungarian parliament, had set out for the Apuşeni Mountains with Kossuth's instructions and money to negotiate a peace with Iancu (see chapter 6). The governor had offered the Romanians what he felt were generous concessions: amnesty in case of surrender; state support to Romanian schools; unrestricted use of the Romanian language in all the primary schools, the courts of law and local administration; and the promulgation of governmental decrees in all the languages of the country.[2] Iancu was willing to talk with Dragoş; and even though he insisted on Romanian territorial autonomy (a concession that Hungary's emissary was not empowered to grant), the climate of negotiations was definitely improving—until a Hungarian blunder put an end to the discussions. Kossuth had neglected to order the local Hungarian commanders to stop their operations. One of the Hungarian free corps attacked the Romanians early in May; it was soundly beaten; and the outraged Romanians, suspecting treason, arrested and executed Dragoş. The war continued in the mountains with further defeats for the Hungarian militia.

On June 6 the Council of Ministers in Buda-Pest again authorized its agents to get in touch with Iancu. The tribune professed interest in the talks but he no longer trusted the Hungarians. Now Nicolae Bălcescu entered the scene, a Romanian historian and member of the defunct revolutionary Provisional Government in Wallachia. For Bălcescu, as for all Wallachian liberals, the Turks and the Russians were the enemy, not the Hungarians. Bălcescu had the same exaggerated fear of pan-Slavism as had Kossuth. Russian troops had helped the Turks put down the Wallachian revolution, and Russian armies were swarming all over the Danubian Principalities.

Accompanied by Polish and Romanian emigrés, Bălcescu had come from Istanbul to Debrecen in May and had met repeatedly with Kossuth, following the government on its wanderings across the country. On July 14 at Szeged, Bălcescu and Cezar Bolliac, another Wallachian emigré, signed a *Projet de pacification* with the governor of Hungary. According to the project, Hungary would recognize the Romanians as a nationality, with the right to use their mother tongue in administration, law, and education, and with special rights on the communal level. The project envisaged the final and complete abolition of the *robot* and the remedy of specific Romanian peasant grievances. In a separate agreement the Romanian politicians promised to set up, with Hungarian money, a Romanian legion to fight on the side of the *honvéd* army.[3]

Bălcescu took the peace project to Iancu but reached no agreement; only on August 3 did Iancu finally write to Kossuth. His was a pathetic message. This twenty-five-year-old son of a peasant, an apprentice lawyer who in March 1848 had marched with young Hungarians to celebrate the birth of freedom, and who now could look back to almost one year of useless fighting against Hungary, bemoaned the tragic fate of his ''Hungarian brothers.'' He wanted to help, Iancu wrote, but now it was too late. The Russians were approaching rapidly and the Hungarians were leaving. The best he could offer was to stay neutral.[4] As it turned out after the war, the Romanians truly gained nothing in return for their 40,000 dead and 100 villages razed on behalf of the emperor. Nor had the *Projet de pacification* achieved anything, short of forming the basis for later cordial overtures between the Hungarians and Romanians. But these overtures also came to nothing.

The Szeged National Assembly met between July 21 and 28 and debated the Romanian question, as well as the law on the nationalities, at both public and closed meetings. Kossuth and Szemere favored the nationality law, of course, as did Foreign Minister Kázmér Batthyány, most members of the Peace Party, and one or two radicals. Placing themselves firmly against all concessions to the nationalities were a great many deputies of the center and almost the entire parliamentary Left. Yet Kossuth's prestige prevailed again; and on July 28 at a public meeting of the House, the nationality bill was enacted unanimously. Law VIII of 1849 guaranteed the right of all ethnic groups to free national development within Hungary. While the language of communication in government, legislation, and the army remained Hungarian, members of the county assemblies were allowed to speak in any language. In those counties where one ethnic group formed the absolute majority, minutes of the meetings could be kept in that language, besides being kept in Hungarian; in communal assemblies people were allowed to use their own language, with the minutes kept in the language decided upon by a majority of members. Local National Guards were to be commanded in their own tongue; primary schools, whether public or denominational, were to use the local language. Finally, ability and merit alone were to be the keys to promotion in the civil service.[5]

To crown their work, the deputies on July 28 enacted into law the emancipation of the Jews. "Citizens of the Mosaic faith" were to have equal rights with others; they were allowed to marry Christians before a civil authority; a council of rabbis and selectmen was to be convoked to improve the condition of the Jews; and Jews were to be taught to become artisans and agriculturists.[6] The Jewish bill had provoked no debate in the House. Cabinet and deputies were one in granting equality to a group that had proved more faithful to the revolution than the Christian Magyars themselves had been.

While the Jewish emancipation law was most enlightened by any measurement of the day (it took the Habsburg administration almost twenty years before it would consent to, let alone initiate, a similar bill), the nationalities law was less progressive than the March Constitution of Stadion or the postwar practices of Habsburg absolutism. Still, for general East European conditions, the nationalities law was remarkably enlightened. Historians critical of Hungary have tended to dismiss the law as window dressing or a belated attempt to undo past wrongs. On the contrary, the law was meant most seriously, as the violent parliamentary debates proved, and it was not a last-ditch effort. It had been in the making from the days of revolutionary Hungary's glory; it was understood to be an act of generosity, not of repentance. The Hungarian leaders never felt that their treatment of the national minorities was ever anything but enlightened and progressive.

Today it is hard to imagine the hopeful atmosphere prevailing at Szeged. The government and the army in flight; the prudent deputies absent by the hundreds; two mighty enemies moving inexorably across the land—yet most of those at Szeged were certain that the war was not lost. "From this city the freedom of Europe will radiate," Kossuth informed the assembled peasants in the muddy streets and among the thatched cottages of the provisional capital.[7] In his last parliamentary address at Szeged, on July 28 (the day the nationality law and the Jewish emancipation law were enacted in parliament), Szemere lauded the general military situation and especially General Bem's reckless excursion into Moldavia; he announced that not only British public opinion but the British cabinet itself was on Hungary's side and that, even though France was unfortunately engaged in a shameful Roman expedition, "that situation cannot last a long time." In the same speech Szemere quietly announced that because of the military situation the government would have to move elsewhere, and the parliament adjourned.[8] At the same meeting Minister of Finance Duschek told the deputies that there was no money (the last public loan the government had launched back in Buda-Pest netted only .5 million gulden), and that a new credit of 60 million gulden was needed for the continuation of the war. The deputies granted the credit without asking where the banknotes would come from. The money press was not functioning; small denominations needed to pay the soldiers were missing; and for the first time in the history of the revolution the currency was not trusted. In Buda-Pest merchants now refused to accept the "Kossuth Notes" or else accepted them well under face value.

The main preoccupation of the 200-odd deputies assembled at Szeged was to find a supreme military commander. The names of Kossuth, Perczel, Dembiński, Mészáros, Bem, and Görgey were on everybody's lips. Kossuth was most willing, but neither cabinet nor deputies wanted him, for he was no soldier and many felt that he had in any case outlived his usefulness. No one seemed to fill the bill. Perczel had had to be removed again from his regional command because of insubordination and threats against the government; Dembiński was unpopular; Mészáros would not accept the position (he had resigned as commander-in-chief a short time earlier); Bem was far away and so was Görgey. Yet Görgey became the favorite of a majority of deputies. His military reputation was greater than ever; Kossuth had made the mistake, for reasons of national morale, of keeping Görgey's blunders from the public and of touting his successes. At the secret meetings of the House the deputies acclaimed Görgey as supreme commander despite Szemere's warnings. They also wanted the general to be completely independent of civilian authority; this Kossuth would not tolerate. After feverish debates, a rush of correspondence, and a lot of intrigue, a Council of War decided on July 30 to make Dembiński commander-in-chief, but only until the arrival of Görgey and Bem.[9] In these negotiations Szemere proved himself most unscrupulous by inciting Görgey and Kossuth against one another. It remains unclear why he did so, except for the facile explanation that the prime minister was a born intriguer. Kossuth himself vacillated on the choice of a supreme commander, chiefly because of conflicting reports from the armies. By then the government was as poorly informed of the military situation as Windisch-Graetz had been the previous winter. Now the tables were turned: thanks to traitors in the Hungarian camp, Haynau was privy to most Hungarian moves.

The closed meetings of the House on July 25 and 26 showed that the deputies, so shy in facing Kossuth at public meetings, felt free to criticize him in the exclusive company of fellow parliamentarians. Deputy after deputy blasted the governor for his weakness, sniping particularly at the "women's camarilla" or "the government of skirts" around him. In reality, Kossuth's wife and his sister Zsuzsa— for these were the women the accusers had in mind—were innocent enough, although it must be admitted that Kossuth's wife did incite him against Görgey.

It was clear that within a short time either Kossuth or Görgey would have to step down. It was also increasingly clear that the man would not be Görgey. "You or Görgey!" (Szemere had written to the governor on July 21). "You have better qualities than Görgey but certain traits which he exhibits you lack, and they are essential: rigor, methodicalness and steadfastness. These enable him to stick to the chosen path."[10]

Meanwhile, Görgey's actions were again incomprehensible. Having initially driven his soldiers at a furious pace toward the rendezvous point with the rest of the *honvéd* army, he suddenly settled down to an inexplicably long rest; then he marched again, briskly and brilliantly. During all this time he negotiated with the Russian commanders. Between July 20 and his surrender on August 13, Görgey was constantly in touch with the enemy. At first there were two low-ranking Russian military emissaries; then there was a mysterious lady bearing a letter from General Count Rüdiger, commander of the third tsarist army corps; later there were higher ranking officers. The first Russians asked for a truce, but (as Görgey perceived immediately) only to slow down his army. Hints were dropped that, should there be a surrender, Görgey and his officers would be taken into Russian service. The emissaries were polite and most flattering; they brought gifts which Görgey returned or reciprocated in kind. It later became clear that what the Russians wanted was unconditional surrender, despite their overtures about a possible amnesty. In his messages to the Russians, Görgey insisted that surrender was negotiable only if Hungary's autonomy and the Laws of April 1848 would be guaranteed. He regularly informed Kossuth of the progress of negotiations, but it was impossible to know whether he was telling the whole truth. Moreover, Kossuth was outraged by Görgey's willingness to abandon Hungarian independence. Partly to control the general and partly to further negotiations (Kossuth was as anxious to see them continue as Görgey), the governor sent Szemere and Kázmér Batthyány on July 30 to Görgey's headquarters. They were authorized to offer the Crown of Hungary to a member of the Romanov dynasty.[11]

The negotiations and the offer of the Crown led nowhere. The fate of the army was unconditional surrender. Yet the Hungarians' hope to split the Allies was not completely unfounded, for relations between Haynau and Paskevich were very bad; the Hungarians knew that through the Russian emissaries. Paskevich was furious that his army received too little food from the Austrians; and that Haynau, who in Paskevich's opinion was not pulling his weight, had the arrogance to ascribe all the victories to himself. In addition, the Russian commander worried about the growing cholera epidemic among his troops; and he was determined (as numerous documents testify) to withdraw from Hungary before the onset of the bad weather. On his part, Haynau was hysterically suspicious of the Russians and accused them of treachery.[12] Accordingly, the Hungarian leaders were justified in playing for time: the trouble was, because there was no longer a national will to go on fighting, time had run out.

The rush and confusion of events in the last days of Kossuth's rule were such that nothing but a brief day-by-day account can keep track of developments.

On July 29, while parliament and government were preparing to leave Szeged, the troops were still arriving in the city. Görgey himself was on the way, although still very far; whereas Haynau, who had come on the direct route from Buda-Pest, was ominously close. On the same day, Bem's army, just back from the Moldavian adventure, was badly defeated by the Russians at Segesvár in Transylvania. Sándor Petőfi, an adjutant to Bem and Hungary's greatest poet, disappeared in the battle. His body was never found but no one today doubts, after long disbelief, that he was killed by Cossacks in the wild flight from the field. The image of a fugitive Petőfi, a silent wanderer, waiting for the propitious moment to inspire his people once again to rise to liberty, was projected for decades following his death.

On July 30 Dembiński assumed command of the army at Szeged. He had many more soldiers than Haynau—who had had to leave regiments behind both at Komárom and for the occupation of Buda-Pest—and yet, on the following day Dembiński announced that Szeged was indefensible. He would now march on Arad, some sixty miles to the east of Szeged. Accordingly, the Council of War sent orders to Görgey to change his route of march and move on to Arad.

On August 2 Haynau entered Szeged. On the same day, at Debrecen far to the north of Szeged, one of Görgey's lieutenants was badly mauled by the Russians. But all was not well in the Austrian camp either. Far in the rear of the Austrian forces, General Klapka erupted from Komárom fortress and took the city of Győr. Now Klapka controlled a big chunk of the Upper Danube region from where he would bring in large supplies and many recruits. Haynau's support lines were threatened, but the Austrian commander pushed ahead undaunted. He attacked and drove back Dembiński on August 5, despite the latter's double superiority in numbers. Dembiński now changed his mind about Arad and marched to Temesvár, a city further to the south, that is, closer to the Ottoman border. The change of itinerary allowed the Hungarians and Dembiński's Poles to escape to Turkey should they suffer defeat, but militarily it was a catastrophic decision. Arad fortress had recently passed into Hungarian hands, while Temesvár was still an Austrian stronghold. Even worse, Görgey knew nothing of the new itinerary, nor was it possible to notify him. When Haynau caught up with Dembiński, the latter's army was forced to make a stand without Görgey's assistance.

On August 6 Bem was again defeated by the Russians in Transylvania, this time decisively. Bem now left the ruins of his army in the hands of a colonel and departed alone for Hungary. The campaign in Transylvania was virtually over: the rest was a mopping-up operation.

No sooner did Kossuth learn of Dembiński's defeat near Szeged and of the general's decision to arbitrarily change the instructions of the Council of War than he dismissed Dembiński and appointed Bem in his stead. Now it was for Bem to stop Haynau, an obvious impossibility since he had barely reached the army at Temesvár on the day of the decisive battle.

On August 9 Görgey arrived at Arad but found no army there; there was only Kossuth, the cabinet, and a few members of the parliament. On the same day Haynau attacked the Hungarians at Temesvár. He had 28,000 men against Bem's 50,000 regulars and some 10,000 peasant auxiliaries. The 110 cannons on each side fought the biggest artillery battle of the war, with the Austrian guns deciding the outcome. Thinned by artillery fire and attacked by the Austrian cavalry, the *honvéd* took fright and ran away in chaos. Bem himself fell from his horse and broke a shoulder blade. Austrian casualties at Temesvár were small, a few dozen men killed; Hungarian losses amounted to several hundred dead and 6,000 prisoners. Thousands more threw away their weapons and headed for home. Now there were only two large and regularly constituted Hungarian field armies: Klapka's in and around Komárom and Görgey's at Arad. The blame for the disaster at Temesvár can be laid to Dembiński's excessive caution and to Bem's reckless daring, but above all it should be laid to the unwillingness of the Hungarian soldiers to carry on the war.

On August 10 the government at Arad still knew nothing of Bem's catastrophic defeat at Temesvár. On the contrary, it was fairly certain that a victory had been won. At a cabinet meeting Görgey declared that he would never accept Bem as supreme commander; for even if the battle at Temesvár were lost, the Pole would continue the war in Transylvania and he, Görgey, was unwilling to go there. He was sick and tired of the destruction, Görgey contended; there was no food or ammunition, and the people wanted peace. The Russians should no longer be fought. If he, Görgey, was not able to beat the Austrians—and he was willing to make another attempt—then he would surrender to the Russians. Görgey demanded as well that the Crown of Hungary be publicly offered to the tsar.

During the night of that same day, Kossuth summoned Görgey to a private meeting in Arad fortress. The two participants later disagreed on what had happened there, but it is certain that they discussed the possibility of Bem's defeat at Temesvár. And if Bem were defeated? "Then I shall surrender," Görgey claimed he had said. "And I shall shoot myself," Kossuth allegedly replied, a conversation that he hotly denied later.

August 11 was the most pathetic and crowded day in the history of the revolution. During the night Kossuth had learned that the army at Temesvár was no more. With Görgey's army as the only solid force left, several members of the cabinet, and Görgey, saw no point in Kossuth and the government continuing in office. Using some ministers, especially Csányi, as his intermediaries, Görgey forced Kossuth to abdicate and to name him—Görgey—not only commander-in-chief but also dictator of Hungary. On the same day several members of the government, but not all, resigned.

Kossuth's manifesto of abdication, addressed to "The Nation," bore his inimitable stamp. He had, he wrote, decided to give full military and civilian authority to Görgey, because now only the army could safeguard the future of the nation, and he included a passage that was to serve as the basis for all of his future self-exculpations: "I expect from him [Görgey]—and I make him responsible for it before God, the nation and history—that he use this power according to his best ability, to save the independent existence of our poor nation, and to secure its prosperity and future. May he love his fatherland as unselfishly as I have loved it, and may he be more fortunate than I was in securing the happiness of the nation."[13]

With full responsibility thrust on the shoulders of the not unwilling general, Kossuth made preparations for his own immediate departure. He feared arrest not so much by the Allies, who were still far away, as by Görgey. Later he bitterly reproached himself for not having arrested and executed Görgey. How this was to be done without any military force at his disposal he never explained.

Kossuth now shaved his legendary mustache and beard, restyled his coiffure (which revealed his baldness), and equipped himself with two false passports, one in the name of a Hungarian, the other in the name of an Englishman. Leaving his wife behind, Kossuth, alias Tamás Udvardi, alias James Bloomfield, left Arad on August 11.

Surrender

After his abdication Kossuth went directly to Bem's camp southeast of Arad, although it is not quite clear what he wanted to achieve there. Some say that he hoped to rally the soldiers, to rekindle national resistance; and only when he saw how small Bem's army was, and how discouraged the officers, did he decide to leave Hungary. There is not much evidence to support this contention. His disguise, the forged passports, his insistence that he was now only an ordinary citizen indicate that as early as August 11 he had decided to go abroad. What is more, he was determined to make his exit, not as the man responsible for defeat, but as the victim of intrigue. These were ugly days in Kossuth's career.

On August 12 Kossuth again wrote to Görgey, accusing him of tyrannical ambitions and warning him not to surrender. "I should consider it treason if you were not to exploit every reasonable opportunity to save the nation. I should consider it treason if you began negotiations, not in the name of the nation, but in the name and the interest of the army."[14]

When he had made Görgey dictator, Kossuth must have known that the general's authority did not extend far beyond Arad, that negotiations in the name of the nation were impossible, and that the general was planning to surrender to the Russians. If he did not know it, as he later claimed that he had not, then Kossuth was both deaf and blind. But since he was neither, his letter to Görgey must be seen as a calculated move to find a scapegoat, to provide the nation with the traitor its broken pride so badly needed. The move was fully successful, for Görgey was never to rid himself of the blame.

Squabbles between Kossuth and the other would-be emigrés began immediately. Prime Minister Szemere, who for the most part had kept silent at Arad and had not resigned, was now also in Bem's camp, the Holy Crown in his baggage. Szemere announced that while Kossuth's resignation was constitutionally valid, the transfer of power to Görgey was not; and that he, as prime minister, was now Hungary's legitimate leader. Szemere's claim did not amount to much, for a few days later he fled to Turkey, having first buried Saint Stephen's Crown in a case at Orsova, on the Hungarian-Ottoman border.*

With Kossuth out of the way, Dictator Görgey acted swiftly. On August 11 he too addressed the nation in a style far removed from that of the governor. "Citizens! Hungary's Provisional Government is no more. . . . Citizens! I shall do all I can for the fatherland in its grave crisis, with force or by peaceful means, as necessity dictates, but always so as to alleviate the heavy sacrifices you have already endured, and so as to put an end to the persecutions, brutalities, and murders."[15]

Görgey's manifesto did not mention surrender but it was difficult not to see that this was what he had in mind. Again on August

---

* Subsequently the Crown of Saint Stephen had an adventurous history. Unearthed by the Austrians a few years later, it was jealously guarded by them until 1867, when Francis Joseph was crowned with it on Castle Hill at Buda in a glittering ceremony to defy all ceremonies. Charles, the last Habsburg ruler, wore it on his head at the same place in 1916, and Admiral Nicholas Horthy placed his hand on it in 1920, to take his oath as regent. It was produced once more, in October 1944, for the Arrow Cross leader Ferenc Szálasi to be sworn in as Hungary's *Führer*. In the spring of 1945 its custodians took the Crown to Germany and handed it over to the U.S. army. For the next thirty-three years it was in American custody, mostly at Fort Knox—an even more unlikely place for this medieval masterpiece than its burial place on the Ottoman border. In January 1978 Secretary of State Cyrus Vance returned the Crown and the other coronation regalia to the Hungarian people at Budapest in a moving ceremony in which the writer of these lines had the pleasure to participate as a member of the U.S. presidential delegation to Hungary.

11, Görgey drafted a letter to Russian General Rüdiger. Acknowl-
edging that it was he who had forced the hand of the government,
Görgey offered to surrender unconditionally, so as "to free my
fellow-citizens from the miseries of the war." He appealed to the
generosity and assistance of the tsar, requested protection for his
fellow officers, and offered himself as the sole victim. In the final
passage he described the itinerary planned for his army in the following three days: "I desire that you lead your forces between the Austrian troops and mine—that you surround me, and cut me off from
the Austrians." If the Austrians were to catch up with him, he would
fight them.[16] Görgey submitted his draft to all the subcommanders,
who debated it in council in the general's absence. It was approved
unanimously, save by two officers who preferred surrender to the
Habsburg army. The letter was then dispatched to Rüdiger, but the
lower ranks were not informed.

On that same August 11 the National Assembly met for the first
and only time at Arad. Minutes were not kept, but we know that
there were only twelve deputies present. The meeting was brief, with
the oldest of the deputies announcing Kossuth's abdication and
Görgey's appointment. The War of Independence was declared lost
and the parliament suspended. (Not for another twelve years would
the representatives of the nation meet again.) The deputies then embraced and headed for a life of exile or imprisonment.[17]

Görgey's surrender went according to schedule. On August 13 at
Világos, a small town not far from Arad, he finally informed the
lower ranks of what was happening and threatened to have anyone
shot who tried to desert. He then distributed all the cash he had
among the soldiers.

Why did Görgey forbid the officers to make a break for freedom? He was particularly callous and contemptuous toward the Poles
and other foreigners, who faced the worst retribution. The fact is that
Görgey himself shared in the illusions widespread in the camp. He
knew better than anyone else that the Russians had promised nothing,
yet he could not conceive of the tsar washing his hands of an army
that had thrown itself on his mercy. Some of Görgey's officers were
so hopeful that they were prompted to ask the general for a last-
minute promotion so as to occupy a higher rank in the tsarist officer
corps. With a massive and orderly surrender, Görgey wished to
please Paskevich and to enhance the Russians' glory. An orderly sur-

render was also required, Görgey felt, by "the honor of the army." To hand over to the Russians the officers and the fugitive civilians in his camp was a gamble, but a gamble worth playing in Görgey's estimation. He did not fear death; nor did he see any reason for his officers to feel differently. Finally, by laying down his arms, he wished to save the lives of the common soldiers.

The surrender was staged according to military tradition and the expectations of a sentimental age. On the morning of the thirteenth, with the two armies lined up as on a *Paradeplatz*, Görgey and Rüdiger met on horseback, shaking hands cordially. The two commanders then rode past the phalanges of the *honvéd*. Flags were lined up on the ground, the muskets assembled in neat pyramids. Görgey was still, pale, cold, immovable; Rüdiger smiled amiably. Only once, when some soldiers raised the cry, "Hurrah, Görgey," did the general let his head fall, for an instant, toward the neck of his white horse. Following the inspection, many old hussars smashed their sabres; others shot their horses, weeping. By nightfall the ceremony was over: 11 generals, 1,426 officers, 32,569 other ranks, 144 guns, and 60 battle flags fell into Russian hands.*

The Russians lionized the captive Hungarians. Toasts were drunk to Hungarian bravery, and there was joint sneering at "Austrian cowardice." Russian enthusiasm for the Hungarians was understandable. The tsar's officers were embarrassed by a campaign that had brought no great victories and that served no ostensible Russian national purpose; Russia had never had any quarrel with Hungary whereas it had never trusted the Germans; finally, the Hungarian officers, mostly noblemen, resembled their Russian counterparts more than did the often *bürgerliche* Austrian officers. All this did not prevent the Russian command from marching the Hungarians straight off into Haynau's camp. Still, Russian surveillance was lax, and thousands escaped during the transfer. Görgey himself was taken to Paskevich's headquarters for another round of celebrations. There he learned that, of all his army's commanding officers, he alone had been amnestied by Francis Joseph; he would have to settle in Carinthia as a free man, but without the right to travel.

The Russians had not consciously trapped the Hungarians, nor

* Subsequently, the flags had a curious history: they were returned to Regent Horthy's Hungary in 1940 by Stalin in exchange for such Communists as Hungary's post–World War II tyrant, Mátyás Rákosi. Re-captured by the Red Army at the end of the war, the flags were again returned to Hungary in 1948.

had Görgey; yet this is what the events amounted to. The Russian generals sincerely admired Görgey and his army: Paskevich, nay the tsar himself, tried to secure amnesty for all Hungarian soldiers. The tsar had put in the strongest plea for Görgey, and it was Görgey alone whom he succeeded in helping.[18]

The Görgey tragedy could now unfold in all its romantic trappings. Soon few Hungarians would doubt that Görgey had always been a traitor, that he had forced Kossuth's abdication with the false promise of Russian support to Hungary, and that he had delivered the officers to Austrian vengeance for his personal safety and for heaps of Russian money. (It was true that Gögey had accepted a purse of gold from Paskevich as a token of the latter's admiration.)

Following his surrender, Gögey wrote to every Hungarian field commander still at large, and to every fortress commander, urging them to follow his example with the plea that the country needed peace and the sooner the war was over, the less the rebels would be prosecuted. Görgey's appeal was effective. Soon all the field commanders capitulated, if possible to the Russians. Bem alone did not surrender, but he had very few soldiers. Most troops went meekly into Russian or Austrian captivity; a minority fled to Ottoman territory. The fortresses also opened their gates, so that by the end of August only Pétervárad and Komárom flew the Hungarian flag and after September 5 only Komárom.

Without Görgey's capitulation the war would certainly have lasted somewhat longer. Did the general harm Hungary's cause with his surrender? If we are to believe Paskevich, then he assuredly did. Writing to Haynau three days after the surrender at Világos, the prince of Warsaw stated that the Hungarians could have gone on fighting and that, if they had, the consequences for the Allies could have been disastrous.

Malgré les échecs que Görgey a successivement éprouvés, il avait encore avec lui près de 30 mille hommes des meilleures troupes de l'insurrection et 140 pièces de canon. Il pouvait donc se défendre, se réunir avec les autres corps rébelles, faire verser encore beaucoup de sang et prolonger une guerre qui en automne et à cause du climat aurait pu être funeste à nos deux armées.[19]

Either Paskevich was misinformed regarding the Hungarians' ability and willingess to carry on for a considerable length of time (the battle of Temesvár should have shown him otherwise), or he deliberately overestimated this capacity in order to make his own success at Világos appear greater. He might also have wanted to emphasize Görgey's services to the Allied cause (and thus win him amnesty), and to excuse his acceptance of Görgey's surrender behind the Austrians' backs. Haynau was in a rage. He sent scores of letters to Vienna denouncing the Russians, and he demanded reasons why the Russians had interposed themselves between the Austrians and the enemy.

It is hard to see how Hungary could have fought on effectively, even until the "onset of the bad weather." And if it could have, and if the Russians had departed, Haynau still had crushing superiority. He could have terminated the war without help, and quite easily.

Whether the Hungarians could still have won the war is not the pressing question, some nationalist and marxist Hungarian historians notwithstanding. It is sheer fantasy to pretend that Hungary could have regained military superiority, or that a European revolution would momentarily erupt anew. The question is whether by dragging out the war for just a few weeks, for a few days even, Görgey could not have won more favorable conditions for the rebel leaders. And to this question the answer must be a hesitant "yes." The revolutionaries, as individuals, might have profited from even the briefest continuation of the war.

Erzsébet Andics, a Hungarian marxist historian, has shown on the basis of documents she uncovered in Vienna that on August 15, 1849, Schwarzenberg recommended to Francis Joseph that something akin to a general amnesty be offered to the Hungarian military commanders through the good offices of Haynau.[20] On the following day an Austrian cabinet meeting approved the proposal, specifying that those "rebel leaders" who had been officers in the Imperial-Royal army should be allowed to rejoin His Majesty's forces or to retire on a pension. Yet four days later, the cabinet meeting adopted a very different and far more brutal resolution, which was then communicated to Haynau.

The reason for this change is clear, Andics argues. On August 16 the Viennese did not know of Görgey's capitulation; on August 20 they did. Therefore on August 20 they saw no reason to make a conciliatory gesture. They no longer worried about the Russians leaving Hungary; nor did they fear European public opinion or the possibility of a new European revolution.

Andics's thesis is convincing indeed, except for one thing overlooked by the author. In his Order of the Day issued at Temesvár on August 18, Haynau specified what the terms of the retaliation would be against the Hungarian rebels. These terms conformed exactly, not to the Vienna resolution of August 15–16, but to that of August 20. Now either Haynau had a precise premonition of what the Habsburg government would decide to do upon learning of Görgey's capitulation, which is rather unlikely; or he spoke in accordance with earlier Austrian resolutions, which would be more likely the case. Therefore the August 15–16 amnesty proposals of the Vienna cabinet must be seen as a sign of temporary weakening, a weakening that, it is true, the Hungarians could conceivably have exploited.[21]

That prolonged resistance could sometimes pay off was proven by developments at Venice and at Komárom. Following a very long siege, Venice capitulated to Austria on August 22, and the insurgents were allowed to go wherever they wished. Komárom surrendered more than a month later, and the terms of the capitulation were favorable to the garrison. The conclusion is inevitable: by capitulating, Görgey made it easier for Haynau to send many Hungarian politicians and officers to jail or to the gallows. But this still leaves open the question whether the blood and the suffering of a few hundred leaders were not amply compensated for by the lives of the thousands of common soldiers and civilians who would have perished in a prolonged conflict. If we consider that Görgey always felt that revolutionary leaders, including himself, should shoulder the consequences of their actions, whereas the people should be protected as far as possible, we may say that he had achieved his goal.

When Görgey capitulated at Világos, Kossuth was still in the country, disguised for a change as servant of a Polish count. Bem had urged him to stay, to reassume supreme power, and to continue the war in the Transylvanian mountains. Writing from near the Ottoman border, Kossuth refused to go back and advised the Polish general to take over at the head of a "committee of people's representatives." As for Kossuth himself: "À présent je suis un simple citoyen et rien de plus."[22] Yet no sooner was Kossuth out of Hungary, than he again called himself governor-president and expected unconditional obedience from the nation.

Kossuth crossed the border into Turkey at Orsova, on the Danube, on August 17. He was again wearing his sword and was dressed as befitted his status. The Turkish generals received him respectfully and took him to Vidin, in what is today northwestern Bulgaria. There he was interned with thousands of other Hungarian refugees, among them Szemere and Bem.

The August days were days of celebration for the Allies. "Hungary lies at the feet of Your Majesty," Paskevich informed Nicholas with some exaggeration, for the unfortunate country lay rather at the feet of Francis Joseph. For his own part, Haynau did not even mention the Russians in his victory Order of the Day of August 18: "The triumphant Imperial-Royal arms have smashed the thousand-headed hydra of the Hungarian revolution. . . . The whole of Hungary has now been occupied by the Imperial-Royal armies."[23] This, too, was an exaggeration, not only because the Russians had been more than a negligible factor, but also because on August 18 the whole country had not yet surrendered. Komárom especially was to fight on for many more weeks.

The Austrian siege forces around Komárom grew to almost 50,000 in September. Klapka had to give up the areas he had conquered earlier and withdraw to the fortress. His and his officers' determination weakened when they heard of the *seriatim* surrender of all the other Hungarian strongholds. Negotiations dragged on into September, while Haynau indicated to Klapka that the capitulation of the fortress would put an early end to the prosecution of the other rebel leaders. The Austrians were in a hurry to end the war and they offered generous terms. Under the instrument of surrender of September 27, the entire garrison, including the civilian rebels in town, was granted amnesty. Those who wished to go abroad were to be provided with passports. Officers were allowed to keep their side-arms; officers and men would receive a few weeks' pay from the Austrians; the sick and the wounded were to be taken care of; personal property was not to be confiscated.[24] Between October 2 and 5 Komárom lowered the Hungarian flag and the troops marched out of the fortress. The last bastion of the European revolution had fallen; the Springtime of the Peoples was over.

No sooner were the troops out of Komárom than Haynau began to sign orders to execute revolutionaries condemned in earlier trials. He had duped Klapka; later many Hungarians reproached the general for not having made Haynau's vague promises of good will toward the revolutionaries more binding, and still more, for not having secured an amnesty for the whole country. This, however, was impossible. Klapka achieved the maximum for his 20,000 men. To expect more from an isolated fortress was unrealistic.

We know very little about the casualties of the war. The Austrians kept inadequate records, the Hungarians kept almost none. It seems that about 50,000 Hungarian soldiers died and about the same number of Austrians. The Russian expeditionary forces lost only 543 killed in battle and 1,670 wounded. On the other hand, Paskevich's army buried 11,028 cholera victims.[25]

Nor can we tell much about the cost of the war. According to one source, the Hungarian government spent 84 million gulden between the spring of 1848 and the fall of 1849. This is not such a great sum if we consider that just before 1848, the king's annual income from Hungary amounted to 34 million gulden, of which 26 million were spent in the country. What the Hungarian campaign cost the Austrians remains unclear; it must have been larger than the Hungarian expenditure. Austria's military budget in 1849 alone totaled 145 million gulden.[26] Destruction in Hungary was heavy but not irreparable. Pest was badly damaged; a few small cities and many villages had been burned to the ground. All were reconstructed within a few years. The most pathetic loss was the violent death of thousands of peasants of all nationalities in the worst ethnic conflict of the Danube Basin.

Retribution

Austrian retaliation was selective, but for those who were victims of the selection, it was quick and brutal. The August 20 resolution of the Vienna cabinet had granted amnesty to the revolutionary rank-and-file, from sergeant down, provided they were born in the lands of the Crown of Saint Stephen. A similar amnesty awaited the junior officers of the rebel army, from captain down, but only if they had not previously been officers of His Majesty. Freedom from prosecution did not mean personal freedom, however. All those fit to serve were to be enlisted in the Imperial-Royal army as ordinary soldiers. In practice, all these privates could not be accommodated and most were discharged immediately. All higher ranking rebel officers, and all who had been officers before the war, were to be tried by military courts. The same fate awaited the leading civilian administrators and deputies. Those who had joined the insurgents from the other Crown lands of the Monarchy were to be tried, or if they were of the rank-and-file, sent to penal companies. This was a horrible punishment, especially for members of the Vienna Student legion, since it meant forced labor in heavy chains. Foreigners were sent back to powers friendly to Austria, thrust into penal companies, or prosecuted. The Council of Ministers entrusted Haynau with the execution of the resolution; as Imperial-Royal plenipotentiary he was empowered to approve death sentences or to grant pardon.[27]

Military courts had begun to operate in Hungary well before the end of the war. After Görgey's surrender the courts at Pest and Arad emerged as the most important, with the former trying both officers and civilians and the latter trying most of the captured rebel generals. The courts took their instructions from Haynau who, in turn, took his general instructions from Schwarzenberg and from Francis Joseph. The emperor was firmly resolved to extirpate Hungarian rebelliousness, an endeavor in which he was staunchly seconded by many ultra-conservative Hungarian magnates. Given the power, the latter would have ordered many more executions.

Haynau sincerely hated the Hungarian revolutionary *Lumpen* who, in his opinion, had brought untold misery upon the innocent masses. "I shall make order here," he wrote to Radetzky, "and I shall have hundreds shot with the best of conscience."[28] He considered the Hungarians, by whom he meant mainly the nobility, an incorrigible lot—which did not prevent him from being attracted to them and to their country. He boasted of the splendid balls he gave in Buda-Pest, and of his popularity in better circles.[29] Following his enforced retirement in 1850, he bought an estate and settled, of all places, in Hungary. As a landowner, Haynau considered himself a member of the Hungarian aristocracy and fretted at being snubbed by his fellow landowners. His plight became so well known that Hungarians had no difficulty recognizing him in a *roman à clef* written by an ex-revolutionary, the famous Mór Jókai.

According to an Austrian report published in 1851, Habsburg courts tried the cases of 4,628 Hungarian rebels between November 1, 1848, and the end of 1850. Among them were 24 generals of the Imperial-Royal army who had served in Hungary in 1848. None of the generals had stayed with the National Defense Committee beyond January 1849, yet several were harshly punished.[30]

Feldmarschalleutnant Baron János Hrabovszky, knight of the Military Maria Theresa Order (for services rendered during the Napoleonic wars), holder of many other distinguished orders, "owner" of the 14th Imperial-Royal Infantry Regiment, royal commissioner under Batthyány in Croatia in May 1848, and subsequently commander-in-chief of the Buda General-Commando, had gone over to Windisch-Graetz in January 1849. The Austrian court rewarded him with ten years in chains to be spent in a fortress prison. Hrabovszky lived until 1852, having been amnestied just before his death. *Feldmarschalleutnant* János Móga, commander of the Hungarians at Pákozd and at Schwechat, had resigned from Hungarian service on November 1, 1848, and two months later he was with the Austrians. Still, he was given five years in a fortress. Released before the expiration of his sentence, Móga died in 1861. His two officer sons had never swerved from serving His Majesty.

The trials of the true rebel officers—those who stayed with Kossuth in 1849—took place in September. They were accused of having disobeyed the emperor's October 3 manifesto. This, as we remember from chapter 4, had dissolved the Hungarian parliament and had placed the country under military jurisdiction. Anyone who had continued on the Hungarian side after that date was considered a rebel and a traitor. The trials were marked by indifference and bureaucratic formality. The courts were in a hurry, and absolutely no attempt was made to uncover the causes of a mass mutiny unprecedented in Habsburg history. Nor have historians attempted, so far, to investigate the motives of the officers, or to create a typology of the rebel commander. Nevertheless, a few things are clear.

In the course of the war, Hungary enlisted about 200,000 men, among them about 10,000 officers. The vast majority of officers were former civilians or noncommissioned officers; up to 1,500 were professionals. After the war, not all the regular officers could be tried: hundreds had retired or surrendered earlier; hundreds escaped to Turkey with Kossuth; and over a hundred surrendered in Komárom and Pétervárad, thus benefiting from negotiated amnesties. Altogether, 498 former Habsburg officers were court-martialed in Hungary: 231 were condemned to death, and about 40 were executed.[31] Two-thirds of those who were tried had belonged to the Imperial-Royal infantry and almost one-third to the cavalry. In age they ranged from twenty-one to sixty-nine; only 6 percent had held higher rank than captain in the old army. The vast majority were Hungarians, but there were also a few dozen Germans from Hungary and from elsewhere, as well as some Poles and other nationalities.

The most famous trial of rebel generals took place at Arad, where fourteen were sentenced to death at the same time. With the exception of General Gáspár, whose sentence was commuted to imprisonment, they were executed on October 6, the anniversary of Count Latour's death. Their lives are well known for they were idolized by generations of Hungarians. Their composite portrait is remarkable for its lack of uniformity.

The ages of the fourteen ranged from thirty to fifty-seven, their old army ranks from lieutenant to colonel. Five were infantrymen, one was an army engineer, and eight were from the cavalry. Most had been in active service before the war, three had resigned earlier but rejoined service in 1848 at the behest of the Hungarian government. One was Greek Orthodox, one a Calvinist, all the others were Catholics. One of the generals, Count Leiningen-Westerburg, came from a princely family in Hesse; he was related to the British Royal house. Another general belonged to the Hungarian aristocracy; yet another was an enormously wealthy landowner; the rest of the defendants had little or no private wealth. One was a German from outside Austria, one a German-Austrian, one a Serb, and one a Croat; the rest were Hungarians, although not all the Hungarians were familiar with the language. Several had brothers in the Austrian army; two had fathers and uncles who were Habsburg generals. None of the Arad defendants was politically active before the war. Some were promoted rapidly in the old army; most had moved slowly. None had had any trouble with the Habsburg military authorities. Their *Conduite-Listen,* drawn up annually in the old army, were favorable. Almost all were married and had children.[32]

What then motivated these officers? One definitely was a republican; another, Leiningen, was a liberal who felt that the fight for a united Germany and the fraternity of peoples would best be advanced by serving in Kossuth's army. All officers professed patriotic sentiments, but only vaguely in the majority of cases. Mostly, the generals argued that they were doing their duty at the point in which the king had placed them. No doubt while in the Hungarian army many were dazzled by the opportunity for glory and quick advancement; certainly they badgered Kossuth for promotion, spending a good deal of time arguing their seniority. But one or two among them were exceedingly modest.

All in all, it was not a particular type of professional officer who fought on the Hungarian side, but many types. More often than not, their regimental assignment had landed them in the Hungarian ranks. Young men were more likely to stay there than older men. While their seniors agonized, the young officers grabbed the opportunity for promotion, adventure, the chance to command army corps rather than platoons. When in doubt they consoled themselves with patriotic sentiments and progressive slogans.

On the Austrian side the situation was in many ways similar. Thousands of officers, among them many Hungarians, did their duty wherever they happened to be. Quick promotion and glory were distinct possibilities in the Austrian army too. In addition, the Austrian officer had clear advantages over the Hungarian. There was safety in numbers—nine out of ten professional officers remained on the Imperial side in 1848–49; there was the lure of time-honored loyalty to the monarch; and finally, there was the comforting feeling that by fighting the Hungarians the officer was fighting for peace among the peoples of Central Europe. Imperial propaganda pointed out again and again, and most skillfully, that before 1848 the many peoples of the Monarchy had lived at peace with one another; that Hungarian nationalism had led to ethnic wars; that the Hungarian nobles were progressive only in theory, but in practice they had been and would remain the oppressors of peasants; that the emperor had always protected the weak among the nationalities and the social classes. Did not the good emperor himself guarantee civil rights and equality to all his peoples? Did not he too emancipate the serfs? There was no reason (the leaflets insisted) why even greater peace and prosperity should not ensue once the Hungarian rebels had been defeated. For the German, Slavic, Italian, and Romanian officers of the Habsburg army, many among them of peasant origin, these arguments were more convincing than any Hungarian appeals for national liberation; and it was the dynastic loyalty of these officers, encouraged by the seemingly safe haven of an invincible Empire, that allowed the House of Austria to survive the greatest crisis in its history.

Although contemporary statistics are contradictory, it seems that at least 500 rebels, soldiers, and civilians were sentenced to death by Austrian military courts, and about 120 were actually executed. In addition, there were some summary executions of guerrillas. Among those who were hanged or shot, there were (besides the Arad thirteen) several other Hungarian officers, the commander of the German legion, a Polish prince and several other Polish revolutionary nobles, the president of the Hungarian Upper House, some high-ranking administrators (among them Kossuth's loyal friend László Csányi), an astonishing number of Catholic priests, a luckless lower civil servant who had been mistaken for a journalist with a vaguely similar name and, finally, Prime Minister Count Lajos Batthyány. He had been arrested, as we remember, at Windisch-Graetz's orders in January 1849. Dragged from one prison to another, questioned endlessly, confronted by many witnesses, he was finally sentenced by a military court at Olmütz in August 1849. At Schwarzenberg's direct command the verdict was death by hanging; but the judges unanimously, and most warmly, recommended clemency. In Austrian practice this had always meant a commutation of the death sentence to imprisonment, but Schwarzenberg and Haynau were not to be influenced by tradition. On October 5 Haynau confirmed the death sentence. By then Batthyány was in a military prison at Pest. On the same night he stabbed himself in the throat with a dagger smuggled in by his wife. His life was saved by military doctors, but it was impossible to hang him properly. The local commander therefore commuted the sentence, on his own authority, to execution by powder and lead. On October 6 he was dragged before the firing squad; he refused to have his eyes covered, and he himself gave the order to the soldiers to shoot. Characteristically for a Hungarian aristocrat, he pronounced this fatal sentence in words taken from three languages: "Allez Jäger, éljen a haza!" ("long live the fatherland"). Haynau was outraged when he learned that Batthyány was not dangling from a rope.

The charges against the prime minister had been ridiculous. He had been accused, among other things, of having contributed to the murders of Lamberg and Latour, and of having financed the October revolution of the Viennese.[33] Obviously, the Austrian leadership needed a supreme scapegoat for the humiliations suffered in 1848. The sentence brought enormous damage upon the House of Austria. All through the life of the Dual Monarchy, the place where Batthyány had been executed was the scene of anti-dynastic demonstrations; and Count Mihály Károlyi, who in November 1918 proclaimed the first

Hungarian republic, brought to his post a hatred of the Habsburgs acquired from his family, which was closely related to the Batthyánys.

In addition to those executed, at least fifteen hundred people were sentenced to long years of imprisonment, either directly or as a result of the commutation of their death sentence. Ten or twenty years in chains was the usual verdict; the Catholic bishop of Nagyvárad was given twenty years—as an act of mercy.

There is a printed Austrian contemporary report containing the names and brief description of 759 condemned revolutionaries.[34] The list is understandably incomplete, yet it sheds some light on the social composition, occupational distribution, and geographic origin of Hungary's revolutionary elite. The report is an abridged *Who's Who* of the Hungarian middle nobility, with a generous sprinkling (33) of high aristocratic names. Almost 9 out of 10 condemned rebels were born under the Crown of Saint Stephen; 199 out of these 666 were born in Transylvania, a respectable proportion. A total of 71 condemned revolutionary leaders came from the other Crown lands of the Monarchy, among them 25 Galician Poles. The latter apparently had not been handed over to the Russians after all. There were also 10 Germans from the non-Habsburg lands of the German Confederation, as well as a handful of Italians, British, and French. If we consider that foreigners were more likely to be sentenced for revolutionary activity than Hungarians, it becomes clear that, Habsburg propaganda to the contrary, the Hungarian revolution was not truly an international affair.

Fully two-thirds of those sentenced were soldiers, among them the great majority of the 199 Transylvanians, all the condemned Poles, and most non-Hungarian rebels. On the other hand, those born in Hungary proper made up a disproportionately large section of the civilian leaders. The average age of the civilians was higher than that of the soldiers, proving that while the typical rebel commander was a fairly young subaltern from His Majesty's army, revolutionary administration was in the hands of those with considerable political and administrative experience. There were among the civilians 8 former county lord-lieutenants and 11 deputy lord-lieutenants, 34 practicing lawyers, 1 Catholic and 2 Greek Catholic or Uniate archbishops, 2 Catholic bishops, 21 Catholic priests and monks, 11 Calvinist ministers and preachers, 35 landowners by profession (the number of those who owned land was of course much higher), but only 1 medical doctor, 1 engineer, 1 barber and 4 peasants.

The condemned were sent to such notorious fortress prisons as the Spielberg at Brünn, Kufstein, Theresienstadt, Josephstadt, Olmütz, Komárom or Munkács. All had to wear chains ranging from the monstrously heavy to the symbolic. Unlike the Viennese students, who were commoners, the Hungarian prisoners were treated as befits noblemen. Instead of the wet and icy cold casamates, they occupied large cells with windows; they could both buy and receive food; they were not obliged to work; they were allowed an occasional visitor and they could generally obtain books. Amnesties came in waves in the 1850s, and by the end of the decade not a single revolutionary was in prison—unless he had engaged in conspiratorial activity following his release.

Today no historian is ready to apologize for Haynau's behavior; and, truly, there is no excuse for his extraordinary show of brutality. One need only recall the history of the Rákóczi rebellion early in the eighteenth century to appreciate the wisdom of generosity; then, too, there had been a Hungarian surrender, yet not a single rebel was punished. Prince Rákóczi himself was free to return to his country but he refused the amnesty. Wise Habsburg policy led to an immediate political compromise between the Court and the Hungarian nobility. It gave the Empire domestic peace and the Hungarian landlords undisputed economic dominance for well over a hundred years.

Now, too, there was to be a compromise between Court and nobility, but only in 1867 and only after great humiliations were to be endured by the Monarchy. Nor were the martyrs of the revolution ever forgotten. If the Hungarians were to cause the Dual Monarchy so many headaches after 1867, and so much actual damage, this could be traced partly to the butchery perpetrated by Haynau and his employer.

In 1851 the Austrian government decided to try the emigrés, too. Following a solemn admonition for them to come home and to meet their fate, the best known exiles were tried in absentia by military courts. In September 1851 the army executioner in Buda-Pest ceremoniously posted the names of Kossuth, Szemere, Kázmér Batthyány, Count Gyula Andrássy, Richard Guyon, László Madarász, Móricz Perczel, and dozens of others on individual gallows.[35]

The news of his hanging in effigy reached Kossuth only after considerable delay. On the day his name was nailed to the first gibbet of the Pest military prison, Kossuth was busy receiving the delirious homage of the people of Marseilles from aboard an American frigate.

Epilogue

WHEN HE HAD crossed the Turkish frontier, Kossuth was forty-seven years old. He was to stay abroad for the remaining forty-five years of his life. It was in exile that his fame assumed titanic proportions, and his political role was never to cease, not even when he was ninety and life in Hungary had gone on without him for many decades. The story of the emigré Kossuth would make another biography, for this *Homo politicus* incarnate remained active to the end, and the Habsburg Monarchy could never rid itself of the menacing shadow of its most illustrious enemy. In this work, the story of Kossuth's exile can serve only as part of the epilogue.

Kossuth had gone abroad without his family. His three children had been hidden long ago in Austrian-occupied western Hungary; his wife had gone from Arad to rejoin them. Why this exemplary husband and father had left his family behind belongs to the many mysteries surrounding his private life and feelings.

There were in Vidin more than 5,000 refugees, most of them soldiers. Unhesitatingly, Kossuth assumed their leadership. Explaining away his resignation at Arad as having been imposed by mortal threats from Görgey, Kossuth again called himself governor-president. He insisted on being treated with the respect due to a head of state. The admiring Turks were far more eager to accord him such treatment than Kossuth's companions in exile, who—following the time-honored emigré tradition—immediately began to squabble and to intrigue, both for and against Kossuth. But while the generals and politicians bickered, the vast majority of the refugees, enlisted men who had trudged obediently behind the commanders, had only one wish: to escape as soon as possible from their filthy open-air encampment near the shore of the Danube. This proved to be relatively easy, for Austrian representatives soon appeared in Vidin with the promise of amnesty to the lower ranks. And since the Austrian offer was reinforced by immediate pay whereas Kossuth had no money in his coffers, at least 3,000 soldiers embarked on the return trip to Hungary within a few weeks. By October, by and large, the only ones remaining with the governor were those to whom the Austrians had not promised clemency. These were some 800 Poles, 200 Italians, and 400 Hungarians, about half of the latter officers. Just as the majority of the Magyar nation had deserted Kossuth's cause before the final defeat, now the majority of the exiles threw themselves on the mercy of Francis Joseph. And of those who remained with Kossuth, the great majority would return to Hungary in the following two decades when it became clear that what awaited them at home was not prison or the gallows but a respected place in Hungary's rejuvenated political life. Even though thousands of Hungarians, other than the Vidin refugees, left the country in 1849, only Kossuth himself and a few hundred others were never to conclude their "compromise agreement" with the House of Austria.

As governor and commander-in-chief, Kossuth diligently prepared for his triumphant reentry into Hungary. He confidently expected a second Hungarian revolution. Also, the international situation was tense, the presence of the Poles and Hungarians in Ottoman territory having created a diplomatic crisis far greater than the stir once caused by the War of Independence. An armed conflict between Russia and Austria on one side and Great Britain, France, and the Ottoman Empire on the other seemed from Vidin a distinct possibility. Kossuth felt it his duty to prepare the Magyar nation for the coming historic confrontation. As a first move, he pointed an accusing finger at the arch-traitor, Görgey. In an open letter dated September 12, 1849, Kossuth made that "accursed man" solely responsible for the temporary defeat of Hungary. This famous Vidin Letter, or rather manifesto, was more anti-Russian in tone than it was anti-Austrian. With an eye on Russophobic public opinion in England and France, Kossuth concentrated his hatred on Görgey's protector, the tsar. He also made clear in the letter that a member of the British royal family would be acceptable as king of free Hungary.[1]

While an international war was at least conceivable, Kossuth's political actions in support of this war betrayed pathetic naiveté. When an enthusiastic British journalist, Frederick Charles Henningsen, arrived in the camp to offer his services to the Hungarian lion, Kossuth majestically appointed Henningsen his plenipotentiary in what had remained of independent Hungary. The Englishman was to travel in disguise to Komárom, there to assume supreme power in the name of Kossuth with the right to order executions.[2] Henningsen did not get very far: he was in Belgrade when he learned that Klapka had surrendered the fortress to Haynau.

Kossuth and his companions had become the center of a great controversy. Russia and Austria demanded the immediate extradition of the refugees; the Porte hesitated; France, and especially Great Britain, pressed for categorical refusal. By October relations between St. Petersburg and Istanbul had reached the breaking point over the question of the Polish refugees. British public opinion, even Palmerston's *Globe*, threatened Russia with war if the Ottoman Empire was attacked. In a letter addressed to his wife, which Henningsen was to smuggle across the border, Kossuth confidently informed the Hungarians that the sultan would rather fight than surrender the exiles.[3]

The position of the Turks was very difficult. According to previous peace treaties concluded between Austria and the Sublime Porte, the two powers were forbidden to grant asylum to each other's "bandits and rebels." The Russo-Turkish treaties had gone farther and required mutual extradition. Even worse, consular agreements had authorized the consuls of Christian powers to arrest and try their own citizens, with the assistance of Turkish authorities.

There was only one legal way out of the dilemma and the Turks tried it. If the exiles were to convert to Islam, none of the treaties would apply to them. Turkish generals harangued the refugees, promising them high ranks in the Ottoman army. Generals Bem and Guyon and a few other Poles and Hungarians decided to undergo the rather formal ceremony of conversion. In becoming Muslims and Turkish generals, they hoped to lead the Ottoman army for the liberation of Poland and Hungary. Kossuth himself would not hear of conversion and, in a bitter letter to "Murad Pasha" (Bem), he denounced those who had given in to the Turks.[4]

The Austrians and Russians continued to press for extradition by mobilizing their forces on the Turkish border, and the British answered in kind. Without waiting for authorization from London, the

British ambassador to Istanbul, Redcliffe Canning Stratford, requested that Admiral Parker bring his Mediterranean fleet close to Turkish waters. The British cabinet belatedly approved the move; the French joined them, and by late October there were twenty-four British and French warships near Istanbul. Meanwhile, the Austrians, especially Alexander Bach, had concocted rather harebrained plans with the approval of Francis Joseph to kidnap or, if necessary, to murder Kossuth. But the plans failed because of the Turks' vigilance and the unreliability of the Austrian secret agents in Kossuth's immediate surroundings. The Polish Countess Dembiński, then an intimate of Kossuth (and possibly his mistress), was one of those unreliable secret Austrian agents. With their violent plans openly aired, the Austrians finally came to their senses, and in November orders were sent from Vienna to the Austrian Ambassador in Istanbul not to press for extradition. Since the Austrians were the first to back down, Tsar Nicholas was furious. He who had condemned the Austrian persecution of Hungarians now reproached Schwarzenberg for having given in to the Franco-Anglo-Ottoman threat. But Nicholas himself had little choice; and at the urging of his chancellor, Count Nesselrode, he stopped reclaiming the Polish rebels.

By the end of 1849 the international crisis was over. Neither Palmerston nor French Foreign Minister de Tocqueville had had the slightest intention of restoring the Hungarian constitution. What they had wished to achieve, and had succeeded eminently in doing, was to protect the Ottomans from Austro-Russian intervention.

Kossuth himself was to pay a heavy price for the success of his protectors. In order to conciliate the emperor and the tsar, the sultan had agreed to intern Kossuth in Asiatic Turkey. In February 1850 Kossuth, his wife (she had meanwhile escaped from Hungary and had rejoined her husband to the great pleasure of the Hungarian refugees, who had frowned on Kossuth's suspected tryst with Countess Dembiński), and a few other Hungarians were escorted to the Anatolian city of Kiutahia (Kütahya). The Turks kept them under heavy guard but surrounded them with all the pomp and circumstance befitting distinguished guests. They were to remain in this miserable town for more than a year. The other exiles had been allowed to stay behind in Sumla (now in Bulgaria), whence they gradually left for the West. Palmerston publicly admonished the Turks for having made a concession to Vienna with regard to Kossuth but made no move to end the internment of the Hungarian leader. Palmerston was a friend of both Ottoman and Austrian integrity, and certainly no friend of Hungarian independence.

Although the Turks respected and honored Kossuth, he was now their prisoner. Of course, he was not the man to give up hope. Plans were hatched for an escape from Kütahya with Henningsen's help, and feverish correspondence was carried on with László Teleki, Ferenc Pulszky, and other Hungarian representatives in Western Europe. From Kütahya, Kossuth authorized and encouraged a conspiracy for revolution in Hungary concocted by Colonel Mack, a brave but probably deranged Hungarian officer. The conspiracy, the first in a number of similar schemes engineered by Kossuth, was immediately betrayed to the Austrian police; several conspirators were executed, and others imprisoned. Kossuth's own sister, Zsuzsa, who had remained in Hungary, was among those taken prisoner; but this had no effect on her brother. He refused to shoulder any portion of the blame.

An invitation from the U.S. government came as a heaven-sent gift: Kossuth would be welcomed in America. The Turks were overjoyed to rid themselves of this responsibility, and so were the British. The Austrians publicly protested the end of Kossuth's internment, but probably did not mind either. In September 1851 Kossuth, his wife, and a few aides-de-camp boarded the pride of the U.S. fleet, the frigate *Mississippi*. When the ship weighed anchor in the Dardanelles, a triumphant journey began the likes of which the world had never seen. Kossuth moved from Turkey to La Spezia, to Marseilles, to Southampton and to London. Wherever he appeared, Hungary's governor-president was acclaimed by the multitude as the hero of the free world and the enemy of tyrants.

Kossuth's unique reputation had preceded him to the United States; so had the news of his political opportunism. "Vive la République," he had shouted at Marseilles, and "God Save the Queen," at Southampton. He was still on the high seas when southerners in the U.S. Senate questioned the authenticity of his republicanism, though the senators did not know he had offered the Hungarian Crown to every reigning house in Europe. In any case, it was not his lack of sincerity that worried them, but the effect the Great Liberator's visit might have on the issue of slavery. The American political situation was already very tense; and while anti-slavery radicals, Freemasons, and Protestants expected substantial political assistance from Kossuth, anti-slavery forces and the Catholic press (especially the Irish press) attacked him well before his arrival.

Americans expected Kossuth to settle in the United States, and they were generally proud to offer a new home to the world's most famous refugee. But as Kossuth came to America not to settle but to secure financial, diplomatic, perhaps even military aid for Hungary, these widely divergent views about the purpose of his American trip could not possibly be reconciled, and the visit—to last from December 1851 to July 1852—was bound to lead to mutual disappointment. Secretary of State Daniel Webster, who wanted Kossuth to help him win the coming presidential elections, said such encouraging things as "we shall rejoice to see our American model upon the lower Danube and the mountains of Hungary,"[5] (a curious territorial extension of Webster's Manifest Destiny theory); but President Millard Fillmore, who, unlike his predecessor Zachary Taylor, knew nothing of Hungary and was not even interested, immediately apologized to the Austrian chargé d'affaires in Washington for the secretary's "individual, unofficial opinion."

The American people themselves simply wished to celebrate Kossuth, and they did so at countless meetings, banquets, and parades, where he was the object of extravagant adulation. He was greeted with a hundred-gun salute when his ship passed by Jersey City; and hundreds of thousands welcomed him when he disembarked in New York. He was called the Hungarian Washington and "the greatest man on earth since Jesus Christ." Banners raised in his honor bore such legends as "Washington and Kossuth—the Occident and the Orient," and at banquets speakers offered "Three cheers for Saint Stephen." He was continually asked to make speeches; and his listeners waxed delirious over the elegance of his manners, his costume, his beard, his hat—and his dignified, faultless, and thoroughly antique English. At the Congressional Banquet held in his honor on January 7, 1852, this is what Kossuth said:

As once Cyneas, the Epirote, stood among the Senators of Rome, who, with an earnest word of self-conscious majesty, controlled the condition of the world, and arrested mighty kings in their ambitious march; thus, full of admiration and reverence, I stand before you, legislators of the new capitol—that glorious hall of your people's collective majesty. The capitol of old yet stands, but the spirit has departed from it and come over to yours, purified by the air of liberty. The old stands a mournful monument of the fragility of human things—yours as a sanctuary of eternal rights. The old beamed with the red lustre of conquest, now darkened by oppression's gloomy night—yours beams with freedom's bright ray. The old absorbed the world by its own centralized glory—yours protects your own nation's absorption, even by itself. The old was awful with unrestricted power—yours is glorious with having restricted it. At the view of the old, nations trembled—at the view of yours, humanity hopes. To the old, misfortune was only introduced with fettered hands to kneel at the triumphant conqueror's heels—to yours, the triumph of introduction is granted to unfortunate exiles, invited to the honor of a seat. And where kings and Caesars never will be hailed, for their power, might, and wealth, there the persecuted chief of a down-trodden nation is welcomed as your great Republic's guest, precisely because he is persecuted, helpless and poor.[6]

Besides his official reception at the White House and the House of Representatives, Kossuth was invited to all the larger American cities. Unbounded enthusiasm greeted him everywhere, even in the Deep South. He gave at least six hundred major addresses, many of them improvised, blasting the emperor, the tsar, frequently even the pope; and requesting U.S. recognition of Hungary, an Anglo-American alliance to counteract the alliance of despots, funds to buy weapons, and volunteers.

In view of America's geographic location, its diplomatic and military weakness, and its foreign policy principles, no official steps could be taken on Hungary's behalf. Money was collected through private efforts, but most of it was spent on the fund-raising campaign and on the maintenance of Kossuth and his large Hungarian retinue. What weapons were bought never left the United States, and the few volunteers who embarked for Europe never got beyond England.

Anti-slavery radicals badgered Kossuth, the emancipator of serfs, to speak up against slavery; he refused, being well aware of the political influence of the South. Yet, while this stand did not make the pro-slavery forces less suspicious of him, it infuriated the radicals. The abolitionist leader William Lloyd Garrison addressed a book-length open letter to Kossuth, calling him a criminal for avoiding the slavery issue in speeches that Garrison described as "characterized by astonishing versatility and copiousness, as well as charged with the electric flame of an oriental eloquence." Again, Kossuth had fallen into his own trap. He had said in New York: "Humble as I am, God, the Almighty, has selected me to represent the cause of humanity before you! My warrant to this capacity is written in the sympathy and confidence of all who are oppressed!"[7] Yet he was no more free to stand up for the rights of Negroes and Indians than he had been free and willing to stand up for the rights of all the oppressed in Central Europe.

The Kossuth craze had begun to wane before the end of his stay. When he left New York for England, traveling with his wife under the name of "Mr. A. Smith and Lady" (for he feared an Austrian assassination attempt), seven Hungarians saw the couple off at the pier.[8] His visit had at least one beneficial effect: Hungarians remained popular in America for a long time; and during the American Civil War several former Hungarian revolutionaries were elevated to the rank of brigadier general or colonel in the Union army; others became U.S. diplomats.

When Kossuth arrived in England in July 1852, the Kossuth fever there had not yet abated. He gave hundreds of speeches and collected fees which were to be used to purchase weapons. The interest in Kossuth was such that in England alone, over a hundred books and several thousand articles were devoted to the activities and personality of the Hungarian hero.[9] While in England, Kossuth cooperated with Italian, Russian, and French democratic emigrés; and from his exile base directed clandestine movements in Hungary. But these movements were all betrayed to the Austrian police, and their leaders were hanged. Kossuth's embarrassing involvement with Mazzini's tragi-comic Milan uprising in 1853, as well as the constant bickering among the emigrés, drove him gradually away from international revolutionary politics and toward Great Power diplomacy. As so often in the past, he again sought alliances with the powerful, an endeavor which earned him the enmity of democrats, especially of Marx and Engels.

The founders of marxism, especially Engels with his racist hatred of the Slavs, had at first been enthusiastic about the emigré Kossuth. Now Marx and Engels denounced Kossuth as a petty bourgeois nationalist, "a swindler" who, "like the Apostle Paul is all things to all men," "a big mouthed charlatan" and, in Marx's inimitably scornful style: "a tight-rope walker who does not dance on a rope but on his tongue." [10]

This kind of critique made little difference to Kossuth—it has only embarrassed Hungarian marxist historians—but his attempt to win Great Power support was not much more successful than this earlier attempt to work with the democrats. His best opportunity came in 1859, when Napoleon III planned an anti-Austrian alliance with Count Cavour, the Sardinian prime minister. The French emperor had a number of meetings with Kossuth; as a result, the Magyar leader undertook to help defeat the pro-Austrian Derby cabinet in the coming British parliamentary elections (an undertaking in which Kossuth was apparently quite successful!), as well as to bring about an armed uprising in Hungary, but only after the Franco-Sardinian forces had landed on the Hungarian Littoral. In exchange, the emperor promised to give Hungary her independence.

Following the outbreak of the Franco-Sardinian war against Austria, Kossuth, Teleki, and Klapka formed a government-in-exile in Genoa, named it the Hungarian National Directorate, and recruited a Hungarian legion in Italy. In the summer of 1859 the French and the Sardinians defeated the Austrian army at Magenta and Solferino; but instead of his troops appearing on the Hungarian border, Napoleon III abandoned his Italian ally and came to terms with Francis Joseph, at the price of Austria's ceding the major part of Lombardy to Sardinia. There ensued a series of Italian revolutions that led to the unification of nearly the entire peninsula. Hungarians at home feted Garibaldi almost as much as they had feted Kossuth; and in the fall of 1860 Kossuth concluded a military pact with Cavour, in the expectation that a war would again break out between Austria and Italy. But there was no war; and no revolution took place in Hungary.

Kossuth had one more opportunity to tie his country's fate to a Great Power controversy: in 1866, when Bismarck prepared for war against Austria. There was no military pact this time between Kossuth and Austria's enemy, but the Prussian prime minister allowed General Klapka to form an exile legion in Prussia. During the campaign, the Klapka legion entered Hungary from Moravia; but having found no popular support, it withdrew quickly. There followed the Austrian surrender to Prussia and Bismarck's generous peace treaty with the Austrian emperor. Kossuth's international political role had come to an end. [11]

Why had there been no revolution in Hungary in the 1850s and 1860s? Was it because the same generation does not make a revolution twice? Because most Hungarians had learned the bitter lesson of 1848–49? Because life under the Habsburgs had not been overwhelmingly oppressive? The lower classes in Hungary continued to idolize Kossuth from afar (his portrait was a fixture in the humblest cottages), but only a handful of people—intellectuals, priests, ex-*honvéd* officers—were willing to die for him.

Following the War of Independence, Hungary had been divided into Inner Hungary, Transylvania, Croatia-Slavonia, the Serbian Vojvodina, the Banat of Temes, and the Military Border; the counties had been suppressed, but none of the social and economic reforms of 1848 had been undone. Rather, new reforms had been introduced in administration, the judiciary, education, and especially economic policy: reforms that invariably favored bourgeois-capitalist development. The customs barrier between Austria and Hungary had been abolished. Austrian goods and capital had come into the country and had built many railroad lines and factories. Hungarian industrial and mineral production had multiplied within two decades.

There had also been significant progress in agriculture. The abolition of the *robot* and the slow and inadequate compensation paid by the state to the landowners gradually bankrupted the landed gentry. Thousands of landowning peasants went the same way, because of heavy taxes and the lack of credit. Only the large estates flourished, with their unlimited capital resources for modernization and for the hiring of laborers. Declassé gentry and peasants began to flock into the cities, the first in search of administrative posts, the second in search of factory employment—a movement that would assume mass proportions later in the century. Thus while the moderate liberal leadership, in particular Ferenc Deák, advocated and practiced passive resistance to Austrian authority, there were more than enough Hungarian nobles ready to work in the Austrian administration governing Hungary. But as the Habsburg authority had brought in thousands of Austrian (especially Czech) bureaucrats, the reestablishment of Hungarian self-government became a bread-and-butter issue for the Hungarian nobles.

Economic progress had solved none of Hungary's political problems, nor was Francis Joseph able to deal with the political problems of the Empire as a whole. He experimented with everything: military dictatorship, progressive liberal centralism, Josephian absolutist centralism, conservative federalism, and a mixture of all these programs. As part of one of these experiments, in 1860–61 Hungary was allowed to hold elections and parliament was convoked. Almost without exception, the elected deputies had played a role in 1848 as conservatives, liberals, or radicals. Many of them had been emigrés; nearly all were noblemen. The national minorities and the lower classes had again been shortchanged. The nobles' cherished county system was restored; but Hungary had not been united, and relations with the rest of the Monarchy were still unsettled.

Such political leaders as Ferenc Deák and Count Gyula Andrássy held to the 1848 constitution: they refused to ask for more but would not be satisfied with less. In the end, they contented themselves with less. After the disastrous 1866 war, Francis Joseph had no choice if he wanted to save the Monarchy; he had to turn to the Hungarian liberals. This was also Bismarck's wish. The Magyar leaders proved to be accommodating; in the 1867 Compromise Agreement Hungary was made an equal partner with the other half of the Monarchy. In exchange the nation gave up what had been unreasonable and suicidal in the 1848 constitution: the separate Hungarian military establishment, separate finances, and separate foreign affairs. There was again a Hungarian minister of defense and a minister of finance, as well as a small *honvéd* army; but they were overshadowed by the authority of the common ministers of war and foreign affairs. From then on and until the fall of the dynasty, the most important affairs of the Dual Monarchy were administered jointly, not separately.[12]

After several centuries of incessant conflict with Vienna, more often peaceful than violent, the Hungarians had won, but without humiliating or fatally weakening their Austrian opponents. The new liberal government became undisputed master over unified Hungary (Croatia remained separate but was subjected to Hungarian authority); and it shared power with the Court, the Austrian government, and the Army High Command in the common affairs of the Monarchy. The Compromise Agreement was unjust toward the non-Magyars and the non-Germans—the majority of the Monarchy's population—but it was a realistic arrangement. It created the basis for five decades of domestic peace and phenomenal cultural, social, and economic progress.

Kossuth rejected the Compromise, and in his famous Cassandra

Letter to Deák predicted that Hungary, having tied its fate to that of the German nation and the Habsburgs, would go down with them. In the distant future, it was to prove a most accurate prophecy.

In 1867 as well as in his later messages, Kossuth addressed the whole nation; but only a minority listened to him, and his followers distorted what they had heard. In exile he had grown mellower on the nationality question and had developed several schemes for the self-government of the nationalities in Hungary, as well as for a Hungarian-Serbian-Romanian confederation in Central Europe. Had his schemes been accepted, World War I might not have taken place; but it is doubtful whether Kossuth himself meant his plans seriously (he certainly did not insist on them), or that the Romanians and South Slavs would ever have accepted any plan that would have preserved Hungarian territorial integrity. In any case, not even his most devoted followers in Hungary paid much attention to Kossuth's "Danube Federation" project.

There was a Kossuth party in Hungary after 1867 and it was a noisy group, but the party's concern was only for the independence and the greatness of Hungary. Ironically seated on the far left of parliament, most Kossuth party members were more chauvinistic and, on social issues, even more indifferent than the governing liberals. Social questions were rarely aired in parliament in any case—such things were not the proper concern of free-thinking politicians. What preoccupied parliament from 1867 to the end of the Monarchy were relations with the king and with the rest of the Monarchy. Gone were the romantic enthusiasm, the good will, and the reformist activism of 1848. The same politicians who, during the Springtime of the Peoples, had at least advocated the fraternity of nations, now voiced social darwinistic sentiments.

After 1867 Kossuth became a true exile.[13] Klapka, Teleki, and hundreds of other emigrés had long returned to Hungary. Kossuth now lived in or near Turin, barely noticed by the local inhabitants. Yet he never gave up politics. He directed the activities of his party, dispatched messages to his followers, received official delegations and private visitors, answered thousands of letters; when poverty forced him to do so, he contracted with a Budapest publisher to write his memoirs. Often he was alone, especially in the 1870s: "I am learning to bark, as I am conversing aloud only with dogs; I also whisper to flowers the way lovers do."[14] By the 1880s he had become more popular again, presiding over large circles of respectful visitors. His mother, his favorite sister Zsuzsa, his only daughter, and his wife had died (the latter in 1865 in Turin); the "Turin Hermit" now lived in the company of an old revolutionary soldier and visiting relatives. When these also died, others came to share his modest residence. His two sons, Lajos and Ferenc, had become successful engineers in Italy: they saw their father but rarely.*

In 1879, at the emperor-king's express wish, a law was adopted in Budapest obliging all Hungarian citizens living abroad to renew their citizenship every ten years. The law, immediately known as "Lex Kossuth," caused the Hungarian leader the greatest of all his humiliations. He would not set foot in a consulate decorated with the flag and the portrait of the Habsburg ruler, even less would he take an oath of loyalty to the king. In 1890 Kossuth was deprived of his citizenship. He had been elected in absentia again and again to the Hungarian parliament; now dozens of cities, Budapest among them, made him their "honorary citizen." He could have returned to Hungary any time he wished, yet he chose to remain stateless. He would not make his peace with Francis Joseph; nor would the other old man forgive the arch-enemy of the dynasty.

Kossuth loved nature, and he climbed the high Alps when he was well into his eighties. After 1867 he devoted more and more time to natural history (his herbarium and his collection of snail shells are now in Budapest museums), yet he never stopped writing his memoirs or cataloguing his enormous book and archival collection. Almost blind, he remained upright, strong, dignified, and argumentative. He also fell in love with a young Transylvanian-Hungarian girl, to whom he addressed pathetically beautiful letters.[15] He died peacefully on March 20, 1894, when he was ninety-two.

The dead Kossuth suddenly reacquired world fame. The municipality of Turin handed over his body, in solemn pomp, to a delegation from the municipality of Budapest. At the wish of Francis Joseph and despite violent street demonstrations in the capital, the Hungarian government and the parliament abstained from taking official notice of the arrival of Kossuth's remains. He was buried in Budapest in the presence of millions.

---

*Lajos Kossuth, Jr. remained in Italy for the rest of his life; Ferenc returned to Hungary after his father's death, there to become the incompetent leader of the Kossuth party and between 1906 and 1910 a member of a coalition cabinet appointed by Francis Joseph.

The Kossuth cult has never abated. A sincere emotion on the part of poor people and especially peasants, the cult has remained a tool in the hands of politicians. In reality, after 1849 Kossuth had contributed little to the political evolution of his country, or to that of Europe. He had learned little, remaining forever a child of the Enlightenment and of the romantic age. He believed firmly in reason and in the perfectibility of man. He thought that he could improve humanity and his own nation through good will, the power of persuasion, and hard work. It would be foolish to pretend that he failed completely, for he gave hope to the oppressed; he opened the way to the modernization of his country, and by inspiring, causing, or provoking national revolutions, he changed the course of Central European history. But he burdened the shoulders of his compatriots with more problems than he was able to solve. He was a charismatic leader who reinforced the Hungarians' suicidal notion that theirs was a particularly exalted destiny, and that the Hungarian contribution to all mankind was crucial. Yet there was in Kossuth no trace of the cynicism, callousness, and furious brutality of Napoleon I or of the twentieth-century dictators. Poor Széchenyi exaggerated a good deal when, in his growing madness, he shouted to his friends in August 1848: "O! my wasted life! Across the firmament, Kossuth's name is written in flaming letters, *flagellum Dei!*" [16]

Notes

Abbreviations

KLÖM = *Kossuth Lajos összes munkái*
  KLI = *Kossuth Lajos iratai*
  OHB = Országos Honvédelmi Bizottmány

1 / Road to Reform: Kossuth and Hungary before 1848

1. English-speaking readers interested in the history of Hungary during the fifty-odd years preceding the revolution of 1848 should turn to such fundamental works as C. A. Macartney, *The Habsburg Empire 1790–1918;* Ervin Pamlényi, ed., *A History of Hungary,* chs. 4 and 5; Béla K. Király, *Hungary in the Late Eighteenth Century: The Decline of Enlightened Despotism;* and George Barany, *Stephen Széchenyi and the Awakening of Hungarian Nationalism, 1791–1841.*

2. The best analyses of the role of the nobility in Hungary are in Király, *Hungary in the Late Eighteenth Century,* pp. 24–42; Henrik Marczali, *Hungary in the Eighteenth Century;* and Sándor Domanovszky, *Magyar művelődéstörténet,* vol. IV.

3. Kossuth's family origins were thoroughly researched by Domokos Kosáry in his admirable *Kossuth Lajos a reformkorban,* pp. 9–17. An older hagiographic work, Lajos Hentaller, *Kossuth és kora,* pp. 1–18, is also useful in this respect. Kossuth's youth is well presented in István Barta, *A fiatal Kossuth.* Kossuth's complete biography, Zoltán Vas, *Kossuth Lajos élete,* summarizes the information contained in the above-mentioned monographs. Vas's work offers little that is new but it is agreeable. It is written in a novelistic, romantic, and patriotic style which is a bit amazing, for the author is an old Bolshevik. But then old Bolsheviks were born and grew up in superpatriotic pre–World War I Hungary. György Szabad's recent study, *Kossuth politikai pályája ismert és ismeretlen megnyilatkozásai tükrében,* is a spirited defense of Kossuth the progressive statesman, with many citations from Kossuth's works but, unfortunately, with only rare indication of their sources.

4. Kossuth's youthful writings, as far as they could be found, were printed in István Barta, ed., *Kossuth Lajos: ifjúkori iratok, Törvényhatósági Tudósítások,* which forms vol. VI of Kossuth's complete works, entitled *Kossuth Lajos összes munkái,* hereafter cited as *KLÖM.*

5. There are many works on the administrative history of Hungary. The finest and most recent summary in a Western language is George Barany, "Ungarns Verwaltung: 1848–1918," in *Die Habsburgermonarchie 1848–1918,* II, 306–468. Also Győző Ember, *Az újkori magyar közigazgatás története;* and Ferenc Eckhart, *Magyar alkotmány- és jogtörténet.* Hungary's consitutional development in the first half of the nineteenth century is well summed up in Edsel

354 / 1. Road to Reform

Walter Stroup, *Hungary in Early 1848: The Constitutional Struggle against Absolutism in Contemporary Eyes*. The Introduction and chapter 1 deal with the pre-1848 period, the rest with events in the spring of 1848. Charles d'Eszláry, *Histoire des institutions publiques hongroises*, discusses Hungarian constitutional developments as a whole.

6. Kossuth in the Assembly of Zemplén county (Sátoraljaújhely, January 24, 1831), *KLÖM*, VI, 215–19.

7. On the effect of the Polish revolution in Hungary and on Polish-Hungarian relations in the first half of the nineteenth century, see Endre Kovács, *A lengyel kérdés a reformkori Magyarországon*.

8. Kossuth's embezzlement scandal is described in Barta, *A fiatal Kossuth*, pp. 59–80.

9. George Barany's *Stephen Széchenyi* is the definitive work on the first fifty years of Széchenyi's life. Unfortunately, there remain nineteen more years, both exciting and tragic, to account for. The English-speaking reader is advised to turn also to such works as György Spira, *A Hungarian Count in the Revolution of 1848*; and the special Széchenyi issue of the *Journal of Central European Affairs*, which contains both essays and documents. There is a fine little biography in German: Denis Silagi, *Der grösste Ungar. Graf Stephan Széchenyi*. The most challenging Hungarian work on Széchenyi is still Gyula Szekfű, *Három nemzedék*.

10. Kossuth's *Parliamentary Reports* are printed in their entirety in István Barta, ed., *Kossuth Lajos: Országgyűlési Tudósítások*, which forms vols. I–V of *KLÖM*.

11. Kossuth's *Municipal Reports* were reprinted in their entirety in *KLÖM*, VI, 627–1037.

12. The list of subscribers to the *Municipal Reports* is printed in *KLÖM*, VI, 1039–44, with an indication of the subscriber's rank and position.

13. For a complete list of the Monarchy's dignitaries and office holders, both titular and real, as well as for the names of regimental commanders and of civil servants down to janitors, see *Hof- und Staats-Handbuch des österreichischen Kaiserthumes*. The most useful edition for our purposes is that of 1845.

14. Kossuth's writings on behalf of László Lovassy and the other "dietal youth" were reprinted in their entirety in *KLÖM*, VI, 523–39 and passim. The same volume contains all Kossuth's available speeches and writings as well as documents on him between 1819 and 1837.

15. There is a fine and succinct biography of Ferenc Deák by Béla K. Király, *Ferenc Deák*.

16. For a delightful description of the evil roles ascribed to the consorts of monarchs with tragic histories, see Henry L. Roberts, *Four Queens and Several Knaves*.

17. Of the sea of literature on Hungary's peasants in the prerevolutionary period, the reader's attention is drawn to the following works: Macartney, *Habsburg Empire*, pp. 61–75 and passim; Pamlényi, *History of Hungary*, pp. 195–200 and passim; Király, *Hungary in the Late Eighteenth Century*, pp. 51–73 and passim; János Varga, *Typen und Probleme des bäuerlichen Grundbesitzes in Ungarn, 1767–1849*; János Varga, *A jobbágyfelszabadítás kivívása 1848-ban*; Gyula Mérei, *Mezőgazdaság és agrártársadalom Magyarországon, 1790–1848*; and Zsolt Trócsányi, *Az erdélyi parasztság története, 1790–1849*.

18. Because of the tragic death of István Barta, editor of Kossuth's complete works (*összes munkái*), the volumes containing Kossuth's *Pesti Hírlap* articles have not yet been printed. A generous selection of the *Pesti Hírlap* writings is contained in Ferencz Kossuth, ed., *Kossuth Lajos hírlapi czikkei*, which forms vols. XII and XIII of *Kossuth Lajos iratai*, edited by Ignácz Helfy and Ferencz Kossuth, hereafter cited as *KLI*.

19. George Barany, "The Awakening of Magyar Nationalism before 1848," p. 21.

20. The history of Hungary's language problems in the late seventeenth and early eighteenth centuries is best analyzed by Gyula Szekfű in *Iratok a magyar államnyelv kérdésének történetéhez, 1790–1848*. The volume contains a lengthy introduction by the author as well as 170 documents.

21. *Ibid.*, pp. 10–11.

22. Kossuth, "Bánat és gondolkodás" (*Pesti Hírlap*, 1842, nr. 183), *KLI*, xii, 411.

23. *Ibid.*, p. 410.

24. Kossuth's speech at the Diet (December 11, 1847), *KLÖM*, xi, 382.

25. Law ii/1844 on the Hungarian language; Law iii/1844 on the equality of Protestants; Law iii/1844 on the theoretical rights of commoners to own noble landed property, and Law iv/1844 on the equally theoretical right of commoners to all public offices, were reprinted in *Gesetzartikel des ungarischen Reichstages 1843–1844*, translated from the Hungarian original(!).

26. Quoted in Kosáry, *Kossuth Lajos a reformkorban*, p. 302.

27. See György Spira, "Egy pillantás a *Hitel* írójának hitelviszonyaira," *A negyvennyolcas nemzedék nyomában*, pp. 151–71.

28. Hungary's economic development before 1848 has not yet been comprehensively analyzed. Some of the more valuable studies are: Gyula Mérei, "L'essor de l'agriculture capitaliste en Hongrie dans la première moitié du xixe siècle"; and, by the same author, *Über einige Fragen der Anfänge der kapitalistischen Gewerbeentwicklung in Ungarn;* Emil Niederhauser, "The Problems of Bourgeois Transformation in Eastern and South-Eastern Europe," i, 565–80; and B. G. Iványi, "From Feudalism to Capitalism: The Economic Background to Széchenyi's Reform in Hungary," *Journal of Central European Affairs* (October 1960) 20 (3): 270–88. The author is indebted to Professor Andrew Janos of the University of California at Berkeley for various statistical data on Hungarian production and export.

29. See, for instance, John Paget, *Hungary and Transylvania; with Remarks on their Condition, Social, Political and Economical;* and Richard Bright, *Travels from Vienna through Lower Hungary*, pp. 98–113 and passim.

30. Ervin Szabó, *Társadalmi és pártharcok a 48–49-es magyar forradalomban*, p. 44.

31. See Domokos Kosáry, *Kossuth és a Védegylet: A magyar nacionalizmus történetéhez.*

32. Kossuth's several drafts of the Proclamation, as well as the speeches he gave in connection with the Proclamation, were printed in *KLÖM*, xi, 116–30, 137–40, 141–51, and 158–64. The text of the Proclamation itself is on pp. 152–57 of the same volume.

33. Pest county's lengthy instructions to its two dietal deputies, mostly drafted by Kossuth, are in *KLÖM*, xi, 168–96.

34. Anonymous report to Vienna (Pressburg, November 6, 1847), *KLÖM*, xi, 229–34 (in German).

35. Letter of Gábor Földváry, deputy lord-lieutenant of Pest County, to Chief Chancellor György Apponyi (Pest, October 19, 1847), *KLÖM*, xi, 222.

36. Kossuth at the "circular session" of the Lower House (Pressburg, November 29, 1847), first printed in *Pesti Hirlap*, December 5, 1847 and reprinted in *KLÖM*, xi, 337.

37. For details of the February 5, 1848, dietal meeting and the text of Kossuth's speeches given on the occasion, see *KLÖM*, xi, 503–15.

38. Letter of Count Karl Vitzthum, secretary of the Prussian Legation, to his mother (Vienna, February 29, 1848). Printed (in Hungarian) in László Bártfai Szabó, ed., *Adatok gróf Széchenyi István és kora történetéhez, 1808–60*, ii, 641.

2 / Reform Triumphant: March–April 1848

1. The standard histories of the Monarchy in English are C. A. Macartney, *The Habsburg Empire 1790–1918;* Victor-L. Tapié, *The Rise and Fall of the Habsburg Monarchy:* Robert A. Kann, *The Multinational Empire: Nationalism and National Reform in the Habsburg Monarchy, 1848–1918*, 2 vols.; and, Robert A. Kann, *A History of the Habsburg Empire, 1526–1918.*

2. On the Monarchy's economic, social, and financial condition in the pre-March period, see Macartney, *Habsburg Empire*, pp. 255–78; Adolf Beer, *Die Finanzen Oesterreichs;* Julius

356 / 2. Reform Triumphant

Marx, *Die wirtschaftlichen Ursachen der Revolution von 1848 in Österreich;* and for a brief summary Walter Pollak, *1848: Revolution auf halbem Wege,* pp. 34–39, 85–90.

3. Macartney, *Habsburg Empire,* p. 323.

4. Kossuth's March 3, 1848, address was printed in all the major documentary collections dealing with the period. As usual, the most reliable version is in *KLÖM,* xi, 619–28. The specific quotation is on p. 624.

5. For descriptions of Vienna's first revolutionary *journée,* see R. John Rath, *The Viennese Revolution of 1848;* Macartney, *Habsburg Empire,* pp. 325–30; Rolland R. Lutz, "The Aula and the Vienna Radical Movement of 1848"; and Lottelore C. M. Bernstein, "Revolution and Response: Radical Thought in Vienna's Free Press in 1848."

6. See Ervin Szabó, *Társadalmi és pártharcok a 48–49-es magyar forradalomban,* pp. 44–45.

7. The literature on Petőfi would fill libraries. A recent collection of essays, Anna Tamás and Antal Wéber, eds., *Petőfi tüze: Tanulmányok Petőfi Sándorról,* contains among others a selected bibliography of scholarly works on the poet. For an introduction to Petőfi's life (in English) see Joseph Reményi, *Hungarian Writers and Literature,* pp. 84–105. See also *Sixty Poems by Alexander Petőfi,* translated by E. B. Pierce and E. Delmár, with an introduction by J. Reményi (New York: Johannes Press, 1948).

8. The March 15, 1848, events in Buda-Pest have been described many times. Most useful in a Western language is the abundantly documented György Spira, "Le grand jour (le 15 mars 1848)," Also, Heinrich Incze, *Die Geschichte des 15. März in Buda-Pesth;* and Laszlo Deme, "The Committee of Public Safety in the Hungarian Revolution of 1848." The quotations from Petőfi's writings are in *Petőfi Sándor összes művei,* v, 141, 83 (Cited in French in Spira, "Le grand jour," p. 360).

9. The Address to the Throne is contained in Kossuth's March 3 speech. It passed through both Houses of the Diet in its original form. See *KLÖM,* xi, 625–28; and Dénes Pap, ed., *Okmánytár Magyarország függetlenségi harczának történetéhez, 1848–1849,* i, 1–4.

10. The Diet's March 15 instructions to the delegation are in *KLÖM,* xi, 658–60.

11. See Árpád Károlyi, *Az 1848-diki pozsonyi törvénycikkek az udvar előtt,* p. 14. This volume, half of which consists of documents, thoroughly analyzes Hungarian negotiations in Vienna. The draft Reply is printed on pp. 207–9 together with the final Reply signed by the king. The latter document is also printed in Árpád Károlyi, *Németújvári gróf Batthyány Lajos első magyar miniszterelnök főbenjáró pöre,* ii, 604.

12. Kossuth, "Császári hála: császári forradalom és annak céljai," speech given in 1858 in England and printed in L. K., *Irataim az emigráczióból,* 3 vols. (Budapest: Athenaeum, 1880–1881), ii, 186–205. The specific quotation is on p. 187.

13. Széchenyi, March 16, 1848. Reprinted in Gyula Viszota, ed., *Gróf Széchenyi István naplói,* vi (1844–48), 749 (vol. xv of *Gróf Széchenyi István összes munkái*). The Kossuth reminiscences are from notes written in exile. Reprinted in *Irataim az emigráczióból,* ii, 265.

14. The palatine to Batthyány (Vienna, March 17, 1848). Printed in Károlyi, *Batthyány,* ii, 605. Also in Imre Deák, ed., *1848: A szabadságharc története levelekben,* pp. 30–31. The palatine's apologetic letter to Ferdinand, written on the same day, is *ibid.,* pp. 31–32.

15. Teleki to Czartoryski (London, July 26, 1849). Printed in Eszter V. Waldapfel, ed., *A forradalom és szabadságharc levelestára,* iv, 244. On the Camarilla see Gyula Miskolczy, *A kamarilla a reformkorszakban,* a well-balanced analysis.

16. See, for instance, György Spira, *A magyar forradalom 1848–49-ben,* p. 92 and passim.

17. The March 1848 Italian events are best described in Rudolf Kiszling et al., *Die Revolution im Kaisertum Österreich, 1848–1849,* i, 86–122.

18. See Gunther E. Rothenberg, *The Military Border in Croatia, 1740–1881: A Study of an Imperial Institution.*

19. Baron Franz Kulmer, lord-lieutenant of Zagreb county, to Jelačić (Vienna, March 30, 1848). Jelačić Papers as quoted in Rothenberg, *Military Border*, p. 145.

20. On the March events in Croatia, see Kiszling, I, 79–82. On the origins of the Croat problem, see Gyula Miskolczy, *A horvát kérdés története és irományai a rendi állam korában*, with most of the work consisting of documents. On Jelačić, see Ferdinand Hauptmann, *Jelačić's Kriegszug nach Ungarn 1848*. Ferdinand's letter of appointment to Jelačić (Vienna, March 23, 1848), is printed in Erzsébet Andics, ed., *A nagybirtokos arisztokrácia ellenforradalmi szerepe 1848–49-ben*, II, 35–36.

21. Underlining by Széchenyi himself. Széchenyi to Antal Tasner (Pressburg, March 6, 1848) in Béla Majláth, ed., *Gróf Széchenyi István levelei*, I, 600.

22. Széchenyi to Tasner (Pressburg, March 17, 1848) in *ibid.*, p. 602. Also in Deák, *1848*, p. 32. The English translation is borrowed from György Spira, *A Hungarian Count*, pp. 31–32. Spira's work is a thorough analysis of Széchenyi's erratic but fascinating doings in the Revolution.

23. Cited in Spira, *A magyar forradalom*, p. 95. Documents on the March 18, 1848, meetings of the Diet are in *KLÖM*, XI, 667–73.

24. For the Catholic church's less than enchanted reaction to the unexpected magnanimity of its representatives in the Diet, see Erzsébet Andics, "Az egyházi reakció 1848–49-ben" in Aladár Mód et al., *Forradalom és szabadságharc, 1848–1849*, pp. 324–28. This very biased marxist account ought to be compared with the pro-Catholic account of Antal Meszlényi, *A magyar katholikus egyház és állam 1848/49-ben*, pp. 63–87.

25. Kossuth in the Lower House (March 19, 1848), *KLÖM*, XI, 675. For relations between the Diet and the Pest radicals in the spring of 1848, see Laszlo Deme, *The Radical Left in the Hungarian Revolution of 1848*.

26. On Kossuth's defeat in the Lower House over Jewish voting rights see *KLÖM*, XI, 684–85.

27. Kossuth in the Diet (March 22, 1848), *KLÖM*, XI, 688.

28. On the "compensation" debate in the Lower House, see *KLÖM*, XI, 689–91. For the whole issue of peasant emancipation see János Varga, *A jobbágyfelszabadítás kivívása 1848-ban;* and the documentary collection Gyözö Ember, ed., *Iratok az 1848-i magyarországi parasztmozgalmak történetéhez*.

29. Károlyi, *1848* and *Batthyány*.

30. See Esterházy's memorandum to the Court (Vienna, May 1848) printed in Andics, *Nagybirtokos arisztokrácia*, II, 86. Also, István Hajnal, *A Batthyány-kormány külpolitikája*, pp. 21–26.

31. Quoted in Spira, *A Hungarian Count*, p. 67.

32. On Mészáros, see Viktor Szokoly, ed., *Mészáros Lázár emlékiratai;* and Zoltán Sirokay, *M. L. tábornok az első magyar hadügyminiszter*.

33. The best approach to Eötvös, a fascinating personality, is through a fine monograph by the American-Hungarian historian Paul Bödy, *Joseph Eötvös and the Modernization of Hungary, 1840–1870: A Study of Ideas of Individuality and Social Pluralism in Modern Politics*. Many of Eötvös' own writings were published in a Western language, for instance: [N. N.], *Über die Gleichberechtigung der Nationalitäten in Österreich* (Pest, 1850). His complete works appeared in Hungarian as *Báró Eötvös József összes művei*.

34. Some of Szemere's reminiscences appeared in a Western language, for instance, *F. m. Gr. Ludwig Batthyány, Arthur Görgey, Ludwig Kossuth*, 3 vols. (Hamburg, 1853), and *Hungary from 1848 to 1860*. See also his *Összegyüjtött munkái*, 6 vols. (Pest: Ráth Mór, 1869–70).

35. The palatine's letter (Vienna, March 24, 1848) appeared in many printed documentary collections, with slight variations as to its contents. There is a very liberal English translation in the famous work of the U.S. chargé d'affaires to Vienna, William H. Stiles, *Austria in*

358 / 2. Reform Triumphant

1848–49, II, 396–97. The German original is printed in Bártfai Szabó, *Adatok gróf Széchenyi István és kora történetéhez, 1808–1860*, II, 664–66. The Hungarian version is in Pap, *Okmánytár*, I, 28–30, and in Deák, *1848*, pp. 45–46. For a good analysis of the letter's contents, see Károlyi, *1848*, 66–71.

36. Arthur Seherr Thosz, "Emlékezések múltamra," *Budapesti Szemle* (1881), 27, 287–88. Quoted in Spira, *A Hungarian Count*, p. 62.

37. Undated financial statement from the Esterházy estates, prepared during the spring of 1848, printed in Andics, *Nagybirtokos arisztokrácia*, II, 76–79. See also Spira, *A Hungarian Count*, p. 63.

38. See Károlyi, *1848*, pp. 34–44. Documents relative to the debate and resolutions of the State Conference on general taxation and the abolition of urbarial statutes are in *ibid.*, pp. 216–25.

39. The debates and resolutions of the State Conference together with the text of the Royal Rescript are printed in Károlyi, *1848*, pp. 226–43. For an analysis of the problem see *ibid.*, pp. 71–79.

40. On the March 29 events at Pressburg see *KLÖM*, XI, 700–703; and Károlyi, *1848*, pp. 79–84.

41. Zichy to Vice-Chancellor László Szögyén-Marich (Buda, March 29, 1848). Printed in Deák, *1848*, p. 54.

42. On the second Buda-Pest *journées*, see Deme, *The Radical Left*, pp. 40–43; and Alajos Degré, *Visszaemlékezéseim*, II, 10–15 and passim. The March 31 proclamation of the Pest Committee of Public Safety, demanding that people prepare for war "without regard to language or religion," is in Pap, *Okmánytár*, I, 45–47. The report of Klauzál and Szemere to Batthyány on the Pest disturbances of late March is in the Hungarian National Archives. Miniszterelnökség, Országos Honvédelmi Bizottmány, Kormányzóelnökség 1848–1849. Általános Iratok (hereafter cited as OHB), 1848:171. Klauzál, Szemere, and Pulszky to Batthyány (Pest, April 1, 1848).

43. The revised Royal Rescript is reprinted in Károlyi, *1848*, pp. 244–57. The final Hungarian bill on "Responsible Government," modified by Kossuth himself in accordance with the Royal Rescript, is in *ibid.*, pp. 248–50.

44. Kossuth at the plenary meeting of the Diet (March 31, 1848), *KLÖM*, XI, 706–10. The particular quotation is on p. 709.

45. See György Spira, "Petőfi kardja," in Tamás and Wéber, *Petőfi tüze*, pp. 369–71.

46. Kossuth's address to the palatine (Pressburg, April 1, 1848), *KLÖM*, XI, 712–13.

47. There is a fine monograph on the 1848 electoral law: Andor Csizmadia, *A magyar választási rendszer 1848–1849-ben*. Most of my data on the subject are from this source. See also János Beér, ed., *Az 1848/49. évi népképviseleti országgyűlés*. The Diet's debates on the reform of the electoral law are printed in *KLÖM*, XI, 678–79, 703–4 and 711–12. The text of Law V/1848 is in Csizmadia, *A magyar választási rendszer*, pp. 311–21.

48. The debate on the reform of the county structure is in *KLÖM*, XI, 716–26.

49. The king's declaration to the joint meeting of the two Houses of the Diet (April 11, 1848) is in Samu Szeremlei, ed., *Magyarország krónikája az 1848. és 1849. évi forradalom idejéről*, I, 67.

50. The April Laws were published as *1848-dik évi Magyar Országgyűlésen alkotott törvénycikkelyek*. There seems to be no modern edition of these crucial thirty-one laws. Contemporary liberal views of Hungary's achievements in March–April 1848 are approvingly summed up in Mihály Horváth, *Magyarország függetlenségi harczának története 1848 és 1849-ben*, I, 3–15.

51. Mihály Horváth, *Magyarország* I, 19.

52. *Ibid.*, I, 29.

53. Ervin Szabó, *Társadalmi és pártharcok*, p. 96; Gyula Szekfű in Bálint Hóman and Gyula Szekfű, *Magyar történet*, v, 394.

54. See especially József Révai, *Kossuth Lajos;* and *Marx és a magyar forradalom;* reprinted in *Válogatott történelmi írások.*

55. Ervin Szabó, *Társadalmi és pártharcok*, p. 32; Révai, *Kossuth*, pp. 12–14 and passim. The particular quotation is on p. 13.

3 / Between Legality and Rebellion: Kossuth Minister of Finance (April–August 1848)

1. Robert A. Kann, *A History of the Habsburg Empire, 1526–1918*, p. 299.

2. The minutes of the cabinet council of April 12, together with the instructions drafted by Kossuth and others, are printed in István Sinkovics, ed., *Kossuth Lajos az első magyar felelős minisztériumban, 1848 április-szeptember*, which is vol. XII of *Kossuth Lajos összes munkái* (hereafter to be cited as KLÖM, XII), pp. 22–34. The minutes were also printed in Daniel Rapant, *Slovenské povstanie roku 1848–49*, vol. I, part 2, p. 22a. For an excellent analysis of the cabinet meeting, see István Hajnal, *A Batthyány-kormány külpolitikája*, pp. 21–48.

3. Palmerston's letter to Ponsonby (London, April 28, 1848). Printed in English in Éva Haraszti, *Az angol külpolitika a magyar szabadságharc ellen*, pp. 118–19. English-Hungarian relations in 1848–49 are inadequately discussed in this marxist work, which nevertheless contains many valuable documents found by the author in the Public Records Office. See also Charles Sproxton, *Palmerston and the Hungarian Revolution;* and Great Britain, House of Commons, *Sessional Papers*, vol. LVII (1851), "Correspondence Relative to the Affairs of Hungary, 1847–1849." The reports of J. A. Blackwell, Great Britain's permanent agent in Hungary, are also printed in Haraszti's work.

4. See Dezső Nemes, "A munkásság az 1848–49-es forradalomban," in Aladár Mód et al., *Forradalom és szabadságharc, 1848–1849*, pp. 267–314. Documents relative to the workers' movement in 1848 are in Gyula Mérei, ed., *Munkásmozgalmak 1848–49: Iratok a magyar munkásmozgalom történetéhez*. Sources on the historic collective bargaining agreement, won by the printers, are *ibid.*, pp. 196–214. See also Ervin Szabó, *Társadalmi és pártharcok a 48-49-es magyar forradalomban*, pp. 139–55.

5. Documents of the spring 1848 pogroms and the Government's answer to them, are in Jenő Zsoldos, ed., *1848–49 a magyar zsidóság életében*, pp. 47–107. See also Deák, *1848*, pp. 69–70, and Dénes Pap, *Okmánytár*, I, 59–60. The Budapest National Archives contain additional unpublished information on anti-Semitism in Hungary, for instance, the letter by a "landowning burgher of Dinnyés" (Pest, April 22, 1848), OHB, 1848:37; Pál Jászay to Lipót Rottenbiller (Pest, April 25, 1848), OHB, 1848:71; and Klauzál, Szemere, and Pulszky to the Prime Minister (Pest, April 10, 1848), OHB, 1848:115.

6. Kossuth in *Pesti Hírlap*, 1844, pp. 300, 376.

7. Salo W. Baron, "The Impact of the Revolution of 1848 on Jewish Emancipation," p. 213.

8. Ignac Einhorn, *Die Revolution und die Juden in Ungarn* p. 35. The English translation is by Baron, "Jewish Emancipation," p. 241.

9. There are many works on the peasant troubles in the spring of 1848. The most thorough analyses are: István Szabó, "A jobbágybirtok problémái," in *Tanulmányok a magyar parasztság történetéből* (Budapest: n.p., 1948), pp. 311–96; and Győző Ember, "Magyar parasztmozgalmak 1848-ban," in Mód, *Forradalom és szabadságharc*, pp. 189–265. See also the documentary collection in Győző Ember, *Iratok az 1848-i magyarországi parasztmozgalmak történetéhez.*

10. See Ervin Szabó, *Társadalmi és pártharcok*, pp. 156–222; and József Révai, *Kossuth*, 12–20 and passim.

360 / 3. Between Legality and Rebellion

11. Fortunately for the historian, the excellent contemporary statistician Elek Fényes provides us with ample data. See his *Magyarország statistikája; Magyarország leírása;* and *Az ausztriai birodalom statistikája és földrajzi leírása.* The only major flaw in these statistics is Fényes's understandable nineteenth-century confusion of Croats with Serbs. There is a good critique of Fényes's data in Endre Arató, *A nemzetiségi kérdés története Magyarországon, 1790–1848,* ɪ, 299–306.

12. The best general works on the nationality question in Hungary before and during 1848–49 are Arató, *A nemzetiségi kérdés,* with almost half the monograph consisting of an annotated bibliography; Zoltán I. Tóth, "A soknemzetiségű állam néhány kérdéséről az 1848 előtti Magyarországon"; Oszkár Jászi, *A nemzeti államok kialakulása és a nemzetiségi kérdés;* and Tóth, "Kossuth és a nemzetiségi kérdés, 1848–1849-ben," in Tóth, ed., *Emlékkönyv Kossuth Lajos születésének 150. évfordulójára,* ɪɪ, 249–340. There is a fine little summary in C. A. Macartney, *The Habsburg Empire 1790–1918,* pp. 380–91. For the eighteenth-century background of the non-Magyar nationality movements in Hungary, read Endre Arató, *A feudális nemzetiségtől a polgári nemzetig.* In English: Zoltán I. Tóth, "The Nationality Problem in Hungary in 1848–1849," pp. 235–77. For the nationality question in the Monarchy as a whole, see the incomparable Robert A. Kann, *The Multinational Empire.*

13. Kossuth addressing the Serbian delegation of Ujvidék at the circular meeting of the Diet (Pressburg, April 8, 1848). Printed in *Pesti Hírlap* (April 16, 1848) and reprinted in *KLÖM,* xɪ, 732.

14. The May 10–11 Slovak demands are printed in Lajos Steier, *A tót nemzetiségi kérdés 1848–49-ben,* ɪ, 75–78 (in Hungarian), and ɪɪ, 48–52 (in Slovak).

15. The Slovak question in 1848 boasts a large literature. Some of the more important works are: Steier, *A tót nemzetiségi kérdés* (second volume made up of documents) and, by the same author, *Beniczky Lajos bányavidéki kormánybiztos és honvédezredes visszaemlékezései és jelentései az 1848/49-iki szabadságharcról és a tót mozgalomról* (also mainly documents). The Slovak view is best presented in Rapant, *Slovenske povstanie* (thousands of documents). Also, Vladimir Matula, *L'udovit Štúr, 1815–1856;* and Ludwig v. Gogolák, *Beiträge zur Geschichte des slowakischen Volkes,* vol. ɪɪɪ: *Zwischen zwei Revolutionen (1848–1919).* See also Stanley Z. Pech, *The Czech Revolution of 1848.*

16. The protest of Hungarian-Romanians against their subjection to the Serbian Metropolitan at Karlóca (Pest, May 21, 1848) is printed in Pap, *Okmánytár,* ɪ, 146–49. On Eftimie Murgu, see Gheorghe Bogdan-Duica, *Eftimie Murgu.*

17. The minutes, resolutions, and newspaper accounts of the May 15–17 Blaj Congress were printed, in Hungarian, in Benedek Jancsó, *A román nemzetiségi törekvések története és jelenlegi állapota,* ɪɪ, 464–66, and in Pap, *Okmánytár,* ɪ, 115–30. In Romanian, in Teodor V. Păcatian, *Cartea de aur, sau luptele politice-nationale ale Românilor sub coroana ungară,* pp. 330–32. The most thorough history of the Congress is by Victor Chereşteşiu, *Adunarea naţionalǎ de la Blaj.*

18. Ferdinand's reply to the Romanian Petition is in Pap, *Okmánytár,* ɪ, 197–98 (see also *ibid.,* pp. 208–11). Romanian documents on the same subject are in Silviu Dragomir, *Studii şi documente privitoare la revoluţia Românilor din Transilvania in anii 1848–1849,* ɪɪɪ, 13 and passim.

19. The Court's dilemma with regard to the Act of Union is thoroughly described in Károlyi, *Az 1848-diki pozsonyi törvénycikkek az udvar előtt,* pp. 155–98. Documents relative to the problem are *ibid.,* pp. 312–21 and passim. See also Pap, *Okmánytár,* ɪ, 182 and passim.

20. Literature on Transylvania and the Romanian question being very rich, the reader is referred to the works mentioned above, as well as to Keith Hitchins, *The Rumanian National Movement in Transylvania, 1780–1849.* This fine study, a bit lenient toward the Romanians and quite harsh on the Hungarians, contains an annotated bibliography. Some other basic works are: Zsolt Trócsányi, *Az erdélyi parasztság története, 1790–1849;* Silviu Dragomir, *Avram Iancu;* Elek Jakab, *Szabadságharczunk történetéhez: Visszaemlékezések 1848–1849-re;* and Cornelia

Bodea, *The Romanians' Struggle for Unification, 1834–1849.* Aside from the already mentioned documentary collections, see also Deák, *1848;* and László Kőváry, ed., *Okmánytár az 1848–49-ki erdélyi eseményekhez.* The Hungarian National Archives is replete with unpublished documents on the Romanian movement in the spring and summer of 1848, for example: OHB, 1848:179, 344, 409, 456, 536, 549, and 729. On the Transylvanian situation in 1848–49 see also the many valuable articles in Lajos Demény et al., *1848: Arcok, eszmék, tettek.*

21. The March 17–19 and March 27 Serbian petitions are printed in József Thim, *A magyarországi 1848–49-iki szerb fölkelés története,* II, 26–35, 49–56. This monumental work consists of one volume of analysis and two volumes of documents; the latter appear in the original language and in their Hungarian translation. Pap, *Okmánytár,* I, and Deák, *1848,* also contain documents on the Serbian revolt. Deák's volume is especially useful on Hungarian reaction to the Serbian nationalist movement.

22. Documents of the May 13 Karlóca congress are in Thim, *A szerb fölkelés,* II, 198–224.

23. Proclamation of the Serbian Glavni Odbor to the Serbian Nation (Karlóca, May 24, 1848) in Thim, II, 287–93.

24. See Hrabovszky's reports in Thim, II, 408–12. On the Serbian nationalist movement in 1848, see also Vaso Bogdanov, *Ustanak Srba u Vojvodini i Madjarska Revolucija, 1848–49;* and Endre Kovács, *Magyar-délszláv megbékélési törekvések 1848/49-ben.*

25. The best source on Croatian activity before 1848 is Gyula Miskolczy, *A horvát kérdés története és irományai a rendi állam korában,* which consists mostly of documents. On Gaj's Russian connections: see Arató, *A nemzetiségi kérdés,* I, 368–70. For Croatian views of the same period, see the first chapters in Vaso Bogdanov, *Društvene i političke borbe u Hrvatskoj 1848/49;* and, by the same author, *Hrvatska ljevica u godinama revolucije 1848/49.* On Gaj, see the fine biography of Elinor M. Despalatović, *Ludevit Gaj and the Illyrian Movement.*

26. See Great Britain, "Correspondence Relative to the Affairs of Hungary," pp. 48–49, and Despalatović, *Ludevit Gaj,* pp. 189–90.

27. Mijo Krešić, *Autobiografija* (Zagreb: Dionicka tiskara, 1898), quoted by Despalatović, *Ludevit Gaj,* p. 190. Hungarian views of the Croatian delegation are in Mihály Horváth, *Huszonöt év Magyarország történelméből 1823-tól 1848-ig,* II, 693. Croatian events of the spring are best summed up in Rudolf Kiszling, *Die Revolution im Kaisertum Österreich, 1848–1849,* I, 77–84 and passim. Also, Gunther Erich Rothenberg, *The Military Border in Croatia 1740–1881,* pp. 142–48, and Despalatović, *Ludevit Gaj,* pp. 185–95.

28. Rothenberg, *Military Border,* p. 148.

29. Jelačić to the First Deputy Lord Lieutenant of Zagreb County (Zagreb, April 19, 1848), in Pap, *Okmánytár,* I, 51.

30. See Aladár Urbán, "Zehn kritische Tage aus der Geschichte der Batthyány-Regierung (10-20. Mai 1848)." Also, by the same author "A Batthyány-kormány hadügyi politikájának első szakasza (1848). április-május)"; and "Agitáció és kormányválság 1848 májusában."

31. On the government's attempt to prevail upon the king to come to Hungary see the resolution of the Council of Ministers (Buda-Pest, May 20, 1848), *KLÖM,* XII, 159–60. Also the palatine's letter to Esterházy (Pest, May 19, 1848), in Pap, *Okmánytár,* I, 142.

32. On the question of Hungary's sharing in the Monarchy's state debt, see Macartney, *Habsburg Empire,* p. 340; Dániel Irányi and C. L. Chassin, *Histoire politique de la révolution de Hongrie, 1847–1849,* I, 184–85; István Sinkovics, "Kossuth az önálló pénzügyek megteremtője," in Tóth, *Emlékkönyv,* I, 106–10; Ferenc Pulszky, *Életem és korom,* I, 353; and *KLÖM,* XII, 20 and passim.

33. The government's April 16 decision with regard to the *General-Commandos* is in *KLÖM,* XII, 37.

34. On measures taken against Jelačić early in May, see *KLÖM,* XII, 114–15, 122. Royal and palatinal orders are in Thim, *A szerb fölkelés* II, 181, 182; and in Pap, *Okmánytár,* I, 76–79, 89–93.

35. The events of May 10 and the following *journées* are described in Urbán, "Zehn Tage."

36. Minutes and reports of the commission investigating the Lederer incident are in Pap, *Okmánytár*, I, 93–107.

37. On the May 21 decision of the Council of Ministers on the oath to be taken by soldiers in Hungary, see *KLÖM*, XII, 161. Batthyány's appeal to the Székelys and other documents on this affair are in Pap, *Okmánytár*, I, 140–41. The government's May 17 appeal to regular soldiers, exhorting them to join the 10,000-man national army, is in Pap, *Okmánytár*, I, 135–37.

38. Urbán, "Zehn Tage," pp. 120–24.

39. The drafts of the royal proclamation regarding Jelačić's dismissal were written in Kossuth's own hand. See *KLÖM*, XII, 165–71, 247–55. Some of the same documents are also in Pap, *Okmánytár*, I, 159–67, 186–93, and in Thim, *A szerb fölkelés*, II, 380–82.

40. The Austrian cabinet's Transylvania debate is amply analyzed in Károlyi, *1848*, pp. 155–200. The documents are in *ibid.*, pp. 312–21, 327–52. The particular quotation is on p. 335.

41. On the affair of the 100,000 gulden, see Kossuth's correspondence with the Hungarian Foreign Ministry in Innsbruck (July 7 and July 29, 1848), in *KLÖM*, XII, 398–99, 636–38.

42. On the Hungaro-Serbian armed conflict in the summer of 1848 see Thim, *A szerb fölkelés*, I, 125–230, as well as documents in vol. II; Rikhárd Gelich, *Magyarország függetlenségi harcza 1848-49-ben*, I, 60–174 and passim (also with many documents); Kiszling, *Revolution*, I, 167–71 and passim; and W. Rüstow, *Geschichte des ungarischen Insurrectionskrieges in den Jahren 1848 and 1849*, I, 79–87. On Bechtold see Sándor Pethő, *A szabadságharc eszméi*, pp. 67–68; *KLÖM*, XII, 351 and passim; and Thim, *A szerb fölkelés*, II, 493, 531, 549, 579–80, and passim.

43. The German and Romanian inhabitants of Fehértemplom to the emperor (June 11, 1848), in Thim, II, 390–92.

44. Blomberg to Latour, quoted by Thim, I, 167.

45. On the fate of Fehértemplom see Thim, I, 121 and passim. Report on the August 19–20 massacres are in Thim, II, 638–45, 658.

46. Mészáros's proclamation (Budapest, June 6, 1848), in Gelich, *Magyarország függetlenségi harcza*, I, 42. On the illegally returning hussars and on legal troop exchanges see Gelich, I, especially pp. 141–46, and *KLÖM*, XII, 243, 259–60, 453–55, 581–82, 721–22 and passim. The Vienna Kriegsarchiv contains many interesting documents on this unique exchange of troops: Austrian State Archives, 1848 Krieg in Ungarn, Akten der Insurgenten Armee, III–XIII. Fasc. 181 and passim.

47. See *KLÖM*, XII, 706; Árpád Károlyi, *Németújvári gróf Batthyány Lajos első magyar miniszterelnök főbenjáró pöre*, I, 162–63; and Viktor Szokoly, *Mészáros Lázár emlékiratai*, I, 105.

48. On the June elections, Andor Csizmadia, *A magyar választási rendszer 1848–1849-ben*, pp. 57–329; and János Beér, *Az 1848/49. évi népképviseleti országgyűlés*, pp. 12–29.

49. The July 5 Address from the Throne is printed in Beér, pp. 139–40. The debates and resolutions of the Buda-Pest Council of Ministers with regard to the Address are in *KLÖM*, XII, 328–84.

50. Kossuth's July 11 address in the House of Representatives was printed in *KLÖM*, XII, 424–38; Dénes Pap, ed., *A magyar nemzetgyűlés Pesten 1848-ban*, I, 66–88; and, in English, William Henry Stiles, *Austria in 1848–49*, II, 384–94. The quotations are; in Stiles, II, 384–85, 394. For the background and circumstances of Kossuth's speech, see *KLÖM*, XII, 413–16 and 417–18; also Beér, *Az 1848/49*, pp. 150–52. Kossuth's motions became Law XXXIII, "On the Hungarian Army," and Law XXXIV, "On the Printing of New Banknotes." Reprinted in Beér, *Az 1848/49*, pp. 561–76.

51. Kossuth in the House of Representatives, July 20, 1848. Printed in Pap, *Nemzetgyűlés*, I, 135–55, 172–74, 175–76, 178–79; and in *KLÖM*, XII, 588–99—the quotation is on p. 594.

52. Kossuth in the House of Representatives (July 21, 1848), in Pap, *Nemzetgyűlés*, I, 179–81 and passim; and in *KLÖM*, XII, 602–13. The specific reference to the dividing of Northern Italy is in *KLÖM*, XII, 604. For Austrian liberal views on the possibility of such a division, see Károlyi, *Batthyány*, I, 361–62.

53. The debates in the Lower House and in the Council of Ministers on aid to Austria against the Italians are in *KLÖM*, XII, 382–84, 588–99, and 602–13. See also Pap, *Nemzetgyűlés*, I, 135–55 and passim; *KLI*, XI, 200–203, 227–38; and Beér, *Az 1848/49*, pp. 164–66 passim. The issue is best analyzed by György Spira, "Kossuth Lajos forradalmi szövetsége a radikális baloldallal és a népi tömegekkel," in Tóth, *Emlékkönyv*, II, 184–90; Károlyi, *Batthyány*, I, 353–65; and György Spira, *A Hungarian Count*, pp. 244–52. The Széchenyi diary entries of July 18 and July 20 are quoted on pp. 247 and 248.

54. The palatine's confidential instruction to Pázmándy and Szalay are printed in Károlyi, *Batthyány*, II, 1–2.

55. The Széchenyi diary entries of July 18 and 20 are quoted in György Spira, *A Hungarian Count*, pp. 247, 248.

56. See the learned essays by the finance specialist Tibor Nagy: "Költségvetés és költségvetési jog 1848/49-ben"; "Az első magyar pénzügyminiszteri expozé"; and "Kossuth költségvetése." On the finances of Hungary in 1848–49 see Miksa Faragó, *A Kossuth-bankók kora* (many documents). Kossuth's budget reports and proposal of July 18 and August 1 are fully printed in *KLÖM*, XII, 466–581.

57. Documents relative to the issuing of the 2-gulden banknotes are in *KLÖM*, XII, 677–79, 697, 700, 702–3, 710–12, 726–27, 784–85. For the ban on silver export, see *ibid.*, pp. 764–66 and 789–92; Faragó, *A Kossuth-bankók kora*, pp. 120–52.

58. Cited by György Spira, *A magyar forradalom 1848–49-ben*, p. 197.

59. See Beér, *Az 1848/49*, p. 177; and Hajnal, *A Batthyány-kormány külpolitikája*, pp. 59–64.

60. Quoted in Beér, *Az 1848/49*, p. 178. The August 3 resolution of the House with regard to Germany is analyzed *ibid.*, pp. 177–78. See the documents in *KLÖM*, XII, 670–75, and in Pap, *Nemzetgyűlés*, I, 306–13; also Hajnal, *A Batthyány-kormány külpolitikája*, p. 65.

61. Széchenyi diaries (August 7, 1848), quoted in Spira, *A Hungarian Count*, pp. 260–61.

62. For the debates of the House on the employment of recruits, see Beér, *Az 1848/49*, pp. 189–95; *KLÖM*, XII, 602–13, 654–66, 755–61, 775–76; Pap, *Nemzetgyűlés*, I, 179–219, 428–36, and II, 9–13, 20–25, 31–32; also Károlyi, *Batthyány*, I, 260–61, and Gelich, *Magyarország függetlenségi harcza*, I, 101–40, 151–60.

4 / The Month of Defiance: September 1848

1. Jelačić to Rajačić (Zagreb, August 28, 1848), in József Thim, *A magyarországi 1848–49-iki szerb fölkelés története*, II, 651–52 (in Serbo-Croatian with translation into Hungarian); also Deák, *1848*, p. 198.

2. The best succinct summary of Jelačić's doings in the summer and early fall is in Gunther Erich Rothenberg, *The Military Border in Croatia 1740–1881*, pp. 147–54.

3. Ferdinand to Jelačić (Schönbrunn, September 4, 1848). The Rescript is printed in Deák, *1848*, p. 211; Pap, *Okmánytár Magyarország függetlenségi harczának történetéhez 1848–1849*, I, 1, and elsewhere. The English translation is by Stiles, *Austria in 1848–49*, II, 397–98.

4. Divided opinions in the Austrian cabinet on Jelačić's planned invasion of Hungary are shown in, among others, the record of the August 26 meeting of the Austrian cabinet council. Árpád Károlyi, *Németújvári gróf Batthyány Lajos első magyar miniszterelnök főbenjáró*

364 / 4. The Month of Defiance

pöre, II, 3–4. Archduke Francis Charles was definitely against the Croatian military campaign at that time.

5. The reports of the governor of Fiume on the city's occupation by the Croats are in Deák, *1848*, pp. 199–200, and Pap, *Okmánytár*, I, 392–94, 398–99.

6. Jelačić at Szemes (on the shores of Lake Balaton), September 21, 1848. Quoted in Hermann Freiherr Dahlen von Orlaburg, "Ein kleines Tagebuch aus grosser Zeit." Dahlen was an officer of Jelačić; his diary was printed in Ferdinand Hauptmann, *Jelačić's Kriegszug nach Ungarn 1848*, II, 1–103. The quotation is on pp. 18–19.

7. Ferdinand's Rescript to the Palatine (Schönbrunn, August 31, 1848) and the Austrian government's attached memorandum are in Pap, *Okmánytár*, I, 401–8. See also Anton Springer, *Geschichte Österreichs seit dem Wiener Frieden 1809*, II, 495–502.

8. The August 27 decision of the Hungarian cabinet on Croatia is printed in *KLÖM*, XII, 805–6; Károlyi, *Batthyány*, II, 626–29; and János Beér, ed., *Az 1848/49*, pp. 681–83. A succinct analysis of the bill is in Beér, pp. 60–61.

9. On the proposals that Batthyány and Deák took to Vienna, see Kossuth in *Kossuth Hírlapja* (September 19, 1848), *KLÖM*, XII, 976–85. Batthyány's letter to the palatine (Vienna, September 3, 1848) and Deák's letter to the Hungarian cabinet (Vienna, September 5, 1848) are in Károlyi, *Batthyány*, II, 5, 9–11.

10. Kossuth's September 4 address is in *KLÖM*, XII, 881–85; *KLI*, XI, 310–15; and Dénes Pap, ed., *A magyar nemzetgyűlés Pesten 1848-ban*, II, 155–61. See also Anton Springer, *Geschichte*, II, 502–3.

11. The affair of the 5-gulden banknotes and the 61 million gulden loan is discussed in Miksa Faragó, *A Kossuth-bankók kora*, pp. 139–48 and 162–63; also in *KLÖM*, XII, 783–85, 787–88, 892–93; and Pap, *Okmánytár*, II, 1–3.

12. The Address to the Throne delivered by the president of the House of Representatives, Dénes Pázmándy, Jr., and the king's brief reply are reprinted in Ferenc Pulszky, *Életem és korom*, I, 382–84; and in Beér, *Az 1848–49*, pp. 216–18. Excerpts in English appear in Stiles, *Austria in 1848–49*, II, 394. See also Anton Springer, *Geschichte*, II, 503–4.

13. Pulszky, *Életem és korom*, I, 381, 384.

14. See *KLI*, II, 265–69; also in *KLÖM*, XII, 927n–930n.

15. Major Zichy to Unknown (Buda, August 31, 1848), in Eszter Waldapfel, ed., *A forradalom és szabadságharc levelestára*, I, 408.

16. On Széchenyi's mental collapse see György Spira, *A Hungarian Count*, 295–301, 305–11.

17. The complex events of September 11 have been amply described by historians. Kossuth's speeches and the parliamentary proceedings of the day are in *KLÖM*, XII, 905–19; *KLI*, XI, 315–30; Pap, *A magyar nemzetgyűlés*, II, 167–77, 182; and Beér, *Az 1848/49*, pp. 216–20.

18. Jelačić's proclamation to the Hungarians is in Pap, *Okmánytár*, II, 3–4, and Rikhárd Gelich, *Magyarország függetlenségi harcza 1848–49-ben*, I, 174–75.

19. On the Border Guards and on Jelačić's September campaign in Hungary, see Rothenberg, *The Military Border*, pp. 143–55; and Hauptmann, *Jelačić's Kriegszug*, vols. I, II.

20. Priscilla Robertson, *Revolutions of 1848. A Social History*, p. 249.

21. Captured letters on Croatian excesses were printed in Gelich, *Magyarország függetlenségi harcza*, I, 205–6, and Pap, *Okmánytár*, II, 15–16, 91–93, 97–98. See also Rothenberg, *The Military Border*, p. 153.

22. Gelich, *Magyarország függetlenségi harcza*, I, 178.

23. *Ibid.*, I, 179.

24. On Teleki's neutrality scheme and on Hungarian measures against Teleki, see the documents in Erzsébet Andics, *A nagybirtokos arisztokrácia ellenforradalmi szerepe 1848–49-ben*,

II, 146–49. On the Wasa battalion, see the document in Gelich, *Magyarország függetlenségi harcza*, I, 181. With regard to the dilemma of the officers in general, see Rudolf Kiszling, "Das Nationalitätenproblem in Habsburgs Wehrmacht 1848–1918," pp. 83–84.

25. The text of the officers' manifesto is in Gelich, I, 183–84.

26. Kossuth in *Kossuth Hírlapja* (September 14, 1848), p. 295, *KLÖM*, XII, 940.

27. Kossuth's September 15 address regarding the election of the three itinerant commissioners is in *KLÖM*, XII, 956–62. Batthyány's objections were printed in the same place. See also *KLI*, XI, 350–58; Pap, *A magyar nemzetgyűlés*, II, 233–44; Beér, *Az 1848/49*, p. 233.

28. Details of the parliament's decision with regard to the tithe on vineyards and Kossuth's speech on the subject are in *KLÖM*, XII, 955–56. See also Pap, *A magyar nemzetgyűlés*, II, 222.

29. *KLÖM*, XII, 997–99, and Beér, *Az 1848/49*, p. 635.

30. Kossuth's speeches of September 15 and 22 and the parliament's decision with regard to the committee of six are in *KLÖM*, XII, 19–25. *Kossuth Lajos az Országos Honvédelmi Bizottmány élén*, 2 vols., part 1, which is vol. XIII of *Kossuth Lajos összes munkái* (hereafter *KLÖM*, XIII), pp. 19–25. See also *KLÖM*, XII, 961–62, 1006–7, and Beér, *Az 1848/49*, p. 246.

31. From letters by officers of the Croatian army. The letters were captured by the Hungarians. Also from a letter of Jelačić to Baron Franz Kulmer (Kiliti, September 23, 1848), in Pap, *Okmánytár*, II, 27–31, 34–36, 51–53, 66. See also Hauptmann, *Jelačić's Kriegszug*, II, 19–22.

32. Ferdinand to Archduke Stephen (Schönbrunn, September 18, 1848), in Deák, *1848*, pp. 219–220; in German in Károlyi, *Batthyány*, II, 24–25.

33. Archduke Stephen's letters to Batthyány (some in German, some in Hungarian) were printed in Károlyi, *Batthyány*, II, 31–55. See also Deák, *1848*, 228–29.

34. See the report of General Móga in *KLÖM*, XIII, 53–54; and in Gelich, *Magyarország függetlenségi harcza*, I, 228–30. On the role the new Hungarian national army played at Pákozd, see Aladár Urbán, "Die Organisierung des Heeres der ungarischen Revolution vom Jahre 1848," p. 181. On the battle of Pákozd, see Kiszling, *Die Revolution*, I, 226. Aladár Urbán, *A nemzetőrség és honvédség szervezése 1848 nyarán*, is indispensable for an understanding of the creation of the national army.

35. The text of the armistice is in Gelich, *Magyarország függetlenségi harcza*, I, 230–31. See also Móga to the Royal Hungarian Ministry (in German; Martonvásár, September 30, 1848), OHB, 1848:800.

36. Reports of Kossuth's recruiting drive and the text of his own accounts were reprinted in *KLÖM*, XIII, 28–38. See also István Barta, "Kossuth alföldi toborzó körútja 1848 őszén."

37. The King's manifestos of September 25 are in Gelich, I, 210–16; and (in English) in Stiles, *Austria in 1848–49*, II, 398. The manifesto on Lamberg's appointment is also in Pap, *Okmánytár*, II, 78–79.

38. Memorandum of the Austrian ministry to the emperor (Vienna, September 21, 1848), in Károlyi, *Batthyány*, II, 26–29. The background of Lamberg's appointment is well explained, ibid., I, 81–91. See also Pulszky, *Életem és korom*, I, 416–17.

39. Kossuth's speech in the Lower House on Lamberg's appointment is in *KLÖM*, XIII, 39–43. The resolutions of the House with regard to Lamberg are in Beér, *Az 1848/49*, 245–55, Pap, *Okmánytár*, II, 84–86; and Pap, *A magyar nemzetgyűlés*, II, 303–10.

40. Eyewitness accounts of Lamberg's assassination are printed in Gelich, *Magyarország függetlenségi harcza*, I, 223n–226n, and Waldapfel, *A forradalom*, II, 125–27, 128.

41. The resolution of the House and Kossuth's speeches on Lamberg's death are in *KLÖM*, XIII, 45–52. See also Beér, *Az 1848/49*, pp. 256–57.

42. The background of the October 3 manifesto is masterfully explained in Károlyi, *Batthyány*, I, 95–97, 410–25. The king's manifesto is in *KLÖM*, XIII, 114–15; Beér, *Az 1848/49*, pp.

366 / 5. From Defiance to Near-Disaster

267–68; and Gelich, *Magyarország függetlenségi harcza,* I, 293–96. The English translation is in Stiles, *Austria in 1848–49,* II, 399. Kossuth's speech on the subject is in *KLÖM,* XIII, 107–13, 117–19. The Assembly's resolution to reject the king's manifesto is in *KLÖM,* XIII, 113–17; Beér, *Az 1848/49,* pp. 269–72; Gelich, *Magyarország függetlenségi harcza,* I, 305–7; and Pap, *Okmánytár,* II, 117–21.

43. Spira, *A magyar forradalom,* p. 241.

44. Much of the information on the activities of the Hungarian radicals in August and September 1848 is culled from a fine article by László Deme, "The Society for Equality in the Hungarian Revolution of 1848." See also his *The Radical Left in the Hungarian Revolution of 1848,* 87–114.

45. Translation by Deme, "The Society for Equality," p. 78.

46. Petőfi to János Arany (Pest, August 16, 1848), in *Petőfi Sándor összes prózai művei és levelezése* p. 464. Also quoted in Deme, "The Society for Equality," p. 78.

47. On the extension of the National Defense Committee, see Pap, *A magyar nemzetgyűlés,* II, 344, and Beér, *Az 1848/49,* pp. 259, 262.

48. On the final establishment of the Committee as Hungary's de facto government, see *KLÖM,* XIII, 121–26, which includes Kossuth's speech on the subject and the resolution of the House. The resolution is also in Beér, *Az 1848/49,* p. 273.

5 / From Defiance to Near-Disaster: Kossuth Dictator, Part One (October–December 1848)

1. Ponsonby to Palmerston (Vienna, Oct. 2, 1848) in Great Britain, "Correspondence Relative to the Affairs of Hungary," p. 85. The other Ponsonby reports cited in the text are from the same volume.

2. On the Vienna October revolution see R. John Rath, *The Viennese Revolution of 1848,* pp. 317–65; Rudolf Kiszling et al., *Die Revolution im Kaisertum Österreich 1848–1849,* I, 236–96; William Henry Stiles, *Austria in 1848–49,* II, 90–147; Ferenc Pulszky, *Eletem és korom,* I, 421–40; and Anton Springer, *Geschichte Österreichs seit dem Wiener Frieden 1809,* II, 548–86. On the Tabor-bridge incident see Eötvös's eyewitness report to Ferenc Pulszky in Pulszky, *Életem és korom,* I, 425.

3. György Spira, *A magyar forradalom 1848–49-ben,* p. 309.

4. Quoted *ibid.*, p. 301. The National Committee's contradictory orders to General Móga and Kossuth's ambiguous speeches on the subject are in *KLÖM,* XIII, 149, 150–52, 178–80, 183–93, 213–16, 225–28, 289–90, and 296–300. See also István Barta, "A magyar szabadságharc vezetői és a bécsi októberi forradalom."

5. Friedrich Engels, "Germany: Revolution and Counter-revolution," in *The German Revolutions,* edited by Leonard Krieger, p. 197.

6. The emperor's manifesto announcing Windisch-Graetz's appointment and his letters to the Field Marshal are in Rikhárd Gelich, *Magyarország függetlenségi harcza 1848–49-ben,* I, 313–16, and in Dénes Pap, *Okmánytár Magyarország függetlenségi harczának történetéhez 1848–1849,* II, 151–52. The Hungarian parliament's reply to Ferdinand's manifesto is in *KLÖM,* XIII, 271–72, and in János Beér, *Az 1848/49,* pp. 289–90. On the field marshal see Paul Müller, *Feldmarschall Fürst Windischgrätz: Revolution und Gegenrevolution in Österreich.*

7. The battle at Schwechat has often been described. See, for instance, Gelich, *Magyarország függetlenségi harcza* I, 328–32; Pulszky, *Életem és korom,* I, 444–49; Kiszling, *Die Revolution,* I, 284–89; and Arthur Görgei, *Mein Leben und Wirken in Ungarn in den Jahren 1848 und 1849,* I, 74–86. Kossuth's own reports of the battle are in *KLÖM,* XIII, 312–14, 319. Note that Arthur Görgey, unlike his brothers, often spelled his name with an "i" at the end.

8. Domokos Kosáry, *A Görgey-kérdés és története,* is a sympathetic historiography of the Görgey problem. For a bibliography of the Görgey problem, see Zoltán I. Tóth, ed., *Magyar történeti bibliográfia, 1825–1867,* I, 94, 99–100.

9. Arthur Görgey's youth is described and amply documented in István Görgey, *Görgey Arthur ifjúsága és fejlődése a forradalomig.* István Görgey was Arthur's younger brother. On Görgey's youth, see also Lajos Steier, *Görgey és Kossuth: Ismeretlen adalékok az 1848–49-iki szabadságharc történetéhez,* pp. 41–56, and Kosáry, *A Görgey-kérdés,* pp. 14–18.

10. On the imperial-royal military schools before 1848, and on Habsburg military life in general, see Moriz von Angeli, *Wien nach 1848,* pp. 62–163. The title is misleading, for it deals less with Vienna than with the Habsburg army between 1840 and 1866.

11. Angeli, pp. 128–58.

12. Görgey's letters to the National Assembly are in Steier, *Görgey és Kossuth,* pp. 68–73.

13. Documents of Görgey's execution of Count Zichy are in (among others) Steier, *Görgey és Kossuth,* pp. 58–59; Arthur Görgei, *Mein Leben,* I, 7–29, with the author's voluminous apologies; Gelich, *Magyarország függetlenségi harcza,* I, 239–42; and Pap, *Okmánytár,* II, 106–9. See also István Görgey, *Görgey Arthur ifjúsága,* pp. 366–71.

14. Kossuth's reports from army headquarters to the National Defense Committee on Görgey's appointment are in *KLÖM,* XIII, 321–23. See also Arthur Görgei, *Mein Leben,* I, 87–94.

15. See Viktor Szokoly, *Mészáros Lázár emlékiratai,* I, 63, 139–40.

16. The Kossuth-Görgey controversy on army organization and strategy is explained in Gelich, *Magyarország függetlenségi harcza,* I, 431–41, with several documents. Görgey is the subject of innumerable studies. Sándor Pethő, *Görgey Artúr,* is useful. See also Gelich, I, 235n–237n; Kiszling, *Die Revolution,* I, 228–29; Steier, *Görgey és Kossuth;* Lajos Steier, *Beniczky Lajos,* pp. 164–89 and passim; István Görgey, *1848 és 1849-ből: Élmények és benyomások;* and George Handlery, "General Arthur Görgey and the Hungarian Revolution of 1848–49."

17. The best modern works on the Habsburg army are by the U.S. historian Gunter E. Rothenberg: *The Army of Francis Joseph; The Austrian Military Border in Croatia, 1522–1747;* (Urbana, Ill.: University of Illinois Press, 1969); and *The Military Border in Croatia 1740–1881.*

18. See Kiszling, "Das Nationalitätenproblem in Habsburgs Wehrmacht 1848–1918," pp. 82–84, and Nikolaus von Preradovich, *Die Führungsschichten in Österreich und Preussen, 1804–1918,* pp. 42–58.

19. Quoted in Rothenberg, *The Army of Francis Joseph,* p. 11.

20. On Richard Guyon see László Márkus, *Guyon Richárd,* a prejudiced marxist account. Brief biographies of Guyon and other Hungarian generals are in the indices to *KLÖM,* XIII–XIV and to György Spira. *A magyar forradalom.* Even more useful is Gelich, *Magyarország függetlenségi harcza,* I–III, with footnote biographies of several Austrian and Hungarian commanders. Guyon's biography is in II, 285n–286n. The *Magyar Életrajzi Lexikon* (2 vols.; Budapest: Akadémia, 1969) is valuable although occasionally inaccurate.

21. From Leiningen's diary (Cibakháza, March 1, 1849), in Henrik Marczali, ed., *Gróf Leiningen-Westerburg Károly honvédtábornok levelei és naplója, 1848–1949,* p. 107.

22. There is considerable literature on Hentzi's defense of Buda Castle, for instance, István Görgey, *1848 és 1849-ből,* II, 258–94; Arthur Görgei, *Mein Leben,* II, 68–96; and Gelich, *Magyarország függetlenségi harcza,* III, 278–95. Several of the above works quote Görgey's and Hentzi's correspondence. The documents are also in Pap, *Okmánytár,* II, 427–29.

23. Preradovich, *Die Führungsschichten,* pp. 43–44. Also Ferdinand D. Fenner von Fenneberg, *Österreich und seine Armee,* pp. 96–97; Johann Springer, *Statistik des österreichischen Kaiserstaates,* II, 254, 257. On Gáspár see (among others) Albert Bartha, *Az aradi 13 vértanú pörének és kivégzésének hiteles története,* pp. 90–92.

368 / 5. From Defiance to Near-Disaster

24. Szokoly, *Mészáros*, ɪ, 13–16 and passim.

25. Rothenberg, *The Army of Francis Joseph*, p. 10.

26. Detailed information on the structure and composition of the Habsburg army in 1848 is contained in Major Alphons Freiherr von Wrede, *Geschichte der k. und k. Wehrmacht: Die Regimenter, Corps, Branchen und Anstalten von 1618 zum Ende des XIX Jahrhunderts*, ɪ, 18–19 and passim; also Kiszling et al., *Die Revolution*, ɪ, 24–29 and passim. The Hungarian units are specially listed in Elek Fényes, *Magyarország leírása*, ɪ, 145–53. See also *Hof- und Staats-Handbuch des österreichischen Kaiserthumes*, (1845), pp. 308–27.

27. On the Hungarian fortresses in 1848–49, see Mihály Horváth, *Magyarország függetlenségi harczának története 1848 és 1849-ben*, ɪ, 595–610; Gelich, *Magyarország függetlenségi harcza*, ɪ, 360–78; József Thim, *A magyarországi 1848–49-iki szerb fölkelés története*, ɪɪ, 658–59, ɪɪɪ, 140–41, 157–58, 163; Pap, *Okmánytár*, ɪɪ, 153–54 and passim; General [György] Klapka, *Memoirs of the War of Independence in Hungary*, especially vol. ɪɪ, chs. 2–3, and appendix 7; and OHB, 1848:1611, 1748, 1818, 4322, 7133, 1849:5255 and passim. Also, Anton Peter Petri, "Die belagerten Festungen Arad und Temeschwar in den Jahren 1848/49," *Südostdeutsches Archiv*, ᴠɪɪɪ (1965), 113–39.

28. Rothenberg, *The Army of Francis Joseph*, p. 29. On the hussars see Wrede, *Geschichte der k. und k. Wehrmacht*, vol. ɪɪɪ, part 1, and József Balázs, József Borus, and Kálmán Nagy, "Kossuth, a forradalmi honvédelem szervezője," in Tóth, *Emlékkönyv Kossuth Lajos születésének 150. évfordulójára*, ɪ, 354–55 and passim. A list of the imperial-royal troops fighting on the Hungarian side can also be found in Klapka, *Memoirs*, ɪɪ, 163–76.

29. On the organization of the national army, see especially Balázs et al., "Kossuth," in Tóth, *Emlékkönyv*, ɪ, 287–408.

30. On the confusion caused by identical trumpet signals in both camps see Colonel Guyon's report to the National Committee (Ógyala, December 24, 1848), OHB, 1848:6545, with Kossuth's annotations on the margin. On Windisch-Graetz's white ribbon order see "Anonymous Report" from Buda-Pest to Minister of the Interior Szemere and from him to Kossuth (Tokaj, January 22, 1849) OHB, 1849:920.

31. Aladár Urbán, "Die Organisierung des Heeres der ungarischen Revolution vom Jahre 1848," p. 115. See also part 2 of the same article and, by the same author, "Die Bewaffnung der ungarischen Nationalgarde im Sommer 1848," "Honvédtoborzás Pest-Budán 1848-ban," and idem, *A nemzetőrség és honvédség szervezése*, indices.

32. Urbán, "Die Organisierung des Heeres," pp. 168–69.

33. Balázs et al., "Kossuth," in Tóth, *Emlékkönyv*, ɪ, 352–56.

34. Kossuth to Görgey (Pest, November 27, 1848), *KLÖM*, xɪɪɪ, 569.

35. Rothenberg, *The Army of Francis Joseph*, p. 16.

36. Csanád county to the National Committee (Makó, December 19, 1848), OHB, 1848:6509; and Mármaros county to the National Committee (Sziget, December 16, 1848), OHB, 1848:6541.

37. Colonel (later General) Baron István Majthény to the Prime Minister (Komárom, October 3, 1848), OHB, 1848:2109.

38. The contract between Stuwer and Pulszky was printed in Friedrich Walter, ed., *Magyarische Rebellenbriefe 1848*, pp. 59–60. The even-handed recruiting policy is described in Pulszky, *Életem és korom*, ɪ, 414.

39. Balázs et al., "Kossuth," in Tóth, *Emlékkönyv*, ɪ, 366, who culled their statistical data mainly from Fényes, *Magyarország statistikája*, ɪ, 83–85. All modern studies use Fényes for statistical data on 1848. Elek Fényes, an excellent statistician, was an official in the Hungarian revolutionary administration. On production figures see also C. A. Macartney, *The Habsburg Empire 1790–1918*, pp. 266–67.

40. Gelich, *Magyarország függetlenségi harcza,* I, 276.

41. Jenő Wagner to Kossuth (Pest, December 30, 1848), OHB, 1848:7020; Kossuth to Colonel (later General) György Lahner (Pest, December 20, 1848), *KLÖM,* XIII, 824.

42. Mészáros to the National Defense Committee (Buda-Pest, Oct. 24, 1848), OHB, 1848:1641; Mészáros to the National Defense Committee (Buda-Pest, Nov. 3, 1848), OHB, 1848:2515.

43. Balázs et al., "Kossuth," in Tóth, *Emlékkönyv,* I, 378.

44. Gelich, *Magyarország függetlenségi harcza,* I, 268–75.

45. Ministry of War to the National Defense Committee (Buda-Pest, October 23, 1848), OHB, 1848:1538.

46. Tabulation submitted to the National Defense Committee by Károly Kikó, director of the Csáktornya military hospital (November 2, 1848), OHB, 1848:3246.

47. Draft of an order by the Ministry of War, submitted for approval to the National Defense Committee (November 16, 1848), OHB, 1848:3318.

48. Adolph Schwarzenberg, *Prince Felix zu Schwarzenberg,* especially pp. 215–19; Friedrich Walter, ed., *Die österreichische Zentralverwaltung,* part 3, *Von der Märzrevolution 1848 bis zur Dezemberverfassung,* I, 258–66; and Macartney, *Habsburg Empire,* pp. 405–6. But see also Joseph Redlich, *Emperor Francis Joseph of Austria,* pp. 30–39; Anton Springer, *Geschichte,* II, 592–93; and Heinrich Friedjung, *Österreich von 1848 bis 1860,* I, 97–99.

49. Macartney, *Habsburg Empire,* p. 405.

50. See, for instance, Gyula Szekfű in Bálint Hóman and Gyula Szekfű, *Magyar történet,* V, 439–41 and 452–53; and Árpád Károlyi, *Németújvári gróf Batthyány Lajos első magyar miniszterelnök főbenjáró pöre,* I, 12–13 and passim.

51. Schwarzenberg, *Prince Felix zu Schwarzenberg,* pp. 210–15.

52. For a detailed description of the events of December 2, as well as their background and immediate consequences, see Kiszling, *Die Revolution,* I, 311–21; and Anton Springer, *Geschichte,* II, 595–97; also Friedjung, *Österreich,* I, 92–118. The imperial manifestos with regard to the *Thronwechsel* (change of rulers) were printed in every language current in the Monarchy and sent out in innumerable copies. They were reprinted in every major documentary collection, for instance, in Pap, *Okmánytár,* II, 238–42, and Gelich, *Magyarország függetlenségi harcza,* II, 14–17.

53. Kossuth's attempt to form a regular ministry is told in Győző Ember, "Kossuth a Honvédelmi Bizottmány élén," in Tóth, *Emlékkönyv,* I, 223–27. Kossuth's correspondence with regard to the ministry (November 19–27, 1848) is printed in Deák, *1848,* pp. 269–79, and in *KLÖM,* XIII, 503–11. On the Peace Party see (for instance) Lajos Kovács, *A békepárt a magyar forradalomban.* Kovács was a militant member of the party.

54. Kossuth to Szemere (Pest, November 20, 1848), in Deák, *1848,* p. 272, and in *KLÖM,* XIII, 506.

55. The printed warrant for the apprehension of the four revolutionaries is in OHB, 1848:6852 (no date, no place).

56. The events of December 6 are described in Horváth, *Magyarország,* II, 170–175. Horváth, a participant at the parliamentary session, was wrong in asserting that the attack of the Peace Party was led by the blind Baron Miklós Wesselényi. After September 1848 Wesselényi was no longer in Hungary.

57. The solemn decision of the National Assembly with regard to Ferdinand's resignation was reprinted in Beér, *Az 1848/49,* pp. 325–27 and in Pap, *Okmánytár,* II, 261–63. Kossuth's crucial newspaper article on the subject, in the December 5 issue of *Kossuth Hírlapja,* was reprinted in Pap, *Okmánytár,* II, 258–60. and in *KLÖM,* XIII, 652–54. See also Görgey's and

370 / 5. From Defiance to Near-Disaster

Government Commissioner László Csányi's proclamation of December 10 on the same subject. The proclamation was issued in the name of the "Royal Hungarian Army of the Upper Danube": Pap, *Okmánytár*, II, 264–65 and Gelich, *Magyarország függetlenségi harcza*, II, 20–22.

58. Kossuth's correspondence with Stiles is in Deák, *1848*, pp. 280–85 passim. Stiles's own account is in his *Austria in 1848–1849*, II, 155–57. The documents on the subject, including the reports of Stiles to Secretary of State James Buchanan and Buchanan's reply of February 2, 1849, are *ibid.*, II, 402–6.

59. On Schlick's December campaign in northern Hungary see Horváth, *Magyarország*, II, 182–85; Kiszling, *Die Revolution*, II, 14; and Beér, *Az 1848/49*, pp. 332–33.

60. The proclamation of the Hungarian National Committee with regard to Simunich, dated October 14, was reprinted in Pap, *Okmánytár*, II, 143–44. The text of the proclamation had been suggested by Kossuth and was drafted by László Madarász (see *KLÖM*, XIII, 194–95).

61. Hungarian and Romanian marxist historians dislike General Puchner. The former see him as a supporter of the Romanian bourgeoisie and the latter as an instrument of the Transylvanian Magyar aristocracy (see Zsolt Trócsányi, *Az erdélyi parasztág története*, pp. 409–10, 420–31; and Cornelia Bodea, *The Romanians' Struggle for Unification*, pp. 192–220). On the role of the Transylvanian Saxons in 1848–1849 see Carl Göllner, *Die Siebenbürger Sachsen in den Revolutionsjahren 1848–49*, but for a Hungarian marxist view see Zoltán Sárközi, *Az erdélyi szászok 1848–1849-ben*.

62. The report of Count Imre Mikó, president of the Székely assembly, to the Hungarian government is in Pap, *Okmánytár*, II, 149–51. The minutes of the Agyagfalva meeting are on pp. 155–62. See also Elek Jakab, *Szabadságharczunk történetéhez*, pp. 387–401, and Deák, *1848*, pp. 241–42, 264–65, and passim.

63. The text of Puchner's October 18 proclamation is in Pap, *Okmánytár*, II, 165–68. There are many interesting documents on Austrian military preparation in Transylvania in Deák, *1848*, pp. 248–59 and passim.

64. The text of the Romanian Pacification Committee's October 19 proclamation is in Pap, *Okmánytár*, II, 169–71.

65. Trócsányi, *Az erdélyi parasztság*, p. 401.

66. On the two hostile armies in Transylvania see Gelich, *Magyarország függetlenségi harcza*, I, 380–99. There was at that time an interesting exchange of public letters between officers of the Romanian and Székely Border Guard regiments (Marosvásárhely, October 21, 1848, and Nagyszeben, October 28, 1848), Gelich, I, 388–92.

67. Colonel Sándor Nádossy to the National Defense Committee (Pest, December 16, 1848), *KLÖM*, XIII, 709.

68. On Windisch-Graetz's and Görgey's armies in December 1848 see Kiszling, *Die Revolution*, II, 5–11, 327; Gelich, I, 473–78; and *KLÖM*, XIII, 708–9.

69. Too much was written on the Kossuth-Görgey controversy in November–December 1848. The number of printed documents is legion. For some examples see Arthur Görgei, *Mein Leben*, I, 95–144; Steier, *Görgey és Kossuth*, pp. 199–296; István Görgey, *1848 és 1849-ből*, I, 22–120; and Ember, "Kossuth," in Tóth, *Emlékkönyv*, I, 253–61. Kossuth's correspondence with Görgey is in *KLÖM*, XIII, 778–80 and passim.

70. There is considerable literature on, and many eyewitness accounts of, the parliamentary session of December 31. See for instance Gelich, *Magyarország függetlenségi harcza*, II, 152–55; Ember, "Kossuth," in Tóth, *Emlékkönyv*, I, 261–62; Beér, *Az 1848/49*, pp. 533–35; Horváth, *Magyarország*, II, 207–10; János Pálffy, *Magyarországi és erdélyi urak: Pálffy János emlékiratai*, pp. 260–62; Gábor Kazinczy, "Szerepem a forradalomban: Kazinczy védirata a haditörvényszék előtt," pp. 92–93; Kovács, *A békepárt a magyar forradalomban*, pp. 41–42; and *KLOM*, XIII, 933–36, 940–53, with Kossuth's numerous speeches and letters on the subject, but also with speeches made by Batthyány and other members of the Peace Party, as well as with a fiery speech made by László Madarász.

71. Unsigned letter (Pest, December 9, 1848), Deák, *1848,* pp. 285–86, and Károlyi, *Batthyány,* ii, 97.

72. The personal reminiscences of Ferenc Deák on the adventures of the peace delegation, and his written report to the National Assembly in Debrecen, were printed in Manó Kónyi, ed., *Deák Ferencz beszédei, 1842–1861,* ii, 367–80. Windisch-Graetz's report to Schwarzenberg on the same subject is in Deák, *1848,* pp. 289–90, and in Joseph A. Helfert, *Geschichte Oesterreichs vom Ausgange des Wiener October-Aufstandes 1848;* appendix, iv, 47–48. Kossuth's speech of January 14, 1849, with regard to the report of the peace delegation is in *KLÖM,* xiv, 109–18.

73. Pálffy, *Magyarországi és erdélyi urak,* p. 262

6 / Recovery and Ecstasy: Kossuth Dictator, Part Two (January–April 1849)

1. Conditions in Debrecen in 1848–49 were masterfully described by István Balogh, "A város és népe," in István Szabó, ed., *A szabadságharc fővárosa Debrecen, 1849 január-május,* pp. 9–57.

2. The arrival of the Buda-Pest evacuees in Debrecen is told in György Módy, "A menekültek," *ibid.,* pp. 61–100.

3. See, for instance, Sándor Novák to the National Defense Committee (Tiszaújlak, January 2, 1849), OHB, 1849:270.

4. Szemere to the National Defense Committee (Debrecen, January 12, 1849), OHB, 1849:395.

5. Major Wysocki to the "Président du Comité du Salut Public" (no place, no date; the letter was received in Debrecen on January 12, 1849), OHB, 1849:265.

6. On the National Assembly in Debrecen, see András Borossy, "Az Országgyűlés," in István Szabó, *A szabadságharc,* pp. 329–84; Mihály Horváth, *Magyarország függetlenségi harczának története 1848 és 1849-ben,* ii, 223–351, and János Beér, *Az 1848/49,* pp. 80–92, 349–440, and passim. The minutes of the meetings of the Debrecen Assembly were reprinted in Dénes Pap, ed., *A parlament Debrecenben, 1849.*

7. Beér, *Az 1848/49,* p. 83.

8. The wholesale confiscation of Transylvanian Saxon property was proposed in the House of Representatives on January 26, 1849; the Romanian deputy Aloisiu Vlad was shouted down on March 8. See Pap, *A parlament Debrecenben,* i, 52–53, 178–79.

9. Lenke Bleyer, *Gróf Zichy-féle gyémántpör,* finds László Madarász guilty. The memoirs of various participants are divided on the question, depending on the ideology of the writer. See also Beér, *Az 1848/49,* pp. 83–86.

10. Bezerédy in the House of Representatives on May 24, 1849, in Pap, *A parlament Debrecenben,* ii, 216–18 and passim. See also Ervin Szabó, *Társadalmi és pártharck a 48–49-es magyar forradalomban,* pp. 333–49.

11. A typical case was that of the Ministry of Cults and Education, where the highest ranking employee, next to the State Secretary, was that single junior clerk who (unlike his fourteen colleagues in the same rank) had made it to Debrecen. See State Secretary Károly Szász to the National Defense Committee (Debrecen, January 23, 1849), OHB, 1849:919.

12. István Szabó, "A küzdelem szervezése," in *A szabadságharc,* p. 137.

13. R. R. Palmer, *Twelve Who Ruled. The Year of the Terror in the French Revolution* (New York: Atheneum, 1968), pp. 79, 238.

14. There are several different lists of government commissioners extant, all incomplete. See, for instance, Rikhárd Gelich, *Magyarország függetlenségi harcza 1848–49-ben,* ii, 375, and the

372 / 6. Recovery and Ecstasy

Report of the Audit Commission of the House of Representatives to the National Defense Committee (Debrecen, March 22, 1849), OHB, 1849:3683.

15. The best summary description of the functions and problems of the government commissioners is by István Szabó in *A szabadságharc*, pp. 125–31.

16. József Révai, "Marx és a magyar forradalom," in *Marxizmus és magyarság*, pp. 88–89.

17. See for instance the report of Pál Sallay, government commissioner in Austrian-occupied Fejér County, to the National Defense Committee (Dunapentele, March 16, 1849), OHB, 1849:3713.

18. See for instance the report of the government commissioner Ferenc Repeczky to the National Defense Committee on the results of his investigation in Hont County (Ipolyság, January 5, 1849), OHB, 1849:487. On the problem of Austrian and Hungarian military debts to one and the same local authority, see the "Extracts from the Minutes of the City of Jászkisér" (February 6, 1849), OHB, 1849:37. For other examples of the dubious behavior of the counties toward the Hungarian revolution see András Fischer, captain in the National Guards, to the National Defense Committee (Boksa, December 5, 1848), OHB, 1848:5704, and Sándor Zarka, first deputy lord-lieutenant of Vas County to the National Defense Committee (Szombathely, December 26, 1848), OHB, 1848:5799. Once a county had surrendered to the Austrians, every official had to affirm his submission with his signature. See, for instance, the submission of Vas County officials (Szombathely, January 18, 1849), in Erzsébet Andics, *A nagybirtokos arisztokrácia ellenforradalmi szerepe 1848–49-ben*, II, 351–52.

19. Károly Ács, sheriff in Pest County, to Kossuth (Kalocsa, February 13, 1849), OHB, 1849:2257.

20. See for instance the report of Albert Boronkay, government commissioner in Zemplén County, to the National Defense Committee (Sátoraljaújhely, April 2, 1849), OHB, 1849:6083.

21. See the report of Colonel [Ignác] Cserey from Nagyvárad to Kossuth (received in Debrecen on January 12, 1849), OHB, 1849:301. See also the letter of the Pacification Committee of Túróc County to the National Defense Committee, OHB, 1849:115, and the statistical account that Fejér County sent to the National Defense Committee (Székesfehérvár, December 29, 1849), OHB, 1849:439. Finally, see the report of János Muhna, government commissioner to Jász County, addressed to the National Defense Committee (Jászberény, January 12, 1849), OHB, 1849:553.

22. Kossuth's proclamation of December 16, 1848, and the relevant decree of the National Defense Committee of December 18, were reprinted in Dénes Pap, ed., *Okmánytár Magyarország függetlenségi harczának történetéhez 1848–1849*, II, 271–76, and in *KLÖM*, XIII, 767–70, 794–98. On the free corps in general, see István Szabó, *A szabadságharc*, pp. 140–44.

23. Mészáros to the National Defense Committee (Debrecen, February 25, 1849), OHB, 1849:2716; Kossuth to Görgey (Pest, December 23, 1848), *KLÖM*, XIII, 858–60, and in Lajos Steier, *Görgey és Kossuth*, pp. 239–42; decree of the National Defense Committee (Debrecen, March 11, 1849), *KLÖM*, XIV, 638–39; letter of Mészáros to the National Defense Committee and the decree of the Committee (Debrecen, March 21, 1849), *KLÖM*, XIV, 689, Mészáros to the National Defense Committee (Debrecen, March 31, 1849), OHB, 1849:1507, and finally, Gelich, *Magyarország függetlenségi harcza*, III, 181.

24. Colonel György Lahner to Kossuth (Nagyvárad, January 15, 1849), OHB, 1849:618.

25. Kossuth's correspondence with regard to the workers' strike in Nagyvárad is quite voluminous. See especially Director Tivadar Rombauer to Kossuth (Nagyvárad, February 10, 1849), OHB, 1849:1898, and the letter of a number of Nagyvárad blacksmiths to the National Defense Committee (Nagyvárad, April 16, 1849), OHB, 1849:5751, also *KLÖM*, XIV, 421, 431, and passim.

26. Colonel Lahner to Kossuth (Nagyvárad, February 12, 1849), OHB, 1849:2079. Kossuth's letter of February 9 to Lahner is in István Barta, ed., *Kossuth Lajos az Országos Honvédelmi Bizottmány élén*, Part II, which is vol. XIV of *Kossuth Lajos összes munkái* (hereafter *KLÖM*, XIV), pp. 385–86.

27. Cited by István Szabó in *A szabadságharc*, p. 189. This work best summarizes the activities of the National Defense Committee in Debrecen.

28. Ponsonby to Palmerston (Vienna, January 21, 1849). Great Britain, "Correspondence Relative to the Affairs of Hungary," pp. 130–31.

29. On the Hungarian council of war of January 2, 1849, see, among others, Rudolf Kiszling, *Die Revolution im Kaisertum Österreich, 1848–1849*, II, 22–23; István Szabó in *A szabadságharc*, pp. 109–10; Gelich, *Magyarország függetlenségi harcza*, II, 158–62; Arthur Görgei, *Mein Leben und Wirken in Ungarn in den Jahren 1848 und 1849*, I, 140–41; István Görgey, *1848 és 1849-ből*, I, 102–4; and István Barta, "Az 1849. január 2-i haditanács és a főváros kiürítése."

30. On the desertion of the officers in December and January, see Görgey to Kossuth (Pressburg, December 16, 1848), OHB, 1848:6204, and *KLÖM*, XIII, 831. One reason for the officers' desertion from the Hungarian army was Windisch-Graetz's amnesty offer of November 12, 1848, which is in OHB, 1848:6403, and was printed in Pap, *Okmánytár*, II, 209–11.

31. Görgey's Vác Proclamation was reprinted in, among others, István Görgey, *1848 és 1849-ből*, I, 124–27; Mihály Horváth, *Magyarország*, II, 234–39; Gelich, *Magyarország függetlenségi harcza*, II, 170–75; Imre Deák, *1848*, pp. 290–92; Pap, *Okmánytár*, II, 301–3 (in German), and William Henry Stiles, *Austria in 1848 and 1849*, II, 406–8 (in English).

32. Kossuth to Görgey (Debrecen, January 10, 1849), *KLÖM*, XIV, 81-84. Also in Imre Deák, *1848*, pp. 295–98; Kossuth to Szemere (Debrecen, January 19, 1849), *KLÖM*, XIV, 163–165. Also in Eszter Waldapfel, *A forradalom és szabadságharc levelestára*, II, 431.

33. W. Rüstow, *Geschichte des ungarischen Insurrectionkrieges in den Jahren 1848 und 1849*, I, 233.

34. Viktor Szokoly, *Mészáros Lázár emlékiratai*, II, 4, 10–12. See also, Horváth, *Magyarország*, II, 242.

35. W. Rüstow, *Geschichte des ungarischen Insurrectionskrieges*, I, 303–4.

36. Kossuth to Szemere (Debrecen, January 21, 1849), *KLÖM*, XIV, 179–81.

37. Friedrich Engels in the *Neue Rheinische Zeitung*, no. 301, May 19, 1849. Reprinted in Bernard Isaacs, ed., *The Revolution of 1848–49: Articles from the Neue Rheinische Zeitung by Karl Marx and Frederick Engels*, p. 260. On Görgey's winter campaign see also Rüstow, *Geschichte des ungarischen Insurrectionskrieges*, I, 198–215, 221–29.

38. On the circumstances of Dembiński's appointment see *KLÖM*, XIV, 252–54, 265, also Pap, *Okmánytár*, II, 341, and Gelich, *Magyarország függetlenségi harcza*, II, 330–32 and passim.

39. On Dembiński see Alphons F. Danzer, ed., *Dembinski in Ungarn: Nach den hinterlassenen Papieren des Generals*. This work contains many errors in translation and interpretation.

40. Görgey to the Army of the Upper Danube (Kassa, February 14, 1849), in István Görgey, *1848 és 1849-ből*, I, 223, and in German in Arthur Görgei, *Mein Leben*, I, 209. Also in Horváth, *Magyarország*, II, 579, and Kiszling, *Die Revolution*, II, 43.

41. The December 15 manifesto of Francis Joseph was reprinted (in German) in József Thim, *A magyarországi 1848–49-iki szerb fölkelés története*, III, 250–52. For a history of the Serbian Vojvodina in 1849 see vol. I of the same work.

42. Windisch-Graetz's views with regard to Hungary are clearly expounded in his numerous letters, which are in Andics, *Nagybirtokos arisztokrácia*, II, 249–50, 282–84, 294–96, 333–35, 374, 385–86, 406–8, 453–54, 464–65, and 500–501. Also in Rüstow, *Geschichte des ungarischen Insurrectionskrieges*, I, 146–50; Kiszling, *Die Revolution*, II, 69–75; and György Spira, *A magyar forradalom 1848–49-ben*, pp. 372–75.

43. Windisch-Graetz to Schwarzenberg (Buda, January 15, 1849), Andics, *Nagybirtokos arisztokrácia*, II, 333.

44. See the documents reprinted in Thim, *A szerb fölkelés története*, III, 256–57 and passim. See also Kiszling, *Die Revolution*, II, 72–73.

45. Count Emil Dessewffy to Schwarzenberg (Vienna, November 1848), Andics, *Nagybirtokos arisztokrácia*, II, 199–208. Other Dessewffy memoranda are ibid., II, 160–65, 172–78.

46. Count György Andrássy to Baron Alexander Hübner (Pressburg, January 18, 1849), Andics, *Nagybirtokos arisztokrácia*, II, 353–62.

47. Dénes Pázmándy and Kálmán Ghyczy to Windisch-Graetz (Pest, January 29, 1849), Andics, *Nagybirtokos arisztokrácia*, II, 412–17. Also in Friedrich Valjavec, "Ungarn und die Frage des österreichischen Gesamtstaates zu Beginn des Jahres 1849."

48. On the battle of Kápolna, see, among others, Rüstow, *Geschichte des ungarischen Insurrectionskrieges*, I, 253–92; Kiszling, *Die Revolution*, II, 50–54; Arthur Görgei, *Mein Leben*, II, 227–46; and Danzer, *Dembinski in Ungarn*, I, 165–204.

49. Windisch-Graetz's post-Kápolna report was reprinted in Gelich, *Magyarország függetlenségi harcza*, II, 440.

50. C. A. Macartney, *The Habsburg Empire 1790–1918*, p. 417n.

51. The March constitution was reprinted in Gelich, II, 108–25. For characteristic Hungarian views of the constitution see Mihály Horváth, *Magyarország*, II, 399–405, and Spira, *A magyar forradalom*, pp. 449–50. The best appraisal is in Macartney, *Habsburg Empire*, pp. 423–25.

52. There are many, often contradictory, accounts of the Tiszafüred officers' rebellion, and of Kossuth's, Görgey's, Dembiński's, and Klapka's roles in the events. See for instance *KLÖM*, XIV, 590–92; Steier, *Beniczky*, pp. 110–23, 262–98; Danzer, *Dembinski in Ungarn*, I, 230–56; Arthur Görgei, *Mein Leben*, I, 271–78; István Görgey, *1848 és 1849-ből*, I, 295–314; and Gelich, *Magyarország függetlenségi harcza*, II, 451–75.

53. Mihály Horváth, *Magyarország*, II, 317. Kossuth's proclamation to the army on Vetter's appointment as commander-in-chief (Debrecen, March 8, 1849) was reprinted in *KLÖM*, XIV, 601–3 and in Pap, *Okmánytár*, II, 356–59. Kossuth's report to the House of Representatives on the Tiszafüred officers' revolt and on Vetter's appointment (Debrecen, March 9, 1849) is in *KLÖM*, XIV, 609–16. For further details, see ibid., pp. 616–22; Lajos Steier, *Az 1849-i trónfosztás előzményei és következményei: Ismeretlen adatok az 1848–49-i szabadságharc történetéhez*, pp. 130 ff.; Georg [György] Klapka, *Der Nationalkrieg in Ungarn und Siebenbürgen in den Jahren 1848 und 1849*, I, 284–93.

54. Mihály Horváth, *Magyarország*, II, 378–80.

55. Arthur Görgei, *Mein Leben*, I, 301–2, and István Görgey, *1848 és 1849-ből*, II, 52.

56. On Field Marshal Radetzky's Italian campaign in March 1849 and the battle of Novara see Kiszling, *Die Revolution*, II, 133–60.

57. Kossuth to the National Committee (Gödöllő, April 7, 1849), *KLÖM*, XIV, 839.

58. Arthur Görgei, *Mein Leben*, II, 7–19.

59. See Kiszling, *Die Revolution*, II, 77–79.

60. On the radicals' March 24 confrontation with Kossuth, see Zoltán Varga, "A trónfosztás," in István Szabó, *A szabadságharc*, pp. 424–25, and György Spira, *A magyar forradalom*, pp. 461–66.

61. On the politics of the Peace Party in March, 1849, see Varga in István Szabó, *A szabadságharc*, pp. 403–14 and passim; György Spira, *A magyar forradalom*, pp. 457–60; and Mihály Horváth, *Magyarország*, II, 380–89.

62. Kossuth's March 25 address in the House of Representatives was reprinted in *KLÖM*, XIV, 718–26, and in Pap, *A parlament Debrecenben*, I, 259–63. See also Mihály Horváth, *Magyarország*, II, 390–94.

63. Daniel Irányi's March 25 proposal to the House of Representatives was reprinted in *KLÖM*, xiv, 723, and in Pap, *A parlament Debrecenben*, i, 264 (see also Beér, *Az 1848/49*, p. 388); György Spira, *A magyar forradalom*, p. 466.

64. Kossuth to László Csányi (Eger, April 1, 1849), *KLÖM*, xiv, 783–85.

65. Quoted in Arthur Görgei, *Mein Leben*, ii, 10.

66. Ibid., ii, 11–12.

67. Kossuth, *Irataim az emigrációból*, ii, 275–76.

68. Since Kossuth presented his proposals of April 13 at a closed meeting of the House of Representatives, his address was not taken down in shorthand. Eyewitness accounts were reprinted in Beér, *Az 1848/49*, p. 543–46.

69. Kossuth's parliamentary address of April 14 and the speeches of the other deputies were reprinted in *KLÖM*, xiv, 873–87, and in Pap, *A parlament Debrecenben*, ii, 60–76. Of the memoir literature, see Horváth, *Magyarország függetlenségi harczának története* II, 497-527, and the works of the following Peace Party members: Zsigmond Kemény, *Összes művei*, vol xii, *A forradalom után*; János Pálffy, *Magyarországi és erdélyi urak*, pp. 262–66; Szokoly, *Mészáros*, ii, 174–83; and Pál Hunfalvi, "Rövid visszapillantás a forradalomra." The historiography of the April 14 meeting and the subsequent Declaration of Independence is naturally voluminous. See especially Beér, *Az 1848/49*, pp. 400–1; Varga in István Szabó, *A szabadságharc*, pp. 387–473; and Imre Révész, "Kossuth és a Függetlenségi Nyilatkozat," in Zoltán I. Tóth, *Emlékkönyv Kossuth Lajos születésének 150. évfordulójára.*

70. See György Szabad, "Kossuth on the Political System of the United States of America," *Études Historiques Hongroises 1975 publiées à l'occasion du XIVᵉ Congrès International des Sciences Historiques par la Commission Nationale des Historiens Hongrois* (2 vols.; Budapest: Akadémia, 1975), ii, 501–529.

71. The most authentic texts of the Declaration of Independence of April 19, 1849, well annotated, are in Beér, *Az 1848/49*, pp. 720–33, and in *KLÖM*, xiv, 894–912. The Declaration was reprinted in Mihály Horváth, *Magyarország*, ii, 527–45; in Pap, *A parlament Debrecenben*, ii, 89–101; and elsewhere. English translations are to be found in Stiles, *Austria in 1848–49*, ii, 409–19, and in General Klapka, *Memoirs*, ii, 287–316.

72. Dániel Irányi and Charles-Louis Chassin, *Histoire politique de la révolution de Hongrie, 1847–1849*, ii, 399–400.

7 / The Travail and Decline of Independent Hungary: Kossuth as Constitutional Governor-President (April–July 1849)

1. István Görgey, *1848 és 1849-ből*, ii, 166.

2. *Ibid.*, pp. 207–8. Also Arthur Görgei, *Mein Leben und Wirken in Ungarn in den Jahren 1848 und 1849*, ii, 33.

3. There is a short biography of Welden in Rikhárd Gelich, *Magyarország függetlenségi harcza 1848–49-ben*, iii, 250n–51n. See also Baron Ludwig Welden, *Episoden aus meinem Leben: Beiträge zur Geschichte der Feldzüge der österreichischen Armee in den Jahren 1848 und 1849.*

4. Kossuth to Görgey (Debrecen, May 4 and 8, 1849), *KLÖM*, xv, 205–6, 237–39.

5. Kossuth to Görgey (Debrecen, April 16 and 18, 1849), István Barta, ed., *Kossuth Lajos kormányzóelnöki iratai, 1848 április 15 - augusztus 15*, which is vol. xv of *Kossuth Lajos összes munkái* (hereafter: *KLÖM*, xv), pp. 15–16, and 27. See also Arthur Görgei, *Mein Leben*, ii, 204.

6. On Damjanich's accident, see the exchange of communications between Görgey and Kossuth (April 29–May 4, 1849), *KLÖM*, xv, 201–3; Arthur Görgei, *Mein Leben*, ii, 65–67.

7. Görgei, *Mein Leben*, II, 56–63.

8. Görgey's "Castle Hill decision" is the subject of seemingly endless historical controversy. While few writers doubt that the move was disastrous for Hungary, there is disagreement on Görgey's responsibility. For typical comments, see Gelich, *Magyarország függetlenségi harcza*, III, 278–85; István Görgey, *1848 és 1849-ből*, II, 247–57; and Mihály Horváth, *Magyarország függetlenségi harczának története 1848 és 1849-ben*, II, 581–92. Austrian military authors are unanimous in making Görgey responsible for the Hungarians' false move, and they agree that Görgey's blunder had spared the Monarchy further defeats. For a modern summary of the Austrian view, see Rudolf Kiszling, *Die Revolution im Kaisertum Österreich 1848–1849*, II, 169–73.

9. [Friedrich Engels], "Buda," in *The New American Cyclopaedia* (New York: 1858), X, 60.

10. Engels in the *Neue Rheinische Zeitung*, no. 301 (May 19, 1849), in Barnard Isaacs, *The Revolution of 1848–49*, p. 263.

11. See Gelich, *Magyarország függetlenségi harcza*, III, 284–85. Görgey's reply to Klapka was printed in German, in Dénes Pap, *Okmánytár Magyarország függetlenségi harczának történetéhez 1848–1849*, II, 432–33; in Hungarian, in Imre Deák, *1848*, pp. 366–67; and General Klapka, *Memoiren von Georg Klapka*, I, 158–59.

12. Rajačić to the Austrian government (Zimony, May 13, 1849). In German, in József Thim, *A magyarországi 1848–49-ben szerb fölkelés története*, III, 727–32.

13. See, for instance, Government Plenipotentiary Count Kázmér Batthyány to Kossuth (Szabadka, April 6, 1849), OHB, 1849:5463. Also, Perczel to the National Defense Committee (Kiskeér, April 4, 1849), OHB, 1849:5527. Also the account of the contemporary military historian Károly Mészáros in *Kossuth levelezése a magyar szabadságharc karvezéreivel 1848–1849-ben*, pp. 52–64.

14. See, for instance Zsolt Trócsányi, *Az erdélyi parasztság története, 1790–1849*, pp. 474–77.

15. *Ibid.*, pp. 462–64, 469–74. See also Kossuth's instructions to Csányi upon the latter's appointment to Transylvania (Debrecen, January 27, 1849), *KLÖM*, XIV, 248–50; and Silviu Dragomir, *Studii și documente privitoare la revoluția Românilor din Transilvania in anii 1848–49*. III, 295–97.

16. See, for instance, Kossuth's "Official Notice to the Nation," in *Közlöny*, January 21, 1849; reprinted in *KLÖM*, XIV, 172. Also Kossuth to Ioan Dragoş (Debrecen, April 14, 1849), *KLÖM*, XIV, 889–90. Kossuth's instructions to Bem upon the latter's capture of Nagyszeben (Cibakháza, March 17, 1849), *KLÖM*, XIV, 666–68.

17. On Bem's colonization program see Endre Kovács, *Bem József*, pp. 389–93. See also Pál Nyáry to Kossuth (Debrecen, March 17, 1849), *KLÖM*, XIV, 669, and *ibid.*, pp. 573, 694–99.

18. See for instance János Czetz to Ödön Beöthy (Torda, January 16, 1849), OHB, 1849:718.

19. Kossuth to Csányi (Debrecen, April 14, 1849), OHB, 1849:5582, *KLÖM*, XIV, 889–90, Deák, *1848*, pp. 348–49.

20. Bem to Kossuth (Freidorf, April 29, 1849) (in French), OHB, 1849:6470. On the massacres in southern Hungary, see for instance Perczel to Kossuth (Újvidék, April 16, 1849), OHB, 1849:5833.

21. On the siege of Castle Hill see, among others, Kiszling, *Die Revolution*, II, 169–73; István Görgey, *1848 és 1849-ből*, II, 258–94; Arthur Görgei, *Mein Leben*, II, 68–96; Gelich, *Magyarország függetlenségi harcza*, III, 278–95; J. Némedy (alias Colonel József Bayer), *Die Belagerung der Festung Ofen vom 4–21. Mai 1849 durch den k.k. Generalmajor v. Hentzi. Nach hinterlassenen Tagebuchblättern eines Augenzeugen* (Vienna,1893); and Peter Gosztony, "Die Verteidigung der Festung Buda durch General Hentzi im Frühjahr 1849."

22. On Hentzi see Gelich, *Magyarország függetlenségi harcza*, III, 263n–264n. Kossuth's correspondence with regard to Hentzi is in OHB, 1848:1364, 1713, 2000, 2262, 2816, 3396, 5172, 5506, 6003, 6247, and 6694.

23. Kossuth's proclamations to the public (Debrecen, May 16 and May 22, 1849) were reprinted in *KLÖM*, xv, 319–321, 375–76.

24. Görgey's April 29 Proclamation to the Army was reprinted in, among others, Arthur Görgei, *Mein Leben*, II, 52–53; István Görgey, *1848 és 1849-böl*, II, 193–94; Gelich, *Magyarország függetlenségi harcza*, III, 275–76; and Pap, *Okmánytár*, II, 422–23; Görgey to Kossuth (Svábhegy, May 13, 1849), *KLÖM*, xv, 319–20.

25. See for instance Kossuth to Szemere (Debrecen, April 19, 1849), *KLÖM*, xv, 48.

26. For an example, see the exchange of letters between Perczel and Kossuth on May 2 and 9, 1849. Perczel's letter of May 2 was printed in Károly Mészáros, *Kossuth levelezése*, pp. 64–66; Kossuth's reply of May 9 is *ibid.*, pp. 70–74, and in *KLÖM*, xv, 246–48.

27. Szemere's May 2 address to parliament was reprinted in Mihály Horváth, *Magyarország*, II, 562–64, and in Dénes Pap, *A parlament Debrecenben*, II, 153–54. Szemere's subsequent remarks to members of the Peace Party are quoted in György Spira, *A magyar forradalom 1848–49-ben*, p. 506.

28. Mihály Horváth, *Magyarország*, II, 554–61. Horváth's views were repeated by György Spira, *A magyar forradalom*, p. 522.

29. Bem's possible appointment as commander-in-chief, his exchange of letters with Kossuth in May 1849, and the question of his joining or not joining with the main army, are discussed in detail in Endre Kovács, *Bem*, pp. 488–500.

30. Kossuth to Görgey (Debrecen, May 12, 1849), *KLÖM*, xv, 237–38; Kossuth to Görgey (Debrecen, May 12, 1849), *KLÖM*, xv, 284–90. See also the decision of the council of ministers with regard to the authority of the minister of war (Debrecen, May 20, 1849), *KLÖM*, xv, 363–66.

31. Szemere to Kossuth (Miskolc, April 20, 1849), Deák, *1848*, pp. 358–59; See János Beér, *Az 1848/49*, p. 89.

32. Kossuth's May 2 message to the National Assembly was reprinted in *KLÖM*, xv, 181–84; Pap, *A parlament Debrecenben*, II, 150–52; Beér, *Az 1848/49*, pp. 414–16; and Pap, *Okmánytár*, II, 424–27. The minutes of the meetings of the House on May 4 and 5 were reprinted in Pap, *A parlament Debrecenben*, II, 176–82. See also Beér, *Az 1848/49*, pp. 419–21. Kossuth's May 14 oath and his subsequent address to parliament were reprinted in *KLÖM*, xv, 303–4; Beér, *Az 1848/49*, pp. 426–27; and Pap, *A parlament Debrecenben*, II, 190–92.

33. The scope of Kossuth's activities and political influence in the period May–August 1849 is debated, among others, by István Barta in his introduction to *KLÖM*, xv, 5–6, and by György Spira, *A magyar forradalom*, pp. 487–89 and passim. In the opinion of this author, both writers underestimate the scope of Kossuth's rejuvenated activity and influence in the last months of the war.

34. György Spira, *A magyar forradalom*, pp. 487–89 and passim.

35. The text of Kossuth's bill on the fifty-thousand additional soldiers was reprinted in Pap, *A parlament Debrecenben*, II, 130–133; Beér, *Az 1848/49*, pp. 734–35, and *KLÖM*, xv, 79–83. See also Gelich, *Magyarország függetlenségi harcza*, III, 394–401. The June 1 order of the council of ministers to the government commissioners was reprinted in *KLÖM*, xv, 454–55. On the shortage of recruits see (among others) Kossuth to Görgey (Buda-Pest, June 6, 1849), *KLÖM*, xv, 477. See also General Lahner to Kossuth on June 30, 1849, OHB, 1849:8906.

36. The report to Kossuth of József Nagy, government commissioner to Szatmár county (Szatmár, March 31, 1849) is in OHB, 1849:5194. Kossuth's correspondence on landowners' abuses in Szatmár county was printed in *KLÖM*, xv, 46–48. Kossuth's April 19 decree was reprinted *ibid.*, pp. 43–46. The question is discussed, for example, in György Spira, *A magyar forradalom*, 507–8, and in István Barta, "A kormány parasztpolitikája 1849-ben."

37. The dissolution of the special police department is discussed in Mihály Horváth, *Magyarország*, III, 94–95.

38. On the reorganization of the summary courts, see Mihály Horváth, *Magyarország*, III, 98–106. The government's decision on the abolition of the summary courts, with the exception of one, was reprinted in *KLÖM*, xv, 490–91, 554.

39. Perczel's letter to Kossuth (Zsombolya, May 2, 1849) was printed in Károly Mészáros, *Kossuth levelezése*, pp. 64–66.

40. See György Spira, *A magyar forradalom*, pp. 514–15.

41. Görgey's account of the events in May are in his *Mein Leben*, II, 102–21.

42. On the circumstances of the execution of the two officers, Major Baron Mednyánszky and Captain Gruber, and on the Hungarian reaction to the executions, see *KLÖM*, xv, 512–13 and Arthur Görgei, *Mein Leben*, II, 132–34.

43. On the parliament's decision to move to Pest see Beér, *Az 1848/49*, p. 92, and Pap, *A parlament Debrecenben*, II, 250–57.

44. Russo-Austrian relations in the first half of the nineteenth century, as well as Russia's interest in Hungarian events, are thoroughly analyzed in Erzsébet Andics, *A Habsburgok és Romanovok szövetsége*. The author's heavy marxist bias mars the interpretation but not the accurate reporting of major developments. The volume contains 147 documents. Unless indicated otherwise, my treatment of the diplomatic preparation for Russia's intervention in Hungary is culled from Ms. Andics' volume. Of almost equal importance for the study of the Russian intervention are Hugo Kerchnawe, *Feldmarschall Fürst Windischgrätz und die Russenhilfe;* Joseph A. Helfert, *Geschichte der österreichischen Revolution im Zusammenhange mit der mitteleuropäischen Bewegung der Jahre 1848–1849*, and R[evekka] A. Averbuch, *Tsarskaia interventsiia v bor'be s vengerskoi revoliutsiei*. The latter contains many documents.

45. The minutes of the Hungarian Council of Ministers of April 23, 1848, were reprinted in *KLÖM*, xII, 23.

46. On the Romanian political refugees in Hungary see (among other works) Kossuth's memorandum to Minister of the Interior Szemere (Buda-Pest, June 18, 1848), *KLÖM*, xII, 288.

47. See, for instance, the letter of Felix Fonton, Russian chargé d'affaires in Vienna, to Foreign Minister Count Nesselrode (Vienna, June 13, 1848) (in French), in Erzsébet Andics, *A Habsburgok és Romanovok szövetsége*, pp. 230–32.

48. With regard to the Russian intervention in Transylvania, see the correspondence between Kossuth and Csányi, *KLÖM*, xIV, 471–72, 534–37. News of Bem's victory over the united Russo-Austrian army is *ibid.*, pp. 666–68, 672–74, 685–87.

49. For information on Russian eyewitness accounts with regard to the Paskevich-Caboga meeting, see Andics, *A Habsburgok*, p. 146.

50. Dembiński's correspondence with Kossuth on the subject of his plan to invade both Galicia and Russian Poland were printed in *KLÖM*, xv, 115, 219–21. Bem's letter to Kossuth rejecting Dembiński's plan (Freidorf, April 29, 1849) (in French) is in OHB, 1849:6470. Bem also addressed a similar letter to Dembiński (Freidorf, May 6, 1849), Gelich, *Magyarország függetlenségi harcza*, III, 379–80. Dembiński's own views were reprinted in Alphons F. Danzer, *Dembinski in Ungarn*, II, 74–75. For the Hungarian soldiers' mixed reaction to Dembiński's plan, see the reports of government commissioner Pál Luzsénszky to Kossuth (Kassa, May 4 and 5, 1849), OHB, 1849:6619, 6659.

51. On Kossuth's reasoning with regard to the international effect of the Russian invasion see especially Mihály Horváth, *Magyarország*, III, 79–82.

52. The memorandum of the Council of Ministers, Kossuth's and Kázmér Batthyány's solemn protest, and the latter's note to Palmerston are reprinted in *KLÖM*, xv, 341–44, 350–53. The first two of these documents and additional proclamations are reprinted in Pap, *Okmánytár*, II, 447–61.

53. Kossuth's and the government's June 27 appeal for a crusade and their June 28 manifesto to Europe were reprinted in *KLÖM*, xv, 602–06, 611–14, also in Pap, *Okmánytár*, II, 480–90.

54. In this respect see the letter of a teacher to Kossuth protesting the idea of a religious crusade: János Joó to Kossuth (Eger, June 1, 1849), OHB, 1849:7745.

55. Of the many works on Hungary's foreign policy under Kossuth, the most important are Eszter Waldapfel, *A független magyar külpolitika, 1848–1849;* Éva Haraszti, *Az angol külpolitika;* Charles Sproxton, *Palmerston and the Hungarian Revolution;* and István Hajnal, *A Batthyány-kormány külpolitikája.*

56. On Count László Teleki see Zoltán Horváth, *Teleki László, 1810–1861.* See also Tamás Lengyel, *Gróf Teleki László.* Teleki's own works and correspondence are in Gábor G. Kemény, ed., *Teleki László válogatott munkái.*

57. On Ferenc Pulszky see his own *Életem és korom,* which contains many documents.

58. Theresa Pulszky, *Memoirs of a Hungarian Lady.*

59. On Golescu's plan, see Teleki's letter to Kossuth (Paris, October 10, 1848), Deák, *1848,* pp. 245–46.

60. Teleki to Kossuth (Paris, May 14, 1849), Gábor Kemény, *Teleki László,* II, 25–29.

61. The protocol of May 19, 1849, was reprinted in French in Zoltán Horváth, *Teleki László,* II, 177–80.

62. Ferenc Pulszky, *Életem és korom,* II, 495–96.

63. Kázmér Batthyány's June 10 note to the Hungarian diplomatic agents was reprinted in Ferenc Pulszky, *Életem és korom,* I, 543–47, and in Zoltán Horváth, *Teleki László,* I, 283–84.

64. See Ferenc Pulszky, *Életem és korom,* I, 497. Palmerston's remarks to Russian Ambassador Philip I. Brunnov are quoted in Andics, *A Habsburgok,* p. 161.

65. Teleki to Kossuth (London, August 3, 1849), Gábor Kemény, *Teleki László,* II, 31–33.

66. From the reports of Brunnov to Nesselrode (London, June 21 and July 23, 1849). Quoted in R. A. Averbukh, *A magyar nép szabadságküzdelme 1848–49-ben,* pp. 98, 99.

67. On the Prussian offer to Austria see Adolph Schwarzenberg, *Prince Felix zu Schwarzenberg,* pp. 53–54.

68. The text of the Hungaro-Venetian alliance treaty was reprinted in Mihály Horváth, *Magyarország,* II, 574–76.

69. Kossuth to President Taylor (Debrecen, May 6, 1849) (in French), *KLÖM,* XV, 217, and Waldapfel, *A forradalom és szabadságharc levelestára,* III, 300–301.

70. On U.S.-Hungarian relations in 1849, see Waldapfel, *A független magyar külpolitika 1848–1849,* pp. 242–48; and Sándor Szilassy, "America and the Hungarian Revolution of 1848–49.''

71. The Austro-Russian military agreement of May 21, 1849, is quoted in Gelich, *Magyarország függetlenségi harcza,* III, 353–55, and Mihály Horváth, *Magyarország,* III, 132–33.

72. On the Brescia incident see C. A. Macartney, *The Habsburg Empire 1790–1918,* p. 476n., and [Julius Haynau], *Biografie des k.k. Feldzeugmeisters Julius Freiherrn von Haynau von einem seiner Waffengefährten,* pp. 44–47.

73. The Hungarians were aware of the Austrians' ability to recruit good men into their army. See the letter of Government Commissioner János Ludwig to Kossuth (Esztergom, June 7, 1849), OHB, 1849:8291.

74. The June–July–August campaigns of Haynau and Paskevich are dealt with in dozens of contemporary and later studies. Statistical data on the number of soldiers and on guns are unreliable if for no other reason than because the authors generally fail to distinguish between military target figures and the actual strength of the armies, as well as between combat and support units. Some of the standard works used here were *Asbóth Lajos emlékiratai az 1848-iki és 1849-iki magyarországi hadjáratból;* Danzer, *Dembinski in Ungarn,* II, 74–84 and passim; Gelich, *Magyarország függetlenségi harcza,* III, 479–80; Arthur Görgei, *Mein Leben,* II, 187

380 / 8. Defeat

and passim; Mihály Horváth, *Magyarország*, III, 132–68; W. Rüstow, *Geschichte des ungarischen Insurrectionskrieges in den Jahren 1848 und 1849*, II, 75–103; Kiszling, *Die Revolution*, II, 188–89 and passim; and Lajos Steier, *Haynau és Paskievics: Ismeretlen adalékok az 1848–49-iki szabadságharc történetéhez*.

75. See Danzer, *Dembinski in Ungarn*, II, 76–78; Gelich, *Magyarország függetlenségi harcza*, II, 373 and passim; and Steier, *Haynau és Paskievics*, I, 74–75.

76. On the behavior of the Russians and Hungarians toward each other see (among others) Mihály Horváth, *Magyarország*, III, 205, and Gelich, III, 380–92.

77. On Arthur Görgey's "Austrian scheme" see his own *Mein Leben*, II, 187–200. On the June 26 cabinet meeting see also István Görgey, *1848 és 1849-ből*, II, 582–607, and Steier, *Haynau és Paskievics*, I, 62–64. That Kossuth accepted Görgey's recommendation to concentrate all efforts against Haynau's army is proven by the governor's letter of the same day to Bem (*KLÖM*, XV, 597–98) as well as by Kossuth's letter to Görgey, also of the same day (ibid., p. 597).

78. Different parts of the correspondence between Kossuth and Görgey at the end of June were reprinted in Deák, *1848*, pp. 385–88; *KLÖM*, XV, 620–22, 626–27, 633–36; Pap, *Okmánytár*, II, 497; and Steier, *Haynau és Paskievics*, I, 136–55 (the most complete version). The controversy over Görgey's Komárom plan and Kossuth's Szeged plan is one of the most confused and most debated issues of the historiography of the War of Independence. Every major source devotes considerable attention to the question.

8 / Defeat

1. On Hungarian attempts to conciliate the Romanians in 1849, see (among others) Keith Hitchins, *The Rumanian National Movement in Transylvania, 1780–1849*, pp. 263–81; Zsolt Trócsányi, *Az erdélyi parasztság története, 1795–1849*, pp. 458–77; Zoltán I. Tóth, "Kossuth és a nemzetiségi kérdés 1848–1949-ben," in *Emlékkönyv Kossuth Lajos születésének 150. évfordulójára*, II, 325–39; Silviu Dragomir, *Studii şi documente privitoare la revoluţia Românilor din Transilvania in anii 1848–49*, vol. III.

2. For details of Kossuth's instructions to Dragoş and the terms of Hungary's proposed concessions to the Romanians, see Kossuth to Dragoş (Debrecen, April 26, 1849), *KLOM*, XV, 136–39.

3. The complete text of the *Projet de pacification*, in French and in Hungarian, is in *KLÖM*, XV, 723–27.

4. Iancu's letter to Kossuth (Topánfalva, August 3, 1849) was reprinted in Imre Deák, *1848*, p. 409. On Avram Iancu see especially Silviu Dragomir, *Avram Iancu*.

5. The text of the Law on Nationalities of July 28, 1848, was reprinted in János Beér, *Az 1848/49*, pp. 868–69; and in Dénes Pap, *Okmánytár Magyarország függetlenségi harczának történetéhez 1848–1849*, II, 526–27. For further details on the law and on debates in the House of Representatives, see Pap II, pp. 93–97, 469–76, 533–54. Also Mihály Horváth, *Magyarország függetlenségi harczának története 1848 és 1849-ben*, III, 355–60; and Zoltán I. Tóth, "Kossuth és a nemzetiségi kérdés 1848–49-ben," in *Emlékkönyv*, II, 325–39.

6. Law IX of 1849 on "The Jews" was reprinted in Beér, *Az 1848/49*, p. 873; and in Pap, *Okmánytár*, II, 527–28. On the preparations made for this law, see Beér, *Az 1848/49*, pp. 869–73.

7. Quoted in Horváth, *Magyarország*, III, 323.

8. Szemere's July 28 address was reprinted in Beér, *Az 1848/49*, pp. 466–69.

9. The issue of supreme command is presented in (among others) Beér, *Az 1848/49*, pp. 550–52, which contains a summary of later eyewitness accounts; Mihály Horváth, *Magyarország*, III, 371–73; Rikhárd Gelich, *Magyarország függetlenségi harcza 1848–49-ben*, III, 810–12; Arthur Görgei, *Mein Leben und Wirken in Ungarn in den Jahren 1848 und 1849*, II,

317–18; and Lajos Steier, *Haynau és Paskievics*, II, 19–58 and passim. The July 30 decision of the Council of Ministers with regard to Dembiński's appointment was printed in *KLÖM*, xv, 797–800.

10. Szemere's memorandum to Kossuth (Szeged, July 21, 1849) was reprinted in Deák, *1848*, pp. 405–7. This particular quotation is on p. 407.

11. The July 30 decision of the Council of Ministers with regard to the delegation of Szemere and Batthyány to Görgey's camp to pursue negotiations with the Russians was reprinted in *KLÖM*, xv, 797–800. The government's instructions to Görgey on the same issue (Makó, July 30) are in *ibid.*, pp. 801–4, as well as in Steier, *Haynau és Paskievics*, II, 138–45. Görgey's important letter to Paskevich (Sajószentpéter, July 22, 1849), in which Görgey insisted that he would not surrender to the Russians until the Constitution of Hungary was guaranteed, was reprinted in (among others) Steier, *Haynau és Paskievics*, II, 112 (in German). Peace negotiations with the Russians are discussed in Arthur Görgei, *Mein Leben*, II, 283–316, and passim; István Görgey, *1848 és 1849-ből*, III, 185–210 and passim; and Steier, *Haynau és Paskievics*, II, 5–19 and passim. The latter volume contains almost all the letters exchanged between Görgey and the Russians (II, 106–15 and passim). See also Mihály Horváth, *Magyarország*, III, 334–45 and passim.

12. Some of Haynau's typical letters with regard to Russian incompetence and their leniency toward the Hungarians were printed in Steier, *Haynau és Paskievics*, II, 162–63, 350–58, 422–24.

13. Kossuth's manifesto of abdication of August 11 was reprinted in *KLÖM*, xv, 845–46. Following it are other documents, in particular Kossuth's almost identical letter addressed directly to Görgey. The manifesto was also reprinted in Gelich, *Magyarország függetlenségi harcza*, III, 853, Arthur Görgei, *Mein Leben*, II, 388 (in German); Mihály Horváth, *Magyarország*, III, 478–79; Pap, *Okmánytár*, II, 534–35; etc. The August 11 events are discussed *ad nauseam* by every source mentioned above, as well as by many others. The most reliable seems to be Mihály Horváth, whose account, however, must be counterbalanced by Görgey's memoirs and by István Görgey, *1848 és 1849-ből*, III, 468–562. Letters by former colleagues of Kossuth explaining the abdication were reprinted (in English) in William Henry Stiles, *Austria in 1848–49*, II, 421–41.

14. Kossuth's August 12, 1849, letter to Görgey, sent from Lugos, was printed in *KLÖM*, xv, 848–50, and in Deák, *1848*, pp. 418–20.

15. Görgey's August 11 Arad manifesto to the citizenry was reprinted in Gelich, *Magyarország függetlenségi harcza*, III, 854–55; Arthur Görgei, *Mein Leben*, II, 389 (in German); Pap, *Okmánytár*, II, 535; Mihály Horváth, *Magyarország*, III, 483–84; etc.

16. Görgey's August 11 Arad letter to Rüdiger was reprinted (in English) in Stiles, *Austria in 1848–49*, II, 420–21; (in German) in Mihály Horváth, *Magyarország*, III, 487–89; and in Gelich, III, 856–58.

17. On the August 11 meeting of the House of Representatives see Beér, *Az 1848/49*, pp. 97–98, 478–79.

18. The tsar's and Paskevich's correspondence with Francis Joseph and Haynau on clemency to the Hungarians was printed in Steier, *Haynau és Paskievics*, II, 385–92 and passim.

19. Paskevich to Haynau (Nagyvárad, August 16, 1849), Steier, *Haynau és Paskievics*, II, 390–92. This particular quotation is on p. 391.

20. See Erzsébet Andics, "1849 augusztus. Ismeretlen adalékok az 1848–49-es magyar forradalom és szabadságharc végnapjairól," in Andics, *1848–1849: Tanulmányok*, pp. 363–402.

21. Haynau's August 18, 1849, "Order of the Day," issued in Temesvár, was reprinted in *Gyüjteménye a' Magyarország számára kibocsátott Legfelsőbb Manifestumok és Szózatoknak valamint a' cs. kir. hadsereg főparancsnokai által Magyarországban kiadott Hirdetményeknek* (hereafter, *Gyüjteménye*), II, 137.

382 / 9. Epilogue

22. Kossuth to Bem (Teregova, August 14, 1849), *KLÖM*, xv, 851–53. This particular quote is on p. 852.

23. *Gyüjteménye,* II, 137.

24. The terms of Komárom's capitulation on September 27 were reprinted in Gelich, *Magyarország függetlenségi harcza,* III, 919–20; *Gyüjteménye,* II, 149–50; Mihály Horváth, *Magyarország,* III, 535; Pap, *Okmánytár,* II, 553–54 (together with other documents); and General Klapka, *Memoiren von Georg Klapka,* I, 281–83. Komárom's last battle is discussed in Gelich, III, 890–992; Mihály Horváth, *Magyarország,* III, 528–40; W. Rüstow, *Geschichte des ungarischen Insurrectionskrieges in den Jahren 1848 und 1849,* II, 381–408; Rudolf Kiszling, *Die Revolution im Kaisertum Österreich 1848–1849,* II, 284–91; and of course in all of Klapka's works (see Sources).

25. On war casualties, see Kiszling, *Die Revolution,* II, 283, and Péter Hanák, ed., *Magyarország története, 1849–1918,* p. 10.

26. Gelich, *Magyarország függetlenségi harcza,* III, 929; Elek Fényes, *Magyarország leírása,* pp. 153–63; see C. A. Macartney, *The Habsburg Empire 1790–1918,* p. 469. Also the calculations of Heinrich Friedjung, *Österreich von 1848 bis 1860,* I, 236–50.

27. The August 20, 1849, cabinet resolution was reprinted (in German) in Erzsébet Andics, *A nagybirtokos arisztokrácia ellenforradalmi szerepe 1848–49-ben,* III, 390–92.

28. Haynau to Radetzky (Temesvár, August 18, 1849), Steier, *Haynau és Paskievics,* II, 358–62. This particular quote is on p. 359.

29. Haynau to Schwarzenberg (Pest, February 6, 1850), Andics, *Nagybirtokos arisztokrácia,* III, 464–66 (in German).

30. See Kiszling, *Die Revolution,* II, 293.

31. A comprehensive list of Habsburg officers tried and sentenced in Hungary after the War was printed in *Verzeichniss der wegen Hochverrathes durch Theilnahme an der ungarischen Revolution gefällten kriegsgerichtlichen Urtheile.*

32. On the fourteen Hungarian commanders tried at Arad see (among others) Albert Bartha, *Az aradi 13 vértanú pörének és kivégzésének hiteles története;* Milos Dimitrovics and Antal Klocz, *Az aradi 13 vértanú életrajza* (Arad, 1890); Tivadar Hatos, *A 13 vértanú és a magyar szabadságharc többi elítéltjei* (Budapest, 1904); Mihály Horváth, *Magyarország,* III, 569–73; Tábornoki rangjegyzék—1848/1849; and Emil Vajda, *Az 1848/49. szabadságharc vértanúi* (Győr, 1898).

33. Count Batthyány's trial and execution are best told in Árpád Károlyi, *Németújvári gróf Batthyány Lajos első magyar miniszterelnök főbenjáró pöre.*

34. *Verzeichniss der wegen Hochverrathes. . . .*

35. For a list of those condemned in absentia, and hanged in effigy see *Magyar Hírlap* (Buda-Pest), September 23, 1851.

Epilogue

1. Kossuth's "Vidin Letter" to Görgey was reprinted in István Hajnal, *A Kossuth-emigráció Törökországban,* II, 22–24. Most of the information on Kossuth's Turkish exile was culled from this superb book. On the Turkish exile see also Imrefi (Imre Vahot), *A magyar menekültek Törökországban;* and John H. Komlos, *Kossuth in America, 1851–1852,* pp. 33–49.

2. Kossuth to Klapka (Vidin, October 2, 1849), Hajnal, *A Kossuth-emigráció,* II, 495.

3. Kossuth to his wife (Vidin, November 1, 1849), *ibid.,* II, 524–25.

4. Kossuth to Bem (Vidin, October 19, 1849), *ibid.,* II, 510–13.

5. Cited by Sándor Szilassy, "America and the Hungarian Revolution of 1848–49," p. 192. There is considerable literature in English and in Hungarian on Kossuth's visit to the United States. Dénes Jánossy, *A Kossuth-emigráció Angliában és Amerikában*, contains hundreds of documents in the original language, plus almost five hundred pages of text. The documents relate not only to Kossuth's stay in England and the United States, but also to international diplomatic activity connected with Kossuth. József Balassa, *Kossuth Amerikában, 1851–1852*, is a brief chronological account. Komlos, *Kossuth in America*, is a definitive study of the effect of Kossuth's visit on American politics. It is based on extensive archival research, it lists the shortcomings in Jánossy's much longer analysis, and it contains a fine bibliography. Joseph Széplaki, *Bibliography on Louis Kossuth, Governor of Hungary, with Special Reference to His Trip in the United States*, is, of course, very useful. Some of Kossuth's speeches in English are printed in P. C. Headley, *The Life of Louis Kossuth, Governor of Hungary: Including Notices of the Men and Scenes of the Hungarian Revolution. Appendix: His Principal Speeches;* and in *The Life of Governor Louis Kossuth, with His Public Speeches in the United States, and a Brief History of the Hungarian War of Independence.* By an Officer of the Hungarian Army (New York, 1852).

6. Cited by William Lloyd Garrison, *A Letter to Louis Kossuth, Concerning Freedom and Slavery in the United States in Behalf of the American Anti-Slavery Society*, p. 61.

7. *Ibid.*, pp. 5, 17.

8. See Balassa, *Kossuth Amerikában*, p. 112.

9. See Ervin Pamlényi, *A History of Hungary*, p. 300.

10. Karl Marx to Bertalan Szemere (London, September 26, 1859), and Marx, "Patrons and Vagrants," in *Herr Vogt*. Cited in John Komlos, "Karl Marx's Critique of Louis Kossuth," unpublished manuscript.

11. On Kossuth's doings in England, France, Switzerland, and Italy between 1852 and 1866, see Zoltán Vas, *Kossuth Lajos élete*, I, 723–933, and II, 7–383; Lóránt Hegedüs, *Kossuth Lajos, legendák hőse*, pp. 254–321; and Otto Zarek, *Kossuth: Die Liebe eines Volkes*, pp. 578–619. There are numerous documentary collections dealing with Kossuth and the Hungarian emigrés in the 1850s and 1860s: for instance, Jenő Koltay-Kastner, *A Kossuth-emigráció Olaszországban;* and, edited by Koltay-Kastner, *Iratok a Kossuth-emigráció történetéhez, 1859* and *Mazzini e Kossuth: Lettere e Documenti Inediti*. See also Tivadar Ács, ed., *Népek tavasza. Ismeretlen levelek, naplójegyzetek a magyar szabadságharc és emigráció korából.*

12. The literature on Hungary between 1849 and 1867 as well as on the Compromise Agreement is enormous. For a brief and intelligent summary in English, see Pamlényi, *History of Hungary*, pp. 287–320. The book contains a valuable bibliography of works in languages other than Hungarian. See also Béla K. Király, *Ferenc Deák*, pp. 138–72; Paul Bödy, *Joseph Eötvös and the Modernization of Hungary 1840–1870*, pp. 61–97, and, for the period immediately after 1849, Peter I. Hidas, *The Metamorphosis of a Social Class in Hungary During the Reign of Young Franz Joseph.*

13. On Kossuth between 1867 and 1894, see the biographies of Vas, Hegedüs, and Zarek, but especially Gyula Szekfű's scholarly "Az öreg Kossuth, 1867–1894," in Zoltán Tóth, *Emlékkönyv Kossuth Lajos születésének 150. évfordulójára*, II, 341–433. Kossuth's own *Iratai* and *Irataim az emigráczióból* are of course invaluable.

14. Quoted in Szekfű, "Az öreg Kossuth," p. 393.

15. See Lajos Hatvany, ed., *Agg Kossuth levelei egy fiatal leányhoz.*

16. Baron Zsigmond Kemény, "Gróf Széchenyi," in *Báró Kemény Zsigmond összes művei*, IX, 342. English translation in György Spira, *A Hungarian Count in the Revolution of 1848*, p. 289.

Sources

As the reader might have noted already, the notes refer mainly to printed documentary collections. Archival sources are mentioned only when a printed version of the document does not exist or could not be found. Secondary works are mentioned in the notes to indicate the most important monographs and articles on a specific subject, or when they are the sole sources of my information. I have tried to give preference to publications in Western languages, whether they are original contributions or translations from the Hungarian. As many translations are inaccurate, especially contemporary translations of documents, I have improved them when necessary.

The following source list is divided into four parts: (1) archival collections; (2) archival guides and bibliographies; (3) printed primary sources; and (4) secondary works. Articles are listed only when they are printed separately, and not when they form part of a collection of articles. To save space I have abstained from adding the English translation of Hungarian, Romanian, or Slavic-language titles. The most important publisher of Hungarian scholarly works, the Budapest-based Akadémiai Kiadó (publishing house of the Hungarian Academy of Sciences) is abbreviated as "Akadémia."

1. Archival Collections

Austrian State Archives. Haus-, Hof-, und Staatsarchiv. Vienna: Kabinetts Archiv, Geheime Akten. Karton Nr. 10 and Karton Nr. 12. Kabinetts Archiv, Nachlässe Kempfen. Konvolutum 35, 39.

Austrian State Archives. Kriegsarchiv. Vienna: 1848 Krieg in Ungarn. Akten der Insurgenten-Armee. Fasc. III–XIII (1848/Fasc. 181).

Hungarian National Archives. Budapest: Országos Levéltár. Miniszterelnökség, Országos Honvédelmi Bizottmány, Kormányzóelnökség 1848–1849. Általános Iratok and Vegyes Iratok.

—— Tábornoki rangjegyzék—1848/1849.

—— Belügyminisztérium Irattára. Elnöki Iratok.

2. Archival Guides and Bibliographies

The science of bibliography is highly developed in Hungary; therefore, only the most relevant archival guides and bibliographical publications are listed here, together with a sample of Austrian and English-language bibliographies.

Austrian History Yearbook. Austin, Texas: Rice University, 1965–. Continuing listing of recent works in German, English, Slavic languages, Hungarian, etc., on the history of Central Europe.

Bridge, F. R. *The Habsburg Monarchy, 1804–1918. Books and Pamphlets Published in the United Kingdom between 1818 and 1967: A Critical Bibliography*. London: School of Slavonic and East European Studies, University of London, 1968.

"Bibliographie d'oeuvres choisies de la science historique hongroise, 1945–1959." In *Études Historiques*. Edited by Győző Ember, Elemér Mályusz, et al. 2 vols. Vol. II, pp. 463–629. Budapest: Akadémia, 1965.

Ember, Győző. *Az 1848/49-i minisztérium levéltára*. Budapest: Akadémia, 1950.

Kosáry, Domokos. *Bevezetés Magyarország történetének forrásaiba és irodalmába*. Vol. I, Part 1. Budapest: Tankönyvkiadó, 1970.

Magyar (A) történettudomány válogatott bibliográfiája, 1945–1968. Budapest: Akadémia, 1971.

Széplaki, Joseph. *Bibliography on Louis Kossuth, Governor of Hungary, with Special Reference to His Trip in the United States*. Athens: Ohio University Library, 1972.

Tóth, Zoltán, ed. *Magyar történeti bibliográfia, 1825–1867*. Budapest: Akadémia, 1950.

Uhlirz, Karl and Uhlirz, Mathilde. *Handbuch der Geschichte Österreichs und seiner Nachbarländer Böhmen und Ungarn*. 4 vols. Graz: Leuschner und Lubensky, 1927–44. 2d ed.; Graz: Böhlaus, 1963–.

3. Primary Sources

Ács, Tivadar, ed. *Népek tavasza: Ismeretlen levelek, naplójegyzetek a magyar szabadságharc és emigráció korából*. Budapest: Általános Nyomda és Grafikai Intézet, n.d.

Andics, Erzsébet. *A Habsburgok és Romanovok szövetsége: Az 1849. évi magyarországi cári intervenció diplomáciai előtörténete*. Budapest: Akadémia, 1961. Text and documents.

—— (ed.) *A nagybirtokos arisztokrácia ellenforradalmi szerepe 1848–49-ben*. 2 vols. Budapest: Akadémia, 1952–1965. (Only vols. II and III published.)

Asbóth Lajos emlékiratai az 1848-iki és 1849-iki magyarországi hadjáratból. 2 vols. 2d ed.; Pest: Heckenast Gusztáv, 1862.

Averbukh, R[evekka] A. *Tsarskaia interventsiia v bor'be s vengerskoi revoliutsiei*. Moscow: Gos. Sotsialno-Ekonomicheskoe Izd., 1935 (text and documents).

Barta, István, ed. *Kossuth Lajos. See* Kossuth Lajos.

Bártfai Szabó, László, ed. *Adatok gróf Széchenyi István és kora történetéhez, 1808–1860.* 2 vols. Budapest: n.p., 1943.

Bartha, Albert. *Az aradi 13 vértanú pörének és kivégzésének hiteles története.* Budapest: Kellner és Kiss, 1930. Text and documents.

Bay, Ferenc, ed. *1848–49 a korabeli napilapok tükrében.* Budapest: Officina, 1943.

Beér, János, ed. *Az 1848/49. évi népképviseleti országgyűlés.* Budapest: Akadémia, 1954. Text and documents.

Biografie . . . Haynau. See Haynau.

Bright, Richard. *Travels from Vienna through Lower Hungary: With Some Remarks on the State of Vienna During the Congress in the Year 1814.* Edinburgh: A. Constable, 1818.

Danzer, Alphons F., ed. *Dembinski in Ungarn: Nach den hinterlassenen Papieren des Generals.* 2 vols. Vienna: Oesterreichisch-ungarische Wehr-Zeitung, 1873.

Deák Ferencz beszédei. Edited by Manó Kónyi. 6 vols. 2d ed. Budapest: Franklin, 1903.

Deák, Imre, ed. *1848: A szabadságharc története levelekben, ahogyan a kortársak látták.* Budapest: Sirály, [1942].

Degré, Alajos. *Visszaemlékezéseim.* 2 vols. Budapest: Pfeifer Ferdinánd, 1883.

Dragomir, Silviu. *Studii şi documente privitoare la revoluţia Românilor din Transilvania in anii 1848–49.* 4 vols. Sibiu-Cluj: Cartea Românească din Cluj, 1944–46. Text and documents.

Einhorn, Ignac. *Die Revolution und die Juden in Ungarn.* Leipzig, 1851.

Életképek, 1848. Edited by Mór Jókai. Journal.

Ember, Győző, ed. *Iratok az 1848-i magyarországi parasztmozgalmak történetéhez.* Budapest: Közoktatásügyi Kiadóvállalat, 1951.

Engels, Friedrich. "Germany: Revolution and Counter-Revolution." In Engels, *The German Revolutions.* Edited by Leonard Krieger. Chicago: University of Chicago Press, 1967.

Eötvös József (Báró) összes művei. 20 vols. Budapest: Révai, 1901–4.

1848dik Magyar Országgyűlésen alkotott törvénycikkelyek. Kassa, [1848].

Fenneberg, Ferdinand Fenner von. *Österreich und seine Armee.* Leipzig: Cabinet für Literatur, 1847.

Fényes, Elek. *Az ausztriai birodalom statistikája és földrajzi leírása.* Pest: Heckenast Gusztáv, 1857.

—— *Magyarország leírása.* 2 vols. Pest: Beimel, 1847.

—— *Magyarország statistikája.* 3 vols. Pest: Trattner Károly, 1842–43.

Garrison, William Lloyd. *A Letter to Louis Kossuth, Concerning Freedom and Slavery in the United States in Behalf of the American Anti-Slavery Society.* Boston: R. F. Wallcut, 1852. Reprint. New York: Arno Press and the New York Times, 1969.

Gelich, Rikhárd. *Magyarország függetlenségi harcza 1848–49-ben.* 3 vols. Budapest: Aigner Alajos, 1882–89.

Gesetzartikel des ungarischen Reichstages 1843–1844. Pest, 1844.

Görgei, Arthur. *Briefe ohne Adresse.* Leipzig: Brockhaus, 1867.

—— *Mein Leben und Wirken in Ungarn in den Jahren 1848 und 1849.* 2 vols. Leipzig: F. A. Brockhaus, 1852. [*My Life and Acts in Hungary in the Years 1848–1849.* 2 vols. London, 1852.]

Görgey, István. *1848 és 1849-ből: Élmények és benyomások.* 3 vols. Budapest: Franklin, 1885–88.

—— *Görgey Arthur ifjúsága és fejlődése a forradalomig.* Budapest: Magyar Tudományos Akadémia, 1916. Text and documents.

—— *Görgey Arthur a számüzetésben.* Budapest: Magyar Tudományos Akadémia, 1918. Text and documents.

Great Britain. House of Commons. *Sessional Papers,* vol. LVII (1851). "Correspondence Relative to the Affairs of Hungary, 1847–1849. Presented to Both Houses of Parliament by Command of Her Majesty August 15, 1850."

Gyüjteménye a' Magyarország számára kibocsátott Legfelsőbb Manifestumok és Szózatoknak, valamint a' cs. kir. hadsereg főparancsnokai által Magyarországban kiadott Hirdetményeknek. 2 vols. Buda: Egyetemi Nyomda, 1849.

Hajnal, István. *A Kossuth-emigráció Törökországban.* 2 vols. Budapest: Magyar Történelmi Társulat, 1927. Text and documents.

Haraszti, Éva. *Az angol külpolitika a magyar szabadságharc ellen.* Budapest: Közoktatásügyi Kiadóvállalat, 1951.

Hatvany, Lajos, ed. *Agg Kossuth levelei egy fiatal leányhoz.* Budapest: Pallas, 1919.

—— *Igy élt Petőfi.* 5 vols. Budapest: Akadémia, 1955–57.

Hauptmann, Ferdinand. *Jelačić's Kriegszug nach Ungarn 1848.* 2 vols. Graz: Historisches Institut der Universität Graz, 1975. Text and documents.

[Haynau, Julius.] *Biografie des k.k. Feldzeugmeisters Julius Freiherrn von Haynau von einem seiner Waffengefährten.* Graz: August Hesse, 1853.

Headley, P. C. *The Life of Louis Kossuth, Governor of Hungary: Including Notices of the Men and Scenes of the Hungarian Revolution. Appendix: His Principal Speeches.* Auburn: Derby and Miller, 1852.

Hof- und Staats-Handbuch des österreichischen Kaiserthumes. Vienna: Aus der k.k. Hof- und Staats-Aerarial-Druckerey, 1845.

Horváth, Eugene [Jenő]. "Kossuth and Palmerston: 1848–1849," *The Slavonic Review* (March 1931), 9(27):612–31.

Horváth, Mihály. *Huszonöt év Magyarország történelméből 1823-tól 1848-ig.* 3 vols. 3d ed. Budapest: Ráth Mór, 1886.

—— *Magyarország függetlenségi harczának története 1848 és 1849-ben.* 3 vols. Geneva: Puky Miklós, 1865.

Horváth, Zoltán. *Teleki László, 1810–1861.* 2 vols. Budapest: Akadémia, 1964. Text and documents.

Hunfalvi, Pál. "Rövid visszapillantás a forradalomra," *Budapesti Szemle* (1883), 24:273–76.

Imrefi. *See* Vahot, Imre.

Irányi, Dániel, and Chassin, Charles-Louis. *Histoire politique de la révolution de Hongrie, 1847–1849.* 2 vols. Paris: Pagnerre, 1859–60.

Isaacs, Bernard, ed. *The Revolution of 1848–49: Articles from the "Neue Rheinische Zeitung" by Karl Marx and Frederick Engels.* Translated from the German by S. Ryazanskaya. New York: International Publishers, 1972.

Jakab, Elek. *Szabadságharczunk történetéhez: Visszaemlékezések 1848–1849-re*. Budapest: Rautmann Frigyes, 1880.

Jánossy, Dénes. *A Kossuth-emigráció Angliában és Amerikában*. 2 vols. Budapest: Magyar Történelmi Társulat, 1940–48. Text and documents.

Jókai, Mór. *Életemből*. 2 vols. Budapest: Révai, 1898.

Károlyi, Árpád. *Az 1848-diki pozsonyi törvénycikkek az udvar előtt*. Budapest: Magyar Történelmi Társulat, 1936. Text and documents.

—— *Németújvári gróf Batthyány Lajos első magyar miniszterelnök főbenjáró pöre*. 2 vols. Budapest: Magyar Történelmi Társulat, 1932. Text and documents.

Kazinczy, Gábor. "Szerepem a forradalomban," *Hazánk*, 1884, pp. 84–105.

Kemény, Gábor G., ed. *Teleki László válogatott munkái*. 2 vols. Budapest: Szépirodalmi Könyvkiadó, 1961.

Kemény, Zsigmond. *Összes művei*. Edited by Pál Gyulai. 12 vols. Vol. XII. *Forradalom után* (1908). Budapest: Franklin, 1897–1908.

Klapka, General [George] [György]. *Memoirs of the War of Independence in Hungary*. 2 vols. London: Charles Gilpin. 1850. [*Memoiren von Georg Klapka*. Leipzig: Otto Wigand, 1850.]

—— *Der Nationalkrieg in Ungarn und Siebenbürgen in den Jahren 1848 und 1849*. 2 vols. Leipzig: Otto Wigand, 1851.

Koltay-Kastner, Jenő, ed. *A Kossuth-emigráció Olaszországban*. Budapest: Akadémia, 1960. Text and documents.

—— *Iratok a Kossuth-emigráció történetéhez, 1859*. Acta Universitatis Szegediensis Sectio Philologica 18. Ser. nova 3. Szeged, 1949.

—— [Eugenio Kastner] *Mazzini e Kossuth: Lettere e Documenti Inediti*. Florence: Felice Le Monnier, 1929.

Kossuth Hírlapja, 1848. Edited by Lajos Kossuth and József Bajza. Daily.

Kossuth Lajos iratai. Edited by Ignácz Helfy and Ferencz Kossuth. 13 vols. Vols. I–III. *Irataim az emigráczióból* (1880–82). Vols. IV–XIII. *Iratai* (1894–1911). Budapest: Athenaeum, 1880–1911.

Kossuth Lajos összes munkái. 11 vols. Vols. I–III. *Országgyűlési Tudósítások*. Edited by A Keleteurópai Tudományos Intézet Történettudományi Intézetének Munkaközössége (1948–49). Vols. IV–V. *Országgyűlési Tudósítások*. Edited by István Barta (1959–61). Vol. VI. *Ifjúkori iratok, Törvényhatósági Tudósítások*. Edited by István Barta (1966). Vol. XI. *Kossuth Lajos az utolsó rendi országgyűlésen, 1847/48*. Edited by István Barta (1951). Vol. XII. *Kossuth Lajos az első magyar felelős minisztériumban, 1848–április–szeptember*. Edited by István Sinkovics (1957). Vol. XIII. *Kossuth Lajos as Országos Honvédelmi Bizottmány élén*. Part I. *1848 szeptember–december*. Edited by István Barta (1952). Vol. XIV. *Kossuth Lajos az Országos Honvédelmi Bizottmány élén*. Part II. *1849 január 1.–április 14*. Edited by István Barta (1953). Vol. XV. *Kossuth Lajos kormányzóelnöki iratai: 1849 április 15.–augusztus 15*. Edited by István Barta (1955). Budapest: Magyar Történelmi Társulat, 1948–66. NOTE: Vols. XI–XV of *Kossuth Lajos összes munkái* are also called *Kossuth Lajos 1848/49-ben*. Vol. XI = Vol. I, Vol. XII = Vol. II, Vol. XIII = Vol. III, Vol. XIV = Vol. IV, Vol. XV = Vol. V.

390 / Sources

Kovács, Lajos. *A békepárt a magyar forradalomban.* Budapest: Révai, 1883.

Kőváry, László, ed. *Okmánytár az 1848–49-ki erdélyi eseményekhez.* Kolozsvár: Demjén László, 1861.

Közlöny. 1848–49. The official daily of the Hungarian government.

Majláth, Béla, ed. *Gróf Széchenyi István levelei.* 3 vols. Budapest: Athenaeum, 1889–91.

Marczali, Henrik, ed. *Gróf Leiningen-Westerburg Károly honvédtábornok levelei és naplója, 1848–1849.* Budapest: Budapesti Hírlap, 1900.

Marx és Engels Magyarországról. Cikkek, levelek, szemelvények. Budapest: Kossuth, 1974.

Mérei, Gyula, ed. *Munkásmozgalmak 1848–49: Iratok a magyar munkásmozgalom történetéhez.* Budapest: Népszava, 1947.

Mészáros, Károly. *Kossuth levelezése a magyar szabadságharc karvezéreivel 1848–1849-ben.* Ungvár: Jäger Károly, 1862.

Miskolczy, Gyula. *A horvát kérdés története és irományai a rendi állam korában.* 2 vols. Budapest: Magyar Történelmi Társulat, 1927–28. Text and documents.

Paget, John. *Hungary and Transylvania; with Remarks on Their Condition, Social, Political and Economical.* 2 vols. New ed. London: John Murray, 1850. Reprint. New York: Arno Press and the New York Times, 1971.

Pálffy, János. *Magyarországi és erdélyi urak: Pálffy János emlékiratai.* Kolozsvár: Erdélyi Szépmíves Céh, n.d.

Pap, Dénes, ed. *A magyar nemzetgyűlés Pesten 1848-ban.* 2 vols. Budapest: Ráth Mór, 1881.

—— *A parlament Debrecenben.* 2 vols. Leipzig: Köhler, 1870.

—— *Okmánytár Magyarország függetlenségi harczának történetéhez 1848–1849.* 2 vols. Pest: Heckenast Gusztáv, 1868–69.

Perényi, J[ózsef]. "Documents relatifs à l'intervention armée russe de 1849 en Hongrie," *Revue d'Histoire Comparée* (1946), 4(3–4): 319–45.

Pesti Hírlap. 1848–49. Edited by Antal Csengery and Zsigmond Kemény. Daily.

Petőfi Sándor összes prózai művei és levelezése. Budapest: Szépirodalmi Könyvkiadó, 1960.

Pillersdorf, Baron [Franz Xaver]. *Austria in 1848 and 1849: The Political Movement in Austria during the Years 1848 and 1849.* Translated by George Gaskell. London: Richard Bentley, 1850.

Pulszky, Ferenc. *Életem és korom.* 2 vols. 1st ed. 1880. Here: Budapest: Szépirodalmi Könyvkiadó, 1958. [Franz Pulszky. *Meine Zeit, mein Leben.* 3 vols. Pressburg-Leipzig: C. Stampfel, 1880–83.]

Pulszky, Theresa. *Memoirs of a Hungarian Lady.* Philadelphia: Lea and Blanchard, 1850.

Rapant, Daniel. *Slovenske povstanie roku 1848–49.* 5 vols. Turciansky Sväty Martin and Bratislava, 1930–50.

Rüstow, W. *Geschichte des ungarischen Insurrectionskrieges in den Jahren 1848 und 1849.* 2 vols. Zurich: Friedrich Schulthess, 1860–61.

Sinkovics, István, ed. *Kossuth Lajos.* See Kossuth Lajos.

Springer, Johann. *Statistik des österreichischen Kaiserstaates.* 2 vols. Vienna: Fr. Beck's Universitäts-Buchhandlung, 1840.

Steier, Lajos. *Beniczky Lajos bányavidéki kormánybiztos és honvédezredes visz-szaemlékezései és jelentései az 1848/49-iki szabadságharcról és tót mozgalomról.* Budapest: Magyar Történelmi Társulat, 1924. Text and documents.

—— *Az 1849-i trónfosztás előzményei és következményei: Ismeretlen adatok az 1848–49-i szabadságharc történetéhez.* Budapest: Genius, 1925. Text and documents.

—— *Görgey és Kossuth: Ismeretlen adalékok az 1848–49-iki szabadságharc történetéhez.* Budapest: Genius, [1924]. Text and documents.

—— *Haynau és Paskievics: Ismeretlen adalékok az 1848–49-iki szabadságharc történetéhez.* 2 vols. Budapest: Genius, n.d. Text and documents.

—— *A tót nemzetiségi kérdés 1848–49-ben.* 2 vols. Budapest: Magyar Történelmi Társulat, 1937.

Stiles, William Henry. *Austria in 1848–49.* 2 vols. New York: Harper and Brothers, 1852. Reprint. New York: Arno Press and the New York Times, 1971.

Széchenyi István (Gróf) összes munkái. See Viszota, Gyula, ed.

Szekfű, Gyula, ed. *Iratok a magyar államnyelv kérdésének történetéhez, 1790–1848.* Budapest: Magyar Történelmi Társulat, 1926.

Szemere, Bartholomew [Bertalan] de. *Hungary from 1848 to 1860.* London: Richard Bentley, 1860.

Szeremlei, Samu, ed. *Magyarország krónikája az 1848. és 1849. évi forradalom idejéről.* 2 vols. Pest: Emich Gusztáv, 1867.

Szilágyi, Sándor. *A magyar forradalom férfiai 1848–49-ből.* Pest: Heckenast Gusztáv, 1850.

Szokoly, Viktor, ed. *Mészáros Lázár emlékiratai.* 2 vols. 2d ed. Budapest: Ráth Mór, 1881.

—— *Mészáros Lázár külföldi levelei és életirata.* Budapest: Ráth Mór, 1881.

Táncsics, Mihály. *Életpályám.* Budapest: Révai, 1949.

Thim, József. *A magyarországi 1848–49-iki szerb fölkelés története.* 3 vols. Budapest: Magyar Történelmi Társulat, 1930–40. Text and documents.

Vahot, Imre [Imrefi]. *A magyar menekültek Törökországban.* Pest: Heckenast Gusztáv, 1850.

Verzeichniss der wegen Hochverrathes durch Theilnahme an der ungarischen Revolution gefällten kriegsgerichtlichen Urtheile. n.p., n.d.

Viszota, Gyula, ed. *Gróf Széchenyi István naplói.* 6 vols. Budapest: Magyar Történelmi Társulat, 1925–39. Also published as *Gróf Széchenyi István összes munkái,* vols. x–xv.

Vukovics, Sebő. *Emlékiratai.* Budapest: Athenaeum, 1894.

Waldapfel, Eszter, ed. *A forradalom és szabadságharc levelestára.* 4 vols. Budapest: Közoktatásügyi Kiadóvállalat-Művelt Nép-Gondolat, 1950–65.

Walter, Friedrich, ed. *Magyarische Rebellenbriefe 1848.* Munich: R. Oldenbourg, 1964.

Welden, Freiherr Ludwig von. *Episoden aus meinem Leben: Beiträge zur Geschichte der Feldzüge der österreichischen Armee in den Jahren 1848 und 1849.* Graz: Damian und Sorge, 1853.

Wrede, Major Alphons Freiherr von. *Geschichte der k. und k. Wehrmacht: Die Regimenter, Corps, Branchen und Anstalten von 1618 zum Ende des XIX. Jahrhunderts.* 5 vols. Vienna: L. W. Seidel, 1893–1900.

392 / Sources

Zsoldos, Jenő, ed. *1848–49 a magyar zsidóság életében.* Budapest: A Pesti Izr. Hitközség . . . 48-as Ifjúsági Bizottsága, 1948.

4. Secondary Works

Acsády, Ignác. *A magyar jobbágyság története.* 2d ed. Budapest: Faust Imre, 1944.
Andics, Erzsébet. *Az egyházi reakció 1848–49-ben.* Budapest: Szikra, 1949.
—— *1848–1849: Tanulmányok.* Budapest: Kossuth, 1968.
—— *Kossuth en lutte contre les ennemis des réformes et de la révolution.* Studia Historica Academiae Scientiarium Hungaricae, 12. Budapest: Academia Scientiarium Hungarica, 1954. [*Kossuth harca az árulók és megalkuvók ellen.* Budapest: Szikra, 1955.]
—— *Metternich und die Frage Ungarns.* Budapest: Akadémia, 1973. [*Metternich és Magyarország.* Budapest: Akadémia, 1975.]
Angeli, Moriz von. *Wien nach 1848.* Vienna and Leipzig: Wilhelm Braumüller, 1905.
Arató, Endre. *A feudális nemzetiségtől a polgári nemzetig.* Budapest: Akadémia, 1975.
—— *Kelet-Európa története a 19. század első felében.* Budapest: Akadémia, 1971.
—— *A nemzetiségi kérdés története Magyarországon, 1790–1840.* 2 vols. Budapest: Akadémia, 1960.
Averbukh, R. A. *A magyar nép szabadságküzdelme 1848–49-ben. Revoliutsiia ia natsional'no-osvoboditel'naia bor'ba v Vengrii, 1848–1849.* Translated by József Perényi. Budapest: Akadémia, 1970.
Bach, Maximilian. *Geschichte der Wiener Revolution im Jahre 1848.* Vienna: Erste Wiener Volksbuchhandlung, 1898.
Bakó, Imre. *A magyar állami "Országos Fegyvergyár" működése 1848–49-ben.* Budapest: 1942.
Balassa, József. *Kossuth Amerikában, 1851–1852.* Budapest: Gergely R., 1931.
Barany, George. "The Awakening of Magyar Nationalism Before 1848." *Austrian History Yearbook,* II (1966), 19–54.
—— *Stephen Széchenyi and the Awakening of Hungarian Nationalism, 1791–1841.* Princeton, N.J.: Princeton University Press, 1968.
—— "Ungarns Verwaltung: 1848–1918," in Adam Wandruszka and Peter Urbanitsch, eds., *Die Habsburgermonarchie 1848–1918.* 2 vols. Vienna: Verlag der Österreichischen Akademie der Wissenschaften, 1975. Vol. II, *Verwaltung und Rechtswesen,* pp. 306–468.
Baron, Salo W. "The Impact of the Revolution of 1848 on Jewish Emancipation." *Jewish Social Studies* (July 1949), 11(3):195–248.
Barta, István. "Az 1849. január 2-i haditanács és a főváros kiürítése," *Hadtörténelmi Közlemények* (1955), 2(2):66–100.
—— *A fiatal Kossuth.* Budapest: Akadémia, 1966.
—— "István Széchenyi," *Acta Historica* (1960), 7(1–2):63–102. In English.
—— "A kormány parasztpolitikája 1849-ben," *Századok* (1956), 90(1–2):4–68.

—— "Kossuth alföldi toborzó körútja 1848 őszén," *Századok* (1952), 86(1):149–66.

—— "A magyar szabadságharc vezetői és a bécsi októberi forradalom," *Századok* (1951), 85 (3–4):443–85.

Beer, Adolf. *Die Finanzen Oesterreichs*. Prague: F. Tempsky, 1877.

Beksics, Gusztáv. *Kemény Zsigmond. A forradalom s a kiegyezés*. Budapest: Athenaeum, 1883.

Bernstein, Lottelore C. M. "Revolution and Response: Radical Thought in Vienna's Free Press in 1848." Ph.D. dissertation, Columbia University, 1972.

Bleyer, Lenke. *Gróf Zichy-féle gyémántpör*. Debrecen, 1931.

Blum, Jerome. *Noble Landowners and Agriculture in Austria 1815–1848: A Study in the Origins of the Peasant Emancipation of 1848*. Baltimore: Johns Hopkins Press, 1948.

Bodea, Cornelia. *The Romanians' Struggle for Unification, 1834–1849*. Bucharest: Academy of the Socialist Republic of Romania, 1970.

Bödy, Paul. *Joseph Eötvös and the Modernization of Hungary 1840–1870: A Study of Ideas of Individuality and Social Pluralism in Modern Politics*. In *Transactions of the American Philosophical Society* (1972), n.s. 62(2).

Bogdan-Duica, Gheorghe. *Eftimie Murgu*. Bucharest: Imprimeria naţională, 1937.

Bogdanov, Vaso. *Društvene i političke borbe u Hrvatskoj 1848/49*. Zagreb: JAZU, 1949.

—— *Hrvatska ljevica u godinama revolucije 1848–49 u svijetlu naše četrdesetosnaške štampe*. Zagreb: Matica Hrvatska, 1949.

—— *Ustanak Srba u Vojvodini i Madjarska Revolucija 1848–49*. Subotica: Gradska Stamparija, 1929.

Cheresteşiu, Victor. *Adunarea naţională de la Blaj*. Bucharest: Editura Politică, 1966.

Csabai, Tibor. *Kossuth Lajos és az irodalom*. Budapest: Gondolat, 1961.

Csizmadia, Andor. *A magyar választási rendszer 1848–1849-ben: Az első népképviseleti választások*. Budapest: Közgazdasági és Jogi Könyvkiadó, 1963.

Deme, Laszlo. "The Committee of Public Safety in the Hungarian Revolution of 1848," *Canadian Slavic Studies* (Fall 1971), 5(3):383–400.

—— *The Radical Left in the Hungarian Revolution of 1848*. Boulder, Colo: East European Quarterly, 1976. Distributed by Columbia University Press.

—— "The Society for Equality in the Hungarian Revolution of 1848," *Slavic Review* (March 1972), 31(1):71–88.

Demény, Lajos, et al. *1848: Arcok, eszmék, tettek (Tanulmányok)*. Bucharest: Kriterion, 1974.

Despalatović, Elinor M. *Ljudevit Gaj and the Illyrian Movement*. Boulder, Colo.: East European Quarterly, 1975. Distributed by Columbia University Press.

Domanovszky, Sándor. *Magyar művelődéstörténet*. 4 vols. Budapest: Magyar Történelmi Társulat, n.d.

Dragomir, Silviu. *Avram Iancu*. Bucharest: Editura Ştiinţifică, 1965.

Eckhart, Ferenc. *Magyar alkotmány- és jogtörténet*. Budapest: Politzer A., 1946.

Ember, Győző. *Az újkori magyar közigazgatás története*. Budapest: "Budapest" Irodalmi, Művészeti és Tudományos Intézet, 1946.

d'Eszlary, Charles. *Histoire des institutions publiques hongroises.* 3 vols. Paris: Marcel Rivière, 1959–65.

Faragó, Miksa. *A Kossuth-bankók kora. A szabadságharc pénzügyei.* Budapest: Nyugat, n.d.

Fejto, François, ed. *The Opening of an Era 1848: An Historical Symposium.* Introduction by A. J. P. Taylor. New York: Howard Fertig, 1966.

Friedjung, Heinrich. *Österreich von 1848 bis 1860.* 2 vols. Stuttgart and Berlin: J. G. Cotta'sche Buchhandlung, 1908.

Gogolák, Ludwig von. *Beiträge zur Geschichte des slowakischen Volkes.* Vol. III. *Zwischen zwei Revolutionen (1848–1919).* Munich: R. Oldenbourg, 1972.

Göllner, Carl. *Die Siebenbürger Sachsen in den Revolutionsjahren 1848–1849.* Bucharest: Verlag der Akademie der Sozialistischen Republik Rumänien, 1967.

Gosztony, Peter. "Die Verteidigung der Festung Buda durch General Hentzi im Frühjahr 1849," *Allgemeine Schweizerische Militärzeitschrift* (August 1967), pp. 474–80.

Hajnal, István. *A Batthyány-kormány külpolitikája.* Budapest: Akadémia, 1957.

Hanák, Péter. "Rapporti storici italo-ungherese verso la metà del secolo XIX," *Acta Historica* (1955), 4(1–3):211–34.

Hanák, Péter, ed. *Magyarország története, 1849–1918.* Budapest: Tankönyvkiadó, 1972.

Handlery, George. "General Arthur Görgey and the Hungarian Revolution of 1848–49." Ph.D. dissertation, University of Oregon, 1968.

Hegedüs, Lajos. *Kossuth Lajos, legendák hőse.* Budapest: Athenaeum, n.d.

Helfert, Joseph A. *Geschichte der österreichischen Revolution im Zusammenhange mit der mitteleuropäischen Bewegung der Jahre 1848–1849.* 2 vols. Freiburg-Vienna: Herder, 1907–9.

—— *Geschichte Oesterreichs vom Ausgange des Wiener October-Aufstandes 1848.* 4 vols. Leipzig: G. E. Schulze; Prague: F. Tempsky, 1869–86.

Hentaller, Lajos. *Kossuth és kora.* Budapest: Athenaeum, 1894.

Hidas, Peter L. "The first Russian Intervention in Transylvania." In *Eastern Europe. Historical Essays.* edited by H. D. Schlieper. Toronto: University of Toronto Press, 1969, pp. 67–79.

—— *The Metamorphosis of a Social Class in Hungary During the Reign of Young Francis Joseph.* Boulder, Colo.: East European Quarterly, 1977. Distributed by Columbia University Press.

—— "The Russian Army in Hungary, 1849," *The New Review* (December 1971), vol. 11, pp. 73–83.

Hitchins, Keith. *The Rumanian National Movement in Transylvania 1780–1849.* Cambridge, Mass.: Harvard University Press, 1969.

Hóman, Bálint, and Szekfű, Gyula. *Magyar történet.* 5 vols. Budapest: Királyi Magyar Egyetemi Nyomda, 1935–36.

Incze, Heinrich. *Die Geschichte des 15. März in Buda Pesth.* Budapest: Sigmund Deutsch, 1900.

Jancsó, Benedek. *A román nemzetiségi törekvések története és jelenlegi állapota.* 2 vols. Budapest: Lampel R., 1896–99.

Jászi, Oszkár. *A nemzeti államok kialakulása és a nemzetiségi kérdés.* Budapest: Grill Károly, 1912.

Kann, Robert A. *A History of the Habsburg Empire, 1526–1918.* Berkeley and Los Angeles: University of California Press, 1974.

—— *The Multinational Empire: Nationalism and National Reform in the Habsburg Monarchy, 1848–1918.* 2 vols. New York: Octagon Books, 1970.

Kerchnawe, Hugo. *Feldmarschall Fürst Windisch-Graetz und die Russenhilfe 1848.* Innsbruck: Wagner, 1930.

Király, Béla K. *Ferenc Deák.* Twayne's World Leaders Series. Boston: Twayne, 1975.

—— *Hungary in the Late Eighteenth Century: The Decline of Enlightened Despotism.* New York and London: Columbia University Press, 1969.

Kiszling, Rudolf. "Das Nationalitätenproblem in Habsburgs Wehrmacht 1848–1918," *Der Donauraum,* (1959), 4(2):82–92.

Kiszling, Rudolf, et al. *Die Revolution im Kaisertum Österreich 1848–1849.* 2 vols. Vienna: Universum Verlag, 1948.

Komlos, John H. *Louis Kossuth in America, 1851–1852.* Foreword by C. A. Macartney. Buffalo, N.Y.: East European Institute of the State University of New York, College at Buffalo, 1973.

Kosáry, Domokos. *A Görgey-kérdés és története.* Budapest: Magyar Egyetemi Nyomda, 1936.

—— *Kossuth és a Védegylet: A magyar nacionalizmus történetéhez.* Budapest: Athenaeum, 1942.

—— *Kossuth Lajos a reformkorban.* Budapest: Antiqua, 1946.

Kovács, Endre. *Bem József.* Budapest: Hadtörténelmi Intézet, 1954.

—— *A Kossuth-emigráció és az európai szabadságmozgalmak.* Budapest: Akadémia, 1967.

—— *A lengyel kérdés a reformkori Magyarországon.* Budapest: Akadémia, 1959.

—— *Magyar-délszláv megbékélési törekvések 1848/49-ben.* Budapest: Akadémia, 1958.

Kukiel, M. *Czartoryski and European Unity, 1770–1861.* Princeton, N.J.: Princeton University Press, 1955.

[Laurian, August Treboniu.] *Die Romänen der österreichischen Monarchie.* 3 vols. Vienna, 1849–51.

Lengyel, Tamás. *Gróf Teleki László.* Budapest: Franklin Társulat, n.d.

Lukács, Lajos, Mérei, Gyula, and Spira, György. *Kossuth Lajos: Rövid életrajz.* Budapest: Művelt Nép, 1952.

Lutz, Rolland R. "The Aula and the Vienna Radical Movement of 1848." Ph. D. dissertation, Cornell University, 1956.

Macartney, C. A. *The Habsburg Empire 1790–1918.* New York: Macmillan, 1969.

Marczali, Henrik. *Hungary in the Eighteenth Century.* New York: Arno Press and the New York Times, 1971.

Márkus, László. *Guyon Richárd.* Budapest: Művelt Nép, 1955.

Marx, Julius. *Die wirtschaftlichen Ursachen der Revolution von 1848 in Österreich.* Graz-Cologne: Hermann Böhlaus, 1965.

Matula, Vladimir. *L'udovit Štúr 1815–1856.* Bratislava: Verlag der Slowakischen Akademie der Wissenschaften, 1956.

Mérei, Gyula. "L'essor de l'agriculture capitaliste en Hongrie dans la première moitié du xixe siècle," *Revue d'histoire moderne et contemporaine* (January–March, 1965), 12(1):51–64.

—— *Mezőgazdaság és agrártársadalom Magyarországon, 1790–1848.* Budapest: Akadémia, 1948.

—— *Über einige Fragen der Anfänge der kapitalistischen Gewerbeentwicklung in Ungarn.* Budapest: Studia Historica no. 30, 1960.

Meszlényi, Antal. *A magyar katholikus egyház és állam 1848/49-ben.* Budapest: Szent István Társulat, 1928.

Miskolczy, Gyula. *A Kamarilla a Reformkorszakban.* Budapest: Franklin, n.d.

Mód, Aladár, et al. *Forradalom és szabadságharc, 1848–1849.* Budapest: Szikra, 1948.

—— *Pártharcok és a kormány politikája 1848–49-ben.* Budapest: Szikra, 1949.

Müller, Paul. *Feldmarschall Fürst Windischgrätz: Revolution und Gegenrevolution in Österreich.* Vienna: Wilhelm Braumüller, 1934.

Nagy, Tibor. "Az első magyar pénzügyminiszteri expozé," *Pénzügyi Szemle* (1963), 8:121–215.

—— "Költségvetés és költségvetési jog 1848/49-ben," *Állam és Igazgatás* (1955), 3/4:221–32.

—— "Kossuth költségvetése," *Pénzügyi Szemle* (1955), 5:341–50.

Niederhauser, Emil. "The Problems of Bourgeois Transformation in Eastern and South-Eastern Europe," *Nouvelles études historiques publiées à l'occasion du XIIe Congrès International des Sciences Historiques par la Commission Nationale des Historiens Hongrois.* 2 vols. Vol. i, pp. 565–80. Budapest: Akadémia, 1965.

Păcaţian, Teodor V. *Cartea de aur, sau luptele politice-nationale ale Românilor sub coroana ungară.* Sibiu, 1904.

Pamlényi, Ervin, ed. *A History of Hungary.* London and Wellingborough: Collet's, 1975.

Pech, Stanley Z. *The Czech Revolution of 1848.* Chapel Hill: University of North Carolina Press, 1969.

—— "The Nationalist Movements of the Austrian Slavs in 1848: A Comparative Sociological Profile," *Histoire sociale/Social History* (Ottawa) (November 1976), vol. 9, pp. 336–56.

Pethő, Sándor. *Görgey Artúr.* Budapest: Genius, 1930.

—— *A szabadságharc eszméi.* Budapest: Az "Élet," 1916.

Pollak, Walter. *1848: Revolution auf halbem Wege.* Vienna: Europa-Verlag, 1974.

Preradovich, Nikolaus von. *Die Führungsschichten in Österreich und Preussen (1804–1918): Mit einem Ausblick bis zum Jahre 1945.* Wiesbaden: Franz Steiner, 1955.

Rath, R. John. *The Viennese Revolution of 1848.* Austin: University of Texas Press, 1957.

Redlich, Joseph. *Emperor Francis Joseph of Austria.* New York: Macmillan, 1929.

Reményi, Joseph. *Hungarian Writers and Literature*. Edited and with introduction by August J. Molnar. New Brunswick, N.J.: Rutgers University Press, 1964.

Révai, József. *Kossuth Lajos*. Budapest: Szikra, 1945.

—— *Marx és a magyar forradalom*. Budapest: Szikra, 1953.

—— *Marxizmus és magyarság*. Budapest: Szikra, 1946.

—— *Válogatott történelmi írások*. 2 vols. Budapest: Kossuth, 1966.

Roberts, Henry L. *Four Queens and Several Knaves*. Introduction by Radmila Milentijević. New York: Institute on East Central Europe and Russian Institute, Columbia University, n.d.

Robertson, Priscilla. *Revolutions of 1848. A Social History*. Princeton, N.J.: Princeton University Press, 1952.

Rock, Kenneth W. "Felix Schwarzenberg, Military Diplomat," *Austrian History Yearbook* (1975), vol. 11, pp. 85–109.

—— "Schwarzenberg versus Nicholas I, Round One: The Negotiation of the Habsburg-Romanov Alliance against Hungary in 1849," *Austrian History Yearbook* (1970–71), vol. 6/7, pp. 109–41.

Rothenberg, Gunther Erich. *The Army of Francis Joseph*. West Lafayette, Ind.: Purdue University Press, 1976.

—— "The Habsburg Army and the Nationality Problem in the Nineteenth Century, 1815–1914," *Austrian History Yearbook* (1967), 3(1):70–87.

—— *The Military Border in Croatia 1740–1881: A Study of an Imperial Institution*. Chicago: University of Chicago Press, 1966.

Sarlós, Béla. *Deák és Vukovics: Két igazságügy-miniszter*. Budapest: Akadémia, 1970.

Sárközi, Zoltán. *Az erdélyi szászok 1848–1849-ben*. Budapest: Akadémia, 1974.

Schwarzenberg, Adolph. *Prince Felix zu Schwarzenberg: Prime Minister of Austria, 1848–1852*. New York: Columbia University Press, 1946.

Silagi, Denis. *Der grösste Ungar. Graf Stephan Széchenyi*. Vienna and Munich: Herold, 1967.

Sirokay, Zoltán. *Mészáros Lázár tábornok az első magyar hadügyminiszter*. Mátészalka, 1928.

Spira, György. "Le grand jour (Le 15 Mars, 1848)," *Études historiques 1970 publiées à l'occasion du XIII Congrès International des Sciences Historiques par la Commission Nationale des Historiens Hongrois*. 2 vols. Budapest: Akadémia, 1970.

—— *1848 Széchenyije és Széchenyi 1848-a*. Budapest: Akadémia, 1964.

—— *A Hungarian Count in the Revolution of 1848*. Translated by Thomas Land. Translation revised by Richard E. Allen. Budapest: Akadémia, 1974.

—— *A magyar forradalom 1848–49-ben*. Budapest: Gondolat, 1959.

——. *A negyvennyolcas nemzedék nyomában*. Budapest: Magvető, 1973.

Spira, György, and Szűcs, Jenő, eds. *A negyvennyolcas forradalom kérdései*. Budapest: Akadémia, 1976.

Spira, Thomas. "Aspects of the Magyar Linguistic and Literary Renaissance during the Vormärz," *East European Quarterly* (Summer, 1973), 7(2):101–24.

Springer, Anton. *Geschichte Österreichs seit dem Wiener Frieden 1809*. 2 vols. Leipzig: S. Hirzel, 1863–65.

Sproxton, Charles. *Palmerston and the Hungarian Revolution.* Cambridge: At the University Press, 1919.

Stroup, Edsel Walter. *Hungary in Early 1848: The Constitutional Struggle against Absolutism in Contemporary Eyes.* Foreword by Steven Béla Várdy. Buffalo, N.Y., and Atlanta, Ga.: Hungarian Cultural Foundation, 1977. Detailed bibliography.

Suciu, I. D. *Revoluția de la 1848–1849 in Banat.* Bucharest: Editura Academiei Republicii Socialiste România, 1968.

Szabad, György. *Forradalom és Kiegyezés válaszútján (1860–61).* Budapest: Akadémia, 1967.

—— *Kossuth politikai pályája ismert és ismeretlen megnyilatkozásai tükrében.* Budapest: Kossuth Könyvkiadó, 1977.

Szabó, Ervin, *Társadalmi és pártharcok a 48–49-es magyar forradalomban.* Vienna: Bécsi Magyar Kiadó, 1921. 2d ed. Budapest: Népszava, [1945]. 3d ed. Budapest: Szikra, 1949.

—— "Aus den Parteien und Klassenkämpfen in der ungarischen Revolution um 1848," *Archiv für die Geschichte des Sozialismus* (1919), vol. 7, pp. 258–307.

Szabó, István, ed. *A szabadságharc fővárosa Debrecen, 1849 január-május.* Debrecen: Debrecen város és a tiszántúli református egyházkerület, 1948.

Széchenyi issue of the *Journal of Central European Affairs* (October 1960), vol. 20, no. 3.

Szekfű, Gyula. *Három nemzedék és ami utána következik.* Budapest: Királyi Magyar Egyetemi Nyomda, 1934.

Szekfű, Gyula, ed. *Iratok a magyar államnyelv kérdésének történetéhez, 1790–1848.* Budapest: Magyar Történelmi Társulat, 1926.

Szilassy, Sándor. "America and the Hungarian Revolution of 1848–49," *Slavonic and East European Review* (January 1966), pp. 180–96.

Szőcs, Sebestyén. *A kormánybiztosi intézmény kialakulása 1848-ban.* Budapest: Akadémia, 1972.

Tamás, Anna, and Wéber, Antal, eds. *Petőfi tüze: Tanulmányok Petőfi Sándorról.* Budapest: Kossuth-Zrinyi, 1972.

Tapié, Victor-L. *The Rise and Fall of the Habsburg Monarchy.* Translated by Stephen Hardman. New York: Praeger, 1971.

Tóth, Zoltán I. *Az erdélyi és magyarországi román nemzeti mozgalom, 1790–1848.* Akadémia, 1959.

—— "The Nationality Problem in Hungary in 1848–1849," *Acta Historica* (1955), 4(1–3):235–77.

—— "A soknemzetiségű állam néhány kérdéséről az 1848 előtti Magyarországon," *MTA Társadalomtörténeti Tudományok Osztályának Közleményei* (1956), 7(4):259–79.

Tóth, Zoltán I., ed. *Emlékkönyv Kossuth Lajos születésének 150. évfordulójára.* 2 vols. Budapest: Akadémia, 1952.

Trócsányi, Zsolt. *Az erdélyi parasztság története, 1790–1849.* Budapest: Akadémia, 1956.

—— *Wesselényi Miklós.* Budapest: Akadémia, 1965.

Urbán, Aladár. "Agitáció és kormányválság 1848 májusában," *Történelmi Szemle* (1970), pp. 344–66.

—— "A Batthyány-kormány hadügyi politikájának első szakasza (1848. április-május)," *Hadtörténelmi Közlemények* (1971), 18(2):211–35.

—— "Die Bewaffnung der ungarischen Nationalgarde im Sommer 1848," *Annales Universitatis Scientiarum Budapestinensis . . . Sectio Historica* (1966), 8:115–37.

—— "Honvédtoborzás Pest-Budán 1848-ban," *Tanulmányok Budapest múltjából* (1963), 15:403–43.

—— *A nemzetőrség és honvédség szervezése 1848 nyarán.* Budapest: Akadémia, 1973.

—— "Die Organisierung des Heeres der ungarischen Revolution vom Jahre 1848," part 1, *Annales Universitatis Scientiarum Budapestinensis . . . Sectio Historica*, (1967), 9:105–30.

—— "Die Organisierung des Heeres der ungarischen Revolution vom Jahre 1848," part 2, *Annales Universitatis Scientiarum Budapestinensis . . . Sectio Historica* (1972), 13:159–82.

—— "Zehn kritische Tage aus der Geschichte der Batthyány-Regierung (10–20. Mai 1848)," *Annales Universitatis Scientiarium Budapestinensis . . . Sectio Historica* (1960), 2:91–124.

Valjavec, Friedrich. "Ungarn und die Frage des österreichischen Gesamtstaates zu Beginn des Jahres 1849," *Historische Zeitschrift* (1941), pp. 91–98.

Varga, János. *A jobbágyfelszabadítás kivívása 1848-ban.* Budapest: Akadémia, 1971.

—— *Typen und Probleme des bäuerlichen Grundbesitzes in Ungarn, 1767–1849.* Budapest: Studia Historica Academiae Scientiarum Hungaricae, 1965.

Vas, Zoltán. *Kossuth Lajos élete.* 2 vols. 2d ed. Budapest: Magvető, 1965.

Waldapfel, Eszter. *A független magyar külpolitika 1848–1849.* Budapest: Akadémia, 1962.

Walter, Friedrich. "Die Beteiligung der magyarischen Protestanten an der Revolution 1848–49." in *Gedenkschrift für Harold Steinacker,* pp. 267–76. Munich: R. Oldenbourg, 1966.

Walter, Friedrich, ed. *Die österreichische Zentralverwaltung.* Vol. I, Part III. Vienna: Adolf Holzhausen, 1964.

Walter, Friedrich, and Steinacker, Harold. *Die Nationalitätenfrage im alten Ungarn und die Südostpolitik Wiens.* Munich: R. Oldenbourg, 1959.

Zarek, Otto. *Kossuth: die Liebe eines Volkes.* Zurich: Bibliothek Zeitgenössischer Werke, 1935. [Translated as *Kossuth* by Lynton Hudson. London: Selwyn and Blount, 1937.]

Index

Absentees' deputy (*ablegatus absentium*), 23-24, 29

Academic Legion, *see* Vienna University students

Academy of Sciences, Hungarian, 26, 69

"Administrators," county, 54, 59, 98

"Affair of the Diamonds," 220-21, 257

Agriculture, *see* Peasants

Agyagfalva assembly, 208-9

Albrecht, archduke, XX, 77

Alexander, tsar, 25

Alispán (deputy lord-lieutenant), 16, 228, 283, 335

Allgemeine Hofkammer (General Treasury), 14, 179

Andics, Erzsébet, historian, 219, 326-27

Andrássy, Count György, 245-46

Andrássy, Count Gyula (Julius), 248, 299, 336; prepares Compromise Agreement, 347-48

Apponyi, Count György, 54, 57, 59, 67

April Laws, 91-106, 127, 183, 192, 212, 234, 269, 317; historically evaluated, 99-106

Arad, fortress and city: as an Austrian stronghold, 193-94, 232, 236, 304; as Hungary's temporary capital, 318-23, 338; Austrian military court at, 246, 330, 332, 334

Arany, János, 143

Aristocrats, *see* Nobles, Hungarian

Armenians, 51

Army of the Upper Danube, 211, 232-34, 305, 308

Arndt, Ernst Moritz, 44

Artisans, *see* Workers and artisans in Hungary

Aula, *see* Vienna University students

Austria, Austrian Empire, *see* Habsburg Monarchy

Austrian army, *see* Habsburg army

Austrian government before 1848, *see* Habsburgs

Austrian government in 1848/1849, xiii, 89, 246; created in March, 79; changes in, 108, 132; its policy of centralization and its August 31 memorandum to Hungary, 138-40, 149-51, 156-57; endorses Lamberg's appointment, 171-73; flees to Olmütz, 179; Schwarzenberg cabinet created, 201-3; and the Stadion Constitution, 249-52; its Russian alliance, 285-90; and punitive measures against the Hungarians, 326-27, 329-37; its efforts to get the revolutionaries extradited from the Ottoman Empire, 340-41

Austrian parliament, *see* Reichstag

Bach, Dr. Alexander, 105, 202, 341

Baillet von Latour, General Count Theodor, 152-53, 213, 332, 334; his ambiguous policy toward Hungary, 139-42, 165; supports Jelačić, 156, 171-73; assassinated, 179

Bălcescu, Nicolae, 313

Balogh, Kornél, 66

Banat, 273, 277, 347

Barany, George, historian, 41-42

Bărnuţiu, Simion, 126

Baron, Salo, historian, 115

Bastide, Jules, 294

effectives during the spring campaign, 255, 266; and the Declaration of Independence, 259-60, 263; and the siege of Castle Hill, 268-70, 273-74; army bill of April and the failure of the conscription, 280-81; generals against Kossuth, 283-84; Polish legion in, 290-91; Hungarian legion in Italy, 299; effectives in the summer of 1849, 302-5; at the battle of Temesvár, 319-20; surrender and disbandment, 323-25, 328-29; total casualties, 329; retribution against, 329-37; soldiers in exile, 338-39; *honvéd* officers in the American Civil War, 345

Horthy, Admiral Regent Miklós (Nicholas), 183, 264, 322n

Horváth, Bishop Mihály; on the April Laws, 101, 103; on Kossuth and his wife, 253-54; enters second Hungarian cabinet, 277

Hotel Lambert, 295-96

House of Austria, *see* Habsburgs

House of Representatives, *see* National Assembly, Hungarian

Hrabovsky, General Baron János: attacks Serbs at Karlóca, 129; royal commissioner in Croatia-Slavonia, 134-35, 137; imprisoned, 331

Hugo, Victor, 294

Hungarian army, *see* Honvéd

Hungarian chancellery, 6, 14-15, 54, 93, 112

Hungarian constitution of 1848, *see* April Laws

Hungarian Diet, *see* Diet, Hungarian

Hungarian government, 192, 281, 307; constituted in March 1848, 87-91; its meeting of April 12, 110-12; and the non-Magyar nationalities, 122; creates national army, 134-35; attempts reconciliation with the Croats, 157-58; second government formed, 276-77, 279; reorganizes judiciary and system of government commissioners, 282-83; first government's relations with Russia, 286-87; launches crusade against Russians, 291-93; moves from Budapest to Szeged and submits bills on nationality and the Jews, 311-15

Hungarian language laws, 16, 20, 28, 35, 42-47, 56, 97

Hungarian legion in Italy, 299, 346

Hungarian National Assembly, *see* National Assembly, Hungarian

Hungarian National Directorate, 346

Hungarian nationalism, xiii, xv-xvi, 27-28, 41-46, 53, 56, 59, 61

Hungarian Noble Guards in Vienna, 184

Hurban, Jozef M., 123, 167, 242

Iancu, Avram, 125, 272; his relations with the Hungarians, 312-14

Illyrian movement, *see* Croats

Imperial-Royal army, *see* Habsburg army

Imperial Treasury *see* General Treasury

Indigenae, 4

Innsbruck, 109, 126, 129, 132, 137-38, 149

Insurrectio of the Hungarian nobles (1809), 4

Iowa state, 221n

Irányi, Dániel, 259

Istanbul, 299, 341; *see also* Ottoman Empire

Italy, Italians, Italian revolution, xvii, 60, 79, 109, 142, 145-48, 189-91, 197, 203, 259, 299, 301, 335, 339, 346; *see also* Lombardy; Milan; Piedmont-Sardinia; Rome; Venice

Jacobins in France, 220, 224-25, 227

Jassy, 121

Jászok, see Jazygi

Jazygi (*Jászok*), 5

Jelačić, General Baron Josip, xix, 139, 150, 175, 185, 193, 287, 294, 302, 304; appointed *ban*, 79, 81; ordered to Budapest, 112; incites Croats against Hungary, 131-32; defies Hrabovszky, 134-35; denounced by king, 137; rehabilitated, 155-57; invades Hungary, 161-65, 168-71; royal plenipotentiary in Hungary, 173

Jersey City, N.J., 343

Jesuits, 42

Jews, xv, 10, 22, 35, 45, 119-20, 240; their numbers and condition, 51; and the pogroms, 86; excluded from the franchise, 97; their situation as a result of the April Laws, 101-2, 113-16; excused from the National Guard, 113-14; their patriotism and services to the Revolution, 115-16; emancipated, 314-15

John (Johann), archduke, xx, 77; opens Reichstag, 149

Jókai, Mór, 330

Joseph, archduke-palatine, 46

Joseph II, emperor-king, xix, 3, 7, 44; frees the serfs, 38; his language ordinance, 42-43; his Edict of Toleration, 114

and the Galician peasant revolt, 54-55; in the Pest county elections, 57-58; their continued franchise under the April Laws, 97-98; dominate National Assembly, 143; in the Habsburg army, 189-190; Windisch-Graetz and Schwarzenberg on, 202-3, 241-43; in the Debrecen House of Representatives, 219; aristocrats in the *honvéd*, 219; Hungarian conservatives on, 244-46; their declining support of the war after April 1849, 264; their proportion among those sentenced after the war, 332-33, 335; their postwar economic position, 347

Non-Magyar nationalities, xiii, xvi, 42, 45-46, 348; their situation as a result of the April Laws, 103; their policies in 1848, 119-31; and Windisch-Graetz, 243; and the nationality law of July 1849, 314

Nyáry, Pál, 136, 220, 224, 245; and message to the Frankfurt Assembly, 152

Obergespann (lord-lieutenant), 5, 15-16, 54, 227, 335

Oberste Polizey- und Censur-Hofstelle (Highest Police and Censorship Office), 14

October 3 Manifesto, (Royal Manifesto), 173-74, 192, 206, 208, 331

Olmütz, 179, 206, 243, 336; the Court at, 179, 201, 249; military court at, 334

Opposition, *see* Party of United Opposition

Orsova, 327, 332

Országgyűlési Tudósítások (*Parliamentary Reports*), 29-30

Osborne, Bernwall, 298

Ottinger, General Baron Franz, 164

Ottoman Empire, 1, 3, 42, 64, 111, 127-28, 299, 313, 319, 331; and the Russian intervention in Hungary, 288; receives the Hungarian revolutionaries, 327-28; and the international crisis over the revolutionary exiles, 338-42

Ozora, Surrender at, 169, 266

Pákozd, Battle of, 169-70, 182, 185, 331

Palacký, František, 121

Palatines, 15, 93-95, 101, 151; *see also* Joseph, archduke-palatine; Stephen, archduke-palatine

Pálffy, János, 214

Pálfi, Albert, 245

Palmerston, Henry John Temple, viscount, 147, 178, 288, 290*n*, 292; replies to Hungarian note, 111; his policy toward Hungary, 297-98; and the revolutionary exiles in the Ottoman Empire, 341, 342

Paris, 20, 25, 43, 60, 66, 68, 174, 224, 253, 294-97, 299

Parliamentary commissioners, *see* Government commissioners

Parliamentary Reports (Kossuth's), 29-30

Parker, Admiral Sir William, 341

Partium, 100

Party of United Opposition, 55-57, 59, 70, 143

Paskevich, Field Marshal Prince Ivan, 289, 300-2, 305; accepts Görgey's surrender, 318, 323, 325-26

Pázmándy, Dénes Jr., 147, 205; on the postwar reorganization of Hungary, 247-48

Peace Party, 59-60, 235, 244, 254, 260, 276, 279, 314; plans for reconciliation with the dynasty, 204-6; activities in Debrecen, 218-22; attempts to influence Kossuth, 257-58; and Declaration of Independence, 262-63; negotiates with Görgey, 283-84

Peasants, xv, 4-5, 10, 17, 96, 167, 216, 302, 310, 315, 336, 347, 351; uprisings of 1831, 21-22; Széchenyi on, 27; the peasant question at the Diet of 1832-36, 28, and at the Diet of 1839-40, 34; their duties and condition, 36-40, 48-50; uprising of 1846, 54-55; the peasant question at the Diet of 1847-48, 59; and the March revolutions, 70; their emancipation in the April Laws, 83-84, 86, 92-93, 97, 100, 102-4; peasant upheavals as a result of the April Laws, 116-18; and the Hungarian revolution, 118-19; peasants in Transylvania, 124-26; Serbian peasants, 127-28; Croatian peasants, 130; peasant deputies in the National Assembly, 143; and the Croatian invasion, 162-64, 169-70; Romanian peasant guerrillas, 209-10; and Windisch-Graetz, 242; Kossuth's decree on behalf of peasants' rights, 280-81; and the Russian invasion, 293

People of the Orient, The, 41

Perczel, General Mór, 232, 245, 276, 283, 316; defeated at the battle of Mór, 212-13; defends the Tisza line, 235-37, 238*n*; vic-